Appropriate Building Materials For Low Cost Housing

Appropriate Building Materials for Low Cost Housing

African Region

Proceedings of a Symposium
held in Nairobi, Kenya, from 7 to 14 November 1983

*Hosted by the Government of the Republic of Kenya
Ministry of Works and Housing & University of Nairobi
and organized by
CIB and RILEM
in co-operation with
UNCHS, UNESCO, UNIDO, UN ECA and CEC*

This publication was undertaken with the financial help of UNESCO

LONDON NEW YORK
E. & F. N. SPON

First published 1983 by
E. & F. N. Spon Ltd
11 New Fetter Lane, London EC4P 4EE
Reprinted 1985

Published in the USA by
E. & F. N. Spon
733 Third Avenue, New York NY 10017

© 1983 CIB, PO Box 20704, 3001 JA Rotterdam and
RILEM, 12 rue Brancion, 75737 Cedex 15, Paris

Printed in Great Britain
at the University Press, Cambridge

ISBN 0 419 13280 5

British Library Cataloguing in Publication Data

Appropriate building materials for low cost housing.
  1. Underdeveloped areas – Dwellings –
Congresses
  2. Building materials – Congresses
  I. International Council for Building Research
Studies and Documentation   II. RILEM
  691   TH4805

  ISBN 0-419-13280-5

Library of Congress Cataloging in Publication Data

Main entry under title:

Appropriate building materials for low cost housing,
African region.

  1. Building materials – Africa – Congresses.
  2. Dwellings – Africa – Congresses. I.
International Council for Building Research,
Studies, and Documentation. II. International
Union of Testing and Research Laboratories for
Materials and Structures.
  TA402.5.A35A66 1983   691'.096   83-14529
  ISBN 0-419-13280-5

2 ◊

◊

CONTENTS

Preface

These are the Proceedings of the Symposium held in Nairobi, Kenya from 7th to 14th November 1983 on

Appropriate Building Materials for Low Cost Housing
African Region

The present Symposium is the first of a planned series to be held in Africa (1983), Asia (1985) and Latin America (1986). The principal aims of this first Symposium may be stated as follows:

(i) To assist in the development of a building materials industry in the African region as an integral part of a construction industry geared to low cost housing.

(ii) To promote the utilization of locally available building materials.

(iii) To identify research priorities with a view to improving the quality of products by better knowledge of building materials.

(iv) To foster in the near future effective cooperation among research institutes, testing laboratories, governmental and non-governmental agencies and professional organizations within and outside Africa.

The main objective was to provide an opportunity for experts in the field of building materials and low cost housing to meet and exchange views and experiences and to formulate recommendations for the further development of appropriate materials for low cost housing in Africa.

This publication presents the first results of the endeavour to bring together the information which will enable us to meet the objectives and draw up as complete a review as possible on the subject.

SECTION I

Pierre, argile, terre, latérite

Stone, clay, soil, laterite

ADOBE BLOCKS STABILIZED WITH GYPSUM

R. KAFESÇİOĞLU, E. GÜRDAL
A. GÜNER, M.S. AKMAN
Istanbul Technical University

1. Introduction

Adobe has not lost its indispensability as a building material since
the primitive ages of civilization. For centuries, mankind has tried
to find remedies for its two major deficiencies: its non-resistance
to water and comparatively low mechanical strength. The greatest
merits of adobe are its low cost, easy availability and possibility of
production by unqualified workmen. The question is how to minimize
the two deficiencies of adobe without impairing these merits. The
efforts for improvement comprise the improvement of the process of
production and/or addition of suitable admixtures. Present work is
mainly a similar effort aimed at using in combination soil and gypsum
plaster, the two archaic building materials; or, in more precise terms,
stabilizing adobe with gypsum and improving the production technology
of this material.

Although there are reports of innumerable works on the subject of
stabilization of soil with cement and lime, there is very limited
accumulation of information on stabilization with gypsum |1|.
The employment of cement and lime stabilization of soils in engineering practices such as highway, air-port runway and embankment dam
construction, where the stabilization increases the strength and
lowers the permeability, have influenced this accumulation. However,
adobe stabilized with gypsum is only a building material for housing,
and the improvement in the water sealing property of the material is
yet small.

Adobe Blocks Stabilized with Gypsum plaster (ABSG) provide the
following advantages |2|:

- Gypsum plaster requires less energy and industrial equipment for
production when compared with lime or cement; it is cheaper. Gypsum
is abundantly available on the earth.
- With ABSG, it is possible to start the construction of walls
short after production without waiting for drying.
- ABSG have low shrinkage, sharp and smooth appearance, high
mechanical strength, low strain under load.

2. *The production technique of ABSG*

In the production of ABSG, care was taken not to depart from primitive methods. However, it may be subject of another work to investigate the effects of ramming or pressing, cajon production and additions of straw or rice husk.

The soil used is of the kind considered suitable for other stabilization purposes |3|. The particle size distribution is of particular importance in this respect. The amount of particles finer than 2 µm should be between 28% and 9%. The amount finer than 74 µm should be about 40%. The coarse fraction of soil has improving effects. In fact, siliceous sand finer than 4000 µm was added to the soil used in this work to improve the grading. The grading curve of the raw material obtained as a mixture of 10% sand and 90% soil is shown in Fig. 1. It is seen that the clay content of the mixture is somewhat low. Nevertheless, in a previous investigation, it was clearly observed that soils used in the brick manufacturing industry with higher clay contents (about 35%, 42% and 48%) were definitely unsuitable for ABSG production |2|.

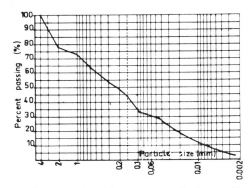

Fig. 1.   Grading curve of the soil

The liquid limit of the soil is 33%, the plastic limit is 24%, the shrinkage limit is 15%; hence, the plasticity index is 9%. It is claimed that soils with somewhat higher plasticity indices, that is, with higher clay contents, are more suitable for stabilization |4|.

The most convenient method for the mixing of the gypsum plaster and soil was found to be that in which the soil is wetted and made into a mud and left to stand until mixing. This method, which is the conventional adobe production practice in Anatolia, also makes it possible to obtain a more homogeneous and workable mix. The amount of water added to the soil was about the plastic limit of the soil. Then the approximately 1:1 gypsum-water slurry was prepared and added to the mud, and soon after that, the operations of mixing and moulding were started and completed. As more precise measurement is possible in a laboratory, the total water content of the mix was calculated so that the water contents were 60% for the gypsum plaster and 24% (plastic limit) for the soil.

The mixture of mud and gypsum sets within 5-10 minutes. This is a critical period of time and, therefore, should not be exceeded. If the mixing and moulding is prolonged beyond this time, the mixture softens again and the advantage of early usability of the blocks is impaired. To prevent this, adequate quantities of slaked lime may be added to retard the setting of gypsum thus postponing the above-mentioned critical time of instability.

It is possible to demould the blocks within half an hour and use the blocks in the construction in less than two days after production. As will be explained below, the blocks attain sufficient mechanical properties without necessitating drying in the sun.

3. *Optimum gypsum/soil ratio*

The optimum gypsum/soil ratio was dealt with in a previous work by the authors 2 . Properties such as compressive and flexural strengths, shrinkage, the rate of capillary absorption, rain resistance, and thermal expansion were taken as the criteria in the determination of the optimum ratio. Mixes with gypsum/soil ratios of 0%, 5%, 10%, 15% and 20%, and lime/soil ratios of 5% and 10% were produced, and the effect of additions of 2.5% and 5% lime to mixes with 10% gypsum was also investigated.

The improving effects of gypsum become apparent for gypsum contents of 10% and over, the change in mechanical properties getting smaller above this ratio. In order to obtain a significant decrease in the water susceptibility of the ABSG, it was observed that gypsum/soil ratios greater than 10% (about 20%) were necessary. The addition of gypsum-lime causes a slight decrease in the strengths, while the production becomes easier and also the deformability increases.

4. *Mechanical properties of the ABSG*

After a pilot investigation of the influence of various gypsum/soil ratios, the properties were studied in more detail on the blocks produced with the minimum (10% gypsum/soil) ratio which yielded significant stabilizing effect. Properties such as the mechanical strengths, shrinkage, creep, toughness etc. were determined on 70x70x280 mm prisms and 70 mm cubes. The specimens were not sun-dried but left to dry in a humidity and temperature controlled room at 65% relative humidity and 20°C temperature. Different curing conditions were of course adopted depending on the property under investigation.

4.1. Compressive and flexural strengths

The compressive and flexural strengths of ABSG were studied as functions of time and water content. It is observed that the two mechanical strengths follow similar trends. The rate of strength development increases between the 5th and the 15th days while the water content decreases from 12.0% to 5.8% and remains constant thereafter. This increase may be attributed largely to the drying of the gypsum adobe. When the drying process is accelerated in a 70 °C oven, the ABSG reaches its ultimate strength in 3 days and no increase in

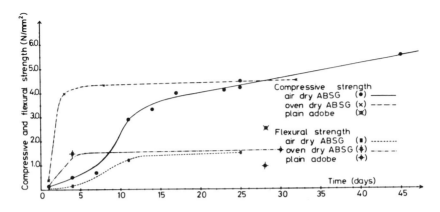

Fig. 2.   Strength versus time relations.

strength is recorded afterwards. However, in the ABSG dried slowly,
the increase is strength continues. The experimental results are
shown in Fig. 2. In plain adobes the compressive strength is
2.42 N/mm^2 and the flexural strength is 0.76 N/mm^2 at 28 days while
the corresponding strengths of the ABSG with 10% gypsum/soil ratio are
as high as 4.45 N/mm^2 and 1.75 N/mm^2 respectively, at the same age.
It is interesting to note that in the specimens tested under compression after being subjected to creep test the compressive strength
reached 5.55 N/mm^2. It was also observed that the compressive
strength of these specimens with 5.50% water content rose to
9.81 N/mm^2 when tested after being oven dried for two days. This
increase is very probably due to the formation of smaller gypsum
crystals as a result of lower rate of hydration extending over a longer
period of time, and suggests an interaction between the soil and the
gypsum. A mineralogical study of the material based on electron
microscopy and electron microprobe analysis could reveal the nature of
this interaction.

4.2. Deformability and toughness
The deformability of ABSG was studied as a function of time and water
content by short- and long-term tests performed on the prismatic
specimens cured under the above-mentioned conditions.

    o Short-term deformation tests
The ABSG prims were tested under compression at 2, 3, 4, 7, 10, 17, 22
and 25 days after production and the strains were measured using
inductive transducers. The results are shown in Fig. 3. The water
contents were also determined on the specimens of the same age by
accelerated drying. The decrease in the water contents are depicted
in Fig. 4. The water content of air-dried specimens decreases to
5.8%, its ultimate value, in 10 days. Until the 10th day when it
reaches its ultimate water content, the material exhibits high strain
but low strength characteristics. As the material ages, a complete

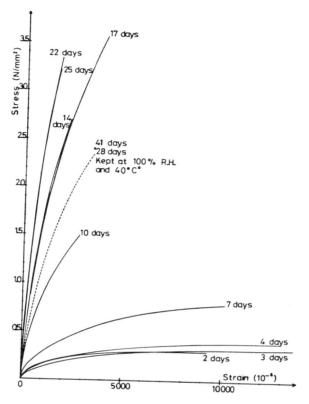

Fig. 3. Stress—strain relations.

reversal of this behaviour occurs. However, the increase in the
strength and the decrease in strain at maximum stress continues after
the end of drying.

The change of toughness of the ABSG with time is shown in Fig.4.
It is not possible to speak of any consistent change. However, it
can be observed that there are two peaks, one at 7 days and the other
at 17 days, which indicate the presence of two materials with distinct
mechanical behaviour. The first material with excessive ultimate
strain can be said to gain strength almost only as a result of water
loss, and the increase in the toughness is due to this increase in
strength, which is similar to the behaviour of plain adobe. The
second material is a brittle one in which the strength development is
independent of water content. But, at later ages, this increase in
strength is compensated by the decrease in ultimate strain, and the
toughness shows another decrease. This phenomenon is an indication of
the fact that ABSG gets more brittle with time. As a matter of fact,

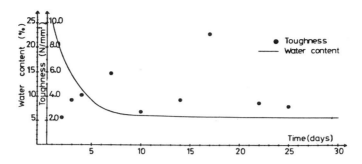

Fig. 4.   Water content and toughness versus time.

the ratio tensile strength/compressive strength, based on the tensile
strength estimated from the flexural strength, is about the order of
1/6, which is an evidence of quite a high brittleness.

   ● Long term deformation tests
The shrinkage and creep tests were continued for 45 days.
   The shrinkage measurements were started one day after production.
The test results are shown in Fig. 5. It is evident from the
affinity of the shrinkage and weight loss curves, and from the
constancy of shrinkage values beyond 10 days, that the shrinkage is
purely a "drying shrinkage". In fact, the water content of the
specimens remains constant after ten days under the curing conditions
adopted in this work. The final value of shrinkage is 2.6%, which is
comparatively low. In a previous work, total shrinkage was found to
be 1.7% in 10% gypsum/soil specimens, whereas that of the plain adobe
was 5.0%, about three times as great |2|. It is thus shown that the
addition of gypsum decreases the shrinkage to a great extent, that the
shrinkage is mainly due to the presence of clay, and that it reaches
a final constant value within a short period of time.
   The specimens were loaded for creep tests at the 14th day after
production. The sustained stresses corresponded to 27% and 56% of
the   14-day compressive strengths. The test results are shown in
Fig. 6. Since the shrinkage had come to an end when the creep tests
were started, the results are pure creep. The deformations were
measured using mechanical extensometers. Under 27% relative sustained
stress, the final creep is achieved within 15 days, the final creep
being about 4 times the instantaneous strain. As for the 54%
relative sustained stress, the creep continued, though at a very
low rate, even after 30 days, in this case the final creep being
approximately 3 times the instantaneous strain. The primary creep is
completed within 10 days. The creep strength may be estimated to be
greater than 60% of the compressive strength.
   The specimens on which creep tests were performed were then tested
under compression, and the compressive strengths were found to be
considerably high. Because of the lack of sufficient comparable data,

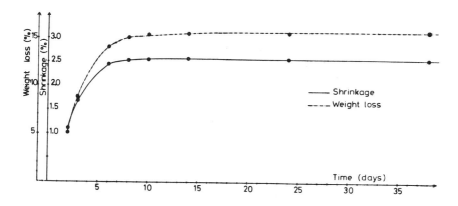

Fig. 5. Shrinkage and weight loss versus time.

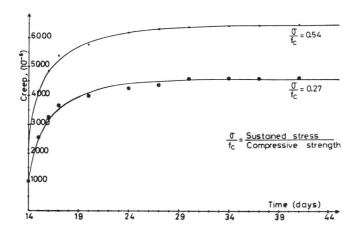

Fig. 6. Creep versus time relation.

it is not possible to give a feasible explanation whether this
increase is effected by ageing or consolidation.

   The experimental work revealed that the ABSG exhibited viscoelastic
behaviour even at comparatively low water contents, that the delayed
strain could be as high as four times the instantaneous strain, that
the material has a creep strength, which is greater than 60% of its
compressive strength determined by   short-term compression tests.

5. *Resistance to water and humidity*

It was mentioned above that an addition of 10% gypsum did not
remarkably decrease the water sensitivity of adobe. A more significant amelioration may be expected by increasing the amount of
gypsum to 20%.

It can be said that apparently the ABSG were not damaged by the
rain effect when compared with plain adobe. In addition to this,
the rate of capillary water absorption decreased from 7.5×10^{-3} cm/s
in the plain adobe to 0.3×10^{-3} cm/s in the ABSG by the addition of
10% gypsum, and also the ABSG remained standing intact after 24
hours in the capillary absorption test while the plain adobe fell
down and disintegrated within 4.5 hours. But, the above findings do
not guarantee that the ABSG could be used without being properly
protected from water |2| .

The ABSG specimens were tested for volume stability by keeping in
special ovens at 100% R.H. and a temperature of 40 $^{\circ}$C. The specimens
were left to dry at 65% R.H. and 20 $^{\circ}$C during the 13 days following
their production, and then subjected to humid curing for 28 days.
The weights increased by 1.20% and the lengths by 0.32% during the
initial six days of humid curing and remained unchanged afterwards.
Stress-strain relations were determined on the specimens subjected
to the above-mentioned treatment. The average test result is
depicted in Fig. 3. The ABSG has become somewhat ductile but the
compressive strength is 48% lower than that of the specimens of the
same age previously subjected to creep tests, and the water content
has risen to 7.3%.

6. *Conclusions*

Gypsum stabilized adobe is a much more suitable low-cost building
material than plain adobe provided that it is not in direct contact
with water.

Compressive and flexural strengths increase 2-3 times and shrinkage
decreases by 3-4 folds when compared with plain adobe while also the
demoulding and curing periods are very short. The strength development continues in the material used in the construction of a wall and
the material transforms into a building stone with higher strength
and lower deformability. Creep does not entail any problems. High
humidity of the atmosphere decreases the compressive strength of the
material to that of the dry plain adobe.

At this stage of the investigation, the topics of primary
importance are development of the production techniques and
improvement of the water resistance by increasing the amount of
gypsum added without impairing the economical character of the idea.
The possible problem of biological corrosion of anaerobic kind is
another point that deserves due consideration. Especially, some
organisms present in soils may have such corrosive effects which will
be studied in a future investigation.

Acknowledgements

The experimental work was carried out in the Materials Laboratory cf
the Faculty of the Architecture and the Building Research Laboratories
of the Faculty of Civil Engineering, Istanbul Technical University.
The help given by Ş. Dilmaç, M.A. Taşdemir and T. Kaymakçı and the
other staff of the Building Materials Unit is acknowledged.

References

1. Eyre, T.T. (1935), *The Physical Properties of Adobe used as a
    Building Material*. The University of New Mexico Bulletin,
    No. 263, Albuquerque.
2. Kafesçioğlu, R. ; Toydemir, N. ; Gürdal, E. ; Özüer, B. (1980),
    Gypsum Stabilized Adobe as a Building Material. Research
    Project MAG-505, Sponsored by Turkish National Research
    Council (TÜBİTAK), (in Turkish).
3. Schwalen, H.C. (1935), *Effect of Soil Texture upon the Physical
    Characteristics of Adobe Bricks*. University of Arizona,
    College of Agriculture Technical Bulletin, No. 58, Tucson,
    Arizona.
4. Derya, E. (1982), *Experiments for using Stabilized Soil as a
    Building Material*. Middle East Technical University,
    (in Turkish).

THERMOMECHANICAL ANALYSIS OF SOME
EGYPTIAN CLAYS AND CLAY/SAND MIXTURES

FATHY HELMY MOSALAMY,
General Organization for Housing Building and
Planning Research, Cairo, EGYPT

1. Introduction

Since long ago, the clay brick industry in Egypt had depended on the Nile-Silt raw materials which used to be deposited in huge quantities on the Nile-banks particulary during flood seasons. After the construction of Asswan High-Dam in 1965, this industry became faced with a series problem. In order to solve it, attempts were made to find a major substitute for Nile-Silt in the building brick industry. Obviously, shale/clay deposits occuring in the neighbourhood areas of potentiality would be the major substitute provided that such a raw material would be suitable for this industry. Accordingly, extenive research work was directed to the exploration of such deposits and their evaluation for the brick industry (1)

Thermal analysis is a group of techniques in which a physical property of a substance is measured as a function of temperature whilst the substance is subjected to a controlled temperature programme.

One of the most important factors generally affecting the brick industry is the volume changes as a function of temperature. Thermomechanical is a technique whereby all these changes can be measured. This technique has been applied since long time ago on clays (2).

In more recent investigations of siliceous sand, it was founded that the negative expansion associated with the a→ B transition quartz strongly influences the dilatometric curves of the whole clay body (3). This technique was also applied to the study of the sintering of metal powders, detection of polymorphic and allotropic transformation and control of the quality of industrial ceramics (4). Recently, this technique was applied for identification of raw materials and sometimes in solid-state chemistry for drawing the phase diagrams (5 & 6). In mineralogical investigations there has been little application of dilatometric procedures, which is surprising, in view of their ability to detect solid-liquid and other phase changes with great accurancy.

The changes in volume by heat are often of great technical importance, especially when substances which undergo such changes are made into articles which are required to be of define size within very narrow limites. The presence of non-plastic materials such as grog, quartz or alumina greatly reduces the firing shrinkage of chays, apparently by acting as a non-reactive skeleton during firing. By addition of such materials an extensive shrinkage in clay body can be avoided (7).

Silica occurs in clays generally either in the free state as quartz, amorphous and colloidal silica or in combination with alumina in the form of clay minerals, felspars and soluble silicates (7).

The aim of this work is the development of an emperical relationship between the percentage of total silica content and the percentage of shrinkage for different clays and clay/sand mixtures thermomechanically analysed for different temperatures, i.e. 900°C,950°C & 1000°C.

2- Experimental Work and Results.

The whole of the experiments described in this study has been carried out using Thermal Analyzer DT-30 (Shimadzu Co. Kyoto-Japan) attached with R-122T bench type automatic balancing recorder.

Each sample or mixture was grinded in an agate mortar to - 73 microns. The resultent material was mixed with the correct amount of water and shapped as a cylinder using a special mould. Samples were then dried at   100°C for 24 hours. Dimentions of the samples after drying were $\sim$ 7 mm. long and $\sim$ 2 mm. diameter. Throughout the .. whole work, thermomechanical analysis was carried out under nitrogen atmosphere (30 ml./min.) and a load of 40 gm/cm^2 was applied to the sample.

Chemical analysis of the four clay samples are given in table 1, and the percentage of the uncombined silica in clay samples calculated using rational analysis method (8) are given in table 2. The seventeen mix compositions and shrinkage up to 900°C, 950°C and 1000°C are given in table 3. The relationship between shrinkage and total silica content of clays and clay/sand mixtures thermomechanically analysed up to 900°C, 950°C and 1000°C is shown in Fig.1.

Table 1. Chemical Composition of Shale/Clay Samples

Oxide	Clay Sample (No)			
Content	1	2	3	4
SiO_2	50.37	48.76	49.14	55.00
Al_2O_3	17.35	19.51	16.78	9.75
Fe_2O_3	8.67	8.53	9.99	6.36

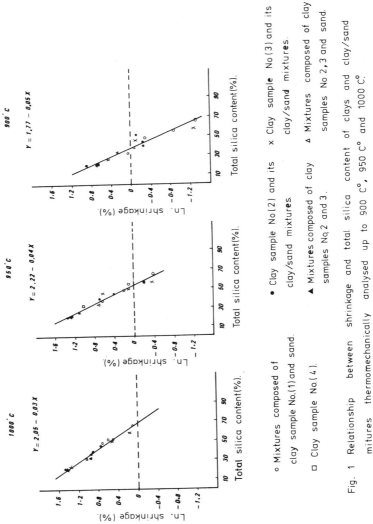

Fig. 1 Relationship between shrinkage and total silica content of clays and clay/sand mixtures thermomechanically analysed up to 900 C°, 950 C° and 1000 C°.

Con.

TiO_2	1.36	1.86	1.94	0.96
CaO	2.66	5.57	6.12	9.45
MgO	2.20	3.10	3.61	2.05
Na_2O	2.82	0.81	0.78	2.77
K_2O	1.25	1.35	1.11	1.49
SO_3	0.11	3.36	3.73	2.39
L.O.I.	12.75	7.34	7.25	10.60
Total	99.54	100.19	100.45	100.82

Table 2.   Percentage of the Uncombined Silica in the Clay Samples.

Clay Sample (No)			
1	2	3	4
19.55	20.30	24.56	32.64

Table 3.   Mix Compostions and Shrinkage of the 17 mixtures.

Clay Sample No.	Percentage of free silica	Mix Composition (Wt %)		Actual mix Composition (Wt %)		Ln. Shrinkage (%)		
		Clay	Sand	Clay	Sand	up to 900°C	up to 950°C	up to 1000°C
1	19.55	71	29	51.45	48.55	−0.29	0.21	0.74
		65	35	45.45	54.55	−0.87	0.095	0.60
		54	46	34.45	65.55	−1.34	−0.41	0.095
2	20.30	100	–	79.70	20.30	0.90	1.38	1.43
		80	20	59.70	40.30	−0.26	0.71	0.90
		75	25	54.70	45.30	−0.25	0.39	0.74
		66.5	33.5	46.20	53.80	−1.00	−0.22	0.52
3	24.56	100	–	74.40	25.60	0.44	1.12	1.39
		80	20	55.40	44.60	−0.11	0.46	0.75
		75	25	50.40	49.60	−0.63	0.16	0.53
		66.5	33.5	41.90	58.10	−1.27 − 0.38		0.18

Con.

		No (2)	No (3)						
4	32.64	100		–	67.36	32.64	0.077	1.04	1.04
2+3		80	20	–	78.80	21.20	0.73	1.29	1.41
		75	25	–	78.70	21.30	0.67	1.31	1.43
		66.5	33.5	–	78.30	21.70	0.67	1.31	1.44
2+3		50	35	15	66.25	33.75	0.28	0.77	0.95
		50	30	20	62.50	37.50	-0.07	0.65	0.89

3. Discussion.

Clays are natural silico-aluminates which present during their thermal evolution, dehydration reactions then solid-solid and crystallisation reactions at high temperatures. The registering of contractions or expansions associated with these reactions has been used for many years for identification of these minerals (5). Changes that occur during firing process are related either to changes in grain size and shape or changes in pore shape and pore size.

Free silica which in most clays, is comparatively coarsegrained (up wards of 10 M). It was reported that (7) the content of this sandy component is variable, ranging from 0 to as much as 50 percent. In this work, and as shown in table 2, the free silica content in clay samples ranging between 19.55 to 32.64 percent.

In addition, this work is cevering the range of total free silica content from 20.3 to 65.5 percent, by adding sand to clay as shown in table 3. It was agreed that, the presence of free silica is lessens the shrinkage (drying and firing), and reduce the plasticity and strength (7) (unless it is of small particle size). From table 3, it can be observed that, generally by increasing the total free silica content, the firing shrinkage is decreasing at all temperatures. It was also observed that, increasing the firing temperature from 950°C to 1000°C, the shrinkage rate has been decreased by half approximatly comparing with that from 900-950°C. This is may be due to that most of the sintering processes take place in these samples up to 950°C.

The shrinkage in clays when fired at high temperatures is mainly the result of the reaction which occur within and between the minerals present (7). These are either crystallisation to form mineral type or liquid formation arising from the combination of fluxing elements with the clay body to form low melting-point euticties. Both reactions reduce the volume of ceramic materials.

From table 3, clay sample No. 4 show no difference in shrinkage at 950°C and at 1000°C. This may be due to the high content of fluxes, especially CaO as shown in table 1. These fluxes combine with alumina and silica to form low melting point liquids.

The relationship between shrinkage and total silica content of clays and clay/sand mixtures are shown in fig. 1. By applying the least square method three different emperical equations can be developed. These are; at 900°C y = 1.77 - 0.05X whereas at 950°C y = 2.22 - 0.04 X and at 1000°C y = 2.05 - 0.03 X (y = percentage of shrinkage "ln" and X = percentage of total free silica content).

These three emperical equations was founded to be in good agreement with the data present in this work.

References

1- Ramez, M.R.H. and Imam, H.F. (1975), The optimum solutions of current problems in locat clay brick industry. Egypt. Acad. Scien. Res. & Tech. (in Arabic).

2- Geller, R.F. and Bunting, E.N. (1940), J.Res. natn. Bur. Stand. <u>25</u> , 15

3- Benleke, M.P. and Edmonds, C.S. (1967), Bull. Kansas Geol. Surv. <u>191</u> , 13.

4- Murat, M. (1971), C.R. Acad. Sci. Fr, 270, 1657 - 60.

5- Mentzen, B. (1971), Bull. Soc. Fr. Mineral. cristallogr., <u>2</u> , 138-140.

6- Bars, J.P. and Carel, C. (1969), C.R. Acad. Sci. Fr, <u>269</u> , 1152-54

7- Searle, A.B. and Grimshaw, R.W. (1959), The chemistry and physics of clays and other ceramic materials, Ernest Benn Limited, London

8- Worrall, W.E. (1975), Clays and ceramic raw materials, Applied Science Publishers Ltd. London.

A NEW LOW ENERGY - INTENSIVE BUILDING MATERIAL BASED ON LATERITIC
SOILS FOR LOW COST HOUSING IN DEVELOPING NATIONS

Dr. B.V. Subrahmanyam,
N.P. Rajamane, &
N. Balasubramanian, Structural Engineering Research Centre,
                    Madras-600 113, India.
Prof. G.S. Ramaswamy, University of Arizona, Tucson, USA.
V. Nagaraju,
A. Narayanaswami &
A. Chakravarthy, Central Mechanical Engineering Research Institute,
                 India.

1. Introduction

The shortage of housing is very acute around the world, more particularly in the developing nations. The spiralling growth of population, the relatively low Gross National Produce and the general lack
of purchasing power are factors which contribute to the progressive
deterioration of the housing situation in the developing nations.
In the typical case of India, the current shortage of housing is estimated to be some 24 million dwelling units. Atleast 5 million
dwelling units are to be built every year from now, if the housing
problem were to be solved atleast by the year 2000 A.D. The situation is equally grim in the other developing nations.
    An impediment to the solution of the problem of housing is the
scarcity and/or high cost of building materials. Ideally, building
materials for low-cost housing must be produced from the locally
available raw materials. Further, these raw materials must be abundantly available or they should be renewable in nature. Materials
such as mud and thatch have been quite popular in the construction
of 'low-cost' and 'no-cost' housing. Such constructions are, however, of reduced, if not poor, quality. The more popular construction materials such as clay bricks and concrete blocks are of good
quality but are high-energy intensive, expensive,and/or are based on
heavy industry. Quite often clay of good quality, required for the
manufacture of burnt clay bricks,is not available.
    It is incidental that most of the developing nations are in the
tropical or subtropical regions of the world. Laterite, a product of
tropical or subtropical weathering, occurs abundantly in such regions
in the continents of Africa, Asia, South America, and Australia. The
term Laterite ('Later' means brick in Latin) was coined by Buchanan
in 1807 to indicate an indurated soil - locally called "Ittica Kallu"
(brick stone) - that he discovered at Angadipuram, Kerala, in India.
Laterites have been defined differently depending on the property of
induration (hardening on exposure to atmosphere), on the basis of
morphology, and based on the chemical composition. While there is as
yet no generally accepted definition, one could tentatively accept
the description given by Gidigasu (1) whereby Laterite denotes all

reddish, residual and non-residual tropically weathered soils, which genetically form a chain of materials ranging from decomposed rocks through clays to sesqui-oxide rich crusts. The main constituents of Laterites are oxides of Aluminium, Iron and Silicon. Laterites occur in forms ranging from soils, pisoliths (pea gravel) to soft rock masses. The world-wide distribution of laterites is indicated in Fig.1.

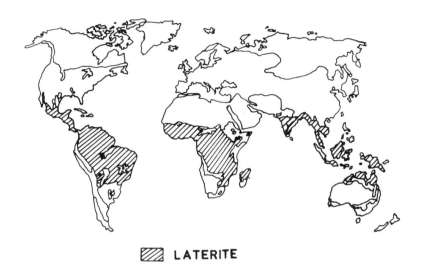

LATERITE

Fig. 1. World-wide distribution of Laterite (After Gidigasu)

In general, Laterites do not have any important mineral or other value or use. They are sometimes used for road-dressing. An exception is where it occurs as large, soft rock masses (as in South-Western India), where it is quarried, cut and dressed to desired size and shape, allowed to air-dry and harden (indurate), and is then used as a masonry block. Since age immemorial, such Laterite stone masonry blocks have been used in the construction of even monuments besides houses and other structures. A notable example is that of the temple structures at Angkorwat in Cambodia. In recent times, due to the non-availability of skilled dressers and increasing labour costs, this type of application is on the wane. Adobe bricks made of Lateritic soil, and soil-cement (or soil-lime) blocks have been used in low-cost housing in Africa and India. Nevertheless, all the above types of masonry blocks require heavy protection, by way of thick water-proofing plaster, from natural elements and are to be rated as substandard construction materials. They also possess low compressive strengths no better than 2.5 MPa (2).

2. Latoblocks

The Structural Engineering Research Centre, Madras, India, developed
a new, low energy intensive process whereby high quality building
blocks could be produced from Lateritic soil and lime. According to
the process (3), a reactive mixture containing primarily Lateritic
soil and lime is mixed, and is moulded under pressure. The blocks
are then subjected to low temperatures of the order of 100°C to produce strong and good quality blocks. These blocks, named
'Latoblocks', possess the typical properties given below.

(a) Wet compressive strengths of the order of 5 to 15 MPa.
(b) Water absorption of about 12%.
(c) The blocks possess sharp corners and smooth faces.
(d) The blocks possess very good dimensional stability.
(e) No warping of the blocks is possible as in the case of burnt
     clay bricks.
(f) The blocks pass the drop test, when dropped from a height of
     2 metres on hard surface.
(g) Inspite of the smooth surfaces the blocks possess very good
     plasterability.

The colour of the Latoblocks is very pleasing, with shades ranging
from cream to light crimson, depending on the source of Laterite.

An important advantage in favour of Latoblocks is that their production is not energy-intensive. This is in contrast to the conventional clay bricks, which are produced by burning at 1000-1200°C for
several days. The energy required for the production of Latoblocks
is also far less than the requirement for autoclaved products, which
are produced by high pressure steam curing (autoclaving). Latoblocks
are thus ideally suited for production and use in countries which are
not self-sufficient in terms of their energy requirement. The other
major advantage of Latoblocks relates to the value addition to a raw
material (viz., Laterite soil) which had hitherto no other significant use or application.

3. Latoblock Machines

In the field of low-cost housing in developing nations, two contrast-
ing situations occur. In the first, occuring primarily in rural
areas, the beneficiaries of the low-cost housing schemes themselves
can contribute manual effort in the various phases of construction.
These schemes are rightly termed self-help schemes. In the second
situation, either governmental or other bodies plan mass-scale, time-
bound schemes for the construction of low-cost houses, accent being
on the early mitigation of the problem of housing shortage. To cater
to both the above situations, two Latoblock making machines were developed by SERC in collaboration with the Mechanical Engineering
Research and Development Organisation.

The first machine costs approx. U.S. \$ 3500. It is labour-inten-
sive and is meant for rural, self-help housing schemes and has a
production capacity of 60 blocks per hour. The second machine is an

automatic block making machine and has a production capacity of 600 blocks per hour.   The cost of this machine is approx. U.S. $ 40,000. This machine, which can be scaled up for larger production capacities, is suited for large scale, commercial production of Latoblocks. It is estimated that the total capital outlay for a small scale industry with a production capacity of 2.7 million Latoblocks per annum is only about U.S. $ 70,000 (4).

4. Field Trials

A low cost demonstration housing unit with a plinth area of 26.5 sq.m. was built in 1976.   Latoblocks were utilised for the foundation and walls of this house.   The walls were plastered on the inside but were not plastered, but only painted, on the outside, to study the long term weathering characteristics.   Latoblocks were also used in the shell roof which was funicular shape.   The shell roof was only 75 mm thick and did not contain any reinforcement (see Ref.5 for details).   The cost of construction was only U.S. $ 525 (approximately) in the year 1976.   The house was adjudged to be the best out of 24 demonstration units and was awarded the first prize during the International Seminar on Low Cost Housing held at Madras, in January 1977.

The house has been under occupation for nearly 6½ years now,has stood the test of time,and is giving very good service to the occupants.

5. Closure

Considerable interest has been evinced by the construction industry in India in the production of Latoblocks.   Proposals are afoot for the establishment of industrial units for the large scale production of Latoblocks.   The low-energy requirement for manufacture, relative economy over construction materials of comparable quality, and the utilisation of a waste, abundantly available natural mineral, are the advantages which are appreciated.   However, the highly conservative nature of the construction industry is an important, impeding factor that has been found to come in the way of popularising the new technology of Latoblocks.

Latoblocks have a very good potential for use in low cost housing in the developing nations especially in the continents of Asia, Africa and South America.

6. Acknowledgements

This paper is published with the kind permission of Dr. M. Ramaiah, Director, Structural Engineering Research Centre, Madras.   The process of manufacturing Latoblocks was invented by the team from SERC and the block making machines were developed jointly by the SERC and MERADO teams.

References

1. Gidigasu, M.D., (1976) Laterite Soil Engineering – Pedogenesis
    and Engineering Principles, Elsevier Scientific Publishing
    Company, Amsterdam, 554.
2. Gresillon, J.M., (1976) Etude Sur la Stabilisation et la Compre-
    ssion des Terres Pour Leur Utilisation dans in Construction,
    (in French), Annales de l'Institut Technique du Batiment et
    des Travaux Publics, V.29, 5, 23-34.
3. _____, A Process for the Manufacture of LATOBLOCKS, Building
    Blocks from Lateritic Soils, (Patent Pending).
4. _____, (1980), Building Blocks (Latoblocks) from Lateritic
    Soils, J.National Buildings Org. & UN Regional Housing Centre
    ESCAP, V. XXV No.1, 4 , 9-10.
5. _____, (1977), Houses for Economically Weaker Sections, Struc-
    tural Engineering Research Centre, Madras, India.

IMPROVEMENT AND USE OF EARTH CONSTRUCTION PRODUCTS FOR LOW COST
HOUSING

J.K. KATEREGGA, Housing Research and Development Unit (HRDU)
                University of Nairobi

1. Introduction

The utilisation of earth in house construction is one of the oldest
and most common methods used by a bigger percentage of the developing
countries' population as of now. This is because earth has several
advantages to offer as a building construction material especially
for the poor and the rural population.

It is the most readily available and cheap material found everywhere. It is easy to work with, requires less skills and as such, it
encourages and facilitates unskilled individuals and groups of people
to participate in their house construction on self-help basis. It
offers a very high resistance to fire destruction of houses and
provides a comfortable built living environment due to its high
thermal and heat insulation value. It also offers other important
factors all of which attribute to the achievement of a good house
planning/design and construction solution.

However, despite all these good qualities earth offers in house
construction, the material has remained unpopular and in many
countries officially unacceptable as a building material. This is so
because it has a lot of weaknesses or poor qualities too when used
as a building material. This paper will therefore try to deal with
some of these poor qualities and to outline some of the possible
methods of reducing them to make earth a more suitable material for
house construction especially for low-cost housing projects.

2. Poor Qualities of Earth Products

One of the main reasons why soil does not feature prominently in
building construction works is because of its poor qualities. If any
developer wanted to put up a housing scheme and during the design
stage he is advised to use soil blocks for wall construction of the
houses, he would definitely raise several questions. These questions
would reflect the inner fears, hesitation and doubts many people have
in using soil blocks as a building material for permanent houses and
other buildings. This also indicates that most people are vaguely
aware of the poor qualities of soil as a building material.

There is one example of a church community in Kenya which approached the HRDU for technical advice in putting up a rural health clinic and when a proposal was made to use stabilised "Brepak" soil blocks for wall construction of the building, the people were "terrified."

Infact, they would not accept this proposal and they decided to use the conventional type of materials. This illustrates that we do not trust earth for constructing our permanent houses or other buildings. However, we ought to ask ourselves one major question ; "why do we distrust earth as a building material for our houses and yet we trust it to be the sole and permanent support of all the houses and other huge buildings we erect on it?" If earth can sustain such high pressure from these heavy structures, surely it should be able to support just a roof and its weight as a wall material without much difficulty unless there is something wrong we tend to overlook when applying it as a building material. This also indicates that whatever weaknesses soil may have can be reduced or even eliminated if properly treated.

2.1 Weaknesses of Earth in Building Construction Works
No doubt earth has a number of weaknesses when used as a building material, these include among others:

- i)   its poor and very low load bearing capacity which makes it unsuitable for supporting heavy roofs from large span buildings;
- ii)   its low resistance to moisture (water) destructive effect resulting in crumbling of its products and leading to structural failure once exposed to moisture;
- iii) it has a very low binding strength for its particles and this contributes to its low compression strength;
- iv)   it has a very high moisture (water) absorption ratio which also contributes to its structural failure stated in (ii) above;
- v)   it has a very high shrinkage/swelling ratio resulting in major structural cracks of its products when exposed to different weather conditions and therefore rendering them unsuitable for building construction purposes;
- vi)   it has a low resistance to wear and tear, less durable and calling for frequent repairs and maintenance when used in building construction works.

These are the main weakness which put earth products to a disadvantageous position when compared with other modern conventional building materials such as concrete products, stones, etc. It is these very weaknesses which cause a lot of fear, doubts and hesitations among designers, developers, users, decision makers, financiers, etc. in trying to accept soil products for building construction works. These are justified reasons and no one should be blamed for not accepting the material. However, the real criticism should be on, why no serious consideration has been given to find ways and means of reducing or even eliminating most of the

above listed soil weaknesses in order to make it more suitable for
building permanent houses for the poor population especially in
developing countries. We are all aware that most of the modern and
conventional materials we tend to accept and use in construction
without question, fear or doubt were developed after undergoing a
lot of experimental work to improve on their qualities, this is
supplemented by keeping very high quality control standards during
their production process. We therefore stand to blame ourselves for
being unjust to earth by not extending similar experiments to
improve on its qualities.

3. Good Qualities of Earth Products

Before going into the techniques of earth products improvement, we
ought to be aware and appreciate a number of good qualities earth
has as a building material which makes it to be one of the common
and most favourite building materials for the poor. In fact, the
good qualities of earth out number its weaknesses and should out-
weigh them too. These include among others:

  i)   its high and perfect resistance to fire destruction which
       is one of the most important qualities required in any
       building material;
  ii) it has a very high heat/thermal insulating value that
       enables it to keep the inside of buildings cool when the
       outside is hot and vis-a-vis thereby creating a comfortable
       living environment in houses;
  iii) it is a good noise absorbent which is also another desirable
       quality in house design and planning;
  iv) it is cheaper than most alternative walling materials and is
       readily available at most building sites;
  v)   it does not require much transportation which contributes
       to its low costs when used in building construction works;
  vi) it is easy to work with using simple tools and less skills;
  vii) it encourages and facilitates self-help and community
       participation in house building due to its qualities (iv)
       and (vi) above.

These qualities, if supplemented by research to reduce the weaknesses of earth products could make them one of the most suitable
and appropriate materials for low-cost housing construction.

4. Some Specific Methods of Improving The Qualities of Earth

There are basically three methods of improving on earth qualities in
order for it to offer better performance in building construction
work. However, the choice of one method against another depends on a
number of factors which include:

  i)   the type of soil being considered for use in construction;
  ii) the intended use and therefore the required improvement;
  iii) the climatic conditions of the area where the products are
       to be used;

iv)   the desired quality to be attained for the end product;
v)   the alternative stabilisers available for improving the earth;
vi)   the available equipment to be used during the improvement process, etc. The three methods are:
- by application of protective measures against weathering;
- by application of high compressive and compaction forces on the earth products while being produced or used in construction work;
- by application of both stabilisers and compaction on earth products.

4.1 Application of Protective Measures
As stated in 2 (ii) above, one of the major defects of earth as a building material is its low resistance to moisture destruction. It is therefore possible to improve on its performance in buildings by protecting it against any possible moisture exposure. This can be done by either constructing thick walls and dome shaped roofs supplimented by rendering the external surfaces with less permeable materials. This is a common and successful method used in dry hot climatic zones.

In wet humid areas, the protection is achieved by the provision of very deep overhangs over buildings supplemented by short walls rendered with water proof materials externally and by raising the ground floor slabs of the building to over 200 mm. above the ground level. Such structures are normally supported on treated poles and in between, mud and wattle used for wall cladding. This is termed mud and wattle wall construction. An elevated moisture resistant splash apron sloping away from the walls is at times constructed all around the house to protect the building against possible floods and splushing rain water from the ground which could otherwise damage the lower parts of the walls. The same splash apron also serves as a sitting base for the occupants of the houses.

4.2 Application of High Compaction and Compressive Pressure
Earth products can perform better if high compaction pressure is applied during their production or actual application in the con-struction process. This includes ramming and compacting of moistured murram soil for floor slabs and walls, production of unstabilised soil blocks using block making machines such as the "Cinva-ram" and the "Brepak" block presses. These exert extra compaction pressure during the production stage and binding the soil particles more to increase on the compression strength of the blocks to give a higher bearing capacity than the ordinary mud (adobe) blocks when kept dry.

It is essential to clearly understand the difference between mud (adobe) blocks and soil blocks. A mud (adobe) block is obtained from soil with unregulated moisture content, usually containing too much water almost to the saturation point for easy workability. The block is made by just filling a wooden mould with mud without compaction at all. The block is sun dried in unregulated curing conditions and in most cases, its bearing capacity is hardly over $1N/mm^2$.

On the other hand, a soil block is made out of a properly mixed moistened soil mixture with regulated moisture contents. The block is properly compacted during the production stage and cured in regulated conditions. Its bearing capacity can go up to 2N/mm2 without any stabilisation. When different stabilisers are added to such soil mixtures the blocks produced are termed stabilised soil blocks. They are far better in quality and stronger than both the mud blocks and the unstabilised compacted soil blocks.

4.3 Application of Stabilisers to Earth

This is the most efficient and effective method that gives a more direct quality improvement of earth products for construction purposes. A combination of earth stabilisation and high compaction during the production or application stage can give the required quality and strength from most soil types. Appropriate stabilisers in their correct quantities can reduce the listed poor qualities of soil to a minimum. Experiments have revealed that different stabilisers assist in reducing or even eliminating different soil weaknesses. (See Table I below.)

Table I: Effect of Different Stabilisers on Different Earth Weaknesses

Stabiliser	Different Poor Qualities of Soil						Remarks
	A	B	C	D	E	F	
Cement	✓	✓	✓	✓	✓	✓	most effective of all
Lime	✓	✓	✓	✓	✓	✓×	suitable for soils with fine particles
Bitumen	✓×	✓	✓	✓	×	✓×	very hard to mix and not common
Gypsum	✓×	✓×	✓	✓×	✓	✓×	not readily available
Ash & sand	x	x	x	x	✓	✓×	reduces movement and cracking
Murram soil	✓×	x	x	x	✓	✓×	suitable for fine soils
Grass, Sisal Straw, etc.	✓×	x	✓×	x	✓	✓×	reduces cracking of the products
Cow dung	✓	x	✓×	x	✓	✓×	in limited supply

Key: ✓ ÷ stands for very effective in reducing the indicated defect

✓÷ partly effective in reducing the indicated weaknesses
×÷ not effective in reducing the indicated weaknesses
A stands for law bearing capacity of earth products
B stands for poor resistance to moisture (water) destructive effects
C stands for low binding capacity of earth particles
D stands for high moisture (water) absorption ratio
E stands for high shrinkage/swelling ratio
F stands for low resistance to wear and tear.

Table I shows that cement and lime are the most effective stabilisers in reducing the six (6) poor qualities of earth listed above. They are also the most readily available stabilisers in Kenya especially cement.

4.3.1 Different Stabilisers are more Effective with Different Soil Types

As stated in 4 (i) above, one of the factors effecting the quality of earth products is the type of soil. Experiments have shown that not all soil types are suitable for stabilisation. There are soils which are structurally too poor for construction purposes and any attempts to reduce their weaknesses tend to give unsatisfactory and uneconomical results. These are soils with very fine particles and high clay contents, over 30% by volume. Such soils tend to have very high shrinkage/swelling ratios, over 18% which result in major cracks of their products at different moisture contents. They require very high propotions of stabiliser contents, over 15% by volume or a combination of more than one stabiliser to reduce such weaknesses. They at times produce unpredicatble results due to some chemical reactions of clay with some of the mineral stabilising agents such as cement, lime, etc. Such soils are termed "bad soils", and "Black Cotton Soil" which is found in many areas in Nairobi is one example of such soils. However, the majority of the soil types are structurally good and are suitable and economical to stabilise and obtain very strong and high quality soil products for construction.

Table II: Some common soils and effects of different stabilisers

Stabiliser	Soil Types					Remarks
	Murram Soil	Red Coffee	Sandy Soil	Clayish Soil	Black Cotton	
Cement	✓✓	✓	✓✓	✓ˣ	✓ˣ	best for coarse soil types
Lime	✓	✓✓	✓	✓	✓	best for fine soil types
Bitumen	✓	✓	✓	✓ˣ	✓ˣ	hard to mix manually

Table II continued....

Gypsum	√	√	√	√ˣ	√ˣ	in limited supply
Ash/Sand	x	√ˣ	x	√	√	reduces shrinkage of soils
Murram Soil	x	√ˣ	√ˣ	√	√	same effect
Cow Dung	√	√	√	x	x	best for surface finishes & plastering
Fibrous Type	x	√	x	√	√	reduces shrinkage ratio too

Key: √√ :- stands for most effective stabiliser for that soil type
 √ :- stands for suitable stabiliser for that soil type
 √ˣ :- stands for partly suitable for that soil type
 x :- stands for not suitable/effective for that soil type

From Table II, the best combination comes from cement with murram soil and sandy soil, while lime is best with red coffee soil and clayish soil. Soils with 50% sand, 30% silt and 20% clay are the best of all.

4.3.2 Optimum Contents of Stabilisers for Different Soil Types

Table II also indicates that most soil types are suitable for stabilisation using different stabilisers. However, for actual production and application, the optimum/economic mix ratios of stabilisers with the different soil types have to be determined through experiments to give the required strengh and qualities. In Kenya, the building by-laws currently require among other things a building block to have a minimum bearing capacity of 3N/mm^2 for single storey building construction purposes. Experiments indicate that once a 140mm thick block attains that bearing capacity, it tends to satisfy most, if not all other requirements external walls are expected to meet.
3N/mm^2 is therefore being taken as the basis for experimental work by HRDU/BRE in improving soil products for use in building works. Table III shows that most of the good soils give the required minimum bearing capacity using cement as stabiliser with contents of between 4%(1:25) and 5.6%(1:18) by volume when using the "Brepak" machine or 9%(1:11) to 12%(1:8) if the "Cinva-ram" machine is used to produce the blocks. In the same table, it is indicated that though clayish and black cotton soil blocks attain more than the minimum bearing capacity (3N/mm2) with similar cement contents, they would fail and/or develop major structural cracks when exposed to moisture. However, when other appropriate stabilisers are combined with cement, they eliminate these other defects and good blocks are produced. Experiments have indicated that a combination of 5% cement or 6% lime and about 25% sand

or murram soil with about 70% black cotton soil by volume would produce just as good blocks as those from a 5% cement content with the
good soil types using the "brepak" block press. Experimental work is
still going on with this soil and if concluded, it would be a break
through to this most difficult soil to deal with in building construction works. This would mean that excavation of black cotton soil from
building sites would be reduced and whatever is excavated could be
reused in making building blocks on site from the same soil with the
above combined stabilisers.

5.   Identification of Different Soil Types

As indicated in Tables II & III, some soils are more suitable for
stabilisation than others. It is therefore essential to have an idea
of how to idenfity these soils. There are basically five (5) methods
of soil identification all based on the physical and structural features of the soils, there are:

   a) by examining the physical appearance and the structural
      composition of the soil particles,
   b) by using the container and soil settlement method,
   c) by using the shrinkage ratio box test method,
   d) by using the graduated clear wide month jar and water method,
   e) by using the soil sieve curve method using a 3x3 mm   ø sieve
      size.

   Any of the above five methods can assist to identify the type of
soil which then leadsto the next stage of preparing it for stabilisation.

5.1   Quality Control in Preparation & Production of Earth Products

Just like any factory produced building materials, quality control can
affect the expected good qualities and strength of earth products when
overlooked even if the appropriate stabilisers in their correct propotions are used. It is therefore essential to follow the specified
precautions and procedures in the preparation and production/utilisa-
tion process of any earth products. These include:

a) removal of all the top soil containing organic matters,
b) using relavtively dry and sieved soils before mixing with stabilisers,
c) using the correct soil and stabiliser propotions and mixing them
   thoroughly well before and after adding the correct moisture(water),
d) utilising the mixture when still fresh(within 2 hours) & protecting
   the products against direct sunshine, dry hot wind & rain during
   the first two days(48 hours)of production/casting to facilitate
   gradual curing and settling,
e) construction elements such as rammed floor slabs, and walls should
   also be given similar protection during their first two days of
   settling and curing.

Table III: Optimum cement contents (mix ratios) for different soil types using the "Brepak" and "Cinva-Ram" presses in soil block production

Type of machine used in block production	Soil types	Mix ratio/% of cement content by volume	Bearing capacity N/mm²	Moisture absorption ratio	Shrinkage ratio	Remarks
"Brepak" block press NB: "Brepak" block press produces six(6) times more compaction force on a block than the "Civa-ram" press	a) Murram soil	1:24 or 4.2%	3.8	7.5	6.7	best blocks without cracks
	b) Red coffee soil	1:20 or 5%	3.9	9.3	8.8	good blocks with minor cracks
	c) Sandy soil	1:20 or 5%	4.2	8.2	7.5	very good blocks no cracks
	d) Clayish soil	1:20 or 5%	4.1	* – *	* – *	**some blocks disintegrate in water
	e) Black cotton soil	1:18 or 5.6%	4.1	9.2	16.4	too high shrinkage ratio and major cracks on blocks
"Cinva-Ram" block press	a) Murram Soil	1:11 or 9%	3.4	7.7	6.9	same as (a) above
	b) Red coffee soil	1:9 or 11%	3.6	9.5	9.1	" as (b) above
	c) Sandy soil	1:9 or 11%	3.9	8.4	7.8	" as (c) "
	d) Clayish soil	1:9 or 11%	3.8	* – *	* – *	" as (d) "
	e) Black cotton soil	1:8 or 12.5%	3.7	10.1	16.7	" as (e) "
	f) Lake sand	1:7 or 14%	6.7	7.6	6.6	too strong blocks

6.   Comparative Costs of Soil Products to Other Conventional Building
     Materials

The main reason for advocating the use of soil products in low-cost
housing projects is because of their cost effectiveness which cannot
be overlooked in this paper. As indicated in the introductory part,
the cost effectiveness of using earth products in house construction
would be most maximum when the following conditions apply:

- when good soils are readily available at or nearby the building
  site,
- when house owners participate in the production of the soil products
  and actual construction of their houses on self-help basis.

     The figures in Table IV are therefore based on **the above** two
conditions being applied and are for the 2nd half of 1982 Nairobi
area prices.

Table IV: Comparative Costs and Strength of Different Building Blocks

Type of block	Size in mm	Avg.bearing capacity, N/mm^2	Avg.cost per m^2, KShs.	Remarks
1.Mud(adobe)blocks	150x150x300	0.9	33.50	below min.b/c of $3N/mm^2$
2.Unstabilised machine made soil blocks	125x140x292	1.8	36.00	still below $3N/mm^2$
3.Stabilised "Cinva-Ram" made soil blocks	125x140x292	3.2	54.00	min. b/c attained
4.Stabilised "Brepak" made soil blocks	100x140x292	3.4	50.00	min. b/c attained
5.Interlocking burnt clay blocks	110x140x292	2.4	76.00	below min.b/c
6.Exaggerated standard burnt clay bricks	90x140x292	3.2	90.00	min. b/c attained
7.Standard burnt clay bricks	80x100x220	7.5	135.00	too strong blocks and walls
8.Concrete blocks	180x140x390	7 to 9	110.00	too strong blocks and walls
9.Building stone blocks	190x140x390	8 to 10	125.00	too strong blocks and walls

     From the above table, it is indicative that wall construction costs
can be reduced tremendously even more than half by sustituting the
conventional wall construction materials such as concrete blocks,
stone blocks,etc. with appropriate low-cost walling materials such as
stabilised soil blocks,etc. The conventional materials as indicated
above are too strong and costly and not appropriate for the low-cost
housing requirements. It should also be noted that though the first
two types of blocks in Table IV do not meet the minimum bearing

capacity for load bearing wall construction, they are actually being
used to build better houses structurally and appearance-wise especially in rural areas. They are the cheapest of all and as such,people
should be encouraged to use them with more quality control during
their production process to improve on their qualities without
introducing any stabilisers so as to keep their cost to the minimum.

7. Conclusion

It is apparent that of late, there has been growing concern by many
developing countries including Kenya to find cheaper solutions to the
problem of providing decent affordable shelter to their poor population. Several steps have already been taken by Kenya including the
review of its current restrictive building by-laws and planning
regulations to facilitate the utilisation of cheaper local building
materials in its low-cost housing projects and programme.

As indicated in Table IV, the use of appropriate cheaper local
building materials in low-cost housing projects is one of the key
solutions to the provision of adequate decent shelter to the poor.
However, the task of getting the concept accepted by the diffferent
groups involved in the implementation of such programmes is not light.
It calls for joint efforts from all the groups namely, the researchers,
the planners/designers, the policy and decision-makers, the developers
the financiers and the users to adopt a positive attitude towards
using such materials including earth products in low-cost housing
projects. This calls for intensified practical research projects
supplemented by the erection of demonstration structures to serve as
examples for all the groups to see and judge for themselves what such
materials can offer in terms of quality of products, durability,
comfort, cost effectiveness, etc., remember, "to see is to believe."
It also calls for much more financial inputs in research programmes
than what is currently being provided by most developing countries,
international bodies, private and professional firms to facilitate
such research projects to be carried out to their conclusions and
applicability stages.

8. References

1. Improved Stabilised Soil-Cement Blocks for Low Cost Wall Construction (interim report by J.K. Kateregga - HRDU & D. Webb - BRE);
2. Appropriate Technologies for Development, a Peace Corps
   Information Collection and Exchange, by Peter Gallant Dec. 1980;
3. Cost of Concrete Block Walls, by J. Eygelaar & G. Ochola - HRDU;
4. Habitat News No.3 Vol.3, Report on Mud;
5. Stabilised Soil Blocks; An Indian Technology Report;
6. BRE Overseas Building Notes 184;
7. Cinva-Ram Booklets and Brepak Manual;
8. Earth Wall Construction in Tanzania, by P. Moriarty;
9. The Sanufacture of Asphalt Emulsion Stabilised Soil Bricks,
   by The International Institute of Housing Technology.

A STUDY OF THE ACTIVITY OF A VOLCANIC POZZOLANA IN NORTHERN TANZANIA

W.J. ALLEN, Ove Arup and Partners, London
R.J.S. SPENCE, Cambridge University, Architecture Department

1. Introduction

In common with other developing regions, East Africa suffers from
shortage of Portland cement, and that which is available is often too
expensive for the individual builder. There is an urgent need to
develop and utilise whatever local resources are available to extend
existing output of cement, and make it more cheaply available.

Pozzolanic materials have the property of combining with lime in
the presence of water to form cementitious compounds; they can be
used either in conjunction with lime as pozzolime cements, or in
replacement of up to 30% of Portland cement in Portland-pozzolana
cements.

Pozzolanas are finely divided siliceous and aluminous materials
which can either be derived from naturally occurring materials such
as volcanic ash, or. artifically by grinding calcined clay or the ash
of agricultural wastes such as rice husk. The volcanic ash deposits
of the East African rift valley system are one widely available
source of pozzolanic materials which has already been used to a small
extent for building purposes, but which could be much more widely
exploited. In many places this ash is uncemented and easily accessible, and could be used for mixing with cement or lime with only very
limited processing and thus with great economy. One such deposit
lies on the western slopes of Mt. Meru in Northern Tanzania where a
small village industry to produce pozzolime and pozzolime building
blocks has been started with the assistance of the Tanzania Small
Industry Development Organisation and Oxfam. (1,2).

To develop the full potential of these volcanic pozzolanas, however, much more needs to be known about the physical processes and
material properties which affect the pozzolanas' performance as a
building material. This paper describes a study which was made of
the Meru volcanic ash deposits referred to, with the intention of
evaluating and understanding the variations in its pozzolanic
activity. It attempts first to explain the reasons for observed
variations in pozzolanic activity, and goes on to establish a
relationship between pozzolanic activity and geographical and topo-
graphical features of the deposit which could be used to locate the
most suitable materials for use in building.

2. *The measurement of activity*

Pozzolanic action is a chemically complex phenomenon, which can be
observed by chemical tests. However, it has been found that the
chemical tests are not reliable indicators of the performance of a
pozzolana as a building material, which is best measured by compressive strength tests. Alternative compressive strength tests have been
adopted as national standards in different countries, and Allen and
Spence (3) have proposed a variant on these, based on 25mm cubes,
which is suitable for rapid evaluation of a pozzolana in a field
survey. The cubes are moulded from a lime-pozzolana sand mortar,
and after a period of accelerated curing at 50°C, the cubes are
crushed at 7 days. The results of this test have been shown to
correlate very well with those of cubes cured at ambient temperatures
for a period of 63 days. The measurement of activity used in this
paper is the average strength value obtained from this test.

3. *The volcanic ash deposit and sampling*

The location of the W. Meru ash deposit studied is shown in Figure 1.
The ash consists of both vitreous and mineral fragments, is brown in
colour, and lies in beds of up to 20m depth. The bulk of it forms a
'terrace' at an altitude around 2000m to the North West of the
Western peak of Mt. Meru, and between the lower hills of Oldonyo
Sambu and Lengijawe to the NE and SW. A feature described in
geological reports as an old lake bed forms the central part of the
deposit; and as this was also the most accessible part, sampling
was concentrated here. The location of 11 initial sampling sites
S1-S11 are shown. At each of these locations a sample was taken from
approximately 2m below the surface (so as to avoid contamination with
vegetable matter). At sample site S6, in addition, a further 10
samples were taken to establish variation in activity and material
properties with depth.

4. *Material properties and pozzolanic activity*

The activity test results are given in Table 1 and 2 together with
surface area, sieve test analysis, chemical composition, and density
test results. In an attempt to identify the important determinants
of pozzolanic activity correlation coefficients between activity and
the various material properties have been calculated and are also
presented. The following conclusions can be drawn from this analysis:

(a) the sieve test analysis revealed that the ash has three component parts. The 1.18mm sieve retained fragments of a glassy grey
pumice while the 300 and 90 micron sieves retained a black prismatic
mineral. The predominant component is a finely divided, amorphous,
brown glass (the active ash fraction) which nearly all passed the 90
micron sieve. The coefficients of correlation between activity and
percentage passing the 90μm sieve are 0.70 and 0.92, demonstrating
the importance of this parameter.

(b) the surface area of the samples was determined by the Blaine
air permeability method (4), the results of which measure the exter-

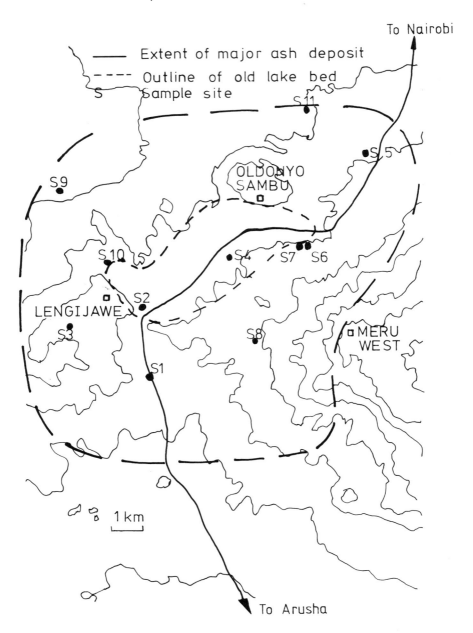

Fig 1   Extent of major ash deposit and sample site locations

TABLE 1: Properties of area distributed samples

Sample	Activity N/mm²	Surface Area cm²/gm	Sieve analysis (% passing)		Density gm/cm³	Chemical Analysis						
			1180 μm	90 μm		SiO_2	Al_2O_3	Fe_2O_3	MgO	CaO	Na_2O	K_2O
S1	4.47	5140	97.8	52.9	2.38	45.4	15.2	9.3	2.6	7.0	3.5	2.6
S2	4.77	6050	99.5	75.0	2.39	43.3	15.9	9.1	2.5	6.8	3.7	2.1
S3	4.41	5060	99.5	69.6	2.42	43.8	16.7	11.3	2.2	6.5	4.2	2.3
S4	5.31	5970	98.8	66.8	2.50	40.6	14.4	9.1	2.5	6.5	3.6	2.3
S5	4.31	4670	94.8	61.3	2.18	44.9	16.0	8.9	2.6	6.5	3.5	2.6
S6	4.67	5370	97.3	62.5	2.41	46.9	17.1	8.7	2.3	5.9	4.3	2.7
S7	4.94	4960	96.8	66.7	2.41	46.9	19.6	7.2	1.4	4.4	3.5	3.2
S8	3.75	4690	90.1	48.1	2.45	46.7	17.7	8.5	2.2	5.8	3.5	2.9
S9	2.32	4330	89.2	48.4	2.30	50.4	20.0	6.5	1.1	2.6	4.4	3.9
S10	6.40	6080	99.6	71.6	2.43	44.0	17.1	9.4	2.4	6.3	4.6	2.8
S11	3.60	1660	97.6	61.1	2.57	45.9	13.1	8.6	2.1	6.2	5.2	2.4
C_1		0.62		0.70	0.05	-0.70	0.20	0.47	0.53	0.58	-0.15	-0.47

C_1 = coefficient of correlation between activity and property indicated

nal surface of the material. The surface area is obviously closely
related to the ash fraction of the sample, although when the ash
fraction and surface area results were correlated together the coefficient was only 0.40. The correlation between surface area and
activity is much stronger (coefficients of 0.62 and 0.86) indicating
that surface area is not simply related to active fraction and has an
individual influence on pozzolanic activity.

(c) The proportions of the different chemical constituents were
found to correlate with activity across the area of deposition, but
these results can be attributed to the different chemical compositions
of the basic components of the pozzolana.

(d) The chemical composition shows identifiable correlations with
depth (Table 2). The soluble elements of the analysis, sodium, potassium, magnesium and calcium, have correlations consistent with redistribution by the passage of groundwater. The proportions of these
elements do not correlate with activity indicating that the observable
weathering effects have little influence on the reactivity of the
pozzolana.

(e) The density of the samples does not correlate with activity.
Density variations largely reflect pumice content.

5. *Material Properties and Topography*

In considering the available data it is helpful to take separate
account of the distributed samples (Table 1) and those indicating
variations with depth at S6 (Table 2).

The sieve test analysis results from the distributed samples give
an indication of the mineral, pumice, and ash fraction variation across
the area of deposition.

Those samples from the area of the old lake bed (S2, S4, S10 Figure
1) all have high active fractions while those at the extremes of the
deposit (S5, S8, S9, S11) have either high pumice or high mineral content. The indications are that the active fraction has been concentrated in what must have been a lacustrine environment, implying that the
ash has been transported and sorted by water action. The idea is
supported by the air permeability test results, those samples taken
from around the old lake bed having very high surface areas.

Photographic evidence was also consistent with the action of surface
water in redistributing the ash. Those sample locations around the old
lake bed are well sorted and show clear divisions between successive
sequences. Those deposits on the lower slopes at the mountain (S5, S9
and S11) are also associated with water courses and show evidence of
sorting. The one exception occurs at S8, high up on the slopes at Mt.
Meru, where ash and pumice are well mixed. This deposit is presumed
to be primary (air fall) material and close to its source, whereas
those lower down are created by the action of surface water removing
ash from the upper slopes to form secondary deposits.

As a result of the water deposition of the ash from the profile at
S6 (on the edge of the old lake bed), the ash fraction has become
separated from the other components of the pozzolana. By virtue of
its high surface area the ash settles slowly, preceded by the mineral
fragments, and followed by the vesiculated pumice, which tends to
float until saturated. The profile spans two sequences with the divid-

TABLE 2: Properties of samples from location S6 at varying depth

Sample Depth, D (m)	Activity (N/mm²)	Surface Area (cm²/gm)	Sieve analysis (% passing)		Density (gm/cm³)	Chemical Analysis						
			1180μm	90μm		SiO_2	Al_2O_3	Fe_2O_3	MgO	CaO	Na_2O	K_2O
0.5	4.51	3840	98.9	62.8	2.15	46.9	15.7	9.1	2.9	7.1	2.3	2.2
1.0	6.64	6055	98.0	66.2	2.26	47.9	17.1	8.9	2.8	6.7	2.3	2.5
1.5	6.70	6515	98.7	69.0	2.25	47.6	16.4	8.9	2.7	6.7	2.1	3.0
2.0	6.37	6940	99.1	67.8	2.45	44.6	16.6	10.0	3.2	7.5	3.2	2.4
2.5	7.46	6550	98.7	71.8	2.47	46.4	16.9	9.5	2.8	6.6	3.0	2.5
3.0	4.93	4925	97.4	59.1	2.40	46.6	17.0	9.2	2.7	6.4	3.9	2.8
3.5	4.38	5175	97.6	57.7	2.47	46.6	17.6	9.1	2.2	5.9	3.6	2.8
4.0	3.30	4470	96.4	57.3	2.46	47.2	17.6	8.5	2.0	5.9	4.2	3.1
4.5	4.87	4400	98.9	54.9	2.44	49.0	16.8	7.8	2.0	5.7	4.9	3.7
5.0	6.19	6310	92.1	53.7	2.35	46.2	15.5	8.2	2.3	7.3	4.4	3.1
5.5	8.39	6390	99.0	66.7	2.28	46.2	15.5	8.0	2.0	6.1	3.4	3.1
C1		0.86		0.92	-0.39	-0.02	-0.45	-0.04	0.23	0.31	-0.35	0.12
C2						0.28	-0.67	-0.51	-0.81	-0.82	0.95	0.79

C1 = Coefficient of correlation between activity and indicated property for restricted group excluding D = 0.5, 5.0, 5.5m.

C2 = Coefficient of correlation between chemical analysis and depth

ing line at a depth of 4.5m characterised by a pumice/mineral rich band.
Surface area results amplify the division and the chemical analysis
further emphasises the distinct nature of the sequences.

The evidence supporting the action of surface water in redistributing the ash is convincing. At its simplest, S8 provides an example of
primary, intermixed ash and pumice while S6 is typical of a reworked
well sorted deposit set down in a lacustrine environment. Other sample locations are intermediate between the two.

6.   *The Relationship Between Activity and Topography*

The most important property of the ash in relation to its activity was
found to be the proportion of active material contained within it and
to a lesser extent, its surface area. These properties, and hence
activity, can be expected to have a defined relationship with the
topography deriving from the mode of deposition of the ash. Areas
where a great deal of sorting has occurred should be repositories of
both highly active and relatively inert pozzolana. In other areas
activity should be a function of the degree of sorting, being intermediate between the primary deposits of S8 and samples from the
lacustrine environment of the old lake bed.

The variation of activity with depth should be particularly distinct with the top of the deposit showing reduced activity (high
pumice content, contamination), the middle band showing gradually decreasing activity with depth, reaching a low as mineral content increases to a maximum. Figure 2 shows the variation with depth of
activity for samples at S6. There is a clear sequence, with the top
of the deposit showing reduced activity (due to the reasons already
mentioned) the middle band showing gradually **decreasing** activity
with depth, reaching a low as (inactive) mineral content increases to
a maximum. A second ash sequence, marked by a rise in activity,
begins at a depth of 5m.

7.   *The selection of active pozzolana*

The pozzolanic activity of the ash in the deposit studied is related
both to its ash fraction and specific surface area as measured by an
air permeability test. From the nature of the deposition of the ash,
it has been shown that active pozzolana can be expected to be
associated with:

  i)   lower slopes of the mountain
 ii)   water courses or visibly lacustrine deposits
iii)   deposits showing thick distinct stratification
 iv)   strata having low pumice and mineral content

These characteristics may be used to locate active pozzolanas in
the field and provide a means to optimise the selection of raw materials for the building industry. In a second phase of the investigation, described elsewhere (5), the indicators of pozzolanic activity
were used to plan a search for active pozzolanas, from which material
with higher activity values than any located in the initial search
was located. The definite connection between activity and ash
fraction also provides a simple means of maintaining quality control
during manufacturing operations using ash pozzolana. The ash fraction

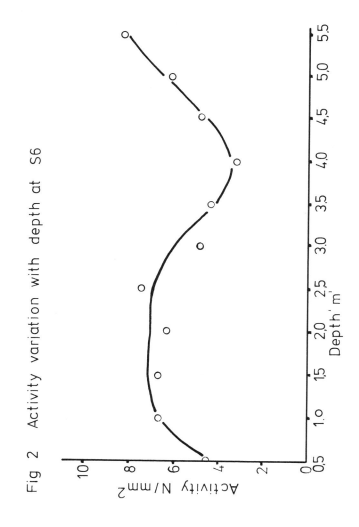

Fig 2   Activity variation with depth at   S6

is closely related to the proportion passing the 90-micron sieve, which could therefore be used for this purpose. A requirement that more than 65% of the sample should pass this sieve, for instance, would eliminate all samples in Tables 1 and 2 with activity values less than $4.4N/mm^2$.

Conclusion

Where volcanic ash deposits are widespread, water transportation, sorting and secondary deposition after initial deposition from air-fall are common phenomena. A precisely analagous process was observed during the 1982/83 eruption of the volcano Mt. Gulangung in Java (6). The results of this investigation, though relevant in detail only to the West Meru ash deposit, can be expected to be relevant to the investigation and selection of volcanic pozzolanas in other parts of East Africa and elsewhere in the world.

References

1. SPENCE R.J.S., and SAKULA J.H. "Lime-pozzolana as an alternative cementing material" in Appropriate Technology in Civil Engineering, Institution of Civil Engineers, 1981.

2. SAKULA J.H., and SAUNI J.T.M., "The SIDO lime-pozzolana project" in Nilsen (ed) Pozzolana and pumice as construction materials, Dept. of Geology, University of Dar es Salaam, 1979.

3. SPENCE R.J.S., and ALLEN W.J., (1981) "Simpler Tests for Lime Pozzolana" Building Research and Practice, May-June p. 180-189.

4. BLAINE R.L., (1943) "A Simplified Air-Permeability Apparatus" Bulletin of the American Society for Testing Materials No. 123, p. 51-55.

5. ALLEN W.J., and SPENCE R.J.S. "The Activity of a Volcanic Pozzolana" to be published.

6. Asian Building and Construction January 1983, pp. 23-25.

FABRICATION DE MATERIAUX DE CONSTRUCTION A PARTIR DE MATIERES PREMIERES ZAÏROISES PEU ONEREUSES

PAUL FIERENS, JOZEF ORSZÁGH, Université de Mons (Belgique)
LUHONDA MAKITU, SELANA MAMBU, SUDI ABDALA, Université de
Lubumbashi (Zaïre)

1. *Introduction*

La présente communication est relative aux premiers résultats des
recherches sur la fabrication de matériaux de construction à partir
de mélanges latérite-chaux qui constituent une partie d'un programme
plus vaste impliquant d'autres matières premières zaïroises abondantes
et peu onéreuses.

Ces recherches sont menées par des équipes belgo-zaïroises dans le
cadre du jumelage entre la Faculté Polytechnique de l'Université de
Lubumbashi au Zaïre et la Faculté des Sciences de l'Université de
Mons en Belgique. Cette coopération interuniversitaire est couverte
par un accord bilatéral entre les gouvernements belge et zaïrois.

T. RINGSHOLT (1) a réalisé une étude sur le développement d'un
matériau de construction obtenu par réaction hydrothermique, en-
dessous de 100°C, de mélanges latérite-chaux.

Le but de la recherche entreprise par les équipes belgo-zaïroises
est d'appliquer et d'optimaliser les intéressants résultats de ce
travail aux latérites de différentes régions du Zaïre. Il est étendu
à l'élaboration d'un projet de petites unités de fabrication industrielle mobilisant une main-d'oeuvre locale abondante en évitant
l'écueil d'une technologie automatisée non appropriée. Il comporte
également la mise au point d'un procédé de fabrication artisanale
susceptible d'être mis en oeuvre en milieu rural africain.

Les matériaux de construction qui seront issus des résultats de
cette recherche seront destinés non seulement aux zones urbaines mais
surtout à développer l'infrastructure et l'habitat des campagnes,
contribuant de cette manière à enrayer l'exode rural.

Le premier stade de la recherche rapporté ici constitue une étape
exploratoire effectuée sur des latérites de la région de Lubumbashi.

Les essais ont été effectués soit à la pression atmosphérique à
95°C, soit en autoclave aux températures de 110°C, 120°C et 130°C.

Les diverses mesures ont été effectuées dans les laboratoires de
l'Université de Lubumbashi et de l'Université de Mons.

2. *Etude à la pression atmosphérique*

2.1. Préparation des échantillons de latérite
La latérite utilisée dans cette partie de l'étude a été prélevée
aux environs immédiats de la Faculté Polytechnique à Lubumbashi.
Elle a été séchée à l'étuve jusqu'à poids constant, broyée et séparée
en fractions granulométriques (série standard de tamis Tyler).
    Les résultats de l'analyse granulométrique font l'objet du
tableau 1.

Tableau 1 - Analyse granulométrique de la
            latérite séchée et broyée

Fractions (mesh)	% Poids des fractions	% Poids des refus cumulés
20	0,46	0,46
24	0,31	0,77
28	0,92	1,69
32	1,04	2,73
35	3,04	5,77
42	2,96	8,73
48	7,52	16,25
65	13,08	29,33
80	10,78	40,11
100	10,78	50,89
115	10,90	61,79
150	1,04	62,83
170	8,24	71,07
250	10,32	81,39
325	11,00	92,39
400	5,00	97,39
>400	1,60	98,99

    Pour la poursuite des essais, trois échantillons de latérite
ont été sélectionnés.

    A - latérite broyée non tamisée.
    B - fractions passantes du tamis 150 mesh et le refus du tamis
250 mesh. La dimension moyenne des particules retenues dans cet
échantillon est d'environ 84 microns.
    C - fractions comprises entre les tamis de 250 et de 400 mesh.
La dimension moyenne des particules est d'environ 51 microns.

2.2. Caractérisation des échantillons de latérite
La perte au feu a été déterminée par chauffage des échantillons à
1100°C pendant 1 heure.
    Pour les dosages chimiques, les échantillons ont été soumis à une
attaque alcaline. SiO_2 insoluble a été déterminé par gravimétrie
tandis que SiO_2 soluble, Fe et Al (exprimés respectivement en termes
de Fe_2O_3 et de Al_2O_3) ont été dosés par colorimétrie.

Tableau 2 - Analyse chimique quantitative et surface spécifique

Echantillon	Perte au feu (%)	SiO_2 (%)	Fe_2O_3 (%)	Al_2O_3 (%)	Surface spécifique (m^2/g)
A	10,8	58,1	11,9	19,0	33,1
B	13,2	50,5	13,8	22,5	44,7
C	13,9	46,3	13,9	25,8	45,4

La surface spécifique des échantillons de latérite a été mesurée par la méthode mise au point à l'Université de Mons (2). Les résultats sont rapportés dans le tableau 2.

2.3. Préparation des éprouvettes

Les éprouvettes ont été confectionnées en mélangeant les échantillons de latérite A, B ou C, de la chaux chimiquement pure et de l'eau distillée[*] dans les proportions requises.

La latérite et la chaux ont été mélangées à sec, pendant 30 minutes, dans un mélangeur du type Turbula T2C.

La quantité d'eau de gâchage du mélange sec a été fixée pour toutes les éprouvettes au rapport pondéral :

$$\frac{eau}{solide} = 0,22$$

La pâte homogène obtenue a été moulée sous une pression de 600 Kg/cm^2. Les éprouvettes crues cylindriques présentent les caractéristiques suivantes : poids = environ 24 g., diamètre : 2,05 cm, hauteur : 3,70 cm.

2.4. Détermination de la teneur optimale en chaux

Dans cette série d'essais, toutes les éprouvettes ont été chauffées, dans une atmosphère saturée de vapeur d'eau, à 95°C pendant 24 heures. Après ce traitement, on a mesuré la résistance à la compression des éprouvettes cuites, à l'aide d'une presse du type AMSLER graduée par 5 Kg. Le tableau 3 résume les résultats.

2.5. Effet de la variation de la durée de cuisson

Les données du tableau 4 sont relatives à des résultats obtenus avec des éprouvettes de l'échantillon de latérite A titrant 16 % de $Ca(OH)_2$. Elles montrent l'influence de la durée de cuisson sur les résistances à la compression. Cette relation est illustrée par la figure 1.

---

[*] Pour certains essais on a utilisé de l'eau de pluie sans influence notable sur les résultats.

Tableau 3 - Résistance à la compression et taux de réaction de la
chaux en fonction de la teneur en chaux de l'éprouvette
crue. Traitement : 95°C pendant 24 heures.

% $Ca(OH)_2$ éprouvette crue	Résistance à la compression (Kg/cm^2)			Taux de réaction de la chaux (%)		
	A	B	C	A	B	C
12	102	115	108	14,0	21,6	15,0
13	120	124	–	16,3	24,6	–
14	131	139	133	16,7	26,9	19,8
15	135	148	–	20,7	29,5	–
16	143	150	154	24,0	31,2	32,0
17	133	153	159	21,4	36,3	36,4
18	128	169	158	17,8	41,0	25,7
19	103	176	148	16,8	46,0	19,4
20	94	180	148	12,6	48,4	16,7
21	–	176	–	–	37,6	–
22	–	172	127	–	32,6	13,7
24	–	152	108	–	28,3	10,0
26	–	140	–	–	24,8	–

Tableau 4 - Résistance à la compression et taux de
réaction de la chaux en fonction de la
durée de cuisson. Echantillon A -
16 % $Ca(OH)_2$

Durée de cuisson (jours)	Résistance à la compression (Kg/cm^2)	Taux de réaction de la chaux (%)
1	143	24,0
2	149	27,5
3	175	37,0
4	203	44,0
5	217	47,5
6	221	48,3
7	228	49,4

2.6. Taux de réaction de la chaux pendant la cuisson
La teneur en chaux non transformée a été dosée dans les différentes
éprouvettes soumises à la cuisson.
   Le mode opératoire suivant a été mis au point.
   Une prise de 100 mg de l'éprouvette cuite réduite en poudre est
placée en contact avec 50 ml d'éthylèneglycol. On chauffe en agitant
pendant 30 minutes entre 65 et 70°C. On ajoute 25 ml de HC1 (0.1 N).
On chauffe 5 minutes. Après refroidissement (15 minutes) on filtre
et on lave le résidu sur le filtre à l'alcool absolu. On titre

l'excès de HCl par NaOH (0.05 N) en présence de l'indicateur constitué par un mélange de 0,1 g de phénolphtaléine et de 0,15 g
d'α-naphtol dans 100 ml d'alcool absolu.

Le taux de réaction de la chaux τ est défini par la relation :

$$\tau = \frac{Q_o - Q_1}{Q_o}$$

où Q_o est la quantité de chaux dans l'éprouvette crue,
Q_1 est la quantité de chaux dans l'éprouvette cuite.
Ces déterminations ont été faites sur des éprouvettes contenant les
échantillons de latérite A, B ou C et des teneurs variables en chaux,
cuites pendant 24 heures à 95°C, dans une atmosphère saturée en
vapeur d'eau (cf. paragraphe 2.4.). Les résultats sont reproduits
dans le tableau 3.

Elles ont également été effectuées sur des éprouvettes contenant
l'échantillon de latérite A et 16 % de Ca(OH)$_2$, cuites dans les
mêmes conditions pendant des durées variables (cf. paragraphe 2.5.).
Les résultats font l'objet du tableau 3 et de la figure 1.

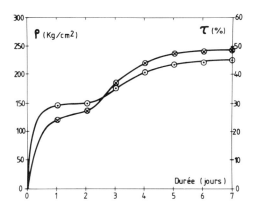

Fig. 1 - Résistance à la compression (ρ) ⊙ et taux
de réaction de la chaux (τ) ⊗ en fonction
de la durée de cuisson - Echantillon de
latérite A, 16 % Ca(OH)$_2$, 95°C.

3. *Etude à l'autoclave*

3.1. Préparation des échantillons de latérite
Trois prélèvements différents de latérite de la région de
Lubumbashi ont été recueillis. Ils ont subi le même traitement
que celui mentionné au paragraphe 2.1. On obtient respectivement
les échantillons I, II et III.

Tableau 5 - Analyse granulométrique des échantillons de
latérite séchés et broyés I, II, III

Fractions (mesh)	I		II		III	
	% Poids des frac- tions	% Poids des refus cumulés	% Poids des frac- tions	% Poids des refus cumulés	% Poids des frac- tions	% Poids des refus cumulés
20	12,4	12,4	7,12	7,12	7,92	7,92
24	1,3	13,7	0,69	7,81	1,14	9,06
32	3,8	17,5	2,50	10,31	1,56	10,62
48	16,2	33,7	5,63	15,94	3,13	13,75
65	31,3	65,0	8,75	24,69	8,75	22,50
80	11,2	76,2	9,68	34,37	9,37	31,87
100	3,8	80,0	9,69	44,06	12,19	44,06
115	3,6	83,8	9,38	53,44	8,44	52,50
170	2,5	86,1	20,93	74,37	17,50	70,00
325	2,0	88,1	8,44	82,81	11,25	81,25
>325	11,9	100,0	16,35	99,16	18,31	99,56

On remarque que la broyabilité de l'échantillon I est inférieure
à celle des échantillons II et III.
Pour les essais à l'autoclave, on a retenu, pour chaque échan-
tillon I, II et III, les fractions passantes du tamis 32 mesh.
On définit ainsi, respectivement, les échantillons de latérite C,
D et F.

3.2. Caractérisation des échantillons de latérite : analyse
chimique quantitative
Les analyses chimiques quantitatives ont été réalisées par spectro-
photométrie d'absorption atomique et ont donné les résultats
rassemblés dans le tableau 6.

Tableau 6 - Analyse chimique quantitative

Elément	Echantillon		
(%)	D	E	F
SiO_2	49,66	49,00	49,61
Fe total	3,25	4,30	3,60
Al_2O_3	17,40	17,00	16,40
CaO	0,04	< 0,01	< 0,01
MgO	0,35	0,38	0,33

3.3. Préparation des éprouvettes

Les éprouvettes ont été préparées selon la méthode exposée au paragraphe 2.3. Elles ont toutes la même composition pondérale suivante : latérite 74 %, chaux 16 %, eau 10 %.

3.4. Effet de la variation de la durée de cuisson et de la température

Les éprouvettes ont été cuites à l'autoclave à 110°C, 120°C ou 130°C, dans une atmosphère saturée en vapeur d'eau, pendant des durées variables. Les résultats font l'objet du tableau 7.

Tableau 7 - Résistance à la compression (Kg/cm^2) en fonction de la durée de cuisson et de la température

Durée de cuisson (heures)	110°C	120°C			130°C
	D	D	E	F	D
1	87	141	138	130	145
2	94	143	142	132	153
3	104	144	148	136	179
4	113	155	170	145	198
5	124	172	194	170	219
6	137	197	220	203	242
7	150	231	240	227	270
8	167	263	250	242	280

3.5. Taux de réaction de la chaux pendant la cuisson

La méthode de dosage de la chaux des éprouvettes cuites est celle décrite au paragraphe 2.6.

Les mesures ont été effectuées sur des éprouvettes contenant l'échantillon de latérite D ayant subi une cuisson faite dans les mêmes conditions qu'au paragraphe précédent. Les résultats se trouvent dans le tableau 8.

Tableau 8 - Résistance à la compression et taux de
         réaction de la chaux en fonction de la
         durée de cuisson et de la température -
         Echantillon D.

Durée de cuisson (heures)	Résistance à la compression (Kg/cm^2)			Taux de réaction de la chaux (%)		
	110°C	120°C	130°C	110°C	120°C	130°C
1	108	136	147	25,9	30,9	37,6
2	114	142	153	27,2	32,4	38,9
3	124	150	168	29,7	35,6	42,3
5	167	191	203	38,1	45,0	49,3

La comparaison de ces résultats avec ceux relatifs à l'échantillon D du tableau 7 donne une idée de l'erreur commise lors de
la mesure de la résistance à la compression d'éprouvettes ayant
subi, en principe, le même traitement au cours d'essais indépendants.

4. *Discussion des résultats*

L'ensemble des déterminations rapportées dans ce travail appelle les
commentaires suivants.

Les données des tableaux 3, 4 et 8 ont été reportées dans le
graphique de la figure 2 en exprimant le taux de réaction de la
chaux en fonction de la résistance à la compression. L'examen de
ce graphique montre, en dépit d'une certaine dispersion, qu'il
existe indéniablement une relation entre ces deux grandeurs. Notons
qu'aucun résultat n'a été écarté et que les 49 points sont relatifs
à des éprouvettes de compositions diverses préparées avec des
échantillons de latérites différentes, cuites à des températures
variées pendant des durées plus ou moins longues, à des pressions
inégales. La grande variété des conditions expérimentales confère
au graphique de la figure 2 un caractère assez remarquable.

Remarquons que lorsque les conditions expérimentales mettent en
jeu moins de variables la dispersion est plus faible. On constate
même que, pour les résultats du tableau 8, les deux grandeurs sont
à peu près proportionnelles. Dans ce cas particulier il est possible
de définir une vitesse réactionnelle et, sur la base des résultats
expérimentaux, de calculer l'énergie d'activation apparente
(8,7 Kcal mole^{-1}) approximative. Toujours dans le même cas
particulier, les données du tableau 7 relatives à l'échantillon D,
compte tenu de la proportionalité entre le taux de réaction de la
chaux et la résistance à la compression, permettent de déceler
l'existence d'au moins deux étapes réactionnelles successives. La
première semble conduire à un équilibre après une durée de l'ordre
de deux heures. La seconde démarre ensuite mais développe une
vitesse plus faible. La position de l'équilibre étant fonction de

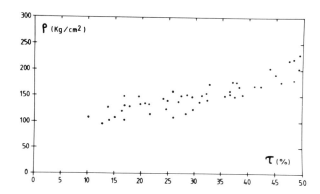

Fig. 2 - Relation entre le taux de réaction de
la chaux (τ) et la résistance à la
compression (ρ)

la température, il est possible d'estimer l'enthalpie de la première
étape à partir des données expérimentales. On trouve $\Delta H = 9,1$ Kcal
$mole^{-1}$ ce qui correspond à une réaction légèrement endothermique,
donnée importante pour le calcul du bilan énergétique d'étuvage pour
une application industrielle à envisager. Au stade actuel de la
recherche, l'énergie d'activation apparente et de l'enthalpie calculées ne peuvent pas faire l'objet d'une interprétation fondamentale.
Le raisonnement développé succintement à propos du cas particulier
a pour but, entre autres, de montrer les possibilités d'une étude
plus élaborée et plus complète.

L'examen du tableau 3 indique que pour les éprouvettes contenant
les trois échantillons de latérite A, B et C, la variation de la
résistance à la compression en fonction de la teneur en chaux des
éprouvettes crues n'est pas une fonction croissante et monotone ;
elle présente un maximum variable selon la nature de l'échantillon
de latérite : 16 % de $Ca(OH)_2$ pour A, 20 % pour B, 17 % pour C.
Cette remarque met en évidence l'influence de la granulométrie
(paragraphe 2.1.), de la surface spécifique (tableau 2) et de la
composition chimique (tableau 2) des échantillons de latérite, ainsi
que la nécessité d'optimaliser les conditions de travail en passant
d'une latérite à l'autre. Les mêmes conclusions peuvent être tirées
de l'examen des données relatives au taux de réaction de la chaux
(tableau 3).

Les tableaux 4, 7 et 8 montrent que la réaction globale latérite-
chaux-eau progresse en fonction du temps et comporte - comme dit plus
haut - au moins deux étapes, l'une rapide débouchant sur un palier,
l'autre plus lente tendant également vers un palier. A titre
d'exemple, la figure 1, relative à des cuissons à 95°C, illustre bien
ces faits. Il serait évidemment intéressant de prolonger la durée

de cuisson,RINGSHOLT ayant mis en évidence une nouvelle accélération
pour des temps plus longs.

En ce qui concerne la nature des différentes étapes de la
réaction globale, il est difficile de conclure à ce stade précoce
de la recherche. Cependant, les spectres de diffraction de rayons X,
pris sur des éprouvettes crues et sur des éprouvettes cuites, montrent
la disparition et l'apparition progressives de raies, dont bon
nombre sont non identifiées pour le moment, au cours des diverses
étapes de la réaction globale. Il est de peu d'utilité de reproduire
ces spectres dans la présente communication. Cet aspect de l'étude
sera évidemment poussé ultérieurement.

5. *Conclusions*

Dès à présent, on retiendra de cette étude exploratoire sur des
latérites de la région de Lubumbashi que même à pression atmosphérique, à 95°C, le niveau des résistances à la compression obtenues
est très satisfaisant, comparé à celui des briques d'argile cuites
actuellement à Lubumbashi (15 - 25 Kg/cm^2) et des briques ordinaires
importées (60 - 80 Kg/cm^2).

Ces premiers résultats incitent à poursuivre, à étendre et à
approfondir l'étude.

Bibliographie

1. T. RINGSHOLT, J. Am. Cer. Soc., 57, 510-518 (1978).
2. F. CAMBIER, P. FIERENS, G. LAMBIN, Silicates Industriels, 39,
    21-26 (1974).

CONSTRUCTIONS EN TERRE STABILISEE EN COTE D'IVOIRE
BILAN ET PERSPECTIVES

ABRAHAM OUATTARA LBTP (COTE D'IVOIRE)
SIMONNET JACQUES LBTP (COTE D'IVOIRE)

1. Introduction

L'emploi de la terre stabilisée (géobéton) a fait l'objet depuis une dizaine d'années d'études et de réalisations concrètes en Côte d'Ivoire.

Sous l'impulsion de divers organismes dont le LBTP (laboratoire du bâtiment et des travaux publics), le PNUD, l'AVB (Autorité pour l'aménagement de la vallée du Bandama), les F.R.A.R. (Fonds régionaux pour l'aménagement rural) et à l'initiative de certains cadres, plusieurs centaines de bâtiments ont été construits.

Bien entendu l'introduction du géobéton s'est heurtée aux problèmes inhérents à toute innovation dans le domaine du bâtiment :

- absence de normes
- préjugés contre le matériau
- main d'oeuvre non formée à son emploi
- difficultés de trouver des presses pour sa mise en oeuvre
  etc...

Après les tâtonnements des premières années on peut estimer que le géobéton est entré maintenant dans une phase opérationnelle.

Deux orientations semblent se dégager nettement pour son emploi en Côte d'Ivoire :

- les constructions rurales dans le Nord du pays, là où le coût du ciment est le plus élevé.
- les constructions à vocation touristique pour lesquelles on recherche l'originalité et une bonne intégration dans le site.

Bien que certaines actions restent à entreprendre pour en développer l'usage, il a semblé utile de retracer les différentes étapes de la politique de promotion du géobéton, à laquelle a participé activement le LBTP au cours des dix dernières années.

2. Principales étapes de la politique de promotion du géobéton en Côte d'Ivoire au cours des dix dernières années.

2.1 Origine des interventions du LBTP.

L'origine de ces interventions se situe dans le courant de l'année 1973. L'AVB qui était assistée par une mission PNUD, se trouvait engagée dans un vaste programme de relogement des populations expropriées par suite de la construction du barrage de KOSSOU.

Après le relogement des personnes "déguerpies", s'est posé le problème de l'amélioration de l'habitat dans les villages non inondés, qui avaient échappé de ce fait à l'opération de reconstruction et de modernisation entreprise par l'AVB.

Les villageois disposant de ressources très modestes, le PNUD a créé à leur intention une cellule d'aide à l'autoconstruction (ACA).

Le responsable de ce projet, Mr BOUJASSON avait antérieurement réalisé au SENEGAL un programme de logements économiques en terre stabilisée.

Il a pensé que ce matériau pouvait être introduit en Côte d'Ivoire dans la région du Centre et permettre des économies sur le coût des constructions.

Afin de connaître les ressources et les caractéristiques des matériaux disponibles dans la région de KOSSOU, la cellule ACA du PNUD s'est appuyée sur le LBTP pour les raisons suivantes :

- tout d'abord le LBTP avait acquis depuis sa création, en 1953, une bonne expérience de la prospection des graveleux latéritiques pour la construction des routes. Or ce matériau semblait bien adapté à la confection de blocs pour la construction.

- il disposait ensuite de personnel qualifié et de moyens d'essais.

- enfin ses interventions recouvraient l'ensemble du territoire ivoirien, et notamment le Centre Bandama, à partir de son laboratoire régional de BOUAKE.

2.2 Première étape:Recherches en Laboratoire

La réalisation d'un programme d'essai sur la terre stabilisée nécessitait la mise en place d'un financement. Celui-ci a été assuré par le PNUD sous la forme de contrats annuels passés avec le LBTP.

Ces contrats prévoyaient notamment la construction d'un petit laboratoire spécialisé dans les problèmes de la terre au sein du laboratoire régional de BOUAKE, la prise en charge d'un ingénieur expert et du personnel chargé de la prospection et des essais.

Ce personnel était également à la disposition de la cellule ACA afin de prospecter et de contrôler les matériaux dans le cadre des opérations menées sur le terrain par le PNUD.

Au cours de la période 1974-1979 le LBTP à réalisé tout d'abord à BOUAKE, puis au laboratoire central d'ABIDJAN, un programme très complet d'essais sur la terre stabilisée.

Les résultats de ces essais ont été présentés au Séminaire Régional sur l'amélioration de l'habitat spontané en 1979 à Lomé (Togo) (1).

Ils ont permis de connaître parfaitement l'influence, sur les propriétés mécaniques et la durabilité des blocs, de divers paramètres tels que :

- les caractéristiques géotechniques de la terre
- le dosage en ciment
- le dosage en eau
- le degré de compactage

Les travaux ont porté également sur les mortiers de montage, les protections des murs, les moyens de compactage.

Des essais de compression en vraie grandeur ont été réalisés de façon à définir les coefficients de sécurité à adopter pour les constructions en terre stabilisée.

Enfin une étude économique est venue compléter ces travaux permettant ainsi de préciser sous quelles conditions il était avantageux de remplacer le parpaing de ciment par le géobéton.

2.3 Deuxième étape:constructions pilotes
Parallèlement aux études de laboratoire, la cellule ACA entreprenait des actions d'auto-construction dans la région du Centre avec l'appui technique du LBTP.

L'introduction de la terre stabilisée dans la construction s'avérait en fait plus difficile que prévu.

L'aspect du matériau était loin en effet de faire l'unanimité chez les villageois. Ils ne voyaient pas de différence entre ce matériau et le "banco" qu'ils employaient auparavant pour l'érection des cases.

Pour eux la terre signifiait un retour au passé qu'ils rejetaient par opposition au modernisme que symbolisait le parpaing de ciment synonyme de construction en "dur".

C'est dans le but d'améliorer l'image de marque de la terre stabilisée, en suggérant l'idée qu'il s'agissait d'un produit nouveau,résistant et durable, qu'est venue l'idée d'employer le terme "géobéton"

Plus concrètement, au niveau des réalisations dans les villages, la promotion du matériau a été réalisée suivant différentes voies.

Dans le village de KOSSOU II les maisons comprenaient une aile en parpaingsde ciment et une aile en géobéton.

Au village d'AKA N'GUESSANKRO là aussi,une technique mixte a été employée à la demande des villageois. La moitié inférieure des constructions jusqu'à 1 m du sol était constituée de parpaings de ciment et la moitié supérieure était en géobéton.

Dans certains villages ce sont les latrines et les douches qui étaient construites en géobéton.

Pour d'autres, l'emploi du matériau était limité aux bâtiments communautaires (écoles ou lieux de réunion).

Enfin le siège du projet PNUD-AVB à YAMOUSSOUKRO comportant plusieurs bâtiments à usage de bureaux a été entièrement réalisé en géobéton.
Finalement, malgré les efforts d'imagination déployés par le personnel de la cellule ACA et la qualité des prestations fournies, on peut dire que l'introduction du géobéton dans la région du Centre de la Côte d'Ivoire s'est soldée par un échec relatif.

Les préjugés de la population à l'encontre du matériau n'ont pu être
entièrement surmontés.

A l'origine de ce demi-échec on trouve, à notre avis, les raisons
suivantes :

Tout d'abord un sentiment de frustration provoqué par le fait que
la reconstruction des 70 premiers villages inondés a été réalisée par
l'AVB en parpaings ciment et non en géobéton. Ce sentiment a été ren-
forcé par la proximité des deux zones urbaines de YAMOUSSOUKRO et de
BOUAKE dont les habitations servaient en quelque sorte de modèle de
référence pour les villageois.

Enfin l'étude économique du LBTP et l'expérience acquise sur les
chantiers ACA ont montré qu'il fallait un prix du ciment élevé, découlant d'une distance de transport importante, pour que le géobéton apporte des économies conséquentes dans les constructions. Ces
conditions ne se rencontraient que dans le NORD du pays.

Compte tenu de cette analyse, définissant d'un point de vue économique le Nord du pays comme une "zone cible" pour le géobéton, le
LBTP a entrepris la construction avec ce matériau de son antenne régionale à KORHOGO.

Cette opération pilote visait à suggérer aux populations que la
terre stabilisée constituait un produit de qualité puisqu'elle était
utilisée par un établissement contrôlé par l'Etat.

D'autre part, le LBTP étant un lieu accessible au public, ses responsables pouvaient apporter des renseignements, voir un appui technique aux personnes intéressées par le géobéton.

Contrairement à ce qui s'était passé dans le centre du pays, l'opération a reçu un accueil très favorable de la population, le personnel du LBTP s'est trouvé assez rapidement débordé par les demandes
d'assistance formulées par des artisans ou des particuliers.

Les causes de ce succès tiennent à plusieurs raisons :
. La région Nord est caractérisée par la survivance d'une très longue
  tradition en matière de construction en terre dont témoignent particulièrement certains monuments vieux de plusieurs siècles, tels
  que les mosquées de KONG et de KAUARA.
. Le climat de la zone Nord, de type Sud→Soudanien, conduit à des
  écarts entre les températures diurnes et nocturnes plus importants
que dans le reste du pays.
. Le géobéton qui confère aux murs une plus grande inertie thermique
  que le parpaing de ciment semble apporter aux constructions un meilleur confort thermique dans cette zone climatique.
. Enfin comme il est montré au paragraphe 3 l'économie apportée par le
  géobéton dans la zone Nord est loin d'être négligeable comme dans
  la zone Centre.

2.4 Troisième étape : Normalisation
Si l'opération pilote menée par le LBTP dans le Nord du pays a sans
nul doute atteint son objectif, elle a montré également ses limites.
En effet, malgré l'intérêt manifesté par les populations et certaines
entreprises pour le géobéton, son utilisation continuait de se heurter
avec juste raison aux réticences des différents organismes intervenant dans le processus de la construction, du fait de l'absence de
normes relatives à son emploi.

C'est dans le but de lever cet obstacle que le LBTP a entrepris en 1980 l'élaboration d'une Recommandation sur l'emploi du géobéton (2). Ce document visait à faire la synthèse des résultats obtenus au laboratoire et des enseignements apportés par les opérations pilotes.

Il ne s'agit pas à proprement parler d'un document de vulgarisation mais plutôt d'un ouvrage de référence destiné aux architectes, bureaux d'études, bureaux de contrôle, services de la Construction, etc.., leur permettant de rédiger des cahiers des charges, de calculer et d'assurer le contrôle de bâtiments construits en terre stabilisée.

Sans entrer dans le détail de cette Recommandation qui a été présentée en 1981 au séminaire Régional sur l'habitat spontané et l'habitat économique à YAOUNDE (CAMEROUN), on peut toutefois rappeler les principales dispositions constructives préconisées pour la Côte d'Ivoire.

Ces dispositions sont valables pour des bâtiments en rez-de-chaussée.

Matériau de base :
> graveleux latéritique ou sable argileux
- % d'éléments fins < 0,08 mm de 15 à 30 %
- diamètre maximal des plus gros éléments < 20 mm
- produit F x Ip compris entre 250 et 900
  (avec F pourcentage d'éléments fins et Ip indice de plasticité).

Epaisseur des murs : 14 cm (blocs confectionnés à la presse CINVA-RAM)

Dosage en ciment :
- 5 % en poids pour les murs en parties courantes
- et 10 % en fondations et soubassements jusqu'à 20 cm au-dessus du sol.

Résistances en compression à 28 jours :
- blocs en parties courantes, 25 bars (conservation dans l'air)
  12 bars (conservation 24 jours dans l'air et 4 jours dans l'eau)
- blocs pour fondations 50 bars et 25 bars dans les mêmes conditions. (1 bar = 0,1MPa)

Coefficient global de sécurité à prendre dans les calculs :
> Coefficient 12 sur résistance après conservation à l'eau.
> (ceci autorise un taux de travail de 1 bar dans les murs, valeur largement suffisante pour supporter un toit en tôle).

Montage et protection des murs :
> Les murs sont montés sans enduit extérieur. Le mortier de montage est dosé à 200 kg de ciment/m^3 et l'étanchéité des joint assurée par un mortier de rejointoiement de 2 cm d'épaisseur dosé à 400 kg de ciment/m^3. De plus, un lait de ciment mélangé de terre ou d'oxyde de fer constituant une barbotine, est badigeonnée sur les murs pour améliorer leur durabilité. La barbotine, d'épaisseur très faible, permet aussi de rattraper les imperfections dans l'aspect des blocs.

Chaînages :

> Les chaînages verticaux sont à éviter. Un chaînage léger en
> béton à la partie supérieure des murs sert à répartir le
> poids de la couverture et surtout à améliorer sa résistance
> aux efforts d'arrachement dus au vent. Il sert également de
> "linteau filant" pour les ouvertures.

Ces dispositions constructives donnent des parements dont l'aspect est
très proche de celui obtenu avec les briques de terre cuite. La durabilité semble aussi bonne que celle procurée par des parpaings creux
de ciment recouverts d'un enduit.

Ajoutons que les façades ne nécessitent pratiquement aucun entretien. Tout au plus peut-on envisager le passage d'une nouvelle couche
de barbotine tous les sept ou huit ans. Les bureaux du LBTP à BOUAKE
construits en 1978 avec cette technique ne montrent aucune dégradation
en 1983. Des murets expérimentaux similaires, réalisés à DAKAR en
1953 par le CEBTP, étaient parfaitement conservés 10 ans après leur
construction.

2.5 Quatrième étape : phase opérationnelle
On peut dire que depuis 1982 le géobéton est entré en Côte d'Ivoire
dans une phase opérationnelle.
Cette phase est caractérisée par le fait que les initiatives privées
ont maintenant relayé celles des organismes nationaux ou interna-
tionaux seuls concernés initialement par le développement de cette
technique.

C'est ainsi que certains Cadres Ivoiriens, ont entrepris des opérations de rénovation de leur village d'origine dans le Nord du pays,
en employant le géobéton, avec ou sans l'appui du Laboratoire.

Les actions menées par le LBTP tiennent compte de ces nouvelles
données et s'orientent de manière à faciliter la mise en oeuvre de
telles initiatives.

Il s'agit maintenant de lever les derniers obstacles techniques ou
administratifs qui freinent encore le développement du géobéton.

Les blocages techniques tiennent à deux facteurs principaux :
- le manque de maçons familiarisés avec le matériau
- la qualité médiocre des presses disponibles sur le marché ivoirien pour la confection des blocs.

En ce qui concerne le premier facteur, le LBTP appuyé par le syndicat
des Entrepreneurs a pris contact avec l'ONFP, (office national de
formation professionnelle) pour que soit dispensée aux maçons sortant
de cet organisme, une formation complémentaire sur la terre stabilisée.

Pour résoudre le problème des presses à géobéton, le Laboratoire a
élaboré un cahier des charges définissant des spécifications pour la
mise au point d'une presse manuelle économique et performante.

L'étude de la conception de cette presse a été confiée à l'IPNET
(Institut pédagogique national d'enseignement technique).

La dimension des blocs a été fixée comme suit :
- hauteur : 13 cm
- largeur : 14 cm
- longueur : 29 cm

La pression finale de compactage sera au moins égale à 1,5 MPa.

Le poids du bloc devrait être voisin de 12 kg, valeur proche du poids d'un parpaing creux de ciment de 15 x 20 x 40 cm. L'augmentation de la dimension des blocs par rapport à ceux confectionnés à la presse CINVA-RAM permet des gains de temps à la fabrication et au montage, (moins de blocs au m^2 de mur) ainsi qu'une diminution de la quantité de mortier de pose (gain de ciment).

En dehors des problèmes techniques qui viennent d'être soulevés, il reste à vaincre certaines réticences d'ordre administratif dues principalement à un manque d'information.

A cet effet, avec l'accord de ses deux ministères de tutelle, le LBTP a prévu de donner en 1983, trois conférences dans des villes de la zone Nord, dans le but de sensibiliser les autorités politiques et administratives locales, à l'intérêt présenté par le géobéton dans cette région.

3. *Conclusions*

Les problèmes rencontrés pour l'introduction de la terre stabilisée en Côte d'Ivoire sont à notre avis exemplaires de ceux posés par la mise en oeuvre d'un nouveau matériau de construction dans un pays en voie de développement.

On peut en tirer les enseignements suivants :

- tout d'abord le matériau choisi doit apporter une économie réelle dans la construction. Une étude technico-économique préalable nécessitant généralement un financement est donc essentielle.

- le choix du matériau doit tenir compte du contexte culturel, historique, socio-économique, climatique et du niveau technologique acceptable.

- il est nécessaire ensuite de réaliser des constructions pilotes, de façon à vérifier la faisabilité de la technique et d'affiner l'analyse économique. Le choix d'une construction pilote doit être guidé par le fait que le nouveau matériau ne doit pas être imposé pour éviter un phénomène de "rejet". Le bâtiment doit pouvoir être vu par un grand nombre de personnes et être accessible au public. L'idée de construire en géobéton un laboratoire dans la zone Nord de la Côte d'Ivoire s'est avérée de ce fait judicieuse.

- dès que la technique est parfaitement au point, il convient d'élaborer un document à caractère officiel définissant parfaitement les modalités d'emploi du produit.

- la dernière phase qui est celle du développement du matériau, nécessite la mise en place d'une politique de formation du personnel, d'approvisionnement en matériel spécifique et de sensibilisation des divers intervenants dans la construction.

Comme on le voit, l'introduction d'un nouveau matériau nécessite des moyens importants additionnés d'une certaine dose d'enthousiasme et de ténacité.

A titre d'exemple on estime que dans un pays industrialisé comme la France, il faut de trois à huit ans pour qu'une innovation effectue une réelle percée dans le secteur du bâtiment...

Pour revenir au cas de la Côte d'Ivoire, il ne faut pas considérer que le géobéton puisse apporter une solution générale aux problèmes de l'habitat. D'autres solutions faisant appel à l'industrialisation de la construction sont en cours d'étude pour les zones urbaines.

Il s'agit plutôt d'un matériau d'intérêt régional, pour lequel l'étude économique donnée dans la Recommandation (2), avait montré que l'on pouvait escompter une réduction des coûts de l'ordre de 5 % par rapport à une construction classique en parpaings de ciment.

La solution géobéton permet en gros de diviser par deux la consommation de ciment au prix d'un doublement des heures de main-d'oeuvre.

Depuis 1979 date à laquelle cette étude avait été faite, le coût du ciment est passé de 16 800 FCFA la tonne départ ABIDJAN à plus de 35 000 FCFA en mars 1983, soit une augmentation de 100 % environ.

Dans le même temps le salaire d'un ouvrier spécialisé augmentait de 21 % passant de 207 FCFA à 251 FCFA de l'heure (1 FCFA = 0,02 FF).

Ces chiffres permettent d'envisager maintenant des économies globales de 7 à 10 % avec la solution géobéton dans la zone Nord. Une nouvelle réduction des coûts est envisagée lorsque seront mises au point les presses étudiées par l'IPNET pour la confection de blocs de 13 x 14 x 29 cm.

Bibliographie

1. Simonnet et Serey, Emploi du béton de terre (géobéton) pour la construction économique en Côte d'Ivoire. Annales ITBTP n° 386 Septembre 1980.

2. LBTP (Côte d'Ivoire), Recommandation pour la conception et l'exécution de bâtiments économiques en géobéton.

SECTION II

Ciments, chaux, pouzzolane, briques, béton

Cement, lime, pozzolana, bricks, concrete

REINFORCEMENT OF CONCRETE BEAMS WITH LOW-MODULUS MATERIALS IN FORM OF TWINES

B.L.M. MWAMILA, Department of Building Engineering,
The Royal Institute of Technology, Stockholm, Sweden

1. *Introduction*

The lack of adequate tensile strength in concrete is what makes the
tensile reinforcement of concrete a necessary condition even when no
more than only incidental tensile stresses are expected. The reinforcement employed is defined by two main mechanical properties,
namely, the modulus of elasticity and its tensile strength. In addition to these two, the stress–strain characteristics of the reinforcement up to failure point and the amount employed for a given cross
section, are decisive with regard to the performance behaviour and
failure mode. The fact that steel has the monopoly as the sole reinforcement material may tempt one to overlook the significance of the
modulus of elasticity of the reinforcement phase in general.

Since concrete has negligible exploitable tensile strength, in
flexural and tensile members the necessary provision is required
right from commencement of loading. For economical and practical con-
venience there is desire to keep the amount of reinforcement as low as
possible. This desire is apparently only satisfied by a material of
higher modulus of elasticity than that of the concrete matrix.

A higher E-modulus reinforcement material is capable of providing
added stiffness to the composite with the result that the cracking
strength is raised. Upon cracking, the effect of the high reinforcement modulus overshadows the weakening effect of cracking, thus producing a smoother change in the composite stiffness. The gradual
change results in the occurrence of small and closely spaced cracks.

Ultimate strength and the occurrence of failure are mainly governed
by the stress–strain characteristics and the ultimate strength of both
the reinforcement and the matrix materials. Adequacy with respect to
amount is also an important factor. For steel the amount of reinforcement employed determines the eventual mode of failure. Thus, we
have the categories, over- and under-reinforcement.

In this paper a proposal is being advanced to the effect that materials with E-modulus less than even that of the concrete be employed
as reinforcement for concrete matrix. One reason behind the proposal
is the fact that among countries of the third world, the dominant reinforcement material, steel, is becoming too expensive to afford and
too difficult to acquire for all construction purposes. The other is

the abundance of natural fibres, which can be spun into twines, in many countries of the world. These natural fibres have low E-modulus, of the order of that of concrete and much less when spun into twines. If, in these countries, the importation of steel for construction purposes could be limited to amounts needed by only that class of buildings whose structural demand is more than what locally available materials can offer, a significant relief of economic strains and frustrations would ensue.

2. *Behaviour of elements reinforced with sisal twines*

2.1 Properties of the reinforcement material

The primary reinforcement material chosen for this study is sisal in the form of single-strand twines of approximate mean equivalent diameter of 1.6 mm. The twines have an average ultimate tensile strength of 265 N/mm^2 under room conditions ($20^{\circ}C$ and about 50% r.h.). The E-modulus and the corresponding ultimate strain are around 7 GN/m^2 and 4% respectively. It should be mentioned here that increase in number of strands in the twine yield inferior properties because of the resulting bundle effect, as illustrated in table 1. The stress-strain curves for both the single fibre and the single-strand twine are straight to the point of ultimate failure, signifying their perfect elasticity. The curves for double- and subsequently higher-strand twines depict a series of peaks and troughs corresponding to discrete failures of the individual strands. Thus, it is indicated that the strands don't effectively act in unison and hence, the choice of the single-strand twines for this study.

When acted upon by repeated load the occurrence of residual strain at zero load and slight reduction in the ultimate strain are evident. The residual strains diminish in magnitude with increasing number of load cycles and by amounts dependent on the peak load. This response is quite typical except for the relatively high magnitudes of the residual strains, a characteristic attributable to a tendency, by individual fibres, to slip over each other. This tendency, however, enhances the grip between the fibres which in turn improves the twines E-modulus, see figure 1.

Table 1. Tensile Strength of Twines

Equivalent twine diameter, ϕ (mm)	Ultimate tensile strength f_t (N/mm^2)	Ultimate tensile strain e_t (%)	Modulus of Elasticity E_t (kN/mm^2)
0.19 (single fibre)	≥ 400	2-3	≥ 26
1.6 (single-strand)	265	4.2	7.1
2.3 (double-strand)	230	5.4	4.4
2.8 (treble-strand)	217	6.1	4.2

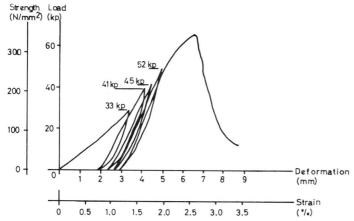

Fig. 1.   Load-deformation relationships for the single-strand twine
          partially submitted to slow repetitions.

2.2 Behaviour of reinforced beams under static load
Beam specimens of dimensions 100 x 130 x 800 mm have been used in the
studies of the performance properties of concrete reinforced by twines. The mix employed was 1:2:0,5 (cement:sand(max 2,0mm):water) and
the amount of twines used in the main study was 2% of the gross section area. A few specimens were also made for the purpose of establishing the effect of varying the amount of reinforcement to include
0,5 and 1,0%. Control specimens in form of cubes and beams have also
been tested.
     For the loaded specimens the occurrence of cracks is usually sudden
and the propagation rapid. By the time failure occurs only two or
three primary cracks have formed with an average spacing of about 10
cm between them.
     Before the occurrence of the first crack the strength-deflection
curve is linear with a relatively steep slope corresponding to the
high flexural stiffness (EI) of the uncracked element. The appearance of the wide and deep first crack greatly reduces the average
flexural stiffness. As the crack grows further the twine in the open
crack and close vicinity gain strength through increased local
strains. Thus the strength-deflection curve gradually rises. A point
is reached at which the strength offered by the twines at the critical
section exceeds that offered by a potential second crack region and a
second crack occurs followed by another drop in the strength-deflection curve. The process repeats itself until when the demand of twine
strength, at the critical section, required to create a new potential
crack is so high that either the twine begins to yield or the resulting crack propagation leads to the yielding of the matrix in the compression zone. As this is incipient the strength-deflection begins
to flatten, as is evident in figure 2.

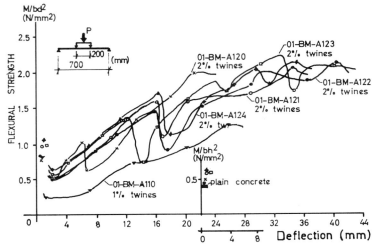

Fig. 2.   Strength-deflection relationships for specimens reinforced
with twines only.

The strength capacity of the element is governed by those of the critical sections. It therefore varies depending on which stage of the
strength-deflection curve the element has reached. Right from incipience of a crack, the strength capacity is governed by the section of
potential crack. It has been observed that the maximum capacity before occurrence of the first crack is slightly higher than that of
corresponding plain specimens, fig. 2. The minimum strength capacity
following the occurrence of the first crack is about 0,5 to 0,6 of
the maximum precracked strength. Corresponding ratios for subsequent
cracks tend to be higher depending on their actual positions in the
strength-deflection curve. This results from the relative decrease
in increase of the peak values as the matrix in compression starts
yielding. The maximum strength capacity is above 2 times the maximum
precrack strength.

     Failure of the elements has mainly been observed to occur through
matrix failure by crushing, wedging off or buckling of the shallow
compression zone. To a less extent the twine has also been observed
to just start yielding. Wedging-off and buckling of the compression
matrix have often been preceded by the formation of horizontal and/or
inclined extensions to existing main cracks.

2.3 Behaviour of reinforced beams under repeated and sustained loads
The performance properties for repeated loading have been studied by
submitting beam specimens to six slow load cycles, at constant load
amplitude, after initial cracking had occurred. The magnitude of
this peak load, 550 kp, was arbitrarily chosen to approximately equal
the cracking load of corresponding plain concrete specimens. From
the tests, in additional to the usual strength-deflection relationships, crack width variations with the number of cycles were noted

and are shown in table 2. As is evident from the table, there is significant residual width and deformation upon load release. Upon subsequent reloading the strength-deflection curves are less steep and as a result the load repetitions yield the famous hysterisis loops. The resulting relative increases in residual crack widths and deflections at zero load diminish as the number of cycles increases.

Table 2. Growth of crack width as slow load cycles are administered - specimen 01-BM-B126

Crack width (mm)	Peak	Residual	Increase upon loading	$\dfrac{\text{Residual in } n^{th} \text{ cycle}}{\text{Residual in first cycle}}$
Cycle 1	5.00	3.95	1.05	1.00
Cycle 2	5.35	4.35	1.00	1.10
Cycle 3	5.45	4.50	0.95	1.14
Cycle 4	5.65	4.70	0.95	1.19
Cycle 5	5.85	4.85	1.00	1.23
Cycle 6	5.90	4.95	0.95	1.25

As the loading continued beyond the cycling stage, normal response resumed. Further cracking, increase in strength and further deflection occurred. The eventual extend of cracking was not quite different from that observed for specimens subject to static load. There was, however, an apparent drop in the ultimate strength and a slight amputation of the ultimate deflection. These deteriorations were a result of the fatigue suffered by the twines and culminated in the modification of the mode of failure of the specimens to one by rapture of the twines.

The effect of the test of time on the crack width, midspan deflection and surface strains, has been studied by submitting pre-cracked specimens to constant load of magnitude of 500 kp. Surface strains on the compression surface directly above the crack were obtained with aid of "foil" strain gauges with gauge lengths of 60 mm. Changes in the deflections and crack widths were obtained by direct measurements between properly marked points and the floor surface and between tack pins securely glued on the opposite sides of each crack. Figures 3 to 5 show the results of these measurements with respect to time. It will be seen that the effects of the sustained load on the different measured parameters for approximately hygral equilibrium are very similar to those normally observed for conventionally reinforced concrete. But in this case in additional to creep of the concrete there are the very high creep strains of the twines, and whose effects are additive. Since the twines are hygroscopic, marked variation in the atmospheric conditions, especially that of humidity, induced increased creep both in the twines and the concrete, which are reflected in the form of indentations on the otherwise smooth curves. An increase in relative humidity from about 35% to about 70% for 2 weeks yielded the indentations shown in the diagrams.

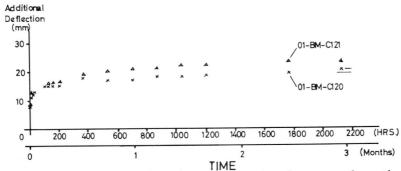

Fig. 3. Additional deflection against time for up to 3 months.

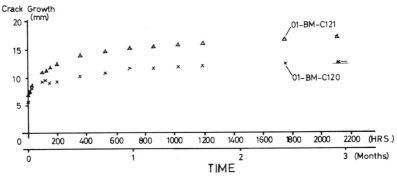

Fig. 4. Crack growth against time for up to 3 months.

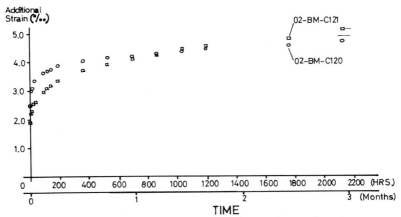

Fig. 5. Additional compressive strain against time for up to 3
months.

2.4 The deficiency

As indicated earlier deficiencies in the performance of elements reinforced with the twines exist and they affect both the short and the
long term performances. In conventional reinforced concrete, for
example, 0,3 mm is about the limit of acceptability of crack widths.
Though not for exactly the same reasons, for similar reasons bigger
cracks are not desirable even for the case in question. Such cracks
give room for biological attack, among others.

One of the most serious deficiencies lies with the fact that big
strength capacity losses accompany the occurrence of each crack.
This characteristic makes it difficult to define the safe strength of
an element. It also makes the knowledge of the ultimate strength
relatively unimportant.

The ultimate deflection and the ductility of the member are un-
questionably high. So, although it has been pointed out that failure
occurs by crushing of the matrix, it does so at a stage when all symp-
toms of imminent failure have long appeared.

The susceptibility of the twine material to moisture conditions, of
the atmosphere, and the effects on performance behaviour, are some of
the other undesirable features, especially in the light of the existence of wide cracks.

To enable favourable consideration of this mode of reinforcement,
for practical use, adaptations are necessary to minimise some of these
deficiencies.

3. *Adaptation techniques*

3.1 Theory

It is today quite well established that concrete is not as brittle as
it was earlier thought to be. It is, actually, proved that concrete
has significant tension toughness. On a cracked beam the effects of
tension toughness are in the areas between the tips of the visible
cracks and the neutral axis. The effects are a result of the action
of aggregate interlock and the bridging action of the aggregate across
the crack behind the visible crack tip. Tension toughness effect is
only transitional and quickly diminishes to zero in the absence of reinforcement, so that in a plain beam once imminent failure cannot be
prevented by it. In reinforced concrete, however, the effect of tension toughness has very significant values, especially in cases where
the safety and performance of a structure depend on the ability of the
concrete to take tension stresses. One such case is when the reinforcement is of low modulus of elasticity. In this case the action
of the concrete between the crack tip and the neutral axis helps to
bring about a smoother transition to a stage where the reinforcement
is fully mobilised to take stresses earlier carried by the matrix.
In figure 6 the effect of tension toughness is illustrated.

In a reinforced concrete beam with one or more flexural cracks,
the matrix in the tension zone of the uncracked regions is under tension so that the tensile stresses carried by the reinforcement in
these regions are lower than those at the cracked sections. This way
the average flexural stiffness of the beam element is higher than the
corresponding value at the cracked section. This stiffening effect

of tension carried by concrete between cracks is of great significance in cases where the difference between the maximum and the cracking moments is not considerable, as it is for the case in question.
The magnitude of the tension stiffening effect depends on the extent
of mobilization of the matrix between the cracks, through bond, to
carry the tensile stresses; or what is the same the extent of reinforcement stress relief in the region of the uncracked concrete between the cracks. The tension stiffening effect is also illustrated
in figure 6.

Before cracking the tensile stresses at the level of the reinforcement are shared between the matrix and the reinforcement in the ratio of their E-modulus. The significance of the total contribution
of the reinforcement before cracking is governed by the magnitude of
the modular ratio, $E_{reinf.}/E_{matr.}$. Considering the strain magnitudes
before matrix cracking, the corresponding reinforcement stress levels
are very low. Upon cracking, across the crack, the reinforcement
remains the main tension carrier, supplemented by the transitional
effect of tension toughness. The immediate stresses in the reinforcement when the crack forms are still very low. It has to increase
many times before the original strength at incipience of cracking
can be restored. It is thus, at this stage that the tension toughness
effect is of utmost importance. As the reinforcement tensile strength
at the crack increases, the combined effect of tension toughness (to
diminishing degrees) and tension stiffness become the supplementary
component of the flexural resistance mechanism.

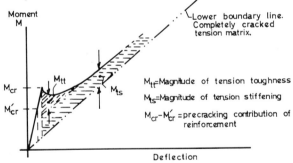

Fig. 6.   Illustration of the effects of tension toughness (M_{tt}) and
tension stiffness (M_{ts}).

3.2 Adaptation
In the light of the foregoing discussion, the ideal way of eliminating
the deficiencies inherent with the reinforcement of concrete using low
modulus materials, demands a combination of matrix modification and
modification of the reinforcement technique and may be increase in the
amount of reinforcement. Modification of the matrix should be geared
towards improving tension toughness of the matrix while modification
of the reinforcement technique is aimed at enhancing the tension
stiffening effect of the uncracked portions of the matrix. Increase
in the amount of reinforcement on the other hand, is a direct substi-

tution of the effects of high E-modulus by increasing the cross section area of the reinforcement to yield the same force at a given strain, i.e. $E_1A_1 = E_2A_2$ so that $E_1E_2 = A_2A_1$.

Practically, however, there are limitations regarding the extent of modifications or amount of reinforcement that can be accommodated. On the other hand there are many possibilities of acquiring the same or similar results.

As mentioned above, it is principally the action of the aggregate in the concrete that is responsible for the tension toughness it possesses. Incorporation of short fibres will definitely, through the inherent sliding friction as they pull out, improve the composite tension toughness. The extent of improvement is, however, governed by the type, length and texture of the fibres among others. In this study, fibres of the type of the primary reinforcement have been chosen. The introduction of reinforcement of high E-modulus in the area between the neutral axis and the primary reinforcement will not only supplement but greatly complement the tension toughness effect offered by the aggregates. Because of the high modulus a kind of "pinch-in" effect on the cracks will result. This way, they act as supplementary reinforcement to the low modulus primary reinforcement.

Tension stiffening effect is mainly governed by the ability on the part of the main reinforcement to induce tensile stresses into the uncracked matrix. Improved bond characteristics will lead to improved tension stiffening effect. The use of secondary reinforcement in form of fibres, can also improve the effect through the resulting redistribution of stresses into and within the matrix. Tension stiffening effect can also be improved by use of supplementary reinforcement applied between the primary reinforcement and the neutral axis. The establishment of new fronts at which transfer of stresses from the reinforcement to the matrix occur may well lead to improved tension stiffening effects.

Finally, it is possible to adopt the solution demanding direct increase in the amount of reinforcement employed. In such case the demand in space is so high that the beam section has to be modified. The introduction of a flange enclosing the reinforcement, in the tension zone, is one possibility.

3.3 Some experimental results

In adoption of the solution of incorporating short fibres, fibres of the same material as the primary reinforcement have been opted for the same reasons favouring the use of the natural material, sisal. The length of the fibres has been maintained at around 35 mm, while the amount incorporated, in volume percentage, has been 1,0% and 2,7%. The water-cement ratio of the matrix has been 0.60. Figure 7 shows some of the results of the effort. In tests whose results are shown in the diagram, the amount of the primary reinforcement was varied so that specimens 02-BM-A111 and -A117 had 0,5%bh, specimens 02-BM-A110 and -116 had 1,0%bh and specimens 02-BM-A120 and -A121 had 2,0% bh. The fibre content in specimen 02-BM-A130 was 2,7% by volume while the twine content was 2,0%bh. Looking at figure 7 in the light of the preceding discussions and figure 2 it is clear that the ability of the short fibres to seal the strength deficiencies mentioned earlier is quite significant. The minimum strength capacity following first crack is now above 0.85 of the maximum precrack strength.

Figure 8 shows a first attempt to verify the suitability of the solution employing small quantities of high E-modulus materials as supplementary reinforcement. It is evident that the strength deficiencies and cracks are sealed and also the initial cracking and ultimate strengths are significantly improved.

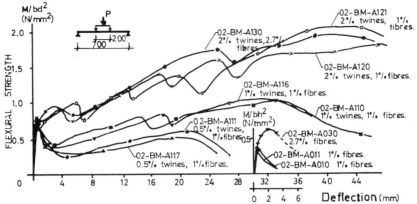

Fig. 7.   Strength-deflection relationships for specimens with twines and fibres.

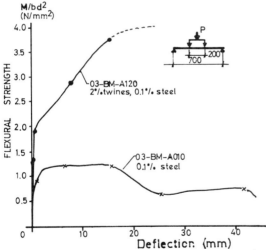

Fig. 8.   Strength-deflection relationships indicating the combined effect of twines and steel.

4.   *Conclusion*

The paper suggests that it is possible to partially and wholly substitute steel as a reinforcement of concrete. Studies are required to establish the possibilities and practice.

POZZOLANA CEMENTS FOR LOW COST HOUSING

A A HAMMOND, Head, Materials Division, Building and Road Research
Institute (Council for Scientific and Industrial Research), Kumasi

1. *Introduction*

The need for establishment of building materials industry in developing countries has long been recognised by the United Nations and
many world bodies. The United Nations, in particular, through many
of her organizations has advocated for development of building
materials industry as part of her economic development programme for
the developing countries. In 1965, a General Assembly resolution
recommended that developing country governments should take all
necessary measures to develop a building materials industry by
utilising local raw materials to the maximum (1). Later, at the
International Symposium for Industrial Development held in Athens in
1967, it was recommended that developing countries should, where
appropriate, give high priority to the development of building
materials industries in order to achieve a greater efficiency in
their construction activities (2). Since then various meetings and
conferences have adopted many resolutions and recommendations dealing
with the great need for improvement in the construction industry and
in the building materials industry subsector.
    The most recent International Conferences at which important
decisions regarding the construction and building materials industries were taken include the United Nations Conference on Human
Settlement held in Vancouver in May and June, 1976, the Fourth
Conference of Ministers of E.C.A. held in Kinshasa in February, 1977
and the Fourth Conference of African Ministers of Industry held in
Kaduna, Nigeria, in November, 1977. In pursuance of these recommendations and resolutions, E.C.A. in co-operation with UNIDO, UNCHS and
O.A.U. initiated a multi-phased programme for the development of
building materials and construction industries in Africa (3).
    Many African countries have enthusiastically adopted this pro-
gramme and have established or are in the process of establishing
building materials industries. Their main problem, however, has
always been in the choice of which material industry to establish and
what level of technology to adopt. Linking the development of a
building materials industry, therefore, with the construction of
improved and affordable low-cost housing in this symposium the
organizers have helped to throw more light on the problem.
    Apart from lime, Portland Cement is virtually the only cementi-
tious product used in Africa for construction, and as it has a high

foreign exchange content, it is obvious that any local substitute
that will bring savings in foreign exchange will be welcome.
Pozzolana cement is such a material.

2. *Historical background*

Many centuries ago, the ancient Greeks and Romans knew that certain
volcanic deposits, if finely ground and mixed with lime and sand,
yielded a mortar which had superior strength and good resistance to
water. The Greeks used the volcanic tuff from the island of Thera,
known as Santorin Earth, and the Romans used the red or purple
volcanic tuff found at different points on and near the Bay of Naples
for this purpose.
    As the best variety of this earth was obtained from the neighbour-
hood of Pozzuoli (in Latin Puteoli) the material acquired the name
pozzolana, a general term covering similar materials of volcanic
origin found at other deposits in Italy, Greece, Germany, France and
Spain. Later the term was employed throughout Europe to designate
any material, regardless of its geologic origin, which possessed
similar properties. At present, however, it is variously called
puzzolana, pozzolan, puzzuolana and pozzolana. The term pozzolana is
adopted throughout this paper, (4-8).
    The purpose of this paper is to discuss the properties and types of
pozzolana and their cements, their manufacture and uses in construction, thereby showing their usefulness in utilizing them for low-
cost housing.

3. *Definition*

In 1938, Lea, defined pozzolanic materials as silicious materials
which, though not cementitious in themselves, contain constituents
which at ordinary temperatures will combine with lime in the presence
of water to form compounds which have a low solubility and possess
cementing properties.

3.1 The ASTM standard on cement (1971), designation 618-71 also
states that pozzolana shall be a siliceous or siliceous aluminous
materials, which in itself may possess little or no cementitious
value, but will, in finely divided form and in the presence of
moisture, chemically react with calcium hydroxide at ordinary temperatures to form compounds possessing cementitious properties.

3.2 In 1956, Srinivasan (10) proposed a modification of Lea's
definition as a result of an extensive work carried out on laterite
and other red soils thus:- "a pozzolana is a siliceous, aluminous or
ferrugenous material, which by itself is not cementitious, but which
under certain states of crystallinity and structure, could react with
lime in the presence of moisture at normal temperature and pressure,
to yield cementitious products". Srinivasan's modification includes
ferrugenous materials. It also takes into consideration the mineralogical and crystallographic conditions of the oxides and pressure at

which the reaction should take place. This definition makes it possible to include laterites and other red and yellow soils which have been known to possess pozzolanic properties.

3.3 The first two definitions which have been universally accepted, however, make no references to the structural condition of the material but to its ability to combine with lime (calcium hydroxide), in the presence of water, to form compounds of cementitious proper- ties. Pozzolanic activity, therefore, depends on the fixative property of the material in respect of calcium hydroxide and its ability to harden under water as a consequence of the changes the above reaction produces. These characteristics may be separate, and it may happen that while large quantities of lime are fixed by the material having pozzolanic activity the accompanying cementitious properties are quite moderate. Malquori, (11) in 1960, therefore, suggested that materials having pozzolanic activity should be defined, in respect of their use, as cementitious materials, quite apart from the interpretation of the chemical and physico-chemical phenomena which are responsible for the hardening of the hydraulic binder.

4. *Classification*

Pozzolanas are grouped under two main classes - natural and artifi- cial. Though the natural and artificial materials have similar pozzolanic activity they differ greatly from one another in origin, chemical composition and mineralogical constitution.

4.1 Natural pozzolanas may further be divided into two main groups:

  (a) There are those derived from volcanic rocks in which the amorphous constituent is glass produced by fusion. These are, for example, volcanic ashes and tuffs, pumice, scoria and absidian.
  (b) The others are derived from rocks or earth for which the silica constituent contains opal, either from precipitation of silica from solution or from the remains of organisms. Example of these are diatomaceous earths; cherts, opaline silica, lava contain- ing substantial amount of glassy component and clay which have been naturally calcined by heat from a flowing lava. Table 1 summarises types, sources and areas where these materials abound (9, 11, 12).

  In Africa, natural pozzolans of volcanic origin may be found in Cameroon, Ethiopia, Tanzania and most probably in Kenya and other places in East Africa.

4.2 The most important artificial pozzolanic materials are "fly ash" or pulverised fuel ash (P.F.A.), burnt clays and shales, spent oil shales, burnt gaize, burnt moler, burnt bauxite, rice husk ash, and granulated blast furnace slag.
  Fly ash is a most widely used artificial pozzolana in U.S.A. and Britain under numerous commercial names. It is a residue from the combustion of solid pulverized fuels in big thermo electric power plants. Its essentially vitreous physical state and low alkali

Table 1. Origin and location of some natural pozzolanas

Type of pozzolana	Origin	Where found
Phlegraean, pyroclastic and alkalitrachytic	Volcanic	Near Naples (Bacoli, Baia and Pozzuoli)
Roman, pyroclastic and leucitic	Volcanic	Near Naples
Santorin Earth, pyroclastic of granular isotropic material mixed with pumic, obsidian, pyrozones, fragment of crystalline, feldspar, quartz, etc.	Volcanic	Grecian isle of Santorin
Rhenish "trass" pyroclastic, alkalitrachytic, zeolitic and metamorphic	Volcanic (Tufaceous rock)	Eifel quarries, Notte and Brohl Valleys close to Neuwied and Andernach.
Tosca, alkalitrachytic, light yellow and compact (Metamorphic)	Volcanic (Tufaceous rock, Ash)	Teneriffe - Canary Islands
Trass, pyroclastic, auto-metamorphic or alteration by hydrothermal or pneumatolytic action	Volcanic (Tufaceous rock)	Bavaria
Tetin	Volcanic Ash	Azores, Japan and New Zealand
Danish "Moler" pyroclastic, amorphous silica	Volcanic (Tufaceous rock)	Holland
French "gaize and tripel" pyroclastic of amorphous silica		Briansk (France)
Romanic "trass" pyroclastic of amorphous silica	Volcanic (Tufaceous rock)	Rumania
Crimea "trass" pyroclastic of amorphous silica	Volcanic Liparitic tuff	Karadagh (Crimea)
Diatomaceous earth (Kieselguhr, infusorial earth), white resembles chalk.	Silicious Skeletons of diatoms	California (U.S.A. Canada, Algeria, Denmark, Germany.

content makes it a useful pozzolana material, provided it contains
admissible amounts of unburnt carbon matter. Where coal is used as
fuel for industrial purposes the ash can profitably be used as
pozzolana.

Burnt clays and shales have been used as pozzolana for a long time.
The Romans had used ground clay bricks and tiles as substitutes where
there was no natural pozzolana. Additions of ground burnt clay,
bricks and tiles to lime have also been extensively used as pozzolana
in India and Egypt where they are respectively known locally as surhki
and homra (6, 10, 13). Practically, there are clays everywhere in
Africa which could be used if they are suitable. The oil-spent
shales in Nigeria, Gabon and Ivory Coast could also be used in
producing pozzolana.

Burnt bauxite is known to make an excellent pozzolana but it
appears the use of this material for the manufacture of aluminium
out-weighs its use for producing pozzolana particularly in those
countries where clays, shales, fly ash and rice husk are readily
available as substitutes. In Ghana, extensive work has been done on
conversion of bauxite-waste to pozzolana (14).

Another source of pozzolana is rice husk. When rice husk is burnt
at appropriate temperature the ash that comes out of the burning is
predominantly silica which reacts with lime to form cementitious
products. In those African countries such as Liberia, Gambia,
Senegal and Ghana where rice is grown the husk can be used in manufacturing rice husk ash pozzolana,

Table 2. Percentage composition of some pozzolans

Pozzolana	Si_2O	Al_2O_3	Fe_2O_3	CaO	MgO	Na_2O & K_2O	SO_3	Ignition Loss
Burnt Clay	62.8	17.2	7.6	2.3	2.5	4.5	2.7	1.7
Spent Oil Shale	52.0	22.2	11.2	4.4	1.2	3.6	2.3	3.0
Diatomite (burnt)	72.0	14.5	8.2	1.5	2.2	3.2	-	7.8
Fly ash	44.8	18.4	11.2	11.6	1.1	3.1	2.0	8.0
Rice husk ash	85.6	2.5	0.3	1.0	1.0	2.5	1.5	-
Burnt bauxite-waste	14.4	48.9	30.0	0.2	0.13	1.2	-	3.8
Santorin earth	65.2	13.0	5.5	3.6	2.0	6.8	-	4.0
Rhenish trass	54.7	16.8	4.1	2.8	1.4	9.0	0.3	9.0
Pumicite	72.3	13.3	1.4	0.5	0.6	7.6	-	4.2

5. *Pozzolana activity*

The most important active chemical ingredients of pozzolanas are silica and alumina as shown in Table 2. It can be observed that although there are differences in origin, composition, constitution and structure of both natural and artificial pozzolanas, they all react with lime in the presence of water to form compounds with cementitious properties. In assessing the ability of a pozzolanic material to react with lime, it is essential to consider its chemical bonds and its physical state.

Silica and alumina are, in effect, vulnerable to calcium hydroxide when their structural bonds are weak and unstable in the original material, as is the case with volcanic glass, in the zeolitic structure deriving from their alteration. The same applies to clay materials when, through total dehydration by heat treatment, the bonds between silica and alumina are relaxed or annihilated. If, instead, Si, Al, and O are bound in the lattices of the individual minerals formed by crystallization of the magma, or in those of the silico-aluminous materials when constitute natural clays, the calcium hydroxide acts far more slowly or not at all.

In case of cementitious action, the parts played by silica and alumina cannot be considered separately since there are silicious materials with very little or no alumina which have high and rapid lime fixing properties but with poor hardening and strength proper-ties when made into mortars or concrete (10, 11, 12).

In fact, Murakami in 1952, observed that the presence of reactive alumina considerably enhances the strength properties of pozzolanic cements, particularly during brief curing. Little is known about the effect of minor components such as iron and alkali on the activity of pozzolana. Iron oxides however are known to lower calcining tempera-ture of artificial pozzolanas (11 & 12).

In 1960, Malquori (11) showed that the zeolitic structures that are found in the examined volcanic tuff - chabazite, herchellite, analcite and phillipsite are attacked more quickly by calcium hydroxide than are the real glassy pozzolanas. These zeolites have high capacity for lime fixation and good cementitious properties.

This observation confirms what Lea (9) has asserted for some time, that the pozzolanic activity of "trass" is not correlated with its ability for base exchange. It is, therefore, the zeolitic structure and its instability that make the zeolitized material more reactive to lime than the glassy pozzolanas (11).

Again, Lea (9), describes the work of Baire, Sestini and Santereli and Malquori, all of whom studied variations in the combined acid-alkali attack and concluded that the determination of soluble SiO_2 and R_2O_3 has some value in comparing materials of the same type, but does not indicate the quality of pozzolanas as a whole.

6. *The evaluation of pozzolanic activity*

Since by definition pozzolanic materials must have the ability to combine with lime to form cementitious compounds, to measure these properties, it is desirable for these actions to take place as rapidly

and intensely as possible. Unfortunately, there are as yet no satisfactory tests for predicting either the ability of the material to
fix calcium hydroxide or the ability to form cementitious binder.

6.1 Many attempts made to assess the value of pozzolanas by the
solubility of their content in acid or alkali solution have all
failed to give results that showed correlation between solubility and
strength developed by pozzolana in lime or concrete. It means that
in evaluating pozzolana both properties of the strength and lime
fixation of the material should be considered separately. This
requirement means determining under standard conditions the mechanical strength of the mortars of concrete and the extent to which free
calcium hydroxide is reduced. These tests must be practical and
quickly performed to give results for acceptance or rejection of the
pozzolanic material (11).

The evaluation of the ability of the pozzolana, however, to combine
with calcium hydroxide in the paste, mortar or concrete after reasonably short curing period, is inaccurate, whether this test is
performed by dissolving extraction of chemical agents or whether by
D.T.A. and thermogravimetric analysis. This inaccuracy arises
because when pozzolanic binders harden, a portion of the calcium
hydroxide remains embodied and protected by the newly formed pseudo-
gelatinous products which impede its passage into the solution.

Attempts have, therefore, been made by a number of investigators,
particularly Frantini and Rio, to devise means whereby these problems
could be avoided. Frantini, proposed a test designed to determine
whether the pozzolanic material added to portland cement, whatever
may be its nature and mix ratio, will actually fix the calcium
hydroxide freed by hydrolysis of the Portland cement. The type of
pozzolana mixed with the Portland cement and the mixture ratio are
satisfactory if the point representing the analysed solution comes
below a solubility isothem. (11 & 12).

In 1968, this method was included in the Italian specification
for pozzolanic cements. It was also included in the International
Standards Organisation recommendation (R863 - 1968). It takes at
least 8 days to obtain results for this test. The results of this
test may afford an index to chemical resistance, but not to the
strength the pozzolana will contribute at long ages.

Lea (12) proposed strength tests in which the pozzolana cement
mortar cubes are cured at $50^{\circ}C$ and $18^{\circ}C$. The difference between the
strengths developed at $18^{\circ}C$ and $50^{\circ}C$ affords a measure of the value
of the pozzolana present. The same method of tests is supposed to
detect pozzolanas with resistance to sulphate attack for pozzolanas
of high $\dfrac{SiO_2}{R_2O_3}$ ratios, but for those pozzolanas with high R_2O_3 it is
doubtful if this method will be adequate.

6.2 Compression or tension tests of sand lime - pozzolana mortars
have been used for evaluating pozzolana activity. Many investigators
have used various ratio of lime to pozzolana and have cured the specimen under several different types of curing conditions. Maximum
strengths are obtained at the early stages with a lime - pozzolana

ratio of about 1:4. For longer periods, however, higher ratios of
lime tend to give high strength. Ratios of 1:2 and 1:3 give maximum
strengths at one year.

Since the activity of a pozzolana is measured by its ability to
react and form a cementitious material with lime, the quality of the
lime will obviously affect the rate of strength development. Temperature is another important factor which affects the rate of strength
development as it is with Portland cement concrete. A little rise in
temperature, however, shows a marked increase in the rate of strength
development in lime-pozzolana mortars.

In terms of strength of test cubes the activity of pozzolanas has
been measured as good, moderate and poor. Table 3 shows classification of surki by the compressive strength of lime - surki mortars
cured at 50°C for 8 days (9). In general, active pozzolana tested to
ASTM C595-71 specifications will give a compressive strength of 100C
psi (7.0 N/mm^2) and above at 7 days, whereas poor or intermediate ones
will range from 400-800 psi (2.6-5.6 N/mm^2) and inactive ones will
range well below 400 psi (ASTM - C595-71). It is clear from this
discussion that all the tests do not give a complete evaluation of
the material. However, the compressive strength method is found most
suitable for evaluating pozzolanas for construction purposes.

Table 3. Classification of Surki by compressive strength
          (after Srinivasan, 1956)

Lime reactivity strength		Activity
LB/SQ.IN.	N/MM^2	
200 and below	1.38	Very inactive
200 - 400	1.38 - 2.76	Inactive
400 - 600	2.76 - 4.14	Poor activity
600 - 800	4.14 - 5.52	Intermediate activity
800 - 1000	5.52 - 6.90	Active
More than 1000	6.90	Very active

7. *Pozzolana manufacture*

Natural pozzolanas may be used directly without any processing. But
they are generally more reactive when heated for a few hours at temperatures ranging between 300-700°C and are more reactive when finely
ground. The artificial ones like burnt clays and shales however,
require prolong heating at temperatures ranging between 500-1000°C.
The temperature for maximum reactivity depends on the type of the
predominant clay mineral present in the sample. The temperatures for
maximum activity for the three main groups of clay minerals, montmor-
illonite, kaolinite, and illite are respectively 600-800°C; 700-800°C
and 900-1000°C. At these temperature ranges the chemically bond
hydroxyls are lost resulting in the collapse of the structure. Consequently large amount of free surfaces are released for reaction.

7.1 The heating can be conducted in either a rotary kiln, vertical shaft kiln or in a fluidized bed calciner. There are many other simple technologies available for calcining clays and shales. In all of these technologies the control of the calcining temperature is crucial. For converting rice husk to pozzolana special burners or stoves where temperatures can be controlled are required. Much work has been carried out in the designing of suitable stoves by many countries in Asia. The work carried out by the Cement Research Institute of India and that by Mehta of the University of California, Berkeley, U.S.A. are worth mentioning (15-22).

7.2 Energy requirement for manufacturing a kilogram of Portland cement clinker is considerably high as compared to that for pozzolana. The energy ranges from 1220-1440 kcal/kg. Energy requirements are higher for the wet process than for the dry one. Favourable energy consumption conditions are obtained with modern rotary kilns which are equipped with special devices for achieving complete utilization of all available sources of heat. Energy requirement for manufacturing a kilogram of clinker can be as low as 840 kcal for such kilns. But for pozzolana production this type of technology is not required. Table 4 shows energy consumed during the manufacture of lime, pozzolana and cement. It is clear from the table that much more energy is required for producing clinker even if energy consumed in grinding is not taken into consideration. This means that pozzolana can be produced at relatively low-cost. There is therefore some cost-benefit to be derived in using pozzolana cements locally produced for low-cost housing.

Table 4. Energy inputs of materials (adapted from 23)

Material	Solid Fuel K.cal/kg	Electrical Energy K.cal/kg.	Total Energy K.cal/kg
Lime	722	3	725
Hydrated lime	547	50	597
Fly ash	0	0	0
Surhki (Broken bricks)	0	50	50
Burnt clay pozzolana	228	56	286
Rice husk ash	0	50	50
Portland cement	1440	120	1560

8. *Uses of pozzolanas*

The main uses of pozzolanas are for lime-pozzolana mortars, for blended pozzolanic cements and as an admixture of concrete mix. Lime-pozzolana mortars are found to be resistant if exposed to water and have been for a long time the only known cements suitable for such exposures. There are many Roman monuments standing today which were built with lime-pozzolana mortar.

Pozzolanic Portland cements have been found useful for improved durability combined with some economy in concrete in marine, hydraulic and underground structures. Their greatest use is in mass concrete where heat of evolution is reduced with consequent elimination of excessive cracks. Pozzolanic cements also inhibit expansion caused by reaction of alkali-aggregates. They are also used to increase the resistance to sulphate attack or to leaching by soft water.

Lime-pozzolana-sand mortars develop adequate strengths for masonry purposes. Replacing up to 30% of Portland cement in concrete with pozzolana 65-95% of the strength of the unsubstituted Portland cement concrete could be obtained at the same age. The strength development normally improves with age.

The manufacture of lime-pozzolana will provide a substitute for cement in mortar for construction. The pozzolana cement is suitable for most non reinforcement work. Using these two products in construction will extend the limited supply of cement, thereby releasing more cement for other construction purposes. Where there is availability and sustained supply of these products, they will be immensely beneficial to a low-cost housing scheme.

9. *Conclusions and recommendations*

This paper has attempted to discuss the properties, types, manufacture and uses of pozzolana cements so as to encourage its production and use for low-cost housing in Africa. It concludes that since pozzolana materials, one type or another, abound in many areas in Africa, efforts should be made by African governments to exploit them for their low-cost housing programmes.

On the basis of the discussions in this paper, it is recommended that in order to encourage and accelerate the production and use of pozzolana cements in Africa, the E.C.A. with the co-operation of UNIDO and UNCHS should establish pilot-cum-demonstration centres in selected African countries for the production of pozzolana cements. It is further recommended that African governments should co-operate in the establishment of these centres.

References

1. United Nations, 1965. Official Records of the General Assembly, Twentieth Session Supplement No.14 (A/6014) Resolution 2036(XX) adopted 7th Dec. 1965. Page 39 para(c).
2. UNIDO, 1968. The development of clay building materials industries in developing countries (Report of Interregional Seminar of clay building materials industries) Copenhagen 12-25 Aug. 1968, pp. 7-9.
3. E.C.A., 1978. Report of the meeting of African experts on building materials. Addis Ababa E/CN.14/HUS/24, 28th July, 1978.
4. Symposium on the use of pozzolanic materials in mortar and concretes. A.S.T.M. Special Technical Publication No.99, 1949.
5. Davey Norman, 1961. A history of building materials. Published by Phoenix House, London, pp. (102-104).
6. Lucas, A., 1948. Ancient Egyptian materials and industries. Edward Arnold (3rd Edition).

7. Knight, B.H. & Knight, R.G., 1955. Builders materials. Edward Arnold Ltd., pp. 29-49.
8. Horstmann, F.C., 1957. History of building (Bk II) Isaac Pitman & Sons, London.
9. Lea, F.M. 1938. The chemistry of pozzolana proceedings: Symposium Chemistry of cement, Stockholm. pp. 460-490.
10. Srinivasan, N.R., 1956. Surkhi as a pozzolana, Road Research Paper I - Central Rd. Research Institute, New Delhi, India.
11. Malquori, G., 1960. Portland-pozzolana cement. Fourth International Symposium, Washington, Vol.II pp. 983-10006.
12. Lea, F.M., 1970. The chemistry of cement and concrete. Edward Arnold Ltd., pp. 141-453.
13. Stephens, G.H., 1904. Barrage across the Nile at Asynt. Proceedings of the Institution of the Civil Engineers Vol.CLVIII of minutes Paper No. 3462.
14. Hammond, A.A., 1974. Pozzolana from bauxite-waste. Conference on cost reduction in public construction sector, Accra, June June 25-28, 1974. Building and Road Research Institute, Kumasi.
15. Chopra, S.K., 1979. Utilization of rice husk for making cement and cement-like binders. Proceedings of the Joint Workshop organised by UNIDO, ESCAP, R.C.T.T., and PCSIR, Peshawar.
16. Anon, 1979. Rice husk ash cement. Proceedings of a Joint Workshop Production of cement-like materials from agro-wastes. Regional Centre for Technology Transfer, Bangalore 5600 52. India.
17. Karasudhi Pisidhi & Nimityongskul Pichai, 1979. Use of rice husk ash as building materials in Thailand. Division of Structural Engineering and Construction, Asia Institute of Technology, Bangkok, Thailand.
18. Cook, D.J. & Pama, R.P. and Paul, B.K., 1977. Rice husk ash - lime cement mixes for use in masonry units. Building & Environment, Vol.2. pp. 281-288.
19. Mehta, P.K. 1977. Properties of blended cements made from rice husk ash. J. American Concrete Inst. Vol.74 No.9, pp.440-442.
20. Mehta, P.K., 1979. The chemistry and technology of cements made from rice husk ash. Dept. of Civil Engineering, University of California, Berkeley, California, U.S.A.
21. Mehta, P.K., 1981. Technology alternatives for producing cements from rice husks. Third Workshop on R.H.A. Cement. 2-6 Nov. 1981., New Delhi, India.
22. Hammond, A.A., 1976. Evaluation of bauxite-waste for cement production. International symposium on new horizons in construction materials, Vol. 1. Lehigh University, Bethlehem, U.S.A.
23. Anon, 1977. Consultation: Lime-pozzolana papers and proceedings New Delhi, 8th-9th Dec. National Buildings Organization and UN Regional Housing Centre, ESCAP.
24. Labahn Otto and W.A. Kaminsky, 1971. Cement engineers handbook (3rd edition). Bauverlag GMBH. Wiesbaden.

PORTLAND-BASALT MIXED CEMENT

A.F. GALAL & M.A.SHATER
General Organization for Housing & Building
and Planning Research Centre, Cairo

H.EL-DIDAMONY
Faculty of Science, Zagazig University,
Zagazig, Egypt.

1. Introduction

Pozzolana as a siliceous or siliceous and aluminous material which in itself possesses little or no cementitious value but will, in finely divided form and in the presence of moisture, react with calcium hydroxide at ordinary temperatures to form compound possessing cementitious properties (1). It is essential that pozzolana in pozzolanic cement be in a finely divided state that silica can combine with calcium hydroxide (liberated during the hydration of portland cement).

Pozzolana is a natural or artificial material containing silica in a reactive form. The natural pozzolanas are of volcanic origin as volcanic ashes, tuffs, basalt but include certain diatomaceous earths, whereas the artificial pozzolana is fired clays or shales (2).

It is not possible to make a generalized statement on the portland pozzolana cements because the rate of strength development depends cn the activity of the pozzolanas and on the proportion of portland cement. Portland-pozzolana cements gain strength very slowly and require, therefore, curing over a long curing period. The ultimate strength is approximately the same as that ordinary portland cement alone (3).

Pozzolanic cements are largely used because of the advantages deriving on their lower heat of hydration and higher durability against aggressive waters. At some localities near Cairo, Abou-Zaabal, some basaltic extrusions are being quarried. At these quarries, basalt powder is produced as a by-product. This has no significant value and known as altered basalt. Thus, during the gradual advance of the quarry faces, in addition to the cost of its removal, introduces a space problem. Therefore, it can be used with portland cement as mixed cement.

In the present investigation the preparation of mixed cement from
portland cement and altered basalt was studied. The compressive
strength as well as the kinetics of the hydration of the hardened
pastes were also investigated. The free $Ca(OH)_2$ and chemically-
combined water contents were estimated up to 90 days of curing.

2. Experimental

The starting materials used were portland cement and altered
basalt (Abou-Zaabal, Cairo, Egypt). Table 1 shows the chemical
analysis of these materials. The fineness of the portland cement

Table 1. Chemical Analysis of Portland Cement
and Basalt, in weight %.

Material	SiO_2	Al_2O_3	Fe_2O_3	FeO	TiO_2	CaO	MgO	SO_3	Na_2O	K_2O	I.L.
Port.Cem.	21.7	5.65	2.95	---	---	62.7	3.12	2.05	0.35	--	1.96
Basalt	49.3	13.63	6.70	3.87	1.54	9.10	4.60	---	3.11	0.95	7.02

was 3150 cm^2/g whereas the basalt was sieved in sieve 170 mesh.
Different pozzolanic cements were prepared from 10, 30 and 50 weight
per cent basalt with portland cement. The constituents of each mix
were mechanically mixed together for one hour in a porcelain ball
mill using one ball in order to ascertain complete homogeneity.

The mixing of the pastes was done as described in a previous work
(4). The water/cement ratio used was 0.26 by weight. The pastes
were moulded in 2x2x2 cubic moulds, cured in humidity chamber for 24
hours then demoulded and cured under water till the time of testing.
The compressive strength measurements were done at the intervals of
3, 7, 28 and 90 days. After any hydration period, the hydration of
the hardened cement pastes was stopped (2, 4). The dried samples
were stored in air-tight bottles to prevent carbonation. The chemically-combined water content, Wn, was determined by the ignition of
the paste at 1000°C for one hour. The free $Ca(OH)_2$ was also estimated using ammonium acetate method (5). The hydration kinetics was
also followed by the aid of X-ray diffraction apparatus. Philips
apparatus PW 1390 diffractometer, Ni filter CuK$_\alpha$ radiation at 40 KV,
20 mA was used.

3. Results and Discussion

3.1 Compressive Strength

The results of the compressive strength of the hardened pozzolanic
cement pastes in comparison with the portland cement pastes are

graphically plotted in Fig. 1. These strength value shows that the substitution of pozzolana for portland cement reduces the compressive strength obtained for all basalt-containing cements. The compressive strength of all hardened pastes increases with the increase of curing time up to 90 days. It is clear that the addition of basalt leads to a reduction in compressive strength of about 12 - 15 %, 25 - 30 % and 40 - 50 % for 10, 30 and 50 % of basalt respectively. This decrease is attributed to the presence of basalt as a non-cementitious material. The hydration kinetics of basalt is very slow and this is mainly due to the crystallinity of the basalt.

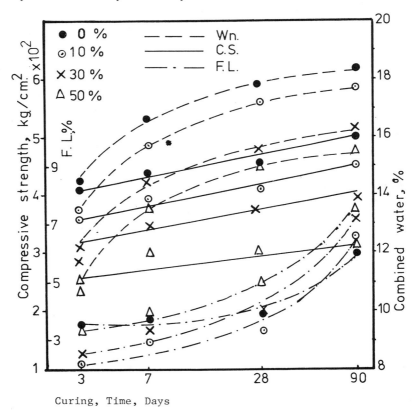

Curing, Time, Days

Fig 1: Compressive strength, combined water and free lime of hardened portland basalt cement pastes.

Wn. = Combined water ; F.L. = Free lime and
C.S.= Compressive strength.

3.2. Free Ca(OH)$_2$ Content:

The free calcium hydroxide as well as the chemically-combined water contents, Wn, can be taken as a measure of the degree of hydration. The results of free Ca(OH)$_2$ of different cement pastes are shown in Fig. 1. It is clear that for any cement paste the free Ca(OH)$_2$ increases with the curing time. At early ages of hydration, the portland cement paste liberates more Ca(OH)$_2$ than the portland basalt mixed cements. In the other hand, as the basalt increases the amount of liberated calcium hydroxide increases. This may be attributed to the liberation of Ca(OH)$_2$ from the basalt itself. The calcium ions of basalt go in solution. This can be seen from the X-ray diffraction pattern of hydrated cement pastes in Figs. 2 and 3.

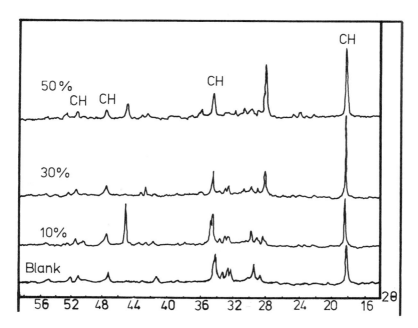

Fig. 2 : X-Ray Diffraction Patterns of Portland Basalt Cement Pastes Cured for 90 Days.

CH = Ca(OH)$_2$

Fig. 2 illustrates the X-ray diffraction patterns of different pozzolanic cement pastes cured for 90 days in comparison with portland
cement. It is clear that the pattern of $Ca(OH)_2$ increases with the
increase of basalt in cement, i.e. cement paste of 30 % basalt gives
more free $Ca(OH)_2$ than the portland cement. Fig. 3 shows also the
X-ray diffraction pattern of hardened cement paste made from 70 %
portland cement and 30 % basalt cured for 3, 7, 28 and 90 days. As
the hydration progresses the peak of $Ca(OH)_2$ increases. The amount
of calcium hydroxide increases with the curing time, i.e. the basalt
portion liberates free calcium hydroxide. The pozzolanic activity
of basalt is very small or negligable.

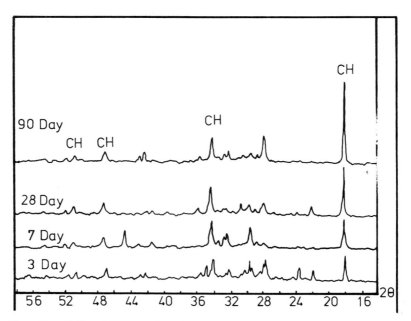

Fig. 3 : X-Ray Diffraction Patterns of Hydrated Portland Basalt
(70:30) in Relation With Curing Time
CH = Ca (OH)$_2$

3.3. Chemically-Combined Water Content, Wn:

Fig. 1 shows the degree of hydration as measured from the chemically-combined water contents of the different pastes cured for 3, 7,
28 and 90 days. As can be seen from the figure, at any age of hydration, the chemically-combined water contents of portland cement paste

has higher values than the mixed cement paste. The increase of basalt content was accompanied by a marked decrease in the chemically-combined water contents at all ages of hydration. The results show that for any cement paste, its degree of hydration increases markedly with curing time. It is clear that the substitution of portland cement by basalt somewhat retards the hydration of the cement paste which leads to lower chemically-combined water contents than of the portland cement paste.

It can be concluded that the altered basalt can be used as pozzolanic material in the preparation of mixed cement. Mixed cement prepared from 30 % basalt gave a suitable compressive strength. Therefore, we can prepare mixed cement for different purposes by mixing basalt by ratios ranging from 10 to 30 %.

References

1. Lea, F.M. (1970), The Chemistry of Cement and Concrete, London Arnold.
2. Taha, A.S; El-Didamony, H.; Abo-El-Enein, S.A. and Amer, H.A. (1981), Zement-Kalk-Gips, 34, 351-53.
3. Neville, A.M. (1981), Properties of Concrete, 3rd. Edn. Pitman Publ. Ltd., London.
4. El-Didamony, H.; Haggag, M.Y. and Abo-El-Enein, S.A. (1978), Cem. Concr. Res., 8, 351-58.
5. Kondo, R.; Abo-El-Enein, S.A. and Daimon, M. (1975), Bull. Chem. Soc. Japan, 48, 222-26.

DEVELOPMENTS IN SISAL FIBRE REINFORCED CONCRETE

A.S. MAWENYA, University of Dar es Salaam, Tanzania

Summary

The inflationary trends of the world economy have escalated the costs of building materials to the extent that in many developing countries many of the conventional building materials can no longer be considered as reasonable propositions for the construction of low cost housing schmemes. In particular the cost of roofing materials like corrugated iron sheets, aluminium and asbestos sheets is disproportionately high and far beyond the means of an average wage earner who is finding it more and more difficult to afford decent housing.

In the search for alternative building materials Sisal Fibre Reinforced Concrete (SFRC) proves to be an attractive proposition. Sisal fibre is a cheap and abundant locally produced material in many tropical countries. Its mechanical and physical properties are comparable to those of many modern fibres that are currently being used for the reinforcement of brittle materials. When sisal fibre is used as reinforcement for concrete it inhibits early cracking and imparts flexural strength and ductility to the composite.

This paper gives a review of the research work carried out so far in the field of SFRC. The review covers the characteristics of sisal as a reinforcing fibre, manufacture of SFRC, behaviour of SFRC members under tensile and flexural loads and durability of SFRC. Prospective applications of SFRC with special reference to SFRC roofing sheets are also discussed. The paper concludes by noting that the use of sisal and other natural (vegetable) fibres as reinforcement for brittle materials has many prospects in the development of low cost housing on a self-reliance basis. Therefore developing countries are advised to pool their resources together and set up collaborative facilities for research and development in the field of natural fibre reinforced materials.

1. Introduction

Sisal, like many other agave plants, is a tropical freshly-leaved plant cultivated for its fibre. The fibre is ordinarily used for the production of cordage, rope, twine, cloth, carpets and similar products. However, with the fast development of the concept of fibre reinforcement the idea of testing the feasibility of using sisal fibre as reinforcement for concrete is quite attractive for various reasons:

- the mechanical and physical properties of sisal fibre are comparable with those of many fibres that are currently being used for reinforcement of brittle materials;

- sisal fibre is a cheap and abundant locally available material in many tropical countries;

- sisal is a renewable resource which requires comparatively little energy and simple technology to process;

- sisal has acceptable environmental characteristics and can replace asbestos which is a health hazard.

Sisal fibre can be used as reinforcement of both organic materials such as plastics and inorganic materials such as gypsum and concrete. Gypsum is perhaps the oldest matrix material that has been used with sisal fibre as its reinforcement (1). On the other hand, the reinforcement of concrete with sisal fibres is a more recent development. A study carried out by Nilsson in 1975 (2) demonstrated that there was great potential of using Sisal Fibre Reinforced Concrete (SFRC), thus the keen interest among a number of researchers who have invested a lot of effort on research in SFRC. The purpose of this paper is to review this research effort. The paper attempts to answer the following questions:

- What are the essential mechanical and physical properties of the sisal fibres?

- How do the fibres affect the properties of the concrete matrix during mixing?

- What are the optimum practical amounts of fibres that can be incorporated into the matrix?

- How do the fibres interact with the matrix? Does the composite material produced exhibit better elasto-plastic properties under loading than the matrix alone?

- What is the durability of the composite under various environmental conditions?

- What are the possible applications of SFRC?

2. Properties of Sisal as a Reinforcing Fibre

In order to evaluate the potential of sisal fibre as reinforcement for concrete data is required on the physical and mechanical properties of the fibre. Extensive information is available in the technical literature concerning these properties (3,4). However, most of the data available relates to the textiles and cordage industries.

The most important mechanical properties to be considered are density, tensile strength, modulus of elasticity and stress-strain characteristics. These properties are dependent on the type of fibre and vary

somewhat with moisture content and rate of stress application. The
values usually quoted for these properties are:

- Density: 12.05 kN/m^3 when dry (3). The lowest value reported for
  the density is 7.0 kN/m^3 (5) and the highest is 15.0 kN/m^3 (6).

- Tensile strength: 330 - 820 N/mm^2 (6,7).

- Modulus of elasticity; 2.6 x 10^4 N/mm^2 (6). The lowest value
  reported is 1.32 x 10^4 N/mm^2 (7).

- Ultimate strain: 3.2 percent when dry and 3.4 percent when wet with
  extreme values of 1.0 and 5.8 percent (8).

- The stress-strain relationship is linear upto failure. On
  unloading, linear relaxation occurs but the strain is not completely recovered. In subsequent loading cycles, hysteresis may be
  avoided by slow rate of stress application.

Since most information in the technical literature is based on tests
carried out in the textiles and cordage industries, there is a danger
of misinterpretting the data. For instance Nutman (6) gives the
tensile stress of sisal at failure as 820 n/mm^2. However, this value
refers to the fibre material only rather than to the fibre as a
whole. When the whole fibre is considered the tensile strength
reduces to 278 N/mm^2(7).

The important physical properties of sisal fibre are its absorptivity
and the ability to withstand degradation due to alkatine cementitious
environment and bacteriological decay. Sisal fibre has a high water
absorption. Percent absorption of upto 105% relative to the weight
of dry fibres has been observed to take place within a relatively
short wetting time of 20 minutes (9). This fast water absorption
has important consequences in the manufacturing process of SFRC.

Sisal fibres, like other vegetable fibres, may biologically deteriorate if not treated. On the other hand the alkanility of the
concrete matrix will prevent the fibres from being attacked. Thus
the fibres, when embedded in concrete, will have a good durability
against biological attack. However, the alkalinity of the concrete
may attack the fibres chemically by decomposing the lignin that
holds the constituent parts of the fibre together (10). This
process reduces the strength and ductility of the fibres. Nilsson
(2) has reported results that indicated a significant reduction in
strength (74% reduction) after the fibres were immersed in lime.
However,Swift and Smith (7) argue that Nilsson's test conditions were
probably too severe. They reported that fibres removed from an 18
month old mortar block which was stored dry after 28 days curing in
fog room showed no reduction in strength.

In comparison with other fibres commonly used as reinforcement of
brittle materials, sisal can be considered as a low modulus high

elongation fibre. The price to strength ratio is the lowest and is likely to remain low for a long time to come (3,5).

3.   Manufacture of Sisal Fibre Reinforced Concrete

There are two main ways in which the concrete matrix can be reinforced with sisal fibres. The sisal fibres can be used as discontinuous chopped short sisal fibres (15-75 mm in lenth) or as continuous long fibres (>75 mm in length). Sometimes both short and long fibres can be used together. The manner in which the fibres are incorparated into the matrix will affect the properties of the composite both in its fresh state as well as in the hardened state. The properties which affect SFRC during mixing are the workability of the mix, blending of concrete, the balling tendency of the fibres and the rate of cement hydration. Not much research has been carried out to determine the influence of sisal fibres on these properties. However, reported results (2,12,13) show that the incorporation of sisal fibres in the concrete matrix has the following effects on the fresh properties of the composite.

- Sisal fibres absorb water when introduced into the mix. This seffens the mix and thereby reduces the workability of the composite relative to that of the unreinforced matrix. To maintain good workability additional water is required. It has been shown that the amount of extra water required varies linearly with the fibre volume content as shown Fig. 1.

- Sisal fibres reduce the bleeding tendency of the concrete. This is advantageous as it results in a more stable material.

- Chopped sisal fibres tend to ball up if their volume content and length exceed certain limits. This results in the production of unworkable and segreagated mix which in turn result in a highly porous and honey-combed composite. The risk of balling, which determines the maximum amount of fibres that can be incorporated into the matrix, can be defined by a parablic relationship between the fibre length and fibre volume content, as shwon in Fig. 2.

- Sisal fibres retard the rate of cement hydration. This is a phenomenon which is peculiar to sisal fibres. More time is needed for complete hydration when the fibres are incorporated into the concrete matrix. This is not necessarily a disadvantage.

While recognizing the above drawbacks many researchers have shown that a suitable composite can be achieved by adopting innovative mixing procedures. For instance, Nilson (2) adopts a procedure of mixing the ingredients with about half the water before adding the dry fibres and the remaining water. Smith and Swift (7) precoated the fibreswith cement paste and placed them in layers that alternated with the concrete mix.

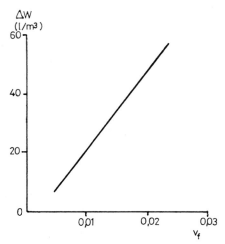

Fig. 1: Additional water (△W) necessary to maintain
constant workability.

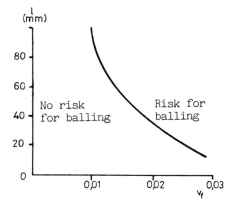

Fig. 2: Influence of fibre length (l) and volume on
risk for balling.

The quantity of fibres that can be incorporated into the matrix depends on the usual factors, i.e. maximum aggregate size, cement content, fibre length, type of mixer and method of fibre incorporation. In order to achieve the best results the concrete matrix should be of rather high quality (fcu $\geqslant$ 30 N/mm^2) with a small maximum size aggregate ($\leq$ 10 mm). Normally shorter lengths of chopped fibres given better workability and quite a high fibre volume content can be achieved with such fibres. However, the most practical fibre volume content does not normally exceed 10 percent.

4.   Strength and Toughness of SFRC members

4.1 Tensile Strenth
A fibre reinforced concrete element which is subjected to gradually increasing tensile load will pass through three more or less distinct stages. These stages correspond to the uncracked, cracked and postcracking stages. At low stress levels the fibre reinforced concrete element is uncracked and the applied load is shared between the concrete matrix and the fibres. In the post cracking stage the concrete matrix ceases to contribute to the tensile strength of the composite and the fibres become the sole resistors of the tensile load.

According to Ref. 11, the incorporation of sisal fibres will enhance the tensile strenth of the composite if

$$\sigma^c_{cr} - \sigma^m_u = v_f(E_f - E_c)\,\epsilon^m_{cr} > 0 \qquad\qquad (1)^*$$

while the ultimate tensile strength of the composite will be enhanced if

$$\frac{\epsilon^f_{max}}{\epsilon^m_{cr}} > \frac{E_m}{v_f E_f} \qquad\qquad (2)$$

Since Ec and Ef are nearly equal for all practical purposes it is clear from equation (1) the incorporation of sisal fibres would not normally improve the cracking strength of the composite. Also, since v_f does not normally exceed 10 percent, the fibres must be able to withstand strains at least ten times as large as those of the matrix at cracking if they are to enhance the ultimate tensile strenth of the composite. This is quite possible, but serviceability requirements may not permit such large strains.

4.2 Flexural Strength
For members subjected to flexure, it is necessary to consider the effect of stress redistribution including movement of the neutral axis which is caused by changes in stress-strain behaviour of the composite during loading. An exact interpretation of the mechanism offlexure presents considerable theoretical problems and certain approximations are necessary. Fig. 3 depicts a simple model, based on conventional beam theory, for representing the strain and stress

*Symbols used in equations are explained in the Appendix

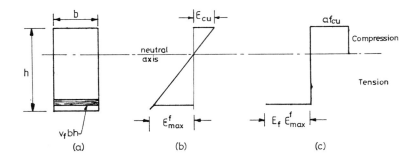

Fig. 3: Flexural Failure Model
        (a) Cross-section (b) Strain (c) Stress

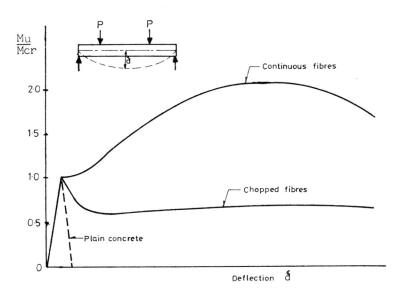

Fig. 4: Typical Load-deformation of SFRC Beam
        (Mu = ultimate flexural moment, Mcr = cracking
        moment)

distribution at failure. Using this model it can be shown that the
incorporation of sisal fibres will enhance the ultimate flexural
strength if (11)

$$v_f > \frac{\alpha f_{cu}}{E_f \epsilon_{max}^f} \cdot \frac{\epsilon_{cu}}{(\epsilon_{cu} + \epsilon_{max}^f)} \tag{3}$$

On the other hand the first cracking moments of the matrix and
composite will be essentially the same.

Typical load-defromation behaviour of a SFRC beam is as indicated in
Fig. 4. In the case of the beam reinforced with short discontinuous
fibres there is normally very little improvemnt in the ultimate load
carrying capacity of the beam, but the beam exhibits considerable
plastic deformation. When continuous fibres are used a very pronounced strengthening effect is obtained.

4.3 Fracture toughness
By examining the areas under the load-deformation characteristics,
Fig.4, it is evident that SFRC has a higher energy absorbing
capacity i.e. toughness than plain unreinforced concrete. The increase in toughness could be as high as 750% (7). This superiour
toughness of SFRC coupled with the increased flexural strength and
ductility make the material attractive for many structural and
semi-structural applications.

5. Applications

5.1 Roofing sheets
There are not many feasible alternatives for roofing materials in
many developing countries, especially in the rural areas where modern
housing has to rely almost exclusively on the use of corrugated
aluminium or asbestors sheets. Due to the high prices of these items,
this makes roofing to be the single most expensive item in rural
housing schemes. Current research shows that roofing sheets made
fromSFRC can provide a cheap alternative to the conventional corrugated aluminium sheets. SFRC roofing sheets are fire resistant and
durable. They also have good themal and sound insulating properties.
Three types of roof sheets have been reported to be promising i.e.
roof tiles, corrugated sheeting and folded plate roof panels (10,13).
SFRC roofing sheets can be produced in small scale industries,
thereby offering opportunities for improving the quality of life in
rural areas (10).

5.2 Light Walling and Cladding
Sun screens and cladding for multi-storey buildings can be manufactured from SFRC, while hollow SFRC blocks can be used for making
light load bearing wall elements.

5.3 Plastering
SFRC surfacing can protect mud-brick walls and mud-and-pole constructions from destruction by rain

5.4 Other applications
SFRC can also be used for the manufacture of paving slabs and as
surfacing for concrete bridge decks. There are also wide possibilities for semi-structural applications of SFRC in the form of light
beams, frames and trusses and as permanent formwork for cast-in-situ
concrete.

6.   Conclusions

Based on the available research information on SFRC, the following
conclusions can be drawn.

- Sisal fibres have significant mechanical properties that make them
  them eligible as   reinforcement for concrete.

- The sisal fibres impart tensile strength, ductility and toughness
  to the concrete matrix. When the fibres are used as short discontinuous fibres (15-75 mm in length) there is normally little
  improvement in the ultimate tensile strength, but the fibres
  inhibit early cracking and improve ductility. When continuous
  fibres are used there is a very pronounced strengthening effect.

- There is strong indication that SFRC, if properly protected, can
  achieve good resistance against normal environmental exposures.

- There are several potential applications of SFRC, particularly in
  low cost housing, for example for the manufacture of roofing
  sheets, cladding mud-brick walls, etc.

Research in SFRC will benefit many developing countries. However,
there seems to be a lot of fragmented effort invested on research
in SFRC in these countries. Perhaps there is a need to pool their
reseources together and establish collaborative facilities for
research and development in SFRC.

7. References

1. Brotchie, J.E and Urbach, G. (1962). Flexural Behaviour of
    fibrous plaster sheets. Australian Journal of Applied Sciences,
    14 (1), 68-93.
2. Nilson, L.(1975). Reinforcement of concrete with sisal and other
    vegetable fibres. Swedish Council for Building Research
    Report D.14.
3. Mawenya, A.S. and Mwamila, B.L.M. (1980). Characteristics of
    sisal as a reinforcing fibre. Uhandisi Journal, 5 (1), 24-34.
4. Lock, G.W. (1969). Sisal. Longmans, Second Edition

5. Mutuli, S.M. Bessell, T.J. and Talitwala, E.S.J. (1982). The potential of sisal as a reinforcing fibre in cement base materials. African Journal of Science and Technology, 1, 5-6.
6. Nutman, F.J. (1936). Agave Fibres. Empire Journal of Experimental Agriculture, 5, 77-111.
7. Swift, D.G. and Smith, R.B.L. (1978). Sisal fibre reinforcement of cement paste and concrete. Proceedings, Int. Conf. pm Materials of Construction for Developing Countries, Asian Institute of Technology, Bangkok, pp. 221-234.
8. Chaudri, M.A., Jamil, N.A., Sandila, D.M. and Shamin, M. (1972). Pakistan Jounal of Scientific and Industrial Research, 15, p. 405.
9. Castro, J. and Naaman, A.E. (1981). Cement mortar reinforced with natural fibres. ACI Journal Technical Paper 78-6 Jan-Feb.
10. Skarendahl, A. (1982). Natural fibre concrete for roofing. Paper presented at the National Construction Council Seminar on Building Materials, Arusha, Tanzania, 27-29 April.

11. Mawenya, A.S. and Mwamila, B.L.M. Mechanics of Sisal Fibre Concrete. Internal Report, Department of Civil Engineering/UDSM.
12. Mawenya, A.S. and Mwamila, B.L.M. (1980). Rheological Properties of sisal reinforced concrete. University Science Journal (Dar es Salaam University), 6 (1) 177-189.
13. Persson, H. and Skarendhal, A. (1978) Sisal fibre concrete for roofing sheets and other purposes. SIDA Industrial Division.

Appendix

The following symbols have been used in the text.

E_m, E_f, E_c, : Young's moduli of concrete matrix, sisal fibres and composite respectively.

f_{cu} : Cube crushing strength of concrete

v_f : Fibre volume content

α : Stress block factor

ϵ_{cr}^m, σ_{cr}^m : Strain and stress in composite at first cracking

σ_u^m : Ultimate tensile strength of concrete tatrix

ϵ_{max}^f : Maximum tensile strain in fibres

ϵ_{cu} : Maximum compressive stress in composite

THE USE OF AGGREGATES OF LATERITIC ORIGIN IN NEW STRUCTURAL CONCRETE

Dotun Adepegba, *Department of Civil Engineering, University of Lagos, Nigeria.*

INTRODUCTION

The word 'laterite' was derived from the Latin 'later' which means brick. Laterite is a highly weathered material, rich in secondary oxides of iron, aluminium, or both. It is nearly void of bases and primary silicates, but it may contain large amounts of quartz and kaolinite. It is either hard or capable of hardening on exposure to wetting and drying (1). The weathered materials include crystalline igneous rocks, sediments, detrital deposits, and possibly volcanic ash (2,3). For engineering purposes laterites are divided into two groups: sensitive and stable laterites (4). The sensitive laterites are generally found in the regions of recent volcanic activity, and because evaluation of their properties is unreliable sensitive laterite is unsuitable for engineering purposes. Stable laterite is amenable to standard laboratory tests and yields reproducible test values.

Laterized concrete is defined as concrete in which stable laterite is used as part or all the coarse and fine aggregates. The work in Lagos which began ten years ago concentrated on the replacement of sand with laterite fines, and the coarse aggregate was either washed river gravels or crushed granites. The effect of using laterite fines instead of sand has been studied (5) in relation to the compressive strength, tensile strength, modulus of elasticity, and resistance to exposure to high temperature. The effect of varying the quantity of laterite fine in a mix (using partly sharp sand and partly laterite fine) on the compressive strength, the slump test and stress - strain characteristic has also been studied (6). The effect of water content on the compressive strength of laterized concrete is clearly shown (7) in Figs. 1,2 and 3, for the standard mixes 1:2:4, 1:1½:3, and 1:1:2.

The main differences between laterized and normal concrete may be attributed to (a) the absorbent and non-granular characteristic of laterite compared with sand, which is granular and non-absorbent and (b) the plastic nature of wet laterite due to its clay content, which is between 20-45 per cent in most deposits. For these reasons laterized concrete requires more water than normal concrete for equal proportions and weights of dry normal concrete and of dry laterized concrete mix. Laterized concrete is, however, not different to the adverse effect of excessive water on the mechanical properties of concrete.

It is not necessary to consider the grading curve of fine aggregate in laterized concrete since the particle sizes of laterite fines may be assumed to be essentially uniform, especially in the pulverized form. The sizes of coarse aggregate recommended for laterized concrete do not differ from those of normal concrete suggested in the manuals of design of concrete mixes of many countries.

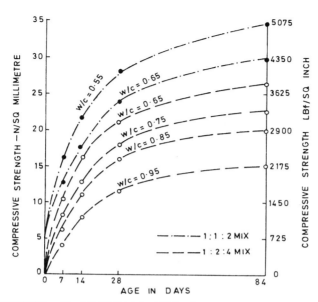

FIG.1 VARIATION OF COMPRESSIVE STRENGTH FOR VARIOUS WATER/CEMENT RATIOS FOR 15·24 cm (6 in) CUBE SPECIMENS OF FULLY COMPACTED LATERIZED CONCRETE

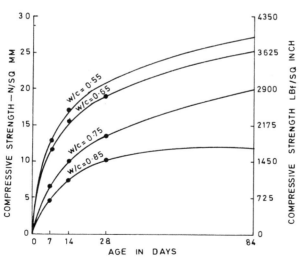

FIG.2 VARIATION OF COMPRESSIVE STRENGTH WITH AGE FOR VARIOUS WATER/CEMENT RATIOS FOR 15·24 cm (6 in) CUBE SPECIMENS OF FULL COMPACTED LATERIZED CONCRETE (1:1¹/₂:3 MIX BY WEIGHT)

EXPERIMENTAL PROCEDURE

The coarse aggregate was crushed granite of maximum size 19mm and the fine aggregate was made up of various proportions of sharp sand and laterite fines. The grading curves for sand and the gravel and the wet and dry analyses of the laterite fines have been reported (6). The size and total analyses of laterite fines were reported already (7)

The reinforced laterized concrete beams reported in this paper were 360cm long, 30 cm deep by 15cm wide. The beams with the cube specimens were kept under wet sack for 28 days when they were tested with point load at the mid-span. The distance from support to the load point was 155cm.

The beams were reinforced with plain bars. Some beams were reinforced with bars with hook at the ends (marked B) while others were reinforced with straight bars (marked A) to investigate the effect of hook or bond. Deflection was measured under the central point load and the load at which the first visible crack appeared is defined as the diagonal cracking load provided the crack later developed diagonally as a shearing crack.

EVALUATION OF RESULTS

The results of the tests in this series are compared with the results of the test of Taylor (8) in which normal reinforced concrete beams without shear reinforcement were tested. It should be noted straightaway that Taylor tested beams 26cm depth and 19cm width whereas the laterized concrete beams were 30cm deep and 15cm wide. Taylor's beams with greater width should carry more loads even under identical conditions. There was little difference between the ultimate loads of Taylor's normal concrete beams and the ultimate loads of the laterized concrete beams. This observation confirms that the shear strength of laterized concrete at the ultimate load compares well with that of normal concrete.

Laterized concrete beams developed diagonal crack at much lower load than normal concrete. This may indicate that the bond property of laterized concrete is poorer than that of normal concrete. This could be expected because the clay in the matrix of laterized concrete may hardly develop enough bond to prevent premature tensile failure at the interface of the matrix and the coarse aggregate. It has to be determined by further research work to what extent the early diagonal crack in laterized concrete beams as compared with normal concrete beams, could be arrested by shear reinforcement. Steel fibres may be one of the several materials that may be tried in such tests.

Observation of Table 1 shows that laterized concrete beams with hooks at the ends of the tensile reinforcements sustained lower loads at diagonal cracking and at failure than laterized concrete beams without hooks at the ends. This behaviour was reported by Kani (9) in which he remarked thus: "for two beams, identical in every respect except bond resistance, the one with poor bond will have a higher load - carrying capacity than the beam with good bond. The surprising result is

Beam Mark	Percentage Reinforcement $p = \dfrac{A_{st}}{bd}$ %		28 days Cube Strength N/mm^2	Load – kN		$\dfrac{P_{ult}}{P_{cr}}$	Deflection Under load at visible crack (mm)
	Straight Ends	Hooked Ends		Diagonal Cracking P_{cr}	Ultimate $P_{ult.}$		
1A	1.0		23.9	48.0	80.0	1.7	9.0
1A	1.0		27.2	47.0	80.4	1.7	8.4
1B		1.0	24.0	38.0	50.0	1.3	8.8
1B		1.0	26.0	40.00	51.2	1.3	8.3
2A	1.3		26.2	47.0	80.0	1.7	7.7
2A	1.3		25.2	47.0	80.4	1.7	6.3
2B		1.3	24.1	40.0	74.0	1.9	4.5
2B		1.3	24.9	40.4	73.6	1.8	5.5
3A	1.6		26.2	47.0	87.0	1.9	8.1
3A	1.6		26.6	47.0	87.0	1.9	7.0
3B		1.6	23.7	40.4	73.6	1.8	6.4
3B		1.6	23.7	40.4	74.0	1.8	7.5
4A	1.7		27.5	47.0	73.4	1.6	7.1
4A	1.7		27.1	46.7	80.2	1.7	5.4
4B		1.7	23.2	45.0	75.0	1.7	8.1
4B		1.7	26.2	45.0	75.0	1.7	7.1
5A	2.1		25.3	47.0	87.0	1.9	9.0
5A	2.1		24.5	47.0	87.0	1.9	9.8
5B		2.1	23.4	53.8	87.0	1.6	9.8
6A	2.6		26.2	46.8	86.8	1.9	6.1
6A	2.6		26.7	46.1	86.8	1.9	9.1
6B		2.6	25.7	46.7	73.6	1.6	10.5
6B		2.6	26.2	46.0	80.4	1.8	7.0

Table 1: Shear Strength of Laterized Concrete Beams without Shear Reinforcement

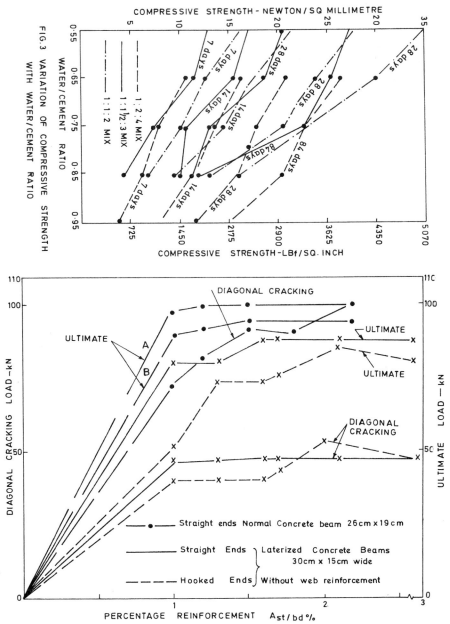

FIG.3 VARIATION OF COMPRESSIVE STRENGTH WITH WATER/CEMENT RATIO

FIG.4 VARIATION OF DIAGONAL CRACKING AND ULTIMATE LOAD WITH PERCENTAGE TENSILE STEEL REINFORCEMENT FOR LATERIZED CONCRETE AND NORMAL CONCRETE

that the better the bond the lower the diagonal cracking load-carrying capacity". Similar observation was reported by Leonhardt and Walther (10).

The variation of percentage tensile reinforcement appears to have little or no effect on the diagonal cracking load and the ultimate load of laterized concrete beams without shear reinforcement. The explanation to this observation may be due to the fact that diagonal tension crack appears when the principal tensile strain which acts perpendicularly to the direction of the diagonal crack exceeds the limiting value for the material. This limiting value does not depend on the percentage tensile reinforcement. Fig. 4 shows the curves for the loads against percentage tensile reinforcement. The curve marked "A" is for the ultimate load of Taylor's normal concrete beams without shear reinforcement and the curve marked "B" is derived by the application of a correction factor to take into consideration the difference between the cross-sectional dimension (26 cm by 19 cm) of Taylor's normal concrete beams and the cross sectional dimension (30 cm by 15 cm) of the laterized concrete beams. The curve marked "B" is closer to the curve for the ultimate load of laterized concrete beams.

CONCLUSIONS AND RECOMMENDATIONS

The result of the tests of laterized concrete beams without shear reinforcement compares favourably with similar test of normal concrete beams without shear reinforcement. The shear strength of laterized concrete beams without shear reinforcement is therefore not inferior to similar normal concrete beams without shear reinforcement. If the laterite content was reduced from 40% to 30% of the total weight of fine aggregate the results could be much better as indicated by the results in Table 1.

Since reinforced laterized concrete columns have been tested under static loading (11) and under repeated loading (12), and the results were comparable with similar reinforced normal concrete columns, and since the results of the series of tests reported in this paper show that reinforced laterized concrete beams are structurally sound as similar normal reinforced concrete beams in shear resistance, it could be concluded that laterized concrete has therefore made its mark in the areas of new structural materials.

REFERENCES

1. Alexander, L.T. and Cady, J.G. "Genesis and Hardening of Laterite in Soils, " U.S. Department of Agriculture Technical Bulletin 1282, Washington, D.C. 1962, pp. 1-90.

2. Maignien, R. "Review of Researches on Lateritie" UNESCO Publications, National Resources Research, Vol. 4, 1966, pp. 1-148.

3. Evans, J.W., "The Meaning of the Term Laterite," Geological Magazine, Vol. 5, No. 7, pp. 189-190.

4. Gidigasu, M.D., "Degree of Weathering in the Identification of Laterite Materials for Engineering Purposes. A Review, "Engineering Geology, Vol. 8, 1974, pp. 213 - 266.

5. Adepegba, Dotun, "A Comparative Study of Normal Concrete with Concrete which contained Laterite Fines Instead of Sand". Building Science, Vol. 10, August 1975, pp. 20-28.

6. Balogun, L.A. and Adepegba, Dotun, "Effect of Varying Sand Content in Laterized Concrete", The International Journal of Cement Composites and Lightweight Concrete, Vol. 4, No. 4, November 1982. pp. 235-240.

7. Adepegba, Dotun, "The Effect of Water Content on the Compressive Strength of Laterized Concrete". Journal of Testing and Evaluation, Vol. 3, No. 6, November, 1975, pp. 449-453.

8. Taylor, R. "Some shear tests on reinforced concrete beams without shear reinforcement". Magazine of Concrete Research No. 36, Vol. 12, November 1960, pp. 145-154.

9. Kani, G.N.J., "The Riddle of Shear Failure and its Solution". Journal of the American Concrete Institute No. 4, Proceedings V.61, April 1964, pp. 441-466.

10. Leonhardt, F., and Walther. "Contribution to the Treatment of Shear Problems in Reinforced Concrete", Beton-und Stahlbetonbau (Berlin) V.56 No. 13, December 1961, and V.57 No. 2, February 1962; No. 3 March 1962, No. 6, June 1962; No. 7 July 1962; and No. 8, August 1962 (in German).

11. Adepegba, Dotun, "Structural Strength of Short, Axially Loaded Columns of Reinforced, Laterized Concrete". Journal of Testing and Evaluation, Vol. 5 No. 2, March 1977, pp. 134-140.

12. Adepegba, Dotun "Random Axial Loading of Short Reinforced Laterized Concrete Columns". Journal of Testing and Evaluation, Vol. 5, No. 6, November 1977, pp. 494-498.

EXPERIMENTAL AND DEMONSTRATION LOW COST HOUSE BUILT WITH RICE HUSK
ASH AND LIME AS CEMENT BUILT AT BUILDING RESEARCH STATION

DR. M. SULAIMAN, NADIR MANSOOR & KHALIDA KHAN, Building Research
Station, KARACHI, PAKISTAN.

Summary

A unique experimental and demonstration Low Cost House has been built
in the compound of Building Research Station, Karachi, using Rice
Husk Ash and Lime as cement in the fabrication of hollow load bearing
blocks and in mortar and plaster.
  The roof is prefabricated and consists of battons, tiles and
screed. In the roof portland cement has been replaced by rice husk
ash to the extent of 30%. The foundation and base-course of floor
are soil cement stabilized; and pre-fabricated door and window frames
have been used. The mosaic floor has been done by a mixture of slag,
portland cement, and lime.
  Load test in accordance with the British Standard Code of Practice C.P:110:1972 (the structural use of concrete) has been performed
on the roof of the house and the house passed the load test, and as
such is fit for habitation.

1.   Introduction

A house has been built for the first time in Pakistan, moreover no
report has been seen that such a house had been built elsewhere.
(Professor D.G.Cook of Australia reported that a room has been built
in India with burnt clay bricks using rice husk ash and lime as
mortar).
  In this house lime mixed with rice husk ash in the proportion
of 1:2 by weight has been used in mortar, in plaster and in the fabrication of load bearing hollow blocks with Malir mix aggregates. The
weight of mixture of lime and rice husk ash form only 8.55% by weight
of the blocks. Moreover battons, tiles and screed have been used in
the prefabricated roof of this house, in which also portland cement
has been replaced by 30% rice husk ash.
  The proportion of lime and rice husk ash has been (1:2 by weight)
determined by a series of experiments and this composition gave the
optimum strength of cube casted in accordance with ASTM-C-109.
  The foundation provided in the house is also different in as
much as the principle of soil stabilization has been employed.
  The house has a covered area of 678 Sq. ft. It consists of two
rooms, two varandahs, a kitchen, a bathroom and a W.C. (Drawing No.1).

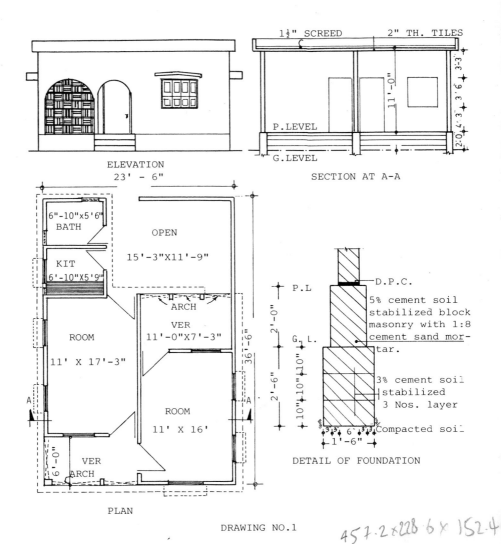

ELEVATION
23' - 6"

SECTION AT A-A

1½" SCREED   2" TH. TILES

11'-0"

P.LEVEL

G.LEVEL

6"-10"x5'6"
BATH

KIT
6'-10"X5'9"

OPEN

15'-3"X11'-9"

ARCH

VER
11'-0"X7'-3"

ROOM

11' X 17'-3"

ROOM

11' X 16'

VER
ARCH

6'-0"

36'-6"

2'-0"

2'-6"

A

A

PLAN

P.L

D.P.C.

5% cement soil
stabilized block
masonry with 1:8
cement sand mor-
tar.

G.L.

3% cement soil
stabilized
3 Nos. layer

10"10"10"

Compacted soil

6"

1'-6"

DETAIL OF FOUNDATION

DRAWING NO.1

457.2ᵪ228 6 ⊬ 152.4

The blocks have 22% hollowness and the size is 18"x9"x6" and
this has been used for load bearing walls providing 6" thickness.
The roof has been prefabricated by placing battons over which C.C.
tiles with nominal reinforcement of 1/8" Ø bar has been placed and
the later covered by a screed of 1½".

The details of each component of the house is discussed below :-

2.   Foundation

The foundation has a depth of 2½' from the ground level, the bottom
of which was compacted with a mechanical compactor to give a density

of 90% of maximum dry density. Then the foundation was filled upto
ground level in three equal layers having 3% cement mixed with soil
and compacted upto 95% of maximum dry density.

The properties of soil used for stabilization and field density
result are given in Table-1.

Table-1. Properties of soil used in stabilized
foundation and base course of floor

Maximum dry density (m.d.d.)	=2.285 gm/cm^3
Optimum moisture content (o.m.c.)	=5.2%
Liquid limit	=20.0
Plastic limit	=Non plastic
Unit weight	=1570 Kg/m^3
Field density	
a) Dry density	=2.201 gm/cm^3
b) Percentage of compaction	=96.3%
Soil classification	
Gravel [+4.76 mm]	=41.8%
Sand [-4.76 mm] [+0.074 mm]	=43.8%
Silt [-0.074 mm] [+0.002 mm]	=41.4%

Particle size analysis

ASTM Sieve No.	Percentage Passing
1"	88.6
½"	75.9
4	58.2
16	34.0
50	23.4
200	14.4

Compressive strength of soil cement(30:1) mixture

Age (days)	Compressive strength of 6" cubic specimen Kg/cm^2(p.s.i.)
3	20.9 (297)
7	32.2 (458)
28	51.5 (732) 5.05 N/mm^2

3.   Plinth

The plinth was made two feet high from the ground level and soil
cement blocks, stabilized with 5% cement, and having the size of
11½"x5½"x3½ inches, were used upto the plinth level. The blocks were
made by a hand operated machine popularily known as Cinvaram machine
and had an average weight of 8.2Kg. per block. The block were joined
together with a mortar which consisted of cement and Malir sand in
the ratio of 1:8 by volume. The properties of soil used to cast the
blocks and the compressive strength of blocks are given in Table-2 &
grain size distribution of soil is diagramatically shown in Fig-1.

Table-2 Properties of soil used in soil cement blocks

Maximum dry density (m.d.d.)	=2.188 gm/cm^3	
Optimum moisture content (o.m.c.)	=6.0%	
Unit weight	=1426 Kg/m^3	
Specific gravity	=2.64	
Liquid limit	=20.8	
Plastic limit	=14.9	
Plasticity index	=5.9	

Soil classification

Sand	[-4.76 mm] [+0.074 mm]	=74.4%
Silt	[-0.074 mm] [+0.002 mm]	=15.4%
Clay	[-0.002 mm]	=10.2%

Particle size analysis

ASTM Sieve No.	Percent Passing
No. 4	95.8
No. 8	78.1
No. 16	62.8
No. 30	56.0
No. 50	50.7
No.100	39.2
No.200	25.6

Compressive strength of soil cement blocks

Age (days)	Compressive strength Kg/cm^2 (p.s.i.)
3	29.9 (425)
7	43.7 (621)
28	80.0 (1137)

7.85 N/mm^2.

4.   Damp proof course (D.P.C.).

D.P.C. has been provided with a mixture of portland cement. Malir sand and coarse aggregate of ½" maximum size in the ratios of 1:2:3 by volume. The mortar was spread over the top of plinth to give a ½" thick layer, smoothed off with trowel and then a sheet of polythene was laid. On this a similar second layer of concrete was given.

5.   Walls

Hollow block masonary has been used in load bearing walls. The blocks were made of rice husk ash and lime as cement & Malir mix aggregate. Rice husk ash & lime formed only 8.55% of the aggregate's dry weight. The blocks were made with hand operated egg laying type of machine and the size of each block was 18" x 9" x 6" and its average weight was 26.5Kg.

The blocks were joined together with mortar of rice husk and lime with Malir sand in the proportion of 1:4 by volume (Rice husk ash - lime:Malir sand).

The properties of mix aggregate and compressive strength of blocks are given in Table-3.

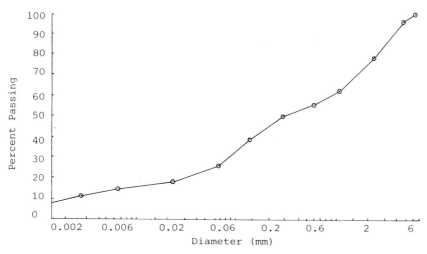

Fig. 1 Grain size distribution of soil used
in the soil-cement stabilized blocks

Table-3   Properties of Aggregate used in Hollow
load bearing blocks

Source of Aggregate   =Malir River
Los Angeles Abrasion loss   =30.2%
Specific gravity   =2.66
Absorption   =0.8%
Sodium soundness loss in five cycles =3.6%
Organic impurities   =Nil
Unit weight   =1836.5Kg/m^3
Particle size analysis

ASTM Sieve No.	Percent Passing
3/4"	100.0
No. 4	91.8
No. 30	20.0
No.200	1.2

Compressive strength of hollow blocks

Age (days)	Compressive strength Kg/cm² (p.s.i.).
7	21.9 (311)
28	29.8 (423) 2.92 N/mm².

* Strength of hollow block (gross area)

6.   Lintels

R.C.C. lintels were cast on the ground and were placed over the opening of doors and windows. The cross sectional dimension of lintels
are 4"x6". The weight of lintel per running foot comes to 11.2Kg.
The concrete used to cast the lintels contained 210Kg. portland
cement and 90Kg. rice husk ash per cubic metre of concrete. The

details of aggregates & concrete are given in Table-4, 5 & grain size distribution of aggregates is diagramatically shown in Fig. 2.

Table-4 Properties of Aggregates used for Concreting.

Properties of fine aggregates
a)	Source of aggregate	=Malir River
b)	Specific gravity	=2.63
c)	Absorption	=1.23%
d)	Organic impurities	=Nil
e)	Sodium soundness loss after five cycle	=3.6%
f)	Unit weight	=1723Kg/m^3

Properties of coarse aggregates
a)	Source of aggregates	=Hub River
b)	Specific gravity	=2.67
c)	Absorption	=0.6%
d)	Aggregate crushing value	=24.0%
e)	Los Angeles Abrasion loss	=21.0
f)	Sodium soundness loss after five cycle	=Nil
g)	Unit weight	=1450Kg/m^3

Table-5 Properties of concrete used for casting Beams and Lintels.

Quantities per cubic meter
Cement	=210.0 Kg
Rice husk ash	= 90.0 Kg
Fine aggregate	=836.2 Kg
Coarse aggregate	=1045.4Kg
Water	=181.6 Lit.

Fresh concrete analysis
Slump		=3.5 cm
Temperature	a) Air	=29°C
	b) Concrete	=27°C
Unit weight		=2349Kg/m^3

Compressive strength of concrete

Age (days)	Compressive Strength of 6" cubic specimen Kg/cm^2(p.s.i.)
3	166.7 (2371)
7	243.7 (3466)
28	301.7 (4418)

[handwritten: = 0.098 N/mm^2]

[handwritten: 29.6 N/mm^2]

7.   Projection slabs (sun-shades).

Sun-shades have been provided over windows by placing 2" thick and 14" wide projections made of cement concrete slabs which were placed over lintels. The concrete had similar proportion of portland cement and rice husk ash as used in lintels. The details pertaining to aggregate and concrete are given in Table-4, Table-6 and grain size distribution of aggregates is diagramatically shown in Fig. 3.

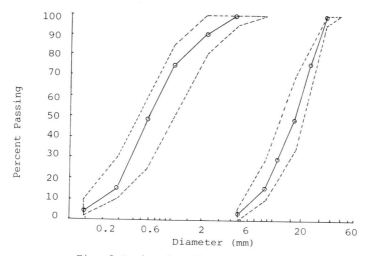

Fig. 2 Grain size distribution of fine and coarse aggregates in (lintels & beams) with curves which indicates the limits specified in ASTM C-33.

Table-6 Properties of Concrete used for casting roof tiles and sun shades (chajjas).

Quantities per cubic meter

Cement	=210.0 Kg
Rice husk ash	= 90.0 Kg
Fine aggregate	=836.2 Kg
Coarse aggregate	=1045.4Kg
Water	=181.6 Lit.

Fresh concrete analysis

Slump		=5.0 cm
Temperature	a) Air	=30°C
	b) Concrete	=30°C
Unit weight		=2360 Kg/m3

Compressive strength of concrete

Age (days)	Compressive strength of 6" cubic specimen Kg/cm2 (p.s.i.)
3	155.1 (2205)
7	225.1 (3201)
28	299.3 (4256)

8.   Floor

The plinth is filled in four layers i.e. (i) soil layer, (ii) soil cement layer, (iii) cement concrete and (iv) mosaic floor with slag.

8.1 Soil layer
Plinth is filled with soil and compacted with by a mechanical

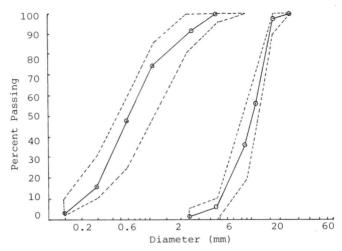

Fig. 3 Grain size distribution of fine and coarse aggregates (used in roof tiles and sun-shades) with curves which indicates the limits specified in ASTM C-33

compactor to give a height 1'.7½".

8.2 Soil cement layer
A three inch thick layer of soil-cement (30:1) by volume is laid on the compacted soil and also compacted with mechanical compactor upto 95% density.

8.3 Cement concrete layer
On the soil cement stabilized layer a 1" thick 1:9 cement concrete has been laid.

8.4 Mosaic floor
Mosaic flooring has been done by a mixture of slag. Portland cement and lime mixed with marble chips. The slag, portland cement and lime mixture was mixed with marble chips in the ratio of 1:2(Mixture:Chips by volume). The compressive strength and composition of mixture of slag, portland cement and lime is given in the Table-7.

9. Roof

The roof is prefabricated and consists of three parts i.e. (i) Rectangular R.C.C. beams or battons (ii) C.C. tiles having nominal reinforcement of 1/8" ∅ bar (iii) in situ screed.

9.1 R.C.C. Beams
The length of beam is 12ft. and clear span is 11 ft. and its cross sectional area is 4"x7". Weight of beam per running foot is 13.1Kg. These beams were placed at a distance of 3 ft. centre to centre and are designed to carry a live load of 30 lbs. The concrete used to cast the beam is similar to what has been used in lintels. The details of concrete and aggregates are given in Table-4, Table-5 and

grain size distribution of aggregates diagramatically shown in Fig-2.

9.2 C.C. tiles with nominal reinforcement
Tiles having the size of 36'x15"x2" were placed on the beams. The weight of tile comes to 42Kg. The concrete used is similar to as used in the prefabrication of sun-shades. Details are given in Table-4, Table-6 and grain size distribution of aggregates diagramatically shown in Fig-3.

9.3 Screed
Over the tiles a screed of 1:3.5:5.5 (cement:sand:aggregate) in situ was placed to a thickness of 1½". However the cement used contained 30% rice husk ash. This was spread properly to give a slope for drainage.

Table-7 Compressive strength of the mixture* of slag, portland cement and lime used in mosaic floor.

Age (days)	Compressive Strength** Kg/cm^2 (p.s.i.)
3	85.8 (1220)
7	108.3 (1540)
28	176.5 (2510)

* Composition of mixture
      Slag   =65%
      Portland cement =20%
      Lime   =15%
** Strength of 2" cubic specimen casted in accordance to ASTM C-109, but instead of graded Ottawa sand, similarly graded Malir sand was used.

10. Doors and Windows

R.C.C. doors and window frames have been provided. The concrete used to cast the frame had 250Kg. cement per cubic metre of concrete. The weight of a door and window frame comes to 7.3Kg. per running foot.

11. Water supply and Sanitation

Overhead water tank of 870 gallons capacity has been constructed with rice husk ash, lime, Malir aggregate blocks and portland cement plaster. The house has four taps, wash basin, shower and kitchen sink. An Indian style W.C. has been provided.

12. Electric connections

Concealed electric wiring has been provided with 16 points.

13. Finishing

½" thick rice husk ash-lime and sand in the proportion of 1:4 by volume in plaster have been provided on both sides of the walls. However, ½" thick portland cement sand (1:6) plaster have been provided on the inside of the roof. Two coats of white wash were applied on the inside of the roof, and one coat of white wash & two coats of distemper

have been applied on the both sides of walls. Enamel paint has been
applied on the door and window shutters.

14. Cost and Comparision

The total cost of the house at market price comes to Rs.44,741.50.
The covered area is 678 Sq. ft. Therefore the cost per Sq. ft. comes
to Rs.66.00. A similar house built with traditional material and
method of construction would cost Rs.71,061.56 i.e. Rs.105.00 per
Sq. ft. The comparative statement of cost is given in Table-8.

Table-8 Comparative statement of different items of Low Cost
House (built with Rice Husk Ash and Lime as cement) and conventional house (built with traditional material and technique).

S. No.	Item	Low Cost House Rate(Rs.) Unit	Cost(Rs.)	Conventional House Rate(Rs.) Unit	Cost (Rs.)
1.	Foundation	3.90/cft.	2925.00	12.48/cft.	9359.33
2.	Plinth	11.34/cft.	4594.48	17.50/cft.	7088.92
3.	Super Structure	2.90/sft.	4494.96	6.10/sft.	9461.75
4.	Roof	7.18/cft.	5423.00	13.00/cft.	9821.70
5.	Plaster	0.90/sft.	4427.10	1.16/sft.	5706.00
6.	Flooring	6.10/sft.	6273.85	8.50/sft.	8738.00
7.	Door & Window	25.11/sft.	6548.11	41.53/sft.	10830.86
8.	Water supply & sanitary	Lump sum	3200.00	Lump sum	3200.00
9.	Elec. & Coloring	Lump sum	6855.00	Lump sum	6855.00
		Total Rs.	44741.50	Total Rs.	71061.56

15. Conclusion

It clearly demonstrates that rice husk ash which is more or less a
waste material can be used for constructing cheap and durable houses
resulting in saving of 37%.

References

1. Soil cement, its use in buildings, United Nations New York, 1964.
2. D.J. Cook, R.P. Pama & B.K. Poul, rice husk ash lime cement mixes
    for use in Masonary units. Buildings and Environment, Vol. 12,
    PP.281, 1977.
3. ASTM standards in Building Codes - 1970.
4. M. Sulaiman & Others. "Pre-fabricated roof and soil stabilized
    block masonary - An answer to low cost housing".
5. M. Sulaiman, Khalida Khan & Nadir Mansoor, "Two experimental low
    cost rooms at Building Research Station, Karachi".

PROPRIETES DE CIMENTS POUZZOLANIQUES OBTENUS PAR CUISSON
DE MINERAUX ARGILEUX A MOYENNE TEMPERATURE. CAS DES CIMENTS
DE METAKAOLIN (x)

MICHEL MURAT[+], JEAN AMBROISE[++], JEAN PERA[++]
Institut National des Sciences Appliquées de Lyon (France).
(+) Laboratoire de Chimie-Physique Appliquée et Environne-
ment ; (++) Laboratoire des Bétons et Structures

1. Introduction

Cette étude a été entreprise dans le but d'adapter l'énergie solaire à la cuisson (ou activation thermique) des argiles en vue du développement de ciments pouzzolaniques
dans les pays du Tiers Monde à fort ensoleillement, disposant de matières premières locales (argiles, latérites) en
quantité abondante.
    Suite aux travaux préliminaires effectués à l'Université
de Toulouse (1), on a cherché à répondre aux questions suivantes :
- Qu'en est-t'il de l'hydraulicité et des propriétés de
durcissement des produits de cuisson des alumino-silicates
et minéraux associés (argiles, latérites) et quelle est l'
influence de la composition minéralogiques et des caractéristiques cristallochimiques des matières premières sur
ces propriétés?
- Peut-on améliorer les résistances mécaniques en jouant
sur les conditions d'hydratation (mode de conservation,
valeurs des rapports Eau/Solide et Minéral calciné/Activa-
teur d'hydratation) et la nature des hydrates formés?
- Quel est le procédé de cuisson de la matière première
le mieux adapté : en lit fixe, en lit brassé (four rotatif) ou en lit fluidisé?
- Comment adapter l'énergie solaire à ces procédés?
    On s'est essentiellement attaché à répondre aux trois
premières questions en choisissant comme matière premiète
le kaolin, minéral dont la calcination dans le domaine de
température 600-950°C conduit à la métakaolinite, laquelle
est reconnue présenter une hydraulicité optimale par rapport aux autres argiles calcinées (1).

(x) Recherche subventionnée par le P.I.R.D.E.S.(Programme
Interdisciplinaire de Recherche et de Développement de l'
Energie Solaire) du Centre National de la Recherche Scien-
tifique. A.T.P. "Thermochimie et Génie Chimique Solaires"

2. *Résultats expérimentaux et discussion*

2.1. Première série d'essais.
Trois kaolins commerciaux pulvérulents (Tableau 1.) ont servi de base aux expérimentations

Tableau 1. Caractéristiques des kaolins utilisés

	K_1 (Hostun, Drôme)	K_2 (Montguyon, Charente)	K_3 (St-Brieux, Côtes du Nord)
Granulométrie	$\langle$ 20 μm	$\ll$ 20 μm	$<$ 30 μm
% Kaolinite	63	98	85
% Quartz	37	1 - 2	5
% Mica	--	--	10
Etat de cristallisation	moyen	très mauvais	bon

Trois types de réacteurs chauffés électriquement et permettant des cuissons en discontinu sur des masses d'échantillon de 80 à 160g ont été utilisés : réacteurs en lit fixe, en lit brassé (four rotatif) et en lit fluidisé. Les deux derniers, comportant un élément chauffant axial, ont été mis au point au Laboratoire et déjà décrits (2,8).
Les kaolins de départ, les produits de cuisson et les produits résultant de l'hydratation du métakaolin additionné d'hydroxyde de calcium comme activateur, ont été caractérisés par spectrographie d'absorption IR, diffraction des rayons X, analyse thermique différentielle et microscopie électronique à balayage.Les produits d'hydratation ont fait l'objet pour leur part, de déterminations de résistances mécaniques en compression à la rupture sur minicylindres ($\emptyset$ 20mm et L 40mm). L'hydratation du métakaolin a été réalisée à 20 $\pm$ 1°C après mélangeage avec l'activateur et l'eau.Le démoulage est effectué à 24h et les échantillons sont ensuite conservés en boites étanches jusqu'à l'échéance choisie.
Les données antérieures (1,3) montrent qu'en présence d'hydroxyde de calcium, les trois hydrates formés au cours du durcissement du métakaolin sont essentiellement la géhlénite hydratée $2CaO.Al_2O_3.SiO_2.8H_2O$, le silicate de calcium hydraté $CaO.SiO_2.xH_2O$ ou CSH_I de la classification de Taylor (4) et l'aluminate tétracalcique hydraté $4CaO.Al_2O_3.13H_2O$. La formulation des réactions d'hydratation conduisant à la formation de ces différents hydrates permet de définir la valeur du rapport théorique Métakaolin / Hydroxyde de calcium (MK/CH) nécessaire à une transformation totale à long terme du métakaolin. La valeur de ce rapport doit être voisine de l'unité (5) ce qui nous a conduit à

choisir un mélange massique 50/50 de métakaolin et d'hydroxyde de calcium.
    La première série d'essais a permis de faire les obser-
vations suivantes :

    (a)   indépendamment du fait que, comme pour tout liant
hydraulique, les résistances mécaniques qui se développent
au cours du durcissement sont très sensibles aux conditions
expérimentales dans lesquelles est réalisée la réaction d'
hydratation (valeurs des rapport E/S et MH/CH, ajout de
sable au mélange, conditions de conservation des éprouvettes, ...), on a constaté que le processus de durcissement
dépendait de plusieurs facteurs difficilement dissociables
et qui sont essentiellement l'état d'amorphisation du métakaolin (déterminé par spectrographie d'absorption IR)(2),
les caractéristiques minéralogiques de la kaolinite de départ (état de cristallinité, présence d'impuretés) et le
mode de cuisson.
    Ainsi l'évolution des résistances mécaniques des pro-
duits d'hydratation des mélanges 50/50 métakaolin/chaux
est fonction de l'état d'amorphisation du métakaolin si la
matière première soumise à cuisson est une kaolinite pratiquement pure, très fine et très mal cristallisée (éch.
K_2). Les résistances en compression mesurées à 28 jours
sont généralement supérieures à celles des pouzzolanes
naturelles très réactives et présentent les valeurs optimales (environ 100 bars) pour une cuisson en lit fixe dans
le domaine de température 700-800°C (figure 1.).Les hydrates formés au cours du durcissement sont essentiellement
la géhlénite hydratée et en quantité plus faible, le CSH_I
et l'aluminate tétracalcique hydraté, ce qui confirme les
résultats antérieurs (3).
    La cuisson en lit fixe dans le domaine de température
700-800°C de kaolinites fines mieux cristallisées et contenant des impuretés (éch. K_1 et K3 contenant du quartz
ou de la muscovite), produit des métakaolins moins désor-
ganisés dont l'hydratation avec la chaux conduit, comme
précédemment, à la formation de géhlénite hydratée mais
d'une quantité plus importante de silicate de calcium hydraté CSH_I, ce qui confère théoriquement au matérieu des
résistances mécaniques aussi élevées sinon supérieures à
celles des produits de durcissement d'un métakaolin préparé dans les mêmes conditions mais à partir d'une kaolinite
pure et très mal cristallisée (figure 2.)(7). Une mise en
forme aisée des éprouvette (coulage) nécessite cependant
l'emploi d'un taux de gâchage élevé (E/S = 1,25), ce qui
pénalise les résistances mécaniques.

    (b)   La cuisson du kaolin en four rotatif est beaucoup
plus rapide que la cuisson en lit fixe mais elle conduit
à un métakaolin un peu moins désorganisé présentant cependant après durcissement des résistances mécaniques encore
élevées. Mais ce mode de cuisson peut poser des problèmes
technologiques tel que le collage du matériau à la paroi

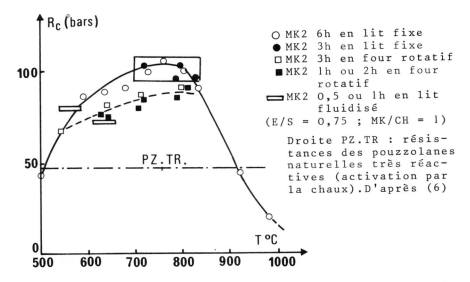

○ MK2 6h en lit fixe
● MK2 3h en lit fixe
□ MK2 3h en four rotatif
■ MK2 1h ou 2h en four
      rotatif
▭ MK2 0,5 ou 1h en lit
      fluidisé
(E/S = 0,75 ; MK/CH = 1)

Droite PZ.TR : résis-
tances des pouzzolanes
naturelles très réac-
tives (activation par
la chaux).D'après (6)

Fig. 1. Variation des résistances mécaniques à 28j des ci-
        ments de métakaolin (éch. MK2) en fonction de la
        température finale de traitement thermique de la
        kaolinite. La partie encadrée correspond aux méta-
        kaolins les plus désorganisés.

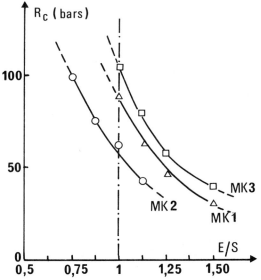

Fig. 2. Résistances à 28j des ciments de métakaolin (éch.
        MK1, MK2, MK3) en fonction de E/S (MK/CH = 1)

pendant la cuisson, avec formation d'un anneau provoquant une surchauffe importante dans le four si l'apport énergétique est de type axial. Ce phénomène, observé avec les échantillons pulvérulents K1 et K3 est tributaire de la composition de la matière première (présence de silice fine ou de micas)(8).La technique de cuisson en lit fluidisé, bien que séduisante au niveau de l'homogénéité de la température dans le matériau, pose bien des problèmes avec les argiles pulvérulentes qui se mettent assez mal, voire pas du tout en fluidisation, même mélangées à un matériau granulaire inerte de granulométrie plus élevée (sable par exemple)(8).

(c) La plupart des résultats de cette première série d'essais ont été obtenus dans des conditions expérimentales qui ne sont pas forcément optimales au niveau de l'obtention, à court terme (28j), de résistances mécaniques élevées. On a étudié le plus souvent des mélanges Métakaolin/ Chaux dans le rapport massique 50/50 qui est le rapport limite pour réaliser une hydratation totale du métakaolin. Dans ces conditions on obtient des résistances à 28j qui sont acceptables et supérieures à celles des pouzzolanes naturelles les plus réactives. L'emploi de rapports MK/CH supérieurs à l'unite, et en particulier du rapport MK/CH égal à 2 conduit à des résistances en compression à 28j qui sont multipliées par environ 1,5. L'établissement de la microstructure des hydrates dans le liant, bien que ne mettant pas en jeu la totalité du métakaolin présent, est donc plus favorable au développement de résistances mécaniques élevées. On verra plus loin le rôle joué par l'hydrate CSH_I dans cette amélioration des résistances.

Il est possible aussi que le protocole de conservation proposé (démoulage à 24h puis conservation en boites étanches) pour la détermination des résistances mécaniques sur minicylindres puisse être amélioré et complété par un séchage des échantillons à l'air pendant une durée limitée avant d'effectuer les essais mécaniques. Nous avons constaté en effet que ce facteur séchage pouvait influencer sensiblement les résultats, les résistances mesurées sur produits humides étant inférieures à celles mesurées sur produits secs.Ceci nous a conduit à entreprendre une deuxième série d'essais.

2.2. Deuxième série d'essais : optimisation des résistancee mécaniques(9).
Partant de l'échantillon de kaolin K2, on a réalisé des cuissons à 750°C en lit fixe dans un four permettant de préparer plusieurs kg de métakaolinite en une seule opération (montée en température en 3h à 750°C et maintien du matériau pendant 5h à cette température).
Les essais ont porté sur l'optimisation du mode de conservation et des valeurs des rapports MK/CH et E/S pour obtenir des résistances mécaniques maximales à 28j.

(a)   Définition des conditions optimales de conservation.

En complément du mode de conservation adopté pour la première série d'essais, nous avons essayé trois autres modes de conservation décrits dans le Tableau 2. avec essais mécaniques à 28j sur produits tels quels ou séchés 1j à 20°C ou à 50°C. Les essais ont été réalisés avec un rapport MK/CH égal à 2.

On constate que le séchage pendant 1j à 50°C améliore les résistances mécaniques et que le mode de conservation le plus performant consiste à démouler à 7j, à immerger les échantillons sous eau jusqu'à l'échéance (j-1) et à effectuer un séchage de 1j à 50°C. On arrive ainsi à des résistances en compression de l'ordre de 170 bars contre 140 et 155 bars pour les deux autres modes de conservation. On a donc choisi le mode IIc du Tableau 2 pour la suite des essais.

Tableau 2. Evolution des résistances en compression en fonction des conditions de conservation (échantillon MK2; MK/CH = 2 ; E/S = 0,75)

Mode de conservation			R_C(bars) à 28j
jusqu'à 7J	après 7j		
Moules étanches	I Moules étanches	a) 21j sans séchage b) 20j + séch. 1j à 20°C c) 20j + séch. 1j à 50°C	114 121 155
	II Sous eau	a) 21j sans séchage b) 20j + séch. 1j à 20°C c) 20j + séch. 1j à 50°C	125 140 170
	III Boites étanches	a) 21j sans séchage b) 20j + séch. 1j à 20°C c) 20j + séch. 1j à 50°C	137 127 140

(b)   Optimisation des valeurs de E/S et MK/CH

En utilisant un malaxeur RILEM type 32 et une table à choc pour la mise en place du matériau dans les moules, on a pu réaliser et couler des éprouvettes avec un rapport E/S de 0,55 (valeur limite). Avec le mode de conservation IIc on a pu obtenir des résistances en compression à 28j de 240 bars. Des valeurs encore supérieures ont été obtenues en augmentant le rapport MK/CH jusqu'à une valeur voisine de 3 (Figure 3.)

L'analyse thermique différentielle des produits hydratés à 28j a permis par ailleurs de mettre en évidence les deux points suivants :
- pour le mode de conservation de la première série d'es-

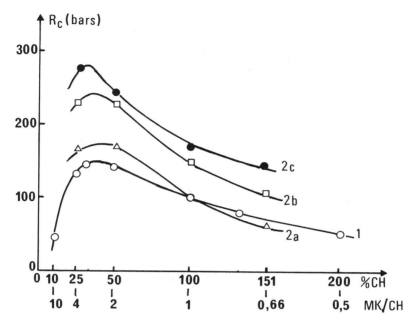

Fig. 3.Variation des résistances mécaniques à 28j en
fonction de la quantité de chaux (CH) ajoutée au métakaolin ou du rapport MK/CH :
    Courbe 1 : démoulage à 24h et conservation 27j en boites
    étanches (E/S = 0,75) (première série d'essais)
    Courbes 2 : mode de conservation IIc (2ème série d'es-
    sais) : 2a : E/S = 0,75 ; 2b : E/S = 0,65 ; 2c : E/S=0,55

sais, la formation de CSH_I (caractérisé par un pic endothermique à environ 120°C, pic"a" Fig. 4.)devient prédominante par rapport à celle de la géhlénite hydratée(caractérisée par un pic endothermique vers 2I0°C, pic"b",Fig.4)
lorsque le rapport MK/CH est compris entre 2 et 4
- pour le mode de conservation IIc, la teneur en CSH_I est
importante quelle que soit la valeur du rapport MK/CH entre
0,66 et 4 aussi bien pour E/S = 0,55 que pour E/S = 0,75.
    La formation de l'hydrate CSH_I joue donc un grand rôle
dans l'établissement des résistances mécaniques, les valeurs maximales observées correspondant systématiquement
à la présence en teneur élevée de cet hydrate dans les
produits d'hydratation du métakaolin.
    L'ensemble de ces observations permet de définir les
conditions d'hydratation conduisant à obtenir des résistances mécaniques optimales à 28j, à savoir :
- conserver les échantillons sous eau après démoulage (ce
qui favorise la formation de l'hydrate CSH_I) , puis les sé-
cher 24h à 50°C avant de réaliser les essais mécaniques

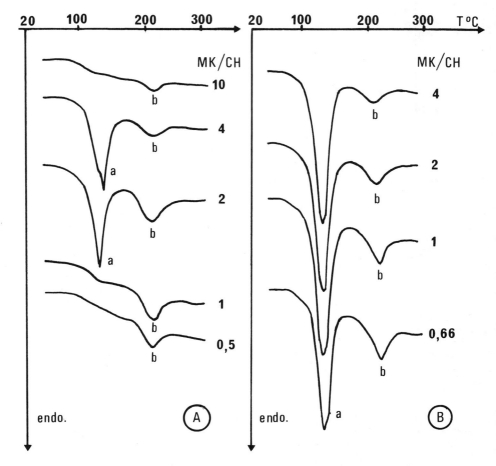

Fig. 4. Courbes d'analyse thermique différentielle du produit d'hydratation à 28j (éch. MK2) pour différentes valeurs du rapport MK/CH et taux de gâchage :
A : conservation première série d'essais ; E/S = 0,75
B : conservation sous eau (IIc) ; E/S = 0,55
Pic "a" : hydrate CSH_I ; pic "b" : géhlénite hydratée

- choisir une valeur du rapport MK/CH comprise entre 2 et 4
- utiliser la valeur minimale possible du rapport E/S.
   Lorsque ces conditions sont remplies on peut espérer obtenir sur pâte pure des résistances mécaniques au moins égales à celles des ciments aux ajouts (CPJ) sur mortier, c'est à dire de l'ordre de 250 à 300 bars à 28j.

3. Conclusion

Il apparait donc que la métakaolinite obtenue par calcination de kaolins relativement purs,dans le domaine de température 700-800°C, présente à 28 jours, après hydratation en présence d'hydroxyde de calcium, des résistances mécaniques très acceptables pour des constructions dans les pays du Tiers-Monde. L'optimisation de ces résistances (280 Bars) a pu être faite en jouant sur les facteurs suivants: mode de conservation, valeurs du rapport Métakaolin/Chaux et du rapport Eau/Solide.

Par ailleurs, la cuisson du kaolin en lit fixe semble conduire à la formation de métakaolin à réseau cristallin très désorganisé, donc à un matériau devant présenter une hydraulicité maximale en présence d'un activateur d'hydratation. Du point de vue pratique la cuisson en four rotatif devrait cependant être mieux adaptée au problème posé, mais dans le cas d'échantillons pulvérulents à granulométrie fine, elle peut conduire à des phénomènes de collage à la paroi du four qui sont tributaires de la composition minéralogique de la matière première. La mise en fluidisation des kaolins pulvérulents pose pour sa part de nombreux problèmes. La cuisson des poudres fines à cependant l'avantage de conduire à un liant prêt à l'emploi, contrairement au cas des ciments portlands dont l'obtention nécessite le broyage du clinker, opération certainement plus coûteuse en énergie que le broyage des kaolins bruts. Mais le métakaolin,en tant que ciment pouzzolanique, est un "modèle" et l'emploi de kaolinites est le plus souvent réservé à l'élaboration de matériaux ou matières premières à haute valeur ajoutée (céramiques,porcelaines,réfractaires,charges pour papier et plastiques,zéolites,...) compte-tenu de son prix élevé.

Ces recherches sont en cours d'extension à d'autres types de minéraux argileux et aux latérites (9), mais il faudra tenir compte des caractéristiques minéralogiques de ces matériaux naturels et faire un choix assez judicieux si on veut obtenir des ciments pouzzolaniques susceptibles de présenter des résistances mécaniques aussi acceptables que celles fournies par de la métakaolinite quasi-pure, laquelle est considérée par rapport aux autres argiles thermiquement activées,comme donnant les résistances mécaniques optimales.

Références

1. Measson, M. (1978),*Etude, en vue d'une utilisation de l'énergie solaire, des propriétés pouzzolaniques dues au traitement thermique des matériaux naturels.* Rapport de D.E.A., Lab. de Minéralogie et de Cristallographie, Université Paul Sabatier, Toulouse.

2. Murat, M. et Bachiorrini, A. (1982), *Bull.Minéralogie,*
    105, 543-55
3. Turriziani, R. et Schippa, G. (1954), *Ric. Scient.,*
    Ital., 24, (12), 2645-48
4. Taylor, H.F.W. (1964), *The Chemistry of Cement,* Acad.
    Press, London and New York, Vol.1, p.167-282
5. Murat, M. (1983), *Cem. and Concr. Res.,*13, (2), 259-66
6. Fournier, M. et Geoffray, J.M. (1978), *Bull. Liaison*
    Lab. Ponts et Chaussées, 93, 70-78
7. Murat, M. (1983), *Cem. and Concr. Res.,*(sous presse)
8. Murat, M. et Comel, C. (1983), *Cem. and Concr. Res.,*
    (sous presse)
9. Ambroise, J. *Thèse de Doctorat* (en préparation).

APPLICATIONS OF FERROCEMENT FOR LOW COST HOUSING IN INDIA

MADHAVA RAO, A.G., Structural Engineering Research Centre, Madras
MURTHY, D.S.R.,   Structural Engineering Research Centre, Madras

Ferrocement is a highly versatile construction material which has
established itself as an appropriate material for socially-relevant
applications in developing countries. It is a composite material
comprising cement mortar which is reinforced with welded and chicken
mesh. There are several reasons which make ferrocement an appropriate construction material for developing countries. The raw materials for ferrocement are available in most countries. Ferrocement
can be fabricated into almost any shape to meet the needs of the
user. The skills necessary for the construction of ferrocement units
are already available in these countries. Ferrocement construction
is labour-intensive and does not need expensive plant or machinery.
The versatile nature of ferrocement is evident from its applications
which range from most sophisticated, such as for boats and load
bearing structures, to the least sophisticated, such as for dust
bins. Its special characteristics have made ferrocement an appealing
and appropriate construction material for socially relevant applications such as for low-cost housing, water storage tanks to provide
hygenic drinking water, economical toilet and bath units, better
storage facilities for food grains and exploitation of alternate
energy sources.
    The potential of ferrocement for low-cost housing has been well
recognised. Attempts have been made to develop ferrocement roofing
to economically replace reinforced concrete and asbestos cement
sheets. Pioneering work on research and development of ferrocement
units has been made by the Structural Engineering Research Centre.
Some of the ferrocement applications described in this paper have
good potential for application in low-income housing and sites-and-
services schemes.

1. Ferrocement service modules

Developing countries are faced with the problem of slums which are
increasing at an alarming rate. Owing to limited financial resources, it has not been possible to clear the slums and replace them
by single or multi-storeyed tenements. Hence, greater emphasis is
now laid on slum improvement programme and sites-and-services

schemes. In the sites-and-services schemes, the low income groups
are provided with a developed plot with a service core unit consisting of a bath and a toilet. Under the slum improvement programme,
the existing slums are improved by provisions of water supply and
sanitary facilities. The Structural Engineering Research Centre,
Madras, has developed sanitary service modules in ferrocement for
bath rooms and toilets (1). These units have been found to be economical compared to those made out of conventional materials. They
have been used in the sites-and-services scheme near Madras which the
Madras Metropolitan Development Authority executed with financial
assistance from the World Bank.

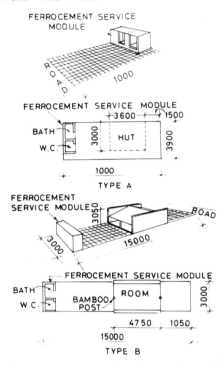

Fig.1 Typical ferrocement core housing units of Madras Urban Deve-
       lopment Project

The salient features of the ferrocement service modules are:

. They can be adopted for bath rooms and toilets.
. The thickness of walls, floor and roof is only 3 cm.
. The toilet units can be constructed directly over compacted
  soil and bath room units can be erected over conventional
  masonry foundation blocks.

. The ferrocement module consists of two layers of 26 g - 13 mm x
13 mm chicken wire mesh tied onto a central layer of 10 g -
150 mm x 150 mm welded wire mesh.

The mesh for the bath room is kept over the 4 pedestals with cen-
tering in between them for floor above. The cement mortar 1:3 is
applied to the cage and finished smooth.

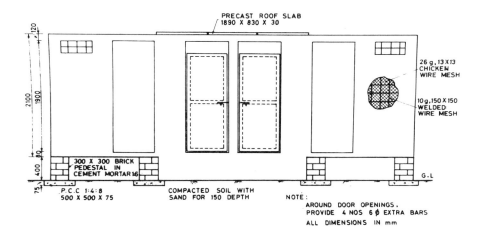

Fig.2   Ferrocement Service Module

The advantages of the ferrocement sanitary modules are:

. Construction is light-weight
. Savings in foundation cost
. The units can be precast or cast at site
. There is a savings in cement upto 30% and upto 15% in the
  total cost of the structure.

The estimated cost of the ferrocement sanitary core units consisting of 4 bath rooms and 4 toilets are given in Table 1.

Table 1. Estimated cost of ferrocement sanitary core units

Description	Rate US $	Qty.	Amount US $
Welded mesh	$1.00/m^2$	$82.5\ m^2$	82.50
Chicken mesh	$0.50/m^2$	$160.5\ m^2$	80.25
Cement	90.00/t	1.05 t	94.50
Sand	$10.00/m^3$	$2.14\ m^3$	21.40
Mild steel rods	600.00/t	0.052 t	31.20
			309.85
Labour for fabrication and casting			205.00
Foundation blocks in brick masonry			25.00
Total (for 4 bath rooms & 4 toilets)			539.85

Cost of one bath room and toilet $= \dfrac{540}{4} =$ US $ 135.00

2. Cyclone resistant core units in ferrocement

The East Coast of India is frequently subjected to cyclones and
floods which cause extensive damage to hutments and loss of tools of
trade of the hut dwellers. Many dwellings along the coastal areas
are not strong enough to resist the forces caused by these high
winds, and floods. Consequently a large proportion of the buildings
are destroyed and many lives are lost each year. Records indicate
that from the beginning of this century about 400 cyclonic storms
have been formed in the Bay of Bengal and about 80 in the Arabian
Sea. A fourth of the former and half of the latter being severe
ones. The loss caused by disasters in Tamil Nadu State of India is
estimated to be about US $ 40.00 per capita and indicate huge loss
that are being imposed by such disasters every time they strike.

As part of the anti-disaster planning strategy, the Governments
of Tamil Nadu, Andhra Pradesh and Orissa have built a chain of
cyclone shelters all along the coastal regions within easy reach of
habitations which are being affected by cyclones. These shelters
have been conceived so as to provide safe and secure shelter during
the cyclonic periods and to be useful fully during the normal
periods for various community purposes.

Often after getting the cyclone warnings, the people have only a
short time to move to the cyclone shelters and they have to leave
behind their personal belongings including working tools like fishing nets and other tools of trade in their huts. These are likely

to get damaged and lost during cyclones, with the result people find it hard to start their professional work immediately on their return to their homes. The cyclone resistant core units developed by the Structural Engineering Research Centre, Madras, in collaboration with the Directorate of Town and Country Planning, Government of Tamil Nadu would serve to protect the belongings of the poor and enable the people to start their work without any loss of time.

Based on the survey of typical villages in coastal areas, the capacity and dimensions of core units have been arrived. The cyclone resistant core units have been designed with capacities ranging from 1.10 cu.m to 2 cu.m and to withstand a wind load of 200 kg/m^2. Two types of core units have been developed:

1. Core units at floor level. These are rectangular or cylindrical ferrocement units.
2. Attic type core units – These are precast ferrocement attic type core units supported on 4 precast RCC columns.

A plan of a hut showing three alternate types of units is shown in Fig.3.

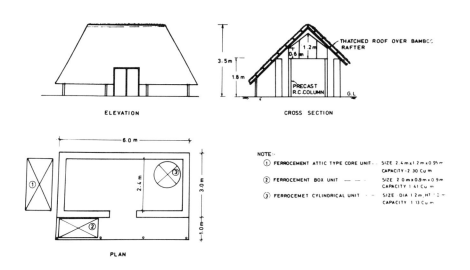

Fig.3   A hut with 3 alternate types of ferrocement units

Fig.4 shows a view of the ferrocement box unit. The size of the unit is 2 m x 0.9 m x 0.9 m. The box unit weights about 700 kg. These precast ferrocement units can be cast in central yards along coastal areas and erected in the huts. Alternately the cages can be transported to the site and mortar spraying done at the site for easy handling purposes.

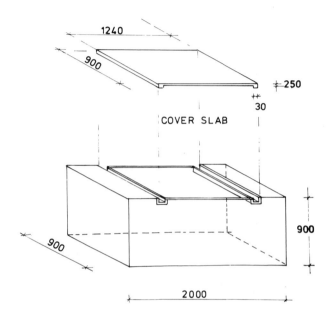

Fig.4   Rectangular ferrocement box unit

Fig.5 shows a view of the ferrocement cylindrical unit. The precast ferrocement cylindrical unit is of diameter 1.2 m, height 1 m, and 1 cm thickness. The cylindrical units can be cast using a semi-mechanised technique. The process consists of continuous winding of wire mesh in a stretched condition from a wire mesh roll onto a cylindrical mould and hand plastering of cement sand mortar onto the mesh and when it is found on the mould. Stretching of wire mesh during winding, application of mortar with trowel over a firm backing, enables achieving high degree of mortar compaction and good thickness control. The unit consists of a reinforced concrete base slab of 4 cm thickness, central ferrocement cylindrical unit and a precast ferrocement top cover slab of 1.5 cm thickness. The total weight of the unit is about 300 kg.

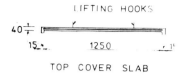

TOP COVER SLAB

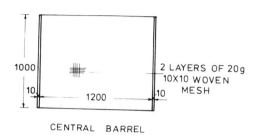

CENTRAL BARREL

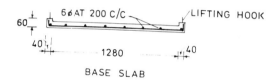

BASE SLAB

Fig.5 Cylindrical ferrocement core unit

Attic type ferrocement core units

   This system consists of a three dimensional ferrocement core unit
of 3 cm thickness. The weight of a core unit is about 900 kg and
these core units are supported on 4 precast concrete columns and are
fixed with in-situ concrete joints. Fig.6 shows the details of an
attic type unit. This simple core unit can be used also as an emergency shelter. The core is designed to be permanent and more hazard
resistant.
   In coastal areas experiencing high winds, floods and tidal waves,
attic type of core units can be used. In areas subjected to high
velocity wind only, box or cylindrical type of units at floor level
are recommended. Ferrocement has been selected for this type of construction because of its superior impact properties, crack resistance,
easy method of casting and mouldability to any desired shpe.

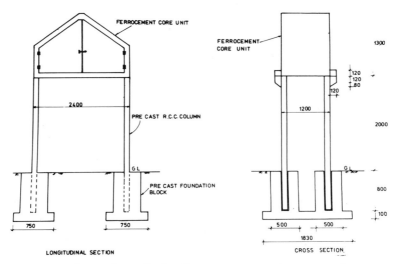

Fig.6 A view of the ferrocement attic type unit

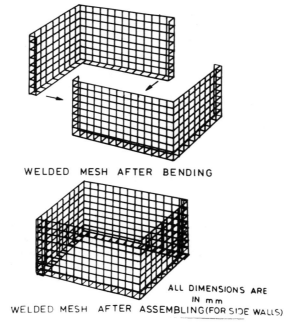

WELDED MESH AFTER BENDING

WELDED MESH AFTER ASSEMBLING (FOR SIDE WALLS)

ALL DIMENSIONS ARE
IN mm

Fig.7 Details of reinforcement for ferrocement water tank

3. Ferrocement water tanks

The demand for small capacity water tanks is as large as the demand for the houses themselves. Designs have been developed for tanks 800, 5000, 7500 and 10,000 litres capacity. Tanks fabricated according to these designs have been subjected to extensive tests to study their short-term and long-term behaviour. The cost analysis made on ferrocement water tanks shows a saving to the extent of 40 percent in the total cost compared to the traditional brick-walled water tanks (2).

Ferrocement small capacity water tanks 800 litres capacity can be made with a wall thickness of 2.5 cm using cement mortar 1:2. The reinforcement consist of a central layer of 10 g x 10 g - 10 cm x 10 cm welded wire mesh and 2 layers of 26 g - 13 mm x 13 mm chicken wire mesh. Fig.7 shows the details of a ferrocement water tank reinforcement.

Both the welded mesh and chicken mesh must be tied together along with fittings such as scour and inlet and outlet and over-flow pipe connections and lifting hooks in the correct positions. The unit can be finished manually or using a spray gun. It is preferable to paint the interior of the water tanks using a tank mastic paint. The weight of the 800 litres water tank is about 340 kg and the cost as per 1982 rates is about US $ 45.00.

Against this a conventional water tank with brick walls cost about US $ 90.00.

The advantages of the ferrocement water tanks over the other types of tanks are:

. They are thin, light, amenable precasting and easy
  transportation.
. They can be cast by labour having skills required for
  normal building construction.
. They do not require the use of shuttering and have a
  high degree of impermeability.
. They are economical compared to tanks built with steel,
  concrete or brick walls.

Conclusions

Low income housing poses a challenge to the policy makers, planners, architects and engineers in view of the several parameters that are to be looked into in finding an economical and viable solution that can be executed within the available resources and time. The process of rapid and uncontrolled urbanisation in developing countries has resulted in the proliferation of vast slums and squatter settlements. Owing to limited financial resources, greater emphasis is now laid on slum improvement programmes and sites-and-services schemes. Use of local materials and technical resources and self-help schemes can only produce economically viable housing and a safer environment. The study has revealed that ferrocement is an appropriate construction material for developing nations for socially

relevant applications like sanitary service core units, water
storage tanks to provide hygenic drinking water and for pre-disaster
housing programmes in cyclone-prone areas.

References

1.   Madhava Rao, A.G., Ramachandra Murthy, D.S., Jayaraman, R., and
      Paul Joseph, G., (1979), American Concrete Institute Publica-
      tion SP-61, 8, 133-142.

2.   Small capacity ferrocement water tanks, (1979), Technical
      Report, Structural Engineering Research Centre, Madras, India.

THE USE OF BLENDED CEMENT IN CONCRETE

IBRAHIM A. ELDARWISH, Ph.D.
Prof. & Director, Testing of Materials Laboratories
MOSTAFA E. SHEHATA, Ph.D.
Assistant Prof., Structural Engineering Department

FACULTY OF ENGINEERING, ALEXANDRIA UNIVERSITY, EGYPT

1. Introduction

Blended cement is a mixture of ordinary Portland Cement Klinder together with active or inactive material ground finely to produce the required cement. It is being produced in many countries all over the world. Different materials being added are pozzolana, slag, fly ash and sand. In Egypt is being produced under the trade name of Karnak cement which is obtained by blending together ordinary Portland Cement Klinder with 25% silicous sand after being finely ground. The blended cement has less mechanical properties but it is cheaper in cost.

2. Effect of sand content on the properties of standard mortar

Fig. (1) represents the effect of sand content on the compressive strength of standard mortar, for stage (1). In fig. (2) the effect of sand content ground or unground on the compressive strength of mortar has been plotted. In fig. (3) the effect of %age of sand on the 28 days compressive strength of mortar has been shown. It was found that the addition of 20% of sand in the form of ground materials represent the most effective percentage regarding the mechanical properties of cement mortar.

3. Properties of fresh concrete

Fig. (4) shows the relation between entrained air and slump for Karnak Cement. In fig. (5) the relation between the entrained air and the compacting factor is being plotted. The relation between slump and compacting factor is shown in fig. (6). A normal relation between different parameters as ordinary cement is noticed.

4. Properties of Hardened Concrete

Fig. (7) shows the relation between compressive strength of standard 15 X 15 X 15 cms cubes and the water cement ratio. Such relation has been plotted again for concrete cylinders 15 X 30 cms. In fig. (9) the relation between indirect tension and W/C is shown. In fig. (10) the relation between bond strength and W/C is clear. The relation between the modulus of rupture and W/C is shown in fig. (11). Normal relations between different parameters are clear. The summary of these relations are plotted in fig. (12) while fig. (13) represents the stress distribution for the splitting tensile test.

5.   Properties of reinforced concrete elements.

Figures (14, 15, 16, 17) show the details of some of the reinforced concrete elements made of Karnak cement that have been
tested. Figures (18, 19, 20) represent the relation between
load and deflection for the same beams. The relation is what
would normally be expected from reinforced concrete beams with
ordinary portland cement.

6.   Conclusion

If the concrete mix is carefully designed with good graded aggregate, low water cement ratio perhaps by the use of plasticizers and good compaction, a concrete cube compressive strength
that ranges from 206 to 325 kg/cm2 has been achieved. Splitting
cylinder tensile strength of maximum value of about 27 kg/cm2
has been obtained, while the maximum modulus of rupture was about
27 kg/cm2. Bond strength of concrete with steel reinforcement
was virtually independent of the compressive strength of concrete
and was in the range of 24 kg/cm2. The fresh concrete properties
were similar to those exhibited by concrete made with ordinary
portland cement. It is possible that the sulphate resistance
of the blended cement is higher than the ordinary one. Tests on
reinforced concrete columns and beams made with blended cement
showed that they can withstand an ultimate load that ranges
between 9.7% to 32% for R.C. columns and between 10% to 25.9%
for R.C. beams as compared to the values obtained when computed
by the plastic theory.

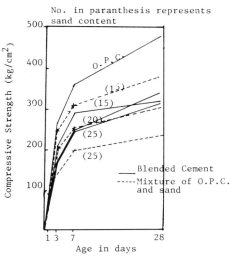

Fig (2) Effect of Sand Content
on the compressive strength of
mortar – Stage (2)

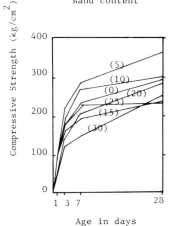

Fig. (1) Effect of Sand Content
on the compressive strength of
Mortar – Stage (1)

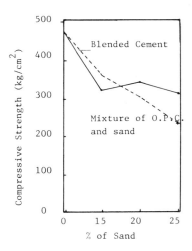

Fig (3) Effect of % age of sand
on 28 days compressive strength
of mortar

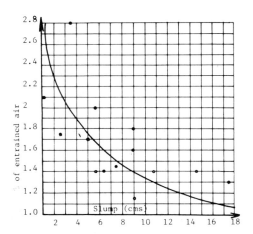

Fig (4) Relation between entrained
air and slump

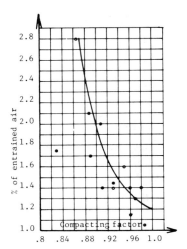

Fig. (5) Relation between
entrained air and compacting
factor

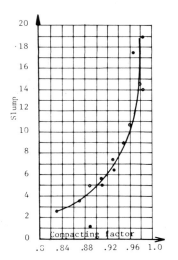

Fig (6) relation between
slump and compacting factor

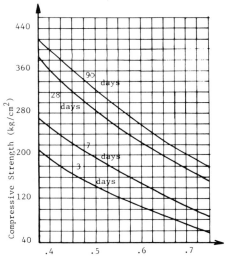

Fig. (7) Relation between compressive
strength and W/C ratio

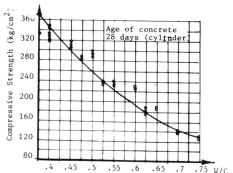

Fig. (8) relation between compressive strength and W/C

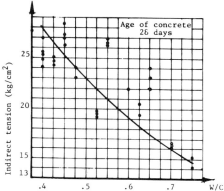

Fig. (9) relation between indirect tension and W/C

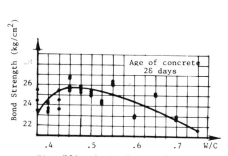

Fig. (10) relation between bond strength and W/C

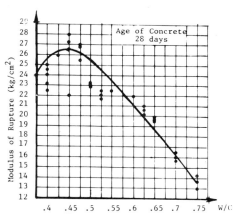

Fig (11) relation between modulus of rupture and W/C

E_c = Modulus of elasticity of Concrete
        Cylinder
f_b = Bond strength

f_t = Splitting tensile strength

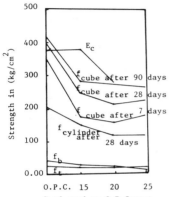

Fig. (12) strength of concrete
made of blended cement stage (2)

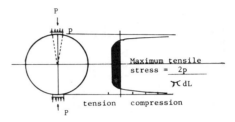

Fig (13) Stress distribution for splitting
tensile test.

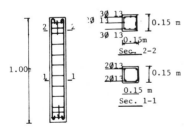

Fig. (14) Details of tested
reinforced concrete column.

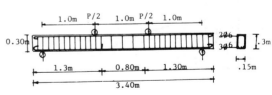

Fig. (15) details of tested reinforced
concrete beam.

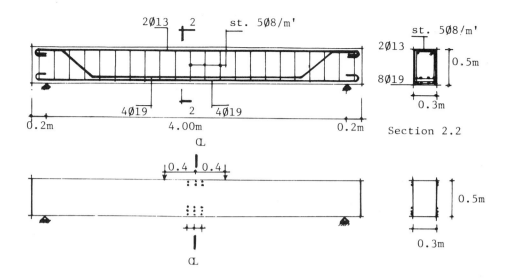

Fig. (16) – Details of the 4.0m tested Reinforced Concrete beam

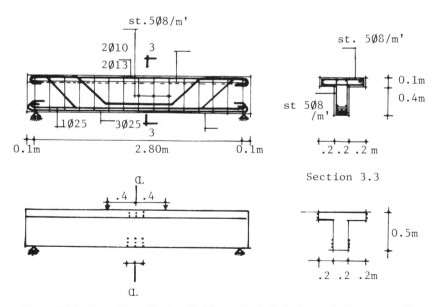

Fig. (17) Details of the 2.80 tested Reinforced Concrete T --
Section beam

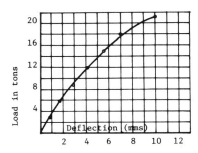

Fig (18) Relation between load
deflection for beam (15)

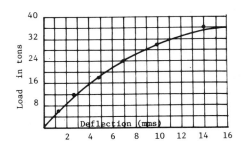

Fig (19) Relation between load deflection
for beam (16)

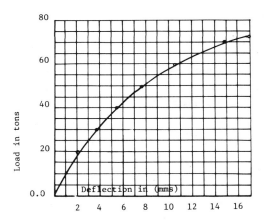

Fig (20) Relation between load and
deflection for beam (17)

PROPERTIES OF PASTES, MORTARS AND CONCRETES MIXED WITH SEA WATERS AND CONTAINING TURKISH CEMENTS

ASIM YEGINOBALI, Yarmouk University, .Irbid, Jordan

1. *Introduction*

The water used for mixing concrete should not result in harmful chemical reactions with the cement, aggregate, reinforcing steel and should not accelerate the deterioration of the concrete properties with time. Considering the complexity of such reactions 'drinkable' water is usually recommended for this purpose. On the other hand, water of such quality can be rather scarce and in countries with coastal regions sea water is occassionally used for mixing concrete.
Considerable research has been done to identify the chemicals in mixing water that can be harmful to concrete and to determine their tolerable limits. Sea waters or waters with similar composition were usually included in these studies. A survey of the literature in-dicated disagreements among the findings of various investigators on. the effects of sea waters on certain concrete properties. For in-stance, in an early study using a sea water with 35 g/l salinity, Abrams reported some decrease in compressive strength after 7 days (1). According to another study even with much higher salinities increased 28 day strengths could be obtained (2). Concerning the effects of sea water mixing on the corrosion of steel reinforcement there were conflicting opinions (3,4). Effects on setting times and durability were also subjects of discussion.
Building codes and specifications usually contain some clauses on the quality of the mixing water for concrete and directly or in-directly remark on the use of sea water for this purpose. Some bring specific limitations on the composition of the water such as allowable total salt and sulfate contents and/or state permissible reductions in strength. Others permit the use of any water encountered in nature providing that it will not cause adverse effects in concrete and in reinforcing steel. Both approaches are reflected in the current Turkish standards (5,6).
In the light of such different approaches by the specifications and considering the somewhat conflicting results from the previous studies, it was felt worthwhile to initiate a comprehensive experi-mental study with the local materials. The experiments were conducted at the Middle East Technical University in Aukara, Turkey.

2. *Materials and experimental program*

The experimental program involved the use of three different sea
waters as mixing water for preparing the paste, mortar and concrete
specimens and a tap water for mixing the control specimens. Four
different portland cements were considered and the type and grading
of aggregate were kept constant.

Sea waters were obtained from western Black Sea, southern Marmara
and eastern Mediterranean shores of Turkey. The locations were
chosen to obtain a wide range of salinity. The compositions of sea
waters used in the experiments are shown in Table 1.

Table 1.   Composition of the sea waters

Principal ions (mg/1)	Black Sea	Marmara Sea	Mediterranean Sea
Na	4,900	8,100	12,400
K	230	340	500
Mg	640	1,035	1,500
Ca	236	328	371
Cl	9,500	14,390	21,270
SO_4	1,362	2,034	2,596
HCO_3	217	182	158
Total	17,085	26,409	38,795
pH	7.4	7.9	8.0

The tap water was the water used at the campus of the university
with the following composition: Cl: 70mg/1, SO_4: 14 mg/1, pH: 7.0.

The four different portland cements were selected among the commonly produced types in Turkey. Together with an ordinary portland
cement, slag cement with 30% blast furnace slag addition, trass cement with 20% trass addition and admixed cement with 10% trass adi-
tion were used in the experiments. Their properties are shown in
Table 2.

The aggregate for the concrete mixes was natural sand and gravel
with maximum particle size of 30mm. It was combined from four different size groups to provide uniform and proper grading. For most
of the mortar mixes standard sand was used to minimize variations in
aggregate properties.

The experimental program involved the tests on different properties
of pastes, mortars and concretes mixed with the sea waters and comparing the results with those obtained by using the tap water. The
tests and investigated properties were as follows:

Cement pastes: normal consistency, soundness, setting times,
heat of hydration, porosity.
Mortars: consistency, flexural strength, compressive strength,
sulfate resistance, reinforcing steel corrosion.

Table 2.   Properties of the cements

Chemical (%)	Ordinary	Slag	Trass	Admix.
SiO_2	20.5	23.8	24.6	23.8
Al_2O_3	7.0	8.4	6.4	7.3
Fe_2O_3	2.6	2.4	2.8	3.2
CaO	51.8	48.0	45.1	50.8
MgO	3.9	4.8	1.6	1.6
SO_3	3.3	2.8	2.1	2.2
Ignition loss	4.0	3.5	4.9	4.7
Insoluble	0.9	0.8	19.5	9.1

Physical				
Specific gravity	3.10	2.96	2.89	3.03
Specific surface (cm^2/g)	3,622	3,254	3,687	3,444
Normal consistency (%)	28	27	30	28
Initial set (hr:min)	2:55	3:10	3:05	4:40
Final set (hr:min)	5:10	5:10	8:10	6:55
Le Chatelier (mm)	2	3	3	4

Strengths (kfg/cm^2)				
7-day flexural	56	49	50	45
28-day flexural	72	73	63	68
7-day compressive	237	213	210	213
28-day compressive	374	350	299	334

Concretes: air content, workability, compressive strength, splitting tensile strength, reinforcing steel corrosion.

Tests were performed according to Turkish standards wherever applicable, which were mostly similar to the standard procedured in U.S.A. or in Germany. At least three repetitions or three test specimens were used for each property tested to obtain the final average value. Full combination of the mixing water - cement variables resulted in 16 mixes which were prepared and tested for most of the properties.

For brevity, different mixes were designated as follows:

To: tap with ordinary, Bo: Black Sea with ordinary, Mo: Marmara with ordinary, Meo: Mediterranean with ordinary.

Ts: tap with slag, Bs: Black Sea with slag, Ms: Marmara with slag, Mes: Mediterranean with slag.

Tt: tap with trass, Bt: Black Sea with trass, Mt: Marmara with trass, Met: Mediterranean with trass.

Ta: tap with admixed, Ba: Black Sea with admixed, Ma: Marmara with admixed, Mea: Mediterranean with admixed.

3.   *Procedures and results of experiments*

3.1   Experiments with cement pastes

The normal consistency of the paste mixes was determined by using
the Vicat instrument. Percentages of water to bring the pastes to
normal consistency varied between 27-30 according to the type of cement. Mixing with sea waters did not affect this property significantly.
    The soundness of the pastes was determined by measuring the total
opening between the needles of the Le Chatelier molds after accelerated curing. The results ranged between 1-4mm for different mixes,
sea waters causing slight or no effect.
    Initial and final setting times for the pastes were determined by
the Vicat instrument. The results are shown in Table 3.
    Heat of hydration evolved from the pastes at the end of 7 and 28
days was determined by using a calorimeter and Beckmann thermometer.
The results are given in Table 3.
    The effect of sea water mixing on the porosity of hardened cement
pastes were investigated by determining the absorption capacity on
5x10cm cylindrical specimens after 60 days of moist curing. Only
four different mixes were used. The results are included in Table 3.

Table 3.   Setting times, heat of hydration and porosity of pastes

Mix	Setting times (hr:min)		Heat of hydration (cal/g)		Porosity (%)
	initial	final	7 day	28 day	
To	2:55	5:10	68	76	29
Bo	2:45	4:50	70	76	--
Mo	2:30	4:45	70	76	--
Meo	2:20	4:35	73	76	27
Ts	3:10	5:10	64	71	30
Bs	2:55	4:55	63	71	--
Ms	2:50	4:50	67	68	--
Mes	2:40	4:40	68	73	28
Tt	3:05	8:00	64	68	--
Bt	2:45	7:45	64	68	--
Mt	2:35	7:30	66	68	--
Met	2:25	7:10	64	69	--
Ta	4:40	6:55	60	67	--
Ba	4:30	6:45	68	70	--
Ma	4:20	6:50	65	69	--
Mea	4:05	6:35	62	70	--

3.2   Experiments with mortars

The consistency of the mortar mixes was determined by measuring the
increase in the base diameters of the mortars molded over a flow
table. The mixing ratio was 1 part cement, 2.75 parts standard sand
and 0.485 part water. The effects of mixing with sea waters were

slight and inconclusive.

Prismatic mortar specimens 4x4x16cm in dimensions were loaded at center points to determine the flexural strength. The mixing ratio was 1 part cement, 3 parts standard sand and 0.5 part water. Moist curing was applied. The results are shown in Table 4.

The compressive strength of the mortars was determined over the broken halves of the flexure specimens by applying the load through 4x4cm steel plates. The results are given in Table 4.

Table 4.　Flexural and compressive strengths of mortars

Mix	Flexural (kgf/cm^2)			Compressive (kgf/cm^2)		
	7 day	28 day	90 day	7 day	28 day	90 day
To	65	80	91	256	324	432
Bo	72	84	90	311	347	458
Mo	72	85	90	297	420	449
Meo	67	85	96	283	413	473
Ts	56	74	80	226	337	432
Bs	69	83	87	270	350	469
Ms	64	76	82	237	325	447
Mes	63	79	89	276	348	516
Tt	46	60	69	184	252	343
Bt	56	66	68	217	290	354
Mt	51	63	72	200	280	364
Met	59	69	73	246	293	401
Ta	49	56	61	183	248	308
Ba	53	64	70	225	263	369
Ma	49	63	70	238	300	380
Mea	65	70	75	256	324	393

The sulfate resistance of mortar mixes were investigated over cubic specimens having 5cm dimensions. Material proportions were same as in consistency test. For each mix the specimens were moist cured for the first 28 days. At this age one group of specimens were tested for compressive strength, the second group was immersed in the mixing water used and the third group was immersed in 10% sodium sulfate solution. The specimens in the last two groups were tested for compressive strength at the end of 316 days. The results are shown in Table 5.

The corrosion of steel bars embedded in mortar was studied over cubic specimens having 15cm dimensions. They were prepared from 1 part cement, 6 parts coarse sand and 0.55 part water. Each contained two steel bars having 12mm diameters and 14cm lengths. The bars were arranged so that one had 2cm and the other 4cm mortar cover. Due to mix proportions and loose compaction the specimens were relatively porous. After 28 days of moist curing they were placed in 3.5% sodium chloride solution up to their mid depths with bars in vertical position.

Table 5.   Compressive strengths in sulfate resistance test (kgf/cm^2)

Mix	28 day	316 day in water	316 day in sulfate	Mix	28 day	316 day in water	316 day in sulfate
To	227	323	193	Tt	186	263	225
Bo	237	328	225	Bt	196	280	242
Mo	279	377	232	Mt	203	268	254
Meo	280	364	212	Met	200	279	250
Ts	221	327	228	Ta	180	258	220
Bs	223	328	239	Ba	194	272	230
Ms	225	324	220	Ma	212	301	248
Mes	230	335	229	Mea	221	312	214

The specimens were removed from the solution after 285 days.   The
bars were cleaned off any rust and weighed to determine the weight
losses.   The results are given in Table 6.

Table 6.   Corrosion of steel bars in mortar

Mix	Mortar Cover (cm)	Weight loss (%)	Mix	Mortar Cover (cm)	Weight loss (%)
To	2	0.733	Tt	2	0.536
	4	0.688		4	0.405
Meo	2	1.516	Bt	2	1.095
	4	1.040		4	0.925
Ts	2	0.391	Met	2	1.120
	4	0.390		4	1.053
Bs	2	0.939	Ta	2	0.527
	4	0.871		4	0.464
Mes	2	1.336	Ba	2	0.933
	4	1.260		4	0.870
			Mea	2	1.177
				4	1.143

3.3   Experiments with concretes

For all concrete properties tested the material quantities in the
mixes, in kg/m^3, were as follows: cement: 300, net water: 150,
fine sand: 377, coarse sand: 453, fine gravel: 491, coarse gravel: 566.
    The air content of the fresh concrete was determined   by the pres-
sure method, using an air meter.   Mixing with sea waters did not
effect the results.
    The workability of the fresh concrete was determined by the slump
test.   The values ranged from 2.5 to 5cm according to cement type.
Again, mixing with sea waters did not have significant effect.
    For determining the compressive and splitting tensile strengths
15x30cm cylindrical specimens were cast from each mix.   They were

moist cured until the day of testing. The results are shown in Table 7.

The corrosion of steel bars embedded in concrete was studied over prismatic specimens having 15x15x30cm dimensions. Each specimen contained four 12mm diameter bars which were arranged along the 30cm dimension to have 2, 3, 4 and 6cm concrete covers. The specimens were cast and compacted carefully and moist cured for the first 48 days. Later, they were subjected to wetting-drying cycles in 3.5% sodium chloride solution, each cycle lasting about one week. After two years, there were no visual signs of corrosion such as staining or cracking over the surface of the specimens. The test is still in progress.

Table 7.   Splitting tensile and compressive strengths of concretes

Mix	Splitting (kgf/cm^2)			Compressive (kgf/cm^2)		
	7 day	28 day	90 day	7 day	28 day	90 day
To	13	19	21	109	179	200
Bo	17	23	24	167	225	275
Mo	15	20	24	168	231	278
Meo	17	20	23	175	248	289
Ts	11	18	21	101	184	220
Bs	13	17	22	137	203	222
Ms	14	18	22	139	192	225
Mes	12	18	20	152	215	265
Tt	8	12	16	83	125	174
Bt	8	14	18	101	147	177
Mt	8	14	15	89	139	176
Met	10	14	19	107	155	187
Ta	11	14	17	111	162	215
Ba	10	14	20	113	164	223
Ma	11	16	20	132	175	241
Mea	12	16	19	141	196	258

4.   *Discussions and conclusions*

The sea waters used in the experiments represented a good cross section of the sea waters existing on earth. The cements generally complied with the related Turkish standards. However, SO_3 content of ordinary portland cement was slightly higher than 3% allowable. Trass cement had a lower 28-day compressive strength than the minimum required 325 kgf/cm^2. Its ignition loss was also higher than 3% allowable. The chemical compositions from Table 2 indicate unusually low CaO and high Al_2O_3 contents, especially for ordinary portland cement. This could be due to improper raw materials, additions and insufficient calcination. All cements were ground much finer than the minimum required values of 2200-2800 cm^2/g.

Mixing with sea water did not have significant influence on the consistency of pastes, mortars and workability and air content of concretes. Sea waters also did not affect the soundness of the pastes indicating that they did not have volume-expanding effects on cements.

A study of Table 3 indicates that with all cements sea waters accelerated both the initial and the final setting times and caused slightly higher heats of hydration. They also reduced the porosity of the hardened pastes slightly. Shortening of the setting times were in proportion with the salinity and could be as much as by 22% in the case of Mediterranean water mixed with trass cement.

Mixing with sea waters increased the mortar and concrete compressive strengths at 7, 28 and 90 days by 15-25%. As seen from Tables 4 and 7, larger increases were obtained with Mediterranean water indicating some proportionality with the salinity. No definite relation could be established between cement type and strength increase. Sea waters caused smaller increases in the indirect tensile strengths of mortars and concretes.

Above effects of the sea waters could be explained by the presence of NaCl as the main salt in the sea water. An x-ray diffraction analysis of the pastes mixed with sea waters indicated its separate crystallization without changing the regular hydration products (7). It was also reported that when NaCl was present in the medium tricalcium silicate could hydrate faster (8). Although the effect of NaCl on heat of hydration and strength is variable (9), the test results confirm its role as an accelerator at least for the salinity ranges and cements involved in the program. Faster hydration with sea water produces more hydration products which start filling the pores in the paste earlier contributing to relatively higher strengths. Smaller increases in the indirect tensile strengths indicate that NaCl crystals forming in the pores may also contribute to larger increases in compressive strength.

According to the strength changes in Table 5 mortars seem to have higher sulfate resistance with trass cement and lower with admixed cement. The effect of sea water mixing is not very conclusive, possibly due to a balance between the chemical reactions involved. Sodium chloride in the sea water increases the solubility of free lime and calcium sulphoaluminates thus, decreasing sulfate corrosion. On the other hand, sulfate concentration in the medium is increased because of the sea water.

Mixing with sea waters increased the corrosion of steel bars embedded in loosely compacted mortars. As shown in Table 6 weight losses were highest with Mediterranean water. Increasing the bar covers from 2 to 4cm was not sufficiently effective. However, steel bars embedded in dense concrete did not exhibit visual signs of corrosion after two years. It is known that normally a protective iron oxide or hydroxide layer forms over the steel bars embedded in concrete due to alkalinity of the medium. Penetration of chlorides lowers the pH value of the medium and the protective layer is destroyed. Test results obtained so far can be explained by a similar mechanism.

In conclusion, it can be stated that as mixing water sea waters do not have significant influence on the consistency, workability and air content of mortars and concretes. They shorten both setting times, cause slightly higher heat of hydration and some acceleration in the formation of hydration products, followed by increased strengths up to 90 days. Strength increases are not very much on the average and such concretes may be proportioned in the usual manner. As in all marine environments concrete should be dense and sufficient bar cover must be provided. In hot climates precautions may be required against accelerated setting.

The results are applicable to the types of cements used in the experiments. Therefore, additional research with local materials would provide basis for the local specifications. Additional studies are also recommended on sulfate resistance and strength developments beyond 90 days.

References

1.   Abrams, D. A. (1924), *Effect of Impure Waters when Used in Mixing Concrete*, Proc. ACI, 20, 442-486.
2.   Taylor, M. and Kuwairi, A. (1978), *Effects of Ocean Salts on the Compressive Strength of Concrete*, Cem. Con. Res., 9.
3.   Griffin, D. L. and Henry, R. L. (1963), *Proc. ASTM*, 63, 1046-1078.
4.   Shalon, R. and Raphael, M. (1959), *Influence of Sea Water on Corrosion of Reinforcement*, J. ACI, June, 1251-1268.
5.   TS 1247. (1973), *Mixing, Placing and Curing of Concrete*, Ankara, Turkey.
6.   TS 500. (1981), *Building Code Requirements for Reinforced Concrete* Ankara, Turkey.
7.   Yeginobali, A. and Cebeci, O. (1981), *TBTAK, Report No. 508*, Ankara, Turkey.
8.   Young, J. F. and Tong, H. S. (1977), *Compositions of Solutions in Contact with Hydrating Tricalcium Silicate Pastes*, J. Am. Ceram. Soc., 60.
9.   Neville, A. M. (1977), *Properties of Concrete*, Pitman, 97.

EMPLOI DE BETONS A FAIBLE DOSAGE EN CIMENT POUR LA CONSTRUCTION
ECONOMIQUE EN COTE D'IVOIRE

JACQUES SIMONNET LBTP (COTE D'IVOIRE)
MICHEL TITECAT   LBTP (COTE D'IVOIRE)

1. Présentation du béton à coût minimum et premiers essais :

C'est en janvier 1982 que sur la demande d'une Entreprise Ivoirienne
a été abordée l'étude de composition d'un béton à très faible dosage
en ciment. Cette Société (Société Ivoirienne pour le Développement de
la Construction Industrialisée-SIDECI) dispose d'un important parc de
matériel de pompage de béton et de banches en fonte d'aluminium (procédé CON-TECH) qu'elle n'a pas pu jusqu'à présent utiliser dans des
opérations économiquement adéquates. Aussi et dans le but de descendre
les coûts, le Laboratoire du Bâtiment et des Travaux Publics était-il
pressenti pour l'étude d'un béton à très faible dosage en ciment (inférieur à 200 kg/m^3), de consistance plastique (affaissement 10 cm) de
façon a être pompable et à permettre une mise en oeuvre correcte en
murs banchés de 10 cm d'épaisseur.
   Au point de vue des résistances l'idée était de faire un mur de béton non armé de capacité portante au moins égale à celle d'une maçonnerie de parpaings creux en 10 cm d'épaisseur, telle que couramment
utilisée dans l'habitat économique à Abidjan.

1.1 Les bétons sous-dosés en ciment :

Les premiers essais ont montré que dès que l'on descendait sous
250 kg/m^3, la qualité du béton diminuait très rapidement. Les résistances devenaient très faibles et surtout l'ouvrabilité du béton
s'avérait très insuffisante : le ciment, en trop faible proportion ne
pouvait plus jouer son rôle lubrifiant dans la pâte. Ainsi le béton
très rêche mais sans tenue, avec des affaissements au cône presque
nuls, perdait-il toute cohésion dès qu'on le vibrait, ne retenant
absolument pas l'eau avec en conséquence de très forts ressuages.

   Il convient de signaler que les sables et granulats utilisés dans
la région d'Abidjan ne constituent pas des matériaux propices à de
faibles dosages en ciment. Notamment les sables se caractérisent par
une granulométrie très étroite avec absence de fines (sables de mer,
sables de lagune). Quant aux concassés de granite ou de quartz, leurs
coefficients de forme sont médiocres.

1.2 Le recours au filler :

Les premiers résultats n'étaient pas très encourageants jusqu'au moment où il a été imaginé de compenser partiellement le manque de ciment par du filler. L'idée allait de soi si l'on considère que les problèmes se posaient au niveau du béton frais, avant prise, auquel visiblement faisait défaut la lubrification apportée par les particules de ciment. On pouvait espérer que les particules de filler de granulométrie proche rempliraient ce rôle.

Ceci a été confirmé dès les premiers essais en laboratoire où l'on observa un saut qualitatif déterminant dans le domaine de l'ouvrabilité. Ainsi alors que les affaissements au cône d'Abrams étaient précédemment en deçà de 2 cm (béton très ferme) même pour de forts dosages en eau (210 l/m^3), l'adjonction de filler (environ 100 kg/m^3) permettait d'obtenir aisément des affaissements de 12 à 15 cm (béton mou) pour les mêmes dosages en eau.

De plus ces bétons avaient une meilleure tenue ; leur vibration ne s'accompagnait pas de ressuage excessif ni de remontée de laitance, laissant bien augurer de leur comportement vis-à-vis de la ségrégation.

1.3 L'utilisation de tout-venant :

Les essais en laboratoire avaient consisté en l'adjonction d'un filler, extrait préalablement de sable fillerisé, et que l'on avait introduit dans une composition classique de béton, comprenant un sable et deux granulats concassés : un 5/15 et un 15/25, le tout dosé suivant la méthode DREUX. Le dosage en filler avait été choisi afin de retrouver la proportion d'éléments fins habituelle dans les bétons, soit 100 à 150 kg/m^3 de filler pour des dosages de 200 à 150 kg/m^3 en ciment.

Or l'examen de la courbe granulométrique du mélange filler-sable-granulat nous a naturellement conduit à envisager l'utilisation d'un simple tout-venant concassé de carrière, ce qui amenait alors des économies importantes.

Sur la région d'Abidjan, compte tenu du différentiel de prix départ carrière entre les tout-venant et les concassés criblés, le recours aux premiers permet une économie de l'ordre de la moitié de celle obtenue en réduisant le dosage en ciment, la seule visée au début.

Ainsi les études préliminaires avaient-elles abouti à un béton à coût réduit, permettant des économies de 35 % à 45 % sur le prix hors oeuvre (fourniture et confection) par rapport au béton classique dosé à 350 kg/m^3 de granulats concassés criblés.

Ce béton d'une ouvrabilité satisfaisante, d'un dosage en ciment de 150 kg/m^3 environ offrait des résistances à 28 j de l'ordre de 2 à 4 MPa, suivant le dosage en eau.

2. Les perspectives d'emploi du béton à coût minimum :

Compte tenu des performances économiques de ce type de béton, compte tenu de leurs caractéristiques mécaniques, un domaine d'utilisation assez large semblait s'ouvrir ; on peut immédiatement le passer en revue.

2.1 Le logement économique :

Il se caractérise le plus souvent par des bâtiments en bande, à simple rez-de-chaussée et couverture légère, ou plus rarement par des constructions en R + 2. Dans les deux cas on rencontre des maçonneries en parpaings avec chaînages en béton armé, porteuses mais très peu sollicitées, que l'on peut songer à remplacer par un béton à coût minimum, banché, non armé (chaîné éventuellement). Les dallages, semelles et longrines de ce type de bâtiment sont également très peu sollicités dans la majorité des cas, et donc envisageables comme domaine d'emploi.

2.2 Les petits ouvrages routiers et de voirie urbaine :

Là encore on rencontre nombre d'ouvrages usuellement conçus en béton ou en maçonnerie, qui sont le plus souvent très peu sollicités : perrés, fossés maçonnés, petits dalots, murs de soutènement de hauteur inférieure à 1 m 50, bordures de trottoir.
    Il faut signaler ici que des propositions concrètes ont été faites dans le cadre d'une "Recommandation sur l'exécution des fossés", où l'on a pu montrer que le recours à des fossés maçonnés en béton à coût minimum pouvait représenter une économie de 45 % par rapport aux ouvrages actuellement utilisés.

2.3 Les impératifs technologiques pour l'emploi des bétons à coût minimum :

2.3.1 Les critères de résistance :

L'expérience de bureaux d'études montre que si l'on exclut les ouvrages d'art (ponts, silos...) et les bâtiments exceptionnels (tours, stades, salles de spectacles...), on rencontre le plus souvent des sollicitations de compression très modérées dans le béton.
    Dans le domaine du bâtiment courant avec des portées (< 5 m), des hauteurs (< 4 à 5 niveaux) et des surcharges (< 2 kN/m^2) modérées, seules les poutres présentent des compressions dans le béton de l'ordre de la dizaine de MPa. Dans les dalles et hourdis les contraintes sont plus souvent en deçà de 5 MPa.

Ainsi si l'on se place dans le cadre du Règlement Français (ccBA), une contrainte en flexion de 5 MPa nécessite un béton de résistance nominale égale à :
    5 MPa/ (5/6 x 0,6) = 10 MPa
    Or les résistances nominales à escompter pour les dosages usuels sont :

2.3.2 Les critères minimaux de qualité :

Nous nous sommes préoccupés jusqu'ici du critère de résistance. Nous avons développé l'idée que nombre d'ouvrages en béton ne nécessitent en fait que des résistances mécaniques modestes, d'où il y a lieu d'utiliser d'une part de plus faibles dosages en ciment, d'autre part des granulats de qualité inférieure.

Il s'ensuit une diminution des résistances mécaniques, mais également une altération plus ou moins prononcée des autres caractéristiques du béton. On peut passer en revue les plus importantes.

. Ouvrabilité :

Lorsque le dosage en ciment décroît, il en est de même de la maniabilité. On sait qu'une des fonctions du ciment est de jouer un rôle de lubrifiant entre les granulats dans le béton frais. On constate aux bas dosages en ciment à la fois des affaissements très faibles au cône et un comportement fortement thixotropique : le béton en apparence très rêche se fluidifie fortement sous la moindre vibration, avec une forte ségrégation et un ressuage brutal (le béton n'a aucune tenue à la main). Les ajouts d'eau seraient donc intempestifs afin d'atteindre les maniabilités désirées. Cependant le recours aux matériaux fillerisés vient résoudre ces difficultés. Nos expériences ont en effet montré que les fines venaient efficacement compléter le ciment dans le rôle de fluidifiant.

. Compacité, porosité :

Les deux propriétés sont étroitement liées à la précédente, c'est-à-dire aux conditions de mise en oeuvre (teneur en eau, énergie de vibration). Elles ont des implications cruciales sur l'étanchéité (dans une perspective économique il faut éviter le recours aux enduits) et sur la protection contre la corrosion des aciers.

. Retrait :

Les risques de fissuration dus au retrait augmentent avec la teneur en eau, la faiblesse des résistances en traction, mais décroissent avec la réduction des dosages en ciment et la diminution des modules d'élasticité. Le problème est donc complexe et les meilleurs enseignements seront fournis par l'observation du comportement de murs en vraie grandeur (voir les études de faisabilité ci-après).

. Corrosion, adhérence des aciers :

L'augmentation relative de la porosité dans ce type de béton risque de rendre plus sensible à la corrosion les armatures. Cependant il est probable qu'une légère majoration des enrobages suffira à écarter ce danger. En ce qui concerne la liaison mécanique entre l'acier et le béton, de nombreuses précautions seraient à prendre :

dosage : 300 kg/m^3 σ'_{28} = 20 MPa.
          350   = 24
          400   = 27

Il est donc possible d'envisager l'utilisation de bétons à carac-
térisitiques mécaniques réduites dans le bâtiment moyennant éventuellement certaines précautions d'emploi.

En fait, le problème principal en ce qui concerne le béton armé
risque de surgir au niveau de la liaison avec l'armature : il faudra
envisager des contraintes d'adhérence notablement réduites et attacher
la plus grande attention à la corrosion (en prévoyant des épaisseurs
d'enrobage majorées).

Un autre domaine possible d'emploi est constitué par le béton non
armé, notamment le béton banché pour murs porteurs. Ici, encore plus
nettement, les taux de sollicitation de la matière sont limités à des
valeurs très faibles (de l'ordre de 1 MPa). Les murs porteurs en béton banché sont à comparer du point de vue mécanique aux murs en ma -
çonnerie classique, plus précisément à la maçonnerie en agglomérés
creux.

Si l'on se réfère aux textes réglementaires applicables en Côte
d'Ivoire (DTU 20.11 et 23.1) on obtient comme contraintes admissibles:

. pour une maçonnerie en blocs creux type B 40, en façade :

  C = $\dfrac{40}{8}$ = 5 bars = 0,5 MPa en compression,

. pour une maçonnerie en blocs pleins, type B 120 :

  C = $\dfrac{120}{8}$ = 15 bars = 1,5 MPa,

. la contrainte de traction admissible est égale au tiers de la
  contrainte d'adhérence du mortier. En pratique on peut admettre
  σ_t = 4 bars = 0,4 MPa (d'après GUERRIN, Béton Armé tome 4),

. pour le béton banché, le DTU 23.1 donne comme contrainte admis
  sible en compression simple :

$$\overline{\sigma'_{bo}} = 0,33 \; \alpha \; \beta \; \gamma \; \sigma'_{28}$$

On peut prendre comme valeur moyenne α = 0,5 ;

  β = 0,6 ; γ = 0,83 ce qui fait :
pour $\overline{\sigma'_{bo}}$= 0,5 σ'_{28} = 6 MPa
              = 1,5   =18 MPa.

On peut donc en conclure :
. que la maçonnerie en blocs de béton peut être remplacée par du
  béton banché à coût minimum.
. que les capacités portantes de ces murs peuvent être reliées à
  la résistance du béton sur éprouvettes par une formule proche
  de : $\overline{\sigma'_{bo}}$ = σ'_{28} /12
. qu'en conséquence les résistances constatées à ce jour, entre
  2 et 4 MPa, autorisent des taux de travail entre 0,17 et
  0,33 MPa en compression dans les murs banchés en béton à coût
  minimum. Ces chiffres semblent suffisants pour de l'habitat
  économique jusqu'à deux niveaux.

- utilisation de ronds lisses,
- minoration des contraintes dans l'acier,
- augmentation des longueurs d'ancrage,
- utilisation de barres de petit diamètre.

Disons tout de même que l'appréciation de ces inconvénients doit être tempérée par le fait qu'à l'évidence les bétons économiques, faiblement sollicités, seront faiblement armés.

. Aspect de surface, résistance superficielle :

Ces qualités, en connexion étroite avec l'ouvrabilité et la compacité, sont essentielles si l'on veut absolument éviter la pose d'un enduit, qui annulerait tout les avantages économiques éventuels de cette technologie. Ici encore il s'avère nécessaire de se référer à des essais en vraie grandeur.

3. Les essais de faisabilité :

Les premiers essais en laboratoire avaient permis de définir un béton à dosage minimal en ciment. Il s'agissait d'un domaine technologique nouveau, peu exploré à notre connaisance. Il convenait de s'assurer de la faisabilité de ce béton dans les conditions de chantier, avant même d'entreprendre toute nouvelle campagne d'étude en laboratoire.

Aussi a-t-il été décidé de la confection d'une série de murs d'essai en vraie grandeur. L'opération a été menée en collaboration avec la SIDECI. Les objectifs majeurs étaient de tester les difficultés éventuelles à la fabrication, au transport et à la mise en oeuvre, de s'assurer de l'ouvrabilité et des possibilités de transit par une pompe à béton, de contrôler l'aspect au décoffrage, la tenue aux intempéries et les fissurations de retrait.

Les bétons ont été confectionnés en centrale, livrés en camion malaxeur, mis en oeuvre par l'intermédiaire d'une pompe. Le coffrage était constitué de banches type CON-TECH, espacées de 10 et 15 cm. Les murs, de 2 m 75 de hauteur dessinaient en plan un H avec un élément central de 2 m 50 et des retours de 1,20m. Les murs d'essais constituaient donc des éléments auto-stables de dimensions comparables aux ossatures usuelles des logements en bande. Cinq murs ont été réalisés, pour des dosages en ciment variant de 200 à 100 kg/m^3. Seul le mur n° 5, qui constituait une tentative de sous-dosage à 100 kg de CPA, ne présentait pas un aspect convenable. Il faut ici retenir que le mur n° 4 a permis de définir un béton entièrement opérationnel. Il se caractérise par :

C = 150 kg/m^3	E = 270 1	σ_7 = 0,8 MPa	σ_{28} = 1,9 MPa	σ_{50} = 2,9 MPa

Il était ainsi établi la possibilité de réaliser des murs en bétons banchés de faible épaisseur (10 cm) et d'une capacité portante suffisante pour des constructions à 1 ou 2 niveaux. Après avoir établi la faisabilité technologique il restait à étudier le bilan économique du recours à un béton sous-dosé en ciment.

On peut tout d'abord estimer les économies réalisées sur la fourniture du béton, en prenant comme base de référence un béton "classique", dosé à 350 kg de CPA par mètre cube. Les prix ci-dessous sont des prix hors taxe sur la place d'Abidjan, au mois de mars 1983, exprimés en francs CFA (1 000 F CFA = 20 FF $\simeq$ 2 $ 75 c)

Hypothèse :

. Prix des fournitures :

ciment :	:	29 900 F/tonne départ usine
granulat concassé	:	5 000 F/tonne départ carrière
sable :	:	1 150 F/tonne départ carrière
		(soit 1 700 F/m^3)
tout-venant	:	2 200 F/tonne départ carrière

. Transport et fabrication :

On estime à 40 F/tonne/km le coût du transport et on admettra une distance de transport de 30 km en moyenne, soit un coût forfaitaire de 30 x 40 = 1 200 F/tonne. Par ailleurs on évaluera les coûts de fabrication (dosage, malaxage) et le transport à pied d'oeuvre du béton à 3 000 F/m^3 pour le béton classique et à 2 500 F/m^3 pour le béton de tout-venant.

Béton classique : prix sec H.T. à pied d'oeuvre :

Composition :
Granulats concassés criblés : 900 1/m^3 soit 1,2 tonne/m^3 (d = 1,33)
Sable   : 420 1/m^3 soit 0,62 tonne/m^3 (d = 1,48)

Coût :
Ganulat 1,2 x 1,05 x (5 000 + 1 200) = 7 812 F
Sable   0,62 x 1,05 x (1 150 + 1 200) = 1 530 F
                                          ─────────
                                          9 342 F
Ciment 0,350 x 1,07 x (29 900 + 1 200) = 11 647 F
Fabrication   3 000 F
                                          ─────────
       Le mètre cube de béton :   23 989 F

nota : On a adopté des coefficients de perte de 1,05 pour les agrégats et de 1,07 pour le ciment.

Béton à coût minimum :

Composition : 1,920 tonne/m^3 de tout-venant

Coûts :
Tout-venant : 1,920 x 1,05 x (2 200 + 1 200) = 6 854 F
Ciment   : 0,150 x 1,07 x (29900 + 1 200) = 4 992 F
Fabrication :   2 500 F
                                               ─────────
       Le mètre cube de béton   14 346 F

On constate ainsi une économie globale de 40 % qui se décompose en 28 % d'économie due au sous-dosage en ciment et 12 % due à l'utilisation de tout-venant.

La consommation de ciment est de 15 kg au mètre carré de mur alors qu'il faut compter 16,5 kg pour des murs en géobéton non enduits et 26 kg pour des murs en parpaings creux avec un enduit extérieur.

4. L'opération pilote de YOPOUGON-KOUTE :

Les essais de faisabilité ont été achevés en janvier 1983, avec les résultats probants que nous venons de mettre en évidence et des perspectives économiques prometteuses. Il a donc été décidé d'entreprendre une campagne d'essais au LBTP, à la Direction de la Recherche, de façon à aller plus avant dans la connaissance de ce matériau, à la charnière entre les graves ciment bien connues dans le domaine routier et le béton hydraulique. Il conviendrait peut-être de désigner ce produit sous l'appellation "GRAVE-BETON". Les premiers objectifs de ces études sont de préciser l'influence des dosages en eau, ciment et filler sur les résistances, l'ouvrabilité, le retrait et la porosité.

Parallèlement la SIDECI, grâce à laquelle ont été réalisés les murs d'essais, confirmait sa détermination à utiliser cette "grave béton" et décidait d'entreprendre une opération pilote visant à s'assurer de la rentabilité du procédé dans le domaine de l'habitat économique. La Direction de la Recherche s'y trouvait naturellement associée et s'il est encore tôt pour en tirer des conclusions sûres, nous pouvons néanmoins espérer à terme de nombreux enseignements sur la résistance, l'ouvrabilité, l'aspect, la fissuration, le retrait de ces murs en grave béton à 15 kg de ciment par mètre cube. L'aspect économique du procédé est également suivi de près.

Disons simplement que l'opération consistera à terme en la construction de 88 logements en bande, à YOPOUGON-KOUTE à la périphérie d'ABIDJAN (20 km environ du centre ville). Les logements sont construits sur des parcelles de 150 m^2 (12 m x 13 m) viabilisées par la SETU (Société d'Equipement des Terrains Urbains); le prix du terrain est de l'ordre de 2 000 à 3 000 F/m^2. Deux types de logements ont été retenus :

. Un modèle minimum comprenant deux pièces, une cuisine et un wc-douche (surface couverte 52 m^2, surface habitable 45 m^2).

. Un modèle standard comprenant trois pièces, une cuisine, un w-c et une douche (surface couverte 81 m^2, surface habitable 70 m^2).

Ces deux modèles sont susceptibles d'une extension future à charge de l'acquéreur. Ils sont livrés avec équipement minimum. Du point de vue technologique on a a adopté pour le gros-oeuvre :

. Fondations : semelles filantes faiblement armées ; grave béton à 200 kg/m^3 de ciment (GB 200),
. Dallage : grave béton non armée en 6 cm d'épaisseur sur terre compactée (GB 150),
. Murs : grave béton à 150 kg/m^3 de ciment, banchée non vibrée, cadres des portes et des fenêtres incorporés au coffrage ; ces murs ne sont pas armés, mais "chaînés" comme une maçonnerie dans les angles, en pied et en tête, aux extrémités et, bien sûr, dans

les linteaux. La consommation d'acier est donc
très faible

. Couverture : la couverture en bac d'aluminium, épaisseur 6/10 mm,
est fixée sur une charpente en bois rouge local très
sommaire et sur des tasseaux noyés en tête de mur.
Pas de faux plafonds.

Estimation prévisionnelle des coûts pour le logement cellule minimum:

1) Métrés :

Fondation : béton propreté   : 0,5 m^3 en GB 150
            semelle   : 1,2 m^3 en GB 200
            acier pour semelles : 35 kg en Fe E22 ou TS 3.3

Dallage   : bétons   : 3,85 m^3 en GB 150

Murs   : béton banché   : 8,50 m^3 en GB 150
            acier pour chaînage : 50 kg en Fe E22 ou TS 3.3

Couverture : charpente   : (pour mémoire)
             bac alu 6/10   : 70 ml en 0,75 m de largeur
                                  utile.

2) Prix Unitaires : (francs CFA)

Acier   :   320 F/kg   prix secs,HT)
Béton GB 150 :
            fourniture, fabrication : 15 000 F/m^3
            mise en oeuvre   : 2 000
                                      ----
                                      17 000 F/m^3

Béton GB 200 :   18 500 F/m^3

Coffrages   :
            banches   18 000 F/m^3
            semelles   12 000 F/m^3
Soit au total :
            GB 150 dallage   = 17 000 F/m^3
            GB 200 semelle : 18 500 + 12 000 = 30 500 F/m^3
            GB 150 banché : 17 000 + 18 000 = 35 000 F/m^3

3) Prix Secs Hors-Taxe :

Fondations : 0,5 x 17 000   = 8 500 F
              1,2 x 30 500   = 36 600 F
              35 x   320   = 11 200 F
                                      ----
                                      56 300 F

Dallage   : 3,85 x 29 000   =   111 650 F

Murs   : 8,50 x 35 000   =297 500 F
              50 x   320   = 16 000 F
                                      ----
                                     313 500 F

Couverture : 70   x 2 500   =   175 000 F
                                               ----
                                               656 450 F CFA

On peut estimer à 100 000 F CFA le reste du gros-oeuvre (équipements, clôture) et à 200 000 F CFA le second-oeuvre et l'équipement (toujours en prix secs hors taxe) soit un prix sec HT total de 1 000 000 F CFA par logement.

Sous condition que l'entreprise arrive à maîtriser ses coûts et ses marges, le "chapeau" peut-être compris entre 1,85 et 2,10 soit avec le coût du terrain un prix de vente de l'ordre de 2 500 000 à 3 000 000 F CFA par logement. Ramené au m² habitable cela fait un prix de 55 000 à 67 000 F/m². Soit 150 à 180 ¢/m² (terrain compris).

En estimant à 9 500 F/m² (cf paragraphe 3 ci-dessus) l'économie réalisée en remplaçant le béton usuel par de la grave béton, l'économie est de 134 000 F/logement sur le prix sec soit une économie de 18 % sur le gros-oeuvre, de 14 % sur le coût total du logement (terrain non compris), de 12 % sur le coût total

Conclusions.

L'opération pilote que nous venons de décrire sommairement ne doit pas être considérée comme un modèle achevé de logement économique. A notre avis seul le gros-oeuvre porteur (fondation, dallage, mur) qui est innovant a fait l'objet d'une étude approfondie. Celle-ci permettra de juger de l'avenir possible de la grave béton dans le domaine de la construction. Nous pensons avoir montré qu'il peut-être riche d'espoirs.

SECTION III

Bois et fibres naturelles

Timber and natural fibres

USE OF KENAF FIBRES FOR REINFORCEMENT OF RICH CEMENT-SAND CORRUGATED SHEETS

OMER M. E. FAGEIRI, Building & Road Research Institute, University of Khartoum

1. *Introduction*

Natural fibres, such as sisal, coir, wood pulp, elephant grass, wood wool etc., were used in some parts of the world to reinforce a low tensile strength matrix to produce low cost building components, e.g., sand-cement corrugated sheets and tiles. Research and development on techniques used for fabrication of building components reinforced with some natural fibres, their physical and mechanical properties and their environmental and structural behaviour in service, was carried out in some countries, i.e., England (2), India (4), Kenya (16, 17, 18), Sweden (10), Tanzania (13), Zambia (3,7), Zimbabwe (18), etc. A review of fibre-cement research and development with particular reference to third world applications was given by Swift (15).

Kenaf which is the vernacular name given to the fibres from the plant *Hibiscus cannabinus* has not been investigated for reinforcement of a low tensile strength matrix to produce low cost building components. The need to produce durable and low cost building components using local building materials and simple technologies, is of great importance to the Sudan as this will help in solving some of the problems of low cost houses related to cost and availability of imported materials and skilled labour in urban and semi-urban areas. The use of kenaf fibres to reinforce rich cement-sand mortor to produce durable and low cost corrugated sheets and roofing tiles will help in lowering the roofing cost of low cost houses which constitutes about 30% of the cost of a low cost house in urban and semi-urban areas of the Sudan (5).

Realizing the success of using natural fibres for reinforcement of rich cement-sand mortar to produce corrugated sheets in some countries, as mentioned before, a project was formulated in the Building and Road Research Institute (BRRI) of the University of Khartoum to investigate the possibility of using kenaf fibres to produce cement-sand building components. The project was divided into three phases:

Phase 1: To investigate the possibility of using kenaf fibres to reinforce rich cement-sand mortar to produce corrugated sheets.

Phase 2: To investigate the techno-economic aspects and long term behaviour of kenaf reinforced cement-sand corrugated sheets and roofing tiles produced by employing simple manual techniques.

Phase 3:   To develop a simple technology to produce kenaf reinforced
corrugated sheets and roofing tiles on a small factory
scale and to carry out the techno-economic feasibility
study of setting such a factory near some urban and semi-
urban centres.

This paper summarizes the findings of Phase 1 of the project. The
results of this phase gave BRRI the green light to pursue the project
into Phase 2 and probably Phase 3. The findings of these phases,
when completed, will be reported in due time.

2.   *A description of kenaf fibres*

Kenaf fibres are extraced from the stalks of the plant *Hibiscus
cannabinus* using mechanical or manual (wetting and retting) techniques.

Hibiscus cannabinus grows naturally in the Tong area of the southern region of Sudan, refer to Fig. 1, where local people extract
manually the fibres from its stalks to make ropes. It is also
cultivated in Abu-ne'ama area of the central region of the Sudan where
the extracted fibres are used to produce sacks in a factory near
Abu-ne'ama, refer to Fig. 1. The plant requires about 125 mm of rainfall or its equivalent per month for the first 2/3 of the growing
period which ranges between 3 and 5 months. The plant's stalks, when
they are ready for harvest, may reach a height varying between 1.50 m
to 2.5 m. (14).

Kenaf fibres are graded before they are used to manufacture sacks.
While best grades are used to produce sacks, inferior grades may be
used to make ropes. The principal characteristics that are considered in determining the fibres grades are their tensile strength,
cleanliness, size, length and colour. These characteristics are
dependent on several factors such as the maturity of the plant when
harvested, size and length of stalks and quality of extraction.

In this project best grade kenaf fibres, similar to those used for
the manufacture of sacks, were used. The size, length and tensile
strength of the fibres were determined and reported hereinafter. The
long term behaviour of the fibres when subjected to repeated wetting
and drying (rot susceptibility) and alkalis (lime) was decided to be
investigated within the scope of phase 2 of this project when the
fabricated sheets will be subjected to long term environmental
conditions.

2.1 Fibre Size and Length: It was found somewhat difficult to
identify a single fibre of kenaf. An apparently visible single long
fibre was found to divide into many shorter fibres when rolled between
fingers and that the lesser the diameter, the shorter was the fibre.
A single kenaf fibre was found to range in diameter between 0.04 μm
and 0.085 μm and in length between 0.03 m and 0.75 m. Thus, kenaf
fibres were found occurring in strands of varying sizes which were
further subdivided by hand into smaller strands of desirable sizes
and lengths.

2.2 Fibre Tensile Strength: Tensile tests were carried out on single
kenaf fibres conditioned approximately to 12% moisture content. The

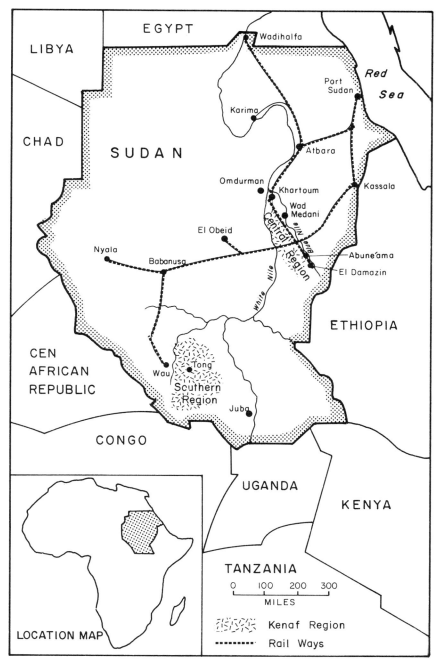

Figure 1. Map of Sudan.

tests were carried out on an Instron Universal Machine at a rate of
0.0254 mm per minute and a maximum load range of 4.45 N. The lengths
of test fibres were about 30 mm which was the maximum fibre length
obtainable when separating single kenaf fibres from fibre strands
using fingers. Load-deformation relationships for individual test
fibres were recorded and the fibres' cross-sectional dimensions
(assumed square) were measured at failure positions using a high
magnification measurement microscope. Also measurements for the
variation in each test fibre cross-sectional dimensions at 10 positions along its lengths were made for modulus of elasticity calculations. Calculated mean values of ultimate tensile stress and modulus
of elasticity and their coefficients of variations are reported in
Table 1 compared with other natural and synthetic fibres. All the
tested fibres were found to have linear load-deformation relationship.
Also, it was found that kenaf fibres have a mean ultimate tensile
stress comparable with those of sisal and polypropylene fibres and
comparatively higher than that of elephant grass, but much lower than
those of glass, asbestos and steel fibres (10% - 30%). Kenaf fibres
were also found to have a mean modulus of elasticity higher than those
of sisal and polypropylene fibres, but much lower than those of glass,
asbestos and steel fibres (10% - 25%).

Table 1. Ultimate tensile stress and eleasticity modulus of kenaf
fibres and other natural and synthetic fibres.

Fibre type	Ultimate Tensile Stress MN/m^2	Modulus of elasticity GN/m^2
Kenaf fibre	Mean = 295 St. deviation = 62 COV = 0.21	Mean = 22 St. deviation = 5 COV = 0.23
Sisal fibre (16)*	Mean = 331 St. deviation = 65 COV = 0.2	Mean = 13.2 St. deviation = 0.3 COV = .023
Elephant grass fibre (3)*	180	--
Polypropylene fibre (6)*	400	8
Glass fibre (15)*	3000	80
Asbestos fibre (15)*	1000 ~ 3000	170 ~ 195
Steel fibre (15)*	1000 ~ 3000	200

*( ) refers to list of references.

3. *Preparation of sheets and testing program*

3.1 Preparation of Sheets: A total of 10 rich cement-sand corrugated
sheets reinforced with long and/or short kenaf fibres were produced
using a technique similar to that adapted by the Appropriate
Technology Centre of Kenyatta College, Nairobi (20). Also 5 plain

Table 2. Data summary on corrugated sheets produced.

Sheet Class	Description of Fibres (at 12% m.c.)	Number of Sheets**	Mean Thickness of Sheets (mm)	Mean Corrugation pitch (mm)	Mean Corrugation depth (mm)	Cement/ Sand Ratio	Water/* Cement Ratio	Short Fibre/ Total wt. Content (%)	Long Fibre/ Total wt. Content (%)	Total Fibre/ Total wt. Content (%)
Cate- gory A	Long fibres + short fibres	5	10.8	148	55	1.5	0.42	0.65	0.91	1.56
Cate- gory B	Short fibres only	5	10.7	148	53	1.5	0.41	1.6	--	1.60
Cate- gory C	Nil	5	10.7	148	53	1.5	0.39	--	--	--

* W/C ratio was decided such that comparable workabilities of mortar mixes of sheets Category A, B, and C were achieved.

** Sheet size is 0.70 m x 1.20 m.

rich cement-sand sheets were produced for control. Figure 2 summarizes the main steps necessary to prepare these sheets. The data adopted for preparation of sheets is given in Table 2.

3.2 Testing Program: Specimens from the sheets were used to determine some of their physical and mechanical properties: namely, density, water absorption, bending and impact capacities. Three specimens from each sheet, i.e., 15 specimens from each category, were tested to determine each of the properties mentioned above.
All tests, except impact tests, were carried out according to ASTM, C 221-77 (1). The falling ball method (constant weight and increasing height) was used to determine the comparative impact resistance of the produced sheets in categories A, B, and C. In this method a steel ball weighing 0.44 kgs was dropped on 3 specimens derived from each sheet from increasing heights at 50 mm intervals. The height travelled by the ball when the first visible crack had developed was recorded. The test was carried out on 2 crests and 2 vales of corrugations of each specimen. Impact energy absorbed by each specimen was then calculated from the work done by the ball to produce first visible crack.
The test results for the three categories of the produced sheets are summarized in Table 3.

Table 3. Summary of mean tests results compared with other corrugated cement sheets.

Sheet type	Density kg/m^3	Water* Absorption %	Bending Moment Capacity KN-m/m	Bending Maximum Deflection mm	Impact Energy Absorbed (Joule)
Category A	1640	16.8	0.75	1.03	3.29
Category B	1650	16.4	0.53	0.98	2.81
Category C	1690	14.4	0.45	0.08	1.01
Corrugated Asbestos ASTM (1)	A -	⊁ 25.0	⊁ 0.556	-	-
	B -	⊁ 25.0	⊁ 1.401	-	-
Corrugated Sheet India (4)	7mm coir. 6mm Asb.	- - -⊁ 25	0.44 1.222	-	-

*Based on dry weight.

4. *Discussion of results*

Results of tests carried out on the three categories of sheets produced are given in Table 3 and show that some of the physical and mechanical properties of plain cement-sand corrugated sheets are

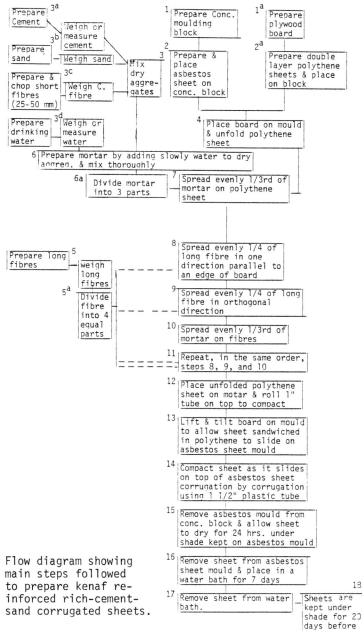

Figure 2.   Flow diagram showing
main steps followed
to prepare kenaf re-
inforced rich-cement-
sand corrugated sheets.

substantially improved when reinforced with kenaf fibres and are comparable with ASTM specifications for Class A asbestos-cement corrugated sheets (1) and also comparable to 7 mm coir-cement corrugated sheets produced in India (4).

4.1 Flexural Properties: It is noted that the moment carrying capacity was improved by 66% by reinforcing plain rich cement-sand corrugated sheets with long and short kenaf fibres (Category A: 1.56% fibre content). On the other hand, a slight improvement of the moment carrying capacity of the sheets was achieved by using short kenaf fibres only (Category B: 1.6% fibre content).

The use of kenaf fibres (long and/or short) greatly increased the ductitility of plain sheets (Category C), such that an increase of about 800% in central deflection at ultimate load was noted, and that, unlike plain and asbestos sheets, minor cracks started early and tended to increase with increasing load (no sudden failures).

4.2 Impact Resistance: The ability of sheets to resist impact forces during transportation, handling and erection is of great importance. It is found that the impact resistance of plain cement-sand sheets was improved by about 300% when these sheets were reinforced with long and/or short kenaf fibres.

4.3 Water Absorption Capacity: The results of water absorption tests carried out on the three categories of sheets show that the water absorption capacity of the plain cement-sand sheets was increased by 16.67% by intoruding long and short fibres in the matrix and by 13.89% when only short fibres were introduced. However, the water absorption capacity of sheets reinforced with short and long or short kenaf fibres was found to lie within the specifications of ASTM:C 221-77 for sand-cement corrugated asbestos sheets (1) and the Indian standards (4).

4.4 Density: The density of plain cement-sand sheet was not affected substantially by introducing such a low content of fibres (1.6%) in the matrix. A decrease of about 2.9% and 2.4% in the density of plain sheets was achieved when reinforced with long and short kenaf fibres (Category A) and with kenaf short fibres only (Category B), respectively.

5. *Summary and Conclusions*

An experimental investigation on the possibility of using kenaf fibres to reinforce rich cement-sand mortar to produce corrugated sheets was carried out. The findings of the investigation revealed that the tensile properties of kenaf fibres are comparable to those of some natural fibres (sisal) and synthetic fibres (polypropylene) that are used to reinforce a low tensile strength matrix. It, also, revealed that the addition of these fibres (1.6% by wt.) to rich cement-sand mortar (1 1/2:1 by wt.) to produce corrugated sheets has substantially improved the bending moment capacity and impact resistance of similar corrugated plain rich cement-sand sheets, but has slightly increased their water absorption capacity. The effect of these fibres on the density of plain sheets has been found to be very slight. It is, also, worth mentioning that the bending moment and water absorption capacities of the 10.7 mm thick kenaf reinfroced corrugated rich cement-sand sheets are found to lie within the ASTM specifications for Grade A corrugated asbestos-cement sheets (1).

The findings of the investigation were assessed at BRRI and were found promising to pursue phase 2 of the kenaf-reinforced building components project at BRRI.

In phase 2 of this project investigations will be carried out to determine an optimum sheet size (width-length and thickness), optimum cement/sand and water/cement ratios for the sheets to comply with the bending moment and water absorption capacities standards specified by ASTM for Grade A corrugated asbestos-cement sheets (1). Also the investigation shall include the long term structural and environmental behaviour of kenaf fibres and sheets in service, a comprehensive evaluation for their physical and mechanical properties and a techno-economic appraisal for a small project to produce these sheets using simple manual techniques.

Acknowledgements

The author wishes to acknowledge that support for this study was provided by the Building and Road Research Institute of the University of Khartoum, Sudan, as part of a research programme on roofs for low cost houses and that all work pertaining to fabrication and testing of kenaf-reinforced corrugated sheets was carried out in its laboratories.

Acknowledgement is extended to Dr. J. Bodig, Professor of Wood Science and Civil Engineering in the College of Forestry and Natural Resources, Colorado State University, USA, for availing facilities to carry out tensile strength tests on kenaf fibres and, also, for his advice to conduct successfully these tests.

References

1. American Society for Testing and Materials (1978), Standard Specifications for Corrugated Asbestos-Cement Sheets. ASTM Designation: C221-77, Philadelphia, PA.
2. Arnaouti, C. and Illston, J. M. (1979), Research into the Strengths of Cements Reinforced with Natural Fibres. Unpublished Report, Hatfield Polytechnic, England.
3. Ayyar, T. S. R. and Mirihagalla, P. K. (1976). Elephant Grass Fibres as Reinforcement in Roofing Sheets. Appropriate Technology, Vol. 6, No. 1, pp. 6-8.
4. Central Building Research Institute (1979). Corrugated Roofing Sheets from Woodwool or Coir Waste and Portland Cement. Project Proposal No. 53, Roorkee (U.P.), India.
5. Fageiri, O. M. E. (1981), Unpublished Report on Development of Low Cost Roofs Using Local Building Materials in the Sudan. BRRI, University of Khartoum, Sudan.

6. Hannat, D. J., Zonsveld, J. J., and Hughes, D. C. (1978), Poly-propylene Film in Cement Based Materials. Composites, pp. 83-88.
7. Inglis, M. (1981), Social Aspects of Introducing Natural-Fibre-Cement Materials in Zambia. Regional Workshop on Natural-Fibre-Cement Construction Materials, Appropriate Technology Centre, Kenyatta University College, Nairobi.
8. Nichlson, N. (1981), Sisal-Cement Building Materials: A Study of Production Techniques and the Market Potential in Zimbabwe. Regional Workshop on Natural-Fibre-Cement Construction Materials, Appropriate Technology Centre, Kenyatta University College, Nairobi.
9. Parry, J. P. M. (1979), Low-cost Handmade Roof Sheets of Fibre Reinforced Cement. Apprpriate Technology, Vol. 5, No. 4, Feb.
10. Persson, H. and Skarendahl (1980), Sisal Fibre Concrete for Roofing Sheets and Other Purposes. Monograph on Applied Indust-rial Technology, No. 12, Applied Industrial Technology for Construction and Building Materials, United Nations, New York.
11. Rilem Symposium 1975, ed. Neville, A. (1975), Fibre Reinforced Cement and Concrete. The Construction Press Ltd., London.
12. Rilem Symposium 1978, ed. Swamy, N. (1978), Testing and Test Methods of Fibre-Cement Composites. The Construction Press Ltd., London.
13. Sirioney, I. M. (1981), Sisal Reinforced Roofing Sheets for Low-Cost Housing in Tanzania. Regional Workshop on Natural-Fibre-Cement Construction Materials, Appropriate Technology Centre, Kenyatta University College, Nairobi.
14. Sudan Industrial Research Institute. Unpublished Report on the Technical and Economic Feasibility of Kenaf Project at Abu Ne'ama. Ministry of Industry, Khartoum, Sudan.
15. Swift, D. G. (1981), Review of Fibre-Cement Research and Develop-ment with Particular Reference to Third World Applications. Regional Workshop on Natural-Fibre-Cement Construction Materials, Appropriate Technology Centre, Kenyatta University College, Nairobi.
16. Swift, D. G. and Smith, R. B. L. (1979), The Flexure Strength of Cement-Based Composites Using Low Modulus (Sisal) Fibres. Composites, pp. 145-148.
17. Swift, D. G. and Smith, R. B. L. (1979), Sisal-Cement Composites as Low Cost Construction Materials. Appropriate Technology, Vol. 6, No. 3, pp. 6-8.
18. Swift, D. G. and Smith, R. B. L. (1978), Sisal-Fibre Reinforce-ment of Cement Paste and Concrete. International Conference on Materials of Construction for Developing Countries, Bangkok, pp. 221-234.
19. Turabi, M. A., El-fadul, M. D. and Gasm-elseed, K. M. (1982), Use of Kenaf Fibres in Sand-Cement Corrugated Sheets. Final Year Project in Partial Fulfillment for the Requirements of the degree of B.Sc. (Hon.) in Civil Eng., Civil Eng. Dept., Faculty of Eng., University of Khartoum, Sudan.
20. Undugu Society of Kenya (1980), A Report on Building for the Katangi Agricultural Project. Undugu Society of Kenya, Nairobi, Kenya.

UTILIZATION OF BAMBOO AS A LOW COST STRUCTURAL MATERIAL

ABANG ABDULLAH ABANG ALI, Universiti Pertanian Malaysia

1. *Introduction*

The construction industry, by far the largest consumer of engineering
materials, has been snatching up every available supply of construction materials. The shortage and rising prices of the traditional
materials such as cement, steel and timber is obliging those in the
construction industry to look for alternative materials. This is
necessary not only from the point of view of maintaining a lower
construction cost but to relieve pressure on the existing supply.
Steel is expensive in many countries and with the current rate of
deforestation, timber may face depletion in the near future. Bamboo
being a very common resource in the Asian region presents an interesting alternative to steel and timber. It has a high strength to
weight ratio, especially in tension, and its supply can be easily
replenished due to fast growth. Provided proper attention in given
to its durability, bamboo may replace steel and timber is the near
future, especially in low cost construction.

2. *Low cost structural material*

The need to produce cheap structures from expensive materials have
discouraged many housing developers from low cost construction. To
overcome this situation, those in the building industry have two
alternatives. Either an engineer or architect produces a smaller
and substandard structure, which is an absolutely unacceptable
solution, or he specifies cheaper materials and construction methods.
An appreciable saving in cost can be achieved through the use of
locally available materials, especially indigenous materials found in
the vicinity of the construction. The saving comes in both materials
as well as transportation costs.

The proper utilization of an engineering material entails a
thorough understanding of its properties and suitability for a particular form of application. This is necessary so that materials are
chosen for specific jobs in a structure. Bamboo as a minor forest
product has a long history of applications especially in the rural
areas. But due to the past and perhaps current good supply of timber,
the potential of bamboo as a structural material has often been

ignored. This situation is temporary. In Malaysia, it is anticipated that by the end of this decade, timber resources would be depleted if the present rate of deforestation is continued. There is already growing awareness of a shortage of log supply in the country. It is therefore important that the utilization of other forest products is maximised, in order to save the forest based industry.

From observations made during field trips to bamboo growing areas, bamboo is infact growing in areas where timber has been felled. Bamboo generally takes two to five years to grow to maturity before it is suitable for use as an engineering materials. This growth period is relatively short when compared to timber which normally requires at least ten years. And at the rate timber is being felled today, bamboo may in the coming years, be the only available structural material in the clearings left behind by timber logging operations.

The use of materials which has not been popular in the past, can in turn encourage supply. Bamboo are not normally cultivated due to the current neglect or lack of demand. But once the potential of bamboo is realised and demand is created by the construction industry which usually consumes a large amount of materials, the cultivation of bamboo may be encouraged. Bamboo can be cultivated on a large scale. Such plantations have been established in India and Japan. Mechanization of growing and collection is possible. Proper cultivation would in turn mean that good quality bamboos would be available.

3. *Material and structural properties of bamboo*

Provided its material and structural properties are well understood, bamboo can be effectively utilized as a structural material. This demands a systematic documentation of experimental test results based on an established standard of testing. Unfortunately the first standard on testing of bamboo was only introduced as late as 1973 and at present very little interest is shown in proper documentation of bamboo strength properties.

In south East Asia there are 220 species of bamboo, and in West Malaysia alone there are 70 species. At present bamboo land is scattered all over the country ; bamboo being found in abundance along river banks and areas cleared of timber. Thin-walled bamboos having diameter less than 125 mm is more common than thick-walled bamboo with diameter in excess of 125 mm.

Factors that influence the mechanical properties of bamboo considerably are the species, age, moisture content and position along the culm. The exterior of bamboo is hard and tough ; bamboo being made up of two fibrous layers. The outer layer contains twice as much fibres as the inner layer and hence is stronger.

Typical material properties of a common Malaysian bamboo obtained from experimental tests conducted at Universiti Pertanian Malaysia is reproduced in Table 1, for comparison with typical corresponding values for mild steel, concrete and timber. It shows that bamboo is as strong as timber in compression, and very much stronger in tension. For some species the tensile strength of bamboo was almost as high as

that for mild steel. However a relatively low modulus of elasticity
was observed especially in compression.

Table 1.   Typical material properties of bamboo in comparison with
mild steel, concrete and timber

| Material | Specific Gravity | Ultimate Strength (N/mm^2) | | | Modulus of Elasticity KN/mm^2 |
		Compression, σ_C	Tension, σ_T	$\dfrac{\sigma_T}{\sigma_C}$	
Mild steel	7.8	–	480	1.0	210
Concrete	2.4	25 – 55	–	0.1	10 – 17
Timber	0.4 – 0.8	50 – 100	20 – 110	1.1	8 – 13
Bamboo	0.8 – 1.4	38 – 65	180 – 440	4.8–7.1	7 – 20

Basic material properties of selected Malaysian bamboo species
are shown in Table 2. As in timber the material properties vary
according to the species and are affected by the presence of defects.
Moisture content which influences the strength properties were in the
range of 12 to 26 per cent, for the specimens tested. *Dendrocalamus
giganteous* were obtained from two different sources which explains
the two different results presented.

Table 2.   Basic material properties of selected Malaysian bamboos

| Species | Dia. (mm) | Thickness (mm) | Specific Gravity | Ultimate Strength | | |
| | | | | Compression | | Tension |
				Load (KN)	Stress (N/mm^2)	Stress (N/mm^2)
Bambusa Vulgaris var. striata	63.9	8.2	1.06	81.3	50.5	295.4
Dendrocalamus asper	76.7	9.2	1.07	139.7	64.7	440.6
Bambusa blumena	78.3	7.4	1.37	106.6	56.2	372.8
Dendrocalamus giganteous						
I	103.8	7.3	1.30	105.1	44.7	319.4
II	159.2	10.6	–	301.1	56.9	–

The compressive strength of bamboo increases with decreasing
moisture content, and increases from the bottom to the top along the
culm. The increase in strength along the culm is due to the percentage increase in sclerenchyma fibres. There is also a significant
increase in compression strength according to the age of the bamboo.

Bamboo is strong in tension. Its tensile strength can be as high
as seven times the compressive strength. An ultimate tensile

strength value of 440.6 N/mm^2 was recorded for *Dendrocalamus asper*.
For this reason, bamboo is sometimes used to replace steel in reinforced concrete construction, provided the problem of swelling and
shrinkage due to high water absorption capacity of bamboo is overcome. Bamboo is sometimes used in suspension bridges for the same
reason. The modulus of elasticity of bamboo is low. Low modulus
concrete may be necessary when using bamboo as reinforcement in reinforced concrete construction and particular attention has to be given
to the problem of bonding.

Hoever, bamboo is weak in shear. Timber would normally have a
shear strength of 20-30 per cent of its compressive strength but the
shear strength of bamboo is only about 8% of its compressive strength.
This property is fully utilized in the basket making industry where
bamboo is split into thin strips. Split bamboo woven in a matrix
mesh is also used in reinforced concrete slabs and wall panels. This
low shear strength of bamboo may infact be a limiting factor in
design and construction ; making it necessary to pay particular
attention to the jointing systems employed.

Another problem that may arise is the tapering of bamboo diameters within a short distance along the culm. For construction which
uses whole bamboo lengths such as in beams, columns and trusses, it
may be difficult to ensure dimensional uniformity along structural
members over a large distance. This may be overcome by appropriate
jointing systems in the structure.

4. *Utilization of bamboo*

Bamboo has been used traditionally for building of houses, rafts and
bridges. But due to lack of interest in this material in the past,
bamboo technology today has not advanced further than rural application. In many countries little is known of the structural application of bamboo, compared to its used for other traditional purposes
such as basket making. However there is now a renewed interest in
its utilization in the construction industry, especially in areas
where it can replace steel and timber.

With proper preservative treatment bamboo can be used as beams
and columns in low cost construction. Flexural tests conducted on
whole bamboo beam specimens over a span of 2.1 m yield ultimate
bending stresses ranging from 32.2 to 75.8 N/mm^2. Table 3 illustrates the results of tests on whole bamboo beam and strut specimens.
Tests on strut specimens of length 0.8 m, 1.15 m and 1.5 m were
conducted on the selected species of Malaysian bamboo and a maximum
ultimate load value of 294.0 KN was recorded. A decrease in ultimate
load of the strut specimens were observed with increase in slender-
ness ratio.

Table 3.   Bamboo beams and columns

Species	Dia. (mm)	Thickness (mm)	Ultimate Bending Stress (N/mm^2)	Ultimate Column Load (KN)
Bambusa Vulgaris var. striata	72.3	7.2	45.3 - 57.0	30.0 - 140.0
Dendrocalamus asper	80.5	8.9	73.4 - 84.3	61.5 - 250.0
Bambusa blumena	80.4	8.0	56.9 - 63.1	28.0 - 157.5
Dendrocalamus giganteous				
I	107.4	7.5	32.2 - 40.8	52.0 - 150.0
II	160.2	10.8	-	215.0 - 294.0

Experimental tests were conducted on full scale fink bamboo trusses using different types of jointing system over a span of 8.0 m to study the behaviour of these trusses under service load conditions. Table 4 illustrates the loads at failure and maximum recorded deflections before failure. All failures occured in the joint at the support where the bottom chord member tapered to a relatively smaller diameter. Assuming a dead load, including truss selfweight of 0.6 KN/m^2 based on asbestos cement sheeting, and a liveload of 0.5 KN/m^2 with truss at 0.75 m spacing centre to centre, a theoritical total service load of 5.2 KN is possible for a single storey building with the truss spaning 8.0 m. Experimental total ultimate load obtained varied between 8.4 to 10.5 KN. With improved jointing system, these value should be much higher as the truss members are able to withstand very high loads.

A good amount of work has been done by other researches on the use of bamboo as reinforcement in concrete. Provided particular attention is given to durability and bond which is related to high water absorption capacity, bamboo can be successfully used in place of steel, especially for slabs and wall panels.

Table 4.   8.0 m span bamboo trusses

	Total Ultimate Load (KN)	Ultimate Load / Service Load
Rattan lashing	8.4	1.62
Plywood Gusset + Screw	9.0	1.73
Steel Bolts	9.6	1.85
Steel Bolts + Ropes	10.5	2.02

5. *Problems associated with the use of bamboo*

The main problem associated with the utilization of bamboo as a structural material is its durability. Bamboo structures has been found
to last provided it is sheltered from moisture and insects. It is
said to last only 1 to 3 years when exposed in an untreated condition.
If properly treated bamboo structures can exceed 10 years.

Bamboo has a major weakness due to high water absorption potential which leads to swelling-shrinking and decay. This creates a
problem in bond between concrete and bamboo in reinforced construction. Simple treatment such as immersing the bamboo for 72 hours
before placing in concrete has been suggested. The low elastic
modulus of bamboo may result in high deflection and its cylindrical
structure may result in poor dimensional stability.

6. *Conclusion*

It is evident that bamboo may become an important structural material
in the near future, especially in low cost construction. However
there is a need to understand this material further and encourage
documentation of strength values before it can be specified for use
in construction. The long term behaviour and performance has to be
investigated. Otherwise, experimental investigation this far, has
proven the potential of bamboo as a structural material.

References

1. Pama, R.P., Nimityongskul, P. and Cook, D.J. (1978), *Proceedings
    of the Internation Conference on Materials of Construction
    For Developing Countries*. Bangkok.
2. Janssen, J.J.A. (1981), *Bamboo in Building Structures*. Doctor
    of Technical Sciences Thesis. Eindhoven University of
    Technology.
3. Lessard, G. and Chouinard, A. (1980), *Proceedings of a workshop
    on Bamboo Research in Asia*. Singapore.
4. Zyed, A.H., (1980), *Strength Properties of A Common Malaysian
    Bamboo.*Unpublished B.E. Project Report, Universiti Pertanian
    Malaysia.
5. Renganathan, G., (1981), *Bamboo Trusses*. Unpublished B.E.
    Project Report, Universiti Pertanian Malaysia.
6. Hamzah, B., (1982), *Structural Behaviour of Bamboo Beams and
    Columns*. Unpublished B.E. Project Report, Universiti
    Pertanian Malaysia.
7. Abdul Razak, A., (1983), *Bamboo Joints*. Unpublished B.E.
    Project Report, Universiti Pertanian Malaysia.

THE ROLE OF FORESTRY RESEARCH INSTITUTE, IBADAN IN THE
USE OF INDIGENOUS RAW MATERIALS FOR LOW COST HOUSING

E. O. ADEMILUYI & S. O. O. BADEJO
FORESTRY RESEARCH INSTITUTE OF NIGERIA,
P.M.B. 5054, IBADAN

1.   Introduction

In the last two decades, Nigeria has experience not only
an enormous urbanisation of its population but also a
phenominal growth in the number of cities. These
phenomina, were catalysed by the boom in the country's
eccnomy over the 1970 decade and more potently by the
quick succession of political and administrative
decentralisation that has taken place since the late
1960s. As a result of this administrative decentralisa-
ticn, each administrative unit created involved the
creation of more urban centres. Hence (with an already
weak base in terms of institutional infrastructure and
utilities) vital infrastructural utility and social
services, for example water supplies, sewage, roads,
transportation facilities and mostly housing supplies
in quantity and qualities have become grossly inadequate.
    Apart from food, adequate housing is one of the major
prcblems facing most developing countries. About 70% of
the Nigerian populace, whose housing problems have been
accorded very low priority in National planning, are
rural dwellers. One of the government's policy statement
is that every Nigerian has a right to adequate, healthy
and habitable accommodation. Infact, various governments
of Nigeria budgeted about ₦4.5 billion under the 1975 -
80 Development Plan Period for various housing units all
over the country and even a greater amount under the
current Plan Period. However the ever increasing cost of
land, building materials, mortgage finance, housing
maintenance and the global inflatory trends in all sphere
of the economy make these obhectives difficult to achieve
in Nigeria.
    In the light of the present soaring cost of housing,
research efforts have been taken in many fields of
building industry to bring down the building cost.

Through wise planning, use of readily available local
materials in preference to imported materials and through
refinement and adoption of traditional method of housing
construction, it will be possible to provide decent homes
at reasonable prices.

2. Vital housing Components in Nigeria

In the rural parts of the country, the traditional
building materials are combinations of wood and mud with
the wood generally used in round form. Example of wood
in poles forms in use include <u>Trema</u> <u>angulensis</u> <u>Harungana</u>
<u>madagascariensis</u>, <u>Diospyros</u> species, <u>Bamboss</u> <u>vulgaris</u>
and splits of Borassus as well as sawn timber which are
used to support their gauge corrugated iron sheets.
    As development improved, the most common material for
walls is cement blocks while sawnwood, corrugated roof
covering, doors and windows frames are generally of wood
although steel frames are being increasingly used in more
expensive designs. In general, wood and wooden component
have become a vital aspect of housing project not only in
Nigeria but even in developed countries of U.S.A., Canada
and some European countries.

3.   The Forest Resources of Nigeria

Nigeria is still one of the largest producers of tropical
hardwoods even through up to half of the wood resource
of the country can be classified as waste. The general
concern for wood waste utilisation in Nigeria has stemmed
from two important and use considerations.

    3.1   (a)   the anticipated future shortage of wood raw
                material to the country's wood based
                industries
    3.2   (b)   the desire to provide alternative source of
                building component of considerable merit for
                low cost housing to the countries rapidly
                expanding building industry sector.

    The dangers and consequences of future shortage of
roundwood supply have been well documented (Okigbo 1964)[1]
(Adeyoju 1975)[2] (Ball 1978)[3] and Badejo and Umeh 1978)[4].
They are attributed to the country's limited timber
resource   which accounted for just about 2% of the
country's total land area as well as for a steady and
upsing growth in the number of operating wood based
industries.

4. Need for Research

Some measure of averting an imminent future shortage of timber in the country have been identified. These include:

    4.1 (a) improved solid wood utilization
    4.2 (b) a fully committed wood wastes utilization
         programme.

    The Forest Product Division of the Forestry Research Institute of Nigeria, Ibadan was set up in 1962 to promote the effecient utilisation of Nigerian forest product especially the so called lesser used species, diversify the use of Forest products, reduce wastage in wood utilisation and also investigate problems associated with forest product utilisation in Nigeria.

5.   Improved Timber Utilisation

The main source of supply of traditional Nigerian timbers such as Iroko (Chlorophora excelsa), the Mahoganies and Obeche (Triplochiton scleroxylon) has been from areas outside the forest resources. As the stockings of timber in these areas become less, it is becoming increasingly difficult to obtain the traditional species. This gives rise to high extraction cost and together with poor and ineffecient conversion techniques which give rise to high conversion waste and costs, explain why building timbers, are expensive in Nigeria today.

    It is only natural that as the sources of supply remain inadequate while the demand for building timbers continues to increase with improving living standards and with no immediate future propect for relief, those species which are at present considered of no use but are still in plentiful supply and which have proven by due processes of research to be suitable for certain purposes will come into the market.

    This is the case in the Forest Resource of Nigeria, moreso, in housing. Research findings have been published on the physical, mechanical, seasoning and preservation properties of these wood species considered as good alternatives to the traditional building timbers. It is well known that the suitability of timber for building in general does not primarily depend only on its working properties but also on its natural durability, ability to permit complete penetration of chemicals, possessing property which will enable it to dry quickly without much degrade. A summary of such timbers with their strength properties and end uses are presented in Table 1.

6. Use of Wood Wastes and Agricultural residues

Due to global decline in roundwood supply, wood wastes have been more extensively used for wood-based panel production. Eupatorium has also become a nuisance weed in the farmlands and forest plantations of the southern states. These are a number of profitable industrial use to which these waste could be put. Important among these include fibre production for the pulp and paper industry, particle board, fibre board and wood-cement board.

Forestry Research Institute of Nigeria, has embarked on a lot of Research into the bounding properties of these agricultural and industrial wastes for the production of particle boards and Wood-Cement board. The recycling of these wood wastes for the production of these panel products, which could serve as substitutes for solid wood and plywood in building, will no doubt reduce the tempo of forest exploitation pressure on the country's high forests, increase monetary net returns to the sawmillers on every volume of log processed and create useful employment through the establishment of wood waste using an allied industries.

A summary of some data obtained on the findings are contained in Tables II, III and IV respectively.

References

1. Okigbo L. C. (1964) Saw-milling industry in Nigeria. Federal Department of Forest Research, Ibadan Nigeria
2. Adeyoju, S. K. (1975) Forestry and the Nigerian Economy. Ibadan University pros 308p.
3. Ball J. B. 1978 Proposals for the development Forestry plantations in Nigeria NIR/71/546. Technical Report No. 3 Federal Department of Forestry, Lagos, Nigeria.
4. Badejo S. O. O. and Umeh L.I. (1978) Meeting the future roundwood needs in Nigeria. Paper presented at the 8th annual conference of the Forestry Association of Nigeria, Ilorin, Kwara State 13th - 16th December 1978

Table 1.

Properties of some Nigerian timber spieces
recently introduced into the building industry

	Density 12% MC	MOE N/MM^2	MOR N/MM^2	CII grain N/MM^2	Durability Ratings
Sterculia rhinopetala	752.3	10.5	84.6	40.6	Durable
Daniellia ogea	512	10.4	73.1	39.1	Non durable
Terminalia glaucesceus	640	7.8	85.2	49.0	durable
Khaya senegalensis	768	7.0	71.7	49.6	durable
Pterocarpus erinaceas	784	8.6	113.0	55.5	Durable
Burkea africana	1041.2	12.0	143.5	70.7	Durable
Ancgeissus leicarpus	913.0	9.8	110.3	55.0	Very durable
Strombosia pustulata	816.9	10.0	95.7	46.1	Non durable
Pterygota macrocarpa	560.6	7.5	57.2	26.7	Non durable
Hildergarelia barteri	288.3	2.7	20.0	9.7	Non durable

Table 2.

Internal Bond and Water Immersion Properties
of Bagasse Particle Board

| Core Resin Content (%) | Pressing Pressure (N/mm^2) | Internal Bond N/mm^2 | 24 Hours Soak in cold water | |
			Water Absorption	Thickness swell (%)
3	0.26	0.16	17.81	7.90
3	0.32	0.25	22.75	8.85
3	0.37	0.23	24.03	9.86
5	0.26	0.35	25.35	9.20
5	0.32	0.27	24.24	7.15
5	0.37	0.50	19.05	6.01
7	0.26	0.44	11.64	1.20
7	0.32	0.43	16.52	4.30
7	0.37	0.44	15.41	4.60

Table 3.

Average Bending strength (M.O.R.), Percent
Water Absorption and Thickness swell of
Bagasse-based Particleboard.

Resin Content (%)	Specific Gravity	Bending Strength	Water Absorption after 24 hours Soak (%)	Thickness Swell after 24 hours Soak (%)
9	0.60	34.53	59	11
9	0.70	44.74	46	11
12	0.60	41.20	55	9
12	0.70	50.62	43	7
15	0.60	44.54	39	9
15	0.70	63.96	38	5

Table 4.

Average Percent Thickness swell values of
wood-cement boards Fabricated from 4
Nigerian hardwoods

	Percent Thickness Swell Values (%)							
Treatments	24 Hours cold soak				48 Hours cold soak			
	A	B	C	D	A	B	C	D
R1C1	3.5	2.8	2.8	0.3	3.5	2.9	2.8	0.44
R1C2	2.7	2.2	2.3	0.2	2.7	2.3	2.6	0.2
R1C3	2.1	1.8	1.9	0.1	2.1	1.8	2.5	0.1
R2C1	2.7	2.2	1.6	0.1	2.8	2.3	2.3	0.1
R2C2	1.8	1.9	1.4	0.1	2.0	2.0	2.1	0.1
R2C3	1.5	1.3	1.3	0.1	1.5	1.4	2.0	0.1
R3C1	1.6	1.3	1.1	0.1	1.8	1.5	1.8	0.1
R3C2	0.5	0.6	0.9	0.1	0.5	0.8	1.5	0.1
R3C3	0.5	0.2	0.8	0.03	0.5	0.2	1.2	0.05

* A - Pycanthus angolensis
   B - Triplochiton scleroxylon
   C - Brachystegia nigerica
   D - Terminalia ivorensis

R1, R2 and R3 denotes wood to cement mixing
ratio at levels of 1=2.0, 1=2.5 and 1=3.0
while C1, C2 and C3 denotes additive
concentration at levels of 1%, 2% and 3%.

MATERIAUX LOCAUX EN TUNISIE : QUELQUES PERSPECTIVES
D'UTILISATION EN GENIE CIVIL

AHMED FRIAA
Departement de Génie Civil, Ecole Nationale d'Ingénieur de Tunis

1. Introduction

En Tunisie, comme dans de nombreux autres pays, les besoins en
matériaux de construction sont de plus en plus grands. Ceci est
dû d'une part à l'important effort consenti en matière d'infra-
structures et d'équipements de base et, d'autre part, à l'importance de la demande dans le secteur du bâtiment.

Or les matériaux classiques (béton, acier, terre cuite,
pierre), ont vu leur prix augmenter d'une manière sensible notamment à cause de la bien célèbre crise de l'énergie. Si bien que,
ces matériaux sont devenus à la fois chèrs et insuffisants.

Dès lors une question se pose naturellement :
existe-t-il des matériaux locaux pouvant constituer une solution
d'appoint ou encore mieux une solution de rechange ?

L'objet de la présente communication est de montrer qu'il est
possible dans certaines situations de répondre par l'affirmative.
Elle présente un ensemble de résultats obtenus dans les laboratoires du département de Génie Civil de l'Ecole Nationale d'Ingénieurs de Tunis.

Les thèmes abordés sont :

- La margine (sous produit de l'huile d'olive) : propriétés
  hydrauliques, mécaniques et perspectives d'utilisation en
  Génie Civil et Bâtiment.
- Le tuf Tunisien ; ses propriétés de liant et applications.
- L'argile expansée et le verre expansé.

2. La margine. Quelques perspectives d'utilisation en Génie Civil

2.1 La margine - Description.

La margine est un résidu polluant et lourd de l'huile d'olive.
Ses caractéristiques physico-chimiques dependent du type d'olivier,
de la région où elle est implantée, de la technique d'extraction
de l'huile d'olive (mode de fabrication, qualité d'écrasement des
olives) etc... . En bref la nature de la margine, sa composition
et donc ses caractéristiques varient selon la région et le type
d'huilerie. Nous pouvons cependant retenir, à titre indicatif la

composition moyenne suivante :
85%   d'eau environ
13%   de matières organiques
2%   de matières minérales

Les matières organiques se composent en général de :
matières grasses, de matières azotés et de sucres. Par ailleurs,
20% des sels minéreaux sont insolubles dans l'eau et comprennent
de la silice et des carbonates. Enfin le PH de la margine est
compris entre 4 et 5. Il s'agit donc d'un PH. Acide.
En Tunisie, la production annuelle moyenne de margine durant
la décennie 1970/1980 est d'environ 250.000 tonne/an. L'intérêt
économique et écologique d'une étude sur la revalorisation de la
margine est donc évident.

2.2 Propriétés hydrophobes de la margine.
Une première étude effectuée aux laboratoire du département de
Génie Civil de l'ENIT avait pour objet la mise en valeur des
propriétés hydrophobes de la margine.
De nombreux sols ont été testés. La figure 1
montre la granulométrie de certains sols testés. Pour tous ces
sols, nous avons observé le phénomène important suivant :
La perméabilité d'un sol traité à la margine diminue sensiblement avec le poucentage de margine ajouté. Pour la plupart des
sols testés, et pour un certain pourcentage de margine, la
perméabilité diminue de 1000% ! Voir fig.2. Ci-après.
La présence de matières grasses dans la margine semble être
à l'origine de ses propriétés hydrophobes.

2.3 Influence de la margine sur les propriétés mécaniques du
sol.
Des études ont été agalement menées pour voir l'influence de la
margine sur les caractéristiques mécaniques d'un sol traité.
Les essais réalisés sont :

1 - l'essai proctor, ou l'essai proctor modifié, utile pour
déterminer la teneur en eau optimale de compactage.
2 - l'essai CBR, utile pour déterminer la portance du sol.
3 - essai de cisaillement à la boite qui permet de déterminer
l'angle de frottement et la cohésion. Ces paramètres jouent un
grand rôle dans les problèmes de stabilité.
4 - Enfin l'essai d'écrasement permettant de déterminer la
contrainte de compression.

Les résultats les plus significatifs sont les suivants :

(a) l'essai proctor montre que la densité sèche optimale d'un
sol traité à la margine est pratiquement conservée tandis que le
pourcentage d'eau optimum diminue avec le pourcentage de margine
ajouté comme le montre la fig.3.

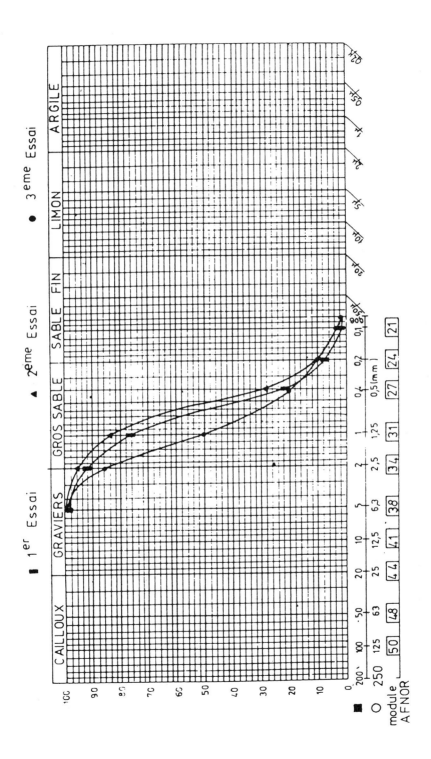

Figure 1 : Granulométrie des sols testés.

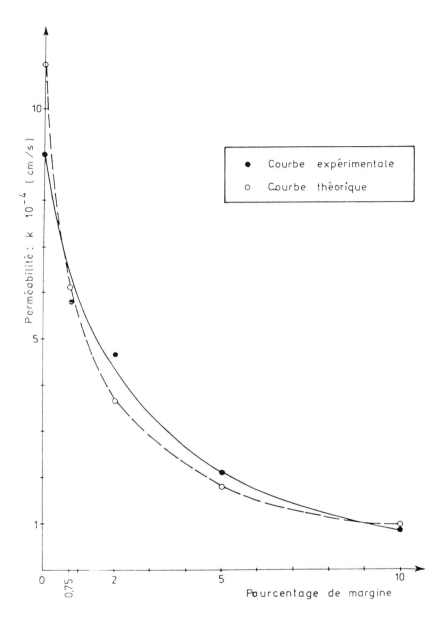

Figure 2 :   Essai de perméabilité.

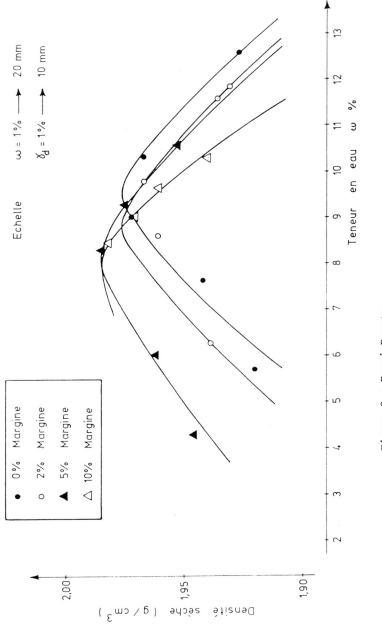

Figure 3 : Essai Proctor

Ceci est normal puisque la margine elle même contient un fort pourcentage d'eau.

(b) Pour les autres essais effectués à l'optimum proctor, les résultats varient sensiblement avec la température et le temps de séchage. A la température ordinaire (20 - 25°c), les caractéristiques mécaniques sont pratiquement conservées - parfois, on observe même une amélioration de l'indice CBR. D'une manière générale, toutes les caractéristiques mécaniques sont améliorées après séchage des éprouvettes, cette amélioration est d'autant meilleure que le temps de séchage est plus long. A 100°c par exemple, la résistance à la compression peut atteindre 50 bars tandis que la cohésion, elle augmente sensiblement - La figure 4 illustre l'évolution de la contrainte de compression.

3. Applications pratiques

3.1 Traitement des sols de fondation des chaussées
Nous avons vu au § 2 que le traitement d'un sol à la margine permet de diminuer sensiblement sa perméabilité et, sous l'effet de la chaleur, il permet d'améliorer sa portance et, d'une manière générale ses caractéristiques mécaniques.

Une première application de ces résultats a consisté en la réalisation pratique de deux tronçons de pistes agricoles par traitement à la margine des sols en place. Deux autres tronçons de pistes sont en cours de réalisation.

Le premier tronçon d'une longueur de 400 m environ et d'une largeur de 4 m a été réalisé dans la délégation de Zarzis dans le sud Est Tunisien. Le sol est constitué de sable très fin difficilement carrossable. Ce sol a été traité à la margine sur une épaisseur de 30 cm en deux couches de 15 cm chacune. Le pourcentage de margine est déterminé par l'optinum proctor.

Les engins utilisés sont : un grader muni d'un scraper, un compacteur à pneux, et une pompe citerne pour le transport et le répandage de la margine.

Une fois les travaux terminés, la piste a été fermée à la circulation durant un mois environ pour permettre son séchage (au soleil).

Le deuxième tronçon de 100 m de long et 4 m de large a été réalisé dans la région de Zaghouan située à 60 Km de Tunis environ. Le sol traité est du type argileux avec une faible proportion de sable. Le traitement a porté sur une épaisseur de 15 cm. Là encore, il a fallu fermer le tronçon à la circulation en réalisant une déviation du trafic constitué enssentiellement d'engins agricoles, pour permettre le séchage de la piste.

De nombreuses visites ont été effectuées aux deux tronçons réalisés et à différentes périodes. Elles permettent de retenir les constatations qualitatives suivantes :

1 - En général la portance est très satisfaisante, même après de

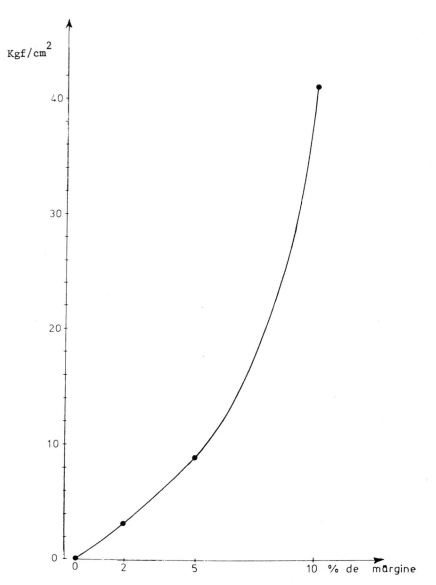

Figure 4 : Augmentation de la résistance à la compression.

fortes pluies !

2 - Sur le tronçon de Zaghouan aucune déflection significative n'a été observée. Par contre sur le tronçon de Zarzis, quelques faibles deflections sont apparues sur à peu près le quart final du tronçon. Il semble que ceci est dû d'une part à l'heterogeneité du sol en place (granulométrie notamment) et d'autre part à quelques difficultés d'exécution à la fin du chantier (mauvais compactage, moindre suveillance du pourcentage de margine, mise en place,...)

3 - Le traitement à la margine n'a pas altéré l'adhérence au contraire celle-ci est même améliorée parfois par la fixation de gravier à la surface.

3.2 Stabilisation des briques de terre à la margine

Une deuxième application des réusltats du § 2 a été essayée dans le domaine des briques de terre stabilisée. En effet, depuis le renchérissement du prix qui a eu pour conséquence une élévation du coût des matériaux de construction classiques, les constructions en terre ont connu un regain d'intérêt.

Or, pour assurer à la construction en terre des caractéristiques mécaniques et physiques satisfaisantes dans le temps, il s'avère necessaire de recourir à des stabilisants. Les plus classiques sont : le ciment et la chaux. Mais ces deux matériaux coûtent chers.

C'est pourquoi, des études ont été réalisées dans le département de Génie Civil de l'ENIT sur les briques de terre stabilisée à la margine.

Différentes caractéristiques ont été étudiées :

- Résistance à la compression à des âges différents : 7, 14, 21 et 28 jours.
- Absorption d'eau
- Erosion par l'eau
- Ramolissement
- Acrochage des enduits.

Nous indiquons ci-après l'essentiel des résultats obtenus :

(a) A températures ordinaires 20-25°c, la résistance à la compression des briques stabilisées à la margine est légèrement plus faible que la résistance des briques stabilisées à l'eau. Néanmoins cette résistance (40 bars environ à 2% de margine) est largement suffisante pour les besoins des constructions usuelles.

(b) Les briques stabilisées à la margine ont une bonne tenue à l'érosion par l'eau (les briques deviennent moins perméables).

(c) L'enduit qui semble convenir le mieux est le mortier au ciment.

(d) Les briques de terre stabilisée à la margine se ramolissent moins vite que les briques non stabilisées. Cependant leur performance vis à vis du ramolissement reste médiocre. L'enduit semble donc necessaire.

Par ailleurs, et pour étudier le comportement d'ensemble et le comportement dans le temps, un local de 28 m2 environ est en cours de construction à proximité de l'ENIT. Ce local à murs porteurs en briques est couvert par une voûte à poutrelles en béton et hourdis en briques de terre.

4. Le Tuf Tunisien. Ses propriétés de liant et application

Le tuf existe en grande quantité dans de nombreuses régions de la Tunisie. Il est utilisé en Génie routier comme matériau de chaussées, il est également parfois utilisé dans la construction, au Sahel notamment, comme matériau de remplissage.

Des études ont été menées au département de Génie Civil de l'ENIT en vue d'utiliser certains tufs comme   liant hydraulique.

Les résultats les plus significatifs de ces études sont :

1. Certains tufs semblent effectivement pouvoir jouer le rôle de liants hydrauliques. Deux facteurs influent sur cette propriété : La composition physico-chimique du tuf et sa surface spécifique.

2. Il est possible dans certaines situations d'obtenir un béton performat du point de vue de la résistance mécanique en utilisant comme liant : 80% de ciment et 20% de tuf.

On présente sur le tableau l les résultats concernant la résistance à la compression et la résistance à la flexion à différents âges pour différents mortiers :

ler et 2ème témoin(100% ciment).
T_1 à T_8:80% ciment et 20% de tuf (8 tufs différents ont été testés).

5. L'argile et le verre expansés

La technique de l'argile expansée ou du verre expansé est devenue classique. On présentera certains résultats montrant que cette technique est bien maîtrisée à l'ENIT.

Références

1. Bouassida,M. et BOUAZIZ,M. (1980), sols traités à la margine application aux fondations de chaussées, mémoire, ENIT.

2. MENSI,R. et KALLEL,A. (1981), Etude des sols traités à la margine, mémoire, ENIT.

TABLEAU Nº 1   RESISTANCES   MECANIQUES   DE   DIFFERENTS   MORTIERS
20%   D´AJOUT

NATURE DE L'AJOUT	SURFACES SPECIFIQUES cm 7G	FLEXION kg/cm			COMPRESSION kg/cm		
		7j	14j	28j	7j	14j	28j
1ªTEMOIN		36,0	46,0	55,4	163	218	280
2ªTEMOIN			37,2	42,9		133	209
T_1	2500	28,3	37,0	44,1	112	150	220
	3220	29,4	39,0	46,4	134	175	273
	3400	30,4	41,0	47,7	130	184	248
T_2	2700	30,8	39,2	44,8	130	186	239
	3500	32,3	38,1	45,6	136	168	227
	3780	31,4	36,9	46,9	138	165	244
T_3	3180	28,5	37,0	43,1	118	159	202
	3450	30,6	37,9	47,1	124	168	233
T_4	1700	29,8	34	44,0	113	154	209
	2500	28,8	36,0	43,1	126	150	218
	3000	31,5	36,8	43,2	140	164	224
	3300	36,0	38,8	49,6	158	176	276
T_5	1570	27,7	32	42,1	116	130	197
	2400	30,0	35	45,2	117	148	220
	2900	30,4	37,0	48,1	123	156	240
	3900	31,9	39	50,3	143	179	253
T_6	1250	28,0	37,3	46,7	97	96	206
	2000	31,0	37,7	45,6	129	168	225
	2300	33,0	40,6	48,5	139	179	238
	3400	34,0	41,6	49,6	151	198	258
	3700	35,0	42,5	44,6	139	189	221
	4000						
T_7	1700	30,1	33	45	125	146	214
	2500	30,2	37,3	46,1	121	167	220
	3400	33,0	36,2	47,2	136	167	234
	3800	32,1	39,4	51,3	117	177	246
	4000	35,2	41,4	49,2	151	191	270
T_8	2080	31,9	34,2	46,3	122	136	203
	3300	34,2	38,3	50,2	135	149	239
	4000	33,5	39,2	50,4	138	163	248

PROGRAMME EXPERIMENTAL REALISE POUR LA REVALORISATION DE LA COUVERTURE VEGETALE EN "SECCO" (Opération expérimentale d'habitat économique au Mali)

M. MARIOTTI, Délégué Technique aux Actions Extérieures au C.E.B.T.P.

La couverture végétale ancestrale est encore largement utilisée surtout dans l'habitat rural de nombreux pays tropicaux, mais dans l'habitat économique urbain, la couverture devenue traditionnelle est la couverture en tôle galvanisée.

La couverture en tôle présente de grands avantages (facilité de pose et de transport, pouvoir réfléchissant important, faible consommation de charpente support, bonne étanchéité) mais elle présente aussi des inconvénients (nécessité d'importation, vulnérabilité aux effets du vent, forte bruyance à la pluie, perte du pouvoir réfléchissant par corrosion, confort thermique discutable par rayonnement, ...).

Dans le cadre des recherches technologiques effectuées pour la réalisation d'une opération expérimentale à Bamako (Mali), un projet de couverture végétale a été envisagé à partir de l'utilisation du "secco", sorte de hauts herbages graminés de savane (herbe à éléphant) couramment utilisé dans l'habitat ancestral.

Le programme expérimental envisagé pour contrôler la validité du projet de revalorisation de cette couverture végétale visait le contrôle des performances et de la durabilité, l'accroissement de la productivité des éléments de couverture, la définition rationnelle des moyens de fixation et de couvrement des points singuliers (faîtage, lisières).

Il a comporté les différentes phases suivantes :
1. Conception des éléments de couverture
2. Caractéristiques mécaniques des tiges élémentaires de secco par essais de flexion
3. Caractéristiques en flexion des nappes de secco cousues sous poids propre
4. Caractéristiques en flexion des éléments de couverture sandwich sous le poids propre, le poids d'eau absorbable, l'effet du vent par chargements répétés, définition de la portée optimale
5. Comportement à l'eau et à la pluie avec effet du vent - longueur de recouvrement minimale et poids d'eau absorbée
6. Contrôle des efforts dus au vent maximum par essai en soufflerie sur maquettes - efforts maximaux et arrachement prévisibles pour le projet des fixations sur la charpente et les ancrages de la charpente dans les murs
7. Résistance des liens de fixation
8. Essais de traitement chimique ignifuge, fongicide et insectifuge.

La présente communication expose sommairement l'ensemble de ce programme et des résultats obtenus.

1. Conception de la couverture et présentation du "secco"

Le secco est un herbage graminé dit "herbe à éléphant" qui pousse abon
damment à l'état sauvage au Mali, sa structure est voisine de celle
des roseaux. Les tiges en pleine maturité mesurant aux environs de 2
mètres à 2,50 mètres de hauteur.

En coupe, les tiges sont constituées d'un anneau rigide présentant
l'aspect du bambou et d'une partie centrale spongieuse tendre. Les
parties latérales feuillues partent de noeuds pleins situés le long
de la tige et distants de 7 à 12 cm.

Le diamètre des tiges à la base est de l'ordre de 7 à 9 millimètres
il cécroit jusqu'à environ 1 millimètre vers le sommet ; la partie
utilisable a un diamètre moyen de l'ordre de 5 millimètres sur environ
2 mètres de longueur.

Le C.E.B.T.P. qui a été chargé de la mission technologique préliminaire devant permettre de sélectionner les matériaux locaux disponibles et de donner des axes de recherches, a ensuite conçu le principe de couverture végétale et a prospecté parmi les P.M.I. françaises
pour trouver une entreprise capable d'apporter les moyens technologiques nécessaires à la fabrication des éléments de couverture (moyens
artisanaux puis moyens mécanisés).

La Société CHARBONNEAU à Corbeil a bien voulu s'intéresser au
problème et a fourni les moyens artisanaux permettant de réaliser la
conception envisagée par le C.E.B.T.P.

Les éléments de couverture ont donc pu être réalisés. Les éléments
sont constitués par un "sandwich" de deux nappes de secco séparées
par une feuille d'étanchéité de polyane traitée pour résister aux
ultraviolets ; les nappes elles mêmes sont constituées par des touffes
comprenant chacune environ 25 à 30 tiges de secco et liées avec serrage au moyen de liens en polypropylène comme le montrent les schémas
n° 1a, 1b et 1c. Les tiges de secco sont orientées de telle sorte que
les bases de tiges de plus fort diamètre se situent vers les lisières
des nappes.

Les nappes proprement dites avaient une largeur pouvant être comprises entre 1,50 mètre et un maximum de 2 mètres, la longueur pouvait être indéfinie mais a été évidemment limitée par les exigences
d'un transport manuel et par les conditions de pose qui ont été minu-
tieusement céfinies.

Les nappes possèdent une file de lien tous les 40 à 50 cm ; les
éléments de couverture sandwich sont, quant à eux, cousus au moyen de
deux files de lien en bordure de chaque lisière, ainsi les perfora-
tions nécessaires de la feuille d'étanchéité n'affectent que les
lisières se situant donc dans la bande des recouvrements de pose. Les
éléments de couverture ainsi constitués pèsent environ 10 kg au m2.

2. Caractéristiques mécaniques des tiges élémentaires de secco par essais de flexion

La résistance à la traction par flexion des tiges de secco dont le
diamètre est compris entre 5,5 et 8 millimètres se situe entre 62 et
131 daN/cm2.

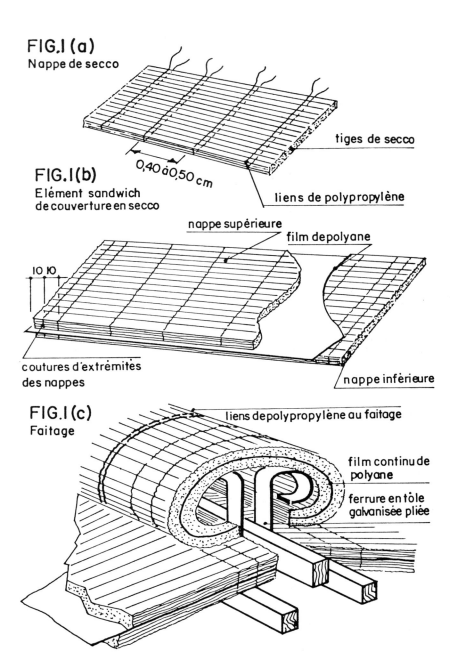

FIG.I (a)
Nappe de secco

tiges de secco

0,40 à 0,50 cm

liens de polypropylène

FIG.I(b)
Elément sandwich
de couverture en secco

nappe supérieure

film depolyane

IO IO

coutures d'extrémités
des nappes

nappe inférieure

FIG.I (c)
Faitage

liens depolypropylène au faitage

film continu de
polyane

ferrure en tôle
galvanisée pliée

Le dispositif d'essai est représenté sur la figure n° 2. Le module élastique des tiges de secco séchées est compris entre 87.000 et 250.000 daN/cm2.

3. *Déformabilité des nappes de secco sous poids propre*

Les essais de flexion de nappe de secco de 4 cm d'épaisseur ont été effectués en faisant varier la portée (portée de 1,70 et portée de 2 mètres). La nappe essayée avait une largeur de 0,38 mètre et une longueur totale de 2,40 mètres.

Les flèches maximales sous poids propre ont été trouvées égales à 33 m/m pour la portée de 2 mètres - 16 m/m pour la portée de 1,70 mètres.

De ces mesures, on a pu tirer le module de rigidité de la nappe :

$$EI = 9,35 \times 10^5 \ daN \ cm2$$

Cette valeur a permis de calculer les flèches à prévoir pour d'autres portées aussi bien sous poids propre que sous un chargement quelconque.

4. *Déformabilité en flexion des éléments de couveture sandwich*

4.1. Ces essais comprenaient en lère phase un essai de flexion sur un élément de 2,30 mètres de longueur et de 1 mètre de largeur ; les appuis étaient distants de 2 mètres et la charge uniformément répartie était réalisée par une couche croissante de sable répandu sur une toile de sac. La déformée de l'élément sous charge croissante a été déterminée, pour chaque intensité de la charge répartie, par des mesures effectuées tous les 20 cm par rapport à une barre de référence fixe. La figure n° 3 montre les déformées obtenues pour les différentes charges réalisées :

Courbe 1 = *poids propre*
    "   *2* = *+ 2 daN/m2*
    "   *3* = *+ 4 daN/m2*
    "   *4* = *+ 6 daN/m2*
    "   *5* = *+ 8 daN/m2*
    "   *6* = *+ 10 daN/m2*
    "   *7* = *+ 12 daN/m2*
    "   *5* = *retour élastique sous poids propre.*

Ces mesures ont permis de calculer le module de rigidité EI de l'élément et les valeurs suivantes ont été trouvées :

Selon courbe 4 $EI = 11,2 \times 10^5 \ daN \ cm2$
Selon courbe 5 $EI = 10,7 \times 10^5 \ daN \ cm2$

donc une valeur moyenne de 11×10^5 daN cm2 peut être retenue. Ce module peut permettre de calculer la flèche pour d'autres portées et pour des charges quelconques.

On constate que les valeurs obtenues ne sont que très peu supérieures à celle de la nappe unique. Les coutures aux extrémités des deux nappes séparées par une feuille de polyane ne modifient pratiquement

FIG. N° 2

Dispositif d'essai en flexion des tiges de secco

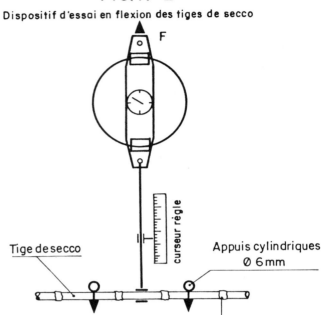

F

curseur règle

Tige de secco

Appuis cylindriques
∅ 6mm

Nœuds

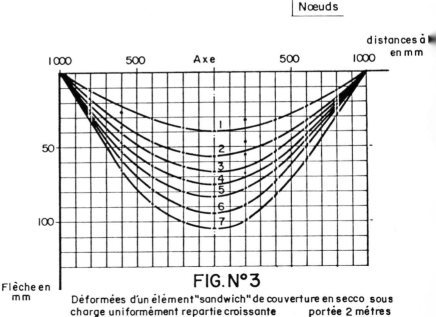

distances à
en mm

1000   500   Axe   500   1000

50

100

Flèche en
mm

FIG. N°3

Déformées d'un élément "sandwich" de couverture en secco sous
charge uniformément repartie croissante   portée 2 métres

pas la rigidité de l'élément par rapport à la rigidité des deux nappes prises séparément ; les coutures d'extrémité ne peuvent donc permettre d'assurer une liaison rigide des deux nappes, comme d'ailleurs l'on pouvait s'y attendre.

4.2. Dans une deuxième phase, nous avons soumis un élément sandwich de couverture à une série de 40 cycles de chargements et déchargements avec deux portées différentes (portées de 1,50 mètre et portée de 1 mètre) suivant le schéma de la figure n° 4 et avons contrôlé le fluage sous charge maintenue constante pendant une heure.

Les valeurs des charges appliquées ont été estimées à partir des considérations suivantes :

(a) poids propre

(b) poids d'eau correspondant à l'absorption du secco après 1 heure d'immersion soit :

$$\frac{\Delta P}{P} = 50 \%, 1/3, 2/3 \text{ et } 3/3 \text{ de ce poids soit } 2 \text{ daN/m3, } 4 \text{ daN/m2}$$

$$\text{et } 6 \text{ daN/2}$$

(c) surcharge due à l'effet du vent qui, en première approximation, a été prise égale à 20,5 daN/m2 (valeur correspondant à la pression dynamique d'un vent de 18,2 m/seconde maximum enregistré à Bamako. Nous verrons cependant que, vu l'importance de l'effet du vent sur le projet des modes de fixation, cet effet a été ensuite spécialement étudié sur maquette en soufflerie.

(d) poids d'eau de percolation dans la nappe supérieure de secco.

Finalement, ces estimations nous ont amenés à retenir les charges de 15, 20 et 30 daN/m2. L'élément de couverture a alors été soumis à 40 cycles de chargements et déchargements avec mesures des flèches instantanées et mesures du fluage sous charge constante pendant 1 heure au 1er cycle, 4ème cycle, 13ème cycle et 40ème cycle.

Les surcharges ont été réalisées par une couche de sable uniformément répartie sur une toile de sac ou par des sachets de sable non jointifs.

Les résultats obtenus sont représentés par les courbes des figures n° 5 et 6.

Ces résultats montrent que :

- Pour une portée de 1 mètre

. *la flèche totale au 1er cycle est quasi linéaire entre les charges de 5 et 30 daN/m2 et atteint un maximum de 10 m/m sous 30 daN/m2*

. *la répétition des cycles jusqu'à 40 répétitions ne donne pas d'augmentation alarmante de la flèche (10 à 11 %)*

. *la mesure du fluage sous charge constante maintenue 1 heure a donné, dans tous les cas, un accroissement négligeable de la flèche*

. *la flèche résiduelle après déchargement à la fin de l'essai atteint 40 % de la flèche totale maximum.*

FIG. N°4

Schéma des essais de chargements en flexion répétés sur deux portées

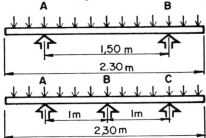

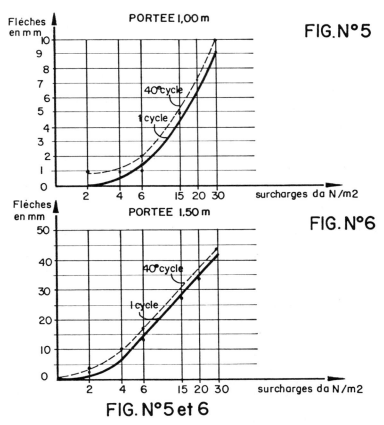

FIG. N°5 et 6

Fléches enregistrées sous surcharges croissantes
répétées (40 cycles) portée de 1.00 et 1.50m

- Pour une portée de 1,50 mètre

. *la flèche totale au 1er cycle est quasi linéaire entre les charges de 3 et 30 daN/m2 et atteint un maximum de 44 m/m sous 30 daN/m2*

. *la répétition des cycles jusqu'à 40 répétitions ne donne pas d'augmentation alarmante de la flèche (14 % sous 30 daN/m2)*

. *la mesure du fluage sous charge maintenue constante pendant 1 heure a donné un accroissement en général négligeable de la flèche*

. *la flèche résiduelle après déchargement à la fin de l'essai atteint 52 % de la flèche totale maximum.*

Ces mesures nous ont conduits à considérer que les charges auxquelles ont été soumis les éléments de couverture sont éloignées de la limite de rupture (linéarité des flèches en fonction de la charge et faible influence de la répétition des charges et du fluage) ; cependant, la mobilisation des liens de serrage des nappes impose un certain glissement par frottement entre tiges du secco, ce que traduit l'importance de la déformation résiduelle après déchargement.

En définitive, ces résultats nous ont conduits à conseiller une portée maximum de l'élément sandwich de secco de 1,30 mètre qui devrait garantir une flèche maximale ne dépassant pas 10 millimètres, soit moins de 1 % de la portée.

5. Contrôle de l'absorption d'eau et de la perméabilité des nappes, exigences du recouvrement

5.1. En vue de pouvoir apprécier l'augmentation de poids propre des nappes de secco sous l'effet de la pluie, nous avons soumis une botte de secco préalablement séchée à un contrôle de l'accroissement de poids par immersion dans l'eau douce pendant une quinzaine de jours. Les résultats obtenus sont représentés par la courbe de la figure n° 7 qui montre que le pourcentage d'absorption d'eau reste constant au bout de 200 heures (environ 8 jours) et atteint près de 160 %. Le poids du secco est donc à multiplier par 2,6 pour atteindre le poids humide à saturation.

Compte tenu de la périodicité des pluies à Bamako, il a été proposé de retenir un accroissement de poids de 50 % correspondant à une immersion complète d'une durée de une heure, cet accroissement étant limité à la nappe de secco supérieure.

5.2. Par ailleurs un essai de perméabilité dans le sens des tiges a montré que le coefficient de perméabilité était largement supérieur à K = 30 cm/sec. et qu'il ny avait pas lieu de supposer que, sur une pente de couverture de 20°, il faille tenir compte d'une nappe suspendue dans la nappe supérieure de secco au cours d'un orage.

5.3. Enfin, un modèle de couverture avec recouvrement de deux éléments sandwich de secco sur longueur variable a été soumis à l'effet d'une pluie artificielle et à l'effet d'un vent horizontal pour pouvoir apprécier la longueur minimale de recouvrement nécessaire pour éviter la pénétration de l'eau sous la couverture.

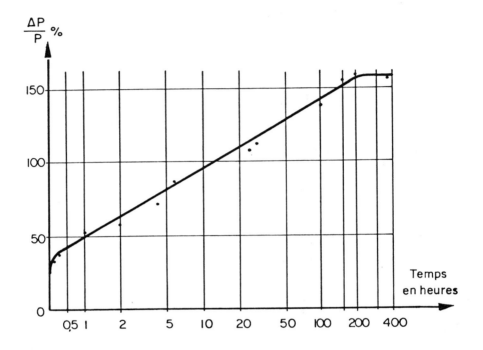

FIG. N° 7

Prise de poids d'un échantillon
de secco immergé

Ces essais ont conduit à constater que la longueur minimum de recouvrement nécessaire était de 35 cm.

6. *Contrôle des efforts dus au vent par essais sur maquettes en soufflerie*

Ces essais importants avaient pour but de définir les liens néces-saires à la fixation de la couverture sur la charpente et les ancra-ges de la charpente dans les murs.

Dans ce but, deux maquettes de maisons types, l'une à une seule pente, l'autre à deux pentes, ont été soumises aux effets d'un vent de référence de 32 m/sec. en soufflerie (soufflerie du C.E.B.T.P. à Saint-Rémy-lès-Chevreuse).

La pente adoptée était de 20° et l'angle d'incidence du vent a été de 0° et 180° sur la façade des deux maquettes.

Les prises de pression installées sur la couverture à l'extrados et l'intrados ont permis de définir les pressions et dépressions moyennes à prévoir sur les couvertures pour un vent maximum moyen de 14 n/sec. et des rafales de 18,20 m/sec. enregistrés à Bamako (soit 50,4 à 65,5 km/heure).

Les valeurs moyennes des pressions et dépressionstrouvées à partir des essais sont les suivantes sur les panneaux A B C D des figures 8 et 9 du toit à une pente unique et du toit à deux pentes, pour le vent à 14 m/sec.

Panneaux	TOIT A UNE PENTE		TOIT A DEUX PENTES	
	Vent à 14 m/seconde		Vent à 14 m/seconde	
	$I = 0$	$I = 180°$	$I = 0$	$I = 180°$
A	− 4,92 daN/m2	− 1,38 daN/m2	− 13,77 daN/m2	− 1,13daN/M2
B	+ 0,43 "	− 6,04 "	− 6,64 "	− 4,86 "
C	− 0,09 "	− 5,87 "	− 3,97 "	− 3,89 "
D	+ 0,95 "	− 5,70 "	− 3,32 "	− 12,15 "

7. *Résistance des liens de fixation*

Les liens envisagés pour la couverture végétale étaient des liens de polypropylène qui ont été essayés à la traction suivant le mode opé-ratoire de la norme NF.G.36.051.

Nous avons trouvé que ce lien de polypropylène avait une résistan-ce de 75 daN à l'état intact avec un allongement de 8,5 % sous 75 % de la charge de rupture.

L'action de l'eau contrôlée sur une éprouvette n'a eu aucun effet.

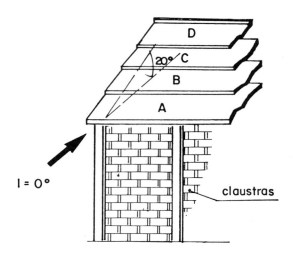

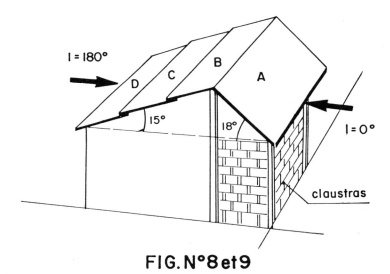

FIG. N°8 et 9

Essais en soufflerie

maquettes de toiture à pente unique et à 2 pentes

Pour l'estimation du nombre de liens nécessaire, il a été tenu compte d'un coefficient de sécurité de 3 pour tenir compte d'une baisse de résistance par vieillissement et un coefficient de sécurité de 3 sur la résistance résiduelle.

Ceci a conduit à prévoir, dans les conditions les plus défavorables, deux liens de polypropylène au mètre carré.

8. Essais de traitement chimique

Dans le cadre du programme expérimental prévu pour revaloriser les couvertures végétales à base de secco, il avait été envisagé un traitement chimique destiné à apporter à la couverture des propriétés fongicides, insectifuges et ignifugeantes.

Il était recommandé de définir un traitement qui soit :

- très simple à réaliser et réalisable de préférence par simple trempage en excluant les procédés faisant intervenir l'imprégnation sous vide ou de hautes températures ;
- capable de laisser persister dans les tiges de secco un produit protecteur non délavable à l'eau, peu toxique et résistant bien aux rayonnements U.V. ;
- économique et de l'ordre de seulement quelques francs au m2.

Nous signalerons que le C.T.F.T. (Centre Technique Forestier Tropical) et la Société Chimique C.E.C.A. ont été associés à la recherche d'une formule de traitement.

Les délais très courts (2 mois) dont on a pu disposer avant le démarrage du chantier ne nous ont cependant pas permis de soumettre toutes les formules envisagées aux contrôles d'efficacité.

Par ailleurs, le coût élevé de la protection ignifugeante nous a conduits, en accord avec l'agence de coopération et d'aménagement responsable du projet, à abondonner l'espoir d'un tel traitement.

Nous présentons ci-dessous les différentes formules qui ont été proposées :

Formule 1

- premier trempage dans la solution suivante :
  - *acide borique à 12   %*
  - *ammoniaque à   1,3 %*
  - *ethanolamine à   1,7 %*
- deuxième trempage dans solution de :
  - *Bactiram CD 30 à 3 %*
    (C.E.C.A.)

Formule 2

- un seul trempage dans une solution de :
  - *acide borique à 12   %*
  - *Noramium à   3   %*
    (C.E.C.A.)
  - *ethanolamine à   1,7 %*
  - *ammoniaque à   1,3 %*

Dans ces formules l'acide borique constitue l'élément ignifugeant, les autres constituants étant des agents de traitement complémentaire et des adjuvants stabilisants.

Formule 3 (après élimination de l'ignifugeant)
. un seul trempage dans une solution de :
- *Bactiram - C85 à 5 %*
  (C.E.C.A.)
- *T.B.T.O. (oxyde de*
  tributyl d'étain) 1 %
  + adjuvants tensioactifs
  + adjuvants anti U.V.

Cette formule, bien que satisfaisante a priori du point de vue de l'efficacité et de la stabilité au trempage, fut éliminée en raison de la toxicité du T.B.T.O.
En définitive, compte tenu de problèmes de licence de transport aérien, il fut décidé d'adopter une 4ème formule.

Formule 4
. trempage dans une solution de :
- *Noramium C 85 à 5 %*

Ce produit à base d'amines quaternaires a des propriétés hydrophobantes, fongicides et bactéricides ; il se présente sous forme d'une micro-émulsion surstabilisée parfaitement miscible à l'eau.
Cependant les délais dont nous avons disposés ne nous ont pas permis de soumettre les éléments traités à un contrôle d'efficacité.

9. Conclusion

La conception adoptée pour revaloriser cette couverture végétale ancestrale en secco au Mali et le programme expérimental qui a été prévu, bien que les délais dont nous disposions n'aient pas été suffisants pour conduire certaines expériences jusqu'à un aboutissement définitif, représentent un exemple intéressant de la démarche à suivre pour revaloriser l'utilisation et la production d'un matériau local traditionnel.
La conception permettait une amélioration de l'étanchéité sans adopter de fortes pentes ; elle permettait aussi d'envisager la production des éléments par des moyens mécanisés pouvant offrir une bonne cadence de production et la création d'une petite industrie nouvelle du bâtiment.
Les produits à importer étaient réduits au minimum (liens de polypropylène et produit de traitement chimique).
Rappelons pour terminer que l'opération expérimentale d'habitat pour laquelle ce programme a été établi, a été financée par le Plan Construction et a été ralisée par l'Agence de Coopération d'Aménagement en étroite coopération avec des organismes et techniciens maliens.

LES SUBSTANCES VEGETALES AU SERVICE

DE L'HABITAT ECONOMIQUE

Cheick Sadibou CISSE
Architecte à la SNED
B.P 1846 - BAMAKO
 M A L I

INTRODUCTION

A Bamako, comme dans bon nombre de pays du Sahel, il n'y
a pas de bidonville tels qu'on en trouve dans les pays
africains côtiers, en Amérique Latine ou en Asie. Les
maisons sont construites en briques d'adobe fabriquées
à la main et séchées au soleil. Elles sont montées à la
hâte, sans grand soin et généralement couvertes de tôles
métalliques ondulées. Les briques, de dimensions et de
forme irrégulières sont noyées dans des joints très épais
(leur volume avoisinant celle des briques), qui affaisent
la construction.

Les enduits au mortier de terre stabilisée au ciment
adhérent mal et se dégradent rapidement. Enfin, la tôle
n'apporte aucune isolation thermique, elle est sonore
sous la pluie.

Les améliorations envisagées dans l'habitat pour le grand
nombre (c'est à ce niveau que je situe l'habitat économique) porte principalement sur deux points qui font l'objet
de cette communication :

- Remplacement des enduits extérieurs par des badigeons
plus faciles à réaliser et plus économique.
- Utilisation de toiture végétales au lieu de la tôle.

Il ne faut pas nourrir trop d'illusions, dans les prochai-
nes années, les habitations de fortune continueront à
proliférer dans les faubourgs des villes. C'est justement
là qu'un effort ede recherche devrait être fait.

Les badigeons et les toîtures végétales en question ont
été testés sur une dizaine de logements expérimentaux en
été 1982 à Banconi, un faubourg de Bamako.

Badigeons
Le badigeon utilisé est un coulis confectionné avec un
poids égal de liant et d'eau. Le liant est un mélange de
ciment et de chaux, à parts égales selon le dosage déterminé au laboratoire. En fait, sur place la mauvaise qualité de la chaux a conduit à privilégier le ciment (2
parts) par rapport à la chaux (1 part). Le coulis est
appliqué à la brosse de peinture : en deux couches.
Théoriquement,

La consommation est de 1,2 Kg de liant sec par m2 de mur.
Dans la pratique elle a atteint 2 Kg/m2.

Pour assurer une bonne adhérence du badigeon, il faut
préalablement humidifier le mur, graté pour éliminer le
glacis formé à la surface des briques au moment du moulage. On a utilisé un pulvérisateur de jardin pour obtenir
l'humidification désitée. D'autre part, pour éviter un
séchage trop rapide du badigeon (farinage, craquelures)
on a recommandé d'appliquer les badigeons en fin de journée. Deux aspersions d'eau sur le mur enduit ont le même
objet.

Des essais de vieilissement acceléré ont été effectués
au laboratoire selon le cycle : aspersion d'eau,
rayonnement actinique.

Le badigeon appliqué sur la brique non stabilisée se
détériore très rapidement : il se forme en effet des
craquelures capillaires, par lesquelles l'eau de pluie
s'infiltre, provoquant le gonflement, puis le retrait de
la brique ; ces variations alternatives du volume de
la brique sont lac cause dub décollement du badigeon.

Pour remédier à ce défaut majeur, il a été proposé
d'appliquer sur le badigeon fraichement appliqué une
solution à 5% d'un hydrophobant (le STABIRAM,677M).Ainsi
traité le badigeon résite à plus de soixante cycles de
vieillissement.

Malheureusement les résultats de ces essais ont été
connus trop tardivement pour pouvoir mêtre mis en pratique sur le chantier, où la mauvaise tenue du badigeon
non traité s'est révélée dès les premières pluies. Le
temps pressant, on a procédé à une application d'enduit
traditionnel au mortier de terre et ciment, sauf sur les
murs les mieux abrités où le badigeon est resté apparent.

Les essais reprendront sur le chantier futur car la mise
en oeuvre du badigeon est aisée et a séduit les tâcherons.
Son aspect est aussi satisfaisant. De plus le badigeon
est économique; même surdosé comme il l'a été sur le
chantier, il coûte (main d'oeuvre non comprise) 3,4FF/m2
alors que l'enduit classique revient à 10,16 FF/m2 s'il
estddosé correctement (350 Kg de ciment par m3) ou à
6,41 FF/m2 s'il est pauvre (et peu résistant). Le temps
de main d'oeuvre est aussi plus réduit.

Enfin l'entretien du badigeon est simple, puisqu'il s'a
s'applique comme une peinture.

Toiture de Secco

Le secco est une herbe qui pousse abondamment dans la
savane. Il est utilisé pour les toitures dans l'habitat
(en couches épaisses) et, tresse en nattes pour réaliser
des clôtures ou des abris.

L'utilisation qui a été proposée est la suivante :

des panneaux de 1,55m (nous recommanderions 1,60 ou 1,65m
pour plus grande facilité de pose) de largeur et de
longueur variable ont été confectionnés en ligaturant
des bottes de secco de 4 cm d'épaisseur. Ces panneaux
trempés dans un bain chimique pour leur conférer une
résistance à l'eau, aux moisissures et aux insectes, sont
superposées deux à deux, un film de polyétylène étant
inséré entre les deux couches pour assurer l'étanchéité
de la couverture. Des coutures aux lisières maintiennent
cet ensemble.

Les panneaux - sandwich sont fixés à la charpente par
des ligatures en attente, ménagées lors de la confection
des panneaux. Des dispositions particulières ont été
prises pour protéger les bords de la toiture sur pignon,
et pour le faîte.

La largeur de 1,55 a été déterminé en fonction de la
résistance à la flexion du secco mouillé. Les ligatures
ont été calculées pour résister à l'arrachement, à la
suite d'essais en souflerie.

L'ensemble de la toiture (pente minimum de 20% pour
assurer un bon écoulement de l'eau) se compose de bandes
superposées avec recouvrement des coutures aux lisières.
La continuité de l'étanchéïté est réalisée par collage
et pliage des bords contigus des films plastiques de deux
panneaux voisins. La longueur des panneaux ne peut en
effet dépasser 3,5o a 4m pour qu'on puisse les porter
à la main.

Les panneaux ont été confectionnés manuellement par quatre
artisans encadrés par un contre-maître. Une produc tion
commercial pourraît être assurée de cette façon, mais il
existe une machine qui peut coudre le secco plus serré,
et bien entendu plus rapidement.

La pose des toitures demande une certaine habilité. Les
tâcherons a qui l'on a appris la technique de pose sur
une première maison n'ont pas eu de difficultés à couvrir
seuls les autres maisons. Le temps de pose est de
l'ordre de 4 à 5 jours (il devrait pouvoir être réduit en
améliorant certains détails qui faciliteraient les opérations). On ne compte pas plus de 2 jours pour la pose
d'une toiture en tôle.

L'avantage des panneaux de secco, produit local, réside
dans la très bonne protection thermique et la ventillation
qu'ils donnent à la toiture. Leur apparence est aussi
beaucoup plus agréable que celle de la tôle.

L'inconvenient principal en est la putrescibilité. A cet
égard, les essais engagés pour vérifier l'éfficacité du
traitement chimique adopté doivent se poursuivre pendant
un an, et l'on ne peut encore se prononcer sur ce point.
On a également mentionné le risque d'incendie. Il est en
réalité assez faible, dans le type de construction peu
dense qui se pratique à Banconi (on notera également que
la plupart des feux de cuisines sont abrités sous des
nattes de secco).

Le prix de revient des toitures (charpentes et couverture) s'établit à 6 495 FM/m2. C'est exactement celui
des toitures en tôles (5,60 Kg par m2) sans sous-face.
l'Adjonction de la sous-face augmente le coût de ces
dernières d'environ 10%.

Le chantier a débuté à la fin de janvier 1982 par la
mise en place de la briquetterie. Il s'est achevé à la
fin de Juin, le dernier mois ayant été géné par
l'arrivée prématurée des pluies.

Fabrication et mise en oeuvre des briques pressées

Deux modules de briques ont été employés :
une brique de 29,5 x 14 x 9, fabriquée à la presse
TERSTARAM (taux de compression 47 Kg/ cm2) ; une brique
de 40 x 20 x 10 mouléeà la presse CINVARAM (taux de
compression de 6 à 12 Kg/cm2). Les premières ont servi
à construire les murs de maisons (murs extérieurs :
14 cm). Les briques de grand module, de moins bonne
tenue ont été réservées à l'édification des clôtures.

La briqueterie installée à proximité du chantier a été
équipée de 3 presses TERSTARAM et de presses CINVARAM.
Elle a occupé 4 équipés, payées au forfait pendant les
quinze premiers jours (période de formation), puis sur
la base de leur production journalière.

L'adaptation a été rapide et les rytmes de production
très satisfaisante : 600 briques par jour à la TERSTARAM
(parfoi jusqu'à 800), 325 briques par jour à la CINVARAM,
dont la maniement est plus lent et plus fatigant.

Après plusieurs essais, on a choisi un mélange de terre
argileuse des bords du Niger et de terre latéritique
locale destinée à apporter les éléments les plus gros
(16mm) pour armer les briques. Le séchage des briques
et leur stockage a été organisé en tas de 10 à 15 niveaux,
à plat.

Incidence du Projet

Une opération de dix logements est assurément trop limitée
pour provoquer un mouvement profond et durable. Elle a
pourtant mobilisé l'opinion et ses prolongements sont
notables.

Localement, elle a suscité une organisation communautaire
que l'on peut espérer maintenir vivace au-dela du projet:
bien que les constructions aient été financées sur un
fonds d'aide, il a été décidé d'en récupérer les coûts
auprès des attributaires et d'utiliser les sommes recou-
vrées pour financer de petits équipements de quartier.
L'apport en capital a été limité à 5%, et les mensualités
calculées sur la base d'un remboursement en 20 ans, à un
taux de 3%. La municipalité de Banconi, fort dynamique, a
créé un Comité de Gestion où sont représentées les principales organisations locales, les bénéficiaires des saisons,
ainsi que des membres du Conseil Municipal. Ce Comité est
chargé de recouvrer les mensualités et de veiller au bon
fonctionnement du groupe de maisons (gestion de la borne-
fontaine, etc...).

D'autre part, le Maire de Banconi a pris l'initiative de
susciter la création d'une coopérative ouvrière qui doit
notamment poursuivre la fabrication des briques compri-
mées. Dès à présent, il est prévu que la production de
briques servira à construire l'extension de l'école du
quartier.

C'est à cette coopérative que seront confiées trois des
presses utilisées sur le chantier, les autres ayant été
été remises au projet Urbain du Mali -(Opération de
trames assainies financées par la Banque Mondiale). Le
Jeune assistant malien qui a participer à l'encadrement
du projet doit prochainement suivre un stage de deux mois
pour parfaire ses connaissances sur la construction en
terre et assurer ensuite le contrôle de la production. Il
participera également au Centre de Technologie Adaptée
que le PNUD est entrain de mettre sur pied au Mali.

Enfin les briquetteries et maçons formés sur le chantier
doivent participer à la mise en route d'un nouveau chantier dans l'opération de la Banque Mondiale.

La fabrication des panneaux de couverture intéresse aussi
une entreprise malienne. La possibilité de passer à un
stade commercial sera examinée lors de la réalisation que
nous espérons prochainement du projet de 220 Logements à
Banconi.

Ainsi, une réalisation limitée a pu éveiller l'intérêt
de la population et des responsables goubernementaux
et locaux. C'est croyons-nous, parce que les habitants
du quartier ont été associés à toutes les phases de la
réalisation, qu'ils en ont vu les progrès aussi bien que
les tatonnement que le peut être faire souche.

SECTION IV

Economie et gestion de la production des matériaux

Organization and economics of the production of materials

TECHNOLOGY ALTERNATIVES FOR PRODUCING BRICKS IN DEVELOPING COUNTRIES

A A HAMMOND, Head, Materials Division, Building and Road Research Institute (Council for Scientific and Industrial Research), Kumasi.

1. *Introduction*

Demand for housing in Africa has always outstripped the supply thereof and this phenomenon has resulted in overcrowding and high occupancy rates, especially in the main urban centres. The obvious solution to this problem is to construct more houses to meet the demand. Unfortunately, unavailability and high cost of building materials, high cost of construction and low productivity of labour, lack of adequate long-term funds for investment in housing and related facilities among others, make it impossible to achieve this goal.

However, many African countries have recognised the need to establish building materials industries to manufacture building materials from local resources so as to ameliorate the present housing situation. But in most cases, some of these industries which are established operate on the basis of technologies imported from highly industrialized countries which are generally unsuitable. Another source of introduction of inappropriate technology to Africa is through foreign aid from developed countries. This gives African countries little chance in the selection of technology for a particular purpose especially when the technology is tied up with foreign aid. The choice is inveriably restricted to the technologies available in the developed country offering the aid. In order to derive maximum benefit from the aid it is desirable to separate financial aid from the acquisition of technology from the donor country. This way, the developing countries would be more likely to shop for more appropriate technology, since they would be in a better position to assess all the technologies available irrespective of their source.

It is true that certain industries such as glass making depend on high technology. In such cases where there are no alternatives to choose from the technology may be adopted. On the other hand, there are other products such as brick, lime and cement which may be produced at different levels of technology. Here there is the need to adopt the most appropriate technology which will enhance large production of affordable durable building materials for low-cost housing.

The purpose of this paper is to identify appropriate technology for brick making bearing in mind the availability of capital and labour. The paper will discuss three methods of production - labour-intensive,

semi-mechanized and fully mechanized methods. The properties of
products from each technology will be discussed in relation to their
requirements for low cost housing and the most appropriate technology
recommended for developing countries.

2.   *Brick making*

In making bricks four main items are required. Availability of
suitable clay and sand, water, fuel and manpower.

2.1 Fortunately for Africa, there is clay in many countries. As
should be expected some countries in Africa have richer deposits of
clay than others and for the same countries some regions may have
more clay deposits than other regions. For example, from data
obtained so far from the Department of Geological Survey in Ghana, the
Western Region has the largest deposits and the Volta Region the
least. Because of these variations existing between countries, and
between regions within the same country, it is difficult to say that
there will be clay in every rural area in any country and that every
country and region should use bricks for housing. This means there-
for that a preliminary search for clay is a prerequisite in
establishing a brick factory even at cottage industry level. Having
found a clay deposit the quantities and qualities of the clay should
be evaluated to establish the technical and economic feasibility of
the project bearing in mind other factors such as availability of
water, fuel and manpower. Generally, when the clay is plastic, sand
should be found nearby the deposit and used in mixing with the clay
so as to reduce its plasticity.

2.2 Water is another important input in brick production. It is
required for mixing and moulding the green bricks and it is important
to find out whether it will be available throughout the year for the
factory. Provision can then be made for storing water during the wet
seasons if necessary.

2.3 Firewood, coal, peat and oil are the main sources of fuel for
brick production. Electricity could be used but it is generally
expensive. It is important therefore to assess the opportunities
available for fuel supply. For example, in the case of firewood and
coal, in fact for all types of fuel, it is necessary to evaluate the
distances involved in carting or hauling the fuel to the factory. In
such places where firewood, coal and peat are not available oil could
be used especially if there is a big market for the product. Other
sources of fuel may be agricultural wastes such as coconut husk,
groundnut shells etc. These sources of fuel are generally suitable
for small scale production at cottage industry level.

2.4 Manpower requirements will vary according to the level of technology adopted. Both skilled and unskilled labour will be required in
addition to technical and managerial personnel. For example, for a

labour-intensive technology the main bulk of labour will be unskilled
with few skilled labour.

3.   *Technology for brick making*

The manufacture of bricks is one of the few industries in which it is
possible to use either very sophisticated methods which require setting up of capital intensive factories or simple ones which are
usually labour intensive. Generally, three methods of production
can be identified. These are manual or labour intensive, semi-
mechanized and fully-mechanized or capital intensive.

3.1 Labour Intensive Technology requires as little capital investment as possible. The winning, mixing, preparation and moulding of
green bricks are undertaken manually. Drying of green bricks, setting up in a kiln, are also manually undertaken. The fuel is usually wood and the firing is either carried out in clamps or in kilns.
The kiln can either be a continuous or an intermittent one. Removal
of burnt bricks from kiln, sorting out and stacking are all done
manually. Equipment and tools required for such a labour intensive
technology are simple and relatively inexpensive. These include
pick axes, shovels and cutlasses for winning the clay; head pans
and/or wheel barrows for transporting the clay to the factory; drums
for storing water if there is no pipe borne water at the factory;
water hose if there is a pipe borne source at the factory; chain-saw
or cutlasses for cutting wood; Wellington boots for clay mixing by
treading with feet; moulding benches and wire cutters, wooden moulds
or metallic moulds and drying and working sheds.
    This technology is recommended for the rural areas where clay,
fuel and water are available and where demand is below 3 million per
year. As the demand for the product increases some aspects of the
process can be mechanized.

3.2 The semi-mechanized technology allows for various degrees of
mechanization or combination of labour and capital. The choice of
relative levels of labour and capital depends on many factors including the required production scale and availability of labour and
capital. There are therefore many levels of semi-mechanization in
the brick industry.
    Generally, however, for a minimum scale semi-mechanized factory
producing about 3-5 million bricks per year, the winning, preparation, mixing and moulding processes are mechanized. These are
extensive operations to ensure greater homogeneity and easier passage of the clay through the die.
    Forming takes place in a pugmill-cum-extruder with constant flow
depending on the plasticity of the clay from any particular deposit.
The machine delivers a continuous "column" of clay which is cut up
into formed bricks of required size by a wire cutter.
    Drying of the green brick may be naturally or artificially under-
taken. Setting up of green bricks into the kiln, removal of burnt
bricks from the kiln, sorting and stacking may be accomplished

manually. The fuel may be wood, coal or residual oil. About 100
tons of residual oil will be required for burning one million bricks.
Electrical power of about 230,000kwh/year will be required for the
preparation of clay and forming of 5 million bricks. One ton of
water will be needed to produce 1000 green bricks.

For a minimum semi-mechanized product the equipment requirement
for the various operations will be clay digging equipment and means
of transport - grab excavator and dumper; clay crusher, feed conveyor;
pugmill-cum-extruder with cutter; wheel barrows and brick barrows;
drying and working sheds, accessories-racks and palette for drying
shed; water and oil tanks; kiln equipments - thermocouples; a
continuous or intermittent kiln; and a pick up. Continuous kiln is
to be preferred to ensure continuous supply of bricks and maximum
utilization of fuel.

For a semi-mechanized brick making factory, a manager, fitter
electrician, mason, carpenter, labourers (skilled and unskilled) and
watchmen are the main personnel required. This type of technology is
not suitable for a small rural community. However, in a situation
where such a community is near to big commercial towns such a technology will be suitable taking into consideration the requirements of
such commercial towns.

3.3 The fully mechanized technology is capital intensive and very
sophisticated. As much as possible all processes that are undertaken
manually in the previously mentioned technologies are mechanized.
From clay winning to the stacking of the burnt bricks every process
is mechanized. This requires a great deal of capital investment, and
it is only where labour is scarce and costly and where production
capacity may be in the range of 15-20 million per annum and above
that it can be viable. Highly skilled personnel will be need -
mechanical and electrical engineers, fitters and skilled labourers,
and an administrative set up will be necessary as well as a workshop
for servicing and repairing of equipment. Presently, this level of
technology is not suitable for Africa. For, these fully mechanized
brick works have not proved very successful in many developing
countries because of many reasons including, lack of sustained demand,
heavy investment, high transportation cost and the like. The
experience with the Prampram Brick Factory in Ghana suggests that
semi-mechanized technology will be more appropriate for the country.

4.   *The properties in relation to the methods of production*

The bricks manufactured by the labour-intensive methods have relatively poorer properties than those made by the semi-mechanized
methods. The Compressive Strengths are low and range between $4-8N/mm^2$
(600-1200p.s.i.) with fairly high water absorption (12-20%), and tend
to have irregular dimensions. They are however economical, are
locally produced, and require little capital investment and transportation cost. The strength properties are adequate for a one-storey
low-cost house. They may be useful for constructing a non-load
bearing structure.

Cn the other hand, the fully mechanized manufactured bricks have more than adequate strength properties for low-cost housing. The strength is high ranging from 17-42N/mm^2 (2500-6000p.s.i.) with low water absorption of about 2-6%. The bricks are uniform with excellent dimensions. Some of such bricks are so good that they may be used for engineering projects. They are however expensive, and the process requires heavy investment and a sustained demand. Transportation cost is generally very high.

The semi-mechanized processes appear to be most suitable since they combine the merits of the labour-intensive and that of the fully mechanized one. The strength ranges between 7-18N/mm^2 (1000-2500 p.s.i.) with water absorption ranging from 5-15%. The uniformity of the products is fair to good and the strength properties are adequate for a two-storey building. For a low-cost housing programme the labour-intensive and the semi-mechanized processes appear to be suitable.

5. *Technology transfer to the urban and rural areas and communities*

To promote low-cost housing with brick in both the urban and rural areas the technology for brick making should be transferred to these communities. Specifically if the low-cost housing programme is integrated with brick making it will enhance the transfer of the technology to these communities. It is therefore important to organise these communities to participate in the low-cost housing programme. Here participation is meant to include conceiving, planning, elaborating, managing and financing industrial projects at village, district, provincial and country levels as well as sub-regional and regional levels.

Experiences available from other parts of the world, notably from Latin America and South East Asia, show that for such a programme to be successful there should be full participation of the local community, "the participation by the people themselves in efforts to improve their level of living with as much reliance as possible on their own initiative; and the provision of technical and other services in ways which encourage initiative, self-help and mutual help and make these more effective"(1) should be the underlying principle. To apply this principle successfully, it is important to organise the community and bringing all its segments into the programme as partners. It is important also that the programme is thoroughly explained to the rural people to avoid any future misunderstanding. There is then the identification of what should be done and allocation of roles to all identifiable groups of the community. Initially, help, both financial and technical, will be required from outside organizations such as the Department of Community Development, the Universities and the Building Research Institutions in either financing some aspects of the programme or providing technical training for both urban and rural people.

In Ghana, for example, the Building and Road Research Institute organizes Brick Making Course for any interested group of people. The course is a practical training of how to make bricks, and it

ensures that the trainees acquire skills in identification and
selection of brick making clays, techniques for preparation, mixing,
moulding of the clays and firing (clamp firing) of the green bricks.
The duration of the training is six weeks. It is advisable for the
trainees to be literates. Tuition is free but the trainees are
expected to provide their own boarding and lodging as well as
transportation to and from the Brick Factory of the Institute. After
six weeks. they go back to their respective areas to train more
people in brick making. Recently, there has been a programme to
link the training in brick making with rural sanitation whereby
rural latrines will be built in bricks. A parallel training programme in brick laying is organized by the Department of Community
Development. This way, construction of low-cost housing in bricks
is being promoted which will eventually result in improvement of
housing and overall improvement of the built environment, which in
turn will enhance socio-economic development of the country.

6.   *Conclusions and recommendations*

Many houses are required to be built every year in Africa in order
to ameliorate the demand/supply situation of housing. To achieve
this, it is necessary to use building materials, such as bricks,
produced from local resources to build more low-cost houses. The
type of technology adopted in producing the bricks is crucial as it
has been found that highly mechanized methods have not been suitable
for most African countries and therefore, labour-intensive and
semi-mechanized methods should be preferred.

On the basis of the discussion on the merits and demerits of the
three levels of technologies, namely, labour-intensive, semi-
mechanized and fully mechanized ones it is recommended that where
there are suitable clays, fuel and water bricks should be produced
by either labour-intensive or semi-mechanized methods to provide
low-cost housing to improve the poor housing situation in Africa.

References

1. Anon, 1956, Twentieth report to the United Nations Economic and
    Social Council, Annex III, New York (Document E/2931).
2. Hammond, A.A. (1979), Development of Building Materials
    Industries in Ghana. Conference of African Experts on the
    Building Materials and Construction Industries in Africa.
    E.C.A., Addis Ababa, 22-27th July, 1979.
3. Hammond, A.A. (1980), Use of selected local Building Materials
    with special reference to clay products and cementitious
    materials. Current Paper No. 36, BRRI, Kumasi, Ghana.
4. Ocran, K.A.G. (1981), Clamp firing for the production of bricks.
    Special Report, BRRI, Kumasi, Ghana, (in press).
5. Anon, 1980, Appropriate Industrial Technology for construction
    and Building Materials. Monograph on Appropriate Industrial
    Technology No. 12. UNIDO, Vienna.

6. E.C.A. Publications.
  i. Policy and strategy for internally self-sustaining
      industrial growth and diversification in the African
      region. 4th Conference of AFrican Ministers of Industry.
      Sponsored by E.C.A., OAU and UNIDO, No.ECA/CM1/FC/A.4/TP/5
      No. ECA/CM14/INR/TP/5 Nov. 22-26, 1977.

 ii. Components of policy and strategy for the Development of
      Construction and Building Materials Industries.
      Meeting of African Experts on Building Materials.
      Addis Ababa (E/CN.14/HUS/23), 17-21 July, 1978.

iii. Building Materials and Construction Industries Develop-
      ment Programme Meeting of Inter-governmental Regional
      Committee on Human Settlement. Addis Ababa.
      E/CN.14/HUS/29, 2-6th Oct., 1978.

BUILDING MATERIALS FOR HOUSING OF LOW-INCOME SECTOR
IN EGYPT

Dr. AHMED A. EL-ERIAN[*] and Dr. MAHMOUD A. REDA YOUSSEF[**]

1. Introduction

This paper presents an overview of the housing problem in
Egypt, and reports the present situation and future trends
and development of building materials used in housing,
especially for low-income sector.
   The basic building materials used in housing construction for low-income sector in Egypt are reviewed, and
related problems and implications are identified.
   Examples are given of recent undertaken research and
development of building materials appropriate for low-cost
housing, and recommended technical solutions and trends
are presented for future development and implementation.
   A special recommendation is given for the immediate
integration of resources and technical expertise within
the African region. A regional research center, chosen
from among the pioneering research institutes and universities in the area, may be established to stimulate and
co-ordinate further research and development, to implement
research findings for practical applications, and to
foster exchanging ideas and expertise within and outside
Africa.

2. Overview of Housing Problem in Egypt

By almost all accounts, Egypt is currently experiencing an
acute housing shortage estimated in 1975 to be approximately 1.5 million units, and expected to reach 3.6
millions by the year 2000. With the present prevailing
constraints, there is no way for the Egyptian government
to provide sufficient housing for this expected demand.

---

* Professor of Building Materials, Structural Engrg. Dept.,
  Faculty of Engineering, Cairo University, Egypt.
**Associate Professor, Structural Engrg. Dept., Faculty of
  Engineering, Cairo University, Egypt.

The total population which is now about 45 millions is
expected to double by the year 2000. While the annual
population growth is 2.4% for the country, the urban rate
of growth is reaching 4% ; of which half is from migration
of unskilled, low-income, rurally oriented families. As
a result, the urban population has increased from 38% in
1960 to 44% in 1976.

The annual rate of built housing units, however, has
declined from an average of 7 units per 1000 population in
1960 to only 2 units per 1000 population in 1976. There
is also a clear indication of the soaring cost of housing
production, especially within the past few years. It has
been estimated that the cost of a square meter of housing
production has increased from a base level of 100% in 1960
to 120% in 1965, 154% in 1970, 278% in 1974, 330% in 1975,
and 574% in 1976.

The problem, in fact, is widespread affecting all
income groups, especially the low-income sector. This
sector already represents 76% of the total Egyptian population and is growing more rapidly than the other income
groups.

The low-income majority of the population comprise and
cause the most severe problems which require immediate
direct actions. It has been estimated by various studies
that 50 to 70% of all new urban housing in Egypt is built
by the so-called "informal sector", in which all those
activities related to the production of shelter are undertaken by individuals outside of - and often in conflict
with - official policies, regulations and laws. Estimates
indicate that 17000 hectares are converted yearly to new
illegal construction where utilities and services are
generally nonexistent.

3.   Overall Situation of Building Materials

One of the major constraints affecting the housing problem
in Egypt is the present situation of building materials.
In the past few years, Egypt has become a net importer of
building materials after having been a net exporter for at
least 25 years.

Cement, steel, and bricks are the basic structural
materials currently used in housing construction in Egypt,
including that for low-income sector. Other major building and finishing materials used in housing include lumber, glass, gypsum, flooring tiles, sanitary fixtures and
lime. Several of these materials are at least in part
imported; lumber being noteworthy as it is almost entirely
imported, while bricks and gypsum are two exceptions for
they are totally produced locally.

Shortage and deficiency are evident in some of the
basic raw materials used for producing building materials.
The Nile silt which has been long used for producing the
familiar "red bricks" is no longer available, resulting in

reduced production and increased cost. Local scrap used
for steel production is in short supply and local iron ore
is of lower quality.

Many obstacles and bottle-necks hinder the production
of the main building materials. The necessary funding for
replacing depreciated equipment and reconditioning old
plants is absent, and the proper maintenance is lacking.
Old fashion techniques and equipment still adopted in some
plants affect the efficiency of production. Lack is evident of the continuous supply of necessary energy sources
needed for the production plants.

Cement prices, like those of most building materials,
have exhibited a highly inflationary trend in recent years.
Official and black market prices, having started out at
the same level, have risen six and ten-fold, respectively,
within the past ten years.

The flourishing existence of the black market, the
imbalance in materials allocation, and the potential
inefficiencies in materials usage, are all detected examples of the present overall situation of building materials in Egypt.

4.   Recent Undertaken Research and Development

Recognizing the massive demands for low-cost housing in
Egypt and the present critical situation of Egyptian
building materials, recent research and development were
directed to this area to alleviate part of the problem.

Research studies were undertaken by many investigators,
including the authors, to assess possibilities for introducing innovative uses and improvements to conventional
building materials, and study potentialities of substituting some of the main construction materials in shorter
supply by available low-cost indigenous materials. This
would include new techniques of construction that would
save in materials consumption and waste, labor time, and
total cost.

4.1 Gypsum

Newly-discovered large deposits of high-grade gypsum in
Egypt make this indigenous material attractive for use in
new applications as building components, other than its
present use as conventional plaster.

Recent studies by the authors investigated the potentialities of locally produced gypsum for use in various
components for walls and roofs in housing units of different cost standards.

Masonry wall units (1) in the form of solid gypsum
blocks were developed for load-bearing walls. The recommended overall dimensions were 29 x 29 x 10 cm and the
compressive strength ranged from 40 to 100 kg/cm^2 according
to the percentage of sand added as a filler. Cored gypsum
blocks of same dimensions, with sawdust filler where light

weight is important, or with sand when cost predominates, are recommended for non-bearing walls and partitions. The corresponding compressive strength ranged from 15 to 30 kg/cm^2, based on gross area of cross section.

Gypsum panels, if reinforced properly, gain a considerable increase in their flexural strength and their impact resistence is largely enhanced. Gypsum panels (2) reinforced with jute, glass wool, galvanized stretched wire mesh, polypropylene fabrics, and Nile reeds were studied for use as partitions and roof planks. Reeds proved to be very promising when used as reinforcement for gypsum planks 60 x 60 x 6 cm, suitable for roofs in rural and low-income sector housing. A recommended thickness of the plank of 6 cm is quite convenient and can safely withstand the expected superimposed loads. Reeds placed in one layer spaced 2 cm on centers are suggested. Native reeds are plentiful and readily available, and no water repellent treatment of any kind appears to be required.

Such applications might help to relieve the pressure on tight supplies of portland-cement concrete products and dwindling supplies of traditional red bricks. The neat surface finish of the gypsum components would also save in the amounts of cement needed for rendering and plastering of conventional red brick partitions.

4.2   Bamboo and Date-palm Mid-ribs

The promising results of bamboo indicated by many research studies in other countries, and the unfailing success of the primitively used mid-ribs of date-palms for roofing Egyptian rural houses, encouraged the authors to undertake extensive studies on both indigenous materials.

Both materials are cheap and locally available. A palm tree produces yearly an average amount of 40 kilograms of mid-ribs. According to the latest census, Egypt has about eight million date-palms distributed allover the country. Bamboo grows very fast without special attention in many rural areas of Egypt and along the Nile and canal banks.

Extensive research studies (3, 4) on both materials indicated their suitability for use, safely and at low cost, as substitutes for steel reinforcement in concrete members of many structural applications. Native bamboo and date-palm mid-ribs exhibited satisfactory high tensile strengths of up to 2600 kg/cm^2 and 1550 kg/cm^2, respectively, while their tensile moduli of elasticity were only about one-tenth of that of conventional reinforcing steel.

Both materials are recommended for use as reinforcement in concrete floors, roof coverings, walls and columns of low-cost housing units subject to moderate loading, and for various precast concrete structural members. No manufacturing process is required beyond splitting the bamboo culms into strips, and treating both materials with a suitable water-repellent agent.

4.3   Shale Bricks
The High Dam at Aswan has stopped the annual flooding of
the Nile and depleted the supply of Nile silt used for
making the traditional red bricks. As a result, the
owners of brick factories resorted to undercutting of the
top layer of fertile soil in the surrounding cultivated
lands, and threatened the agricultural wealth of the whole
nation.
  This necessitated undertaking extensive geological ex-
plorations and research investigations (5) which revealed
the existence of shale deposits allover the country,
suitable as a substitute for the Nile silt in the clay
brick industry. The shale material showed potentialities
for use in producing solid and cored bricks, hollow blocks,
roofing and paving tiles, and lightweight aggregates from
expanded shale.
  The Egyptian government has started the erection of
many shale brick factories with a total annual production
of 240 million bricks.
  The developed brick is considerably superior to the red
brick in strength and general applications, especially in
load-bearing walls of housing units of up to seven storeys.
This would save in cement of concrete beams and columns if
skeleton type of construction is used. A considerable
saving is also achieved in cement mortar and plastering
due to the larger size of the shale brick and the uniformity and quality control of its production.

4.4   Stabilized Earth
Earth construction is widespread throughout the world,
including Egypt. Although primarily used in housing,
there are ancient structures such as the 1100-year old
50-meter high minaret in Samarra, Iraq, that attest to the
capability of earth as a construction material.
  Many materials which are available in Egypt were employed as stabilizers, including portland cement, asphalt,
bitumens, tars, lime and even cow dung. Except for bitumens and asphalts, which can impart dark colors and possible odours, probably temporary, appearance is not unduly
affected. Nevertheless, most earth structures are faced
with stucco or plaster of some sort, often based on mud.
  Stabilized earth blocks and bricks appear to be most
promising for low-cost housing of low-income groups, and
for rural areas and villages. This may be considered as
one solution to the problem of red bricks in shorter
supply in Egypt.

4.5   Surface-bonded Brick Walls
The conventional technique of brick-wall construction by
placing mortar between successive courses of bricks and
between individual bricks of the same course, proved to
have many disadvantages. The erection time including the
process of plastering is relatively long, resulting in

less labor productivity. Considerable amounts of cement are consumed in binding mortar and trowelled plaster, raising final cost. Furthermore, the mortar used usually has low strength properties and poor adhesion to masonry bricks, affecting the service life and bearing capacity of the wall.

A technique of surface bonding brick walls (6), which is new to local practice, is recommended by the authors for construction of walls and partitions in residential units. It proved its practicality, lower cost, speed of construction, and significant saving in cement consumption. The tested surface-bonded brick walls gave twice the flexural resistance and seven times the impact resistance of corresponding conventional brick walls.

The recommended surface-bonding mortar is composed of one part by weight cement, one part by weight sand, and 0.4 part of water, to which 1% by volume sisal fibers of 4 cm length is added. Sisal was chosen for being a commercially available material of low cost, and for exhibiting satisfactory mechanical properties when incorporated with cement mortar.

5. Recommended Future Trends and Technical Solutions

In an attempt to alleviate part of the problem of Egyptian housing shortage, and meet the increasing demands for low-cost housing by the low-income population, the following future trends and technical solutions are recommended :

   a.   More efforts should be directed in the future to study the possibility of substituting some of the main building materials in shorter supply by new available low-cost indigenous materials which are largely known and already applied elsewhere, but still untried in Egypt. A good many of such low-cost materials have not yet been studied for possible innovations and improvements which would meet the aspirations and overall requirements of the low-income population.
   b.   It appears that the potential for increased production and for diversified uses of Egyptian gypsum are attractive. A careful examination of the expanded uses of gypsum is, therefore, recommended to be undertaken. More emphasis should be on applications such as wallboards, fiber-reinforced panels for walls and partitions, planks for floors and ceilings, solid and cored blocks, and veneer plaster. A special consideration must be given to public acceptability and adaptability. Egyptian objections to wallboard are mainly to the passage of sound and the possibility of destruction by vandals or careless occupants. Full-thickness cored panels could help overcoming such problems.
   c.   Possible innovative uses of low-cost indigenous agricultural and agro-industrial wastes need to be assessed.

This includes :
- Using woven matting of bamboo strips as wall partitions.
- Converting cellulosic materials such as refuse paper and cardboard into corrugated sheets for roofing.
- Producing particle boards from wood and agricultural wastes chipped or flaked and bound together with a suitable adhesive.
- Carbonizing indigenous plant materials to obtain low-cost lightweight insulating product.
- Stabilizing earth to produce blocks and dust-proof and water-proof flooring.
- Producing wood-cement boards that are much cheaper than conventional particle boards bonded with polymeric resins. Such boards could be used as infill panels for frame structures, permanent shuttering for concrete, and sound-proof partitions for false ceilings.
- Utilizing sulfur as a binder in place of portland cement in concrete, as an impregnant for concrete blocks to double their compressive strength, and as a matrix in fiber-reinforced composites.

d.   The need has become more urgent to start producing new types of low-cost blended cement of different levels of strength qualities, which would be suitable for many applications. Mortars for brick and tile laying, rendering and plastering of brick walls with cement surface coatings, concrete masonry blocks, and base layer (back) of cement tiles, are all examples of such applications currently utilizing costly portland cement of needless high strength qualities.

e.   New sources for producing lightweight aggregates, of lower cost than currently used conventional sand and gravel, should be investigated. This includes foaming blast-furnace slag, .heat expanding of shales, and burning or sintering silt or fly ash.

f.   More consideration should be given to rationalization of building materials usage through introduced modifications in methods of design, codes of practice, construction and finishing techniques, architectural performance requirements, and means of transportation and site storage of materials.

g.   As a general recommendation, most efforts should be directed towards the immediate integration of resources and collaboration of technical expertise within the African region as an effective means for solving regional problems of general nature geared to low-cost housing.
A regional research center, chosen from among the pioneering research institutes and universities in the area, may be established to stimulate and co-ordinate further research and development, to implement research findings for practical applications, and to foster exchanging ideas and expertise within and outside Africa.

References

1. Youssef, M.A.Reda; and Dietz,A.G.H. (1981),"Potentialities of Egyptian Gypsum for Housing," Journal of
   the Structural Division, ASCE, Vol. 107, No. ST4,
   April.
2. Youssef, M.A.Reda; and Dietz, A.G.H. (1982),"Reinforced Gypsum for Egyptian Housing," Journal of the
   Structural Division, ASCE, Vol. 108, No. ST6,June.
3. Youssef,M.A.Reda (1976),"Date-palm Mid-ribs As a Substitute for Steel Reinforcement in Structural Con-
   crete - Parts I & II," Symposium on New Horizons in
   Construction Materials, Lehigh University, U.S.,
   October, Vol. 1, Papers 31 and 32.
4. Youssef, M.A.Reda (1976),"Bamboo As a Substitute for
   Steel Reinforcement in Structural Concrete - Parts
   I & II," Symposium on New Horizons in Construction
   Materials, Lehigh University, U.S., October, Vol. 1,
   Papers 41 and 42.
5. Imam, H.F.; and Ramez, M.R.H. (1980),"Raw Materials as
   Substitutes for Nile Silt in Building Industry,"
   Scientific Engineering Bulletin, Faculty of Engrg.,
   Cairo University, Vol. 2.
6. El-Erian, A.A.; Youssef, M.A.Reda; and Dietz, A.G.H.
   (1980),"A New Technique of Surface-Bonding Brick
   Walls for Housing," Interim Report of the Housing
   and Construction Industry in Egypt Project, TAP
   Report 80-13, Cairo University/MIT, Fall.
7. El-Erian, A.A.; Youssef, M.A.Reda; and Dietz, A.G.H.
   (1978),"Non-conventional Materials & Non-conventional Uses of Traditional Materials : Their
   Potential for Application in Egypt," Interim Report
   of the Housing and Construction Industry in Egypt
   Project, TAP Report 78-3, Cairo University/MIT,
   Spring.

INTERLOCKING CEMENT AND CONCRETE COMPONENTS FOR LOW-COST HOUSE
CONSTRUCTION: THE BUILDING TOGETHER EXPERIENCE IN THAILAND

A. BRUCE ETHERINGTON, Asian Institute of Technology
                      University of Hawaii

1. Introduction

The construction system described is based on the system successfully
employed in the San Antonio Village Project, Manila (350 units) and
the Building Together Project, Bangkok (202 units). Ease of construction by unskilled labour is achieved through modular interlocking components and the high efficiency of structural design resulting
in permanent structures costing not more than two-thirds of that
usually achieved through conventional construction. The cost of
materials, for example, in the Building Together Project was 375 baht
per square metre (US $1.65 per square foot) in 1981 for two-storey
row housing. The life expectancy of Building Together housing is
estimated at 50 to 100 years.
    Design specifications include fire resistant materials, ease of
fabrication and erection by unskilled labour, long life expectancy
and capability to withstand winds up to 200 KPH and earthquakes up to
7.8 on the Richter Scale in multi-storey construction.

2. The components

The system consists of interlocking dry-laid concrete blocks of hollow core and channel configurations for constructing walls and precast
concrete joists which interlock with the concrete block walls to support floors or roofs.*

2.1 The interlocking block walls
The basic wall block (see Plate 1 - Ordinary Block), measuring 198 mm
wide x 396 mm long x 200 mm high has raised rims (A) surrounding two
hollow cores (B) on the upper surface. On the lower surface are corresponding recesses or depressions (C) to receive the projecting rims
of the block below. Intersecting the rims and depressions are two
small vertical recesses at both ends of the block (D). A smaller

---

*Where soil conditions require sectioned piles supporting a grade
beam may be added to the system.

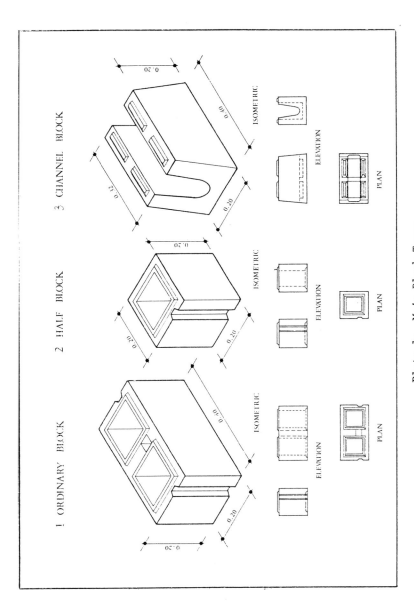

Plate 1: Main Block Types

core (E) is located midway along the length of the block and is aligned with the two end processes.   When the blocks are stacked without
mortar in a running (staggered) bond the end recesses (C) will meet
exactly under or over the centre hole (E) of the blocks above and
below, thus creating continuous vertically aligned holes the entire
height of the wall.   When cement grout is poured into these holes a
vertical seal is achieved and the blocks become permanently locked
together.   A horizontal seal is automatically obtained when the rims
(A) nestle in the recesses (C).   Thus both horizontal and vertical
joints are sealed.

Since the block length is exactly double its width turning corners
is simply solved by continuing the running board around the corner so
that no special corner block shapes are required.

When the walls must end at a door or window, for example, the regular block is simply halved (see Plate 1 - Half Block) while the end
recesses (D) may be retained at one or both ends.

The large hollow cores (B) measuring approximately 15 x 15 cm are
large enough to accomodate small reinforced concrete columns.   This
is especially useful in multi-storey construction in order to support
the additional weight of floors and walls above.

A second block type which forms a continuous channel (see Plate 1-
Channel Block) is used in multi-storey construction to provide a
channel to receive reinforced concrete in order to create beams within the walls.   This block is also provided with abbreviated rims on
the upper surface and depressions (C) in the lower surface similar to
those of the hollow core block to interlock with the hollow core block
so that there is complete continuity in a wall regardless of which
block type is used.

Thus when reinforced concrete columns within the cores of the hollow core block are combined with reinforced concrete beams within the
channel of the channel block, a concrete reinforced concrete framework may be achieved without the use of formwork.   Plate 2 - Block
Assembly - illustrates the combination of both block types to create
columns and beams as well as the method of laying and grouting the
block.   As can be seen, intersection of two walls is easily achieved
with the running bond which will provide a strong horizontal connection by virtue of the interlocking rims of the blocks.

2.2   The interlocking floor system
Precast concrete joists measuring 6 cm wide at the top and 3 cm wide
at the bottom and 20 cm high can span up to 8 metres in length if
spaced at 40 cm on centre and properly reinforced.   Typically reinforcing consists of one 12 mm steel rod at the bottom and two $\frac{1}{4}$ end
span 9 mm rods at the top.   The bars top and bottom extend about 12
cm beyond the end of the joist at both ends so that they may be bent
sideways and anchored into the channel block concrete beam.   This
creates a fixed end condition for each joist which considerably increases its carrying capability

Shear reinforcing consists of 2 to 3 mm wire looped or bent diagonally spaced approximately 10 cm on centre.   The wire loop is
allowed to protrude 4 or 5 cm above the top surface of the joist.

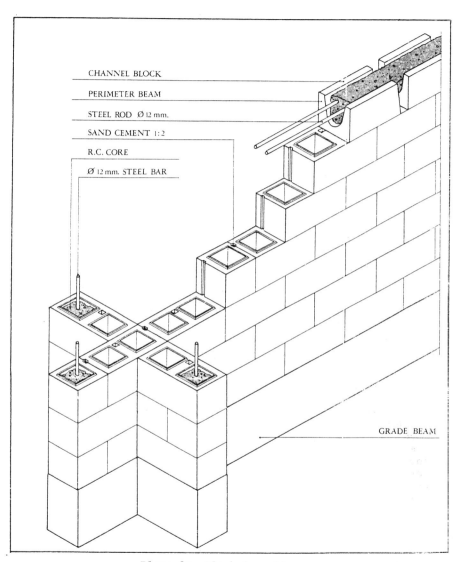

CHANNEL BLOCK

PERIMETER BEAM

STEEL ROD Ø 12 mm.

SAND CEMENT 1:2

R.C. CORE

Ø 12 mm. STEEL BAR

GRADE BEAM

Plate 2: Block Assembly

This is done (a) to provide a shear connection between the joist and the concrete floor to be poured on top of the joist and (b) to provide a means of picking up the joist to carry and place it.

The joists also have a continuous ridge on both sides of the joist running parallel to the top of the joist and about 5 cm below the top. The ridges are used to support cross pieces which in turn support the formwork for the poured-in-place concrete floor (see Plate 3 - Floor Assembly).

The concrete floor slab is nominally 5 cm thick and is reinforced with wire mesh. The concrete mix is 1:2:2 using ¼" aggregate. The wire mesh is 1" x 1" square welded.

3. Assembling the components

If soil conditions do not require piling, then a conventional footing may be used. However, it should be noted that masonry walls frequently fail due to differential settlement of the footing. A grade beam therefore is desirable to carry the masonry walls above regardless of whether piling is used or not.

The concrete block walls are placed on top of the grade beam. If the grade beam is not smooth and level on its top surface it will be necessary to use a mortar bed and string between batter boards as is customary in conventional masonry work. After the first course of blocks has been well and truly set, succeeding courses may be stacked as quickly as the workers can physically lay them with no time lost aligning blocks with string courses or placing mortar beds. It is not uncommon for two or three unskilled workers to lay 500 to 600 blocks in a day. It is advisable to pour the cement grout (1 part cement, 8 parts sand) into the grout holes (see Plate 2) every four courses. When the blocks reach the level upon which floor joists will sit (if a multi-storey structure is being built), reinforced columns may be poured. This is done by placing reinforcing bar steel in the large core (see Plate 2). Concrete is poured up within 2 or 3 inches of the top of the top block course.

The interlocking block must always be laid in running bond, i.e. with the joists in every course or layer staggered in relation to courses above and below. Corners may be turned and interlocked by continuing the running bond around the corner. The same is true for T or cross wall intersections. Openings in walls will require the use of .5 blocks (see Plates 1 and 2) every other course.

If the structure being built is multi-storey, a perimeter beam must be introduced at each floor level in order to tie the walls to the floor system (see Plate 3). This is accomplished by using channel block (see Plate 2) as a mould to hold the reinforcing steel bar and concrete of the perimeter beam. Normally the channel blocks have vertical ends so that they butt together to make a continuous trough. However, where the concrete floor joists intersect the channel block, the channel block is cast with angled ends equal to the angle of the joists (see Plate 3). This permits each joist to

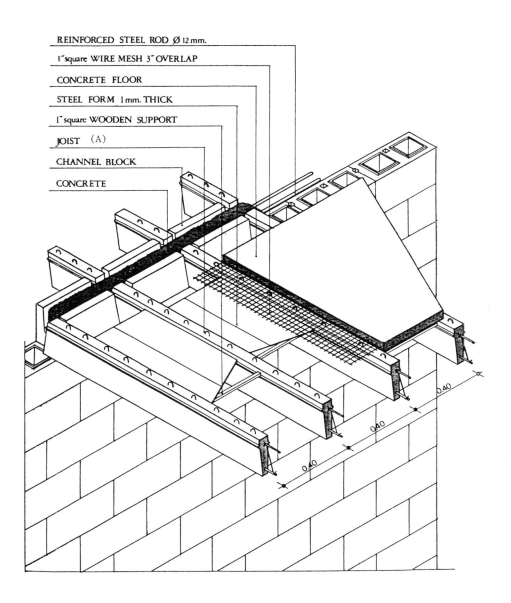

REINFORCED STEEL ROD Ø 12 mm.

1"square WIRE MESH 3" OVERLAP

CONCRETE FLOOR

STEEL FORM 1 mm. THICK

1"square WOODEN SUPPORT

JOIST (A)

CHANNEL BLOCK

CONCRETE

0.40

0.40

0.40

Plate 3: Floor Assembly

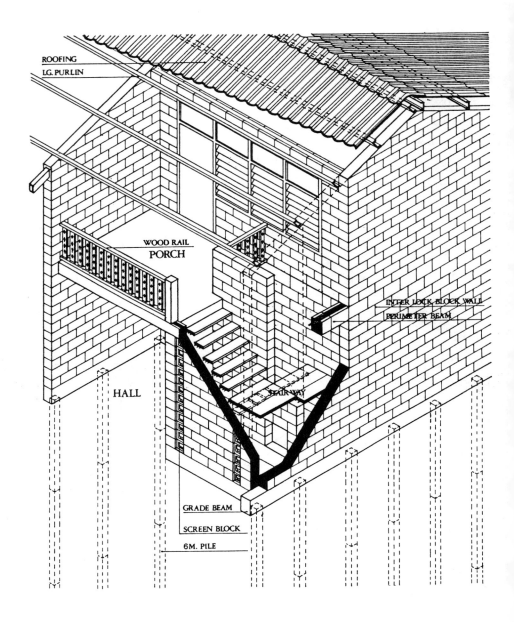

ROOFING
LG. PURLIN

WOOD RAIL
PORCH

HALL

INTER LOCK BLOCK WALL
PERIMETER BEAM

STAIRWAY

GRADE BEAM

SCREEN BLOCK

6M. PILE

Plate 4: House Isometric

nest between adjoining channel blocks.

The ends of the reinforcing steel in the joists are bent parallel to the direction of the channel in the channel block beam. The required concrete beam reinforcing steel is placed in the channel block and concrete poured. The ends of the joists are also canted inward at the top so that reinforcing rods laid in the channel block trough may pass by the ends of the joists.

Five cm thick concrete floors are poured in place. The wire loops on the tops of the joists must be cut and bent over to hold the wire mesh in place. The formwork consists of two panels of wood or steel running parallel to the joist with a continuous joint in the centre. To erect the floor formwork it is simply necessary to rest the cross pieces on the ridges on the sides of the joists, place the formwork on top of the cross pieces and pour the floor. To remove the formwork the cross pieces are knocked sideways so that they come free of the ridges on the sides of the joists and fall to the ground. The formwork, now unsupported by the cross pieces, will also fall downward leaving the exposed underside of the concrete floor slab poured above.

Succeeding walls and floors (up to 5 stories) may be built following the previous procedures providing the walls are reinforced on the lower floors with the appropriate number of columns poured within the concrete block cores.

The top or roof level may be a flat deck in which case the roof is a duplication of the previously described floor system, with the addition of sealed sulphur joints at the intersection of the vertical and horizontal surfaces. A precast self-supporting interlocking pitched concrete roof may also be used but is not described in this paper.

If precast concrete treads are used in conjunction with the concrete block walls, these must be built in the block courses as the wall is laid (see Plate 4). To be modular with the block the treads run and rise are 8 inches (20 cm) and 8 inches (20 cm) respectively. This permits the placing of treads every .5 block for every course, making it easy to locate each tread. Of course the actual tread width is greater than 8 inches (usually around 11 inches) to provide overlap at each step.

Acknowledgements

Collaborators: Jaffrey Zaigham, Chae Ko, Fr. Leo Schmitt, Parid Wardi
Drawings   : Manu Kupadakvinij

BUILDING MATERIALS AND CONSTRUCTION METHODS IN LIBYAN JAMAHIRIYA'

SALEH BARONY, Assoc. Professor
AYAD GALLAL, Assist. Professor
MUSTAFA TAWIL, Assoc. Professor

Civil Engineering Department,
University of Al-Fateh, Tripoli.

1. *Historical review*

The imprints of human civilization in Libya dates back to thousands of years, and some of these represent land marks which are still standing nowadays resisting the effects of nature and other civilizations. Though three quarters of the country is presently classified as desert and scarcely populated, but deep into history it was totally the reverse where land was very rich in plantation and population.

Humans in the past history were more considerate of their living needs and the environment, than what we call the modern era of human civilization, and Libya stands as one of the witnesses on this.

Though Libya is scarcely populated and possesses a good national welath, but as any other developing country it is required to raise up the standard of living of its people in all different spheres of life (social, economical, and cultural). These require more than what the national resources can handle, or stretching them beyond limits. For this reason good planning and economy becomes a must so that the aspiration of the people for reasonable or good housing, education, health, and welfare to be met in a short time. In this we feel that we share the aspiration of the so called developing or third world countries, in the need for developing low cost housing systems depending on local materials and locally developed or well suited imported technology, coupled with the identification and creation of a national or regional architectural and planning identity matching the social and environmental requirements.

Traditional housing systems depending on local materials, expertise, and environment have been widely used in different parts of Libya up to the Italian invasion and occupation of the country at the beginning of this century. Nowadays a large percentage of building materials are imported, though they are expensive and mostly inadequate environmentally and socially. Also traditional home designs which meet the social requirements are being left aside, and the use of modern imported materials and systems become a way of life.

In Jamahiriya the housing program is aimed that at the year 1990 almost every family will have a decent and modern residence. In statistical form and figures, means the construction of over six hundred thousand housing units during a period of twenty years starting from 1970. The realization of ambitious program is carried out through the General Secretariat of Housing, which is directly responsible for design and construction of the major percentage of the required homes, and the smaller part through loans to private individuals to build their own homes.

2. *Types of housing systems*

Types of housing systems may be classified as:

(a) historically: old and new
(b) geographically: rural and urban

In Libya, and upto the early sixties, most of the rural people lived in old types of housing like cloth tents that are made of strips of cloth woven from goat's or camel's hair, and vegetable fibres; and formed on a set of wood poles. Others used huts made of woven reed mats and palm leaves as side walls and roofs. In mountains, however, many lived in cliff dwellings or in digged underground rooms which are really self conditioning: warm in winter and pleasant in summer.

In urban areas the people used rectangular mud or stone walls covered with different kinds of roofs: a flat roof with wood elements, hollow bricks with thin steel rods, steel I-beams arched by three solid or hollow bricks. Domed and cylindrical roofs were also used with stone blocks and mud.

Adjustment to climatic conditions was sometimes incomplete and facilities for sanitation were rare specially in rural areas. All building materials used then along with the house form were dictated primarily by traditional building practice.

Recently, and after the economy of Libya had a break-through when oil was discovered, new housing systems came about. Larger houses made up of sand stone or concrete-block walls with or without concrete columns and beams are commonly noticed. A skeletal type is also being used widely nowadays.

The vast development programs and the centralization of services in the main cities of Libya (Tripoli and Benghazi) made a serious impact on these cities from the population increase point of view, which in the beginning created a relatively large slum areas around them. But the large housing programs undertaken by the government in the last ten years almost eliminated this phenomenon.

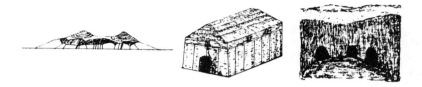

Some old types of housing systems

Some wall types and material

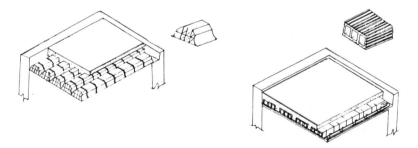

Some roof types and material

3. *Building materials*

When the concept of building materials is taken in a wider sense, it should include all the aspects of materials used in the realization of a building or a house, which may include structural, architectural or finishing, mechanical, electrical and communication materials. But we limit the scope of our consideration to the structural materials with some reference to finishing materials wherever appropriate or necessary. This was done, firstly because of the specialisation and secondly because it constitutes the larger share in construction period and expenses.

In Libya and upto the early sixties, local materials and local traditional systems were mainly used whether in urban or rural areas, these basically are the constituents of sand, clay, lime and gypsom. With the oil discovery which opened the doors of the country to international consultants and construction companies to take part into the vast development programs, the importation of building materials reached unproportional limits, and the local industry could not match neither the demand nor the specifications required by different consultants. This part was most noticeable in the finishing materials, such as glass, wood, windows, doors, tiles, marble, plastering and painting, as well as some of the basic materials such as cement and reinforcing steel.

This concept persisted upto the late Seventies when local industry products took some share in this development, as in the case of cement industry where the country almost reached self-sufficiency and consequently concrete and clay blocks.

In the present construction industry for housing, the materials commonly used can be summarized according to their structural function as follows:

3.1 Wall units
In this part we present the most popular used materials for wall enclosures whether they work as partitions or bearing walls:

(a) Gargaresh blocks: they are natural lime stone blocks quarried on the coastal zone of the western part of the Jamahiriya. Upto now they are the most widely used wall materials, which are used for wall bearing and wall partitions in framed buildings. Its main disadvantages can be summarized as follows: Heavy in weight but still has high permeability; plastering is required inside and outside; and to be widely used it has to be transported for more than 700 kilometers.

(b) Concrete blocks: they are very competitive to Gargaresh blocks and specially as wall partitions. The industry is not fully developed, and the production is done through small and scattered local fabrication, and consequently it lacks standardization in strength and quality.

(c) Clay bricks: these bricks are of light weight hollow bricks and are mainly produced for roof slabs, but specific sizes are commonly used in partition walls specially in framed buildings.

(d) Sand lime bricks: laboratory experiments proved the success of
this product. Plans for production are underway, where it is
believed that it will dominate the market in the future owing to
minimal disadvantages; and the advantages of light weight, good
final texture, and reasonable strength.

(e) Light weight blocks: laboratory experiments on light weight
aggregates proved to be satisfactory. Investigations of national
reserves of local materials are under way, and production will take
place when the system proves to be feasible and economical.

It is a standard procedure in all the housing buildings that walls
are plastered internally and externally then painted with water
emulsion paints.   0

3.2 Roof units
The materials presently used in roof slabs can be divided into two
categories, bearing in mind that all the roofs are of flat type and
no inclination is required:

(a) Reinforced concrete: this type is basically a solid cast in
situ reinforced concrete slabs.

(b) Hollow blocks (Travetti): in this case the hollow clay bricks
are used in the form of precast beams where the blocks are joined
together with steel bars and cement paste, or done in situ.

3.3 Industrialized system
Under this heading all kinds of precast or prefabricated, concrete
or nonconcrete, total system of housing are included. But we
consider the prefabricated concrete systems where two factories one
in Tripoli and the other in Benghazi are in operation for some time.
These two factories work on full prefabrication process of walls and
roof slabs, where walls are of the bearing type.

4. *Construction methods*

Construction methods in Libya covered a wide range through the years.
It started, many years back, the primitive way of construction using
wood logs, rock pieces put together with mud, palm leaves and trunks,
and other locally available materials. Nowadays, methods of construction become more and more a technical art.

The construction method commonly used recently in building a
traditional house of one floor is to construct a continuous footing
on which bearing walls, using Gargaresh lime-stone or cement blocks,
are erected. A flat roof is then constructed by lifting the ready-
made (Travetti) beams and laying them one beside the other. Concrete mix is then put along the top of walls where the beams are
resting to form a restraint of the system. The whole roof is
covered with a thin layer of concrete giving the slope needed and
filling all voids in between those (Travetti) beams.

For those people who can afford to build a house of two or more floors, and for the multi-storey buildings, the skeletal type of construction is the popular. The skeletal system, as known, is formed from footings, columns, beams and/or girders, and slabs; all of reinforced concrete. When these elements are in place, side walls and partitions are then formed using either Gargaresh or cement blocks. In the two-floor housing, some people construct walls and partitions before the columns, beams, and floors; leaving spaces for the columns, and when getting to the desired floor height, the reinforcing steel for columns, beams, and floor roof are put into place and then concreted. In this sense they are overcoming the appearance of hair cracks between the walls and beams, and between walls and columns.

The framework of shuttering is mainly used from wood although some are using the metal posts where available. The using of wood is costly in Libya because it is to be imported from outside, and it will be advisable to use another material that are reusable for a long time like the metal framework.

5. *Discussion and conclusion*

Jamahiriya represents a special case study for developing countries, where it constitutes a vast land which scarcely populated. Less than quarter of a century ago it was considered one of the poorest countries in the world. With the discovery of oil, the country embarked on major transformation programs which have been intensified in the last fifteen years. But as the case of any developing country, many problems have occured and many are lying ahead in the road for development; for money cannot buy everything and determination cannot alter reality and cannot solve problems.

Most developing countries suffer from low standard of living, and then spend large percentage of their national budget in different development programs. Housing takes a large share and the priority in their development programs with the aim of obtaining a decent living accommodation for the majority of the people.

In the housing field, one can say that in Libya we have almost eliminated the slum areas, but the overgrowth of the cities ahead of proper planning created areas which do not match the required standard of living and constitute major settlements around the main cities which necessitate redevelopment.

In Libya upto now we have tried all available systems of construction and types of materials, without a serious look or appraisal for the reason of determining the most suitable from the economy, social and environment points of view. For this matter we try to give our conclusion remarks in the form of appraisal and general recommendations as follows:

(a) for traditional systems, effort should concentrate on specifications and standardization, including improvement of productivity and introduction of new materials with better qualities and performance as in the case of sand-lime bricks and light weight bricks.

(b) insulation against humidity and low and high temperature should be developed and introduced in the building systems for the final production of an energy and economically efficient house.

(c) introduction of natural effects in design and construction, whenever applicable, such as floods, cyclons, tornados and earthquakes.

(d) in situ reinforced concrete skeleton systems, with the necessary exterior and interior nonbearing walls, are expensive as well as material and time consuming. Consequently we feel that this system should be used in highrise buildings only.

(e) industrialization in buildings is a technological necessity for the improvement of standard, speed of work and reduction in man power needed in the construction field, but special considerations to joints and connections are necessary.

(f) it is not necessary to use concrete in housing prefabrication specially when using single or two storey systems, so that reduction in expenses of transportation and erection can be obtained.

(g) social education, for the proper use of living accommodations and proper way of living in an urban area, becomes a necessity and attention of different popular and governmental systems should be concentrated on this line.

(h) the recognized world wide phenomenon of unplanned and unauthorized settlements developing along the main lines of communication and around the urban areas evidently causes serious problems and aggrevations to the authorities to supply them with water, sewerage, roads, transportation, and communication lines in trying to raise the standard of these settlements.

(i) rapid changing pattern of living and its adverse effect of upsetting traditions and creating social problems should be handled with care. Studies on the national and regional basis are required to cope with the main social problems resulting from urbanization and modernization of a country, as well as detailed studies for town planning and proper housing systems.

(j) due to the centralization of services and work in the major towns and cities, coupled with the large requirements for manpower needed for the development programs and construction industry, leads to the rapid growth and urban over crowding, which gives an adverse effect on housing programs and makes it almost impossible to meet the needs for residential accommodations. This aspect requires a serious attention, study, and continuous review for the planners and decision makers to give recommendation for what to do to overcome these difficulties.

(k) a final note of awareness is being raised through this paper to all developing countries, rich or poor, to rely on their own local materials and look deep into their traditional building systems. For we are sure that there is a lot of good sense and probably engineering ingenuity in them, and require only the introduction of systemized or production technology into them.

Acknowledgement

The authors acknowledge the assistance of the Architect Juma Fellah in preparing the sketches presented in the paper, and the National Consulting Bureau (NCB) for typing of the paper.

References

1. Ali, M.H. and Abu-Atwarat, A.A. (1982), *Appraisal of Materials and Methods of Construction in Residential Buildings*, B. Sc. Project, Civil Engg. Dept., Univ. of Al-Fateh.
2. Proceedings of IAHS (1978), *Housing Problems in Developing Countries*, V. 1 and 2., John Wiley and Sons.
3. Secretariat of Light Industry (1978), *Future Forecasts and Suggestions for the Development of Building Materials Industry*, Industrial Research Center Report, Tripoli, Libya.
4. Ministry of Planning (1976), *Economical and Social Transformation Plan 1976-1980*, Tripoli, Libya. (In Arabic).
5. Ministry of Planning and Development (1964), *Housing in Libya*, V. 1 and 2., Document DOX-LIB-A17, Tripoli-Libya.

USE OF RICE HUSK AS FUEL FOR FIRING BUILDING BRICKS

Satya Prakash & F.U.Ahmed
Central Building Research Institute,Roorkee, India

1. Introduction

In India, about 9.8 million tonnes of coal is required
annually for burning about 5000 (1) crores of building
bricks in commercial kilns. Transportation of such a huge
amount of coal is not fully met-with by railways, and more
than half of the coal is transported by road which results
in higher cost at the kiln site. Problem of coal supply is
aggravating due to their diminishing reserve and installation of many other consumer industries.

In India, about 26.5 (2) million tonnes of rice husk is
obtained as waste material every year from agricultural
sector which finds no substantial use so far. This waste
material can be utilised as renewable source of fuel if
some technique is developed for its burning in commercial
brick kilns.

2. Experimental

Rice husk is a hard fibrous material, it has hardly got
any nutritious value and hence is not used as fodder for
cattle feed. It has about 20% silica as mineral content.
The calorific value of rice husk is about 2800 K.Cal/kg
against 7000 K.Cal/kg for best quality coal (3). Field
trials have been conducted for use of rice husk as fuel
for burning building bricks in three ways:

- By burning bricks in small scale kilns having capacity
  upto 15 - 20,000 bricks.

- Partial substitution of coal with rice husk as fuel for
  saving coal in Bull's Trench Kiln.

- Use of rice husk and firewood as fuel in Bull's Trench
  Kiln.

2.1 Use of Rice Husk in Small Scale Intermittent Kiln

Rice husk can be used alongwith firewood for firing 15-
20,000 bricks at a time in small scale intermittent kiln
for individual requirements. The dimensional details of
one such kiln is given in Fig.1.

As indicated in Fig.1, two parallel walls, each of
length 9.14m (30'), were constructed leaving a space of
2.6m (8'). The height of walls were 2.3m (7'6"). The walls
were .91m (3') thick at the bottom and staggered to a
thickness of 0.47m (1'6") at the top. One side wall of(Fig.2)
.91m (3') thickness from top to bottom was made with a
flue hole over which chimney was fitted. Four fire boxes,
two on each of the side walls were made front to front as
shown in Fig.1. These fire boxes were utilised for feeding
firewood and cleaning the ash from the bottom. One sheet
damper was used at the base of the chimney to regulate the
draught as desired. A metallic chimney of 4.6m (14') height
was installed over flue hole in the side wall to create
sufficient draught.

2.2 Setting of Bricks in the Kiln

The setting of bricks was adopted similar to that of normal
Bull's Trench Kiln. The only adjustment that was made,was
to provide the fire wood feeding line after every two rice
husk feeding lines. This helped in proper combustion of
rice husk and movement of flame in the forward direction.
A layer of 15cm thick ash was put on the top of brick
setting to check heat losses.

2.3 Initiation of Fire and Burning of Bricks

To initiate fire, wood is burnt in the very first line to
enable the next fire line to attain temperature up to 900°C
when rice husk feeding in small quantities is started.
About 15-20 quintals of dry firewood is required to initiate the firing. Firewood was fed in wood feeding line which
was repeated after every two rice husk feeding line was
completed. The usual temperature 1000 to 1050°C was obtained. This temperature was maintained for 3-4 hours. For
firing 15,000 bricks, 2 tonnes of firewood and 4 tonnes of
rice husk was used.

3. Use of Rice Husk As Fuel in Bull's Trench Kiln for Commercial Production

For saving coal up to 30-40%, rice husk was utilised in
the commercial Bull's trench kiln. Rice husk was fed in
two successive lines after coal feeding line (Plate 1). In

this type of feeding no change in setting pattern was made. Rice husk was fed in the same feeding hole as was made for coal burning. The temperature was found to be about 1000 ± 20°C.

Fuel Consumption:

(Basis per lakh bricks)

  i)   Coal   7 tonnes
  ii) Rice husk   25 tonnes

When rice husk was used alongwith coal and firewood

(Basis per lakh bricks)

  i)   Coal   7 tonnes
  ii)   Firewood   12 tonnes
  iii) Rice Husk   12 tonnes

4. Use of Rice Husk and Fire Wood Exclusively for Firing Bricks in Bull's Trench Kiln

Field trials were conducted in commercial Bull's Trench kiln where rice husk and firewood were available. In this technique one fire wood feeding line was invariably given after every two rice husk feeding lines. The temperature achieved was 1000 ± 20°C.

Fuel Consumption recorded as:

(Basis per lakh bricks)

  i)   Firewood   12 tonnes
  ii) Rice Husk   30 tonnes

5. When only Coal was Used

(Basis per lakh bricks)

  18 tonnes per lakh of bricks

Quality of the Product

Bricks made of alluvial soil and fired in Bull's Trench kiln using rice husk and firewood were tested as per IS: 3495-1976 for compressive strength and water absorption and reported in Table 1.

Table 1.   Compressive Strength and Water Absorption of
            Bricks

Compressive Strength (kg/cm^2)	Water Absorption (%)	Quality (%)
Above 150	12.14	20-25
100 -150	12.15	60-65
50 -100	13.15	10-15
Below 50	15.20	5-10

Cost of firing bricks directly depends on the availability
of raw materials and their current cost.

6. Conclusions of field trials

-   Rice husk and firewood can be used for firing bricks
    on small scale. The capacity of intermittent kiln may
    be designed for firing 20,000 - 50,000 bricks at a
    time.

-   Rice husk with coal can be employed economically. A
    saving of coal up to 30-40% is achieved in commercial
    Bull's Trench Kiln.

-   Rice husk together with fire wood can eliminate the
    use of coal completely.

-   The technique is simple and can be tried in running
    Bull's Trench Kiln. Other agricultural residues like
    groundnut husk, saw dust and bagasse also may be used.

-   Technique especially is useful in rice growing areas
    where coal is scarce.

-   It can easily be adopted in developing countries.

References

1. 'Brick and Tiles News' Annual Number 1976, pp. 5-12.

2. Tripathi, S.C., and Nanda, S. 'Agricultural Production'
    Yojna, No.8, 1980, pp. 28-30.

3. Govinda Rao, V.M.H. 'Utilisation of Rice Husk a- a
    Preliminary Analysis, Journal of Scientific and
    Industrial Research Vol. 39, No.9, 1980,pp.495-515.

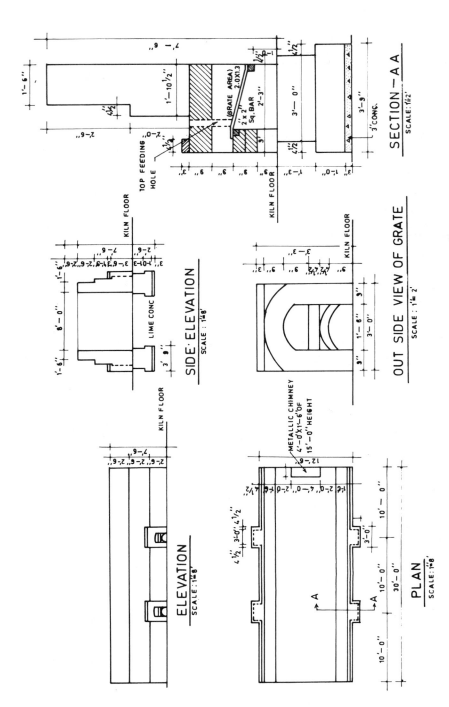

FIG. 1. DESIGN OF BRICK KILN USING RICE·HUSK AS FUEL

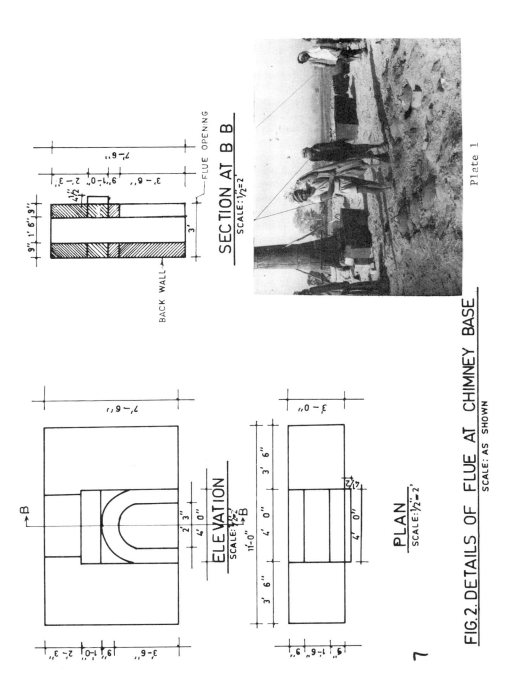

SECTION AT B B
SCALE: 1/2 = 2

FLUE OPENING

BACK WALL

ELEVATION
SCALE: 1/2 = 2

PLAN
SCALE: 1/2 = 2

FIG. 2. DETAILS OF FLUE AT CHIMNEY BASE
SCALE: AS SHOWN

Plate 1

7

LOW COST HOUSING IN CHINA USING INDIGENEOUS MATERIALS

BAN ZHUO, Chinese Academy of Building Research

1. Low cost urban housing in China

China has a large population. To solve the housing problem in urban areas is indeed a great challenge to the
not yet affluent economy of a developing country as
China. Under the present conditions, state-built urban
housing is dictated by the following criteria:

(a) Limited floor area per person. The floor area
of a dwelling for an ordinary urban household is $45-50m^2$
in average.

(b) Simple exterior and interior finishes and service facilities. Water supply and drainage systems,
power supply and sanitary fixtures are provided for
housing in general, with heating systems for housing in
North China only.

(c) Low construction cost of about 100-170 Renminbi
per square meter.

In fact, the majority of urban housing in China are
of low cost. As these building standards will be maintained for a considerable period of time to come, it is
necessary to investigate on the proper ways of using
local materials for housing throughout the country in
order to save construction funds and fully exploit local
resources.

2. A fine tradition of utilizing local materials

2.1 For thousands of years, the Chinese people have
been taking advantage of a variety of local materials,
such as earth, stone, wood and the like, to build
various kinds of buildings and structures. According
to historical records, during the Han Dynasty two thousand years ago, people were able to make all kinds of
burnt-clay eavestiles and bricks with highly artistic
decorative patterns. Now, the Chinese people have

accumulated a wealth of experiences and acquired the mastery of techniques in using timber, brick, tile and stone. The classical Chinese architecture is reknown for its unique style in the world history of architecture.

2.2 Today in China, a large number of traditional houses in the vast rural areas are built of local materials, for instance:

Buildings of earth construction have been in existence for thousands of years throughout the country. The development of the methods of construction may be divided into 3 stages:

(a) Transition from natural caves into man-made grottos, such as cave dwellings dug into the cliffs (Fig. 1) and underground cave dwellings (Fig. 2).

Fig. 1   Fig. 2

(b) Further strenthening of the natural material manually. At this stage, houses were made of rammed earth and walls began to take shape.

(c) Manufactured products such as sun-dried adobe bricks were made by simple process from raw earth, which could be used to build walls, arches or roofs. New forms of building were developed.

These three types of earth buildings can be found all over North China.

Up till now, traditional houses have been built continually on a large scale because local materials are readily available and easy to work with, and expensive long-distance transportation is avoided. Some of these materials, such as bamboos and trees may be planted and raised by the residents themselves. Thus, traditional buildings are viable through their low cost.

3. The importance of using local materials in housing
    construction

The largest portion of material consumption in housing
is for walls. In China, the material used for walls is
still clay brick of small size and the work done by hand
for the most parts. For this, early in the fifties, the
government has put forth the task, "to accomplish gradually the transition to building industrialization".
This task should include: (a) realization of standardization of design, prefabrication of structural
elements and components and mechanization in construction, (b) structural innovation with wall innovation as
the focus. Since 1958, various kind of materials for
wall have been developed in all parts of the country,
creating a fovourable condition for building industrialization. At the same time, many residential buildings
have been built by industrialized methods of construction.

More than twenty years of practice proves that the
requirements of wall innovation promote the development
of building materials, and the production of new building materials speeds up the progress of building
industrialization. Building materials are local
products demanded in great quantities. Many structural
elements and components are of a large size and very
heavy, unsuitable for long-distance transportation.
Economically they are feasible only when produced and
used locally. And this is more important for low cost
housing. Therefore, the problem of using indigeneous
materials must be held in great account. The principle
of "fully utilizing local resources and industrial
wastes" is set down for the development of the building
material industry.

At present in China, the following 3 kinds of materials are most commonly used for walls:

3.1 Brick   Brick houses amount to 90% in the whole
stock of urban housing. The reasons are: (a) Bricks
possess better insulating properties. The production
technologies are well established, simple and easy to
master. Now, the annual output of brick is 160 billion
units, and of which 75% are produced by rural bricklilns.
(b) Brick offers more flexibility in design. (c) Bricks
cost less than any other materials for wall. So brick
houses remain to be widely accepted by residents. In
West China, where there are vast expanses of loess
plateau covered with thick deposits of loess, the production of brick has broad prospects. However, in
densely populated regions, brick production has brought

adverse effects to agriculture. For every one or two
million bricks produced, there will be one mu (0.066ha.)
of farmland laid waste. In recent years, 30-50 thousand
mus of farmland were destroyed annually. It is a grave
problem for China, a country with a large population and
insufficient farmland. There are two approaches to its
solution: (a) to replace brick with products made of
cement and industrial wastes; (b) to improve traditional
brick for high-strength, hollow core and light-weight.
The former has achieved successful results. The cement
industry has gained considerable development. The annual
output of cement reached 90 million ton in 1982, providing a favourable condition for the production of cement
products.

3.2 Block   Concrete block houses have extended from
north to south in China. Every year about 2.5-3 million
m² of residential building of block construction are
built. The blocks may be either solid or hollow, from
small size to medium size. The use of local materials
and industrial wastes results in a great variety of
blocks. Shanghai, which is the first city to use blocks
in residential buildings, has been producing pulverized
fly ash blocks for the past 24 years. In Hangzhou, a
complete set of technology for designing and constructing
with concrete hollow blocks has been developed. Other
areas use different materials of industrial wastes such
as pebbles, crushed stones, colliery shales, slags, etc.,
depending on the particular local condition.
   In the temperate South, where insulation is not so
important, blocks are used in large quantities and have
partially replaced bricks in residential buildings.
Block construction is widely used in small and medieum-

Fig. 3   Fig. 4

sized cities due to the simplicity of manufacturing processes (Fig. 3), ready availability of materials and
ease of construction (Fig. 4).

3.3 Industrialized wall panel   A variety of industrialized residential building systems have been developed
in recent years. Those making the fastest progress are
the prefabricated large panel system (Fig. 5, Fig. 6),
monolithic concrete wall system cast with large forms
(Fig. 7) and monolithic system cast with slip-forms.
These new systems promote the use of concrete walls.
According to the principle "to suit measures to local
conditions and to use indigeneous materials", cities all
over the country carry out researches and experiments on
the use of different kinds of wall panels (hollow-cored,
solid or sandwiched) and different methods of production
(factory prefabrication, on-site prefabrication or cast
in place). In the warm southern regions of China,
hollow-cored wall panels are widely used, because they
are easy to form and economic in the use of materials.
While in the north, the sandwiched types are more often
used. Due to the difficulty in casting the sandwiched
exterior walls, the monlithic system has been changed
from all cast in place to a composite system of cast-in-
site interior walls and some other form of exterior
walls, such as precast panels or brick (Fig. 8) or block
masonry. These composite systems are more suitable to
the actual conditions and easy to use in medium-sized
cities.
   The precast wall panels in different localities are
made by a variety of materials. Solid wall panels include vibrated brick panels, fly ash light aggregate
concrete panels and no-fines light aggregate concrete
panels, etc. Sandwiched wall panels include cement
perlite panels and coal tar-glass wool sandwiched panels,
etc. Aerated concrete is used extensively. An important subject for research is the selection of insulating
materials for exterior wall panels used in the northern
regions, because the performance and thickness of the
insulation layer directly effect the cost of residential
buildings.
   The factories for prefabrication prefer panels made
with a single kind of material, because their production
is more simple and convenient. However, the composite
panel is believed to be the proper approach to fully
utilize local materials and industrial wastes and to
give full play to different qualities of different
materials. Some of the pressing research needs are the
properties of insulating materials, standards of insulation and the molding of bulk materials into required
forms, etc.

Fig. 5

Fig. 6

Fig. 7

Fig. 8

4. New subjects in need of research

4.1 New demands   Generally speaking, the development
of the building material industry in China is far from
meeting the needs of large scale housing construction.
Lumber is in most acute shortage among the so called
"three principal materials", steel, lumber and cement.
The policy adopted to cope with this situation is "to
use steel in place of wood", "to use plastics in place
of wood". Now, steel windows and steel-wood doors are
used in most residential buildings. Plastic doors and
plastic picture mouldings have been trial-produced, but
they have not met the quality standard fully yet.
plastic wall papers and flooring materials are still
too expensive to be used generally. Research and production of light-weight materials for walls are still a

weak link. China is very rich in gypsum deposits, some
modern factories of gypsum products have been set up.
However, light-weight materials are still short in
variety, not good in sound insulation, inadequate for
housing needs and too costly. These factors have hindered the development of residential buildings with
reinforced concrete frame and light-weight cladding
panels. In recent years, along with the rise in family
income and living standard, residents demand higher
qualities for their homes. They want to have colored
wall paints that will not easily fade, and to decorate
their houses with beautiful but low cost plastic wall
papers and waterproofing floor paint. These are some of
the increasing number of new subjects that need research.

4.2 Trend of development and new tasks for the building
     material industry of China

In order to promote industrialized building and raise
the quality of low cost housing, it is neccessary to
improve traditional materials and develop new materials
according to the principle of fully utilizing local
materials and industrial wastes. The main tasks are as
follows.

(a) To process raw materials into industrial products, finished or semi-finished.
(b) To change from producing single-material components to composite components, so as to reduce inplace
construction work and improve efficiency in transportation and erection.
(c) To develop complete sets of materials and components for specific housing systems.

China is a developing country. Faced with this tremendous task of housing construction, we have just made
a start in the development of building materials. We
must hold to the policy of using indigeneous materials
while at the same time learn from foreign advanced
experiences, and make further progress in the development of building materials for low cost housing.

LES MATERIAUX LOCAUX A FAIBLE COUT ENERGETIQUE ET LEURS PROCEDES DE
FABRICATION

SID BOUBEKEUR, GRET
                    ERA-CNRS Lyon

1. Introduction

La substitution des matériaux locaux au ciment représente un véritable
enjeu économique pour le logement social. Selon les experts de l'ONU-
DI, elle permettrait à terme une réduction de 15 à 20 % des coûts globaux des constructions.
    L'industrialisation de ces matériaux entraînerait d'autre part des
effets positifs dans le système productif des pays en développement :
création d'industries nationales, création d'emplois, réduction des
importations en matériaux.
    Cette vision conduit nécessairement à aborder les problèmes de
choix technologiques. A cet égard les travaux du GRET (*) insistent
d'une part sur la complémentarité des matériaux lourds (ciment, acier)
et des matériaux locaux, et d'autre part sur la complémentarité des
technologies modernes et locales. Dès lors, la gamme importante de
matériaux et de technologies disponibles autorisent à faire des choix
en fonction de la nature des travaux. Par exemple, les unités de production de ciment et d'acier peuvent sous réserve d'une maîtrise technologique satisfaire la branche Travaux Publics, alors que la production de matériaux locaux répondrait en partie à la demande de logements. Dans cette optique, la substitution des matériaux locaux au
ciment ne peut être vue que sous l'angle d'un pluralisme technologique. Le problème revient alors à être posé en ces termes : quelque
soit le degré de complexité des procédés (traditionnels, mécanisés,
semi-automatisés), et quelque soit la nature des fabricants (grands
ou petits industriels), quels sont aujourd'hui dans le monde les procédés alternatifs qui permettraient de résoudre en partie les problèmes d'insuffisance, et de coûts des matériaux ?

(*) Y. CABANNES et S. BOUBEKEUR : Innovation et adaptation de technologies pour l'industrialisation des pays africains au Sud Sahara : le
cas des matériaux de construction alternatifs au ciement. GRET -
octobre 1981.

Il existe dans le monde suffisamment de procédés fiables et poten-
tiellement transferables, aussi l'objet de nos travaux a-t-il été de
sélectionner ces procédés sur la base de critères technico-économique :
faible consommation énergétique, faible coût à l'exportation, facile
maîtrise technologique.

La diffusion d'informations sur les procédés fiables permettrait
d'éviter les échecs et d'améliorer l'efficacité des pays en développement. Il faut cependant observer les limites d'une telle sélection,
en raison même de la nature encore exploratoire de nos travaux.

Ainsi, la présentation du procédé "PLATBROOD" fabriqué par un
artisan belge, et du procédé "STRAMIT" produit par une firme hollan-
daise, sera accompagné en annexe d'un tableau d'identification de
procédés de l'engenierie et des expériences qui feront l'objet de nos
futures recherches.

2. Le procédé "PLATBROOD"

La terre crue pour la construction rassemble de nombreuses qualités :
grande disponibilité, faible coût écologique, aptitude au recyclage,
simplicité des procédés de transformation.

Dans la filière de production, les opérations d'extraction de la
terre et de séchage peuvent garder un caractère encore traditionnel.

En revanche, une rationalisation de la production exige une mécanisation des opérations de malaxage et de compactage de la terre.

Nous nous intéresserons ici   à la seconde opération.

Sur 28 presses analysées par le groupe CRATERRE, 6 presses commer-
cialisées sont jugées satisfaisantes. Parmi celles-ci, la presse
TERSTARAM comprend du point de vue technique et économique de nombreux
avantages. Elle a été en particulier utilisée par l'ADAVA.

Cette machine très robuste a été conçue spécialement pour les pays
tropicaux. Les boulons et les barres d'acier sont standard. En cas
de cassure d'une pièce, la machine peut être réparée par un forgercn
de village. Ce procédé n'entraîne donc aucune dépendance vis-à-vis
de l'extérieur en matière de pièces de rechange.

E. COMMISSAIRE et C. FAURE (*) décrivent la facilité d'utilisation
de cette machine : "La démonstration témoigne d'un jeu de levier astu-
cieux. En un seul geste, une pression de vingt tonnes comprime la terre,
façonnant ainsi deux briques. La machine fonctionne avec deux hommes,
un au mécanisme, l'autre au remplissage de la terre et au retrait des
briques moulées. De chaque côté de la presse se trouve un levier de
commande. On effectue ainsi les opérations de moulage et de démoulage. La production moyenne est de 1600 briques par jour de 220x110 mm
ou de 800 blocs de 295x140 mm".

L'utilisation d'une pelle doseuse et d'un malaxeur améliore la
productivité.

"Les malaxeurs à axe vertical ou vis d'archimède sont chers.
Monsieur PLATBROOD qui connaît bien les problèmes de terrain, a étudié le matériel qui évitera le malaxage par piétinement ou l'acquisition d'un malaxeur.

(*) Compte-rendu de la viste faite à Monsieur Fernand PLATBROAD.
GRET - 10 juin 1981.

Ce compromis idéal est une autobineuse BERNARD modifiée avec deux disques arrière montés sur roulement à billes plus un disque plus petit monté à l'avant. Pour l'opération malaxage, il suffit de faire pénétrer le motoculteur dans l'aire de malaxage de préférence ronde au fond cimenté".

La presse PLATBROOD présente un double intérêt. Grâce à l'adaptation de moules, elle permet de fabriquer d'autres produits que la brique (tuiles, tuyaux de drainage, briquettes cylindriques de combustible, pierres à lécher pour animaux). Le coût concurrentiel de la machine (cf tableau 1), la facilité d'utilisation et de transport, ainsi qu'un niveau de production adapté à un marché local sont les principaux atouts de ce procédé.

TABLEAU COMPARATIF DES PROCEDES ET DES PRIX EN 198?

Procédés	Fonction	Caractéristiques techniques	Production	Prix	Remarques
Presse TERSTARAM standard	Machine manuelle pour le compactage de briques de terre stabilisée et de briques cuites	Dimension : 1,4 m x 0,55 m x 1 m de hauteur. Poids : 320 kg. Fixe au piston inférieur 3,6 mm. Rabattement du couvercle dans le moule 15 mm réglage de l'épaisseur du produit par des cales de différentes dimensions - Poussée thermique maximum : 20 tonnes	800 blocs de 295 x 140 mm. 1600 briques de 220 x 110 mm (2 briques à chaque opération)	Presse standard 4 550 FF. moule 29,5 x 14 x 9 : 845 FF moule double : 2 x 22 x 10,5 x 9:936 FF	
Presse TERSTARAM spéciale				Presse 4 875 FF. moule 40 x 20 x 10: 936 FF. 30 x 20 x 10: 936 FF. 29,5 x 14 x 9: 884 FF. moule double 2 x 22 x 10,5 x 9:1 001 FF	
Presse hydraulique terstamatique				65 000 FF à 78 000 FF	Arrêtée depuis quelques années la production de cette presse est reprise du fait de la demande croissante des firmes européennes et des pays africains
Pulvérisateurs système CARR	Broyage et mélange de la terre	1 cuve Ø 1 m largeur 0,4 m 1 disque Ø 0,95 m épaisseur 12 m/m une à deux rangées de barres Ø 28 poids 110 kgs - 1 disque intérieur avec 2 rangées de barres Ø 28 - Poids 105 kgs.2 transmissions.rapport 4//.les 2 disques tournent inversement l'un dans l'autre et la terre y rentre par le milieu doit traverser 4 rangées de barreaux qui pulvérisent la terre. Celle-ci tombe sur un tamis au-dessous duquel est placé la brouette.	Dépend de l'alimentation de la cuve	6 656 FF	Ce procédé a l'avantage de traiter toutes les terres y compris les terres latéritiques fonctionnement continu
Motobineuse Bernard	Malaxage	Disques réglables en hauteur		3 140 FF	

3. Le procédé "Stramit"

Ce procédé a l'avantage d'utiliser des déchets végétaux (herbe à éléphant, paille de blé, d'orge, de riz, tige de coton et de chanvre) et de fabriquer des panneaux qui peuvent avoir diverses utilisations: murs extérieurs, éléments de toitures, cloisons, coffrages.

En Suède, la durée de vie d'une maison réalisée avec ce procédé a été d'une quarantaine d'années. Les murs extérieurs, grâce à l'application d'enduits de ciment ou de chaux, ont en moyenne une épaisseur de 7,5 centimètres.

Le tableau suivant donne les principales qualités des panneaux:

Tableau 2. Caractéristiques des panneaux

Caractéristiques mécaniques	Durabilité	Feu	Flamme	Isolation thermique	Absorption phonique	Termites rongeurs
Panneau en paille	Comprimé, le panneau conserve une excellente résistance à l'humidité	Bonne tenue	Résistance prolongée à la flamme avec un faible échauffement	Bonne	Mauvaise	Inattaquable

Institut Technique des Céréales et des Fourrages (ITCT), étude sur les pailles de céréales, 1975.

Le procédé Stramit est utilisé dans une vingtaine de pays dont le Mexique, la Colombie, le Sri-Lanka, la Thaïlande, le Kenya...

La filière technologique de production se décompose en cinq phases:

Tableau 3. Différentes phases de fabrication des panneaux en paille

Procédé de fabrication	1e phase	2e phase	3e phase	4e phase	5e phase
Panneau de paille	Les pailles sont: nettoyées, secouées, aspirées séparées, des corps étrangers	Déversées dans la goulotte de distribution de la machine principale	Comprimées puis chauffées à 280°C pour former un matelas de 1,20 m de largeur et 5 cm d'épaisseur	Qui est recouvert par un revêtement en carton	Sciage

ITCT, o.p.-cit

La présentation des caractéristiques technico-économiques permettra de
mieux cerner les qualités du procédé.

3.1. Caractéristiques techniques

En ce qui concerne le procédé STRAMIT, les panneaux sont fabriqués en
une seule largeur de 1,20 mètres. L'alimentation de la chaîne de fabrication se fait à partir du stock de paille.Celli-ci est placée sur
le tapis de charge qui amène les fibres dans la machine de préparation.
Les pailles sont secouées et séparées des poussières et des grains.
    A l'extrémité de la machine, les fibres sont déversées dans le gou-
lotte verticale qui alimente directement la machine à fabriquer les
panneaux. La paille est alors comprimée. On obtient un panneau continu
qui reçoit entre deux plateaux-guides un carton de protection sur chacune des faces. La consommation de colle est d'environ 800 grammes
par m2 de panneau produit. Le panneau s'engage enfin entre deux tables
chauffantes portées à une température de 280°C, et le piston le re-
pousse en une nappe continue.
    Après refroidissement, les panneaux sont coupés aux longueurs dé-
sirées au moyen d'une scie circulaire automatique.
    Selon Monsieur PLUVINAGE, ancien directeur de l'unité STRAMIT dans
le LOIRET (France), ce procédé de faible complexité technologique est
facilement maîtrisable. La simplicité d'utilisation ne nécessite
qu'une main-d'oeuvre formée sur le tas, un contremaître, un mécanicien
et un électricien.
    Le tableau 4 fait ressortir les besoins en matières, en matériels
et en main d'oeuvre pour deux types d'unités existantes actuellement
sur le marché.

Tableau 4. Tailles des unités de production

	Investissement	Produits	Matières connexes	Matériels connexes	Main d'oeuvre
Procédé I - 3 000 T de paille par an, - 150 000 m2 par an, - 1 équipe	Moyen	- panneaux découpés sur mesure, - panneaux composés, - panneaux décorés, - éléments avec revêtement, - cloisons de bureaux, - éléments de toitures, - éléments pour coffrage.	Colle	–	Ouvriers spécialisés, un mécanicien, un électricien, un contremaître
Procédé II - 10 000 T de paille par an, - 500 000 m2, - 3 équipes.	Environ un million de francs	Idem plus construction de maisons entières	- colle, - lames en aluminium ou en acier, - bois de charpente	Machine spécialisée dans le travail du bois	Idem plus un directeur de production, des dessinateurs et un service commercial spécialisé dans la construction

3.2. Caractéristiques économiques

Comparativement aux panneaux de fibres et de particules, la fabrication de panneaux "STRAMIT" exige moins d'énergie et le coût à l'emploi productif est faible (cf tableau 5).

Ce panneau représente de ce fait un intérêt particulier pour les pays du Tiers-Monde qui disposent de larges ressources en déchets agricoles. "STRAMIT" se situe d'autre part au carrefour d'activités agricoles et industrielles. En effet, les déchets végétaux peuvent être transformés sur place par la même population qui travaille dans les champs. Dans cet environnement on relève bien une relation étroite entre l'agriculture et l'industrie.

Malgré les avantages du point de vue économique et technique, il n'est pas sans intérêt de faire quelques réserves.

3.3. Réserves

Le procédé STRAMIT est en effet soumis à trois contraintes de taille :

(a) l'approvisionnement en paille : une unité fonctionnant en continu exige un approvisionnement régulier en matériau sous peine d'une rupture de la chaîne de production et partant d'une réduction de la productivité.

(b) le transport de la paille : au-delà de 15 à 20 kilomètres, les coûts des transports greffent sérieusement le coût global des panneaux.

(c) le coût de la paille : ce procédé ne représente un intérêt que si le coût de la paille est nul. A cet égard, il n'est pas inutile de rappeler que l'échec de l'unité STRAMIT dans le Loiret en France est en partie lié au coût de la paille.

En effet, une spéculation sur ce matériau a induit une augmentation très sensible de son prix, entraînant ainsi une croissance du coût des produits. Ces derniers n'étant plus concurrentiels par rapport aux panneaux de particules, l'unité du Loiret a dû fermer.

Tableau 5. Comparaison des filières de production de panneaux utilisant des déchets végétaux. Unités de production minimum.

Type de panneaux	Fibres/Panneaux durs/Panneaux isolation/Procédé humide	Fibres/Panneaux durs/Moyenne densité/Procédé à sec	Particules	Pailles compressées	Agglomérés ciment
Taille des unités minimum	12 T/jour	60 T/jour	20 T/jour à 42 T/jour	16 T/jour	160 plaques/jour
Source ou procédé	ONUDI/Kenya	Sunds defibrator /Indonésie	Chine et France	Procédé Stramit/ Grande-Bretagne, Kenya, Thaïlande	Tropical Product Institut (TPI)
Coût à l'emploi productif(*) en milliers de $	53 M $ (**)	133 M $	Inférieur aux fibres; pas de données fiables	20 M $	6 M $
Coût énergétique (thermique et mécanique)	Elevé 525 KW/T de panneaux	Elevé 450 KW/T de panneaux	Faible	Moyen Chauffe à 280°C	Faible 77 KW/T
Degré d'extraversion (part de produits importés tels que ciment, résines)	Très faible Pas de résines ni de ciment	Moyen 90 kg de résine par tonne de panneaux	Elevé Besoin de résines	Très faible Rien importé	Elevé 524 kg ciment par tonne !
Fiabilité de la filière. Caractère expérimental	Filière au point sur bagasse. Sinon expérimental	Fiabilité élevée pour le bois, faible sur les déchets	Nombreuses expérimentations peu d'industrialisation	Filière très au point	Filière très au point

(*) Calcul à partir des données disponibles. Actualisation + 15 %/an
(**) TPI indique 104 M $/emploi productif

Annexe. Tableau: identification des procédés, de l'ingénierie et des expériences qui feront l'objet de futures recherches

Matériaux	Fabricant ou origine du procédé	Ingénierie	Observations
Terre crue	SUISSE: tamisseurs concasseurs, BELGIQUE: presses-pulvérisateurs, FRANCE: presses Turquin, presses Junas, presses GB2, USA: procédés automatisés de fabrication d'adobes (pondeurs d'adobes)	FRANCE: CRATerre, GRET, Plan Construction	- Expériences en cours: Cameroun, Haute-Volta, Mali, - France: la société "Minérale Technique" travaille sur le durcissement économique de la latérite, - RFA: les sociétés Krupp et Mayer sont spécialisée dans le transfert d'usines de production de blocs de latérite stabilisée à chanal.
Brique cuite	GRANDE-BRETAGNE, BELGIQUE, SUEDE	FRANCE: CERIC	- Projet: mini-briqueterie au Cameroun, Congo et au Rwanda, - Autriche: mise au point d'une briqueterie mobile,
Chaux	RFA, FRANCE	FRANCE: GRET	- Petites et moyennes unités au Burundi et au Rwanda.
Plâtre	RFA, FRANCE	FRANCE: GRET, GEFOSAT, CEBTP, Plan Construction	- Petites et moyennes unités au Cap Vert en Mauritanie et au Mali.
Pierre		FRANCE CEYLAN	- Projets recensés: Cap Vert, Somalie, Djibouti.
Déchets agricoles et végétaux	SUEDE: Sunds defibrator, RFA: Schenk et Siempeltramp, USA, AUTRICHE, URSS		

DEVELOPING A BUILDING MATERIALS SECTOR IN THE CIRCUMSTANCES OF HOUSING FOR THE URBAN POOR

F.I.A. TACKIE, Building and Road Research Institute, Ghana.

1. *Introduction*

It is the intention of this paper to shift the emphasis of a search for a solution to this problem away from the public sector and more to the private sector, especially such traditional sources as the farming community. In order to derive such a conclusion, the current housing situation of the urban poor is discussed. This issue is related to the importance of the building materials sector. The vital question then is, what are the real issues which have tended to hinder the development of this sector in the context of the urban poor.

Finally, major recommendations based on the role of the private sector are discussed with particular reference to the supportive roles of both National and International agencies.

2. *The housing situation of the urban poor*

Using Africa as an example, there is an extreme imbalance in the rural-urban population ratio. Most countries tend to have one or two cities with extreme urban concentrations. It is in such urban areas that the housing problem for the urban poor is acute.
For example, it is estimated that about 53% of the population of Accra live in slums and uncontrolled settlements; Ibadan has 75%, Lome 75%, Cassablanca 70% and Yaounde 90%. (1). Apart from these, there are others in the urban poverty gap who live in non-slum areas Together, they constitute a force in the estimation of needs and demands in the urban housing market.

If the existing trend of urbanization were to remain constant, then the problem may seem well defined and possibly controllable. Unfortunately, predictions for the future are gloomy. (2). It presents a problem of numbers with an equally gloomy prediction about the future of the economies of most of such countries. Apart from their numbers the socio-economic and cultural circum- stances tends to betray the problem. In addition to the indigenous poor, there are two categories of migrant poor - the permanent and the temporary. (3). This migrant group, particularly

the latter type has a value system which tends to influence their
effective demand for housing on the urban market. One of such
value systems is the tendency to have frequent interactions with
their respective villages and above all the extreme desire to
invest more in housing at the place of origin rather than the
respective urban area of abode. In addition to the concept of
external-family ownership of property, these issues tend to potray
the urban poor as an unrealistic group within the urban housing
market.
    On the supply side, there are three major sources of output –
(i) a large group of ageing housing stock, (ii) an insignificant
proportion of dwellings by the public sector; (iii) a small
proportion of new construction by the private sector which has the
highest potential of dominating the supply, barring all the underlying constraints. The main issue here is that apart from the
existing ageing and dilapidated stock there is no other dependable
basis of supply of shelter for the urban poor.

3. *The importance of the Building Materials Sector*

This can be measured by at least two basic parameters – production
of shelter and employment or incomes generation.

3.1 *With regard to output of shelter*

Three major factors can be identified in a matrix of housing output
for the urban poor – (i) public sector output, (ii) individuals
termed the urban poor and (iii) private sector petty-scale
property developers. To complete this model, one can identify at
least five major factors of production of shelter i.e. labour,
infrastructure, land, policy matters and building materials.
Table 1 below shows the interaction between the two sets of
variables.

Table 1 Housing Supply Matrix

Agents of Supply	Factors of Production	Land	Policy matters	Labour	Infra-Structure	Building Material
Public Sector (1)		+	+	–	+	+
Individuals (2)		+	–	+	–	–
Petty-Scale developers (3)		–	–	+	–	–

Building materials for this purpose must satisfy at least two
conditions - (i) minimum cost and (ii) easily available. Apart
from the public sector which has the opportunity to overcome the
constraint of lack of adequate building materials, the other two
actors seem to be cut-off from the supply base due to the
deficiency of one factor. To these latter actors, the remaining
factors of production may not be seen as scarce resources.
The proliferation of an informal building industry in some African
countries explains the easy access to labour (4); policy matters
have been ignored most often; infrastructure may be assumed to be
existing even though insufficient; and Land has never been an
exclusive monopoly of the state. On the above basis one can
measure the importance of the building materials sector by
concluding that if it fulfils the two conditions then actors 2 and
3 stand a chance of out-competing actor 1 and thus increasing the
supply base of housing for the urban poor. Another simplistic
measure of its importance is the fact that building materials
account for over 60% of the total value of construction output (5).

3.2 *Employment generation*

As a component of the construction industry, the building materials
sector can be said to be pivotal to all socio-economic development
projects. In a similar manner, one can measure its importance in
terms of contributions to gross fixed capital formation or G.D.P.
of a country. (6). Unfortunately, all these measures have not been
statistically established when the subject is related to housing
for the urban poor. Rather, the importance can be measured by the
level of contributions made in terms of employment or income
generation. (7). Recent indications even point to benefits
accrued as a result of inter-sectorial multiplier effects.

4. *Constraints facing the building materials sector*

In analysing such constraints, the concept of third world countries
needs to be reclassified on the basis of three different criteria -
(i) Oil producing nations, (ii) countries with size peculiarities
and (iii) countries with technological advantage. By implication,
the level of constraints facing a particular country will tend to
vary with the characteristics imposed by all or any of the criteria
outlined above. Similarly, the term building materials needs to be
re-classified as follows:- (i) key building materials which are
import-based and available on the market but expensive; (ii) key
building materials same as above except that they may be very
scarce or toally unavailable even though they may be popular,
(iii) Indigenous key building materials already in production and
(iv) indigenous key building materials yet to take off from the
experimental stage into commercial ventures.

One fundamental constraint facing the sector it seems, is the
lack of a policy outline on the importance of the subject and
above all stipulating the types of materials with expected targets
to meet the peculiarities of the urban poor. It is possible to
aim at expanding the production basis of import-based key materials
without any special protection for the urban poor. Alternatively,
a policy may hinge on encouraging indigenous key materials to
satisfy a peculiar market. This paper supports the latter option
and consequently, the following have been identified as the major
constraints.

4.1 *Constraints from the demand point of view*
The disorientation of values in recent times may not tend to favour
a shift from key building materials such as aluminium sheets,
cement blocks etc., to local substitutes such as clay bricks,
roofing tiles and timber as a walling material. (8).

To some in the lower income category, small-scale maintenance
of aged buildings is their effective demand and not the
construction of new dwellings. However there is often a
constraint of non-availability of basic building components and
accessories.

Building Codes and regulations as they exist are a misfit
especially given the circumstances of housing for the urban poor(9).
Lack of cheap and easily available materials for construction and
maintenance of basic infrastructure is one major problem facing
the sector.

4.2 *Constraints from the supply point of view*
The basic inputs required for the output of such indigenous
building materials are raw materials, labour, machinery, energy,
infrastructure, finance and entrepreneurship (10). The likely
problem with raw materials is basically lack of data on exact
quantity and performance characteristics. Here, one may ignore
the locations which may often be in undeveloped hinterlands.
Certain specialized skills of labour may tend to pose as
constraints. Energy requirements for the production of lime, clay
bricks and roofing tiles could be high. Conventional energy
sources and their problems need no extra elaborations (11).
Renewable energy sources, on the other hand are getting more
expensive or out of realization.

Of all the factors of production identified, the most striking
deficiency, it seems is the factor of investment or entrepreneurship. Central governments of poor countries are by definition
poor, so one cannot rely on that option. If the private sector
on the other hand has not responded, then the underlying
constraint it seems is two-fold. First the building materials

sector vis-a-vis other sectors is not investment-attractive
i.e. longer-time period for investments to pay back, high
initial capital outlay, risks in fluctuations of demand etc.
Secondly, for indigenous building materials it is a new concept
in the business market and therefore requires special attention.

   Lack of an effective housing policy on behalf of the urban
lower-income category is yet another constraint. Such a policy
if implemented will normally serve as a necessary motivation for
both the supply and demand of building materials.

   Lastly, one may identify several problems related to technology
(12) but of specific importance is the fact that given the present
circumstances, local materials such as timber for walling, bricks
and clay are entirely new materials with a likelihood of
inadequate building technology to support their use.

5. *Recommendations*

The focal point of solutions to this problem is the private
sector - particularly the indigenous private sector. This is
under the assumption that some indispensable roles will be played
at both National and International levels. In the production of
local key building materials, certain factors are required some
of them abundant others scarce. Table 2 below indicates the
factors and the relative scarcity or abundance with the three
complimentary sectors—private, national and international.

Table 2 Factors of production with the sectors of production

Factors	Scarce			Abundant		
	Priv.	Nat.	Int.	Priv.	Nat.	Intern
1. Investor		-	-	+		
2. Finance Local		-	-	+		
3. Finance(Foreign)	-					+
4. Policy matters	-				+	+
5. Raw materials	-		-	+		
6. Land			-	+	+	
7. Machinery	-	-				+
8. Skilled labour	-				+	+
9. Energy	-				+	+
10. Infrastructure	-		-		+	

On the above basis the following recommendations are made:

5.1 *The role of individual governments*
The following items must be the responsibility of each central government.

(a) policy matters:- apart from an overall policy stressing the importance and types of building materials which need priority attention, there is a need for a housing policy which seeks to accept upgrading of run-down housing areas as an immediate programme for the urban poor. This can be supported by a programme of new housing stock by motivating investment efforts of the petty - scale developers. With such a demand base re-activated the next issue is the supply of the appropriate building materials.

(b) raw materials – Here, central government agencies should undertake certain minimum functions on behalf of potential investors from the private sector in the form of incentives. This includes geological surveys, laboratory tests and above all acquiring concessions on land etc.

(c) fiscal policy - An attractive fiscal policy by the central government can achieve at least two things. First, attract loose funds from the individuals in the private sector (especially those in the informal and farming sectors) into special development banks, and secondly guarantee credit facilities from the same banking institutions. Such fiscal measures should be seen as reinforcement to already existing policies such as those on tax concessions, tarrif impositions etc.

(d) basic infrastructure:- As long as production decisions are determined by the location of raw materials, the absence of basic infrastructure may remain a deterent to potential investors. The responsibility of the central government here will be the provision of access to the site, access to water and if possible a means of generating electricity.

(e) energy requirements:- Firewood as an alternative source of fuel in the production of building materials cannot be guaranteed (13). Renewable resources of energy such as biogas seem very feasible given the circumstances of vast agricultural resources in the very location of raw materials for the production of indigenous building materials, yet in being Scientific innovations they may not be attractive to the private sector investor. Hence, the need for central government intervention.

(f) aggressive dissemination:- Research institutions and such central government agencies need a radical shift in the marketing of their findings so as to convince the private sector investor about both technical and commercial viability. For a start, the agencies may prepare full feasibility reports at their own expense and there after identify specific target groups for dissemination.

5.2 *The role of the International Sector*
This should be seen as directly complimentary to that of the National agencies. They include the following:

(a) machinery and equipment:- This issue is a near monopoly of the international sector. There are several possibilities here. First, development agencies such as UNIDO, UNCHS and ILO may select pilot projects and support them with direct aid of machinery and equipments. The second is for monetary and agencies such as the World Bank to guarantee credit facilities directly to both local and external private sector investors on the most favourable terms. The third, which is often prone to abuse, is to supply such items directly to the respective governments as capital aid.

(b) manpower:- At this level the concept of U.N. regional commissions and Regionalization in general becomes useful. By virtue of economic or geographic size some countries cannot support building materials research institutes and may have to depend upon a Regional pull to provide this level of service.

Certain skills may also not be available and may be provided on a
short term basis as an aid or a training programme.
    (c)   getting recipient governments committed. It is by now
obvious that even though much attention is being drawn to the
importance of the subject by International development agencies
such as UNIDO, UNCHS and C.I.B., some governments in the third
world countries do not seem to have reflected this level of
importance or near emergency about the subject. Experience has
shown that it is easier for such countries to respond to a
particular direction of policy from such august bodies as the
World Bank, the U.N. etc. If the role assigned to the National
and International agencies as specified in this paper are to
achieve any results, then the fundamental task is this issue of
getting the respective governments really committed to the task.

5.3 *Conclusions*
The importance of housing for the urban poor has been stressed.
One of the most critical constraints is the absence of a building
materials sector sympathetic to their demands. T his paper has
made an attempt to outline such issues and arrive at a recommendation that private sector investment is the key to any eventual
breakthrough. This however depends on the indispensable inputs
from both national and international agencies.

References

1. United Nations   Human Settlements in Africa
    Economic Commission   E/CN.14/HUS/15. Adis Ababa
                           1976. See also UNIDO monograph
                           on appropriate industrial technology
                           No.12. New Yorl 1980.

2. B. Ward   The Home of Man
                           Penguin 1976 pp.3-5.

3. UNCHS (Habitat)   The residential circumstances of
                           the urban poor in developing
                           countries. Praeger 1981 pp 21-62.

4. F.I.A. Tackie   The informal building industry in
                           the context of urban housing.
                           Unpublished M.Phil thesis.
                           University of Newcastle Upon Tyne
                           1979.

5. D.A. Turin and   Building materials industries -
    T.P. O'Brien   Factors affecting their growth
                           in developing countries.
                           UNIDO monograph 1969 May Vienna.

6. D. Turin   Economic significance of
                           construction. Architects Journal
                           No.42 Oct. 1969 pp 923-929.

7. S. Ganesan   Employment generation through
                           investments in Housing and
                           Construction. Unpublished PH.D.
                           thesis, University College of London,
                            1976.

8. Z. Berhane   The use and development of indigenous
                           building materials and components.

                           U.N. Ad Hoc Expert Group Meeting
                           H.S./Conf.2/81/12. Nairobi Nov. 1981.

9. UNCHS (Habitat)   U.N. Seminar of Experts on Building
                           Codes and Regulations in Developing
                           Countries, Sweden March 1980.

10. D.A. Turin and
     T.P. O'Brien   Op. Cit.

11. UNEP   U.N. Conference on New and
                             Renewable Sources of Energy.
                             Nairobi, August 1981.

12. G.C. Verkerk   Sectorial Survey paper of the
                             Building materials and
                             Construction Industry UNIDO/PC.56
                             Oct. 1982.

13. UNEP   Op. Cit.

A PROPOSED TIMBER FRAME LOW COST HOUSE FOR ZAMBIAN CONDITIONS

MAURI LAAKKONEN, Forest Department, Zambia

1. Introduction

At the moment the relevant examples of low cost houses in Zambia
are made out of concrete blocks, but their price, when produced tc
the standard required by the local authorities, is excessive for a
large amount of people in the low income group. Since plantations
of exotic eucalyptus and pine timber in the country are now well
established, and the plantation timber is moderately priced
compared to indigenous or imported species, an attempt is being
made to utilize these exotics in producing a house, which more
people could afford.

2. Design considerations

Throughout the design highest possible priority was given to the
economy, in order to achieve minimum cost. In practice only
structural safety (strength) had always preference over the cost
factor, and in some essential details minimum cost principle was
abandoned in favour for durability, since the design life span of
the house was set at about thirty years.

For a timber frame house there is not any technically and
economically suitable locally made wood based panel in Zambia to
be used as an external skin, and therefore locally produced
asbestos-cement sheets were chosen.

Major hazard for timber in buildings in Zambia is caused by
subterranean termites, and since neither of the used exotic
species, i.e. Eucalyptus grandis and Pinus kesiya, is naturally
resistant to termites, both structural and chemical methods were
used to eliminate this hazard.

For vertical loads on the roof the following values given in
the Zambian code ZS 016:1975, (1), were used:

-0.25 KN/m² measured on plan or
-1.0 KN concentrated in a square with a 300mm side.

In the absence of Zambian code for windloads, the extreme wind
gust used in design was set at 31.7 m/s (71.0 m.p.h.), from reference 2.

The permissible stresses and deflections for timber were determined according to the draft Zambian code (3).

Data on racking strength (i.e. ability to resist horizontal
inplane shear forces, normally caused by the wind) of the timber
stud wall with flat asbestos-cement sheeting was not available,
so strength testing was necessary to obtain this information.

3.   *Strength testing*

The equations for computing racking strength are independent of
panel size, so both simple lateral nail tests and small scale
racking tests could augment the more expensive full-size panel
tests (4). In this project the first type of test was carried
out, since lateral nail resistance of a single fastener, together
with the geometry of the wall panel and nail spacing, provide adequate data for calculating the racking strength.

Two types of joints illustrated in figure 1. were tested to
failure, using both sawn and planed air-dried Eucalyptus grandis
timber, and semi-compressed flat asbestos-cement sheets, TYPE 2
according to Zambian standard ZS 006:1973, (5), rough surface of
the sheet facing the timber. Galvanized nails in the test samples
were always driven through pre-drilled holes in the sheets. Ten
test pieces in each group were produced, bringing the total number
of tested specimens to forty. After tests the moisture content of
timber was determined.

The ultimate load per one nail required for calculations was
derived by assuming that the normal distribution (Gaussian curve)
holds in the case of the nail resistance, and by setting the lower
tail exclusion limit at 5.5% (i.e. 94.5% of the test results are
likely to exceed the so derived ultimate load).

The nail resistance of the planed timber studs was found to be
considerably higher than that of the sawn timber studs, and therefore planed timber was used in the stud wall design.

4.   *Design of a prototype*

The proposed one family house has two bedrooms, living room, kitchen
(net area of these rooms is 36.6 sqm), and a verandah (7.5 sqm).

The foundation is made out of concrete blocks laid onto concrete
footing, and 75mm thick concrete slab on compacted hardcore filling
is used as a flooring. The ground below the building is poisoned
and termite barrier out of galvanized steel sheet is used around the
perimeter of the building to prevent termite attack.

Timber frame consists of 50x100mm, c/c 575mm studs and 50x100mm
wall and sole plates out of plantation grown Eucalyptus grandis, and
6mm thick and 1200mm wide flat asbestos-cement sheets are nailed
onto the outer face of the frame, overlapping 50mm at every other
stud. Internal skin is excluded, except behind the stove in the
kitchen. The roof is made out of corrugated asbestos-cement sheets
fixed with drive screws onto eucalyptus purlins spanning from gable

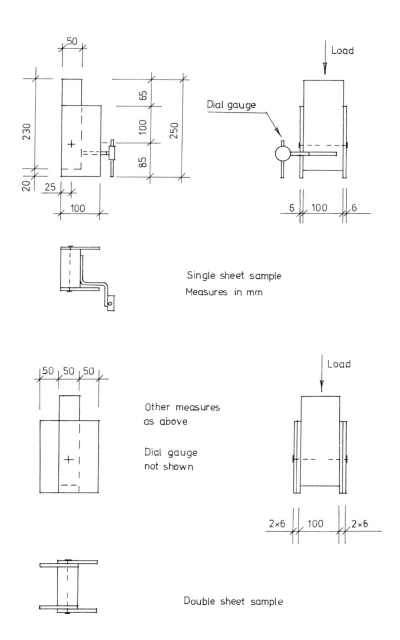

Load

Dial gauge

Single sheet sample
Measures in mm

Other measures
as above

Dial gauge
not shown

Load

Double sheet sample

Figure 1.   Strength test samples

ends to the middle wall of the house. No trusses are used.

Nail spacing in the walls was determined according to the results of the strength tests described above, to achieve the horizontal stability against wind forces, using the following method: One of the asbestos-cement sheets in each external and internal wall is to be fixed with adequate number of nails to resist the windload towards the wall concerned, multiplied by 2.75 (safety factor). All the other sheets are to be nailed using the minimum nail spacing required by the suction of the wind. Since the nailing of these other sheets is also contributing to the rigidity of the whole structure, and since the equation from reference 4 used to calculate the racking strength gives only the resistance afforded by the perimeter nails, omitting the resistance of the field nails, the total factor of safety against racking under the chosen windload is higher, and it is estimated to be above 5.

Figures 2. and 3. show the plan and a section of the prototype house respectively.

5.   *Estimate of the cost*

The price of the building in Kitwe or in Lusaka was estimated at 3,600.- Zambian Kwachas (about 3,600.- US dollars) in the latter half of May 1982, including labour and transport cost. Water and toilet facilities are supposed to be arranged jointly for several houses, and their cost is not included in this estimate. Ventilated pitlatrines and shower units approved by the World Health Organization, originally designed in Zimbabwe, and currently introduced in Zambia, appear to offer a solution to this problem at a very moderate price.

The cost of possible electrical fittings is also excluded from the above estimate.

6.   *Discussion*

The estimated cost of the house indicates that loans are necessary for individuals in order to be able to meet the cost, and therefore the structure needs the official approval by the relevant government bodies, so that loan facilities can be made available.

Together with monitoring of the long term performance of the building, the prototype should be used to observe if any possible asbestos-fiber emission by the structure is within acceptable limit.

It is also envisaged that even if the prototype to be built proves to be technically sound (or can with minor revisions become technically sound), and acceptable to the local authorities, market promotion is necessary to gain users acceptance for this type of a structure in Zambia.

There are recommendations that the price of one family house should not exceed the buyer's net salary of 2 to 3 years. If we adopt 3 years salary as a basis, it is concluded that all families

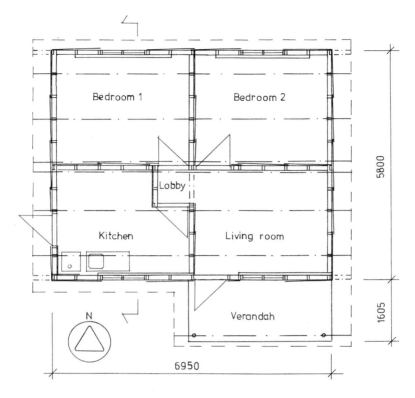

Figure 2. Plan of the prototype house
Measures in mm

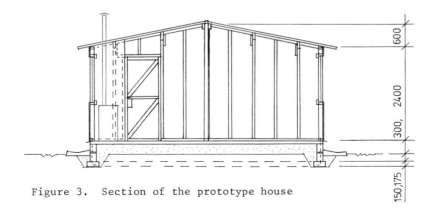

Figure 3. Section of the prototype house

earning about ZK 100.- per month could be regarded as potential
buyers for this kind of a house.

Finally, when compared to the traditional concrete block construction, it is evident that the main advantage of the timber frame
is its viability in prefabricated production. Therefore, if the
prototype house can prove the basic structure to be feasible in
Zambian conditions, the next logical step in the project would be
the design of a prefabricated version.

7.   *Acknowledgements*

The writer wishes to extend his appreciation to the following
Zambian institutes and corporations for their contribution during
the process of design:

  -Kitwe Urban District Council, City Engineer's Department
  -National Council for Scientific Reasearch, Building Reasearch
   Unit, Lusaka
  -National Housing Authority, Lusaka
  -TAP Building Products Ltd, Chilanga
  -University of Zambia, Technology Development and Advisory Unit,
   Lusaka.

References

1.   Zambia Bureau of Standards * (1975), *Loading, Dead and imposed
     loads.* ZS 016:1975, 16.
2.   Hutchinson P. (1976), *Climate data for architects in Zambia.*
     Zambia Geographical Association, Occasional Study No.8, 45.
3.   Zambia Bureau of Standards * (1982), *Draft 2, Zambian standard
     code of practice: Structural use of locally grown timber.*
     9,16.
4.   Tuomi R.L. and Gromala D.S. (1977), *Racking strength of walls:
     Let-in corner bracing, sheet materials, and effect of
     loading rate.* U.S. Department of Agriculture Forest Service,
     Forest Products Laboratory, Madison Wis., USDA Forest Service
     Reasearch Paper FPL 301 1977, 16,3.
5.   Zambia Bureau of Standards * (1973), *Asbestos-cement flat sheets
     and slates.* ZS 006:1973, 2.

*   Former Zambian Standards Institute.

SYMBOLS, SECURITY AND SALESMANSHIP AS FACTORS IN TECHNOLOGY REJECTION

RICHARD MARTIN, Technical Adviser, United States Agency for
International Development, Regional Housing and Urban Development
Office, Nairobi

"After you've searched your soul for an appropriate technology, how do you get people to use it?" Allen Jedlicka

Let us imagine ourselves in an urban squatter settlement, maybe in
Nairobi, Dar es Salaam, Lagos, Gabarone or other large city in
Africa. Looking around one will usually see buildings of three
distinct types: the ones built out of traditional materials, those
built out of junk materials, and those built out of concrete blocks
and corrugated iron. Traditional materials often show signs of deterioration, either because the urban areas no longer provide a good
source of appropriate materials, or because the residents no longer
have the time to maintain them as they do in the rural areas: roofs
leak, and the walls are eroded by the rain. The junk materials look
terrible, and work badly. Only the concrete block/corrugated iron
houses appear to offer a satisfactory solution. But further inquiry
reveals the very high cost of this form of construction, and also
points to the poor insulation of the roof.
   You or I could show the residents of that settlement several
different ways of building that would be little more expensive than
traditional construction but yet would provide a solution more durable. We could therefore demonstrate that if the person building in
concrete blocks had adapted our approach he could have saved a considerable amount of money, which he could therefore use to increase
the amount of covered space in his house to the great advantage of
himself and his family.
   Let us also go to a village and look at the houses there. Although cheap - if not free - and offering good thermal insulation and
other advantages, rural housing requires much maintenance, often
harbours pests and does not respond easily - in many cases - to the
changes demanded by new life styles. Thus we also witness here the
increasing incidence of the concrete block walled, corrugated iron
roofed house. Here too we could demonstrate solutions that would
provide a satisfactory alternative to the concrete block house
without costing the owner nearly as much. As we all know however,
this is, in fact what many have done. Much enthusiasm and dedication
have gone into the task, but the spin-off effect of these efforts to

introduce new technology have been negligible.*

It would not be appropriate here to suggest materials that would
answer the descriptions given above as replacements for concrete
blocks or traditional materials. But it is important to state that
nothing I refer to here or elsewhere in this paper is intended to be
restricted to any particular type of technology: it can be the so-
called "appropriate" "intermediate" or "alternative" technology, or
it can be space-age technology. For the purpose of my general argu-
ment, the specific type of technology makes no difference. THE FACT
IS THAT NEW TECHNOLOGY IS VERY PRONE TO BE REJECTED. My thesis is
therefore that instead of trying to invent ever more and different
types of technology, we should try to understand why existing technologies are not more widely adopted. Only when we understand this
better will we be in a position to know whether it is the material
which is at fault or the methods by which it is introduced.

There are, in brief, three main reasons why building technologies
are rejected:

1. In self help housing** all risks are at the owner/builder's
expense, and adoption of unknown technology therefore causes unwelcome financial risks.
2. Building technologies are almost invariably invented or developed
outside the social and cultural group that will use them. They
therefore have to be "sold" to them, a process that arouses deep
suspicions, and is in itself a source of rejection.
3. In urban housing in Africa, what a house says is at least as
important as what it does.

We shall take these three points one by one.

1. Owner/Builders are not prepared to risk their savings on unproved building methods.

There are good reasons for caution in the field of construction, even
in the so-called technological societies of the north. Windows can
fall out of skyscrapers, bridges can collapse, and routinely houses
crack and leak. Materials such as tiles fall off walls and lift from
floors, and processes that were once highly recommended fall into
disrepute as further study is undertaken on them***.Materials that
have been fully tested and covered by complex Codes of Practice (e.g
high alumina cement) can fail disastrously even under the supervision
of fully qualified professionals.

The literature of building failure runs little risk of being

---

*For example every possible variant of the roof-on-legs scheme has
been tried in Zambia, using different materials and systems. In spite
of obvious technological advantages, none was widely adopted by the
people.
** By the term self-help housing I mean any housing erected under the
supervision of the owner (not necessarily by his owns hands).
*** One of the most dramatic examples of this has been the filling of
cavity walls with insulating foam, which subsequently has been found
to give off toxic gasses.

deprived of raw material. But for the owners who suffer from such failures there is at least a crumb of comfort. The buildings were designed by professionals who hold some responsibility in law for designing a sound product, and who can therefore be sued. Likewise the contractor can be sued, and even the local authority (in English law anyway) can be sued for certain defects if they are covered under the inspections required for compliance with the building regulations. In the field of housing there is often also a fourth guarantor of the quality of the product, the lending institution which may insist on certain standards being adhered to and the building being insured against collapse. Thus if there is a collapse the owner has a number of remedies so that he can be recompensed for his losses.

In spite of all this many building owners are very reluctant to innovate. Should we therefore be surprised that people in a self-help scheme are not very willing to abandon materials that they know well and to try an entirely new product? The house will represent a far bigger investment in comparison to their income than it would in the richer countries, and it is simply imprudent for them to risk their money on an untested material.*

In considering the problem the potential building owner will probably take the advice of the community, and the most important voice will be the builder's**. Builders the world over are notoriously conservative, and in poorer communities in developing countries they are no different. They will recommend the old and tested solutions, not being willing to risk their reputation on untried methods or materials.

If the owner does decide to proceed with building in unconventional technologies, what chance does he have to recover his money in the event of a collapse? There is very little likelihood that he would have either the financial resources or suitable connections to institute legal action. But if he were to have access to these, he will not be able to sue the builder (who has no money anyway) and there are no professionals or insurance companies. He might consider sueing the advisers who 'sold' him the technology in the first place, but as likely as not they will be representing the state or the local administration which he would have little chance of beating in a civil action.

We must therefore not underemphasize the degree of trust required by an ordinary person in a new building method if he is to use it. And here we find an additional factor that will inhibit acceptance of new technologies. By the very nature of things, new technologies for the poor are introduced by public agencies. In the field of housing it is more than likely to be either a specialised state agency (of the National Housing Authority type) or the local administration. Both are subject to much mistrust by the poor. Existing services are mismanaged, officers are reputedly often lazy and arrogant, and their activities are subject to political direction which may not accord

---

* The same problem has been identified with farmers who are reluctant to put their faith in new seeds or methods because of the magnitude of the risk. (Bryant and White 1982:214).
** For a more detailed discussion of the role of builders as advisors see Martin 1978:7-14.

with the interests of the groups in question. Those responsible for
introducing new technologies have a natural tendency to feel proud of
what they have to offer the poor - better housing for lower costs.
But for the poor to be subjected to this may cause them much puzzle-
ment. They will ask "why me?" and supply their own answer, which
which will reflect a healthy scepticism if not suspicion, and which
can be summed up as follows:

2. If a technology has to be sold there must be something wrong with
it.

The problem of trust between public authorities and the poor leads us
directly into the issue of "selling". Within the term selling I
include all forms of advertising and moral pressure to induce people
to change their habits or beliefs.
    I was involved in a complex "selling" programme in a project in
Lusaka, which has been favourably mentioned in a number of articles
and books about low income housing.* We went to a great deal of
trouble to persuade people to use soil-cement blocks or sun-dried
soil bricks instead of concrete blocks, as we believed that the extra
space, which was made possible by using these materials instead of
the widely favoured concrete block, was of great importance socially
and even economically.
    Allow me a few lines to list the components of this "sales drive".
- We built demonstration houses.
- We took the leaders within the communities to see those who had
built houses out of soil-cement blocks in another (rather small)
scheme.
- We engaged a local band to sing songs in favour of soil-cement
blocks: they recorded some of them, and one was even on the top of
the pops and was regularly featured on the radio.
- We had public block-making demonstrations of how to make the
blocks, which we made more attractive by the presence of the same
band, playing the songs.
- We lent the block making machines without charge to anyone who
wanted to use them.
- We printed posters and other hand-outs in the vernacular and distributed them very widely.
- We showed films about people in other towns and countries using the
material.
- We had a large corps of community development workers and technical
assistants who were able to explain the materials in more detail in a
series of small briefing meetings with individuals who were going to
build their own houses.
    Net result? Less than 50 of the roughly 10,000 new units that were
built were in soil-cement blocks, and only one was in sun-dried
brick.
    Now before putting all the blame on the fact that the ideas were
being "sold", it should be understood that there were other factors
involved, such as that using soil-cement blocks took much longer

---

* This was the World Bank aided Lusaka Squatter Upgrading and Site
and Service Project, started in 1974.

because they had to be made by the owner/builder instead of being simply bought*. But in a large measure, I am convinced that it is because a building technology comes from outside a culture or soc- iety, often brought by foreigners, that it is the subject of suspi- cion. The more actively it is "sold", the greater the suspicion might become. This is not to decry proper communications in project administration - they are of the greatest importance, but "how" it is being communicated is at least as important as "what". Anyone who wants to study further the language of suspicion should look at Latin America where there is widespread suspicion of all those in a pos- ition of power. Foreigners are suspected of wanting to extend econ- omic interests by introducing new materials, while governments are suspected of wanting to gain economic or political control.

For the sake of illustration let us take two examples of the way in which suspicion can affect the receptivity of people to new ideas. We have already mentioned the case of public agencies, whose political record and administrative style have earned them distrust or resentment. International agencies are not tarred with the same brush, but suspicions are also attached to them. Probably the most common one is that of imposing outside ideas on projects in order to extend their influence, either economically or polit-ically. In the case of building materials the analysis of their motives may not be very clear, but there will be a big doubt as to why anyone would go to any trouble to introduce a material that none of the beneficiaries perceives the need for. Particularly if the material is cheaper than the norm, suspicion will hinge on the question of why the agencies should want to "condemn" people to "second class" standards (to borrow words in common political parlance in this respect). If it is more expensive, the question will be, why are they trying to force us to use this material - surely they are trying to make money out of us somehow? You will note that in these discussions of suspicion I have made no reference to the factual material that usually accompanies the "selling" of a new material or technology, which aims to demon- strate that in terms of cost and durability it is preferable to other commonly used alternatives. This is because until people have lost their suspicion, such facts and figures are meaningless**.

A second illustration of the problem. Demonstration houses have for long been considered a necessary component in the introduction of new technologies or designs, and early UN publications on self help housing nearly all recommended this as a way of communicating tech- nical information to non-technical people (the potential owner/builders). But how do the potential beneficiaries really per- ceive this act? They witness official lorries delivering the mat erials; they see highly trained official workmen putting the building together; commonly they will also witness a flurry of technical

* But it should be noted here that there later emerged another method of block making which also required that the blocks be made by the residents, which was very popular. This is discussed below.
** I feel obliged to note that having studied dozens of comparisons between new technologies and conventional ones, I am not impressed by the standards of objectivity used: indeed the comparative cost figures used often verge on the dishonest.

advisers who will go to tremendous lengths to make sure that it is
correctly built. Very commonly some parts are taken down and re-
erected. When this activity is all over, the public will be invited
to study the building and to marvel about the economy of the
construction method and/or materials. The reaction of the ordinary
man is one of downright scepticism. "If it is so simple," he tells
himself, "why was there such a fuss in getting it built?" And: "how
do they work out what it would cost us?" He doesn't take it
seriously because he knows that the resources that he has at his
disposal, both technically and financially, are nothing compared to
those of the sponsoring agency, and can see no connection between
their costs and his own. In Lusaka, being aware of this problem, we
decided to use local labour for the construction of both demonstration houses that we put up in one of the squatter settlements. In
one case the local people also made all the soil-cement blocks themselves. But even with this local involvement, the gap remained: it
was, for the people, a case of "if they want to do it like that, let
them: we know enough about building, and do not see the need for
these special demonstration houses".

There is a third element in the suspicions that surround the
attempted selling of a material or construction technique. It is
this: "if this material or technique is so good, why do the people
who are selling it to us not use it in their own houses?" (which they
assuredly do not). And the corollary of this is: "we know we are
poor, but do we want to be classified as poor for the rest of our
lives? The system which we are supposed to use here is specially for
the poor: we want something that's good enough for the rich as well.
We don't want to be categorized as inferior in this respect."

To understand this point of view better, imagine that you are the
resident of a simple but cheap mud hut, with corrugated iron roofing.
The system being proposed for your use is, you are told, more durable
and only a little dearer. It is burnt clay bricks that you can make
yourself, built in a vault form that obviates the need for shuttering. It is thus a much stronger house, and by eliminating the
usual corrugated iron roof is a better insulated one. But for all
its advantages, to you this house has one clear disadvantage: it
looks different. It singles you out as a person who cannot afford
the type of house that you really aspire to: the concrete block
walled, corrugated iron residence with large windows and an imposing
entrance.*

At this point we must re-iterate: even to the poor the objective
of saving money must be placed within a broader framework. If it
means that the owner will be singled out as peculiar and thereby will
loose his self-respect it may simply not be worth it. He would
prefer to build a smaller and conventional house, or postpone the

---

*Similarly, even modern materials (of which concrete is the best
example) can be used in such a way as to single them out as poor
housing. Large panel re-inforced concrete walls, for example, are a
clear indicator, even in developed countries, of mass housing, and
as such become associated with people who can afford nothing better.

task until more money is available*.

This consideration leads us into the third impediment in the introduction of new technology for the poor:

3. What a house says is at least as important as what it does

In Zambia we undertook a number of studies into the way that people perceived their housing, and what they would like to have given either a limited amount of money, or by way of an "Ideal House".** One of the first points we noted about the responses was that the standard of construction is more important than space for the majority of people. In other words they would prefer to have one room that is well built than two that are built of poorer materials, preferring to suffer the constrictions of a single room while they are saving up to build additional ones, to living in comparative comfort in a structure that does not reflect well on them.

The second point we noticed was that certain features were considered very important, while others were hardly important at all. Windows and entrances have a symbolic power that no amount of space has: thus even in poor houses the entrance was often decorated so as to make it appear more important and imposing. Even in houses that did not in fact have any windows at all, windows would be painted on - not, I am sure primarily as decoration, as there were many other forms of decoration within the vernacular - but to associate the house with the moneyed class who could afford windows.

We also undertook surveys into plot use, and found that whereas the area provided in many state-built houses was quite large - enough to provide a regular supply of vegetables - the amount of land cultivated for vegetable growing was rather small, even though the residents were unarguably in need of nutritional and financial supplementation. By comparison a lot of effort was put into planting trees and flowers in front of the house, so as to beautify it and make it more similar to the expensive houses that were very much larger in themselves.

We also studied furnishing patterns (in houses occupied by those who had risen above the lowest income groups, typically those who had a limited amount of secondary schooling) and found that furniture was selected with scant regard to the functional limitations of the space in which it was to be situated. It was not uncommon for the rooms to be so full of furniture that there was practically no room to move in or out of them. Typically, while the living room was stuffed with heavily upholstered three piece suites, the bedrooms were very sparsely furnished, and the children were sleeping on no more than a blanket on the floor. We concluded that these are indicators of the

---

* President Nyerere of Tanzania noted this phenomenon, as this extract from the Arusha Declaration (1977) shows: "People refuse to build a house of burnt bricks and tiles, they insist on waiting for a tin roof and "European soil" - cement. If we want to progress more rapidly in the future we must overcome at least some of these mental blocks." (my emphasis).
** This and other matters discussed in this section are described and illustrated in more detail in Martin:1976 p 626-34

importance of "appearances" and that status symbolism can override functional considerations.*

We came to the conclusion that this phenomenon is a sympton of a highly mobile society. As with urban society in Britain in the 19th century, or suburban life in the US in the 1960s, the urban areas of Africa are places of great stress, where the security of being among life-time family and friends has been replaced by a system in which no one knows who or what you are other than by what they see.

There are other implications for design inherent in this state of affairs, but for the purpose of this paper, we only need to note that housing is a good that attracts considerable attention as a symbol, and therefore we must be aware that building materials and technology may also be selected for their symbolic value.

Technology transfer: are there any solutions?

It is always easier to describe what has gone wrong than it is to prescribe how to do it properly. However, experience has taught us something on which we can build a better procedural model.

In order to explain it I want to refer to the "top down/bottom up" dichotomy, which has unfortunately become cliched and therefore requires some explanation. To understand the problem we shall consider the example of how corrugated iron has become part of the vernacular of the tropics, even though it is in many respects grossly unsuitable. In the colonial period corrugated iron was widely used, because of its ease of carriage, low cost and resistance to water penetration. It was introduced as an imported modern material: a product of the high technology of rolling mills and galvanising tanks; used by the colonial power and its citizens for housing and a multitude of other tasks. Gradually, as incomes rose and building patterns changed, corrugated iron came to be used by much poorer classes of people, until today it is in almost universal use as a roofing material for the urban poor. However it remains a symbol of progress, and there are many households, especially in the rural areas, who aspire to a house roofed with it. This material was, we could say, introduced by a top-down method.

As I have already commented above, however, the present tendency is to introduce materials by a bottom-up method, i.e. by starting with the poor, saying "because you are poor you need special materials: here they are, just get on and use them and you will see the difference". Unfortunately, as I have also pointed out above, this does not work for a multitude of reasons. But there is one overriding cause for the situation: even though the material is being introduced

---

* There is an interesting example from Pakistan f this phenomenon. An organisation in Karachi built a low-cost house at half the current construction costs. Two co-operative societies volunteered to adopt the system, but when detailed consultations were held, the President of one of the societies said that the plans were unacceptable because they did not provide a drawing room. "Where will the workers keep their sofa sets and TV?" he asked. "I was stunned" the director of the organisation said later,"What dawned on me that day was that housing cannot be detached from lifestyle". (Agarwal,1981:p63)

from the bottom up economically, it comes from the top
down politically. In other words the people are not being helped to
find their own solutions but are instead being told what is good for
them.

The two true alternatives are therefore (1) the laissez-faire
approach by which corrugated iron and concrete blocks were introduced, i.e. under which materials are first used by upper income
groups and then filter down to lower income groups as their incomes
rise or as lower cost versions of the technology are developed;* and
(2) not to introduce a new material to the poor but to find out from
them what materials they really want or need, and help them to develop them. This all sounds rather fanciful, but I shall use an
example, again from Zambia, to demonstrate how it can work.

We were working very hard to inculcate into the minds of the
people that concrete block was an extravagant and unnecessarily expensive material, and that soil cement could do the job just as well at
a much lower price. However, as I have pointed out above, this programme was not a success. Meanwhile we noticed that one or two house-
holders had started making their own concrete blocks instead of
buying them from the building materials store that we provided. By
making them themselves they were saving less than 20%, but this
saving was important enough for people to put considerable effort
into it. Within a few days - literally no more - the small group
that had started to make concrete blocks on their own had mushroomed
into a sizeable number, and soon it seemed as if everyone was doing
it. But enthusiasm went too far: while some might have understood
the right way of making concrete blocks, many did not, and the
results were far from good. They made the mix too wet, they allowed
them to dry too quickly, they put them on rough ground after moulding
and they used dirty materials. Doubtless many participants even lost
money by making these mistakes. However the initiative was there,
and it was clear that this was the direction in which innovation
should be helped. We therefore decided to lend official support to
the make-your-own-blocks-movement by doing the following:
1. We hired out steel moulds for making hollow blocks at a nominal
charge thus enabling a considerable saving in materials, as well as a
dimensionally more consistent block as compared with the solid blocks
from wooden moulds made previously.
2. We advised all people who were making the blocks on the correct
mix, the need for proper curing, for flat surfaces to be used during
drying, and on the importance of using clean materials.
3. We made sure that our stores supplied sand and aggregate for
block making, commodities that had not previously been very plentiful or easy to obtain by participants.

While the blocks made by individuals in this way were not as
strong as those supplied commercially, they were nevertheless adequate for the simple buildings erected by the participants. When

---

*A committee set up in Kerala, India, to look at ways of lowering the
cost of houses was aware of this problem. They wrote: "We decry any
move towards Low-Cost Housing for 'the Poor'. Reform, rethinking,
replanning and redesigning must start at the top and spread through
all strata of society."(Agarwal,1981:p57)

we came to re-look at the economics of making soil-cement blocks as
compared to those of making concrete blocks, we had to concede that
there was little to choose between them. Soil cement blocks required
much more care in the mixing and making; they were considerably
smaller, thus requiring more mortar and labour in the wall building;
and they were generally less resistant to rain. Taking these factors
into account concrete blocks, if self made, had a definite, if
slight, advantage.

In the language of community development, this processs of developing a new approach to a building material is called answering a
felt need. Possibly it is because many materials which look good to
a technologist do not answer a felt need that they are not more
widely adopted. But if we KNOW that we have a new and very special
building technology or material, is there any way in which it can be
introduced successfully?

In my view building technologies are like any consumer product:
they have to be tested on the market. This can be done either by the
community development approach of discussing with the people what
their priorities are, and if a technology fits their needs, then
helping them to use it; or by the "vacuum cleaner salesman" approach
of trying to convince people that they DO NEED IT, whether they
really think they do or not, in the hope that once other people see
the new system in operation they will want to copy.

Realistically speaking however, this is the wrong question to be
addressing: it is not how to introduce a new material or technology
that we should be considering, and it is because the question has
been asked in this way that we have so often gone wrong. What we
should be asking instead is: "how can we, with our technological
resources support the house building efforts of the poor?" In order
to do this most effectively we must first better understand the
process by which the poor assemble their housing: their technical
terms of reference, their financial constraints, their priorities,
and their perception of what shelter should really do. It is only
with informed answers to these questions that technologists can fully
fulfil their role. While the understanding of the problems and procedures of low income people has improved dramatically in the last few
years, it is not until this becomes part of the language of technology that technology will be able to fulfil its real role in
helping the poor to obtain better shelter.

REFERENCES

Agarwal, Anil, 1981: Mud Mud, The potential of earth-based materials
for Third World Housing, Earthscan, London

Bryant, Coralie and White, Louise G. 1982: Managing Development in
the Third World, Westview Press, Boulder, Colorado.

Jedlicka, Allen, 1978: Delivery Systems for Rural Development, paper presented at the National Meeting of the American Academy for the Advancement of Science, February 23 1978, quoted in Rybczynski, Witold: Paper Heroes, Prism Press Dorchester, 1980, p125.

Martin, Richard, 1974. The Architecture of Underdevelopment, or The Route to Self Determination in Design. In Architectural Design, Vol XLIV October 1974, pp 626-634.

Martin, Richard, 1978. The Role of the Implementing Agency in Self-Help Projects: A Case Study from Lusaka. In Planning and Administration, Vol 5, No 2 Autumn 1978, pp 7-14.

LOW COST HOUSING BEGINS WITH AN OVERALL ASSESSMENT OF POSSIBLE MATERIALS

NEVILLE R HILL, Consultant, United Kingdom.

1. *Introduction*

Methods and designs for existing traditional dwellings have developed gradually in a manner similar to the evolution of species. They have evolved so as to provide, with whatever resources have been available, reasonably durable shelters that have been livable under the prevailing conditions.

Unless thoroughly thought out, and tried by the local people, attempts to introduce materials or designs which are new to the area are very likely to prove to be inappropriate, as has happened, for instance, with blocks of flats only thirteen years old in Glasgow. Unfortunately, there has arisen among the authorities of many developing countries, a kind of prejudice against traditional materials, such as mud and thatch and even stone.

Another familiar result of the adoption of ideas and materials from industrialized nations is that schemes for so-called low cost housing are providing homes for wage earners and middle class people whilst neglecting the need for improved accommodation for the people who live and work 'on the land'. The Brandt Commission reported that one recent study showed that one-third to two-thirds of even those families living in the cities, such as Hong Kong, Madras, Mexico City and here in Nairobi, could not afford the cheapest new housing currently being built.

This paper proposes that there should be a multi-disciplinary approach to the selection of materials and the designs of the houses in which they are incorporated. There is a wide variety of factors that influences the achievement of a successful low cost housing project, especially in rural areas, and suggestions are made for some of the many possible sources where the necessary information upon which to base the choice of building materials should be sought.

2. *Overall assessment of the possible raw materials*

The factors that affect the successful implementation of a housing project in rural areas are so numerous and diverse that a single person probably will not have the width of experience in the field to achieve the system of construction and selection of materials that will prove most appropriate. Ideally the project manager will be someone having an overall knowledge of building construction and performance of materials, able to appreciate the factors influencing cost and keep them clearly in mind and also be able to gain the co-operation of people ranging from government ministers to village headmen.

2.1 Project team
Except in the smaller projects, the project manager will need to have the full or in some cases perhaps part-time support in the project team of at least the following staff.
    A qualified builder able to adapt to possible unfamiliar materials but with sound construction ability.
    A specialist, usually a geologist, well acquainted with the properties and possible uses of the inorganic and non-metallic natural and waste materials and their likely occurrence.
    A specialist in naturally occurring organic materials and their utilization, especially timber but including bamboo and all other vegetation.
    If the project manager is not already an architect then a person able to design for living under the particular climatic and other local conditions will also be in the team.   This person will work closely with an assistant, co-opted into the team, who speaks the local language(s) and has lived in the area under consideration. Such a person may already be a community worker in the area or be working as a social anthropologist at the university.
    Whoever are recruited to work in the project should have a flexible, free-thinking outlook and be capable of seeking and receiving from anywhere information and ideas that might benefit the aims of the project.   Otherwise there might be further cases arising like the community who preferred to put their cattle in their new houses because of the condensation or those who refused to sleep under roofs covered with clay tiles as to them it signified that they would then be already on the way the their graves.

2.2 Sources for information and co-operation
After the preliminary meetings with the economic planning department and any others dealing with overall development objectives, the project team should carry out as soon as possible an initial recon-naissance of both where the houses may be built and, ideally, also the former home area of the people being re-housed. These are often not the same location and in the case of refugees and transmigration schemes can be separated by hundreds of kilometres. The team has to see the geography of the area, especially in relation to natural resources, such as water, climate, communications, cultivation, type of existing houses, if any, availability of other services such as electricity possibly and so on. The team can then better visualize what is being referred to during subsequent meetings elsewhere.
    At this stage some of the people in the area will be met, includ-ing for instance the headman and schoolteacher, for whom the houses are to be built. Calls can be made on any local mission stations and any other projects or rural development offices located in the area. Nearly always missionaries, such as the White Fathers in Malawi, produced their own bricks and tiles for building their churches and

houses. Sometimes the equipment they used may still exist there.
Obviously, brief inspection should be made of any site where a saw
mill, limekiln, brickworks or quarry operates or formerly existed
and similarly with any present building activity. Places where by-
product materials may be available should be checked and can include
rice mills, sugar factories and abattoirs.

Following the initial visit to the field, there will then be a
series of enquiries, mainly in the capital, to obtain advice and
information concerning conditions in the area under study. As
already mentioned, the bodies working on the national development
plan will advise on the status of the area. It may be that it has
been designated for tourism or be due to be flooded by the waters of
a hydro-electric scheme. There are numerous other departments that
may have significant information.

The lands or survey office will have maps. The geological survey
department will be visited at an early stage for advice on the
occurrence and known characteristics of the non-metallic rock and
mineral resources, i.e. the industrial minerals and fossil fuels.
In addition to the specialist in industrial minerals, much assistance
should be available from the area geologist who has been mapping to
a scale of 1:50,000. Geological survey departments may be able to
test and evaluate some of the potential raw materials. The ones
likely to be of most interest to the project team are stone,
including slate, clays as well as mud and earth, limestones, sulphur,
gypsum, pozzolanas, sands and coarse aggregates, decorating materials
such as ochres and white clays, bitumen, coals and peat. Sometimes
the department of mines will know of quarrying operations and be able
to co-operate but sadly their personnel mostly are engaged on
metalliferous mining projects. Governments still seem to be
reluctant to accept that the numerous small scale operations digging
limestone, clays, sands, gravels, etc. are a part of the mining
industry.

The land husbandry, agriculture and forestry departments and
research stations should know about the available timber and broad
leaf species, the possibility of establishing fast-growing tree
plantations, the bamboo, grasses and reeds, the cereal crop straw
and other agricultural wastes and the saw-milling operations that
exist.

The availability and price of national and imported building
materials, such as cement, iron sheets, nails, etc. can be checked
with the ministry of public works and supplies. The ministry of
industry and the chamber of trade may know of factories having
particular materials available. It was found that a textile factory
in Malawi had 10 tonne a day of boiler ash requiring disposal and
the fishing net factory had a large quantity of offcuts of synthetic
netting material.

There are sometimes so many UN and foreign aid organizations with
specialists and projects in the country that keeping abreast on who
is doing what amongst them, that might have a bearing on the work of
the low cost housing project, may itself be difficult. This is
where briefings by the UN resident representative and his staff can
come up with important contacts. The project manager should see
that such offices are kept advised of their activities, even if the

project is not already being mounted by one of the UN organisations, and opportunities should be taken for bringing the project's work to a wider audience through the media, particularly the local press.

Traditional housing and the materials used are unlikely to make sudden major changes. Centuries of experience have shown people which local materials and methods best provide them with a satisfactory shelter, though its durability may not be all that they would wish. Sometimes, the methods previously used, and which may have been introduced by foreigners, become forgotten. This was the case with the mortar technology including use of pozzolanas brought to Britain when it was invaded by the Romans. Here is where it may pay to get ideas from the museum and the archaeologists. Similarly, the previous history, beliefs, native skills, methods and materials of a particular tribe may be worth discussing with an anthropologist.

Whatever materials and systems are finally selected for low cost rural housing they have to be within the capability of the local people to use and maintain by themselves. Otherwise the numbers of houses required will never be built and their overall cost will be beyond the reach of the people who subsist and don't earn money to pay for a house builder.

3. *Some recommendations*

There has to be a multi-disciplinary approach to the selection and utilization of the materials if there is to be the best chance of finding the most appropriate to use for a particular low cost housing project, especially in the rural areas. A geologist specializing in the evaluation and methods of utilizing the industrial (non-metallic) rocks and minerals should be included in the project team or at least be co-opted part-time at an early stage.

Planning, including the selection of materials, takes place only after a good knowledge has been gained on the ground of the conditions at the proposed site(s) and particularly of the local resources that exist.

One should try and prevent low cost housing ending up as homes for the wage earners and middle class when it has been intended originally for the poorest section of the community who may be those who subsist by cultivating the land. Perhaps those who live in the rural areas would best be provided for by showing them how to adapt and improve upon the traditional methods they have used with locally occurring materials.

Specialists in particular systems and materials should be recruited only when the most appropriate to adopt have been identified and agreed.

Reference

1. Independent Commission on International Development Issues, Chairman: Willy Brandt, (1980). Report:'North-South: a Programme for Survival'.

MATERIALS FOR BUILDING HOUSES - SOME CASE HISTORIES FROM HOME AND
OVERSEAS

NEVILLE R HILL, Consultant, United Kingdom.

1. *Introduction*

This paper aims to illustrate, by case histories from the author's
own experience in a dozen developing countries over the past ten
years, situations that have arisen including examples of ways to
develop and use local building materials. The intention is to show
not only certain inappropriate situations that have developed but
also to give wider publicity to what seem to be correct approaches to
making use of the local resources that exist. Firstly, though, it is
suggested that everyone working in this field should examine, at
least briefly, the materials that have been used for building houses
in one's own home area and see how the present situation may have to
adjust if conditions change in future.

2. *Some case histories*

2.1 Central Southern England

Before the railways were built in the 19th century, the typical
materials used for construction of ordinary dwellings were wattle and
daub, mud block, rammed earth, timber and, for the roof thatch, long
straw. Those who could afford to would also use fired clay bricks
and roof tiles, stone such as flints from the Upper Chalk of the
Cretaceous Period and Oligocene Bembridge Limestone from the 7 m
thick bed that occurs on the north shore of the Isle of Wight.
Numerous lime kilns were located on the Chalk of the South Downs and
the lime was used in mortar and as a decorative and hygienic coating.
   The only materials, apart from smaller, higher cost items such as
nails and other hardware, that were brought in to this area came by
sea and included roofing slate, also used for damp-proof courses,
from North Wales, reed, for a longer lasting thatch, from Norfolk in
East Anglia and coal, for firing the brick, tile and lime kilns, from
the north-east of England ('coals from Newcastle').
   Manufacture of cement in the area began about 1840 on the River
Medina in the Isle of Wight. To begin with an improved Roman cement
was made, though the high lime content 'cement stones' had to be
brought from the Jurassic clays on the mainland coast and later even
dredged from the sea. However, by 1848 the Medina cement works was
experiencing competition for engineering projects from the superior

strength of the true Portland cement then becoming available, the
process for which had been discovered by both William Aspdin and
Johnson a few years earlier. The Medina works then changed to burning chalk mixed with mud or blue clay from beside the Medina river.
Other works in the region were at Newhaven and Shoreham on the Sussex
coast, a small plant on the River Itchen near Southampton and also at
Lyme Regis in Dorset, from 1899, using the Jurassic Blue Lias
argillaceous limestone. The significance of ready access to
transport by water can be noted from the location of these works,
which also were served by railways, e.g. the London, Brighton and
South Coast Railway.

With improved transportation, firstly by the railways and then at
the beginning of the present century by motorized road vehicles, it
became possible to transport building materials by greater distances
overland. This and rising labour costs meant that the manufacture
of building materials came to be concentrated on a few large plants.
Only two small lime plants are still working within the region. In
the county of Hampshire only five brick and tile works are operating
whereas in the late 19th century more than a hundred existed.
Architects like the appearance of hand-made bricks and these can sell
for six times the price of the mass produced wire-cut and machine-
pressed bricks. Production of sand-lime bricks has declined. Gypsum
plaster and board are made in the east of the region. Portland
cement delivered to the middle of the area, say Southampton, has to
come nearly 100 km by road from the nearest factory. Not only is it
being used now in mortars and concrete, much of which is delivered
from ready-mixed plants, but cement-based artificial stone has
displaced natural stone and fired clay roof tiles have been almost
completely substituted by coloured concrete tiles. In addition, the
reinforcing steel for concrete comes from the Midlands of England and
the wood for the timber-frame houses so common now comes mostly from
Scandinavia.

In effect then, and especially since 1973, the building materials
being consumed in central southern England are largely dependent on
one material, Portland cement, of which fossil fuel constitutes a
large proportion of the manufacturing cost and much extra fuel has
to be burnt to deliver it. Presumably, this situation can be
tolerated whilst there are national sources of coal and oil and the
level of per capita income is able to stand the cost – the price of
cement in the U.K. is around £45 (US$70) a tonne.

There are some signs that the trend may not continue. A company
is now doing good business supplying and fixing a stone cladding to
improve the appearance of houses that were built in the first decades
of this century, and people are restoring other older houses or re-
using the materials from those that have to be demolished.

Unfortunately, in many developing countries, especially in Africa,
it is common to find energy intensive materials, such as cement and
corrugated galvanized iron sheets, being transported great distances
to housing projects, despite the absence of an indigenous supply of
fuel for the vehicles and lack of adequate levels of income to pay
for the materials, except for the more wealthy people.

2.2 Caroline Islands (Pacific Ocean)

These islands were administered as a trust territory on behalf of the
United Nations from 1945. They are perhaps the best known example
of what happens when aid is supplied in the form of an administration
with cash but few training programmes or creation of incentives to
develop the natural resources, apart from a little tourism.

There are clays that were used during the Japanese occupation to
make good quality bricks and roof tiles but there has been no
production since then. Coral limestone is abundant but there is no
lime manufacture. Some igneous rock occurs but the quarry was opened
only to produce aggregate for the airport runway. There is a luxur-
iant growth of vegetation but no timber is developed and, apart from
copra production, no local fruit is seen being marketed. The houses
are built of metal; it is rare to see stone used.

A new house, being erected in 1979, had a timber frame of imported
Douglas fir and larch, the walls, doors and roof were made of 26
gauge flat galvanized steel plate from Japan, aluminium window frames
with glass louvres (from Belgium?) and the cement for the concrete
floor was made in Taiwan. The only local material used was stones
from the beach to make up the concrete foundation slab.

These buildings are, of course, very hot to live in. (So are the
few modern tourist hotels when the electric power fails as there is
no provision for cooling breezes to circulate or for the walls to be
shaded as was customary before electricity became available in
tropical countries).

2.3 South-east Asia

A government, with multilateral aid, had a programme to transmigrate
people into areas of very low population density. Original forest
still exists there. There was a standard specification for the
houses: compacted earth floor, timber from the contractor's own local
saw mill for the frame and walls and roofs of corrugated galvanized
iron. Their area is 35 m^2 and the contractor was receiving US$500,
in 1977, for each house completed. Owners said that their houses
were hot and noisy when it rained. Owners own extensions were being
roofed with a type of panel made from palm leaves. Many of the
occupiers would have preferred tiled roofs. Some of them knew how
to make bricks and tiles and clays within 15 km had been used for
that purpose by people native to the area.

In another 'pioneer' region, having one of the few remaining great
rain forests, the local government offices are furnished with
imported chairs, tables and filing cabinets made of steel and plastic.
The residences for government officials were prefabricated houses
delivered from Singapore. The transmigrants houses had an identical
specification to those mentioned already and in 1978 cost US$1200
each, i.e. US$34 per m2. After two years some of the galvanized
iron sheets were already corroding. There were more expensive houses
being erected, having a concrete tile floor, concrete block walls and
asbestos cement roofs and in 1978 these cost US$240 per m^2 to build.
The retail price of the cement was US$135 a tonne. However, this was
less than a quarter of the price reached by the time it had been
delivered to an isolated valley in the mountains, accessible only by
aircraft, where it was used in constructing government buildings and

houses.   In that valley deposits of limestone were well exposed and
there were some disused lime kilns there. Missionaries have
established brick making but roof tiles were said to get blown off
by the wind.   (In Grenada, in the East Caribbean, the 1955 hurricane
stripped off the iron sheets whereas there the tiled and thatched
roofs performed quite well).
     At another location, closer to the capital, a chipboard factory
had been delivered and erected under US$4.8 million of bilateral aid
from a West European government. Its ambassador had proposed this
project as a means of providing low cost housing. The formaldehyde
resins were being imported from Europe. Problems arose in making the
chipboard panels weatherproof and after two years operation it was
decided that the chipboard houses were proving to be too costly.

2.4   East Caribbean
The well established and successful walling material is now concrete
blocks. These are based on Portland cement, imported from the
periphery of the region and retailing in 1980 at US$136 a tonne, but
do of course consume local aggregate. On one island the blocks are
lightweight as the aggregate is a pumiceous tuff. On a neighbouring
island the blocks are very much heavier as a haematite-bearing sand
from stream beds is used, even though, as was demonstrated, huge
resources of good pumiceous tuff exist unexploited there.
     Even so, where the pumice aggregate was being used there had been
no attempt to exploit the local limestone to make lime so as to be
able to produce lime-pozzolana blocks, like the successful 'batako'
blocks in Indonesia. This would have been a far more logical development than the bilateral aid project aimed at introducing a different
product, fired clay bricks, from clay resources that are not of
especially good quality. Not surprisingly, as there was no price
advantage from building with the bricks, they have received little
or no support from the local private building contractors. This
island has plenty of fuel wood available.
     The small islands, several of which have deposits of volcanic ash,
should be, like the Canary Islands, a classic case for the concept of
small cement mills, grinding imported Portland cement clinker and
gypsum together with the volcanic ash, as well as any local limestone,
to make Portland pozzolanic cement and Portland masonry cement. Both
of these would be more appropriate for the type of market than would
ordinary Portland cement. Even so, on one island there are plans to
build a cement kiln with a capacity such that to be fully utilized
it would need an increase in market demand on the island itself and
from neighbouring islands of over 400% and there is no known
indication that such a demand will arise in the foreseeable future.

2.5   Paraguay
Cement and lime kilns should be established as close as practicable
to the limestone quarry because of the substantial weight losses that
occur during firing. One of the few justifiable and successful
exceptions to this rule exists in Paraguay. There the major mineral
resource is the limestone at Vallemi, around 400 km upstream of the
capital Asuncion, on the River Paraguay. On the limestone is the
cement factory and also the centre for lime production. Besides the

transportation of the cement and lime by river barge to the capital, some limestone also is sent there for consuption by lime kilns operating competitively beside the river.

Despite the availability of Portland cement, house building in Paraguay continues to use lime: sand mortars, with the quicklime being slaked in a shallow pit on the construction site. At one time grey, hydraulic lime was made from thin siliceous limestones 165 km by road east of the capital. Although much better located in relation to the market, the industry there has dwindled mainly as a result of prejudice against the colour compared with the white lime made from Vallemi limestone.

2.6 Ethiopia

It is unfortunate that wood is such a satisfactory fuel for lime-making and so much deforestation has been caused. Eucalyptus sp. was introduced into Ethiopia about 100 years ago and large plantations exist near Addis Ababa. The principal lime producing area is around Ambo and Guder 130 km west of the capital but the fuel for the small kilns now has to be charcoal which is brought in on the backs of donkeys. Before being fed in to the kilns, the charcoal is soaked in water to make it burn with some of the advantages of wood. Here is an obvious instance where the possibility of establishing fast growing tree plantations close to the kilns should be investigated. Lime is being used as a whitewash for decorating the exteriors of shops and houses. Rain removes the whitewash from the lower, unprotected parts of the walls. Ethiopia, though, has many cattle and in local butcher's shops tallow could be bought, in 1979, for the equivalent of US$0.25 per kg. The quicklime sells for US$0.10 per kg. By adding about one part of tallow to twelve parts of quicklime during the slaking with water, an effective, water-resistant white paint was produced on site for the equivalent of only US$0.34 for 12 litres. That quantity is adequate to decorate the exterior of a small rural dwelling.

These examples illustrate the wide range of materials and type of problem that have to be dealt with in making appropriate building materials for low cost housing.

2.7 Malawi

Karonga District is in the far north, at the end of Lake Malawi and adjacent to the border with Tanzania. The distance from the national cement factory is around 600 km and only a little less from the nearest lime producing centre in the country. In Karonga, the retail price of Portland cement in 1982 was quite expensive at the equivalent of US$175 per tonne, but white hydrated lime was double this price at US$360. White PVA emulsion paint there retailed at US$17.3 for 5 litres. The Geological Survey Department has been able to demonstrate, by means of small scale field firing and slaking trials, that white limewash can be made from small deposits of limestone in the District. In addition to wood fuel there are shallow deposits of coal there as yet unexploited.

Farmers have improved their homes by re-building with bricks which they fired in field kilns beside the road close to the house. Sufficient extra bricks were burned for sale direct from the kiln.

The rammed-earth method is widely practiced, with good results, for building rural houses. The walls can be constructed very cheaply at the equivalent of US$27 for 28 m² houses to US$50 for 60m² in 1982. 'Plastering', inside and out with a thin slurry of clean sand and mud, cost US$20 to US$32 respectively. The construction of walls is not a problem in this area. Appropriate local alternatives are needed, though, in the materials for the roof, imported corrugated galvanized iron sheets, which with its timber supporting structure, together account for 75% of the total cost of these houses. Grass thatch, though, remains the usual roofing material for traditional rural houses in Malawi but in places it is in short supply. Until recently the authorities were said to be against using thatch for official low cost housing schemes but there are signs that attitudes to choice of building materials may have become more flexible, probably through the influence of a UNCHS low cost housing project started a few years ago.

2.8 Botswana
A common problem with many geological survey departments is that the good work in the field, laboratory and drawing office ends up as maps and reports on shelves in government offices. There is always plenty of interest and offers of funding if the findings relate to possible occurrences of hydrocarbons, copper, nickel and other prestigious materials. On the other hand, the data on the location and performance of non-metallic rocks and minerals, especially the higher bulk volume materials used for building purposes, are seldom transferred into a form that benefits the poorer, and usually illiterate, people who could be prepared to manufacture bricks, tiles, lime and alternative cements, etc. There has to be a unit which can demonstrate to the potential entrepreneurs and village co-operatives how to use the clays, limestones, gypsum, pozzolanic materials and stone in their area. The same seems to be true also for other materials such as boiler ash, agricultural wastes and other by-products.

The work of the Southern Rural Development Association, P.O.Box 343, Kanye, Botswana is one possible approach which seems worthy of consideration by other countries. SRDA is also the type of implementing organisation that can be funded and staffed initially through external aid so as to identify and establish workable projects which can eventually be handed over, when shown to be viable, to local groups or individual entrepreneurs.

Through one of its six trusts, the Mineral Holding Trust established in 1982, SRDA can already claim several successes in the development of small scale production of building materials based on the non-metallic rock and mineral resources in its area. Until recently, slate was being imported from South Africa for paving but this can now be supplied from MHTs own quarry. Production of lime and fired clay bricks has begun, fuelled by Botswana coal, whereas previously there was no manufacture in the Southern District. The villagers digging mineral iron oxide to provide red and yellow pigments have been organized and given an assured market. Dumps of mine waste have been purchased and this is crushed to provide various grades of aggregate. (Talc also occurs in the mine dumps and now is to be upgraded prior to export).

The progress of these projects has been greatly assisted by the Geological Survey Department, especially its industrial minerals geologist, in Lobatse and who made freely available to MHT their information and analysed the materials under consideration. SRDA/MHT has been the catalyst that has converted the geological maps and reports into actual small scale mining which is now achieving local self-sufficiency in building materials.

References

1. Francis, A.J. (1977), The Cement Industry, 1796-1914: A History David & Charles, Newton Abbot, UK.
2. Hampshire Industrial Archaeology: A Guide. (1975). Southampton University Industrial Archaeology Group, Southampton, UK.
3. McHenry, D. (1970 ?), Micronesia: Trust Betrayed. Published in the USA.

THE USE OF LOCALLY AVAILABLE AGGREGATES IN JORDAN FOR THE DEVELOPMENT
OF LOW COST HOUSING, JORDANIAN EXPERIENCE

DR. RUHI SHARIF, Director, Building Research Center,
Royal Scientific Society

1. *Housing Problem*

The shortage of adequate housing is prevailant in most countries of
the world. The problem in the developing countries, is more acute and
it has reached in some countries to a crisis level. The estimated
demand for housing units in the year 2000 is around 730 million units
in the developing countries and 41.2 units in the Arab world(1).

   All suffer from the fact that a majority of their populations live
in substandard housing; characterized by overcrowding, lack of bath-
rooms, inadequate sources of potable water, improper sanitation, lack
of services and general lack of requirements for dignified existence.
All are experiencing high rural migration to the cities and high
population growth. And all suffer, to varying degrees, from the low
income of the people in comparison to housing costs(2).

2. *Factors Leading To The Housing Problem*

   (1) Population growth and social development which increased
demand for more rooms in the house and more houses for big families.
   (2) Increasing urbanization and migration to cities.
   (3) Housing needs a relatively large amount of capital.
   (4) Housing has been given lower priority in the construction
sector and development plans.
   (5) Cost of housing in comparison to family income is too high.
   (6) Lack of a comprehensive housing program that takes into
consideration priority areas, population distribution and needs.
   (7) Rise in land prices.
   (8) Lack of skilled labour or the migration and movement of the
skilled labour to other countries in search of better pay.
   (9) The increase in construction costs due to inadequate supply of
materials and scarcity of labour.
   (10) The building industry and materials producers can not cope
with increasing demand for housing.
   (11) Deterioration of old houses which were built of low quality
material and were left without proper maintenance.
   (12) The non-existence in some countries of private firms or housing societies for housing construction for the limited income groups.

(13) Due to low return on the capital, investors were not willing to invest their money in unproductive sector.

3. *Low Cost Housing*

The main obstacles associated with the sustainable satisfaction of housing needs are the inability of people to pay for required housing arising from limited incomes and high building costs; the shortage of skilled labour and materials; and inadequate and inefficient traditional building technologies which add to the cost and slow down production.

The solution appears to lie in the development of low-cost housing construction systems based mainly: on the employment of alternative cheaper building materials and processes. The low cost house should be a house designed and manufactured as any other house with regard to foundations, structure, strength, etc. The reduction in cost will be in postponing finishings and in implementing them at stages, and in utilizing available building materials and products that are durable, economical, accepted by the public and do not need costly maintenance thus conserving the countries foreign currency holdings. It should aim at increasing the efficiency of workers, minimizing waste in design and space and applying good management. The system should respond to the needs of the community and utilize solar heat.

4. *Approach Adopted By Building Research Center*

The Building Research Center (BRC) of the Royal Scientific Society (RSS) has been able to develop a low cost housing system based on the following principles(3):

(1) The development of a semi-industrialized building construction system arising from indigenous technology and based on the core house approach, where the house is constructed of a sturdy durable carcass and designed such that additional rooms can be constructed and finishes and services improved until an adequate dwelling answering the needs and of good quality is achieved. This is an industrialization on a less comprehensive and less mechanized scale. It is a productive method employing mechanization to a certain extent that is based on organized processes of a repetitive character. The mechanization however, is simple, uncomplicated and easy to operate and to maintain. Moulds and machines required for the manufacture and assembly of components are manufactured locally.

(2) The rationalization and systemization of the building process to increase productivity and reduce waste in man-hours and materials.

(3) Better and more efficient building design and room dimensions to achieve optimum use of floor area and maximum economy, based on function, furniture and circulation.

(4) High technology has been avoided because it is difficult to absorb and it uses high capital. Breakdowns of machinery and shortage of skilled labour, technicians and engineers will cause the system to collapse.

(5) The system includes the manufacturing of moulds and machines and a well designed small factory for the production of components of

good quality and production control. It is an efficient system for
the transport and storage of components and a simple method of erection requiring minimum skills and machinery.

(6) No cost reductions may be made at the expense of quality and
durability. Real cost reductions as related to the construction can
be made in the rationalization of process, elimination of waste and
redundancy and reducing the need for skilled labour.

(7) Modular coordination is an essential requirement for rational-
ized construction.

(8) Future expansion has been provided for, either horizontally
or vertically.

(9) The system has comprised a small number of component types and
a yet smaller number of basic moulds that can produce many types.

(10) The components have been designed to perform several functions
(local bearing, space enclosing).

(11) For manual handling and transport of components, a maximum
weight of 25 kg per man was adopted.

12 different components are used in the system and all 12 components are made of concrete. The basic hollow concrete walling block
is of the modular dimensions 600 mm long, 200 mm thick and 200 mm
high. It is manufactured in a special mould using an ordinary block
making machine. The basic block wieghs 22 kg. Blocks fit on top of
each other without mortar. Instead, concrete is poured in the enclo-
sure between two adjacent blocks, thus forming columns spaced 600 mm
apart which carry slab beams. Other blocks as tie blocks and corner
blocks are used. The slab consists of precast beams spaced 600 mm
apart. These spaces are filled with hollow blocks similar to those
used in traditional ceilings. The walls are covered with special
pieces to close opening in walls thus allowing for pouring concrete
for peripheral beam and topping. Other pieces of precast elements are
used for lintels, sills and stair treads.

5. *Study On The Development And Control Of Cement Blocks Industry*

Traditional buildings in Jordan are: stone bearing walls with concrete
roofs; concrete frames .filled with stone curtain walls, blocks or
concrete; and concrete or block bearing walls with concrete roofs(5).
In the Jordan Valley thick mud walls buildings have been used for a
while. Recently, fire clay bricks and sand lime bricks have been
introduced for curtain and bearing walls at small scale.

Cement blocks industry is an old and important industry which is
distributed all over the country. There are around 700 factories
distributed over cities and villages producing around 75.5 million
blocks of different sizes each year at a cost of 25 million dollars(6).
Building Research Center of Royal Scientific Society in cooperation
with Directorate of Standards and Specifications has started in 1979
a quality control project on cement blocks. The steps and procedures
adopted in this study included a questionnaire inquiring about type
and size of production, equipment used, manpower, prices, materials,
testing etc. Factories producing cement blocks were identified and
visited by a joint team from BRC and Directorate of Specifications.
They were asked to fill in the questionnare. Block samples were taken

from them and these were tested at BRC and results were analysed and published. Cement block factories which were given questionnaires were 435, of which 392 were reclaimed. Moreover, 2025 block specimens were brought from 137 factories and tested.

Study included investigation into dimensions, density, process of manufacturing, areas occupied by factories, block making machines, raw materials used such as cement, aggregates and water, man power, production, strength and cavities.

Results of analysis show that there is little control on propor tioning of blocks ingredients, on water cement ratio, slump, mixing, grading, curing and transporting and shaking of blocks. These caused reduction in strength, improper evenness, and wide variations in dimensions and densities. Densities vary between 1.7 to 2 kg/cm^3. The 28 day compressive strength ranges from 12 - 104 kg/cm^2. This means that although this industry is wide spread and important, yet, production needs more control.

6. *Aggregates Industry*

There are around 265 quarries in Jordan producing 18 million cubic meters of crushed limestone aggregates per year half of which is used in concrete whereas the other half is used in roads. In addition,there are 20 sand pits producing around 2 million cubic meters yearly and 85 building stone quarries. This is apart from wadi gravel taken from rivers and a part from some other types of aggregates such as tuff, trippoli, basalt, barite, sand stone and granite which are used in small quantities. In fact, the main source of aggregates in Jordan is limestone which tend to be very stratified with marl, occur throughout the country and soft. Basalts and granites are very hard, whereas wadi gravels, tend to be small sized and rounded, presenting problems in satisfying specification clauses. Moreover, the sand stones are too weak to be used as coarse aggregates, and they are used after crushing as fine aggregates.

6.1 Quality control on quarries

In 1977, the Building Research Center (BRC) started a joint quality control project with Natural Resources Authority (NRA) on crushed aggregates, building stone and natural sand quarries operating in different parts of the country(7). The ultimate objective of the work is to:

(1) Study the properties of produced aggregates, classify material into different grades, upgrade material at the production site, instead of construction site, thus giving good material for all consumers and save their money and their lives.

(2) Classify quarries according to quality of production(5).

(3) Compile comprehensive data on distribution of quarries, size of production, type of aggregates, man power and equipment.

(4) Upgrade the quality of concrete structure, concrete mixes and blocks which suffered during the last ten years due to the fact that crushed aggregates contained high percentage of soft particles and high percentage of fines passing 75 microns mesh.

(5) Identify problems and suggest solutions that will improve methods of quarrying and increase production.

(6) Develop specifications that take into consideration local materials and conditions.

6.2 Procedures adopted in quarrying

Since limestone quarries are composed of strata varying in strength and depth and separated by thin layers of marl, it is necessary to quarry one layer at a time, discard soft layers and crush hard stones. This should be proceded by cleaning the top soil and removing all un- suitable materials.

This is the ideal situation but, unfortunately, owners of quarries do not always follow this procedure. Instead, they mix all layers together including marl and they dump everything in the crusher. The crushed aggregates are stockpiled on the soil instead of concrete floors. When loading the truck, shovels usually dig into the ground and, consequently, part of the clay is excavated from the ground and mixed with aggregates. This problem is aggrevated during rainy seasons when clay is carried by wheels of shovel and trucks and mixed with aggregates. Producers are seduced to neglect proper procedures of quarrying because there is great demand on aggregates. Many con- sumers are obliged to accept almost any quality because demand is more than supply at a time where construction industry is experienc- ing a boom.

As a result of this, aggregates became weak and filler contents increased to quantities varying from 4 - 40%. High filler contents mean low strengths of concrete mixes unless excessive quantities of cement are used. There are alternative methods open to producers such as prescreening of aggregates before crushing or washing aggre- gates with water.

6.3 Procedure adopted by BRC

Since 1977, each quarry has been visited once or twice a year, where samples are taken and tested at BRC laboratories. Results are ana- lysed and discussed with NRA staff. Measures are taken concerning quarries that are producing bad aggregates. A file is kept for each quarry in which all information concerning that quarry and results of tests of each visit paid to the quarry are filed. The owner and NRA are given copies of results. If the results are not to specifica- tions, the owner is asked to improve the quality. The liscence is renewed anually by NRA after BRC checks the record of the quarry. If there is an improvement, then the owner is given a clearance according to which (NRA) will renew liscence for him. If no improvement is made, he is ordered to stop production until he takes measures to improve production. Meetings are held between officials of BRC and NRA during which the progress of work is discussed, improvement and developments are suggested, measures are taken and the whole process is evaluated. There is an improvement in the quality, but there is still a great deal to be done. Many people are now involved and aware of the situation. There is great hope in improving the quality.

6.4 Analysis of results

(1) There are 270 crushers used in the quarries. Most crushers used are locally manufactured and they vary in capacity from 50 - 400

cubic meters per day. There are some few big crushers varying in capacity from 600 - 1000 cubic meters per day.

(2) Samples brought from quarries are tested with regard to abrasion, grading, specific gravity, absorption, clay lumps and percent fines passing 0.075 mm sieve. Three rounds of visits have been finished and the number of quarries visited were 106, 203, and 212 quarries in the first, second and third rounds respectively.

(3) Results of abrasion tests show that abrasion of aggregates as measured by Los Angelos test varies from 20 - 55 with an average of 36.99, 38.62 and 34.9 for the first, second and third rounds respectively. Only Ministry of Public Works have specified abrasion values for each type of concrete namely, not more than 30%, 35% and 40% for concrete of cube compressive strength after 28 days of 420 kg/cm^2, 350 kg/cm^2 and 265 kg/cm^2 respectively. Moreover, abrasion of 45% was set for concrete of cube compressive strength of 140 and 70 kg/cm^2 (The last type is used for cement blocks).

According to these specifications or requirements, 89.6% of the quarries are not suitable for high strength concrete with regard to abrasion whereas only 17.4% of these quarries are not suitable for any type of reinforced concrete. Moreover, 4.7% of these quarries are not suitable for even the lowest type of plain concrete.

(4) Only NRA specifies minimum specific gravity which is 2.35 and 2.3 for coarse and fine aggregates respectively. Accordingly, results show that 28.3%, 25.4% and 32.5% of the quarries visited in the first, second and third rounds respectively are not to specifications with regard to specific gravity of coarse aggregates. With regard to fine aggregates, however, percentages not complying with specifications are 53.5%, 48.2% and 56.6% respectively.

(5) Directorate of Specifications and Standards and the NRA have set up maximum values for water absorption. These are 4% and 6% for coarse and fine aggregate respectively for the Directorate of Specifications and 3.5 and 4.5% for NRA. With regard to water absorption of coarse aggregates, quarries not complying with specifications are 46.2%, 36.9% and 36.7% for the first, second and third rounds respectively when Directorate of Specifications limits are considered. When the NRA Specifications are considered, however, the figures are 53.8, 48.3 and 46.7% respectively. With regard to fine aggregates absorption, however, the results are 41.8%, 35.3% and 37.9% for Directorate of Specifications and 81.6%, 63.7% and 65% for NRA respectively.

(6) Both Ministry of Public Works and Directorate of Specifications have set up maximum % for filler material. These are 20% and 5% respectively as percentage of fine aggregates. According to these limits, % of quarries not complying with specifications are 54.1%, 33.3% and 48.3% for the first, second and third rounds respectively for Ministry of Public Works and 100%, 97.5% and 98.5% for Directorate of Specifications.

Results have revealed the characteristics and properties of aggregates, both coarse and fine, which are very important for a material used on a wide scale, in construction and in housing sectors. The quality of these aggregates is not completely as required by specifications, but a huge amount of these aggregates could be utilized if the proper material is used for the proper job. Moreover, results show that an improvement in the quality of aggregates from one round to another has occurred. This project has revealed techniques and procedures adopted in quarrying and crushing. Bad quality is attributed to the misuse of these techniques. It is hoped that the proper use of techniques such as cleaning soil over lay, quarrying one layer at a time, removing marl embedded between layers, discarding bad stones, adopting proper use of shovels and proper storage on clean floors could improve quality.

7. *Locally Available Aggregates For Low Cost Housing*

The previous study has concentrated on three major elements moving in the same direction: The first is the need to develop low cost housing system that could   solve the   problem of housing.   This system is based on the use of cement blocks after certain developments are being made in the block.

The second element is the cement block; cement block is durable, employing locally available materials, namely aggregates and cement. It is manufactured by local people who have a wide experience in this field, and the block making machine is locally manufactured. Cement block industry is an old one and it is spread all over the country from north to south. Many people are familiar with it and it is a very easy job. People live in houses built with concrete blocks and they like these houses. Quality control project carried out on blocks have developed methods of making blcoks, improved quality, increased production and compiled information on the industry.

The third element is raw material used in blocks, namely, aggregates. Study has shown the distribution of aggregates all over the country. It showed that 18 million cubic meters of aggregates are produced each year, and these are distributed all over the country from north to south. People have a good experience in quarrying, crushing and handling of aggregates. Quality control project on quarries has developed methods of quarrying, improved quality, increased production and compiled information on the aggregates.

Both block making industry and quarrying industry are local industries employing local building materials, locally made equipment, local experience and local techniques and traditions.

To develop a low cost housing system that utilizes cement block which has great potentials is a move in the right direction. After developing the block to fit the system, the outcome will be a cement block, known by people, accepted and manufactured by people who have a long experience in such a work, and who live in what they manufacture and build. The block used in the system is a cement block manufactured in the same block making machine used for the ordindary block. The differences will be in mix design, in dimensions of moulds and in the cavities. Builders will imagine themselves building old blocks with less effort than what was required.

The system came to make use of two industries and utilize their products in housing with some amendments. It is true that these amendments have taken years of research, but when they came out, they appeared to be very simple changes. For instance, the same block making machine was used and steel moulds used were similar to

traditional moulds. Mixing, compacting, curing and handling did not
change but more control was experienced on these activities. Builders
found the new system easier than the traditional and they increased
productivity.

8. *Recommendations*

To succeed in this system and to be able to increase production and
reduce cost, efforts should be made to:

(1) Improve methods of quarrying and upgrade quality of aggregates.
(2) Utilize other types of aggregates such as ḣezria, tuff,
trippoli, basalt and granite where limestone aggregates are not
available.
(3) Research should continue on studying the properties of available raw materials with the object of maximizing use and reducing
waste in raw materials.
(4) The quality of blocks should be controlled and improved so
that houses remain strong and durable. Initial cost should not tempt
researchers to reduce prices at the expense of quality. Researchers
should keep control on the system during construction and development.
Reduction in cost should be sought in increasing production and reducing waste.
(5) The idea of minimum future needed maintenance should be
emphasized.
(6) Seminar should be held on this system in order to exchange
ideas and help transfer the know-how.

References

1. Sharif, R.L. and Jabaji, D. (1979), Technologies and Organization
       for the Sustainable Provision of Basic Shelter. Aleeso,
       Aspen and UNEP Seminar, Nairoubi Kenya.
2. Sharif, R.L. (1981), The Role of Building Research in the
       Development of Indigenous Construction Sector. Adhoc Expert
       Group Meeting, Nairoubi, Kenya.
3. Building Research Center, (1981), A Proposed System for Housing
       Low Income Groups in Jordan. Technical Report, BRC, Amman,
       Jordan.
4. Sharif, R.L. (1978), Construction Industry Seminar, Amman, Jordan.
5. Sharif, R.L. (1981), Stone Bearing Walls, Seminar in Bagdad, Iraq.
6. Sharif, R.L. and Others (1980), Cement Blocks in Jordan. BRC
       Technical Repeort, Amman, Jordan.
7. Sharif, R.L. and Others (1982), Quality Control of Aggregates,
       Cement and Concrete. Paper Submitted to Seminar held in
       Ryiadh, Saudi Arabia.

THE ECONOMICS OF BUILDING MATERIALS RESEARCH

PETER A. ERKELENS, Eindhoven University of Technology, The Netherlands

0. Summary

This paper analyses the importance of building materials in relation to the G.D.P. Building materials research is a basic requirement for low cost housing solutions. Because of limited funds available this research should be done in close cooperation between developing countries and developed countries.

1. The Importance Of The Building And Construction Industry

According to the Kenya Economic Survey 1978 (1) the analysis of gross fixed capital formation by type of asset at current prices shows that the value of completed building and construction in 1976 by private and public bodies (both residential and non residential, modern and traditional) was KShs 2834 million comprising 48.3 percent of the total investments. The value of completed modern buildings (residential and non residential) was KShs 1059 million, which is 37,4 percent of the total value completed by the building and construction industry. The process of development is therefore closely connected with this industry.

The construction cost, including on-site development cost can be estimated in the order of 70 percent of the total value completed. The construction cost (or the contract sum) can be subdivided into cost for labour, plant, equipment, materials, overhead and profit. A case study of three building projects in Nairobi (2) has revealed that the total labour cost are around 25 percent of the contract sum, while the building materials component can be estimated in the order of 50 percent. Assuming that this is valid for the whole country it can be derived that 16,8 percent (0.483 x 0.7 x 0.5) of the gross fixed capital formation consists of cost for building materials. The gross fixed capital formation is 23% of the Gross Domestic Product (GDP) (1), the building materials are therefore 3.9 percent of the GDP. According to the United Nations Economic Commission for Africa (3) the expenditure on building materials for the whole of Africa can be calculated as some 4-6 percent of the GDP, imported materials 3.6 percent and the total investments in construction is 9.8 percent of the GDP.

2.   *Considerations For Research Into Appropriate Building Materials*

Selection of appropriate building materials is obviously important because of the above conclusions. Intelligent selection depends upon research in which a number of considerations has to be taken into account:

1.   The use of appropriate locally available building materials may lead to heavier construction. This may result in higher cost of other parts of the construction. E.g. a recently developed local roof element of sisal cement is heavier than the more common corrugated galvanized iron sheets and requires, therefore, more and heavier purlins, walls and foundations. However the insulation is better. Therefore, the effects of application of any material have to be calculated thoroughly. (4)

2.   The use of (local) appropriate building materials may be hindered by the people, who don't accept these materials. This may be because they are associated with former poverty. Such, for example, is the reason why windmills with the use of fabric in the wingblades are not accepted, since fabric structures reminds them too much of improvisation as was characteristic of the slums of the past.

      Another example, but now in the housing field: the use of timber has been promoted by the Government of Kenya, but the people were not prepared to apply this material for a number of reasons, such as fire-risk, maintenance problems, and because it was considered to be a 'substandard' material.

3.   For developing countries, foreign currency problems are also tangible in the building - and construction industry. There are frequent cases in which a building project had to be extended due to inavailability of materials, which had to be imported, i.e. strict import quota and licenses. It is therefore of importance to reduce the dependency on importation.

4.   Another consideration is the energy to be used for the manufacturing of a building material. Local production may require much more energy -- and therefore more foreign currency -- than the amount of money required for other, or imported, materials.

5.   There should be a preference for the development of more labour-intensive materials during production as well during erection on site.

6.   In many developing countries transport is in general a difficult, time-consuming and costly affair. This argues for the development of materials which are not bulky, not heavy and preferably available near the construction site. If transport over long distances is required, building materials with a high value/weight ratio are preferred.

7.   In most developing countries there is a great shortage of skilled labour. The materials to be developed should, therefore, not require too much skill when used in building.

8.   Materials have to be durable, maintenance has to be at a low level and materials should not be too sensitive to mechanical damage, rot, fungi etc...

9.   In fact a complete analysis has to be made of a building material by calculating all the cost: from its production to demolition, while taking into account all the previous points.

3.   Example Of Materials/Elements To Be Researched

The analysis of the cost of various low cost housing plans can give an indication of the materials and building elements for which research and/or new development may make a meaningful contribution.

An additional problem, which should be kept in mind, is that the existing building code may not permit certain building materials. For example in Kenya: no walls shall be constructed at a lower standard than that of wattle. Until such codes are altered, application of research results may be hindered.

The Housing Research and Development Unit of the University of Nairobi (HRDU) has developed a series of low income houses types (5) of which fig. 1 gives an example.

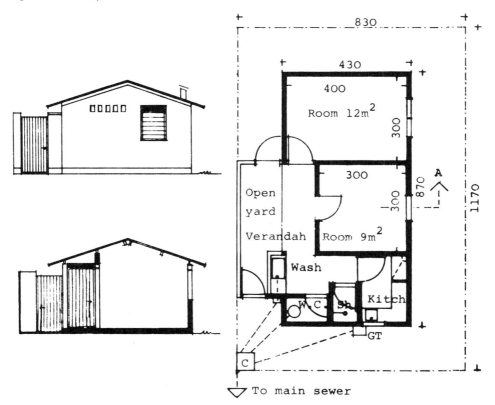

Fig. 1: Low income house type, detached.

The design is very simple: A roof supported by purlins only, loadbearing walls and a minimum of services. This design is meant mainly for the urban situation and the materials choosen are mostly locally produced. It can be assumed that this house type is appropriate for the Kenyan situation.

Table 1 shows a break down in the cost of materials grouped under the input indicators as specified by the Kenya Central Bureau of Statistics (6).

Table 1: Building materials grouped under CBS indicators and in order of cost size

Material	% of the total material cost	Imported
Concrete blocks	26.0	
Roofing materials (cgi)	14.2	+
Cement	14.2	
Drainage works	10.9	
Sanitary fixtures	6.9	+
Doors	5.2	
Hardware	4.1	
Sand	3.6	
Timber	2.9	
Aggregate	2.8	
Trapped gully	2.2	
Paints	1.8	+
Harcore filling	1.8	
Glass	1.7	+
Windows	1.4	
Reinforcing steel	0.3	+
Total material	100.0	

Another ordering of the figures by building elements may give a better impression of the areas where research should be concentrated (table 2):

Table 2: Building elements in order of cost size

Element	% of the total element cost
Superstructure	18.6
Roof	15.4
Finishing	13.1
Foundations	10.2
Doors & windows	9.6
Kitchen furniture	9.2
Floors	7.2
Washplace	6.7
W.C.	6.3
Shower	3.7
Total elements	100.0

From an analysis of both tables it can be concluded that the main cost of materials are from the superstructure, finishing, the roof and foundation. Research into these elements and related materials may lead to a considerable reduction of the total cost of a building. However, the remarks from the previous paragraph have also to be taken into consideration. The materials indicated in table 1 with a + are presently imported. The total contribution of these materials to the cost may be low but the foreign currency component can be very important.

4.   The Location Of Building Materials Research

Building materials research is carried out in both developing and developed countries. Research is a basic requirement for the development of a country. However a developing country's building industry may, in general, lack sophisticated research equipment, highly trained personnel and management. These are some of the reasons why selection of a research location must be done very carefully. The advantages of carrying out research on materials in its country of origin are the (abundant) availability of the materials and the similar climatic conditions during testing as well as construction. The upgrading of the already existing laboratory facilities and the level of skill is a longlasting and costly matter. Housing is furthermore not the most important requirement of human life for most of the developing countries. It comes after food, water, health and education. Therefore the developing countries can only invest limited funds in research. Though not always preferred by these countries, a realistic approach would be to cooperate with the developed countries in the field of research. For the time being research in developing countries should be limited to certain areas, in agreement with the available possibilities.

In such cooperative research programs, the primary research activities of the developing countries can be:
- To set up specifications and standards for building materials,
- To check, if materials comply with specifications and standards,
- Simple tests on materials, not requiring too much equipment and skill.
While the developed countries may concentrate on:
- Research and development of materials. This may require heavy equipment and computer support.
- Capital intensive research.

Cooperation in research will give the best results for the near future. There are a number of good examples of joint research projects between a developing country and a developed country. For example: the British Building Research Establishment (BRE) and the HRDU have an agreement for collaboration in the testing of an improved soil-block making press. This press has been developed in the laboratories of the overseas division of BRE. Field tests were carried out in Kenya under supervision of BRE and HRDU. This has resulted in a number of improvements of the machine.

5.   References

1.   Ministry of Finance and Planning, *Economic Survey 1978*, Kenya.
2.   Erkelens, Peter A. (1980), *CASE STUDIES OF THREE BUILDING PROJECTS IN NAIROBI*, Housing Research and Development Unit, University of Nairobi, Kenya.
3.   United Nations, Economic Commission for Africa (1976), *THE ROLE OF HOUSING AND BUILDING*, Addis Ababa.
4.   Teerlink, Hans in collaboration with Erkelens, Peter A. (1980), *APPROPRIATE BUILDING TECHNOLOGY in Katangi*, Undugu Society of Kenya and the Housing Research and Development Unit, University of Nairobi, Kenya.
5.   Olesen Finn (1979), *LOW INCOME HOUSE TYPES FOR KENYA*, Housing Research and Development Unit, University of Nairobi, Kenya.
6.   Erkelens, Peter A. (1981), *LOW COST HOUSING BUILDING COST INDEX*, Housing Research and Development Unit, University of Nairobi, Kenya.

IS IT LOW COST HOUSING, OR LOWER THE COST OF HOUSING?

A. NAGABHUSHANA RAU (Individual Member - CIB)
Jt. Managing Director, The Hindustan Construction Co.Ltd., Bombay.

1. Introduction

There is so much talk of Low Cost Housing all over the world. Mostly the developed countries, interested in the developing and least developed countries, talk more and more of the 'Low Cost Housing'.

1.1 The basic issue is, what is 'cost' and what is 'low'? Even the most affluent want the 'cost' to be 'low'. Is it the 'cost' to the owner, the government, the society or the entire economy of the country?

1.2 Even the most abundant and economical item like 'earth' which is the basic building and construction material all over the world may be the costliest, if many constraints that are imposed like price of land, quality, cost of recovery, cost of wastage, cost of transport, cost of remodelling the pit to suit the environment and ecology etc. are considered. Then it may be that the 'cement' which is otherwise the costliest, work out to be the 'cheapest'.

1.3 In many countries the natural building materials like, earth, stone, bamboo, grass, timber etc. which are abundant, works out to be 'costly' as there are no suitable technology or technicians to use them properly or even the basic infrastructure does not exist.

These are the areas where research is needed to improve local materials available, local technology and skills available, and to develop houses to suit local conditions, keeping in view the cost levels.

2. A new approach to achieve objectives

2.1 The objective is to improve the standard of living of the people by giving them better shelter in better environments. More people live in rural areas in the developing world. If so, the appropriate building material for low cost housing has to be examined, keeping in view the following factors -

a) Does one compare the standards of living in the developing countries with those of highly developed countries of the West and try
to implant those standards? Or examine what would suit the
region, the country or even part of the country, consistent with
socio-cultural traditions, national economy and the objectives
set by the Government of the country?

b) Should it not be based on self help and self-reliance instead of
always looking to outside grant, aid and help and technology ?
If so, what are the local funds available and what resources are
at hand?

c) How long one expects the 'house' to last with normal maintenance
or what should be the life of the building?

d) The life style of the people for whom the housing is built?

e) What is the pace at which the social conditions of the area is
changing which depends on the exposure the area is subjected to
by outside influences, education, rate of growth of infrastructure.

f) What are the natural conditions like sunshine, weather, wind,
rain, etc. in the region?

2.2 Since the way of life changes so fast now-a-days due to the national and international influence and interaction, is it not worth considering life of a house not on a long time schedule but a short one?
The aim must be to improve the standards gradually by improving the
environments, infrastructure, etc. so that the community adjusts to
changed ways of life. If this approach is accepted, then the specification for material and the rules and regulations by the local authorities and the engineering departments has to change to suit these
and should not be the ones set .by the departments based on urban areas
and systems based on the developed countries. At present, it is so
as most of the developing countries have the rules and codes from the
previous developed country which had control over the same.

3. *Experience on Indian Construction Projects*

3.1 Many housing colonies in the civil engineering project areas,
spread over different parts of India to house between 2000 to 8000
people have been built by my company, with all infrastructure, at our
project sites. In all these cases the objective has been that the
people who work on projects, away from town and in the interior have
better standards of living with a proper environment. In these hous-
ings the specifications and codes of permanent and long life construction were considered to be not relevant, but only safety of structure was kept in view.

3.2 The local materials only have been adopted to suit rainfall,wind,
climate. Some of the houses have stood with normal maintenance, for
periods upto twenty years. Normally they have stood periods of six
to twelve years when buildings have to be dismantled to restore the

site to the Government departments; otherwise life could be more. In all these cases, the roofing has been with galvanised sheeting, as it could be reused from project to project.

a)   Using soil cement blocks 9" thick with various cement content (5% to 2%) from bottom to top. Blocks moulded at site and sun dried.

b)   Plain mud plaster inside with white wash.

c)   Plain mud plaster with a coat of thick cement slurry wash. In some cases, a slurry was given on the face exposed to rain splash once in a year or two years.

d)   The random rubble masonry in mud mortar with joints deep pointed with cement mortar - some cases mud plaster inside.

e)   9" burnt brick pillars in cement mortar with 4½" thick walls with cement pointing in dry climate or cement plaster in wet climates.

f)   Only 9" burnt brick for outside walls in mud mortar with cement pointing with all internal works with sun dried 9" brick in mud mortar.

g)   Stone lintels for windows and door openings.

h)   Use of precast concrete door and window frames instead of timber.

i)   Using of slate and stone slabs for flooring or 4½" burnt brick in edge with 1" to 1½" cement concrete laid inside floor finish.

j)   Use of bamboos and bamboo mattings for building houses with palm leaves for roof.

k)   Use of tubular steel strucutres for roof, as they are light and can be reused.

In many cases, the Company used the services of the Building and Materials Research Institutions of India.

4.   Research to suit local conditions

4.1 It is unfortunate that all research is being concentrated on highly sophisticated methods of production in large quantities with high capital technology. There is so much talk of research on ferrous cement element, prefabrication, use of new plastics, ceramics etc. which are not relevant in the Low Cost Housing in the third countries where more attention to be given to rural housing with local materials, local talent and to the improvement of living conditions and environments, keeping a view to the culture and social habits.

4.2 Another area that is neglected but needs greater attention is the management aspects and training which control costs more than any other aspect. It is not only training of workers but policy makers, project planners and project managers.

5. Conclusion

If a little more attention is paid to improve brick making, soil, cement or lime blocks, burnt clay products, use of stone, gravel, sand, local timber etc. the same will contribute more in building economical and faster houses within the local resources available and local talents available. The objective has to be to improve the living conditions of the people in third countries by lowering the cost of houses, with better management, better use of local materials and change in the approach, change in the specifications and codes and life of building but keeping in view the safety of the structure.

APPROPRIATE TECHNOLOGY AND LOCAL CONTROL: The Development of the
Grenada Indigenous Housing Program

MARY C. COMERIO, University of California, Berkeley

1. *Background*

Grenada, often called the "Isle of Spice" is one of the smallest
nations in the Western Hemisphere, with a total land mass of only
133 square miles. It is the southernmost of the Windward Islands,
located in the Caribbean Sea about 70 miles north of Venezuela.
The island is volcanic in origin and much of the terrain is rugged.
About 75% of the land formation exceeds 20° slopes and is covered
with forests and tropical vegetation.

The total population, as of 1980, is 110,000, with a density of
828 persons per square mile. The ethnic composition is 84% black,
11% mixed, 3% East Indian, and less than 1% white. The four major
cities, St. George, Gouyave, Grenville and Victoria, have a combined population of less than 15,000 people. The majority of
Grenada's people live in rural areas.

Grenada suffers from all the features of small developing island
economies. After 200 years of British colonialism, the country is
almost devoid of industry and economically dependent on tourism and
the export of three crops, cocoa, bananas, and nutmeg. In 1979, the
island's people had a yearly per capita income of US $300, were 50%
unemployed and 40% illiterate. Although one-third of the arable
land lay fallow, two-thirds of its food had to be imported. In fact,
in 1979, exports were valued at $21.67 million while imports totaled
$43.59 million, leaving a deficit of $22.04 million.

The new social democratic government resolved to turn this
situation around. Bernard Cord, Minister of Finance and Deputy Prime
Minister, describes the enormous task: "On March 13, 1979 we took
over a ravaged country, a ravaged economy . . . we found ourselves
without a cent in the treasury. As to the national debt, that was
in excess of 57 million dollars . . . [Yet we knew that] repairing
the road networks around the country will cost $200 million. To
provide a proper water system, that is a water supply in every home
would cost about $175 million. To provide decent homes and to re-
pair those that are dilapidated would cost well in excess of $150
million. Yet we inherited a country . . . in which the entire national budget (recurrent and capital) was less than $60 million. In
this situation, the only way to rebuild our country was to all pitch

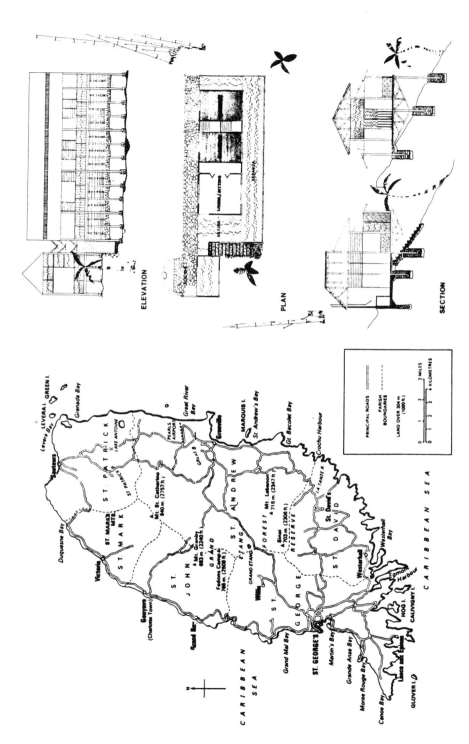

ELEVATION

PLAN

SECTION

Figure 2: Prototypical House Plan

Figure 1: Map of Grenada

in."[1]

With drastic needs in education, health, housing, and economic development, the new government has attempted a number of programs in order to begin to improve the quality of life for Grenadian people. In 1981, for example, the government entered into an agreement with Huck Rorick Associates through the Center for Environmental Change, Inc.[2] to undertake a pilot program in community development and low-cost housing. The program is based on concepts of sustainability, ecological balance, local control, and citizen participation, with energy derived from domestic sources, construction based on local materials, and wastes handled as part of an integrated system, including uses for energy as well as fertilizer. The program is structured to be useful in a, number of ways beyond simple provision of shelter. In particular, it is intended to provide lasting benefits in education, employment, development of local materials and construction industries.

As in most other developing countries, housing in Grenada is a critical problem. The 1970 population census revealed that 46% of the population lived in buildings that were in a state of disrepair. A majority of the households were without the services of piped water (64%), toilet facilities (77%), or electricity (56%). 72% of the housing units were wooden structures and 63% of that total were built more than 20 years ago. No significant new housing has been constructed to meet the increase in population since the 1970 census or to replace those units deteriorated beyond repair.

The rising cost of imports and especially energy has had a further negative impact on the situation. The cost of lumber rose 246% in the last 8 years, and cement, an energy intensive material, rose 480%. With a projected need for at least 1000 units of housing over the next 10 years, it is clear that locally self-sufficient, energy-efficient technologies are the only viable choices that exist.

In the 50's and 60's, housing was seen primarily as a "social issue," as was education or health. This perception was as true in the U.S. as it was in developing countries, and it generated a whole range of policies and programs aimed at the production of "low-cost" housing. Unfortunately, in today's economy, the bottom line is that neither design nor construction technology, nor financing, nor subsidy alone will make housing affordable. Housing for the poor is no longer a social issue; the production of affordable housing is a base-line economic problem for the majority of people in third world countries.

2.   *The Indigenous Housing Approach*

After initial meetings with Grenadian officials, our project team developed a proposal for a comprehensive housing and community development program in which a prototype village would be built. The village would consist of approximately 50 dwellings, a community building, a utility infrastructure, and alternative energy systems. It would incorporate local participation and training in design and construction; use of local materials; and the opportunity for related economic development.

The work was to be broken down into three phases: I. Research,

planning, design, and cost analysis; II. Final design and construction; and III. Evaluation and incorporation of improvements into
the next cycle. The American team was to raise funding for the
technical/research phase based on Grenadian government commitments
for substantial resources for Phase II, including land, access to
raw materials on government land, and financing through low-
interest loan commitments.

In broadest terms, the research that would lead to development
programs for building materials, alternative energy, and construction industries would be supported by housing, and education programs as well as through community participation. Ideally the
proposal hoped for the development of several types of local
building materials and energy sources simultaneous to the design and
construction of the prototype village.

Because the Secretary of the Ministry of Communications and
Works was a strong advocate of the project, some preliminary technical research was able to begin before the project team made its
first working visit in October of 1981. We had some information on
surveys of forest lands and we also knew that the island had significant quantities of volcanic ash. Biogas digesters had already
been experimented with on the island and some preliminary studies
were already completed on the feasibility of small dam construction.
On the policy side, we understood the "Idle Lands for Idle Hands"
program provided a natural match between the need for housing and
unemployment. We also were aware of the fact that land suitable
for cultivation was a scarce resource in Grenada. Only 6% of the
land has slopes less than 10 degrees, and housing should not be built
on this land.

Our agenda for the October 1981 visit was twofold. First we
wanted to gather as much technical information on local materials as
possible, including soil and mineral samples for testing. Secondly,
we wanted to look at land use, analyze costs on recently constructed
"low-cost" concrete block housing, and learn more about government
programs and grassroots organizations. The latter was particularly
important in determining what portion of the population the prototype housing would be aimed at, and in the selection of a site for
the project. It was also critical to ensuring community participation in all aspects of the project.

3. *Research Components*

Technical progress was made in several areas and a great deal of
valuable work was completed during the first month-long work
visit.[3]

3.1 Local Forest Resources. Extensive meetings were held with
Grenadian and outside experts in tropical forestry. Grenada's
Forest Manager has worked in the forest over 25 years. In that time
he has supervised the planting and care of over 30 experimental
plantations dating back to 1955. These plantations contain important information on forest regeneration rates, suitability of
different plant species, effects of maintenance regimes, terrain,
exposure, soils, etc. Unfortunately, it is not written down in a

useable form for future foresters. Documentation of this information is a critical task.

Reference materials were gathered from diverse sources including
the Institute of Tropical Forestry in Puerto Rico. This work has
been drawn together and is available as a resource in Grenada. From
our meetings and site visits we have drawn the following conclusions:

*Forest resources can make a considerable contribution to
Grenada's economy and specifically to housing. These resources can
be utilized in the short term (next 24 months), medium term (next
15 years), and long term at increasing (not decreasing) levels.
That is, we can formulate a program which is the reverse of the
usual quick exploitation of large quantities with a progressively
declining yield.

*The lack of adequate sawmills currently limits the size and
quality of milled lumber to 4"-6" in diameter, steps can be taken
to increase the output of the mills.

*Road engineering assistance is critically needed. Recent roads
constructed for logging are too steep for their intended use by
trucks and are causing radical erosion damage. There is an immediate
critical need for engineering assistance and alternative methods of
logging.

3.2 Pozzolan. We consulted with a materials geologist studying the
quarries in Grenada. That work was in specific reference to
materials for use in road construction, but the assistance will
reduce our project costs. With additional information from previous
geological surveys, the airport engineers and local people, we identified several sites and took volcanic ash samples for testing in
U.S. laboratories.

Pozzolan was used as mortar in colonial buildings and there is a
local craft industry that makes use of lime mortar. Lime, an ingred-
ient in pozzolan cement, is made from seashells and coral. Currently, the local factory uses coral, fired in wood fueled lime kilns.
The lime produced is used for agriculture and for construction.

We also gathered information on stone and clays. Stone quarries
do exist, but transportation has always been a serious problem. We
found out that plans did exist for the development of a brick factory
but the work was never carried out. This is an area that requires a
longer range plan because of the technical research necessary and
the high start-up costs for industrial development.

3.3 Bamboo. We found an abundance of bamboo on the island, but very
little of it was used in construction. The attitude towards its use
did not seem to be extremely negative, despite the fact that it is
used mostly in the poorest structures and is generally used untreated
and in ways that result in its rapid decay. We were surprised to
find, however, that there is significant local knowledge about its
use. It seems that many older craftsmen remember that use of bamboo
in construction of houses was quite common before the 1955 hurricane.
One could surmise that there is a direct relation between the decline
in the use of bamboo and influx of "modern" materials that came as
part of the foreign aid for disaster relief.

3.4 Micro Hydropower. A French firm has prepared a report on the installation of "mini" hydropower which would be capable of replacing the island's current generating capacity. While these installations are of a larger size than we were contemplating for the development of village scale "micro" hydrosystems, the research is invaluable. This area, like the development of earth materials industries, will need a longer range development program because of the front-end capital expense.

3.5 Waste Management/Biogas. We examined current conditions and practices and discussed the problems with numerous officials who were remarkably open to new ways of handling solid wastes and sewage. We observed the current management processes from collection to ultimate disposal (which we would want to change to "utilization"), and we visited a range of facilities, from outhouses to community toilets utilizing septic tanks. We discussed community attitudes toward garbage and human waste as well as personal habits, and we developed some alternatives that could be implemented immediately.

About 77% of the households in Grenada lack indoor toilets. In rural communities people generally have outhouses, but in some areas they have a communal toilet facility with 4-6 toilets serviced by a septic tank. These toilets are used by as many as 500 people and serve homes up to 200 yards away. At night, people use an enamel chamber pot which is then emptied into the outhouse or communal toilet the next day. The facilities are maintained by a person in the community who is paid to clean it on a daily basis.

These communal toilets present an opportunity to convert sewage wastes into a productive resource such as biogas. The cost of constructing a communal facility with biogas construction is comparable to the costs for a septic tank. The problem of excess water in the digester is solved since water borne sewage lines are not used. Most important, however, is the fit with current practices and customs.

4. *Participation and Local Control*

As outside "experts" with a bias toward an indigenous housing program, one of our tasks was to find ways to minimize the need for outside experts. Thus one of the objects of the first working visit was to integrate the project with the public sector budget and to develop local counterparts for each of the research areas. The Ministries of Housing, Health, Communications and Works, and the Central Water Commission all expressed willingness to coordinate planning and personnel in conjunction with the project.

For example, in 1979 the Ministry of Housing initiated a massive housing repair program with a minimum of bureaucracy. Any individual earning EC $150 or less could get EC $1000 worth of building materials from the program. One third of the amount was a grant and the remainder was paid for at the rate of EC $5 per month for 20 years. If the person's earnings were EC $150-$250, they paid back the total amount at EC $17 per month. No interest was paid in either case. (Note that U.S. $1=approximately EC $3.) The material was purchased in quantity by the government and distributed at the parish level. Construction was up to the individual generally through self-help, although some people worked together in their communities, others paid someone else to do the labor. In two years over 1100 houses have been repaired. Clearly this kind of existing program will be incorporated into our development plan.

Several people have been selected to work on each of the technical areas in order to provide continuity in our absence, and to act as the human instruments of technology transfer. As our trainees, these people will become the "local experts." Their work on the demonstration project will enable them to then carry on the work in other villages and to pass-on their knowledge. To help in this effort we set up a small resource center to function as an office meeting space, and central location for all reference materials.

Several significant project changes resulted from the interaction between the project team and local officials.

The Grenadians felt that it would be extremely important for the first phase to produce some immediate concrete results. The original plan was ideal in terms of producing a model for an ecologically sound, low cost, sustainable community, but it required a heavy commitment of "front end" time. Some of the local materials industries and power systems would have to be part of an economic development scheme and the technical research would involve only a limited number of local trainees. As such, none of the results would be visible until the village was finished.

Together we decided that building activity should be incorporated into the first phase, since it would be particularly important in developing community participation, training and educational programs that raise the level of consciousness about house and village design issues could be integrated into this work. Further, the creation of actual models would allow community evaluation and refinement of design ideas for use in the more extensive construction to follow.

In this way, we would develop a strong base of skills, a high level of participation, and a series of examples of new and renoated houses that could be replicated in other locations at the same time that the plan for an integrated village moves foreward. This revised plan also meant that the proposal could be divided into components (three for materials industries, two for energy supply, one architectural, and one for training) which would make funding more manageable.

The revised plan for Phase I allows for technical research to continue but focuses on the construction and/or repair of 16 houses; the construction of a community facility, community education and participatory design. In choosing a site, the Grenadians felt it was important for success to consider a place with a good base of community organization, a high need, and good visibility, both physically and politically. Several towns and new co-operatives were considered. Waltham, in St. Marks parish, was chosen for a number of reasons.

Waltham, which is located on the coast road, just north of Gouyave and Victoria, is one of the poorer communities in Grenada, with an average household income of U.S. $27 per month. There is no sewer system and only four of the approximately 100 households in the vil-

lage have electricity. Few have running water. Most people live in
one-room shacks that are dilapidated and overcrowded.

In the midst of this severe economic environment, the people of
Waltham have an active community and are organizing themselves on a
number of fronts. It has a school, youth and women's organizations,
and a farmworkers union. It is an agricultural area with several
rivers and good access to timber and other raw materials.

We discussed the housing program at a community meeting, and we
found that people were excited about the idea of becoming involved in
the design of their homes and community. Whereas some administrators
had expressed concern that people would find local materials and
technologies "primitive," we found the residents not only open to the
idea, but eager to introduce us to older craftsmen knowledgeable in
the use of bamboo, rouseau (a reed), and native timber. In fact,
people wanted to hear about the methods we were suggesting so that
they could use them in their homes right away.

5. *Work in Progress*

The first working visit in October of 1981 brought about several modifications of the initial large-scale proposal and work has continued
in 1982-83 as funding has permitted. Two issues changed the direction of the project. First, the Grenadians felt it was critical to
develop a plan of action that would produce immediate and visible
results. This meant using materials and construction techniques that
were readily available and establishing programs that would quickly
technical expertise and information out of the hands of the researchers and into the hands of the Grenadians. It also meant putting some
experimental work in developing industries on the "back burner" without losing sight of the long term objectives for ecologically sound,
locally based community development. Second, it was difficult
realistically to fund a full scale research project on the integration of building materials, economic development and housing as set
out in the original proposal, particularly from any one single
source. It is ironic to note that if any large amounts of aid for
housing or economic development were available, it would have probably been designated for more traditional concrete block housing and
other "imported" technologies.

Thus, the need for both immediate and incremental development
shaped the next phase of the work. The project team returned to
Grenada in July of 1982 for several months work. The purpose of the
trip was to initiate community education activities and participatory planning with the people of Waltham. One of our first activities was to conduct village workshops on the construction of Lorena
Stoves. Since most families cook over an open wood fire in small
huts, the Lorena stoves could reduce their fuel consumption by as
much as 50%, which means less work in gathering fuel and greater
protection for the forests. The stoves were built of sand and clay
and had no cash cost. They were built with fitted chimneys made
of scrap materials in order to remove smoke from the kitchen, making
the room cleaner, cooler, and easier to breath in. After several
stoves were built in Waltham, we began to get requests from other
parts of the island. So, in cooperation with the National Science

and Technology council, our Lorena workshop leader is now doing a
stove workshop in each parish in Grenada.

Our biogas technician worked on design of a community biogas
facility. He worked with the Farm School, which has several experimental digesters, and several agricultural cooperatives as well.
Two new units were completed in 1982 and at the same time, one mason
was trained and he will begin construction of another digester on
his own.

Most important in this trip was the community design work with
several families in Waltham. It was useful to get villagers to
think about alternatives in their own housing as well as community
issues like sewage, water supply and communal facilities. It was
also useful for us to develop an understanding of how Grenadians
use their homes and what innovations might work.

We built a small demonstration structure utilizing the construction materials and methods that would be used in the houses. The
total cash cost for the 8' x 12' building was U.S. $5 which was
spent on nails and cement. The labor was voluntary and the other
materials were entirely local. These included stone, sand, light
timber, thatch, plant fiber, and bamboo.

The building, intended as a bus stop, has received constant and
heavy use as a meeting place, hangout, barber shop, milk distribution
point, and climbing structure (by the children), as well as a bus
stop. During our stay, we were never able to visit the structure
when no one was using it, and it has become the model for another
building in the village.

As outsiders, working with the villagers helped us to get some
insight into a number of questions about lifestyle, habits, and
attitudes. For example, in calculating the cost of "low cost" housing, we wondered what could be done with the lowest cost labor.
Although $3 per day was the prevailing wage for agricultural labor
and unemployment was high, it was not easy to find someone to work
for that on a full time basis. We concluded it was unfeasible
to build an economy on the existing wage scales.

The reason is that most people survive by gathering food from
the jungle, fishing, keeping a garden and possibly animals, gathering firewood and making charcoal. If they work full time, they have
little time left over to do these things. But at a laborer's wage,
it is impossible to afford store bought food, which is priced the
same or higher than it is in the U.S. As a consequence, full time
labor is not compatible with survival--one important criteria in
developing an economically feasible housing program.

6. *Lessons from the Approach*

The need for the production of affordable housing and a basic infrastructure in Grenada is not atypical. In developing countries
throughout the world, there is a chronic and critical state of inadequate housing. The United Nations estimates that "over 1,000
million people in Africa, Asia, and Latin America--about half of
the population of these continents--live in housing which is a
health hazard and an affront to human dignity."[4]

"In theory, the solutions to this immense problem are well known;

they include intensified research into low-cost designs that are applicable to the climate, materials, and cultural context of each area; use of the more efficient concepts of mass construction . . . [and] maximum utilization of every resource, especially non-monetized resources in labor and material."[5]   In theory, the concept of ecologically sound community development, utilizing self-help and community participation in conjunction with the development of indigenous materials and local building industries, is not new.   In practice, however, the actual attempts to integrate these concepts at a programatic level are few.

Hassan Fathy's work in Egypt is one of the best examples and yet, we might suggest that the success of that work can be attributed primarily to the perseverance of a single individual--Fathy himself.[6] But in countries like Grenada, woefully short of professional expertise within its population, the common need is in the area of program development which is dependent on outside assistance.   If we can generalize that the main problem with what we call "traditional" low-cost housing assistance programs is affordability in terms of cash costs relative to the users' ability to pay, then we might generalize from the Grenada experience, that the problem with indigenous housing development is also one of affordability, but primarily in terms of time.

The development of programs based on community participation and cottage industry are not particularly efficient by traditional standards that rank success by numbers of units produced per year.   The timeline for a participatory approach must be considerably longer, and there needs to be an up-front investment in "soft costs" for organizing, training, and research.   Thus one cannot make a correlation between cost and housing units on the front end since the investment in personnel and time in the beginning pays off over the long term through the production not only of housing units that are affordable, but also in jobs and economic development.

In Grenada, the contrasts between the cost of quick production housing units and the cost of an indigenous housing program are glaringly apparent.   At the time of our first working visit, they had recently completed 18 typical "low-cost" housing units which stood empty because no one could afford the U.S. $12,000 price tag.   On the other hand, our program has been quite difficult to fund because for the first 3-5 years it is hard to show a significant number of units produced.

Our experience has provided some insight into the time problem, particularly how to streamline the front end of the process.   Typically in developing countries, communications are difficult. Phones don't work, mail is slow, and few people have transportation. With middle level management in short supply, the government bureaucracy is slow and preparations or authorizations not completed tend to impede progress.   In Grenada, a single individual, the Secretary of Communications and Works, took personal responsibility for keeping the project moving forward.   It was only after he left the position and no other individual took sponsorship, that we recognized how critical that kind of intervention was in order to maximize the use of our time and energy.

If some of the "time" problems are manageable, others are more intractable. Given the overworked, understaffed, and probably underqualified management in the government bureaucracy of most underdeveloped countries, it is easy to see that a "planning" process often loses priority over day-to-day crisis intervention. The work of organizing people becomes much more difficult than fixing a road grader because the deadlines are more ephemeral and the consequences of not doing that job are certainly less visible. Further, even the most ardent supporter of a local development process is faced with the ever-present dilemma between the appropriateness of small-scaled, incremental processes and the need for something that politicians can point to, in order to tell their constituencies what they are doing.

If, as Habraken says, "our task is primarily to find a formula for a housing process which allows comfort and human dignity to exist hand in hand,"[7] then to carry out this humanistic approach, we must recognize the importance of appropriate technology and local control in housing programs. We must also give more attention to the process required to operationalize such programs. As much as there is a need for continuing research on indigenous building materials and methods, there is a pressing need for more experience in the process of initiating and implementing integrated community development programs. If we as housing experts recognize the issues to be political and economic, as well as technical, then let us redirect our research to show concern not only for the physical products produced but also for the spirit brought to the work.

References

1. Interview with Bernard Cord, <u>Westindian Digest</u>, March 1980, pp. 24-26.

2. The Center for Environmental Change Inc. is a non-profit corporation associated with the College of Environmental Design at University of California, Berkeley.

3. More detailed information on research components is available in progress reports on the Grenada Indigenous Housing Project dated Nov. 14, 1981, and Nov. 11, 1982, available from the Center for Environmental Change, Inc.

4. <u>The United Nations Development Decade Proposals for Action</u>, United Nations Publications, New York, 1962, p. 59.

5. <u>Manual on Self Help Housing</u>, United Nations Publications, New York, 1964, p. 1.

6. Fathy, Hassan, <u>Architecture for the Poor</u>, University of Chicago Press, Chicago, 1969.

7. Habraken, Nicholas J., <u>Supports</u>, Praeger Publishers, New York, 1972, p. 54.

1. Introduction

La gestion est l'ensemble des décisions destinées à réaliser un certain objectif. Même si les objectifs et les critères servant à qualifier leur degré de satisfaction, ne sont toujours aisés à définir le gestionnaire aura pour principale règle de conduite de choisir parmi toutes les décisions qui réalisent cet objectif, celle qui se traduit par le coût le moins cher. Optimiser consiste à faire au mieux en cas de multiplicité de critère ou en tenant compte d'autres critères que celui de la régle du moins disant. Nous examinons dans les exemples qui suivent les difficultés de mise en oeuvre des techniques d'optimisation.

2. Contradiction entre objectif

C'est le cas notamment des projets de batiments où se rencontrent au moins trois objectifs antagonistes
- confort, qualité, performances, esthétiques
- délais
- coût

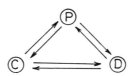

Ils ne peuvent être examinés séparément. Toute décision ne peut résulter que d'un compromis qui n'est jamais facile à établir. En effet si le coût des confort, qualité, esthétique et performance est déterminable, en revanche, la valeur ou la satisfaction procurée par ces mêmes éléments n'est pas mesurable. Le cas est plus favorable lorsque tous les éléments de la décision peuvent être définis par des coûts, car dans ces conditions, il est généralement possible de les synthétiser dans une fonction économique dont on recherche le minimum.

Exemple 1: les coûts de V.R.D. et Fondations constituent un couple de fonctions antagonistes indissociable même paramètre "côte de seuil" fig.1).
Malgré cela, leur dissociation est systématiquement faite dans la pratique :

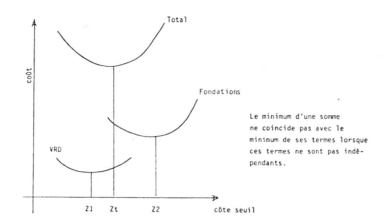

. lotissement et construction réalisés de manière totalement indépendante (opérations désintégrés).
. opération intégrée de lotissement et construction mais recours à plusieurs intervenants non coordonnés.
. opération intégrée et un seul intervenant mais Maître d'ouvrage non averti et BET sacrifiant la conception à l'exécution.

Exemple 2 :   le coût d'un projet et le coût des études correspondantes constituent un couple antagoniste.

Fig. 2. Il est évident que construire plus économique nécessite plus de savoir faire et de temps de réflexion que de construire cher.

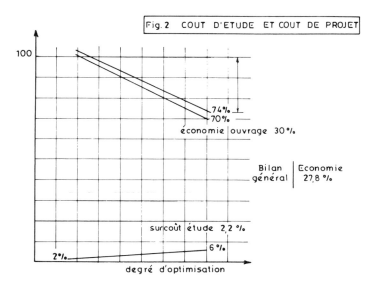

Fig. 2   COUT D'ETUDE ET COUT DE PROJET

	Etude à 2%	Etude à 6%
Taux	2%	6%
Assiette = coût des ouvrages	100	70
Honoraires	2	4,2
Total	102	74,2
Economie		27,8

Malheureusement même pour desintervenants identiquement rétri-
bués il peut exister des différences flagrantes atteignant 25%
des coûts. Le tableau de la figure 3 fournit les variations
observées selon les intervenants pour des ouvrages parfaitement
comparables. Seule une sensibilisation des pouvoirs publics
pourrait améliorer la situation par la mise en place de conven-
tion provant le respect d'objectifs précis.

FIG.3 COMPARAISON DU COUT DES OUVRAGES
- Ouvrages parfaitement comparables
- Quantités tirées des dossiers d'appel d'offres (Septembre 1982 à Novembre 1982) marché au forfait
- L'ouvrage E est pris comme référence
- L'économie est évaluée à raison de 600 Dhs/m3 béton et 8 Dhs/ kg d'acier

Projet	Surface HO	Quantités		Ratio		Economie en	
		Béton	Acier	Béton	Acier	%	Dhs
	m2	m3	kg	cm/m2	kg/m2		
A	28.300	9.511	844.000	33.6	29.8	23	2.850.000
B	28.300	9.430	811.400	33.3	28.7	20	2.540.000
C	25.540	10.250	668.000	40.1	26.2	24.6	2.825.000
D	20.000	6.020	615.000	30.1	30.8	20	1.743.800
E	25.170	7.223	526.650	28.7	20.9	-	-

L'économie à réaliser permettrait de faire un 6ème ouvrage de 29.400 m2.

9.958.000

3. Difficultés d'ordre mathématique

La recherche du minimum se heurte très souvent à des difficultés d'ordre mathématique ou pratique
- elle peut nécessiter la manipulation de nombreuses équations non linéaires dont il est impossible d'étudier analytiquement les variations.
- la fonction économique comporte des variables discrètes : on ne sait plus calculer les dérivées ni déceler les tendances. Il en est ainsi du coût d'une poutre (telle qu'on la rencontre dans un logement économique en fonction de la hauteur qui met en jeu des aciers dont le diamètre varie de manière discontinue selon la série commerciale.
- Les coûts unitaires de la fonction économique sont connues avec une trop grande marge d'erreur. Si on peut assimiler ces coûts à des variables aléatoires normales indépendantes, alors le calcul des écarts type permet de réduire l'erreur globale.

Dans ce cas où la résolution analytique ou le calcul manuel déviennent fastidieux voire impossible, il ne reste plus qu'à se tourner vers l'ordinateur pour procéder par des simulations exhaustives à la recherche de l'optimum.

4. Difficulté de définition des coûts

Les difficultés de l'optimisation ne se limitent pas aux objectifs et critères, la définition même des coûts appelle des remarques.

Généralement pour un Maître d'Ouvrage, le coût d'un projet est celui qui ressort du marché de l'adjudicataire. Mais c'est faire abtraction de tous les évènements qui engendrent des coûts secondaires. Parmi ces évènement, on peut citer :

4.1. L'aptitude et la qualification des Maîtres d'oeuvre et entreprises qui influent directement les :

a) coût d'encadrement plus élevé si l'intervenant est défaillant
b) solution plus onéreuses si le maitre d'oeuvre est insuffisamment compétent.
c) frais financiers sur ressources mobilisées ou recettes de commercialisation différées en cas de retard.

4.2. La notion d'intérêt général est variable d'un décideur à l'autre :

a) ainsi le recours à des intervenants étrangers, même moins disants plutôt qu'à leurs homologues nationaux, se traduit au niveau de la nation par des répartitions monétaires (transfert de devises, taxes), d'emploi, de capitalisation d'expérience, d'investissement etc... différentes et consiste à privilégier le court terme par rapport au long terme pratique qui conduit à la négation de toute politique de développement.

b) l'utilisation de techniques plus ou moins mécanisées permet de raccourcir les délais et souvent le coût mais au détriment de la main d'oeuvre utilisée.

COMPARAISON DE DIFFERENTS MODES D'EXECUTION   FIG. 5

Quantité de mains d'Oeuvre en heures

	1	2	3	4	5
. Exécution de 6 coffrages de poteaux	35	35	35	35	35
. Coulage de 6 poteaux et décoffrage	2	2	2	2	2
. Exécution coffrage pour les poutres	82	82	82	35	32
. Coulage des poutres et décoffrage	10	10	10		
. Exécution de coffrage pour le plancher	43	27	43	25	22
. Coulage des dalles, pose, décoffrage	6	1	4		
	178	157	176	97	91

Solutions :

1 : méthode traditionnel (tout coulé en place)
   plancher nervure en corps creux 16 + 4 coulé en place

2 : dito 1 sauf nervure préfabriqué du commerce

3 : plancher en dalle pleine de 15

4 : dito 3 mais préfabrication totale des éléments horizontaux
   dalle et poutre pose sur étais

5 : dito 4 pose sans étais

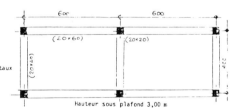

4.3. L'introduction de clauses financières lors des négociations telles que : avance ou préfinancement, caution bancaire ou retenues de garantie, utilisation de formules de révision de prix variables conduit à des distorsions non négligeables qu'il est possible de prendre en compte par la technique du calcul

d'actualisation. Il apparait que le moins disant en terme de soumission n'est pas forcement le moins disant en terme de valeur
actualisée.

Cette méthode traduite par un modèle mathématique à été utilisée
lors du dépuillement d'un projet de 4236 logements. Elle permet
d'aboutir aux conclusions suivantes.

- Le modèle est indifférent à la forme de la courbe des dépenses
  tant que cette courbe reste symétrique, le paramètre déterminant est le centre de gravité des somme dépensées.

- Les formules de révision sont du type

$$\frac{P}{P_0} = 0,15 + 0,85 \ (I/I_0) \quad \text{et plus généralement}$$

$$a + b \ I/I_0 \ \text{avec } a \geq 0 \quad b \geq 0 \qquad a+b = 1$$

Lorsque b varie de + 10 en valeur absolue, la valeur actualisée
varie de $\pm$ 1,36 % (fig. 6)

En particulier pour b = 0 (neutralisation de révision) le gain
ou rabais serait de 9,5 % par rapport à la solution de base
(b = 70) et de 11,4 % âr rapport aux hydothèses de l'Administration (b = 0.85)

Fig. 6 EFFET DE LA REVISION DES PRIX

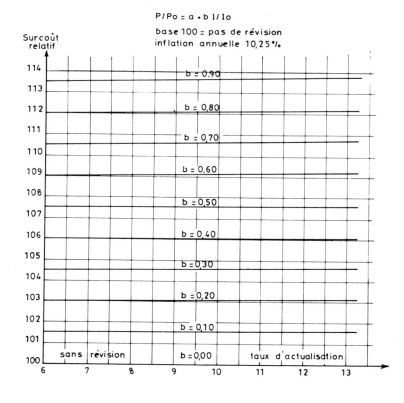

- L'acceptation d'une caution bancaire en place et lieu de la retenue de garantie induit un surcoût de 0,62 % pour le Maître d'ouvrage (Fig. 7)

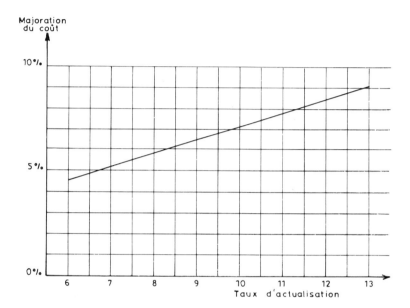

Fig. 7 EFFET FINANCIER DE LA CAUTION BANCAIRE
AU LIEU DE LA RETENUE DE GARANTIE

- L'octroi d'une avance dont le montant est déductible des sommes
  à réviser se traduit par une économie négligéable pour le Maître
  d'ouvrage (fig.8), 0,5 %o pour une avance de 10 % et 1,5 %o pour
  avance de 25 % du montant du marché.

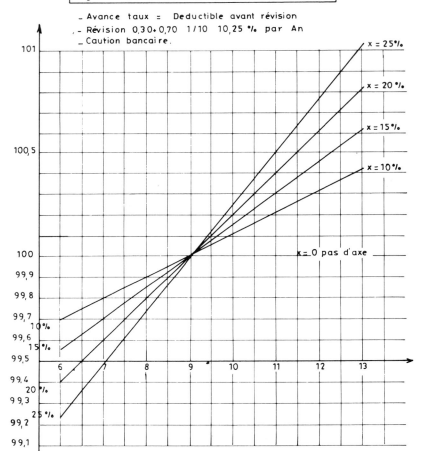

Fig. 8   SURCOUT OU ECONOMIE EN% DU PROJET

- Avance taux = Deductible avant révision
, - Révision 0,30+0,70 1/10 10,25 % par An
_ Caution bancaire.

- Loctroi d'une avance dont le montant n'est pas déductible des
  sommes à réviser se traduit par un surcoût équivalent à 10 % du
  taux de l'avance elle-même soit :
  avance de 10 % surcoût 1% du marché
  avance de 20 % surcoût 2 % du marché (fig. 9)

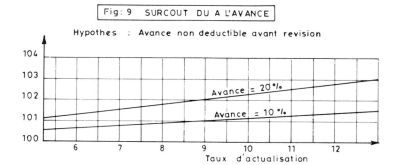

Fig: 9   SURCOUT DU A L'AVANCE

Hypothes : Avance non deductible avant revision

Dans la pratique, les conditions variaient d'une entreprise à
l'autre et mettaient en jeu d'autres paramètres.
- La figure 10 resume l'ensemble des jeux de conditions financières
définitivement arrêtées et les coefficients multiplicateurs par
lesquels il convenait de multiplier les soumissions pour en obtenir les valeurs actualisées.

COMPARAISONS DES DIVERSES HYPOTHESES FINANCIERES   FIG. 10

		(1)	(2)	(3)	(4)		(5)	(6)	(7)				(8)
Entreprises	Hypothèses	% Avances	Revenue de garantie	Coefficient b de la Révision	Origine index		Coefficient finan- cier de nivellement CF taux actualisation 8,5 %	Majorations ou rabais	Coefficient global C6 = CF x MR	Hypothèses retenue	Entreprise retenue		Actualisation par ... d la solution de ...
A		non	oui	70	1.81		0.959.169	1,00	0.959.169				Base Appel d'offre
B	1	10	non	85	1.81		0.998.477	1.00	0.998.477				1.041
	2	20	non	85	1.81		1.007.830	.98	0.9876734	X	X		1.051
	3	20	non	non			0.904.997	1.10	0.9954967				0.944
C	1	15	non	85	1.81		1.003.153	.832325	0.8349493	X	X		1.046
	2	20	non	non			0.904.997	.960	0.86879712				0.944
D		20	oui	non			0.899.345	.931	0.8372901	X	X		0.938
E		non	non	85	1.81		0.989.125	1.	0.989125	X			1.031
F		non	non	70	12,80		0.976.735	1.	0.976735	X	X		1.018
G		non	non	non			0.899.345	.9016	0.810849	X			0.938
H		20	non	70	1.81		0.984.031	.8869	0.872737	X	X		1.026

OBSERVATIONS :(1) (2) (3) non dans ces colonnes signifie pas d'avance, caution au lieu de retenue, marché non révisible
(4) L'origine des index Janvier 1981 ou Décembre 1980 est dûe d un report de la date d'ouverture des plis
(5) CF est le coefficient multiplicateur d utiliser pour transformer le montant de la soumission en valeur actualisée
(6) L'acceptation des conditions financières était selon les scénarios assortis soit d'un rabais, soit d'une majoration
de la soumission. C'est le cas pour B3 la non révision est assortie d'une majoration de 10 %
Pour C2 la non révision se traduit par rabais beaucoup plus faible que pour C1.

f

La dernière colonne montre la plus ou moins value qui résulte de la
seule application du jeu des conditions financières. En toute logique,
l'entreprise devait assortir sont acceptation par un réajustement
symétrique (col.6). La superposition d'un rabais purement
"commercial"fausse cette comparaison.
4.3. Coûts non imputés
Les coûts d'intervention du Maître d'ouvrage au titre d'un projet
sont souvent imputés sur des budgets de fonctionnement et de ce fait
n'apparaissent plus comme des rubriques contribuant à la formation du
coût du projet.

4.4. Coût de la non réalisation d'un projet

Dans de nombreux cas les conséquences financières entre autres de la
décision de non réalisation d'un projet peuvent être plus importantes
que celle découlant de sa réalisation. C'est en ces termes que se
pose le problème de l'édification des grands ouvrages d'équipement.
Plus modestement, dans le domaine du bâtiment, on peut citer le
recours ou non au Laboratoire d'étude de sol, aux bureaux d'études
techniques etc... dont l'intervention se chiffre à quelques dizaines
de pourcents du coût des ouvrages.
Une décision ne peut être arrêtée en pleine connaissance de cause que
si toutes les conséquences de son application sont déterminées et
également toutes celles de sa non application.

La déision finalement retenues est celles qui minimise les dépenses.
Il revient au même de procéder à la différence des coûts des deux
situations en prenant l'une d'elles comme référence. Ce deuxième
critère tout en étant équivalent au précédent procure deux avantages:
le 1er est celui d'éliminer des coûts qui interviennent identiquement
dans les cas.
Le 2ème est de ne pas oublier la situation de référence.

LE PLATRE, UN MATERIAU APPROPRIE A LA CONSTRUCTION ECONOMIQUE ?

MARC NOLHIER : PLAN CONSTRUCTION - FRANCE

1. Introduction

Des actions de recherche et d'expérimentation sur la construction économique à base de plâtre sont menées, depuis 1982, par la France et plusieurs pays africains dans le cadre du programme REXCOOP : "Réalisations Expérimentales en Coopération".

Nourries par l'observation d'une tradition millénaire de construction utilisant le gypse, renforcées par les résultats de recherches et d'expérimentations effectuées au milieu du siècle en Algérie, en Allemagne et en France, ces actions concernent essentiellement les pays à climat chaud et sec et trouvent leurs applications au Sénégal et en Tunisie.

Après une année de travaux, il est possible d'apporter des éléments de réponse à la question de l'intérêt de ce matériau pour la construction économique des pays en développement.

La communication présente l'actualité technique de ce type de construction, et après avoir proposé des critères de définition des technologies appropriées, elle évalue une technique d'utilisation du plâtre en fonction de ces critères.

2. Quelques techniques prometteuses

2.1 Le plâtre résulte de la cuisson, à température modérée, du gypse ou sulfate de calcium bihydraté. Les plâtres sont des matériaux complexes puisque selon les températures et conditions de cuisson, on peut obtenir plusieurs types différents de produits. Ainsi, le plâtre artisanal, préparé sans précaution particulière, est un mélange des différentes variétés et ses qualités sont donc irrégulières. Ainsi, les techniques modernes de cuisson industrielles permettent d'obtenir l'une ou l'autre variété correspondant à des usages spécifiques : plâtre de construction, gros et fin, plâtre pour enduits de haute dureté, plâtre de surfaçage, plâtre à projeter, plâtre pour enduits extérieurs, plâtre médicaux plâtre pour préfabrication, etc...

Gaché avec de l'eau, le plâtre se réhydrate, fait rapidement prise, se cristallise et durcit pour donner un sulfate de calcium bihydraté semblable au gypse initial : $Ca\ SO4,\ 2H_2O$.

Autrefois dans de nombreux pays, le plâtre était utilisé à l'intérieur comme à l'extérieur des bâtiments pour la réalisation du gros oeuvre et des finitions. Actuellement, le plâtre est utilisé principalement dans le second oeuvre, soit pour des finitions intérieures (enduits de mur et plafonds), soit sous forme d'éléments préfabriqués (carreaux de cloison, plaques de parement, éléments de plafond).

Ces utilisations modernes sont désormais classiques dans de nombreux pays industrialisés. Nous ne nous intéresserons dans cette communication qu'à l'utilisation du plâtre dans le gros oeuvre, essentiellement dans les parois verticales.

2.2. Le plâtre a été utilisé massivement comme élément constitutif du gros oeuvre des murs, porteurs ou non, sous pratiquement toutes les techniques : hourdage de blocs de maçonnerie, banchage par lit, banchage de hauteur d'étage, projection mécanisée, petits et grands éléments préfabriqués, plaques minces cartonnées ou simple remplissage d'ossatures à pan de bois.

Deux procédés semblent devoir être privilégiés par les P.E.D. pour la réalisation de constructions économique : les petits blocs et le banchage.

Il est possible de réaliser par moulage ou extrusion pratiquement toutes les formes de petits blocs en plâtre pleins ou creux. Selon la granulométrie du matériaux et la précision des moules on obtient des blocs plus ou moins grossiers. La bonne coulabilité du mélange plâtre-eau, sa rapidité de prise et la facilité d'obtention de produits parfaitement surfacés favorisent la fabrication de blocs de très bonne précision dimensionnelle (1/10ème de mm) présentant tenons, mortaises et deux faces lisses. Ces blocs sont posés collés et ne nécessitent que des enduits pelliculaires de surfaçage. Selon la présence ou non d'agrégats (gypse ou sable), et selon les formes (pleines ou creuses), on obtient aisément des composants présentant des résistances supérieures à 50 Kg/cm^2 en compression. Ainsi, au Sénégal, sont actuellement utilisés des caneaux alvéolés de 60 x 40 x 15 pour la réalisation de murs porteurs (4 au M^2).

Ce mode d'utilisation du plâtre n'est rentable qu'avec une production de qualité régulière nécessitant une unité industrielle (qui peut rester peu sophistiquée)

A l'inverse, si le plâtre est produit par une installation artisanale très frustre c'est la technique du banchage par lits successifs qui semble devoir s'imposer. Le plâtre grossier ainsi produit, mélange irrégulier de semihydrate, de surcuits et d'incuits, est utilisé comme liant d'un béton de granulats gypseux ou non. Cette mise en oeuvre est actuellement utilisée à Nouakchott en Mauritanie par l'ADAUA pour la réalisation d'une centaine de logements économiques.

D'autres techniques sont également utilisables pour la réalisation de toitures. Citons des coupoles en plâtre projeté sur moule polyster réalisées à DAKAR et des formes rondes inspirées de l'architecture classique réalisées en blocs hourdés au plâtre en Mauritanie. Ces dernières utilisations posent avec acuité l'un des problèmes techniques les plus ardus de l'utilisation du plâtre à l'extérieur : celui de la tenue à l'eau.

2.3. Le principal inconvénient du plâtre est sans nul doute sa susceptibilité à l'eau. Un litre d'eau douce peut dissoudre 2 grammes de plâtre. L'humidité ambiante ne provoque pas, pour sa part, de dommage structurel, mais elle peut favoriser éventuellement le développement de micro-organismes. En conséquences, les règles de l'art des pays du Nord prescrivent de soustraire le plâtre aux ruissellements réguliers qui entraînent inéluctablement des pertes de matières par érosion. Il semble bien que les climats des pays chauds et secs permettent d'autres prescriptions.

Il est premièrement possible de concevoir un mur double où la partie porteuse en plâtre située à l'intérieur est protégée par une mince paroi écran. Ces techniques ne nous paraissent pas économiquement adaptées à la construction à faible coût, elles peuvent par contre résoudre certains problèmes d'isolation thermique dans des bâtiments plus coûteux.

La deuxième solution consiste à protéger directement le plâtre par une peinture, un enduit ou un bardage. Les techniques d'enduction d'un film mince, peinture ou badigeon (huile de lin bouillante, chaux aérienne, ...) nous semblent bien adaptés. Pour ce qui concerne les enduits, nous avons le choix entre trois grandes options : les peintures plastiques épaisses, les enduits à base de plâtre hydrofugé, les enduits anciens à base de plâtre, de chaux et de sable.

Nous pouvons écarter les premiers. Ils sont généralement très efficaces mais, étant totalement importés, leurs prix de vente sont incompatibles avec la construction très économique. Il nous semble préférable de prôner l'utilisation de la troisième catégorie d'enduits inspirés des enduits traditionnels parisiens à base de chaux grasse qui ont longtemps donné satisfaction.

La troisième et sans doute plus intéressante solution consiste à laisser le plâtre nu et à adopter des dispositifs architecturaux susceptibles de le soustraire à des concentrations d'eau ruisselante : toits débordants, gouttières, coupure étanche au niveau du plancher bas, soubassements en ciment élevés, etc...

La réalisation la plus démonstrative de cette conception est la fromagerie du monastère de Keur Moussa réalisée près de Dakar en carreaux de plâtre non protégés. Ce bâtiment résiste depuis plus de six ans, sans dommages apparents, à une hygrométrie intérieure très élevée (on y produit des fromages) et aux pluies d'hivernage (575 mm/an).

3. Quelle appropriation?

Après avoir brossé rapidement le panorama des techniques d'utilisation du plâtre les plus prometteuses pour la réalisation de constructions économiques en P.E.D. il convient de définir les conditions d'une bonne appropriation de ces techniques.

3.1. Différentes définitions des technologies appropriées s'affrontent. Daniel BIAU a proposé lors du colloque international M.T.C. tenu à l'UNESCO en Janvier 1983 la classification que nous adopterons. Elle est résumée ci-après.

Les critères sont groupés en deux catégories, ceux qui ont trait à l'offre et ceux qui concernent la demande.

Pour ce qui est de l'offre, on distingue d'une part les ressources disponibles et d'autre part les intérêts des intervenants dans la production de l'habitat :

- Pour les ressources (humaines-emplois, qualifications-matérielles-mines, énergies, équipements de production, de transport, de chantier) la distinction entre locale ou importée est généralement considérée.

- Pour les intérêts des intervenants il est clair d'une part que ces derniers n'ont pas tous le même stratégie et d'autre part qu'aucune technologie ne peut se développer tant que des acteurs économiques suffisamment puissants n'y trouvent pas leur intérêts. On distingue les producteurs directs (ouvriers, tâcherons) qui visent à augmenter leurs revenus, les opérateurs (entrepreneurs, fabricants, négociants) qui entendent rentabiliser leurs investissements et les pouvoirs publics qui agissent à différents niveaux (fonciers, financiers, fiscaux...)

Pour ce qui est de la demande, on fait la distinction entre les ressources (solvabilité) et les aspirations (disposer d'un habitat durable, confortable, adapté au mode de vie...) des différents groupes sociaux.

Une fois clairement énoncés, ces critères doivent être pondérés selon les contextes. C'est ce que nous nous proposons d'effectuer avec l'exemple de la construction de murs porteurs en blocs de plâtre.

3.2

a - Pour ce qui concerne les ressources humaines il faut distinguer la production de la poudre, la fabrication des blocs et la construction.

La production de la "poudre" de plâtre de préfabrication utilise peu de main d'oeuvre (une ou deux personnes par tonne de production annuelle) mais celle-ci doit être qualifiée de façon à gérer correctement une installation industrielle.

Pour sa part, la fabrication de blocs de parfaite régularité (qualité et dimension) peut être effectuée, comme au Sénégal, dans un atelier artisanal à forte consommation de main d'oeuvre (20 m^2/Homme/Jour de blocs de 15cm) peu qualifiée (quelques jours de formation pour un manoeuvre).

Enfin, la technologie de pose des blocs de plâtre s'apparente à celle de la maçonnerie traditionnelle : elle est fortement consommatrice de main d'oeuvre faiblement qualifiée mais présente une productivité supérieure à celle de la pose de parpaings de ciment (+ 30 %). Cette technologie de pose est bien acceptée dans les pays de maçons. Cependant il semble préférable de former des poseurs à partir d'ouvriers non qualifiés plutôt qu'à partir de maçons qui arrivent difficilement à oublier les gestes traditionnels de la pose des parpaings (le maçon recharge un joint épais alors que le plâtrier arrase un joint mince serré au marteau et à la cale).

En résumé, on a affaire à une technologie globalement très consommatrice d'une main d'oeuvre de qualification aisément disponible dans les pays africains.

b - Pour ce qui concerne les ressources matérielles on distingue
la disponibilité en matières premières, en énergie et en équipements.

La gypse utilisable pour la préfabrication est soit d'origine
naturelle soit d'origine industrielle. Les pays à climats chauds et
secs sont généralement bien pourvus de ressources en gypse de
carrière ou éolien. En Afrique on peut citer : la Mauritanie, le
Maroc, l'Algérie, la Tunisie, l'Egypte, le Soudan, etc... D'autres
pays de la même zone disposent d'industries de transformation des
phosphates en engrais dont le principal sous-produit est le phospho-
gypse, c'est le cas du Sénégal et du Maroc.

A l'inverse, le fuel et l'électricité nécessaires pour la cuisson
du plâtre et la fabrication des blocs sont généralement coûteux en
devises. Il faut souligner qu'en comparaison des chaux et ciments,
la production du plâtre exige néanmoins peu d'énergie (64,5 Kg
fuel/t pour la plâtrerie sénégalaise de 25.000 t/an a comparer à 159
Kg fuel/t pour la cimenterie Dakaroise de 380.000 t/an). En outre,
la faible température nécessaire (120°) peut rendre intéressante
l'utilisation de l'énergie solaire (expérience en cours en
Mauritanie). Même si le matériau n'est pas énergétiquement gratuit,
son utilisation massive peut s'avérer intéressante. Au Sénégal on a
comparé les coûts énergétiques des cloisons en carreaux de plâtre
alvéolés et des cloisons en agglomérés de ciment. En 7 cm d'épaisseur, l'aggloméré consomme 5 kg de fuel/m^2, le carreau 3,1, en 10 cm
l'aggloméré consomme 6,2 Kg/m^2 et le carreau 4,2. Cette économie de
32 à 38 % provient essentiellement de l'économie d'enduit autorisée
par le bloc de plâtre parfaitement surfacé.

Enfin, pour ce qui concerne les équipements de cuisson, de
préfabrication, de transport et de chantier, force est de constater
que même s'ils peuvent être relativement peu sophistiqués, les
fours, les moules et les matériels de manutention seront pour la
prochaine décennie encore presque systématiquement importés des pays
industrialisés. Leur entretien par contre ne nécessite généralement
pas de spécialistes expatriés.

Le critère relatif aux "ressources matérielles" doit être examiné, au cas par cas, selon la localisation, la taille de l'installation et le système constructif envisagé. S'il existe des ressources naturelles ou artificielles en gypse il sera sans doute pertinent
de les valoriser. Dans le cas contraire, malgré des coûts de transport maritime en vrac particulièrement avantageux, il est probable
que le bloc de plâtre ne se développera pas.

c - Pour ce qui concerne les stratégies des intervenants dans la
production de l'habitat, des intérêts divers - ceux des ouvriers, de
l'Etat en passant par ceux de l'entrepreneur - se conjuguent ou
s'opposent.

Nous avons déjà mentionné l'intérêt de former des ouvriers
n'ayant pas exercé préalablement le métier de maçon. Ces hommes
neufs dans le secteur du bâtiment seront les promoteurs du nouveau
matériau. Ils se verront opposer une certaine inertie et résistance
au changement par les autres corps de métiers qui devront s'adapter
aux impératifs d'une nouvelle technologie qui tolère mal l'à-peu-

près. Ainsi, il serait souhaitable que tous les travaux de béton-
nage soient achevés avant la pose des premiers blocs de plâtre, afin
que le chantier soit plus conduit comme une oeuvre d'assemblage de
composants finis de qualité que comme un gigantesque travail de
bricolage rattrapé in fine par des enduits épais, comme cela est
trop souvent la règle sur les chantiers de maçonnerie.

Les entrepreneurs de bâtiment devront pareillement remettre en
cause le planning de leur chantier, le recrutement de leur personnel, le mode de formation de leur prix de revient en acceptant
d'acheter des composants élaborés plus performants mais également
plus chers. Ces multiples changements susciteront autant de freins à
l'innovation.

A l'inverse, les industriels producteurs de poudre et de composants devront rentabiliser au mieux un investissement et des frais
fixes de fonctionnement significatifs (environ 8 millions de Francs
sur 10 ans pour l'unité de 25.000 t/an de DAKAR) en menant une rude
concurrence aux monopoles du parpaing de ciment. Cette conquête
d'une partie du marché de la construction peut s'effectuer selon
différentes stratégies privilégiant tel ou tel produit à base de
plâtre. Ainsi, au Sénégal l'industriel producteur établit à un haut
niveau les prix de la poudre, du plâtre à staff, du plâtre à projeter, des dalles de plafond de façon à concurrencer les produits
équivalents (importés ou à base de ciment) et vend les carreaux et
les blocs pratiquement à prix coûtant. Cette péréquation des frais
d'amortissement vise à garantir le maximum de chance au bloc de
plâtre pour effectuer sa persée sur le vaste marché du gros oeuvre.

Enfin, à l'intérieur même des pouvoirs publics différentes
logiques s'affrontent. La diminution des coûts de la construction à
qualité égale prônée par les ministères en charge de la construction
s'appuie le plus souvent sur la rationalisation des techniques
conventionnelles à base de ciment, alors que la rentabilisation du
potentiel des industries et des matériaux nationaux, les économies
d'énergie et de devises mobilisent les ministères de l'industrie et
des finances.

3.3. a - Pour ce qui concerne la demande, sous son double aspect de
solvabilité et d'exigences qualitatives, les premiers critères
intéressant un procédé innovant comme le mur porteur en blocs de
plâtre sont ceux que la maîtrise d'ouvrage publique édicte. En
effet, premièrement le secteur informel de l'auto-construction ne
s'appropriera pas un procédé sans solides réalisations de référence,
deuxièmement la maîtrise d'ouvrage publique est bien souvent le seul
interprète explicite des aspirations populaires autrement informu-
lées et troisièmement c'est souvent le seul type de promoteur qui
acceptera de prendre des "risques" sur la technique ou son accep-
tabilité.

Le critère solvabilité a été partiellement démontré, au Sénégal
par exemple, puisque des bâtiments publics et des logements ont été
réalisés en blocs de plâtre à des coûts comparables à ceux des
logements sociaux habituellement construits (1000 F/m^2). Ces
expériences demandant à être confirmées sur une plus grande échelle
et dans des conditions réellement concurrentielles.

Les aspirations pour un habitat confortable sont largement

satisfaites par les qualités unanimement reconnues du plâtre telles l'isolation thermique, la régulation hygrométrique, la résistance au feu, la facilité de réalisations décoratives et esthétiques.

Enfin, les aspirations pour un habitat durable, c'est à dire, pour ce qui concerne le plâtre, résistant à l'eau, sont satisfaites par les différentes technologies présentées plus haut. Les recherches et expérimentations en cours tentent à améliorer le rapport qualité prix de cette fonction.

4. Conclusion

Il est naturellement difficile de tirer des recommandations précises et exhaustives des considérations qui précédent. Néanmoins, lorsqu'il existe une disponibilité en gypse naturel ou chimique, si un investisseur industriel accepte de s'engager et si des pouvoirs publics soutiennent même modéremment la promotion du plâtre, c'est à dire en résumé s'il existe un potentiel réel de l'offre, il est réaliste de tenter l'expérience. C'est actuellement ce à quoi s'emploient les Sénégalais et les Tunisiens.

Il est clair qu'on ne peut obtenir aucune certitude sur l'intérêt du type de technologie ici présentée à l'aide seulement d'études de laboratoire ou de faisabilité. Seule l'expérimentation à échelle significative, mettant réellement en jeu tous les acteurs de la filière construction peut lever les freins successifs à l'innovation et permettre d'évaluer l'avenir d'un matériau et d'une technique.

Puisque l'on demande, à juste raison, aux chercheurs de sortir de leur laboratoires pour se confronter aux pratiques concrètes, il faut également demander à ce que soient mis en place les moyens correspondant de valorisation et de développement de la recherche. Les responsables politiques doivent prendre conscience de la nécessité de lancer de tels programmes d'expérimentation à grande échelle.

SECTION V

Action du milieu et des intempéries, durabilité et protection

Environmental factors, weathering, durability and protection

METHODS FOR REDUCING THE TENDENCY TOWARDS EMBRITTLEMENT IN NATURAL FIBRE CONCRETE

HANS-ERIK GRAM, Swedish Cement and Concrete Research Institute

1. Introduction

Concrete reinforced with natural fibres has been studied in Sweden since 1971. The aim was to develop a low cost, appropriate and durable roofing sheet made of locally available materials. In collaboration with organisations in Tanzania, roofing sheets of sisal fibre concrete have been developed.

It was found that sisal fibre concrete becomes brittle in tropical climates. Obviously there was a need to study the durability of natural fibre concrete and in 1979 a joint venture research project on this subject was initiated between the Faculty of Engineering at the University of Dar es Salaam in Tanzania and the Swedish Cement and Concrete Research Institute (CBI).

2. Why does sisal fibre concrete become brittle?

Nilsson /1/ among others found that natural fibres which had been conditioned in an alkaline solution lost in tensile strength. Investigations at CBI showed that sisal fibres conditioned in solutions with a pH value in excess of 12 are coloured yellow, see also Gram /2/.

This yellow discolouring of the fibres indicates a reaction between the buffer solutions OH-ions and the lignin in the sisal fibre. The primary cause of the change in the characteristics of sisal fibre in concrete is assumed by the author to consist of a chemical decomposition of the lignin and the hemicellulose in the middle lamella. The alkaline pore water in the concrete dissolves the lignin and hemicellulose and thus breaks the link between the individual fibre cells, see Fig. 1. The long sisal fibre looses its reinforcing capacity in concrete, since it breaks down into numerous small units.

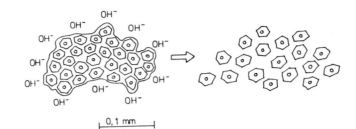

Fig 1. Schematic sketch of the decomposition of sisal
       fibres in concrete. The middle lamella is dissol-
       ved by the alkaline pore water in the concrete.

The rate at which sisal fibre concrete is embrittled
depends on the magnitude of the variation in the relative
air humidity and temperature to which it is subjected.
These variations initiate the transport of alkaline pore
water to the fibre and the removal of decomposition products and neutralized pore water from the fibre - factors
which are essential for the decomposition of the fibre
components.

3. Production and curing of specimens, test methods

Specimens for durability experiments have been manufactured with a mortar composed of binder, aggregate and water
with a weight ratio of 1:2:0.5 respectively. The share by
volume of embedded fibre has been 2%. A thin layer of
mortar has been placed on a plastic mould measuring
400 x 280 mm and 220 mm long sisal fibres have then been
placed on the surface of the mortar, uniformly distributed and aligned parallell to the end of the mould. This
layer of fibres was then worked into the mortar with the
aid of a roller so that each individual fibre was surrounded by mortar.
    A new thin layer of mortar was then placed on the
fibre layer and a second layer of fibres was placed in
position, oriented in the same direction as the fibers in
the first layer. The last layer of mortar was then placed
and levelled off and the mould was vibrated until the
surface of the mortar became smooth and glossy. The 8-10
mm thick specimen was demoulded after 24 hours in a conditioning room with a temperature of +20°C and a relative
air humidity of about 100%. After that the specimen was
placed in a tub full of water for curing for a further
5-7 days. Up to the testing time or the storage in the
intended environment (normally a further three weeks) the
specimen was stored in a conditioning room with a temperature of +20°C and a relative air humidity of 50%.
    Using knowledge about the influence of the external
environment on the embrittlement of natural fibre con-

crete as a basis, a method has been produced for accele-
rating the ageing of natural fibre concrete in this
respect. The method has then been used to determine
whether the measures taken to prevent the embrittlement
of natural fibre concrete have any effect.

The specimens have been stored in a climate cubicle,
see Fig. 2, for 0, 3, 15 and 30 days. The specimens in
the climate cubicle were subjected to moistening and
cooling by spraying them with water from the sprinkler
nozzles. The water which was transported into the climate
cubicle maintained a temperature of $+10^{\circ}C$. Each specimen
was sprayed with 1.5 litres of water a minute for 30
minutes. A period of 30 minutes was selected on the basis
of the capillary suction capacity of the concrete. The
time available permitted the 8-10 mm thick specimens to
have a considerable part of their capillary pore system
filled. After the water spraying the heat and fan were
started in the heat cubicle. The temperature in the
cubicle was permitted to reach $+105^{\circ}C$. The heat was
switched on for five and a half hours before the water
was sprayed into the climate box again. During the heating period, the capillary pore system in the specimens
dried out. As a result, the capillary pore system of the
specimens was both filled with and emptied of water
during the conditioning cycle of six hours. This means
that the fibres embedded in the specimens came in contact
with the alkaline pore water of the concrete during the
moistening phase and that any decomposition products
which were formed as a result of the reaction between the
fibre components and the pore water could be transported
away form the fibre during the drying phase.

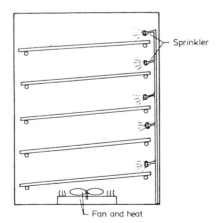

Fig.2. Schematic sketch of CBI climate cubicle.

The embrittlement of sisal fibre concrete has been
studied by following the changes in the behaviour of

the not aged or aged composite during bending. Beams measuring 55-60 x 230-280 x 8-10 mm were sawn out and subjected to flexural strength tests with a load set-up
shown in Fig. 3.

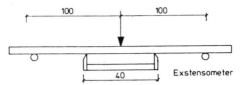

Fig. 3. Load set-up when bending natural fibre concrete
        beams.

The stress-strain curve was produced with the aid of
a XY-plotter and had two different layouts in principle
as illustrated in Fig. 4.

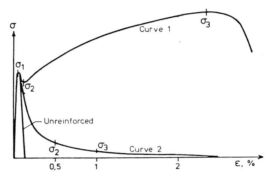

Fig. 4. Principle layouts for stress-strain curve during
        tests of flexural strength of natural fibre con-
        crete beams.

Either the stress, having passed the proportionality
limit (σ_1) and a possible drop (σ_2), increased again
to a maximum value (σ_3) according to Curve 1 or else
the stress decreased the entire time with an increase
in the deformation according to curve 2. For a sequence
in accordance with Curve 2, σ_3 has been selected as the
stress which prevails at a deformation of 1%. The lower
value of σ_3 the smaller the area under the stress-strain
curve and, therefore, the toughness of the composite. The
parameter σ_3 has been selected as a criterion of the
toughness of the composite.
Fig. 5 shows stress-strain curves for specimens of
sisal fibre concrete aged 0, 4, 8 and 120 cycles in the
CBI climate cubicle.

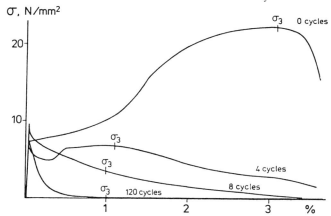

Fig. 5. Stress-strain curves for specimens of sisal fibre
concrete aged 0, 4, 8 and 120 cycles in a climate
cubicle.

4.   Countermeasures against the embrittlement of sisal
fibre concrete

Different approaches to prevent the observed embrittlement of sisal fibre concrete have been tested.

One approach was to use embedded bundles of sisal fibres in concrete instead of individual fibres. The fibres
which are in direct contact with the matrix can be broken
down with time while the inner fibres retain their
strength. A mesh of fabric consisting of sisal fibres
with about 30 fibres in the weave threads was embedded in
a concrete matrix and aged in the climate cubicle. When
specimens which had gone through 0 cycles were subjected
to bending tests it could be seen that the interaction
between the mesh reinforcement and the matrix was not at
all as good as was the case when individual fibres were
embedded and completely surrounded by the matrix, see
Fig. 6.

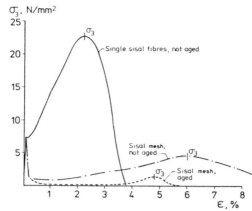

Fig.6. Stress-strain curves for concrete reinforced with
       sisal mesh which had been subjected to 0 and 12
       cycles in the CBI climate box, and unaged concrete
       with individually embedded fibres.

As can be seen from Fig. 6, the value for σ_3 achieved
when the reinforcement was embedded in the form of mesh
reinforcement was not at all as high. σ_3 occurs at a far
greater deformation, in this case at a deformation of
about 6% compared with a normal value of 2-3%. The dis-
placement of σ_3 is due to the fact that the individual
fibres in the mesh have a far longer anchorage length
since they are not in continous contact with the matrix
at the same time as they are not tensioned to the same
extent.
     As can be seen from Fig. 6 the toughness was conside-
rably reduced when the composite had been aged.
     Earlier it was noted that the decomposition of the
sisal fibre in concrete is due to the fact that the fibre is attacked chemically by the alkaline pore water in
the concrete. One way of avoiding or delaying this decomposition could be to impregnate the fibre with agents
which react with certain fibre components and build up
compounds which are difficult to dissolve in an alkaline
environment.
     Table 1 presents some of the investigated impregna-
tion combinations as well as the values for σ_3 for specimens cast with impregnated sisal fibres aged for 0, 12,
60 and 120 cycles in the climate cubicle.

Table 1 Values for σ_3 after a different number of cycles
in the climate box for specimens reinforced with
sisal fibres which have been impregnated with
blocking and water-repellent agents.

Impregnating agent	Number of cycles and $\sigma_3(N/mm^2)$			
	0	12	60	120
Unimpregnated sisal	32.8	2.8	0.9	0.4
Boric acid and PVC_2	0	-	-	-
Borax and chromium stearate	16.1	-	-	3.3
Formine and stearic acid	16.7	-	7.7	4.2;6.3
" "	17.4	3.8	7.2	5.3
" "	13.6	9.7	9.5	5.6
Potassium nitrate and stearic acid	14.0	-	6.4	3.0;4.1
Magnesium sulphate and PVC_2	4.8	-	0.8	0.6
Sodium chromate and fluori-ne-carbon-hydrogen-stearate	18.2	-	3.9	3.7

As can be seen from Table 1, impregnating the sisal
fibre with blocking and water-repellent agents causes the
value for σ_3 for unaged specimens to be lower than for spe
cimens with unimpregnated fibre. Impregnating the sisal
fibres reduces the embrittlement, however, after ageing in
a climate box. Fibres impregnated with formine and stearic
acid, potassium nitrate and stearic acid, sodium chromate
and fluorine-carbon-hydrogen-stearate, and borax and chro-
mium stearate give values for σ_3 after 120 cycles which
exceed 3 N/mm^2.
Table 2 presents the values for σ_3 for specimens conditioned outdoors in Dar es Salaam or Stockholm.

Table 2. Values for σ_3 for specimens reinforced with sisal
fibres which have been impregnated with blocking
and water-repellent agents and which have been
stored outdoors in Dar es Salaam or Stockholm.

Impregnating agent	Lo-ca-lity	Number of days and $\sigma_3(N/mm^2)$		
		0	135	200
Unimpregnated	Sth	10.7	-	6.9
"	Dar	12.4	-	0.3
Boric acid and PVC_2	Dar	$0^1)$	1.8	-
Formine and stearic acid	Dar	11.4	-	6.9
Barium nitrate and stearic acid	Sth	18.2	-	12.2
"	Dar	14.1	-	9.7

1) The 0-value has been taken from Table 1.

The results in Table 2 confirm the results achieved
with specimens aged in the climate box. Impregnating sisal fibres with formine and stearic acid or barium nitrate and stearic acid has a favourable effect and leads to
a retardation of the embrittlement tendencies in the composite.

The transport of alkaline pore water to the fibre and
the removal of neutralized water with the decomposition
products from the fibre which occur when the temperature
and moisture conditions of the composite are changed might
be reduced or eliminated completely by sealing the pore
system in the matrix in some way. This would delay or perhaps completely eliminate an embrittlement of natural
fibre in concrete.

Among the methods which have been tested for sealing
the pore system of the concrete matrix can be mentioned
the use of aggregate with a higher proportion of fines, a
lower water-cement ratio, replacing a part of the cement
with fly ash or slag, changing the binder from ordinary
Portland cement to finely ground blast furnace slag which
is activtated with powerfully alkaline admixtures, admixture of polymer micro-particles and admixing wax beads.
None of the methods which were tested for changing the pore
system of the concrete matrix proved capable of completely
eliminating the embrittlement of sisal fibre concrete. However, interesting results in the laboratory tests were obtained with the admixture of small beads of wax in the
fresh mortar. When the concrete had hardened and dried out
the composite was heated so that the wax melted and flowed
out in the pore system. The sealing by means of wax made
the absorption of water much slower and specimens with wax
amounting to 6.5% of the cement weight do not lose their
toughness after 120 cycles in the climate cubicle.

Sisal fibre concrete with a wax-sealed pore system becomes brittle when it is conditioned outdoors in Dar es
Salaam. One possible reason for the difference observed
in the experimental results for specimens aged in the
climate box and for specimens conditioned outdoors in Dar
es Salaam may be that the moisture content in the Tanza-
nian concrete was excessively high when the pore system
was sealed by melting the wax. The wax may have had difficulty in penetrating water-filled pores and the moisture which may have been enclosed when the pore system
was sealed was, perhaps, capable of transporting OH-ions
to embedded fibres. Further experiments with wax-sealed
sisal fibre concrete should shed light on the suitability
of this method for preventing embrittlement.

The last approach tested to prevent the embrittlement
of sisal fibre concrete has been to reduce the alkalinity of the pore water of the concrete matrix. Attempts to
carbonate the composite rapidly have been carried out,
but were not successful. The alkalinity in the pore water
in the matrix can be reduced considerably by using high
alumina cement as a binder instead of ordinary Portland

cement. Table 3 presents values for σ_3 for specimens manufactured with high alumina cement and aged in the climate box.

Table 3. Values for σ_3 after different numbers of cycles in the climate box for specimens manufactured with ordinary Portland cement or high alumina cement and reinforced with sisal fibres.

Binder	Number of cycles and σ_3 (N/mm^2)			
	0	12	60	120
Ordinary Portland cement	32.8	2.8	0.9	0.4
High alumina cement	30.8	21.3	21.4	13.5

As can be seen from Table 3, specimens manufactured with high alumina cement retain some of their toughness even after they have been subjected to ageing in the climate box. The value for σ_3 after 120 cycles is 13.5 N/mm^2. The tendency of the composite to become brittle canthus be reduced, although not completely eliminated, by using high alumina cement as a binder instead of ordinary Portland cement.

The pH value for the pore water in the matrix is reduced by replacing some of the ordinary Portland cement with a highly active, ultra-fine silica fume. It was noted when carrying out investigations of the alkalinity of pore water that the pH value for the pore water decreases from 13.2 for a matrix with ordinary Portland cement only as binder to 12.9 and 12.0 for matrixes in which 17% and 33% respectively of the binder consisted of silica fume.

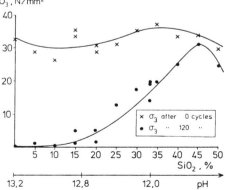

Fig. 7   The stress σ_3 (mean value for three specimens reinforced with sisal fibres) after 0 and 120 cycles in the climate box as a function of the percentage silica fume of the binder weight.

Fig. 7 presents the values for σ_3 for specimens manufactured with varying proportions of silica fume in the
binder and aged in the climate box.

As can be seen from Fig. 7, specimens in which up to
20% of the binder weight consisted of silica fume received comparatively insignificant or moderate increases in
the value for σ_3 after 120 cycles compared with specimens
without an admixture of silica fume. When 30-50% of the
cement is replaced with silica fume, a dramatic improvement is obtained in the toughness of the composite after
ageing.

5. Summary

Thin roofing sheets of sisal fibre concrete stored outdoors in a tropical climate become markedly embrittled
within a period of 6 months. The reason has been found to
be that the alkaline pore water in the concrete dissolves
components in the fibres so that they become decomposed
and lose their reinforcing capacity. Efforts have been
made to find remedies to counteract this embrittlement.
The effects of various countermeasures have been studied
on specimens subjected to accelerated ageing in a climate
box. The laboratory experiments were supplemented with
experiments with specimens stored outdoors in Stockholm
or Dar es Salaam. The experimental results indicate that
the most efficient way of counteracting the embrittlement
of sisal fibre concrete is to reduce the alkalinity of
the pore water. This can be achieved by replacing 40-50%
of the ordinary Portland cement with silica fume. Replacing the binder with high alumina cement also reduces the
alkalinity of the pore water and thus slows down the rate
of embrittlement. Sealing the concrete pore system with
wax and using various fibre impregnating agents have also
reduced the embrittlement somewhat.

References

/1/ Nilsson L: Reinforcement of concrete with sisal and
    other vegetable fibres. Swedish Council for Building
    Research, Document D14:1975. Svensk Byggtjänst,
    Stockholm, pp 1-68.

/2/ Gram H-E: Durability of natural fibres in concrete.
    CBI-research Fo 1:83, Swedish Cement and Concrete
    Research Institute.

LA PROTECTION DES CONSTRUCTIONS EN TERRE ARGILEUSE AU TOGO

EPHOEVI-GA Foli   Ingénieur Chimiste
CENTRE DE LA CONSTRUCTION ET DU LOGEMENT
B. P. 1762 '— Tél. 21-64-03
LOME — TOGO

APERCU GEOGRAPHIQUE SUR LE TOGO

Avec ses 56.000 km2, la République Togolaise est le plus petit Etat francophone d'Afrique de l'Ouest. Elle se présente comme un couloir allongé sur 600 km du Nord au Sud entre le Ghana à l'Ouest, le Bénin à l'Est, la Haute-Volta au Nord. Au Sud, une étroite façade maritime de 55 km lui donne un accès à la mer, dans le golfe de Guinée. De l'Est à l'Ouest, la distance ne dépasse nulle part 120 km.

Au point de vue relief, le Togo présente au Sud, une plaine côtière d'une cinquantaine de km de profondeur tapisé de "terre de barre" (c'est-à-dire argile) d'âge tertiaire. Cette plaine est suivie d'un plateau ancien de 150 à 500 m d'altitude qui offre sur plus de la moitié du pays un paysage de collines et de vallons. Ce plateau est interrompu par une petite chaîne montagneuse orientée sud-ouest/nord-est qui est le prolongement au Togo du massif béninois de l'Atakora et le massif Ghanéen d'Akwapim. La chaîne togolaise atteint ses plus fortes altitudes au Sud, dans la région de Kloto (1.020 m). Elle s'abaisse au Nord, vers la plaine alluviale de l'Oti et à l'Est vers la plaine du Mono.

En raison de sa grande extension en altitude (6è et 11è degré latitude Nord) le Togo jouit de trois zones distinctes de climat.

- entre le 6è et le 8è degré, le Sud a un climat tropical moins humide que ne le laisserait attendre la latitude subéquatoriale avec deux saisons pluvieuses (Mars à Juin, puis Septembre-Octobre) alternant avec deux saisons sèches (Novembre à Mars, puis Août — Septembre). La faible pluviosité, 700 mm au total dans la région côtière malgré un rythme climatique de type équatorial, s'explique par le fait que le littoral est relativement abrité de la mousson océanique par l'écran que forme au Sud-ouest le cap édifié par les alluvions de la Volta. Les précipitations sont plus importantes dès qu'on aborde les reliefs de l'intérieur : 1.600 mm en moyenne.

   - entre le 8è et 9è degré, le centre, abrite des vents pluvieux par la dorsale montagneuse, a un climat sec.

   - entre le 9è et le 11è degré, le Nord a un climat de type soudanien, avec alternance d'une courte saison pluvieuse de Mai à Octobre, et une longue saison sèche. Le maximum de pluies se situe en Août et la moyenne des précipitations ne dépasse pas 1.300 mm.

   Les températures sont partout comprises entre 22 et 32°C. Les écarts thermiques s'accroissent de la côte vers l'intérieur. Le réseau hydrographique comprend : le système lagunaire bordant tout le littoral ; le système du bassin de la Volta constitué par l'Oti et ses affluents ; le système du Mono et le système côtier avec le Sio et le Haho. Les cours d'eau ont tous un régime irrégulier.

L'HABITAT TRADITIONNEL AU TOGO

   Les matériaux utilisés dans les habitations traditionnelles sont tirés directement de l'environnement. Ils sont immédiatement disponibles ; ils ont les avantages certains d'un coût peu élevé et un bon pouvoir d'isolation thermique. On distingue les matériaux des murs de ceux des couvertures.

Le mur

   Les matériaux traditionnels pour les murs comprennent l'herbe, les branchages, la pierre, mais c'est surtout la terre qui domine.

   La terre ou l'adobe appelé aussi banco se présente selon les lieux sous forme d'argile à plasticité variable allant de l'argile limoneuse très plastique à l'argile sableuse. Sa teinte oscille entre le gris et le rouge latérite. Pour être utilisée dans la construction, la terre est préparée par l'addition d'eau suivie d'un pétrissage.

   La construction des murs se fait d'une façon monolithique armé ou non ou bien à partir de bloc séché au soleil. Lorsque le mur est armé, ce sont des branches d'arbres qui constituent les armatures.

   L'épaisseur des murs en adobe varie en moyenne entre 20 et 60 cm ; elle est forte en bas et diminue progressivement vers le haut, ceci pour minimiser l'érosion que pouvait provoquer les eaux de ruissellement à la partie inférieure du mur.

La couverture

C'est du règne végétal qu'est tiré cette fois les matériaux indispensables à la couverture des habitations traditionnelles. En effet, la paille qui est l'élément de couverture très répandu est issu de graminées. Si la paille est un matériau recherché pour son bon pouvoir d'isolation thermique, il est néanmoins très inflammable et ne dure pas assez longtemps. Mais on peut cependant augmenter la durée de vie du matériau en le mettant à l'abri du pourrissement. C'est pourquoi on évite que l'eau de pluie séjourne pendant trop longtemps dans la paille en accentuant la pente des toits de chaume qui, selon les bâtiments, peuvent être ronds ou rectangulaires.

PROTECTION DES MURS EN TERRE ARGILEUSE

Le bâtisseur traditionnel a cherché depuis longtemps à protéger ses maisons des intemperies de diverses manières (drainage des eaux de ruissellement autour des constructions, débordement et pentes accentués des toitures). Mais devant l'insuffisance et la précarité de ces moyens, il est amené à trouver d'autres méthodes de protection des bâtisses en terre argileuse.

C'est souvent au stade de finition que la protection des murs intervient. Les produits hydrofuges généralement utilisés dans les milieux ruraux peuvent se classer en produits locaux et en produits importés.

Produits locaux : Ils sont d'origine minérale ou végétale tout comme les éléments ayant servi dans le gros-oeuvre.

Produits d'origine minérale : Certaines terres extraites des cours d'eau (limon) douées de propriétés hydrofuges sont utilisées comme enduits ou badigeons. Elles protègent contre l'infiltration de l'eau dans le banco et empêche ainsi la dégradation des murs. Leur efficacité, certes, ne dure que quelques années ; mais par un entretien périodique et régulier on arrive le plus souvent à prolonger la durée de vie du matériau.

Produits d'origine végétale : Les décoctions de certaines légumineuses communément appelées le néré sont utilisées dans la finition des sols battus. Ces extraits donnent une cohésion au matériau et lui confèrent une dureté et une étanchéité relatives le mettant pour un certain temps à l'abri de l'érosion de l'eau et de l'usure.

Produits importés : Selon leur nature, ces produits sont
employés soit à l'extérieur, soit à l'intérieur des maisons
d'habitation.

   - Le goudron. Il est employé généralement à l'extérieur
du mur, en plusieurs couches ; il protège la maison des eaux
de pluie. En dehors de l'aspect lugubre qu'on lui reproche,
(il arrache l'attrait, la gaîté et le charme au bâtiment) son
adhérence au subjectile est très mauvaise et c'est ce qui
explique les nombreux corquages sur le mur.

   - La chaux. Elle est réservée d'habitude au badigeon
intérieur des murs. Quoique répandue, elle demeure d'accès
difficile à cause de son coût relativement élevé.

   En conclusion, on peut remarquer que les différentes
méthodes traditionnelles de protection employées dans le
milieu rural par le paysan ont deux inconvenients majeurs.

- d'abord l'inéfficacité quasi totale des produits locaux,
- ensuite le coût excessif des produits importés (goudron,
chaux). Afin de trouver une approche au dilemme devant lequel
le paysan togolais, est confronté, le Centre de la Construction et du Logement à Cacavelli, dès sa création en 1969, s'est
penché sur l'épineux problème de protection des murs en terre
argileuse. L'un des objectifs que le Centre s'était fixé
consiste dans la mise au point de produits hydrofuges qui,
convenablement employés soit dans la masse de l'enduit soit
comme badigeon protègeraient le banco de la pénétration d'eau,
cause essentielle de dégradation du matériau sous nos climats.

EXPERIENCES DU CENTRE DE LA CONSTRUCTION ET DU LOGEMENT (C.C.L)

   Au cours des recherches, certains produits hydrofuges,
jusque là inconnus dans le milieu rural, ont été expérimentés
avec succès au C.C.L. C'est ainsi que les études ont porté
sur les produits tels que l'huile de kapok, le mortier batard
et le palmitate de calcium.

L'huile de kapok

   Elle est extraite des graines du kapokier ou fromager
(Ceiba guineensis) arbre géant des pays tropicaux.

Son utilisation en tant qu'agent protecteur des murs en banco est intervenue depuis 1975 au C.C.L. L'huile de kapok est une huile siccative, d'odeur forte et catéristique d'un jaune doré. L'huile brute préparée artisanalement à une masse volumique de 0,92 g/cm3 à 27°C, un indice de saponification de 193 et un indice d'iode de 98. Tout comme les autres produits hydrofuges, huile de kapok est utilisée dans la masse de la terre qui a servi d'enduit au mur sur lequel le test est porté puis passée en badigeon de trois couches avant le début de l'essai.

Le mortier bâtard

Il est composé de ciment portland artificiel et de chaux grasse dolomitique produite et commercialisée au C.C.L. La proportion des liants constituant le mortier bâtard varie suivant la nature et la granulométrie de la terre. Elle est généralement de 3 parties de chaux grasse pour 1 partie de ciment. Mais, il est parfois nécessaire d'ajouter au mélange terre argileuse + ciment + chaux une quantité variable de sable propre et d'une bonne granulométrie pour faciliter la mise en oeuvre et empêcher la fissuration de l'enduit par diminution les effets de tension que provoqueraient les éléments fins de l'argile. Lorsque l'enduit est bien dosé l'adhérence est bonne et le risque de décrochage qu'on observe généralement à la mise en oeuvre du mortier sable-ciment sur un mur en banco est moindre. L'addition de chaux, produit local fait du mortier batard un matériau à coût réduit et d'une efficacité relativement bonne.

Le palmitate de calcium

C'est le produit qui a donné le meilleur résultat parmi tous ceux qui ont été expérimentés au C.C.L. Le palmitate de calcium est un mélange de chaux grasse et d'acide palmitique. Il ne renferme aucun liant hydraulique (ciment ou chaux).

L'acide palmitique est une masse solide, onctueuse au toucher, obtenue par action de HCl dilué à 25 % sur une solutior de savon local appelé ako_to_ lequel est le résultat de la saponification de l'huile de palme par les cendres de feuilles incinérées de baobab et autres végétaux riches en métaux alcalins. Le rendement est de 1,5 kg d'acide palmitique par kilogramme de savon pour 8 litres d'eau de dilution totale. Il faut rendre l'acide palmitique fluide (il fond à 70°C) avant de pouvoir le mélanger intimement sous agitation, à la chaux

préalablement éteinte. Le mélange chaux acide palmitique
donne le palmitate de calcium qui, bien dosé à la terre, sert
à enduire le mur en banco.

Une fois le produit à expérimenter retenu, des pans de murs
élevés pour la circonstance sont revêtus d'un enduit en terre
argileuse auquel est incorporé l'enduit à tester. Des essais
accélérés d'arrosage par un poste mobile servant à mesurer
l'infiltration de l'air et la pénétration de l'eau dans les
différents éléments du bâtiment ont permis de juger de
l'efficacité des agents hydrofuges expérimentés. Parrallèle-
ment, l'expérience est menée sur un mur témoin ne renfermant
aucun produit protecteur. Les résultats des essais ont permis
de déduire que l'huile de kapok assure une certaine protection
aux constructions en terre argileuse comparativement au matériau dépourvu d'agents hydrofuges mais son efficacité reste
cependant médiocre par rapport au mortier bâtard qui se classe
après le palmitate de calcium.

CONCLUSION

Des enquêtes menées auprès des populations rurales ont
prouvé que le paysan togolais consacre chaque année un temps
non négligeable de ses moments de loisirs à entretenir ses
maisons d'habitation. Or la productivité se trouverait
largement accrue si cette corvée pouvait lui être épargnée
à la fin de chaque saison de pluie. Pour atteindre cet
objectif à court terme, il faudra que des recherches soient
entreprises sur les produits hydrofuges à base des matières
disponibles sur place. C'est pourquoi l'inventaire et l'identification de tous les produits locaux couramment employés
pour protéger le banco dans nos milieux traditionnels doivent
être faits. Puis le chercheur étudiera et vulgarisera une
technologie améliorante des produits, car tels qu'ils sont
actuellement utilisés, ces produits ne donnent pas entière
satisfaction à l'utilisateur.

Enfin, la recherche de nouveaux produits hydrofuges
beaucoup plus efficaces doit être entreprise car, par ses
propriétés d'isolation thermique et son prix de revient
quasiment nul, le banco restera pendant longtemps encore le
matériau de prédilection le plus accessible au paysan dans
l'autoconstruction et le mieux adapté au climat tropical.

ANALYSIS OF SERVICE LIFE OF MATERIALS FOR THE BUILDING ENVELOPE

CHRISTER SJÖSTRÖM, National Swedish Institute for Building Research

1. *Introduction*

Service life prediction of building materials is a troublesome subject
for practical considerations when designing a building or planning
for its maintenance. It is furthermore a vast research area, even
when restricted to materials in the building envelope.

Many test methods exists for assessing the relative performance
over time of materials, but it is a well-known difficulty to use only
data from short term testing to predict a materials service life in
the actual use situation.

Despite the many obstacles to reliably predict service life a lot
can be acheived by a systematic approach when analysing a durability
problem. This paper opens with a short over-view of such systematic
approaches mainly to present a background and to point out the
essential parts of service life prediction.

The first important step in all service life analysis is the
problem definition, that is to identify the performance requirements,
the degradation factors and the possible degradation processes of
the material. In this article are presented examples of important
degradation factors and of general degradation processes for different materials.

2. *Some systematic approaches*

2.1 Terminology and a model of thinking
To start with one has to conclude that there is no uniform terminology in the field of service life prediction. It is not the aim here
to try to solve that problem, but merely for the sake of further
understanding to present the authors view.

In a Nordic report edited by Sneck (1) the different meanings of
expressions like durability and performance over time were presented
and commented. The report concluded that durability can be seen as
the resistance of a material, incorporated in a structure, to the
environmental factors. The surrounding materials form a part of the
environment and effect through the design the service life of the
material in question. The expression performance over time means

the ability of a building product to maintain its initial performance to an acceptable extent.

A way of looking at service life prediction, based basically on the same definitions, is presented in figure 1.

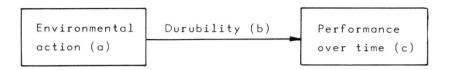

Fig. 1 Service life prediction

Environmental action (a) means all degradation factors, including static and dynamic loadings, affecting a material. Materials in the building envelope are influenced mainly by climatic factors and normal air constituents, pollutants and use factors. It is important to remember that especially for exterior materials the intensity of most environmental factors varies with time, even if one often has to describe a certain factor by some typical value. One important barrier to reliable methods for service life prediction is the poor knowledge of the environmental action on materials in actual use.

Durability (b) means in this context the resistance of a material to deterioration. This material´s quality is quite anonymous until it is pointed out what specific properties (performance characteristics) to measure, that is to use as indicators of degradation.

The performance over time (c) can be defined as the function describing how the measured values of the choosen properties varies with time. With this function established and with a performance criterion that sets the limit of the service life all essentials are known for a service life prediction. It can be stated that service life analysis aims at creating the performance over time functions.

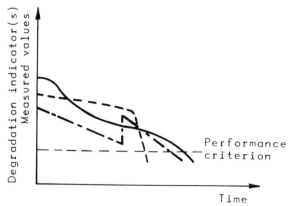

Fig. 2 Hypothetical performance over time functions

2.2 Systematic frameworks

An important and well established systematic approach to treat service
life prediction is the ASTM E-632 Standard Practice for Developing
Accelerated Tests to Aid Prediction of the Service Life of Building
Components and Materials (2). The Standard Practice is divided into
four parts: Problem Definition, Pre-Testing, Testing and Interpretion
and Reporting of Data.

Masters, one of the authors of the Standard Practice, presents in
(3) a review of different systematic frameworks for addressing service
life prediction, one of which is the Standard Practice. He concludes
that though the examples show somewhat different approaches they all
point out the importance of a) understanding the basic degradation
processes of the materials and b) characterizing the environment in
which the materials are used.

An understanding of the principle mechanisms by which a material
deteriorates should constitute the basis for all service life analysis. Ramachandran (4) claims that one reason that some accelerated
weathering tests for organic materials have not proven satisfactory,
is the method of developing the tests by presupposing important
exposure factors and incorporating most of them in a test chamber.
He argues that it is more effective first to determine the degradation processes and then design the test to reproduce them.

3. *Degradation factors and examples of deterioration processes*

3.1 General aspects

A complete listing of degradation factors is given in the ASTM E-632
(2). The main headings in the list are Weathering, Biological,
Stress, Incompatibility and Use factors. Here the prime interest
will be paid to the effects of weathering factors, that is climatic
factors, normal air constituents and pollutants. The use factors,
if one includes the design of a building and the maintenance procedures, have often a decisive effect on the materials service life and
will be separately commented.

From normal meteorological statistics it is possible in most
countries to get information on several climatic variables of interest
for the studies of durability. Some examples are the data obtained
on temperature, precipitation, humidity, wind and in som areas also
solar radiation and air pollutants. It is though important to remember that materials deterioration depend on the micro-climate and
even the conditions within the material. Data on macro-climate might
give some guidance on what weathering factors that are of importance,
but such data are not enough for a service life analysis. The relation between macro-, meso- and micro-climate is a research area in
which a lot needs to be done.

3.2 Solar radiation

Photodegradation by sunlight is one of the most important degradation
processes for organic materials such as plastics, paints and wood.
The breakdown occurring leads to a loss in mechanical and aestethical
properties. It is mainly the ultra-violet part (wave-lengths < 400 nm)
of the solar radiation that, together with oxygen and photoactive

substances in the materials, cause the deterioration. However, it has for wood been shown by Miller (5) that also the visible light plays an important role in the photodegradation. Wood exposed to sunlight gets a degradation of the surface that impaires the paint holding properties.

A general effect of the infrared part (wave-lengths > 800 nm) of solar radiation is an acceleration of ageing through an increase of the surface temperature. How high the temperature gets depends on the colour and the texture of the surface, but as high temperatures as 80-90°C has been recorded for black surfaces. It is not uncommon during high insolation in the winter-time in the Nordic coutries with surface temperatures of 15-25°C when the air temperature is below zero. If the material surface is shadowed the rapid decrease in temperature might cause severe tensions in the material. This might also occur in the summer due to a sudden cold rain. While UV radiation is an important degradation factor for organic materials the infrared radiation has an impact on all materials due to the temperature risning effect.

It is interesting to note that while, for many polymers, through laboratory studies there is a good knowledge of the deterioration mechanisms, the knowledge of the UV-intensity in the nature is limited. One explanation is the difficulty to measure the UV-radiation in a simple and non-expensive way, and these limitations have prohibited measurement programs aiming at characterizing UV dose at different locations in a country and at different spots on a building. Photochemical methods to measure UV that are far cheaper to use than the ordinary physical methods, have been developed by Martin (6) using poly(vinyl chloride)-films and by Davis et al (7) using poly-(phenylene oxide)-films. The degree of deterioration of the films due to accumulated UV dose during a time of exposure is evaluated by using IR- and UV-spectrophotometric analysis. The deterioration of the films are calibrated with data from measurements using known UV pyranometers. Both methods are at the moment being developed for and adjusted to Nordic conditions by the National Swedish Institute for Building Research.

3.3 Temperature
Temperature and its fluctuation is of great importance for durability studies. The main effects are, as already been indicated, an acceleration of ongoing chemical reactions or movements in a material or a component resulting in internal stresses, and thermal degradation at relatively high surface temperatures. Oxidation, photochemical reactions and hydrolysis might get the reaction velocity doubled by a temperature increase of 10°C which means that temperature has a great impact on organic materials. The rate of corrosion of metals and also biological degradation is influenced by temperature.

In cold regions porous materials such as concrete, bricks, wood and also paints are affected by frost action. A destruction of a porous material by freezing and thawing is dependent of the moisture content of the material, of a temperature below 0°C and of the rate of cooling.

3.4 Water and moisture
Water plays an important role in most deterioration of materials,
either directly as involved in the degradation mechanisms or as a
medium for the reactions. A relative humidity of 85 % in the nearest
atmospheric layer of a metal has been shown to be enough for a fast
rate of corrosion. The same importance of the relative humidity is
probably a fact for coatings and other organic materials though the
specific relative humidities necessary for deterioration, for different classes of organic materials, have not yet been specified. The
time of wetness is an important variable for description of the environment and a measurement equipment has been developed by Sereda (8).
    Drivning rain affects porous materials basically in two ways:
a) by wetting a material beyond the surface and thus enclosing water
for a longer period of time which permits the water to take part in
secondary deterioration processes, and b) by erosion. Erosion by
drivning rain is mainly a problem for inorganic materials such as soil
blocks and clay bricks, but it may also influence for example paints
with poor binders.
    The water content in a building material at the time of installa-
tion is a factor that might well be decisive for the materials performance. An obvious material´s example is wood which, to avoid
dimensional changes, after being handled in a saw-mill or otherwised
processed must be allowed to dry before being used. The rate of
drying must be controlled.
    To regulate the rate of drying is one way in a strive of control-
ling the drying shrinkage of different types of soil blocks.

3.5 The effects of pollutants
It can be stated that little is known of the effects of pollutants on
building material´s durability. Atmospheric corrosion of metals
might be the one field in which exists a rather good knowledge of the
influence of sulphur oxides.
    Data on sulphur oxides, soot and other particulate matter and of
sea salts are often available for major cities or industrial areas as
a result of measurements performed by special authorities. There is
though a lack of knowledge on how the pollutants are deposited on
buildings. The negative effect of acid rain, resulting from gaseous
pollutants dissolved in rain water, on metals, marble, renderings and
many other materials has for many years been taken for granted, and
it does most certainly influence the deterioration. But dry deposition of dust, dirt and other particulates on a material might well
form a more acidic environment when the relative humidity is high.
    Pollutants have very different effects on different materials and
, for example, some polymers are only attacked if sunlight and oxygen
are present.

3.6 Normal air constituents
The normal air constituents of main importance for materials deterioration are oxygen and ozone. Oxidative reactions are always accelerated by UV-radiation, by an increase in temperature and by the
presence of some catalyst.

4. *Building design and maintenance procedures*

Most examples of early deterioration of exterior materials leading to
unexpected maintenance are caused by a faulty design. A proper
planning should account for the local environment and the material
properties already at the moment of locating the building at the
building ground.

If aesthetical demands are high and a dominating facade has to be
facing south or east and thus subjected to high doses of UV-radiation
and high temperatures, there is reason to chose the material accordingly, if possible to avoid organic coatings or to perform a careful
study of different formulas.

Porous materials have to be protected against erosion caused by
driving rain. This ought to be done both by taking into consideration the prevailing winds when locating the building and by building
design measures. To protect a wall material important details are the
design of the roofing and of the walls connection to the foundation.
It is also important to prevent water from being capillarily
transported from the ground to the wall material.

It is rewarding to plan for the building maintenance as early as
at the time of building design. How shall the choosen materials be
maintained in order to present an optimum service life? Are well
functioning maintenance procedures available? These questions have to
be answered.

5. *A material's example - coated sheet metal*

Coil coated steel and aluminium are rather common cladding materials
in the Nordic countries. The materials consist of galvanized steel or
aluminium sheets that are coated in factories with different sorts of
paints. The coating has an aesthetical purpose at the same time as
it constitutes a part of the corrosion protection. This kind of
materials are at the moment being used in a methodological study comprising surveys in the housing stock, exposure of the material at
field stations and accelerated laboratory testing (9, 10).

The aesthetical properties of the coatings are mainly the ability
to maintain the initial gloss and colour, that is primarily to withstand the effects of solar radiation. Dirt retention is also an
important property that has not only an aesthetical importance. The
corrosion protective qualities might be described as the coatings
ability to prevent water from penetrating down to the metal.

The following indicators of ageing have been choosen and are being
evaluated: gloss, colour change, chalking, dirt retention, blistering,
cracking, corrosion and paint adherence. The same standardized
evaluative techniques are being used both in the field studies and in
the laboratory studies.

The accelerated tests used upp till now are ATLAS Weather-ometer
(ASTM G26-70), salt spray test (ASTM B117-73) and the so called
Cleveland test (ASTM D2247-68).

The tested coatings are poly(vinylidene fluoride) (PVF_2), acrylic
latex, silicone polyester, alkyd-melamine and PVC-plastisol.

Some very summarized results are the following: The silicone

polyester and the alkyd-melamine react clearly, both in the laboratory test and in the field studies, to UV-radiation with chalking and
change in gloss and colour. The coatings show micro-cracking which
leads to tendencies of corrosion after about ten years in the studied
environments. The tested PVF_2-paint shows a very good durability
against UV-radiation but the corrosion protective ability was not as
good as expected. PVC-plastisol has a good durability to water and
moisture, but reacts to UV-radiation. While these coatings showed
about the same behaviour in the field studies and in the laboratory
testing, the acrylic latex reacted differently. In the field studies
slight tendencies to chalking was noted, implaying that the coating
reacts to UV-radiation. No such tendencies could be observed when
the coating was subjected to UV-radiation in the laboratory using the
weather-ometer. The acrylic latex absorbes water which results in a
softening of the coating, in blisterings and in reduced adherence.

A comparison of the results obtained in the field studies with the
data from the laboratory testing is to some extent promising. It
seems that there are possibilities to use these standardized tests as
parts in a predictive test method for the coatings studied. The
findings however also show the danger of a too general reliance on the
test methods. Test procedures have to be carefully built up with regard to deterioration mechanisms and environmental observations.

6. Evaluative techniques

A lot might be said of different techniques to evaluate durability
and a review of such methods goes beyond the aim of this article. A
summarized presentation is to be found in for example (1).

Most evaluation of materials durability includes, at some stage,
the use of different sorts of short-term test methods. The difficulty
of interpreting the test results is well known, but anyhow such
methods are quite necessary for new materials and old materials in
new applications.

Systematic field studies in the existing house stock as a mean to
establish data on materials performance, is a methodology that is
little developed. In the study of coated sheet metal mentioned above
the technique is being used and has proven to be successful, but
labour intensive. The development of an inspection routine, which
shall include descriptions on what material parameters to evaluate and
on measurement techniques and measurement equipments to be used, is
a vital part when planning a field survey.

It is recommended that field surveys in the house stock are used
as an important complement to other techniques. It is of course
possible to draw conclusions of a materials behaviour by comparison
with the performance of a similar material used in the existing
houses.

7. Concluding remarks

This paper describes some essential deteriorating factors effecting
exterior materials and gives examples of degradation processes. The
important steps in a service life prediction are: to identify the
performance requirements, to describe the environmental action and try
to point out the possible degradation processes of the material in
question, to decide for and design some evaluative techniques.

   The performance over time of a building material is greatly influenced by the building design.

   Systematic collection of data from the existing housing stock might
serve the twofold purpose of presenting data on materials performance
as well as giving indications of which degradation factors to account
for.

References

1. Sneck, T. (1982), editor of *Activities on Durability of Building
    Products*. Research notes 96 and 97, the Technical Research
    Centre of Finland, Espoo, Finland, April.
2. American Society for Testing and Materials (1981), *Standard
    Practice for Developing Accelerated Tests to Aid Prediction of
    the Service Life of Building Components and Materials*, ASTM E
    632-81.
3. Masters, L. (1983), *Service life prediction: the barriers and
    opportunities*. Proceedings of the 9th CIB Congress, National
    Swedish Institute for Building Research, Gävle, Sweden.
4. Ramachandran, V.S. (1983), *New approaches to building materials*.
    Proceedings of the 9th CIB Congress, Nat. Swedish Institute
    for Building Research, Gävle, Sweden.
5. Miller, E. (1981), *The photodegradation of wood during solar
    irradiation*. Proceedings of the 2nd Conference on the Dura-
    bility of Building Materials and Components, Nat. Bureau of
    Standards, Gaithersburg, September.
6. Martin, K.G. (1973), *Monitoring ultraviolet radiation with poly-
    vinylchloride*. Brit. Polymer Journal 5, 443-450.
7. Davis, A. et al (1976), *A world-wide program for the continous
    monitoring of solar UV radiation using poly(phenylene oxide)
    film, and a consideration of results*. Journal Appl. Polym.
    Sci., 20, 1165-1174.
8. Sereda, P.J. et al (1980), *Measurements of the Time-of-Wetness by
    moisture sensors and their calibration*. Nat. Research Council
    of Canada, Div. of Building Research, Ottawa, June.
9. Sjöström, Ch. et al (1979), *Fabrikslackerad plåt - åldrande och
    provningsmetoder (Coil coated sheet metal - ageing and test
    methods)*. Bulletin M79:10, Nat. Swedish Institute for Building
    Research, Gävle, April.
10. Sjöström, Ch. et al (1983), *Studier i husurval och accelererad
    provning. Fasadbeklädnad av fabrikslackerad plåt (Surveys in
    the housing stock and accelerated ageing. Coil coated sheet
    metal as cladding material)*. Bulletin M83:10, Nat. Swedish
    Institute for Building Research, Gävle, March.

COLLAPSE MECHANISMS OF RURAL HOUSE FRAMES IN SOUTHERN CAMEROON

NJOCK LIBII, Josué, Ecole Polytechnique,

University of Yaounde, CAMEROON.

1. Introduction

Building shelters is as old as the world. In each region design, construction and maintenance of houses are reflective of the history, the
environment and the degree of technological sophistication of the a-
rea. As a consequence, there exists a wide variety of dwellings
throughout the world.

Traditionally, in Southern Cameroon, houses were built using wood,
bamboo, soil and variety of leaves and ropes. Nowadays, however, there exist many construction materials to choose from depending upon
one's purchasing power. By and large, the kind of material at one's
disposal determine the kind of house that will be built.

In this paper we study the two most common types of dwellings in
Southern Cameroon for the purpose of Comparing their building procedures, their structures, the factors that lead to their collapse,
their costs and their durabilities.

2. Description of house types

There are different kinds of houses in Southern Cameroon. For simplicity, these houses have been grouped under three different types
which are referred to, respectively, as Basic traditional, modern tra
ditional and modern. We restrict our attention to the first two becau
se they are the most common.

2.1 Basic Traditional houses

Basic traditional houses are rectangular houses, designed and built
by the owner with the assistance of neighbors and friends using local
ly available materials and traditional techniques. They have three
outstanding characteristics. They are : (1) very labor-intensive, (2)
made of more than 90% locally available materials, and (3) made with
local technology and labor.

A typical construction procedure could involve these basic steps :
(1)- choice of a building site. (2)- Clearing of the site. (3)- Laying out the house. (4)- Wooden columns are driven into the ground
(20 to 30cm) and the basic house frame is set. (5)- The roof is built
(sometimes on the ground) using bamboo, leaves and ropes and lifted

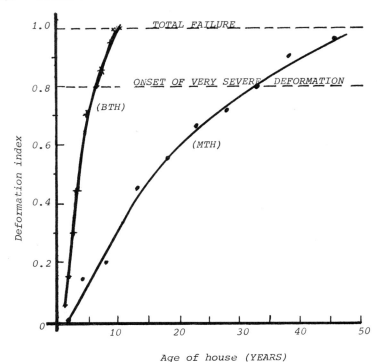

Age of house (YEARS)

Figure 1. Aging curves of houses in southern Cameroon

onto the house frame. If the roof is made of tin sheets they would be
nailed directly onto the roof frame. (6)- an earth foundation is raised and compacted. (7)- a bamboo mesh is built around the house frame
(8)- wet soil is used to fill in the bamboo mesh, thus making the house walls. (9)- After the walls have dried, they are finished using
different varieties of clay.

2.2 Modern traditional houses
Modern traditional houses are ones that have a mixture of basic traditional elements and modern components. (2) They are designed and
built by the owner with much assistance from professionals. They have
three outstanding characteristics. They are : (1) moderately capital-

intensive, (2) made of less than 75% locally available materials, and (3) built with a mixture of local and external technology and labor.

A typical construction procedure **involves** the same basic steps as for a basic traditional house with four new elements added. These are (1) the building of roof trusses where there were none, (2) the use of corrugated tin sheets instead of raphia sheets, (3) the use of cement and concrete instead of "adobe" and clays. (4) the use of nails and metal wires instead of ropes.

The basic structure of the frame has remained traditional. Wood, bamboo and soil have retained their traditional functions and the building steps are mostly the same as above.

2.3   House-type distribution and costs
For the city of Yaounde and surrounding villages, the following data have been obtained (table 1).

Table 1 : BASIC DATA FOR YAOUNDE AND SURROUNDINGS

	Basic traditional	Modern traditional	Modern	Description
FREQUENCY (%)	50	30	20	City of Yaounde
FREQUENCY (%)	77	20	3	Surrounding villages
Cost of a 120-150m^2 House	2-3	5-7	15-20	in 1982 10^6 F-CFA
	7-9	17-24	50-65	in 1982 10^3 Dollars (USA)
	14-18	34-48	100-130	in 1982 multiples of per capita income ($500 USA)
	35-45	56-80	250-325	in 1982 multiples of per capita income ($600 USA)

3.   Collapse mechanisms

After having followed the construction of several houses of both types, we visited 1012 houses in the city of Yaounde and surrounding villages. One hundred of these were studied in detail. During these visits we observed and recorded the most frequent problems. To facilitate our investigation, a house was divided into these basic components which are the foundation, the wall frame and the roof.

In order to describe the status of each component, we needed to identify the most prevalent collapse mechanisms observed, the associated collapse mode, the principal agents and the frequency of occurence of each individual mechanism.

3.1   Definitions
- A collapse mechanism is a physical process of destruction that could potentially lead to the collapse of a building.
- A collapse mode is either the shape, or the appearance of a buil-

ding that results from the application of a collapse mechanism.
- A collapse agent is a force, action or process causing the mecha-
nism to occur.
The frequency of occurrence of an individual mechanism is the total
number of times it was observed expressed as a percentage of total
observations.

3.2   Collapse mechanisms of foundations

Collapse machanism	Collapse mode	Postulated Principal agents	Frequency %	
			BTH	MTH
Cracking	Sideview	- differential settling - impurities - overloading	95%	70%
Erosion	Sideview	- Fluid flow - pets	97%	70%
Separation	Topview	- Poor adhesion - Erosion - Vibration - Variability of humidity	87%	30%
Settling	Sideview	- Poor compaction - Weak soil - Overloading	3%	13%

3.3   Collapse mechanisms of wall frames

Collapse mechanism	Collapse mode	Postulated principal agents	Frequency (%)	
			BTH	MTH
Rotation	$5°<\alpha, \ \beta<23°$	- termites - shallow penetration - inertial imbalance - poor foundation - erosion - wind forces	90%	70%
Differential Sagging	$10<\epsilon<40cm$	- termites - settling - inertial imbalance - rain penetration - rotting		
Warping and cracking		- poor adhesion - shrinkage - non uniformity - inertial imbalance	98%	73%
Separation		- loose connections - material failure - inertial imbalance	67%	22%

3.4   Collapse mechanisms of roofs

Collapse mechanism	Collapse mode	Postulated principal agents	Frequency (%)	
			BTH	MTH
Leakage and rotting	Not drawn	- rains - temperature flux - corrosion	86%	79%
Sheet separation from truss	Not drawn	Wind	50%	32%
Loosening of connections	Not drawn	- termites - vibration - thermal stresses	25%	40%

3.5   Comparison of collapse mechanisms
The frequencies of collapse mechanisms have been tabulated above. Here, they are compiled to compare the relative importance of individual
mechanisms in each house type. These results are shown on table 2.

It is found that the order of importance of the mechanisms is the
same for both types ; but the magnitudes are lower in Modern Traditional Houses than in Basic Traditional ones by 25% or more. The two
exceptional collapse mechanisms for which the frequencies in the former are higher then in the latter are the settling of the foundation
and the loosening of roof connections.

For each house component, the collapse mechanisms have been ranked
in the order of decreasing frequency as follows :
The Foundation : (1) Erosion, (2) cracking, (3) separation and, (4)
                     settling.
Wall Frames : (1) Warping and cracking, (2) rotation, (3) sagging,
                 and (4) separation.
The Roof : (1) leakage, (2) separation and (3) loosening of connecti-
              ons.

Table 2 : Relative importance of collapse mechanisms

House component	Collapse mechanism	Rank based on Frequency importance		Difference in frequency $(\frac{MTH-BTH}{BTH})$
		BTH	MTH	
Foundation	Erosion	1	1	-27%
	Cracking	2	1	-25%
	Separation	3	3	-65%
	Settling	4	4	+330%
Walls	Warping and cracking	1	1	-26%
	Rotation	2	2	-23%
	Sagging	3	3	-25%
	Separation	4	4	-67%
Roof	Leakage	1	1	-8%
	Separation	2	2	-36%
	Loosening of connection	3	3	+38%

4. Global deformation of the houses and aging.

Knowing the collapse mechanisms of individual house components, it would be desirable to determine both their interactions and how they combine to affect the deterioration of the dwelling as a whole through time. Unfortunately, these are hard to establish without good models · In order to shed some light into these interactions, we have sought to determine aging curves independently. These curves display the global state of deformation of the house as a function of time. It is thus assumed tacitly that such curves exist and, while they may not be unique, that they have a unique trend.

4.1 Aging curves

To obtain these curves the following steps were followed :

1. When a house was visited, its global state of deformation was observed and characterized by one of the following words : Normal, Mild, Severe, very Severe, or failure. Subsequently weights were assigned to these words according to table 3, Shown below :

Table 3

Word	Normal	Mild	Severe	Very Severe	Failure
Weight	0	$\frac{1}{4}$	$\frac{1}{2}$	$\frac{3}{4}$	$\frac{4}{4}$

2. For each house type, the houses were subdivided into 10 groups based on their ages. This was necessary because the ages of the houses were not known exactly.

3. For each group, a global deformation index was determined by computing the arithmetic average of its weights. Similary, the average age of the houses in each group was found. These are shown on tables 4 and 5.

4. These indices were plotted against the average ages to yield the aging curves sought (Fig. 1).

4.2 Interpretation of Aging curves

The curves shown on figure 1 display the aging curves that characterize the houses observed. It follows that the global deformation index represents the extent to which the house has aged. Hence, the slopes of these curves are the rates of aging of the house types considered.

From figure 1, one sees that Basic Traditional houses age five times as fast as Modern Traditional ones. The former have a lifetime of ten years. For the latter, these lifetimes are thirty two and fifty years, respectively. Here, too, then, the ratio is one to five. Since both house types are subjected to the same natural elements and since the structure and the building procedure are similar in both cases, the difference in the two curves are mostly due to construction materials. Furthermore the longevity of Modern traditional houses indicate that the traditional house frame which is used in both house types is able to last that long.

BTH'S deteriorate at a constant rate for most of their lifetime. MTH'S, however, do not. Their aging curve presents two distinct portions : the first ten years, and thereafter. During the first ten

Table 4 : GLOBAL STATE OF DEFORMATION OF THE HOUSE (B.T.H.)

	Weight	Normal 0	Mild $\frac{1}{4}$	Severe $\frac{2}{4}$	Very severe $\frac{3}{4}$	Failure $\frac{4}{4}$	Total Weight $\Sigma(Weight)$
Age of House (years)							
0-1		4	1	0			0.25
1-2		3	1	1			0.75
2-3		1	2	2			1.5
3-4		0	1	2	1		2.25
4-5		0	0	2	2	1	3.5
5-6		0	0	1	2	2	4.0
6-7				0	3	2	4.25
7-8		0	0	0	1	4	4.75
8-9		0	0	0	0	5	5.0
9-10		0	0	0	0	5	5.0

Table 5 : GLOBAL STATE OF DEFORMATION OF THE HOUSE (M.T.H.)

Age of House (years)	Normal 0	Mild $\frac{1}{4}$	Severe $\frac{2}{4}$	Very severe $\frac{3}{4}$	Failure $\frac{4}{4}$	Total Weight $\Sigma(Weight)$	Weight
0-2	54	0				0	
2-5	3	1	1			0.75	
5-10	2	2	1			1.0	
10-15	0	2	2	1		2.25	
15-20	0	2	1	1	1	2.75	
20-25	0	0	3	1	1	3.25	
25-30	0	0	2	2	1	3.5	
30-35	0	0	1	2	2	4.0	
35-40	0	0	0	2	3	4.5	
40-50	0	0	0	1	4	4.75	

years, the aging rate is high but constant. Thereafter, this rate decreases to about half of its original value. The first portion, then, is essentially linear while the second is nonlinear.

This decrease of the aging rate with time appears puzzling at first. But it can be explained as follows : the traditional structure develops many small problems early on (the first ten years). While these small problems are noticeable and indeed appreciable (20% of the total deformation of MTH) they act individually and do not yet interact. Hence, the linear behavior in this region represents the rapid accumulation of collapse mechanisms. Thereafter, interaction begins and nonlinearity becomes noticeable. Additional changes in the global state of deformation are slow to develop because most of the problems have appeared, and, there are no more major collapse mechanisms that will cause sudden changes in the global state of deformation.

Deformations during the first ten years represent environmental wear. This environmental wear is too powerful for traditional materials to survive the first decade ; Basic traditional houses are then limited by this inadequacy of construction materials. By being better able to resist this environmental stress Modern traditional houses age much more slowly and last much longer, too.

5. Socio-Economic implications

All cameroonians know in a general way that Basic traditional houses are cheaper to build and have a lower longevity than Modern traditional houses although they may not know the exact reasons why. As a consequence the dream house of most rural cameroonians which is realistic is the modern traditional house. As shown on table 1, it is an expensive project and there is a sizeable group of cameroonians for whom this is an impossible dream. For them the Basic traditional house is the only house that is affordable.

Although this latter is convenient to build, a new one must be built every seven years or so. And any one who has ever tried it can testify to the hardships involved. On the other hand, MTH'S require a large capital at the outset which is a limiting factor, too. In both cases, it appears imperative that a program of maintenance start immediately after the end of construction to delay or slow down the progress of collapse mechanisms. It is estimated that a moderate program of maintenance that is started early can slow down the aging process by 30% and increase longevity by 50%.

6. Conclusions

In this paper, we have studied the collapse mechanisms of Basic traditional and modern traditional house types. By dividing each house into three components : the foundation, the wall frame and the roof, we have identified eleven important collapse mechanisms and associated collapse modes. We have also postulated the Agents responsible for the mechanisms.

By comparing the frequency of occurrence of the mechanisms in both house types it was found that the order of importance of the mechanisms is the same for both but that the magnitudes of the frequencies themselves are, in general, twenty five per cent lower in Modern houses than in Basic traditional houses. Finally, the aging curves have been drawn. From these it is seen that the Basic traditional houses age five times as fast as Modern ones and the latter last five times as long as the former. These differences are due essentially to the nature of the construction materials rather than to the structure of the frame. The exact connection between Aging curves and collapse mechanisms remains the subject of current investigations.

DEVELOPMENT OF MATERIALS OF CONSTRUCTION IN SAUDI ARABIA

ABDUL HAMID J.ALTAYYEB, Department of Civil Engineering,
University of Petroleum and Minerals, Dhahran.
WAJAHAT H.MIRZA, Department of Civil Engineering, King
Abdulaziz University, Jeddah.

1. Introduction

The Royal Kingdom of Saudi Arabia has experienced a very
fast pace of development in which huge volumes of construction materials have been used. The major component of
construction activity revolved round concrete frame structures with partitions being made of masonry. A research
project has been sponsored by Saudi Arabian National
Center for Science and Technology (SANCST) to study the
development of building materials from local resources and
the work being reported in this paper is part of the
progress reports already submitted to SANCST.
    The paper describes the properties of three basic units
of masonry being developed in the Western region of Saudi
Arabia, namely, sand mortars, clay bricks and ceramic
tiles. Because of brevity certain details are being omitt-
ed which are available in [1] . The objective of the
current work is to consolidate information on the locally
made building materials and to make it available to the
users for reference purposes.

2. Development of Building Materials

The present study is restricted to those areas where extensive developmental works are in progress and hence coarse
aggregate, sand and clay samples were collected from the
main towns. Only those sources have been included in the
investigation whose potential reserves/quantities can be
exploited commercially. Table 1 gives information about
the sample sources and their locations. The samples were
brought from the field and their physical characteristics
like shape, size and grading were determined in the laboratory. The data thus obtained was then used in furhter
studies.

Table 1. Sample sources and their Designations

Type of material	Designation	Source Area
Coarse Aggregate	KSA - 4 ⎫ LSA - 5 ⎬	Al-Medina
Fine Aggregate (Sand)	KZS - 1	Jeddah Beach Sand
	KZS - 3	Wadi Fatima, Makkah
	KZS - 4 ⎫ KZS - 5 ⎬	Al-Madina
	KZS - 8	Yanbo Beach Sand
	KZS - 10	Badr Dune Sand
Clay	KZC - 14 ⎫ KZC - 15 ⎬ KZC - 16 ⎭	Bathan Aqul Al-Madinah Aqeeq
Shale	KZC - 18	Wadi Fatimah, Makkah

2.1 Physical Properties of Mortars

The Kingdom of Saudi Arabia has an abundant supply of sand from Wadis (Valleys), deserts and beaches. These sands are of varying particle size and shape and hence behave differently in their flow characteristics and compressive strengths when mixed with cement and water to form mortars. Jeddah and Yanbo sands have been studied and some of the results obtained are discussed here.

The flow table tests were performed on sand samples collected from Jeddah and Yanbo areas. Generally, the mobility of the mortar (1:3 ratio of cement to sand) has been a function of the gradation and the fineness modulus of sands. Thus Wadi sands have shown greater degree of fluidity than fine-grained dune or beach sands for similar water/cement ratios.

Compressive strength tests were also performed on the 70 mm cubes of 1:3 mortar using different sands and the results are presented in Figure 1. The flow characteristics have influenced the strength and the figure shows that highest values of strength are obtained for Wadi sands. The desert sands make a stiff mix at lower water/cement ratios and in order to obtain higher strength, special compaction procedure needs to be adopted. The beach sands produced workable mixes at water/cement ratio greater than 0.55 and hence meaningful strength results below these values could not be obtained. All sands were mixed as obtained from the field and their water absorption capacities may have resulted in an effectively lower water/cement ratio.

Fig.1 Compressive Strength of Mortars

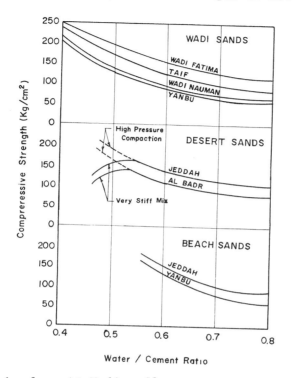

2.2 Bricks from Al-Madina Clays

Madina Al-Monawwara is surrounded by valleys through which natural streams pass with seasonal flow. These streams have been depositing fine, clayer materials over the centuries. Thus considerable deposits of clays are available around Al-Madina, particularly in the valleys of Aqul, Bathan and Aqeeq. In order to study the feasibility of these clays in making bricks and other masonry units, clay samples were collected and then subjected to various laboratory tests. The results obtained from these tests are reported in this section.

2.2.1 Plasticity Characteristics

The plasticity of wet clays is of importance in moulding bricks as the greater the plasticity (fludity), the lesser will be the effort required in making brick specimens. The plastic and liquid limit tests were performed

Table 2.   Plasticity Characteristics of Al-Madina Clays.

Source of Clay	Plastic Limit	Liquid Limit	Plasticity Index	Shrinkage Limit
AQUL	25.8	37.0	11.1	22.0
BATHAN	24.6	35.0	10.4	21.6
AQEEQ	22.9	29.4	6.5	19.4

Table 3.   Proctor Density Values of Al-Madina Clays

Source of Clay	Maximum Dry Density (g/cm^3)	Optimum Moisture content (%)
AQUL	1.67	17.5
BATHAN	1.63	17.0
AQEEQ	1.62	16.0

on the three clay samples and the results are shown in
Table 2. Clays from Aqul and Bathan have a high plasticity
index indicating greater percentage of fine particles. The
shrinkage limit values are also given in Table 2. Since
these values are close to or higher than 20%, their resistance to deformation and warping on heating is expected to
be fair.

2.2.2 Proctor Compaction Density Results

    Proctor compaction tests were performed on clay samples
to determine the maximum dry density and optimum moisture
contents which are used later in casting bricks. The density curves are plotted in Figure 2 and the values of
maximum dry density and optimum moisture content for the
three clay samples are given in Table 3.

Fig.2 Proctor Density Curves of Clays

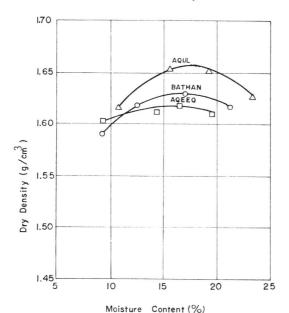

Moisture Content (%)

2.2.3 Compressive Strength of Burnt Clay

The suitability of the use of clay deposits for making bricks was checked by burning the air-dried cylinderical specimens (2" (50.8 mm) dia x 4" (101.6 mm) high) at high tempeatures.

The specimens were burnt in a furnace at temperatures of 800°, 900°, 1000° and 1200°C, separate specimens being fired at each temperature. The ultimate compressive strength obtained for the burnt specimens are shown in Figure 3. It is apparent that the higher the burning temperature the greater is the compressive strength. It was also observed that there was a distinct change in colour of the burnt specimens. Upto 900°C, the specimens remained Light Brown in colour but between 900° and 1100°C, the colour was changed to Red brown. Beyond 1200°C, the clays exhibited excessive deformation and warping and their colours were Dark Brown to Black.

2.2.4 Water Absorption Characteristics

The degree of water absorption after 24 hour submergence in water and the initial rate of water absorption for the burnt clay specimens are shown in Figure 4 and Figure5 respectively.The results seem acceptable as these are are

Fig.3 Compressive Strength of Burnt Clays

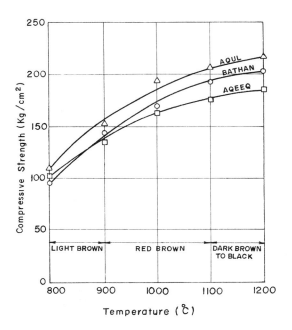

Fig.4 Water Absorption of Burnt Clays

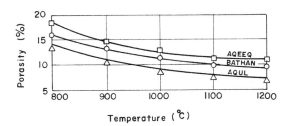

Table 4. Chemical Compositions of Some Tile Bodies

Tile Body	SiO$_2$	Al$_2$O$_3$	Fe$_2$O$_3$	MgO	CaO	Na$_2$O	K$_2$O	TiO$_2$	Ig-loss	Total
T$_1$	49.83	14.53	9.26	4.92	7.04	2.79	1.73	1.53	7.40	99.03
T$_2$	55.57	13.89	7.48	3.85	5.62	3.20	2.21	1.23	5.76	98.81
T$_3$	51.37	20.55	10.24	1.51	1.74	1.63	1.05	1.28	9.52	98.89
T$_4$	56.67	18.19	8.18	1.42	1.84	2.37	1.72	1.05	7.27	98.71
T$_5$	54.26	16.48	7.86	3.93	5.24	3.33	2.09	1.13	6.89	101.21
T$_6$	51.62	16.96	7.82	4.67	5.85	2.72	2.23	0.98	8.37	101.22
T$_7$	50.42	16.00	9.28	4.71	6.93	3.19	1.67	1.57	6.73	100.50

Table 5: Sintering Temperatures for the Tule Bodies

Tile Body No.	Sintering Temperature (^{o}C) (Linear Shrinkage %)				Firing Range
	13 %	11%	5 %	2.5%	
T_1	1082.5 (5.5)	1085.4	1099.2	1105.8 (9.6)	Narrow
T_2	1084.2 (5.8)	1087.5	1090.8	1097.5 (7.2)	Narrow
T_3	-	1082.5	1115.8	1133.3 (6.0)	Wide
T_4	-	-	1130.8	1144.2 (6.2)	Wide

within acceptable limits.

2.3   Ceramic Tiles

. In order to develop a ceramic tile, seven raw materials
consisting of four clays (i.e. KZC-14,15,16,18) two aggregates (i.e. KZA-4,5) and one sand (KZS-5) were selected
from among the mineral samples from the Western region of
Saudi Arabia. The sand and aggregates were chosen for the
use as a source of feldspars.
By using these raw materials, seven tile bodies were
formulated as indicated in Table 5.3. The chemical compositions of the formulated bodies were expected to be as
indicated in Table 5.4
Weighted raw materials in the given ratios were mixed
and ground in a ball mill of alumina porcelain to a fineness of 100 % minus #100 mesh sieve. The ground mixture of
body was pressed into a shaped tile of 60 mm x 60 mm x 7mm
with a pressure of 200 kg/cm^2 by using 5 % of binding
water. After drying, the shaped tile was heated upto a
given temperature at a rate of 200°C/hr and soaked at that
temperature for 2 hrs in an electrically heated furnace.
The soaking temperature adopted in this experiment was
varied from 1075°C to 1150°C with an interval of 25°C. The
fired tile was then cooled to the room temperature inside
the furnace. The degree of sintering attained were compared to each other depending on the criteria defined for
the production of tiles such that the water absorption for
interior wall tiles should be in the range from 11% to 13%
and the water absorption of exterior wall tiles and floor
tiles should be in the range from 2.5% to 7.0%. Result

comparisons are given in Table 5 for four tiles which showed encouraging results. Specimens T_3 and T_4 not only had
a wider firing range but also lower shrinkage on firing
than specimens T_1 and T_2. Therefore these specimens (T_3
and T_4) have been chosen for further developments. The
final target of this development is to produce a tile coated with a white opaque glaze on a red body.

The thermal expansion coefficients measured from the
tile pseçimens T_3 and T_4 ranged from 60 x 10^{-7} cm/cm/$^{\circ}$C to
70 x 10^{-7} cm/cm/$^{\circ}$C.

Conclusions

1. Depending on the source of sand (Wadi, desert,beach
etc), the performance of mortar in terms of flow characteristics and compressive strength can be affected. Thus
Wadi sands show maximum strengths and beach sands yield
minimum strengths with the desert sands falling in between.

2. The abundant supplies of plastic clays in Madina Al-
Monawwara can be utilized for making brick masonry. The
compressive strength and water absorption values of the
burnt clay bricks are within acceptable limits.

3. The results of developing ceramic tiles from local
clays and aggregates have so far proved encouraging.Cert-
ain proportions of these materials have exhibited wide
range of sintering temperatures and their water absorption
and linear shrinkage values are low.

References

1. SANCST Project AR4-Building,(1982),Second Progress
      Report,Riyadh, Saudi Arabia.

2. Budnikov, p.p., (1964), The Technology of Ceramics
      and Refractories, 60-62, The M.I.T. Press; U.S.A.

3. Building Materials, (177), BRE Digests, the Construc-
      tion Press, London, U.K.

4. Smith, R.C., (1979),Materials of Construction,
      McGraw-Hill Book Company, New York.

5. Hornbostel, C (1978), Construction Materials, John
      Wiley and Sons, New York.

PROGRAMME EXPÉRIMENTAL SUR BADIGEONS DE PROTECTION DES MURS EN BÉTON DE TERRE

Par M. MARIOTTI : Délégué Technique aux Actions Extérieures au C.E.B.T.P.

―――――

Ce programme s'inscrit dans les recherches réalisées pour une opération expérimentale d'habitat économique à Bamako (Mali).

Il avait pour but de définir la composition et les caractéristiques d'un badigeon chaux + ciment peu onéreux et d'application facile ainsi que les conditions de préparation du support et les interactions support-badigeon pour la protection de murs en béton de terre.

Le programme envisagé et dont une partie seulement a été réalisée en raison de délais trop limités, comprenait l'étude de :

1) - *la compacité et conditions de compactage du support en béton de terre.*
2) - *la consistance et la composition du badigeon - stabilité en fonction du temps après malaxage.*
3) - *la relation entre consistance et pouvoir couvrant.*
4) - *la force de succion du support suivant sa compacité et son degré de saturation.*
5) - *la perméabilité des badigeons vis-à-vis de la perméabilité du support.*
6) - *l'adhérence du badigeon et la susceptibilité à la fissuration par retrait.*
7) - *la résistance du badigeon à la fatigue (imbibition + séchage) ou durabilité.*
8) - *le traitement du badigeon pour obtenir un effet hydrophobant sans supprimer la perméabilité aux gaz - Durabilité du traitement.*

Dans les délais dont on a disposés pourl'opération expérimentale, seules les investigations 1 - 2 - 7 - 8 ont pu être menées, cependant il a paru intéressant de présenter les modes opératoires et les commentaires correspondant aux investigations n° 1 à 8.

L'opération expérimentale d'habitat économique de Bamako (Mali) a été financée et supervisée par le Plan Construction ; l'étude et la réalisation ont été assurées par l'Agence de Coopération et d'Aménagement avec la collaboration technologique du C.E.B.T.P.

1. *Caractéristiques du support en béton de terre*

Le matériau constituant le support était un béton de terre en limon sablo-graveleux légèrement argileux disponible sur place. Le béton de terre devait être, soit simplement compacté, soit compacté et stabilisé au ciment.

Les conditions de compactage ont été définies par l'essai Proctor normal bien connu du domaine routier ; les caractéristiques optimales étant, pour un indice de compactage de 100 %.

(a) <u>sans ciment</u>

poids volumique sec maximum   = 19,5 KN/m3
teneur en eau optimum   = 11,5 %

(b) <u>avec ciment</u> (2,5 % de ciment CPA 45)

poids volumique sec maximum   = 19,5 KN/m3
teneur en eau optimum   = 12,1 %

Les éprouvettes de béton de terre utilisées pour les essais étaient cylindriques avec un diamètre de 15 cm et une hauteur voisine de 7,5 cm.

Les éprouvettes ainsi destinées aux essais de badigeon ont été conservées préalablement pendant 7 jours dans une atmosphère quasi saturée d'humidité (HR de 95 ± 5 %) puis pendant au moins 23 jours à l'air ambiant (température 30° ± 2° et HR de 50 % ± 5).

2. *Consistance du coulis suivant sa composition et stabilité en fonction du temps après malaxage*

Les coulis à badigeon qui ont été envisagés étaient constitués d'un mélange de chaux et de ciment.

La consistance du coulis dépend essentiellement :

. de la finesse des composants (surface spécifique des éléments) et de leur nature ;
. de la composition du coulis et notamment du rapport entre le poids d'eau et le poids du minéral sec (E/M) ;
. de la nature de l'eau ;
. de la température de l'air ambiant.

Cette consistance a été mesurée par la détermination du temps d'écoulement d'un volume fixe de coulis au cône Marsh (ajutage de 10 mm) bien connu dans la technique des injections.

Les mesures de consistance des coulis associées à des essais d'application sur support avec une "brosse" de peintre, nous ont conduits à définir une consistance optimale correspondant à un temps d'écoulement de 10 à 12 secondes de 1 litre de coulis au cône Marsh (ajutage 10 mm) ; cette consistance traduisait une consistance crêmeuse d'une peinture courante assez épaisse.

Divers mélanges de chaux + ciment + eau ont ainsi été étudiés et le rapport E/M déterminé pour obtenir la consistance optimale, le malaxage se faisant au moyen d'un mixer électrique à palettes.

Avec les matériaux utilisés :
. chaux hydraulique de surface spécifique   = 5600 cm2/gr
. ciment CPJ 45 de surface spécifique   = 3000 cm2/gr
le mélange retenu pour la consistance optimale a été le suivant :
Composition = parties en poids

$$M = \begin{cases} \text{chaux} & 0.85 \\ \text{ciment} & 0.85 \end{cases} \qquad \text{rapport } \frac{E}{M} = 0.59$$

$$E = \text{ eau} \qquad 1.00$$

Les temps d'écoulement au cône Marsh en fonction du temps de repos après malaxage.

Temps de repos en minutes	Consistance Temps d'écoulement au cône Marsh (secondes)
0	12
30	12
60	13
90	13

3. *Relation entre consistance du coulis et pouvoir couvrant*

Bien que cette phase des recherches n'ait pas été régulièrement suivie, le programme prévoyait la mesure du pouvoir couvrant (nombre de mètres carrés pouvant être couverts par 1 kg de coulis) suivant la consistance du coulis et le mode d'humidification du support (voir commentaires ci-après à l'article 4)

Le pouvoir couvrant dépend :
. de la consistance et de la composition du coulis,
. des propriétés de succion du support,
. de l'instrument utilisé pour l'application.

La mesure du pouvoir couvrant devait être obtenue par trempage complet pendant deux secondes de l'éprouvette de béton de terre dans le coulis ; l'éprouvette de béton de terre étant préalablement humidifiée de façon variable.

Si :
Ph est le poids de l'éprouvette du support humidifiée
Ps le poids sec de l'éprouvette du support

PBH est le poids de l'éprouvette badigeonnée et humide (10 minutes après trempage)

PBS est le poids de l'éprouvette badigeonnée et desséchée jusqu'à poids constant.

S est la surface de l'éprouvette.

On a :

- Poids d'eau absorbée par humidification préalable par m2

$$= \frac{Ph - Ps}{S}$$

- Poids de coulis humide retenu par m2

$$\beta h = \frac{PBH - PH}{S}$$

- Poids sec de coulis retenu par m2

$$\beta h = \frac{PBs - Ps}{S}$$

4. Mesures de la succion du support

Aussi bien pour les enduits, pour la pose de carrelages que pour l'application de badigeons, le potentiel de succion du support et sa perméabilité ont une grande importance.

Il influence le pouvoir couvrant, l'hydratation des liants, l'adhérence et donc aussi la durabilité de la protection.

Le béton de terre ayant une fraction argileuse qui est loin d'être négligeable, à l'état sec, le support possède un très fort potentiel de succion. En présence d'une mince pellicule de badigeon, la succion instantanée de l'eau par le support risque de provoquer une rupture des cheminements capillaires et de supprimer une bonne partie de l'eau nécessaires à l'hydratation et au durcissement des liants hydrauliques. Il en résulte une perte d'adhérence et un grave défaut de durcissement entrainant un "farinage" du badigeon (poudroiement du badigeon au frottement des doigts).

Inversement, un support saturé d'eau recevant un coulis de badigeon risque une coulée liquide qui ne laisse subsister qu'une pellicule insignifiante de coulis ; par ailleurs, sur un support non stabilisé au ciment, le phénomène peut être accompagné par l'entrainement de matériaux et l'érosion du support.

Cette interaction entre badigeon et support nous paraît mal maîtrisée et nous avons donc conçu une méthode expérimentale destinée à contrôler le potentiel de succion et la perméabilité initiale du support.

L'appareillage proposé est représenté sur la figure n° 1.

L'essai consiste à déclencher le processus de succion du support à partir d'un instant initial bien défini grâce à l'intervention d'un "bouchon de mercure" réversible.

On scelle au centre de la face de l'éprouvette, au moyen d'un

mastic étanche durcissable, un tube de verre (a) de 6 cm de diamètre
et 10 cm de hauteur en ayant bien soin d'éviter toute salissure sur
la surface ainsi isolée. Sur le tube scellé est ajusté un bouchon
muni d'un petit tube (b) de 7 à 8 mm de diamètre de telle sorte que
le petit tube (b) dépasse du bouchon d'environ 3 cm. Ce petit tube
(b) est raccordé par un tuyau souple mais très peu déformable à un
tube mesureur (c) de 1/2 cm2 de section fixé par une prise coulis-
sante sur une échelle graduée.

Avant démarrage de l'essai, le mercure introduit dans le tube (a)
empêche toute succion ; au moment du démarrage, le niveau d'eau dans
le tube (c) est ajusté de telle sorte qu'il soit situé à 5-10 mm au
dessus de la face de l'éprouvette, et l'éprouvette est retournée
lentement de 180° de telle sorte que le tube (a) se situe sous la
face d'essai et que le mercure ayant dégagé la surface de succion se
trouve rassemblé autour du tube (b) comme l'indique la figure n° 1.

Ainsi, il paraît possible de contrôler le régime du débit de succion en maîtrisant le démarrage pour des supports plus ou moins imbi-
bés.

Du point de vue de l'interprétation de l'essai, désignons par Ho le
potentiel de succion (hauteur maximum d'ascension capillaire de la
frange saturée) :

par K : le coefficient de perméabilité dans les pores saturés

par S : la section de la face d'essai du support ou section du
tube (a)

par s : la section du petit tube mesureur (c)

par n : la porosité = rapport volume des vides au volume total

et reportons-nous à la figure n° 1.

Le débit de succion se traduit par une baisse Z de niveau dans le
tube (c) et par une très légère montée de la frange capillaire **x** dans
le support (a). En se limitant à une durée faible à partir du démarrage de la succion et si Z est la baisse de niveau par rapport au
sommet de la frange capillaire, la loi de Darcy et l'égalité des
débits en (a) et en (c) permettent d'écrire :

$$KS \; \frac{Ho - Z}{\mathbf{x}} \; dt = sdZ \quad ou \quad nK \; (\frac{S}{s})^2 \; \frac{Ho - Z}{Z} \; dt = dZ$$

en notant que $Sn\mathbf{x} = sZ$

$$nK \; (\frac{S}{s})^2 \; dt = \frac{ZdZ}{Ho - Z}$$

ce qui après intégration conduit à l'équation :

$$nK \; (\frac{S}{s})^2 t = HoLog \; \frac{Ho}{Ho - Z} \; - Z$$

ou encore :

$$n \; \frac{K}{Ho} \; (\frac{S}{s})^2 t = Log \; (\frac{1}{1 - \frac{Z}{Ho}}) \; - \frac{Z}{Ho}$$

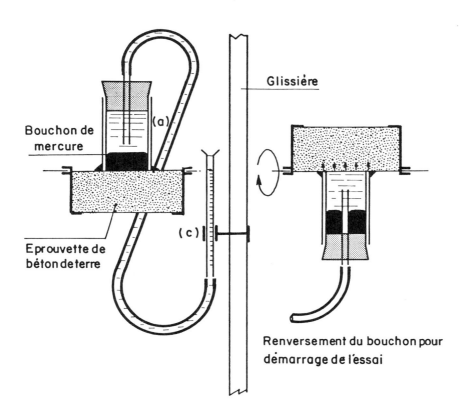

Bouchon de
mercure

(a)

Glissière

Eprouvette de
béton de terre

(c)

Renversement du bouchon pour
démarrage de l'essai

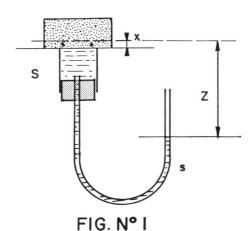

FIG. N° I

Appareil de mesure du potentiel et du débit de succion

Cependant, l'équation comporte deux inconnues K et Ho qui sont les
caractéristiques fondamentales de la succion et nous verrons dans
l'article suivant le processus envisagé avec le même matériel pour
séparer ces deux paramètres.

Bien entendu, cette analyse ne tient pas compte de la diversité
des dimensions des pores qui jouent évidemment un rôle important dans
l'analyse du phénomène de succion.

Cependant, il convient de remarquer qu'au début du phénomène de
succion, les franges capillaires correspondant aux différentes classes de pores sont très concentrées et traduisent donc bien le débit
capable de la frange saturée ; ce n'est que pour un temps assez long
que l'éventail des degrés partiels de saturation se déploie.

A titre d'information, nous donnons ci-dessous les valeurs du second membre de l'équation en fonction de $\dfrac{Z}{Ho}$

$\dfrac{Z}{Ho}$	$Log\ (\dfrac{Ho}{Ho\ -\ Z}) - \dfrac{Z}{Ho}$
0.10	0,004
0.20	0,023
0.40	0,113
0.60	0,315
0.80	0,809
0.90	1,402
0,95	2,045
0.98	2,930
0.99	3,610

5. Perméabilité du support et du badigeon

Comme nous l'avons vu précédemment, il est important de pouvoir séparer K et H pour l'étude du débit de succion.

En dehors d'essais technologiques réalisables in situ pour connaître le débit global percolant au travers d'un mur, nous avons conçu
un essai de perméabilité au laboratoire utilisant un matériel analogue
à celui des essais précédents. Le montage est représenté sur la figure n° 2 et ne diffère du précédent que par le remplacement du tube
(c) par un tube débitmètre de Mariotte permettant d'exercer une
charge constante de hauteur h sur la surface du support.

(a) Support : si l'on désigne par

*K et Ho la perméabilité et le potentiel de succion du support,
le cheminement de la frange saturée supposée limitée
à la section S du tube (a)*

Z   la baisse du niveau dans le tube de Mariotte

*S et s   respectivement la section du tube (a) et la section
effective du tube de Mariotte*

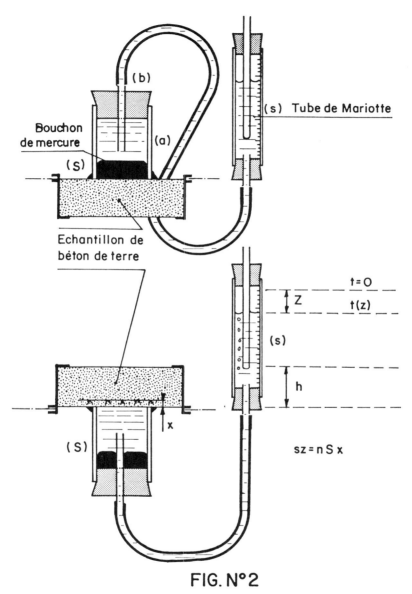

FIG. N°2

Appareil de mesure du débit de succion
sous charge h constante

*h   la charge d'eau maintenue constante sur la surface du
          support*

on a l'écoulement regi par la relation suivante :

$$KS \ \frac{h + /Hc/}{x} \ \ dt = sdz \ \text{notons que } Snx = sZ \text{ ou } x = \frac{sZ}{Sn}$$

soit en intégrant :

$$A \ KS^2 \ n \ (h + /Ho/) \ t = Q^2$$

ou bien :

$$Q = \sqrt{2 \ KS^2 \ n \ (h + /Hd/) \ t}$$

*en effectuant deux mesures avec des charges constantes différentes h_1
et h_2 et en faisant le rapport des valeurs Q_1 et Q_2 obtenues, on fait
disparaître K et l'on peut déterminer Ho*

$$\frac{Q1}{Q2} = \frac{\sqrt{(h1 + /Ho/) \ t1}}{\sqrt{(h2 + /Ho/) \ t2}} \quad ou \quad \frac{Q1}{Q2} \frac{\sqrt{t2}}{\sqrt{t1}} \ \sqrt{\frac{h1 + (Ho)}{h2 + (Ho)}}$$

(b) <u>Support et badigeon</u>

*soit Kβ le coefficient de perméabilité du badigeon supposé
saturé*

e   son épaisseur (voir figure n° 3)

*si l'on désigne par H la charge inconnue d'eau à l'interface
support/badigeon, l'égalité des débits exige, pour une charge
h maintenue constante sur le badigeon, que l'on ait :*

$$K \ \frac{H - Ho}{x - e} = K_\beta \ \frac{h - H}{e}$$

*(H et Ho en valeur
algébrique)*

*(dépression négative
(pression positive)*

d'où l'on tire :

$$H = \frac{K\beta h \ (x - e) + KeHo}{K\beta \ (x - e) + Ke}$$

Le débit à travers le badigeon est régi par :

$$S \ K\beta \ \frac{h - H}{e} \ dt = sdZ$$

ce qui donne après développement et intégration :

$$2 \ K\beta \ KS^2 \ n \ (h - Ho) \ t = K\beta \ s^2 z^2 + 2s \ Sne \ Z \ (K - K\beta \ )$$
$$+ \ s^2 \ n^2 e^2 (K\beta - 2K) + C^{te}$$

*expression qui, connaissant K, Ho et e, permet de déterminer
Kβ*

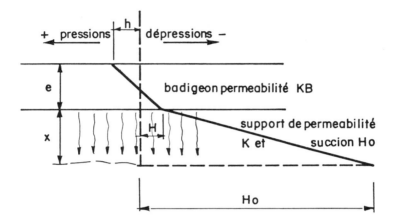

FIG. N° 3

Essai de perméabilité sous gradient
de succion .

Profil des hauteurs piézométriques

au travers du badigeon et du support.

Nous tenons à signaler que ces modes opératoires permettent de contrôler l'efficacité de produits hydrophobants qu'ils soient appliqués en
imprégnation superficielle ou dans la masse du badigeon. Dans l'opération expérimentale qui a été présentement réalisée, le badigeon a
été justement traité avec un hydrophobant superficiel (STABIRAM).

L'hydrophobant, sans obturer les pores, donne aux interfaces des
propriétés anticapillaires, si bien qu'au lieu d'un potentiel de
succion, la surface traitée possède au contraire une résistance à la
pénétration de l'eau, et il faut donc exercer une certaine charge ho
qu'il est bon de contrôler pour forcer la pénétration de l'eau à
travers la barrière anticapillaire. Bien entendu ho dépend de la
finesse des pores et il est nécessaire que ho soit supérieur à celle
de l'effet d'une pluie associée au vent.

6. *Adhérence et susceptibilité à la fissuration*

La susceptibilité à la fissuration dépend évidemment de la finesse
des minéraux constituant le coulis du badigeon et de la teneur en eau,
mais, s'agissant d'un revêtement de très faible épaisseur, elle dépend
essentiellement de l'adhérence.

Ainsi, s'il existe des modes opératoires bien connus pour mesurer
l'adhérence dans le domaine des peintures et enduits, il nous a paru
intéressant de concevoir un essai de fissurabilité par retrait en
s'efforçant de ne pas utiliser une éprouvette indépendante du rôle du
support.

L'éprouvette est de forme cylindrique identique à celle des essais
précédents (Ø diamètre 15 cm et hauteur d'environ 7,5 cm) ; elle est
badigeonnée après une cure normale mais en empêchant l'adhérence sur
une partie bien délimitée de l'une des faces sans toutefois supprimer
la succion du support. Dans ce but, un disque de papier filtre est
disposé sur la face au moment de son humidification préliminaire comme
l'indique le schéma de la figure n° 4 (a).

L'éprouvette ainsi badigeonnée est ensuite introduite dans une en-
ceinte à température et hygrométrie bien contrôlées (par exemple :
t = 30°C et H.R. = 30 %).

Les contraintes parasites dues au retrait se développent en solli-
citant tout particulièrement l'aire non adhérente du badigeon sans
qu'aient été beaucoup modifiées les influences du support.

On note alors le temps d'apparition des premières fissures et le
rapport entre la surface d'essai et la longueur totale des fissurations
(ce rapport qui a les dimensions d'une longueur représente la dimension du maillage de fissuration).

Enfin, on notera la largeur des fissurations et l'évolution du rapport précédent en fonction du temps (voir figure n° 4 (b)).

7. *Résistance du badigeon au vieillissement accéléré - durabilité*

Ces essais ont été réalisés sur les éprouvettes de béton de terre stabilisées et non stabilisées au ciment, et enduites, après humidification du support, du badigeon dont la composition a été définie au début

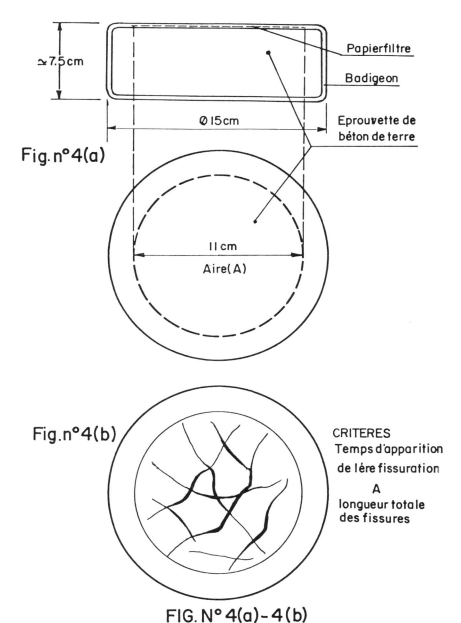

Fig.n°4(a)

≃ 7.5 cm

Papier filtre

Badigeon

Ø 15 cm

Eprouvette de
béton de terre

11 cm

Aire (A)

Fig.n°4(b)

CRITERES
Temps d'apparition
de 1ère fissuration

A
longueur totale
des fissures

FIG. N° 4(a) - 4(b)
Susceptibilité à la fissuration des badigeons dans une
ambiance donnée

soit, en partie, en poids :

$$M = \begin{cases} \text{chaux} & 0.85 \\ \text{ciment} & 0.85 \\ \text{CPJ 45} \end{cases}$$
Rapport $\frac{E}{M} = 0.59$

consistance = 12 secondes

$$E = \quad \text{eau} \quad 1.00$$

après une cure normale comprenant 7 jours en atmosphère saturée et
23 jours de conservation à l'air (t = 30°C et H.R. = 50 %), les éprouvettes ont été soumises à la répétition du cycle suivant :

. aspersion d'eau   1/2 heure
. chaleur sèche 60°C   4   heures
. Aspersion d'eau   1/2 heure
. Rayonnement actinique)
  (chaleur sèche à 60°C }   4   heures
  + U.V.)   )

Les éprouvettes, toujours placées dans la même position, ont été observées au cours de la répétition des cycles.
    Ces observations nous ont montré que le badigeon seul était insuf-
fisant pour soustraire le support à des variations volumiques fissu-
rantes et, dès les premiers cycles, le badigeon seul s'est décollé en
entrainant toutefois une plaque très adhérente du support ; la cause
de ce mauvais comportement n'était pas due, en conséquence, à un manque d'adhérence, mais à une instabilité propre du support par imbibition et séchage.
    Le badigeon a ensuite été traité au moyen d'un hydrophobant appli-
qué en imprégnation superficielle (STABIRAM 677 M de la Société CECA).
Cet hydrophobant s'est avéré très efficace et a permis de soumettre
les éprouvettes de béton de terre non stabilisées au ciment et stabilisées au ciment, à 60 cycles de vieillissement sans désordre apparent.

CONCLUSION

La recherche de moyens économiques pour construire des logements en
faveur des populations à bas revenus, conduit à revaloriser des techniques du passé par des moyens peu utilisés dans les pays industrialisés. Cela doit nous conduire à une certaine reconversion technologique de telle sorte que nos connaissances de base soient rationnel-
lement adaptées à l'étude de nouveaux matériaux particuliers sortant
du cadre des normes habituelles, ou à l'étude de matériaux tradionnels
locaux peu ou pas utilisés dans les pays industrialisés.
    C'est avec cette volonté que nous avons abordé l'étude des matériaux
économiques de l'opération expérimentale de Bamako, notamment l'étude
des badigeons sur murs en béton de terre compactée et stabilisée ou non
au ciment.

Cette étude a abouti en laboratoire à la définition d'un coulis de chaux et ciment complété par un traitement hydrophobant.

La communication a présenté le programme expérimental qui avait été envisagé et dont la réalisation a dû être écourtée par des impératifs de périodes climatiques favorables au chantier.

SECTION VI

Essais, normes et règlements de construction

Testing, codes and standards

CONTRIBUTION A LA DEFINITION DES EXIGENCES REGLEMENTS ET NORMES DE
CONSTRUCTION DANS UN PAYS DONNE ; EXEMPLE DU CAMEROUN

JOSE FONTAN, CENTRE SCIENTIFIQUE ET TECHNIQUE DU BATIMENT -PARIS-

1. Introduction

Concevoir et construire un bâtiment, c'est répondre à un certain
nombre de problèmes d'ordre technique et économique afin de savoir
comment et à quel prix un bâtiment peut permettre aux activités qu'il
abrite de s'effectuer normalement.
  Une démarche classique permettant d'aborder ce problème consiste
d'abord à formuler les exigences fonctionnelles du bâtiment. Ces exigences fonctionnelles peuvent être classées en deux catégories :

  - Les exigences d'habitabilité parmi lesquelles on trouve la
sécurité, l'acoustique, l'hygrothermique, etc...
  - Les exigences économiques qui, en dehors de la notion de coût
de construction, intègrent les exigences de durabilité, d'entretien,
de coût de fonctionnement ; elles peuvent également être d'ordre
macro-économique lorsqu'il y a nécessité d'utiliser des matériaux
locaux même si, dans un premier temps, cette nécessité engendre un
surcoût.

  La formulation de ces exigences n'est en général pas d'une utilisation très commode lors de l'élaboration d'un projet ; c'est pourquoi elles trouvent une expression plus technique sous la forme de
Règles de Qualité telles que les Normes et Règlements de Construction.
  Bien entendu, les exigences fonctionnelles et d'une manière encore
plus forte les Règles de Qualité qui en découlent, dépendent de
l'environnement humain, physique et économique d'un pays ou d'un
groupe de pays donné, et l'application de Règles empruntées risque de
conduire soit à une inadaptation du produit, soit à un surcoût ou
encore à un produit de mauvaise qualité.
  Ce rapport présente les conclusions d'une mission d'étude effectuée au Cameroun à la demande de la Société Immobilière du Camerour.
et financée par le Plan Construction. Cette mission était composée de
Messieurs : J.L. GAILLARD Direction de la Construction (M.U.L.)
              J. NAVILLE   Sté Centrale Immobilière Caisse des Dépôts
              B. PARANT   Centre Technique Forestier Tropical
              J. FONTAN   Centre Scientifique et Technique du Bâtiment

Il s'agissait d'examiner notamment comment et à quel prix était-il
possible de construire des maisons en bois et d'établir un Guide permettant de guider le choix des concepteurs, tant en ce qui concerne
les essences à utiliser que les technologies les mieux adaptées au
pays.

On exposera les méthodes employées pour effectuer l'étude, l'influence des divers facteurs sur la conception des maisons en bois et
enfin, les coûts probables du produit ainsi défini.

2. Méthodes employées

Une étude de ce type ne peut bien entendu pas se faire sans une
étroite collaboration avec les différents intervenants dans l'acte de
construire du pays considéré. C'est donc par de nombreuses rencontres
que cette étude a été conduite. Un entretien avec les différents responsables locaux en matière de politique du logement a permis de dégager les objectifs économiques à atteindre. Les industriels du bois,
les négociants en matériaux ont permis d'examiner le potentiel de
l'industrie et les matériaux disponibles sur le marché. Les maîtres
d'oeuvre et les maîtres d'ouvrage ont, en complément de l'examen du
mode de vie des habitants et des traditions locales en matière d'habitat, défini les exigences d'habitabilité. De nombreuses rencontres
avec les artisans ont donné des indications sur les caractéristiques
et les habitudes de la main-d'oeuvre.

3. Exigences à satisfaire

On examine ci-après les exigences auxquelles on doit satisfaire et,
compte tenu des conditions locales, l'influence de ces exigences sur
la définition de la maison en bois.

3.1 Exigences économiques

Elles sont de deux ordres. Le maître d'ouvrage a fixé le prix au
mètre carré de la construction à ne pas dépasser, sur la base de prix
pratiqués dans ses programmes sociaux. Les responsables locaux ont
souhaité que soient utilisés des bois nationaux et plus particulièrement ceux qui sont sans grande valeur sur le marché international et
la main-d'oeuvre locale. Il a donc été nécessaire d'examiner les po-
tentiels de l'industrie du bois camerounaise.

La production actuelle est de 1.500.000 m^3 de grumes dont 60 %
environ sont transformés sur place. Il existe de nombreuses unités de
déroulage et des scieries qui produisent 300.000 m^3 de sciages dont
la moitié sont vendus sur le marché local. Il a été remarqué que les
stocks dans les scieries sont peu importants et que les bois propo-
sés sont rarement secs. En outre, il existe très peu de séchoirs.
Quant aux usines de contreplaqué, elles produisent environ 64.000 m^3
de placages, dont un peu moins de la moitié est consommée sur place.
Il a été noté l'existence de contreplaqué à collage résistant à
l'humidité.

Les industries de seconde tr..sformation sont essentiellement des entreprises de charpente, menuiseries (portes principalement), carrosserie industrielle. Quelques entreprises ont réalisé des maisons en bois à très petite échelle.

Les principales essences exploitées au Cameroun ont été inventoriées. Compte tenu des objectifs économiques à atteindre, le choix des bois devra tenir compte des critères suivants :

- Le prix : sauf pour les essences ayant une valeur sur le marché international, le coût des bois est déterminé par les frais d'exploitation, d'usinage et de transport. C'est pourquoi, il varie très peu d'une essence à l'autre et il apparaît que, compte tenu également de la faible quantité de stations de traitement, il sera préférable d'utiliser des bois de bonne durabilité naturelle.
- La résistance aux agents extérieurs.
- La facilité de mise en oeuvre.
- Les facilités d'approvisionnement.

En conclusion, il a été possible de déterminer pour chaque cas d'utilisation, les essences les mieux adaptées et donc les moins coûteuses, conformément au tableau ci-après.

Emploi	Essences
Pilotis	Azobé - Padouk - Bilinga
Lisse basse	Iroko - Bilinga
Poteaux cadres	Iroko - Movingui - Bilinga - Fraké *Framiré*
Menuiseries extérieures, Frises et clins	Iroko - Movingui - Bilinga - Tali- Fraké*
Menuiseries intérieures	Iroko - Movingui - Bilinga - Fraké *Olon- Ayous *
Charpentes	Niové - Tali - Iroko - Dabéma - Movingui-Fraké*
* A condition d'appliquer à cette essence un traitement de préservation lorsqu'elle est soumise aux intempéries.	

Le potentiel de l'industrie du sciage, notamment en ce qui concerne les sections disponibles et les possibilités de la main-d'oeuvre locale, en particulier l'inexistence de charpentiers qualifiés, ont orienté le choix de la technologie. Il est apparu, que la mieux adaptée est celle des maisons à murs porteurs en panneaux d'ossature de petite section, assemblés en atelier.

En raison des spécificités qui lui sont propres, l'exigence de durabilité qui intervient dans le coût global de la construction sera examinée dans un autre paragraphe.

Le coût de fonctionnement devra, quant à lui, être le plus réduit possible compte tenu de la destination des habitations ; il est
en particulier exclu de prévoir l'installation de climatiseur. Cette
exigence aura des répercussions sur les choix architecturaux.

Les habitudes et les traditions locales semblent de nature à permettre un certain entretien. Il faut cependant qu'il puisse être
effectué par l'occupant de la maison s'il s'agit d'accession à la
propriété. Dans le cas de logements locatifs, les maîtres d'ouvrage
ont un budget d'entretien.

3.2 Exigences de sécurité

Elles concernent la stabilité des maisons sous les différentes sollicitations et la sécurité en cas d'incendie. Les relevés météorologi-
ques existants, notamment en ce qui concerne les vents et les inten-
sités des précipitations ont permis d'évaluer les sollicitations à
prendre en compte. En l'absence de relevé, c'est par un examen de
l'habitat existant qu'aurait pu être effectué l'approche du problème.

La sécurité en cas d'incendie a été examinée par rapport à la
sécurité des personnes avec comme objectif d'apporter une protection
au moins égale à celle des bâtiments en maçonnerie actuellement construits. Dans ces constructions, c'est l'effondrement de la toiture
qui est l'élément déterminant le délai d'évacuation des personnes et
c'est le délai qui a été pris en considération pour la stabilité au
feu des constructions en bois. Il aurait été possible d'aller plus
loin vis-à-vis de cette exigence, notamment en considérant le risque
de transmission du feu entre maisons voisines comme cela existe dans
d'autres pays, mais les différentes rencontres que nous avons eues
ont contribué à ne pas retenir ce critère.

3.3 Exigences d'habitabilité

Ce sont elles qui déterminent les conditions de confort et d'occupation des locaux. Elles prennent en compte les conditions climatologi-
ques, le mode d'habiter, les évolutions souhaitées par les maîtres
d'ouvrage et les occupants en matière de confort. Leur formulation a
eu pour point de départ l'examen de l'habitat existant.

Dans ce pays, un élément essentiel est le confort thermique.
Comme nous l'avons vu, les contraintes économiques ne permettent pas
d'envisager la climatisation des locaux. La satisfaction à cette exigence aura donc des répercussions directes sur les choix architecturaux et techniques.

On devra en particulier, éviter la pénétration de la chaleur par
les fenêtres. On recherchera pour cela les orientations Nord ou Sud
pour les baies, des protections pour ces baies soit par un débord de
toiture soit par des fermetures.

De la même manière, les pénétrations de chaleur par les parties
opaques devront être réduites. Pour cela, deux moyens ont été envisagés : l'isolation, sans doute trop coûteuse et l'écran avec face
arrière largement ventilée, solution retenue. Pour les parties hori-
zontales, la ventilation ne peut être efficace que si elle est très
importante, ce qui paraît difficile à réaliser compte tenu des habitudes locales. L'isolation apparaît là, comme une solution plus

intéressante mais qui, pour des raisons économiques ne pourra être mise en oeuvre.

Enfin, il s'agit également d'évacuer la chaleur qui pénètre grâce à une large ventilation transversale des bâtiments. C'est pourquoi, on devra préférer les protections solaires trop étanches à l'air et préférer les protections par avancée des toitures. Ceci aura également une influence sur les choix urbanistiques pour éviter les écrans coupe-vent.

Un autre élément du confort thermique réside dans l'inertie du bâtiment. Cet élément est surtout intéressant lorsqu'il y a de forts écarts de température dans la journée. Les conditions du Cameroun, faible écart de température entre le jour et la nuit, rendent inutile l'inertie thermique. C'est pourquoi on peut favorablement envisager la réalisation d'un plancher bas léger construit sur plot. C'est même un élément favorable dans la mesure où il permet également, la ventilation en sous-face.

Une autre exigence d'habitabilité se trouve dans l'étanchéité à l'eau et à l'air. La première peut aisément être satisfaite en partie courante grâce à l'écran avec face arrière ventilée. Pour les habitations à rez-de-chaussée envisagées, l'étanchéité des fenêtres est surtout assurée grâce au large débord de la toiture. Il n'est pas nécessaire que l'on satisfasse à la seconde, car comme il a été remarqué précédemment, la ventilation est une condition indispensable au confort thermique.

Le problème du confort **acoustique** a été également abordé sous les deux aspects d'isolement vis-à-vis des bruits extérieurs et d'isolement entre logements voisins. Le premier aspect est incompatible avec la nécessité de ventilation et l'exigence de confort thermique a été jugée prépondérante. Bien que dans l'habitat traditionnel, l'implantation des maisons est telle, que les bruits en provenance d'un logement pénètrent dans le logement voisin par les ouvertures sur l'extérieur, le maître d'ouvrage a manifesté le désir de voir les murs séparatifs aptes à apporter un isolement acoustique. Une solution devra donc être étudiée dans ce sens.

Il a été nécessaire d'examiner enfin, les exigences liées au mode d'habiter. On a pu noter notamment, la nécessité d'une protection des baies contre l'effraction, la quasi-généralisation de terrasses couvertes. Certaines de ces exigences peuvent être à l'origine de contraintes au niveau de la conception ; d'autres au contraire, en particulier l'habitude de disposer la cuisine dans un local séparé du reste du logement, peuvent faciliter, en limitant le risque, la satisfaction aux exigences de sécurité en cas d'incendie.

3.4 Exigences de durabilité

L'exigence de durabilité est certainement celle dont la transcription sous forme de Règles de Qualité est la plus nécessaire pour pouvoir être facilement prise en compte par les concepteurs. Elle vise aussi bien la qualité des produits mis en oeuvre que les conditions de mise en oeuvre et les conditions de l'utilisation future des locaux. Les conditions climatiques et l'environnement influent largement sur les conditions de cette durabilité et c'est pourquoi les règles applicables en vue de satisfaire à cette exigence peuvent varier notablement d'une région à l'autre.

Dans le cas particulier des maisons en bois destinées à être construites au Cameroun, l'exigence de durabilité a été formulée ainsi : "durer aussi longtemps que les maisons en maçonnerie dont le coût est le même". Les différents ouvrages de la construction ont donc été examinés et des conditions ont été données cas par cas pour que cette exigence soit satisfaite.

La première des conditions a été le choix des bois à utiliser en fonction de leur destination. Le tableau donné en 3.1 indique les essences à utiliser dans les conditions économiques et industrielles actuelles. L'examen des conditions climatiques et du mode de construction a permis de définir les contraintes nécessaires à un bon comportement des ouvrages. Elles sont indiquées ci-après :

- Afin de protéger le pied de mur des rejaillissements importants dus à la violence des précipitations, le pied de mur devrait être situé à environ 30 ou 50 cm au-dessus du niveau du sol.
- Un large débord de la couverture protègera les parois extérieures de l'action de l'eau et du rayonnement solaire et diminuera la fréquence de l'entretien.
- La ventilation importante et l'absence de climatisation, équilibrent les pressions de vapeur entre l'intérieur et l'extérieur et annulent le risque de migration de vapeur et par conséquent, le risque de condensation qui pourrait avoir une influence défavorable sur le comportement des bois d'ossature.
- Les conditions d'humidité et de température ambiantes fixent l'état d'humidité d'équilibre des bois à l'abri des intempéries à un seuil où le développement des champignons est peu probable, et rendent par conséquent inutile, le traitement anticryptogamique.
- La protection contre les termites implique soit l'utilisation de bois résistants soit une conception interdisant la construction de galeries reliant le sol au bois. Pour les autres insectes, un traitement insecticide devra, le cas échéant, être appliqué.
- Dans le cas de plancher bas sur terre-plein, on devra disposer une coupure de capillarité entre le béton et le mur en bois.

4. Conclusion

Après avoir déterminé le système de construction en bois le mieux adapté semble-t-il aux conditions locales et le mieux à même de répondre aux objectifs économiques, une étude économique a été effectuée afin de comparer le coût d'une maison F5 en maçonnerie et celui d'une maison de même surface en bois. Cette comparaison ne peut bien entendu qu'être approximative puisque les prix des bois recueillis chez les négociants ne peuvent pas refléter exactement ce qu'ils seraient dans le cas d'un développement de ces techniques. Il semble, malgré tout, que l'objectif initial puisse être atteint.

Le cas exposé ici est un cas particulier à deux titres : d'une part les exigences ont été formulées pour un maître d'ouvrage donné et avec un objectif économique précis et d'autre part, le passage des exigences aux règles de conception a été fait pour une technologie

de construction particulière. C'est pourquoi le Guide de Conception
qui en a résulté est très détaillé, voire même très directif sur
certains points. Il est évident qu'il ne pourrait avoir un caractère
de document général de conception de maisons en bois au Cameroun.
Des modifications de l'environnement économique pouvant remettre en
cause les choix technologiques effectués.

TESTS AND TECHNICAL SPECIFICATIONS FOR CONCRETES IN SOMALIA

G. AUGUSTI, University of Florence
C. BLASI, Technical University of Milan
A. CECCOTTI, University of Palermo
A. FONTANA, University of Calabria
G. SACCHI, National Somali University

National Somali University - Mogadishu, School of Engineering

Summary

This paper presents the results obtained, over the last two years
by the authors together with C. Polizzotto, G. Sara, H. Mohamud,
A. Adan within the program of Technical Cooperation between Italy
and Somalia.
The research work was entirely carried out at the Laboratory for
Structures and Building Materials of the Engineering School of the
National Somali University in Mogadishu.
After a brief description of the materials commonly used in the
Mogadishu area (Benadir), a standard mortar is proposed to allow
the identification of the cement's strength. Then, results on
destructive and non-destructive tests of concrete, made with the
materials available in Somalia are reported; finally, a cost-strength
comparison is made between commonly used concretes, obtained from
coral aggregates, and concretes made with siliceous materials, which
can only be found outside the Mogadishu area and so are seldom applied in practice.
The present work is intended as a first step towards the establishment of national Somali standards for reinforced concrete constructions.

1. Introduction

No national code for reinforced concrete buildings exists in Somalia.
For major buildings, foreign standards are applied, albeit often unsuited to local conditions; minor buildings, especially those of
private ownership, completely elude any technical control.
The authors felt that the main danger of this situation arises from
the poor quality of most concretes. Three- or four-storey buildings
are no more a rarity in Somalia, but concrete is still mixed by hand,
neither vibrated nor compacted; moreover, weak and porous aggregates
are used, being those most easily found.
It was therefore decided to start extensive tests on concretes commonly used in the Mogadishu area, where most of r.c. building activity
is carried on, from the points of view of both their strength and
durability. The studies on the latter aspect mainly related to the
high permeability of usual concretes and consequent high corrodibility

of reinforcing bars in such a tropical marine climate are still
in the initial stages.
As already said, foreign standards are generally unsuited to Somali
materials and climate. The general aim of the current research is
therefore to provide, as the first step towards a national r.c. code,
tentative recommendations giving general directions to ensure higher
r.c. strength and durability, and to offer a useful tool to engineers
and constructors operating in the Democratic Republic of Somalia.

2. Aggregates

The aggregates commonly used for concrete, coming from a sea-shore
area within 20 Km from Mogadishu, are mostly calcareous with siliceous
traces.
Siliceous aggregates can only be found at 200 Km from Mogadishu
(see fig. 1).

2.1. Sands

Essentially, three sizes of shore sands are available: fine, medium,
and coarse; a small percentage of chlorides and sulphates is included.
Their grading curves are reported in fig. 2, where also the limit
curves of the Italian "normal" sand are shown for comparison.

2.2. Crushed stones

Crushed stones, obtained from shore rocks, mainly of coral origin,
are very porous and weak. Four sizes are usually available: fine,
medium-fine, medium-coarse, and coarse (see fig. 3).

2.3. Size Grading of aggregates used for r.c.

2.3.1. The aggregate traditionally used for r.c. is a mix of medium
sand and coarse crushed stones: this poor grading does not fall within
Fuller's range (fig. 4).

2.3.2. As shown by previous studies performed at the N.S.U. (ref. 2,3)
a richer grading, made of coarse sand and three sizes (medium-fine,
medium-coarse, and coarse) of crushed stones, can correct the distribution, to fall within Fuller's range (fig. 4).

3. Cements and mortars

Quality control of cement is crucial since deliveries often come in
unqualified jute bags.

3.1. A proposal for a "normal mortar"

In order to obtain indications on a possible "normal mortar" for
quality control of cement, the possibility of using a particular
siliceous sand for the Bur Acaba area (fig. 1) has been investigated,

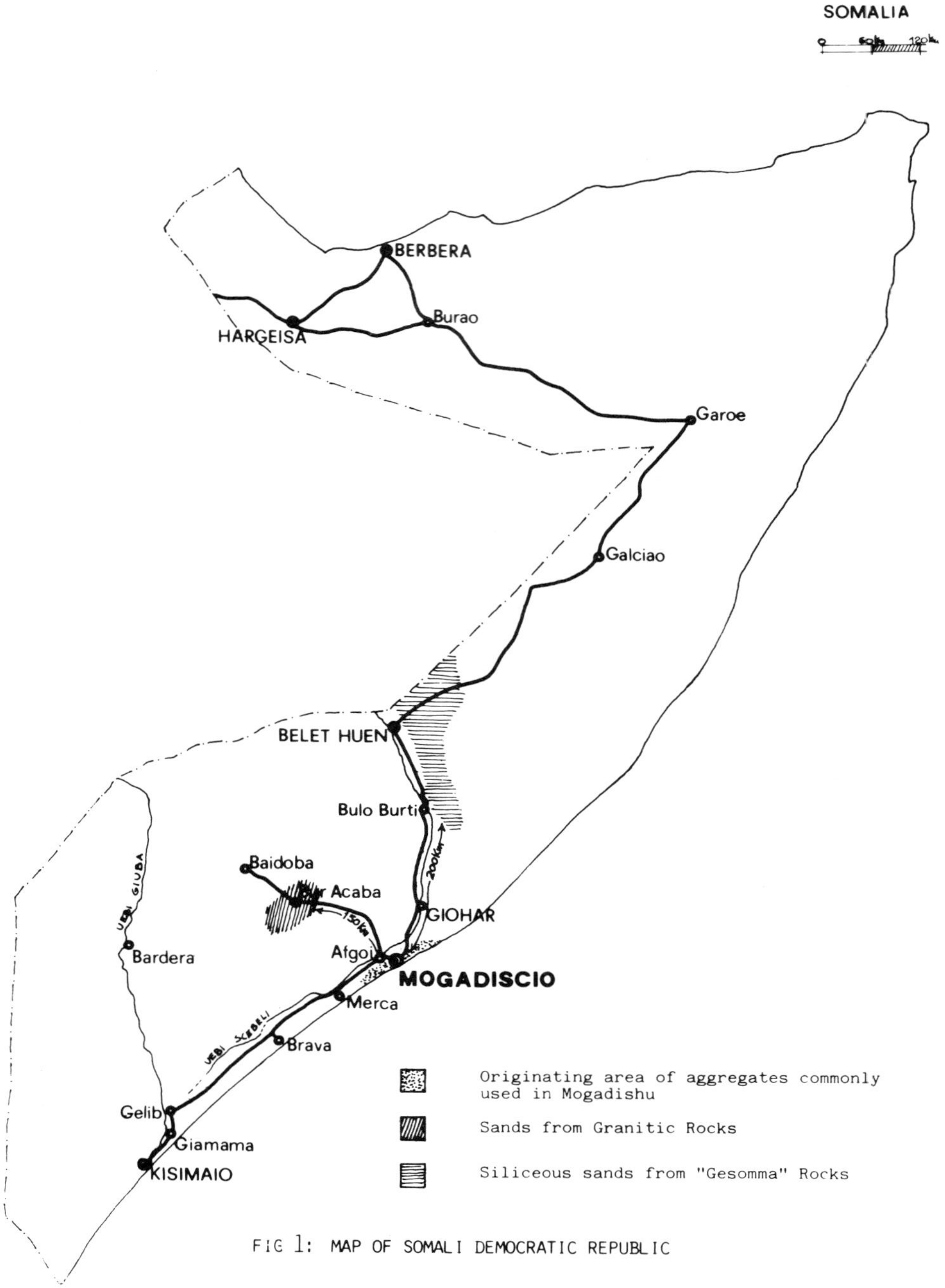

SOMALIA

0   60km   120km

- BERBERA
- Burao
- HARGEISA
- Garoe
- Galciao
- BELET HUEN
- Bulo Burti
- Baidoba
- Bur Acaba
- GIOHAR
- Afgoi
- MOGADISCIO
- Merca
- Brava
- Bardera
- Gelib
- Giamama
- KISIMAIO

USCI GIUBA

USCI SCEBELI

200km

150km

135km

▦ Originating area of aggregates commonly
used in Mogadishu

▨ Sands from Granitic Rocks

▤ Siliceous sands from "Gesomma" Rocks

FIG 1: MAP OF SOMALI DEMOCRATIC REPUBLIC

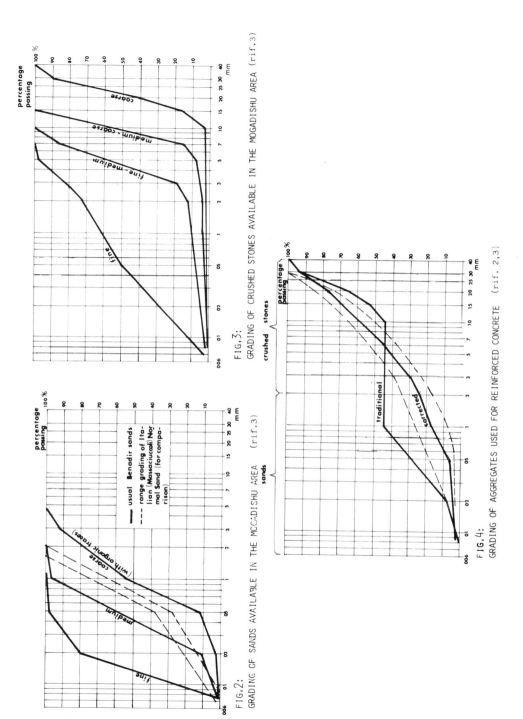

FIG. 2:
GRADING OF SANDS AVAILABLE IN THE MOGADISHU AREA (rif.3)

FIG. 3:
GRADING OF CRUSHED STONES AVAILABLE IN THE MOGADISHU AREA (rif.3)

FIG. 4:
GRADING OF AGGREGATES USED FOR REINFORCED CONCRETE (rif. 2,3)

because the grading of this sand tends to be fairly constant and, as shown in fig. 5, approaches the optimum range fixed by the Italian standards. To this end, mortar specimens were prepared in compliance with Italian standards using either the Bur Acaba sand or the Italian "normal sand" (from Massaciccoli).
The results, reported in Table 1, suggest that, for equal values of all other factors, the strength of the mortar made with Bur Acaba sand is up to 85% of that of the corresponding Italian "normal mortar". It could therefore be proposed that, for Somali standards, test mortar specimens be prepared with the grading and procedure fixed by Italian standards, but using Bur Acaba sand; for quality control of cement, the values given by Italian standards should be reduced by 15% (see Table 1.bis). This reduction, however, should not be adopted for low maturations, to take into account the faster curing, occurring in an environment of temperature +29°C (*) instead of 20°C as considered by the Italian standards.

3.2. Mortar made with shore sand

Fig. 6 shows the strength values of mortar specimen made with shore sands: they are significantly lower than observed when using Bur Acaba siliceous sand.

4. Concretes

Extensive tests on concrete cubes made in the Laboratory with shore aggregates and well water in compliance with Italian standards were carried out, each time varying certain parameters.
Maturation took place in the Laboratory at almost constant temperature 29°C and relative humidity 90%. The most relevant results are reported in the following.

4.1. Water/cement ratio

Fig. 7 shows, for varying water-to-cement ratios, the mean strength curve of concretes made with different gradings.
Note that to obtain the same workability, a 50% larger w/c ratio is needed in comparison with concretes obtained from European standard (non porous) aggregates; below w/c = 0.6 the mix is not workable at all, because of the quantity of water absorbed by the porous aggregate: therefore, the strength that can be obtained using shore aggregates (albeit corrected) has a definite (and rather low) upper limit.

4.2. Hardening time

As for mortars, hardening of concretes is much more rapid than usual at 20°C. (fig. 8)

(*) almost constant throughout the year in Mogadishu

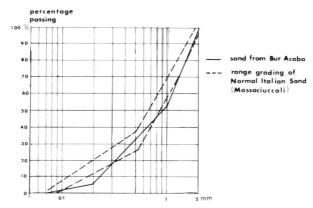

FIG.5:
GRADING OF GRANITIC SAND FROM BUR ACABA

SAND	cem. sand	water cem.	cement type	days		
				3	7	28
MASSACIUCCOLI	1/3	0,5	325	=	37,3	47,1
			425	33,7	40,9	55,0
BUR ACABA	1/3	0,5	325	=	32,0	41,8
			425	31,1	37,1	48,0

TAB 1: AVERAGE EXPERIMENTAL COMPRESSIVE STRENGTH (MPa) OF NORMALIZED
MORTARS (PREPARED AT N.S.U. WITH CONTROLLED CEMENTS)

REGULATIONS	cem. sand	water cem.	cement type	days		
				3	7	28
ITALIAN	1/3	0,5	325	=	17,5	32,5
			425	17,5	32,5	42,5
SOMALI (PROPOSED)	1:3	0,5	325	=	17,5	28,0
			425	17,5	28,0	37,0

TAB 1BIS: MINIMUM ACCEPTED COMPRESSIVE STRENGTH (MPa) OF
NORMALIZED MORTARS

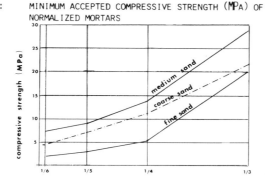

FIG.6: AVERAGE EXPERIMENTAL (28 DAY) COMPRESSIVE
STRENGTH OF MORTARS PREPARATED WITH USUAL
SHORE SANDS AS A FUNCTION OF CEMENT/SAND RATIO

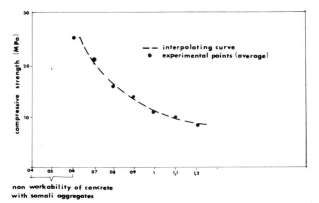

FIG.7:
AVERAGE CONCRETE CUBIC STRENGTH AS A FUNCTION OF WATER/CEMENT RATIO

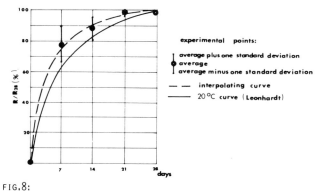

FIG.8:
CONCRETE CUBIC STRENGTH VS TIME FROM CASTING

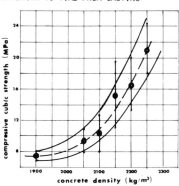

FIG.9:

28-DAY CONCRETE CUBIC STRENGTH VS DENSITY

4.3. Strength-density

Correlation between strength and density appears to be particularly significant: the non linear correlation coefficient gives $r^2 = 0.75$ (see fig. 9).

4.4. Effect of grading selection

In comparison with mixes obtained using traditional gradings, when corrected distributions are adopted (cf. 2.3.2.), lower w/c ratios are needed to obtain the same workability while the mean strength increases by at least 60% (Table 2).

5. Non-destructive control tests

The Model L Schmidt rebound hammer was used, being more suited to test weak concretes made with light aggregates than the Model N more usual in Europe.
Concrete obtained using 300 Kg/m^3 high-strength cement, and correctly distributed shore aggregates, cured for 21 days at 20°C (5 days in water and 16 in the open air at relative humidity 90%), was taken as reference.
A first series of 10 cubes made varying the w/c ratio and cured in the shade yielded the correlation curve (a) plotted in fig. 10 against the calibration curve given by the factory: it can be seen that the latter curve is much steeper than the former.

A second series of 10 cubes, cured in the sun, gave curve (b), which would suggest that, to the same rebound index, a concrete cured in the sun, has a strength 12% lower, i.e. that an "influence reduction coefficient" equal to 0.88 must be applied to any calibration curve obtained in the Laboratory, when concrete cured in the sun is tested by the rebound hammer.

6. Costs of concrete production. Comparisons.

A correct distribution has almost no influence on cost per cubic meter of concrete made using shore aggregates, while resulting in a relevant increase in admissible stress: taking the minimum stress values of Table 2 as a reference and considering a safety coefficient equal to 3, the admissible stress can increase from 3 MPa to 5 MPa. However increased, this value is still very low: moreover the contents in chlorides and sulfates, and the porosity of these aggregates are a main cause of the rapid deterioration of most Somali reinforced concrete constructions. As suggested in Table 3 these problems can only be overcome by using compact siliceous aggregates which are only found in areas which are situated farther away from the capital (Fig. 1).
However higher delivery costs would be balanced by the smaller volumes required, on account of the greater admissible stress (see Table 3); moreover, these kind of aggregates would provide a much better

SHORE AGGREGATES	cement dosage kg/m	$\frac{W}{C}$	cubic strength (MPa)	Eo (MPa)	E4MPa (MPa)
TRADITIONAL	350	0,8	13,6	29.000	23.000
		1,0	11,1		
		1,2	8,7		
CORRECTED	350	0,6	25,3	29.000	23.000
		0,8	18,1		
		1,0	13,5		

TAB 2: CUBIC CONCRETE STRENGTH VS TRADITIONAL AND CORRECTED
SHORE SOMALI AGGREGATES

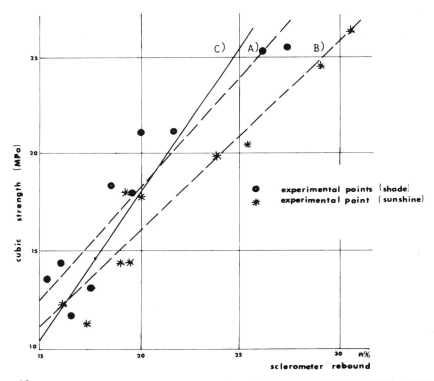

FIG.10: REBOUND HAMMER TESTS, EXPERIMENTAL POINTS AND INTERPOLATING LINES:

A) SPECIMENS MATURED IN THE SHADE
B) SPECIMENS MATURED IN THE SUNSHINE
C) CALIBRATION LINE OF THE INSTRUMENT'S PRODUCER

A

MATERIALS	BASIC COST	TRANSPORT	QUANT.	COST
SHORE SAND	28/m³	72/m³	0,5 m³	50
CORAL CRUSHED STONES	444/m³	56/m³	0,8 m³	400
CEMENT	4/kg	=	350 kg	1400

$$\overline{\sigma} \leqslant 5\,\text{MPa}$$

1850/m³

B

MATERIALS	BASIC COST	TRANSPORT	QUANT.	COST
GRANITIC SAND	36/m³	720/m³	0,4 m³	302
GRANITIC CRUSHED STON.	577/m³	560/m³	0,8 m³	910
CEMENT	4/kg	=	350 kg	1400

$$\overline{\sigma} = 7,5\,\text{MPa}$$

2612/m³

TAB. 3:
COSTS OF CONCRETE PRODUCTION, COMPARISONS (all cost in Somali Shillings

protection against weathering of concrete and corrosion of reinforcement, and therefore require much reduced maintenance costs.
In conclusion, the writers strongly feel that the use of shore
aggregates should be discontinued, and that a prohibition to this
effect should be included in the projected Somali technical code.

7.   Future research

The following research objectives have been set for the immediate
future in the National Somali University:
- completion of investigations into the characteristics of aggregates
  from more remote areas;
- extensive tests on weathering of concrete and corrosion of reinforcement;
- continuation of a program of control tests on construction sites
  of concrete produced, steel used and building procedures followed
  by a statistical analysis.
These investigations will allow to provide within a reasonable perioc
of time, a set of Technical Instructions for acceptance and control
of materials and for design of reinforced concrete structures in the
Democratic Republic of Somali.

References   (Previous N.S.U. Report)

1. G. Augusti, M. D'Adamo, H. Mohamud - La resistenza dei calcestruzzi
                                         cementizi confezionati in So-
                                         malia. U.N.S. Nov. 81

2. C. Blasi, L. Sevino, H. Mohamud   - La resistenza dei calcestruzzi
                                        e delle malte di cemento con-
                                        fezionate in Somalia.
                                        U.N.S. Giugno 82

3. G. Sara, C. Polizzotto, V. Soave,
                           A. Adan   - Ricerca sui calcestruzzi da
                                        cemento armato confezionati
                                        in Somalia. U.N.S. Nov. 82

4. G. Sara, C. Pollizotto, M. Assan,
                           A. Adan   - Il problema della normativa
                                        somala per le costruzioni in
                                        c.a.
                                        U.N.S. Dic. 82

5. V. Amicarelli, G. Sara   - Prove di corrosione dei tondi-
                                        ni di acciaio inglobati nei
                                        provini cilindrici di cal-
                                        cestruzzo.
                                        U.N.S. in preparation

EVOLVING APPROPRIATE BUILDING CODES AND REGULATIONS AS
A BASIS FOR LOW COST HOUSING

F.I.A. TACKIE, Building and Road Research Institute
Ghana.

1. *Introduction*

There are several dimensions to the housing dilemma of
the majority low-income earning population. Inappropriate building codes and regulations may be considered
as one out of many complex network of problems. For a
very desperate group of people in search of an item so
fundamental as shelter yet so far out of reach, any
munimum effort towards in improvement may achieve a
significant impact.

It is with this in the background that this paper
sets out with the following objectives. First, to
identify the relevance of the topic by asking why building codes in Low Cost Housing. Second, to discuss what
items to take into consideration in search of an
improvement and lastly how to realize any proposed
strategies for improvement.

2. *The relevance of codes and regulations to the Low Cost Housing concept.*

One characteristic feature of the Low-cost housing
concept, is the desire to satisfy the housing requirements of the urban majority otherwise known as the urban
poor. The inability of the public sector to respond to
these demands needs no further clarification. In this
manner effective demand for housing to the private
sector. (1) And even here a distinction ought to be
made between new housing stock as against the ageing
existing stock. Slums and squatter settlements which
mainly represent the latter, tend to dominate the
private housing market. (2). But what is more important is the fact that most third world countries are
facing an explosive urban population problem. Especially in Africa, the rate of urban growth is said to be
over 8% a year and mainly attributed to the concept of
migration.

(3). This trend is likely to worsen and at the same
time it is predicted that the economic situation is
not likely to improve. (4). Under these circumstances
the private housing sector remains the only avenue to
absorb such increases in the urban population.

It is precisely here that building codes and regulations become relevant to the concept of Low-cost
housing. In an attempt to increase the intensity of
use of the existing slum, squatter and other low-income
housing areas, the defects of inappropriate codes or
non-existent codes are often made manifest. The
manifestation is in unsafe buildings, unhealthy habitat,
lack of space for economic activities, lack of minimum
publit utilities and in general non-planning.

In contrast, the existing codes have tended to favour
the formal construction sector, represented by civil
engineering works, private and public sector non-residential buildings and public sector housing. Together,
their demands on key building materials lead to a
problem of acute unavailability. This of course
reduces housing output with the most vulnerable being
the lower income group. With adequate measures through
codes and regulations, it is possible to regulate the
supply of such scarce materials with the objective of
protecting reasonable excess to the lower-income
housing sector. Again, the formal construction sector,
seems a more reasible target for innovations on alternative local building materials such that a consolidation there, can help in breaking the resistance likely
to be encountered with the lower - income group.

3. *Some characteristics of the existing codes and regulations.*

Apart from the politico-historical circumstances which
tend to put most of the codes out of place, more serious
controversies have been observed. (5). Two major issues
stand out here. First, the performance concept controversy - most codes are criticized on being functionally
rigid and generally out of line with the performance
concept. (6). When applied to the construction output
of the formal sector it may seem an attractive concept.
But given the complexity of housing especially lower-
income housing, is the concept really a panacea? In
the midst of perpetual inaction, the performance of
alternative concepts can hardly be measured.

The second is the construction output controversy.
This refers to the inability of existing codes to
reflect the rather diverse nature of construction
activities. This implies that different sets of codes
should be applied to equally different construction types.

The user concept is relevant here i.e., whether it is residential, civil works etc. Moreover, it is vital to have a set of codes for the respective levels of construction output under each user group. If such a style is adopted then the story of the low-income housing sector may be given a fair consideration. Similarly, certain geographical diversities especially natural disasters are not adequately catered for in the often-uniform codes.

3.1. *Likely constraints in the review of codes.*

There are first and foremost constraints posed by the existing nature of the codes. These tend to hinder developments in the housing sector more than the other construction sectors if only for the simple reason that they have virtually ignored the presence of the bulk of the housing market.

The more important set of constraints is rather related to the question what are the likely obstacles to be met if the existing codes are to be revised especially to suit a peculiar purpose such as improving upon the housing situation of the lower-income population. There is a relationship between both sets of constraints. However, the second set is likely to originate simultaneously from the "Suppliers" of codes i.e. public agencies etc. and the "consumers" of codes i.e. builders, dwellers etc. The following is a summary of some of the major constraints:-

(a) Socio-economic determinants:- The cultural habits of the lower-income population, their attitudes and value systems are likely to undermine the success of any such enforcement. Especially for the migrants who may outnumber the indigenes in a given system, the notion of temporariness may not encourage the expected response to acceptable housing standards.

Illiteracy or rather the absence of an appropriate mode of communication is yet another hindrance. (7). Underlying all these draw-backs is the economic structure of the urban low-income population. Adherance to any set of codes and regulations implies some minimum cost or spending which to the urban poor may not be an affordable expenditure item.

The summary of all this is expressed in the very complex nature of low-income housing - a subject which has not let itself to easy conprehension. (8).

(b) Data base and the paradox of manpower:- Closely related to the above, is the problem of not only inade- quate data to proceed with any revision, but more fundamentally, the difficulty in deriving an appropriate

methodology for the purpose of such data collection.
Further evidence on this deficiency is the lack of
qualified manpower or the inability of the subject to
attract the attention of qualified manpower. Probably
too, it is so complex that it falls outside the
jurisdiction of every profession.

(c) Legislation and Administrative commitment:-
Codes and regulations tend to demand some legislative
backing. A revision as such requires a legislative
decision. The first possible problem concerns the
often-complex procedures involved in achieving new
legislations (if even in a democratic system). The
second is the dilemma of the technical basis of such a
legislation. (9). What should the legislation seek to
achieve given the circumstances of the urban poor?
Should it risk aggressive enforcement and punitive
measures - the very issues which have proven to be
deterrents in some instances?

Above all this is the issue of apathy from the
administrative set-up of the public sector. How best
can governments get the message of the importance of
low-cost housing and further get committed to details
such as the revision or adoption of codes?

(d) Finance:- To revise or adopt building codes
for lower-income housing situation, implies considerable cost. This may be a deterrent to any central
government of any poor country which by implication is
that poor. At the same time, it seems apparent that
poor countries are that desperately poor in sectors
which do not seem to attract relative importance in the
national socio-economic development frame work.

(e) The building industry:- Building codes and
regulations form a minor yet important component of the
building industry. (10). The nature of the Building
Industry in any given country is likely to reflect on
the appropriateness of codes and regulations. So much
has been said about the characteristics of the construction industry in third world countries, especially
their problems. (11). For the purposes of housing for
the urban poor, the building industry has such peculiar
problems as - inadequate or lack of key building
materials, - an unrecognised yet indispensable informal
sector, - inadequate resources to support alternative
indigenous building materials.

The issue at stake is that the building industry is
so problematic that a revision in codes and regulations
presupposes a radical streamlining of the parent
industry itself.

4. A direction for future codes and regulations.

Most of the existing codes show an interaction of three
parties - the public agencies in charge of codes, the
builders and the dwellers in general. The existing
system has tended to potray a confrontation between
the public agencies on the one hand and the others,
where by it is the responsibility of the latter group
to ensure conformity. Defining the basic parameters
of low-income housing this approach has a fundamental
weakness which needs a radical reversal whereby conformity will be the responsibility of the public agencies.
At least for this subject - matter alone, the concept
of paternalism and intervention can be said to be
acceptable for the lower-income group. (12).
   If this hypothesis sounds reasonable, then some of
the guiding objectives for the future are as follows.
Apart from ensuring minimum public health, safety and
comfort, the codes should aim at (i) promoting the
development and use of lower cost building materials.
(ii) promoting the maintenance of the built environment.
(iii) Eliminating bureaucracy as far as the dweller and
builder are concerned. (iv) Ensuring the cautious
integration of non-residential activities. (v) promoting investment in non-residential facilities by the
public and quasi-public agencies. (vi) Enforcing an
overall comprehensive town planning strategy for lower-
income settlements within the urban framework.

4.1. Factors to be considered for implementation.

On the basis of the above set of objectives an attempt
can be made at prescribing certain strategies which may
eventually influence appropriate recommendations. For
such a purpose it is worth re-emphasizing that apart
from countries with distinct geophysical contrasts in
terms of natural disasters etc., the notion of regional
differentials in codes should be substituted as far as
housing is concerned, with differentials based on
housing classifications. Within the low-income housing
activity, the following classifications can be made. -
(i) private sector slum and squatter settlements. (ii)
Emerging private sector housing. (iii) public sector
housing and (iv) rural type housing. From this
classification, the following factors can be applied
accordingly.

(a) Upgrading programmes.
Especially for private sector slums and squatter settlements, such intervention measures from the public
agencies must be seen as a positive contribution to an
increase and an improvement in the housing situation of

(f) Public utilities (infrastructure)
Walkways, access to water supply, electricity supply,
drainage are some communal utilities which may go a
long way to help in achieving a drastic improvement.
Revised codes should aim at making it obligatory on the
public executing agencies to provide minimum utilities
as a basic prerequisite to shelter construction.

5. *Realizing the strategies.*

There are a complex network of actions involved in
order to realize any targets from the objectives discussed above. One such single set of actions which may
play a very central role in the midst of persistent
inaction is the act of intervention by national governments in conjunction with international bodies. The
following is a summary of the sets of action to be
taken and an indication of the expected level of intervention.

5.1. *Policy formulation.*

This should be the primary concern of all concerned
governments. However, with regard to the eminent
problems which have led to a situation of near-apathy,
there is need for a further level of intervention by
regional bodies such as the E.C.A. Such level of
concern is already being expressed by this body in its
work programme. There is a likelihood that similar
response will emerge from smaller groupings such as
ECOWAS etc.

5.2. *Policy co-ordination.*

There exists several government agencies responsible in
one way or the other for matters concerning either
codes or low cost housing or both. The problem of
inaction it seems has partly been due to the lack of a
clear direction. A policy guideline should go as far
as stimulating restructuring of the system of co-ordination by the respective governments towards better output. In instances where manpower is a constraint, sub-
regional pools may be set out to co-ordinate a region
of countries.

5.3. *Implementation or pilot projects.*

A realistic implementation of the suggested codes and
regulations should involve a high degree of decentrali-
zation or localization but of course with some supportive co-ordination.

the lower-income group. Depending on the homogeneity
of the settlement and the resources available, the
intervention could be direct or act as a catalyst.
Whatever be the case, expected conformity to codes and
regulations will seem to have a better chance with this
approach.

(b) Lower cost building materials
The non-availability of building materials affordable
to the lower-income group is in itself a causative
factor in the neglect and non-functioning of codes.
Much has been said already about strategies for developing indigenous building materials. (13). Of equal
importance is the concept of popularizing their use.
Here, the formal sector is one source of advertisement
and direct pilot projects in the lower-income settlements through upgrading, yet another.

(c) Town Planning strategies.
Both as a curative and preventive measure, but more of
the latter, preparation of appropriate layouts for newer
lower-income housing areas should be considered in areas
adjoining the higher income and medium income private
sector residential zones. The layout in content should
be defensive and protective in order to achieve aims of
public health, safety and comfort. Moreover, such
planning regulations should capture the non-residential
spaces which are often susceptible to abuse. Such a
regulation is a corollary to the suggestion that public
agencies and quasi-public agencies be encouraged to
invest in non-residential activities, especially those
with higher job-generation potential.

(d) The informal building industry.
If the construction industry as a whole remains in its
disjointed form, then obviously any effort to improve
upon codes will be meaningless. The success of codes
and regulations presupposes the availability of expected
materials, building skills etc. Fortunately, housing
output for the lower income group stems largely from the
informal building industry. (14). Certain improvements
are needed in this sector, if it will become useful.
They include, - skill training for artisans, basic
management techniques for materials producers etc. etc.

(e) Rural Housing.
One of the sources of the problems inherent in low-cost
housing with regard to codes emerges from the rural
population. It seems likely that if rural housing is
improved upon through appropriate codes it stands to
achieve two things. First, to retain some future
migrants and secondly to transfer better building and
living habits to the urban zones.

Especially with slum and squatter upgrading programmes,
there is need for the establishment of local project
offices or "planning offices". For such reasons,
implementation should largely fall within national
resources.

5.4. *Code preparation and review.*

Technical constraints of inadequate manpower can be
overcome by external aid in terms of manpower. Regional co-operation and exchange of experiences become
usefull here. Certain processes need not be duplicated
such as that of methodology for data collection;
dissemination techniques etc.

5.5. *Financing.*

From local sources it should be possible to attract
some revolving fund to be used in defraying cost of
administration of codes. In the upgrading programmes,
minimum funds could be realized within the often-
buoyant informal economy. Much bulkier funds especially for capital projects will require some external
assistance from regional bodies such as E.C.A., A.D.B.
etc. and from global sources such as the World Bank.

6. *Conclusions.*

For a subject as complex yet important as this, it is
not easily possible to answer simultaneously the
questions, why?, What? and above all how? The attempt
made so far in this paper may seem marginal yet will
prove very useful if only the barrier of inaction or
apathy covering the subject of housing for the urban
poor is removed. It is nearly a decade since the
famous Vancouver conference was held. There is still
hope that by the period of the decade some response
would have emerged however modest it may.

References

1. UNCHS (Habitat)   The residential circum-
                         stances of the urban
                         poor in developing
                         countries.
                         U.N. 1981 Praeger.

2. United Nations Economic   Human Settlements in
    Commission for Africa   Africa. E/CN.14/HUS/15.
                                   Addis Ababa 1976.

3. Ward, B.   The Home of Man Penguin
                                   1976 pp 3 - 4.

4. Shaw, M.   Towards reformation and
                                   or revolution? Africa
                                   1984-2000 West Africa
                                   Magazine No. 3428 pp
                                   995-998.

5. UNCHS   Overview on building
                                   codes and regulations
                                   in developing countries
                                   U.N. Seminar, Sweden
                                   1980.

6. C.I.B.   The performance concept
                                   and its terminology.
                                   C.I.B. report No. 32.

7. Mallonga, R.   Paper summary. UN
                                   Seminar on building
                                   codes OP. Cit 1980 p 71.

8. Angel, S and Benjamih, S   17 reasons why the
                                   squatter problem cannot
                                   be solved. Ekistics
                                   No. 242 Jan. 1976

9. Boateng, E.   U.N. Seminar on building
                                   codes OP. Cit pp 65-66.

10. UNCHS   Theme paper, UN experts
                                   group meeting, Nairobi
                                   1981.

11. UNCHS   Ibid

12. Angel, S and Benjamin, S   17 reasons why the
                                   squatter problem cannot
                                   be solved OP Cit

13.   Ver Kerk, G.C.   Sectorial survey paper
                                       of the Building materials
                                       and const. Ind. UNIDO/p6.
                                       56 Oct. 1982.

14.   Tackie, F.I.A.   The informal building
                                       industry in the context
                                       of urban housing unpub-
                                       lished M.phil thesis
                                       University of Newxastle
                                       Upon Tyne 1979.

QUALITY ASSURANCE FOR BUILDING CONSTRUCTION

MUSA RESHEIDAT, Yarmouk University, Irbid, Jordan

1. *Introduction*

Building construction today has grown in size, accelerated in pace,
and become so highly mechanized that it is nothing but an outdoor
assembly plant. It is a highly traditional regionally and locally
conditioned activity, bound by a variety of cultural, social, climatic, as well as technical parameters. In this era of rapidly
rising prices of materials, escalating wages forced up by inflation
and increasing energy costs, the initial costs of construction have
been rising at an ever increasing rate. Moreover, the follow-on
costs, such as maintenance and operations have also escalated
rapidly.

The need for an optimal criteria for the use of available local
building materials, selection of structural system, method of construction, and human skills in developing countries should be realized as systematic consideration of cost, time and quality. Such
criteria may termed as quality assurance which is an integrated
system of quality controls, applied to all stages of building process based on the right decision which takes into account the economical, cultural, social, environmental and technical aspects.

2. *Quality assurance system – QA*

QA is a total overall system that deals with the planning and obtaining of the quality level needed for the finished product to perform
the functions and service needed for a particular situation.

2.1 Quality assurance in design

In designing structures, an iterative process is usually followed.
Starting with a preliminary design with specified configuration,
dimensions, and materials, an analysis is made to study the adequacy
of this design in meeting requirements for various limit states.
The preliminary design can be modified or alternated and the new design will be analyzed again. This design analysis cycle can be repeated until satisfaction with the serviceability, safety, and
economical feasibility of the final design is achieved.

2.2   Quality assurance in specifications

A specification is part of a legal contract document between an owner and a contractor and a means of communication at the same time (1). It must say what it means and it must also mean what it says. It should be aimed at getting the quality needed rather than a probability of rejection. It must be practical and realistic and in tune with the nature's laws.

In specifications, the application of practical uses of the laws of probability must be added. The reason for this is variability, a law of life that is found in all material processes and operations. It cannot be completely eliminated, but it can be reduced to managable levels.

2.3   Quality assurance during construction

With the best designs and specifications, one can still have a poor structure if things go wrong in the field. Accordingly, the greatest payoff from quality assurance and quality control may occur during the construction phase of the entire building process.

Quality assurance in this phase must develop convenient procedures to insure that proper records and measures are obtained to monitor pending serious deviations of predetermined quality. Such procedures must be outlined to provide immediate actions to rectify errors so as minimize delays and increased costs. The construction work should be planned so that important parts will be accessible for inspection during the work.

The management on the construction site must apply the quality assurance concept in erection stages. It has the responsibility for the quality control of materials and components produced at the construction site and for the control in connection with the erection of the structure (2).

Perhaps one of the most important quality assurance subsystems is inspection. The quality of inspection makes the difference between a properly constructed structure and one that is full of problems and, in extreme cases, a failure. The activities of inspection should be the same whether they are applied by the contractor or by the acceptance team representing the owner.

2.4   Quality assurance in feedback

The entire building process must be documented and formalized to bring back to all bodies involved in building construction, namely, the designer, the specification writer, the bidding team, the quality assurance and quality control teams the items to be learned for future use (quality assurance) and to make sure that all items are recorded and become part of the feedback subsystem (quality control). The application of the feedback subsystem will be a constructive step in the development of quality assurance system.

3. *Life cycle costing - LCC*

LCC may defined as systematic consideration of cost, time and quality of a given facility. Should the technique of life cycle costing be promoted by the owner and designer, effective utilization of our national resources as a matter of utmost concern to all segments of our socioeconomic system may be realized. Life cycle costing allows assessment of a given solution or choice of alternative solutions on the basis of considering all relevant economic consequences.

3.1 Cost analysis procedure

A number of properly sequenced steps must be taken to rationally arrive at a recommendation. First a facility design must exist. Next, a life cost estimate is produced. Depending on the life cycle study, the costs of real estate, design and review, management and control, move-in expenses, and follow-on costs may included. Initial costs must be organized in a way that will allow design alternates to be compared.

3.2 When timing counts

The element of time plays an important role in making economic comparisons. The concept of engineering economics has been developed for the purpose of equating time and the cost of money. Such an inherent part of life cycle estimating process is applied following one of two approaches. The first, that of "present worth", converts all present and future expenditures into a common point in time (today's cost). The second approach converts initial recurring and non-recurring costs to an annual series of payments. The relevant mathematical expressions used in these approaches could be found in Reference (3).

4. *Design-cost model*

For any structural facility, optimum design may be achieved following a design-cost model which is presented in Fig. (1). Based on the available data and utilizing a conceptual model (state-of-art), a preliminary design is set out. Following quality assurance in design, which has been presented in Section 2.1, a possible final design may be accepted.

This procedure will pass either through modified designs or alternative designs; as shown as design-analysis-cycle. Then the technique of life cycle costing is applied in order to rationally accept the final design. In both the two iterative procedures, one can obtain high quality with minimum total costs for a predetermined economical life of the structure (4).

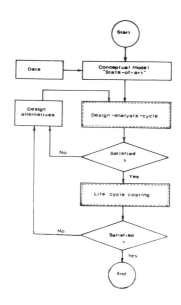

Fig. 1.   Design-cost model

5.   *Quality assurance in acceptance*

An acceptance program must outline the strategy that offers the best
chance of insuring that quality will be adequate for typical construction. This strategy must define the criteria for accepting or
rejecting building materials and/or products. A probabilistic approach which utilize the statistical expressions may be convenient to
define acceptance considering variability of materials.

5.1   Importance of material variability

The importance of material variability in construction materials and
products can be illustrated by analyzing the data on material variability with statistical techniques based on the normal distributions.
The density of individual values is a function of the mean and standard deviation.

Variability exists in all materials we deal with, in all processes,
and in all sampling and testing. Occasionally, these different items
of variability cancel each other, but as a rule they are more likely
to be cumulative.

5.2   Factors influence variability

The variability in the property of a product is dependent on the 4M
factors: Material, Man, Machine and Measuring method. Thus the

quality is directly related to variability, and as a general rule, the higher the quality the lower the variability, and vice versa.

5.3   Illustrative example

Three different probability curves, as shown in Fig. 2, represent three different populations of compressive strength test results. Each curve has a different degree of variability. The statistical information for the test results is presented in Table 1. Considering the limit required by the specifications be equal to 200 kg/em^2, the probability of rejection can be evaluated. All three curves give the same reliability of acceptance. But the curve A will be the best to improve the quality, followed by curves B and C respectively.

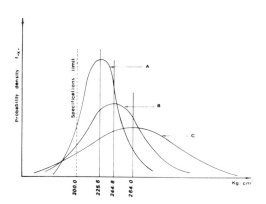

Fig. 2.   Distributions of three testing results

Table 1.   Statistical information

Population	Mean kg/cm^2	Standard deviation kg/cm^2	Coefficient of variation, %
A	225.6	20.0	8.86
B	244.8	35.0	14.30
C	264.0	50.0	18.94

6.   *Construction cost and quality*

Due to the fact that material properties can not be of deterministic
nature but of variable one, an adequate quality should be seeked.
So, the engineering management has to face two challenges:

(a)   materials or products must be of possible high degree
(level) of quality, and
(b)   producing these materials or products with the possible
minimum amount of costs.

The two challenges are often in contract with each other. However, an optimum quality could be obtained to realize a balance between the possible quality and minimum amount of total cost. Fig.
3 illustrates the cumulative cost versus quality.

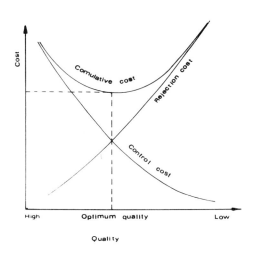

Fig. 3.   Optimum quality and its cumulative cost

7.   *Conclusions*

The following conclusions may be drawn from this paper:

(a)   quality assurance system is the right decision that must be
taken in the frame of predetermined and prepared plan.
(b)   quality controls are subsystems which are applied in the
quality assurance program in order to obtain the economical optimum
quality.
(c)   specifications must be prepared in such a way that they must
be fair and equitable and must be fairly administrated.
(d)   variability should be considered in specifications, procedures of acceptance and rejection, and all that by utilizing the

well-known statistical expressions.

(e)   interaction between quality assurance in design and life cycle costing is an effective model in realizing the optimal design taking into account the economical aspects.

(f)   quality assurance consists in the procedures that tend to answer the question: "Are we doing the right things?", while quality control consists of the steps taken to answer the question: "Are we doing these things right?". The former is involved in the decision making process and how one can be sure that these decisions are properly executed.

References

1.   Abdun-Nur, E. A. (1976), *Transportation Research Record No. 613,* Transportation Research Board, 51-55.
2.   *General Principles on Quality Assurance for Structures,* (1981), *J.C.S.S. Report,* IABSE-AIPC-IVBH, 35, 1-58.
3.   Kirk, S. J., *Life Cycle Costing: Problem Solver for Engineers,* (1979), Specifying Engineer, Architectural Record, McGraw-Hill, Inc.
4.   Resheidat, M. R. (1982), *Reliability-Design-Cost Interaction for Engineering Structures,* 13th J.C.S.S. meeting, Paris, October 26-28, 1982.

Résumés

Abstracts

ADOBE BLOCKS STABILIZED WITH GYPSUM

R. KAFESÇIOGLU, E. GÜRDAL
A. GÜNER, M.S. AKMAN
Istanbul Technical University

Abstract

Adobe Blocks Stabilized with Gypsum plaster (ABSG) provide certain significant advantages:

- Gypsum plaster requires less energy and industrial equipment for production when compared with lime or cement; it is cheaper. Gypsum is abundantly available on the earth.
- With ABSG, it is possible to start the construction of walls short after production without waiting for drying.
- ABSG have low shrinkage, sharp and smooth appearance, high mechanical strength, low strain under load.

In fact it is a more suitable low cost building material than plain adobe provided it is not allowed to come into direct contact with water.

Compressive and flexural strengths increase 2-3 times and shrinkage decreases 3-4 times when compared with plain adobe while also the demoulding and curing periods are very short. The strength development continues in the material used in the construction of a wall and the material transforms into a building stone with higher strength and lower deformability. Creep does not entail any problems. High humidity of the atmosphere decreases the compressive strength of the material to that of the dry plain adobe.
    At this stage of the investigation, the topics of primary importance are development of the production techniques and improvement of the water resistance by increasing the amount of gypsum added without impairing the economical character of the idea. The possible problem of biological corrosion of anaerobic kind is another point that merits further consideration. Especially, certain organisms present in soils may have such corrosive effects which will be studied in a future investigation.

BLOC DE PISE STABILISE AU PLATRE
R. KAFESCIOGLU, E. GURDAL, A, GUNER Istanbul Technical University

Les blocs de pisé stabilisé au plâtre présentent plusieurs avantages
significatifs :
- le plâtre exige moins d'énergie et d'équipement industriel pour sa
  production que la chaux ou le ciment,
- on peut commencer la construction d'un mur peu de temps après la production (inutile d'attendre le séchage)
- les blocs de pisé stabilisé au plâtre subissent peu de retrait, leur
  aspect est agréable et leur résistances élevées, avec peu de déformations sous charge
- le fluage ne soulève aucun problème.
Néanmoins, le matériau craint l'humidité, donc il est impératif de mettre au point les techniques de production et l'amélioration de la résistance à l'eau en augmentant le pourcentage de plâtre sans perdre l'avantage économique. Il faut également étudier la corrosion biologique du
type anaérobique. Certains organismes présents dans les sols peuvent
exercer un effet corrosif qui est actuellement à l'étude.

THERMOMECHANICAL ANALYSIS OF SOME
EGYPTIAN CLAYS AND CLAY/SAND MIXTURES.

FATHY HELMY MOSALAMY,
General Organization for Housing Building and
Planning Research, Cairo, EGYPT.

Abstract

Recently, Shale/Clay deposits in Egypt recieved attention as a suitable substitute to Nile-Silt for burnt brick industry.

Four different clay samples, in addition to therteen different mixtures (by wt %) of clay and sand were studied in this work using thermomechanical analysis. The percentage of the uncombined silica in clay samples were calculated whereas, the total silica content of each mixture was estimated. This work is covering the range of total silica content from 20.3 to 65.5 %.

Three different tecmperatures; 900C° , 950C° and 1000C° were selected for this study. Relationship between total silica content (percentage) and shrinkage (Ln. percentage) for the 17 sample at each of the above temperatures has been developed by the least square method.

The investigation was further pointed out that shrinkage was generally decreased by increasing the total silica content and clay minerals tends to shrink by increasing firing temperature.

On étudie en Egypte depuis quelque temps la possibilité de remplacer le limon du Nil par les gisements de schiste bitumineux et d'argile dans l'industrie de la terre cuite.
Quatre échantillons d'argile, ainsi que treize mélanges d'argile et de sable ont été examinés au moyen d'analyse thermomécanique. On a calculé le pourcentage de silice noncombinée dans les échantillons d'argile, tandis que la teneur totale en silice a été évaluée pour chaque mélange. Ce travail montre une teneur totale en silice entre 20,3 et 65,5 %.
Trois températures sont utilisées pour cette étude : 900 C°, 950 C° et 1000 C°. Le rapport entre la teneur totale en silice et le retrait pour les 17 échantillons à chaque température a été calculé au moyen de méthode des moindres çarrés.
L'étude indique que le retrait diminue avec une augmentation de la teneur totale en silice. Le retrait des matériaux argilleux devient plus significatif avec une augmentation de température de cuisson.

A NEW LOW ENERGY - INTENSIVE BUILDING MATERIAL BASED ON LATERITIC SOILS FOR LOW COST HOUSING IN DEVELOPING NATIONS

Dr. B.V. Subrahmanyam,
N.P. Rajamane, &
N. Balasubramanian, Structural Engineering Research Centre,
                  Madras-600 113, India.
Prof. G.S. Ramaswamy, University of Arizona, Tucson, USA.
V. Nagaraju,
A. Narayanaswami &
A. Chakravarthy, Central Mechanical Engineering Research Institute,
                  India.

Abstract

The spiralling growth of population, low GNPs and lack of purchasing power are all aggravating the housing situation in developing countries. A solution to the problem cannot be forthcoming until there is an abundance of building materials suitable for low cost housing and these should ideally be produced from the locally available raw materials.
Most of the developing nations are in the tropical or subtropical regions of the world.
Laterite, which is a product of tropical or subtropical weathering, occurs plentifully in such regions in the Continents of Africa, Asia, South America and Australia.
The main constituents of Laterites are exides of Aluminium, Iron and Silicon.
The Structural Engineering Research Centre, Madras, has developed a new, low energy intensive process whereby high quality building blocks (Latoblocks) can be produced from Lateritic soil and lime. The paper describes field trials to which the blocks have been subjected and states that proposals are afoot for the establishment of industrial units for their large scale production.

Le centre de recherche des structures de Madras. (Inde) a mise au point un processus de fabrication à faible consommation d'énergie pour la production de blocs de qualité supérieure à base de latérites et de chaux. Appelés "Latoblocks", leur qualité et leurs performances sont comparables à celle des briques en terre cuite. Toutefois leur prix est bien inférieur. Différents niveaux de mécanisation sont possibles grâce à deux machines spécialement mises au point : la première, qui convient à une production industrielle dans un secteur industrialisé à échelle réduite, est automatique et coûte environ $ 40 000. Elle permet une production annuelle de 2,1 millions de blocs ; la deuxième coûte $ 3400 destinée à une exploitation artisanale sur les chantiers d'autoconstruction avec une capacité de 60 blocs à l'heure.

IMPROVEMENT AND USE OF EARTH CONSTRUCTION PRODUCTS FOR LOW-COST
HOUSING - ABSTRACT

J.K. KATEREGGA, Housing Research and Development Unit (HRDU)
                University of Nairobi

This paper touches briefly the current negative attitude towards the
use of earth products in house construction in favour of the conventional building materials mainly within the official circles in most
developing countries.It outlines the poor qualities of earth which are
the main cause of this negative attitude and a reflection of fears
and doubts by those involved in formulating and implementing low cost
housing programmes of the material's suitability/performance in such
programmes.
      The paper also outlines some of the good qualities of earth as a
building material, indicating its advantages such as its cheapness,
availability, etc. which could contribute positively to the provision
of affordable shelter for the poor. Three possible methods of
improving earth qualities and performance are given with soil
stabilisation standing out as the most effective and efficient of all
supplemented with the application of high compaction pressures on the
products.
Specific examples of results from HRDU/BRE joint experiments covering
a number of different soil types with different stabilisers in Kenya
are also given indicating the type of products obtainable, their
qualities, where they can be used in house construction and their
cost effectiveness as compared to the conventional alternatives. An
attempt is also made to identify some of the most suitable common
soils for improvement with the correspondent stabilisers especially
for the production of stabilised soil building blocks using two of
the simple manually operated block making machines, the "Brepak"
and the Cinva-ram" block presses.
      The paper concludes by emphasising the need for joint efforts from
all the groups concerned with low cost housing programmes to
intensify in practical research and demonstrative projects which
would assist to disseminate research findings on improvement and use
of earth in house construction at a practical and applicable level
for easy understanding and quick acceptance of the concept by the
decision-making groups, etc.

AMELIORATION ET UTILISATION DES MATERIAUX DE CONSTRUCTION EN TERRE POUR L'HABITAT ECONOMIQUE.
J.K KATEREGGA Université de Nairobi,

L'attitude négative envers l'utilisation des matériaux et base de terre dans la construction de l'habitat est courante principalement parmi les responsables dans la plupart des pays en voie de développement. L'auteur souligne les propriétés de la terre comme matériau de construction avec des avantages tels que le faible coût, la disponibilité etc qui peuvent contribuer de façon positive à fournir des abris aux populations pauvres. On examine trois méthodes pour l'amélioration des qualités et des performances, surtout la stabilisation et le compactage.
Une étude des résultats de la recherche HRDU/BRE sur différents types de terres et de produits de stabilisation permet de définir leurs qualités, leur emploi et leurs avantages coût/ bénéfice. On s'efforce également d'identifier les terres les plus aptes à la stabilisation pour la production de blocs au moyen des presses Brepak et Cinva-Ram.
Il est essentiel que tous les groupes engagés dans les programmes d'habitat économique intensifient leur travail sous forme de recherche pratique et de projets - pilotes afin de diffuser les résultats pour assurer une compréhension facile et rapide du concept par les responsables.

A STUDY OF THE ACTIVITY OF A VOLCANIC POZZOLANA IN NORTHERN TANZANIA

W.J. ALLEN, Ove Arup and Partners, London
R.J.S. SPENCE, Cambridge University, Architecture Department

Abstract

The paper describes an investigation of the pozzolanic properties
of a volcanic ash deposit from Mt. Meru in Northern Tanzania.
Pozzolanic material of this sort is widely found in East Africa,
and provides a cheap means to extend supplies of Portland Cement
or manufacture alternative cementitious materials.

It is shown that within this one deposit there is a very strong
correlation between the pozzolanic activity (measured by a compressive strength test) and the proportion of fine ash in the sample;
Blaine surface area also correlates strongly with activity. On the
other hand, the properties of the chemical constituents do not
correlate independently with activity, and nor does density.

There is shown to be a strong relationship between the location
of the most active materials and the topography of the deposit, resulting from the method of deposition. The most active material is
associated with lacustrine deposits on the lower slopes where there
is a distinct stratification and where the fine ash has been separated. This information can be used to locate the most active pozzolanas
in the field.

A simple fineness test is proposed as a method of maintaining quality
control during manufacturing operations.

L'ACTIVITE D'UNE POUSSOLANE VOLCANIQUE.
R. SPENCE   W.J. ALLEN , Royaume Uni

L'article rend compte d'une investigation des propriétés pouzzolaniques d'un gisement de cendres volcaniques du mont Meru en Tanzanie
du Nord. Ce type de matériau est répandu en Afrique Orientale et fournit une substitution économique au ciment Portland.

En étudiant ce gisement, on constate une bonne correlation entre
l'activité pouzzolanique (mesurée au moyen de l'essai résistance à la
compression) et la proportion de cendres fines dans l'échantillon ;
ceci est vrai aussi pour la surface spécifique Blaine. Par contre, les
propriétés des constituants chimiques n'accusent pas de corrélation indépendante avec l'activité, de même la masse volcanique.

On constate un rapport étroit entre la localisation des matériaux
les plus actifs et la topographie du gisement, qui résulte de sa formation - le matériau le plus actif est associé avec les dépôts lacustres
sur les pentes inférieures à stratification distincte où la cendre fine
est bien localisée. Un essai de finesse simple est proposé comme méthode de contrôle de qualité au cours de la production.

FABRICATION DE MATERIAUX DE CONSTRUCTION A PARTIR DE MATIERES
PREMIERES ZAIROÏSES PEU ONEREUSES

PAUL FIERENS, JOZEF ORSZÁGH, Université de Mons (Belgique)
LUHONDA MAKITU, SELANA MAMBU, SUDI ABDALA, Université de
Lubumbashi (Zaïre)

Résumé

L'étuvage humide, à la pression atmosphérique ou en autoclave, de
mélanges de chaux, d'eau et d'une matière abondante et peu onéreuse
telle que des latérites, permet l'obtention de matériaux de construction de qualité.

Les variables explorées sont la granulométrie des réactifs solides,
la température, la durée et la composition des mélanges.

La recherche, en cours de réalisation, implique l'investigation
de différentes latérites, la mise au point d'une étuve solaire,
l'étude de petites unités de production industrielle et de procédés
de fabrication artisanale.

Abstract

Steaming of lime, water and laterites mixtures, under normal
atmospheric pressure or in an autoclave, gives good quality and
inexpensive building materials.

The studied parameters are solid state granulometry, temperature,
duration and mixtures composition.

The research, still in progress, involves the investigation of
various laterite samples, the construction of a solar energy vapour
bath, the study of industrial manufacture unities as well as the
study of small-scale production processes.

BUILDING WITH STABILIZED EARTH IN THE IVORY COAST -
PAST ACHIEVEMENTS AND FUTURE POSSIBILITIES
J. SIMONNET A. OUATTARA   L.B.T.P. Ivory Coast

Over the last ten years the L.B.T.P. has pursued a policy
of promoting stabilized earth for construction in the Ivory
Coast. Although this material cannot give a general answer to
the problem of low-cost housing in this country, it is nevertheless of regional interest more particularly for building
in the northern district, where the price of cement is highest.
The difficulties met with in introducing geoconcrete into
the Ivory Coast are typical of those raised by placing a new
material in a developing country. The article outlines the
different actions taken to make this project operational.

Résumé

Depuis une dizaine d'années, le Laboratoire du Bâtiment et des
Travaux Publics (LBTP) a mené activement une politique de promotion
de la terre stabilisée (géobéton) pour la construction en Côte
d'Ivoire.

Bien que ce matériau n'apporte pas une réponse générale aux problèmes
de l'habitat économique dans ce pays, il présente cependant un intérêt régional plus particulièrement pour les constructions en zone
Nord, là où le coût du ciment est le plus élevé.

Les difficultés rencontrées pour l'introduction du géobéton en Côte
d'Ivoire sont exemplaires de celles posées par la mise en oeuvre d'un
nouveau matériau dans un pays en voie de développement.

Il a paru utile de retracer ici, les différentes actions qui ont permis à ce produit de rentrer maintenant dans une phase opérationnelle

REINFORCEMENT OF CONCRETE BEAMS WITH LOW-MODULUS MATERIALS IN
FORM OF TWINES

B.L.M. MWAMILA, Department of Building Engineering,
The Royal Institute of Technology, Stockholm, Sweden

Abstract

In reinforced concrete, practice demands that the reinforcement phase
is of higher E-modulus than the matrix phase and hence the suitability
of steel as the sole reinforcement material. Steel is, however, an
expensive building material let alone the fact that it is imported for
most third world countries. On the other hand, there are many locally
available materials whose applicability as reinforcement materials is
restrictive mainly on grounds of their low-modulus and durability.
   In this paper, the behaviour of beam elements reinforced with sisal
twines under static, repeated and sustained loads is presented and
briefly discussed. Deficiencies in performance are identified followed
by a discussion on how to minimise them without off-setting the advantages. Some results are, finally, presented to demonstrate the effectiveness of two of the possibilities for reducing the deficiencies,
namely, using short sisal fibres and using very small quantities of
small diameter steel.

Dans la pratique du béton armé, on exige que l'armature ait un
module d'élasticité plus élevé que celui de la matrice, d'où le choix
de l'acier comme matériau d'armature. Malheureusement, l'acier est un
matériau de construction coûteux qui doit être importé dans la plupart
des pays du tiers monde. En revanche, il existe des matériaux locaux
dont l'utilisation en tant qu'armature est restreinte à cause de leur
faible module et de leur manque de durabilité.
   Ce rapport étudie le comportement de poutres armées de sisal torsa-
dé sous charges statiques, répétées et de longue durée. On identifie
les défauts de performance et les moyens de les minimiser sans perdre
les avantages. Une présentation de résultats montre deux possibilités:
l'utilisation de fibres courtes de sisal et l'incorporation de faibles
quantités d'acier de petit diamètre.

POZZOLANA CEMENTS FOR LOW-COST HOUSING

A A HAMMOND, Head, Materials Division, Building and Road Research Institute (Council for Scientific and Industrial Research), Kumasi.

Abstract

This paper discusses the manufacture, the properties and the applications of the different types of pozzolana and their cements.
It looks at the energy requirements for manufacturing pozzolana as compared to Portland cement and points out the more favourable positions of pozzolana in this respect.
The paper states that the manufacture and use of pozzolana in construction will increase the amount of housing for the economiccally less well off. The recommendation is made that in order to encourage and accelerate the production and use of pozzolana cements in Africa, the E.C.A. with the co-operation of UNIDO and UNCHS should establish pilot-cum-demonstration centres in selected African countries for the production of pozzolana cements. African Governments should co-operate in establishing these centres.

Cette communication porte sur la fabrication, les propriétés et l'utilisation des différents types de pouzzolanes ainsi que sur les ciments pouzzolaniques. De plus, elle compare l'énergie consommée dans leur fabrication et celle du ciment Portland. Ceci montre les avantages qui découlent de l'économie d'énergie dans la fabrication de la pouzzolane.
La communication affirme que la production et l'emploi de la pouzzolane dans la construction apporteront une amélioration à l'habitat des populations à faible revenu, d'où le souhait de voir s'établir des centres pilotes en Afrique pour étendre la recherche et l'information.

Portland-Basalt Mixed Cement

A.F. Galal. M.A. Shater
General Organization for Housing Building and
Planning Research,
H.El-Didamony
Faculty of Science, Zagazing University,
Zagazig, Egypt.

Abstract

Pozzolana is defined as a material which though not cementing compounds related to those in set portland cement. Pozzolanic materials, irrespective of their origin and composition, must have the ability to combine with calcium hydroxide to form compounds possessing cementing properties at room temperature. Basalt is said to be a natural pozzolana. The pozzolanic cement is made by intergrinding portland cement clinker with a portion of pozzolanic material with 10 - 50 % by weight of cement.

At some localities, on the boarders of the Nile Delta (Abo-Zaabal), near Cairo, extrusions in the form of the sheets are being quarried. At these quarries, basalt powder is produced as a by-product. This powder has no significant value and is usually dumped. The top most layer of the basaltic extrusions is usually altered into a friable rock known as weathered basalt. Therefore, this waste product was mixed with portland cement to prepare a pozzolanic or mixed cement. The aim of this work is to investigate the physico-chemical properties of the portland-Basalt cement paste.

The results showed that the compressive strength decreases as the basalt content increases. 30 % basalt gives a suitable compressive strength. From the results of free lime, it may be concluded that the amount of free lime increases with the addition of basalt than the blank at later ages of hydration (3 months). This may be due to the libration of free lime from the basalt itself. The kinetic of hydration as measured by the chemically-combined water decreases with the basalt content. As the hydration proceeds, the amount of chemicall-combined water as well as free lime increases. The addition of basalt to portland cement leads to a reduction in compressive strength of about 12-15, 25-30 and 40-50 % for substitution, of basalt for cement, respectively.

CIMENT COMPOSE PORTLAND - BASALTE

A.F. GALAL, M.A. SHATER   H. EL. DIDAMONY Housing, Building Research,
Le Caire Université de Zagazig

L'exploitation des gisements de basalte près du delta du Nil fournit
un produit de rebut en poudre qui, mélangé au ciment Portland peut
former un ciment pouzzolanîque. Cet article étudie les propriétés
physico-chimiques de la pâte de ciment obtenu avec ce mélange.

Les résultats montrent une diminution de la résistance à la compression avec une augmentation de la teneur en basalte (une teneur de 30 %
de basalte assure une résistance à la compression convenable). On constate que la quantité de chaux libre augmente avec l'addition du basalte
dans une éprouvette après 3 mois d'hydratation. Ceci peut-être dû au
dégagement de la chaux libre du basalte. La cinétique de l'hydratation
mesurée au moyen de l'eau liée chimiquement, décroit avec la teneur en
basalte. A mesure que l'hydratation progresse, la quantité d'eau chimiquement liée aussi bien que celle de chaux libre manque.

DEVELOPMENTS IN SISAL FIBRE REINFORCED CONCRETE

A.S. MAWENYA, University of Dar es Salaam, Tanzania

Abstract

The inflationary trends of the world economy have escalated the costs
of building materials to the extent that in many developing countries
many of the conventional building materials can no longer be considered as reasonable propositions for the construction of low cost
housing schemes. In particular the cost of roofing materials like
corrugated iron sheets, aluminium and asbestos sheets is disproportionately high and far beyond the means of an average wage earner
who is finding it more and more difficult to afford decent housing.

In the search for alternative building materials Sisisal Fibre
Reinforced Concrete (SFRC) provies to be an attractive proposition.
Sisal fibre is a cheap and abundant locally produced material in
many tropical countries. Its mechanical and physical properties are
comparable to those of many modern fibres that are currently being
used for the reinforcement of brittle materials. When sisal fibre is
used as reinforcement for concrete it inhibits early cracking and
imparts flexural strength and ductility to the composite.

This paper gives a review of the research work carried out so far in
the field of SFRC. The review covers the characteristics of sisal as
a reinforcing fibre, manufacture of SFRC, behaviour of SFRC members
under tensile and flexural loads and durability of SFRC. Prospective
applications of SFRC with special reference to SFRC roofing sheets
are also discussed. The paper concludes by noting that the use of
sisal and other natural (vegetable) fibres as reinforcement for
brittle materials has many prospects in the development of low cost
housing on a self-reliance basis. Therefore developing countries
are advised to pool their resources together and set up collaborative
facilities for research and development in the field of natural fibre
reinforced materials.

L'inflation rend prohibitive l'utilisation des matériaux convention--
nels pour l'habitat économique dans les pays pauvres.
     Le béton armé de fibres de sisal s'avère approprié comme matériau de
remplacement ayant des propriétés mécaniques et physiques comparable à
celles des produits modernes. Le sisal empêche une fissuration précoce
et assure la résistance à la flexion et à la ductilité du composite.
     Ce rapport examine la recherche effectuée dans le domaine du béton
armé de fibres de sisal : fabrication, propriétés au jeune âge et à
l'état durci, résistance à la flexion. durabilité, applications nouvel
les en toiture. On conseille aux pays en voie de développement de créer
leur propre installation de recherche pour l'étude de ces matériaux.

UN NOUVEAU MATERIAU STRUCTUREL : LE BETON DE LATERITE
D. ADEPEGBA   Université de Lagos.

Le béton de latérite est par définition un béton où tout ou partie
des granulats gros et fins sont d'origine latéritique. Il existe de
grands gisements de cette terre en Amérique du Sud, en Asie et en
Afrique, d'où son importance dans les projets d'habitat économique
dans ces régions.

L'auteur précise les caractéristiques principales du béton de latérite : les résistances à la compression à 7,14 jours diminuent avec
une teneur élevée de latérite, tandis qu'à 28 et 84 jours, cette diminution est moins marquée. On constate que le dosage approprié est
1 : 1,5 : 3 avec un rapport eau /ciment de 0,65 à condition que la
teneur en latérite soit inférieure à 50 % du poids total du granulat
fin. Le module d'élasticité avec ce dosage peut atteindre 18 - 20KN/mm2
si la composition est bien contrôlée.

EXPERIMENTAL AND DEMONSTRATION LOW COST HOUSE BUILT WITH RICE HUSK ASH AND LIME AS CEMENT BUILT AT BUILDING RESEARCH STATION.

DR. M. SULAIMAN, NADIR MANSOOR & KHALIDA KHAN, Building Research Station, Karachi, Pakistan.

Abstract

A unique experimental and demonstration Low Cost House has been built in the compound of Building Research Station, Karachi, using Rice Husk Ash and Lime as cement in the fabrication of hollow load bearing blocks and in mortar and plaster.
The roof is prefabricated and consists of battons, tiles and screed. In the roof portland cement has been replaced by rice husk ash to the extent of 30%. The foundation and base-course of floor are soil cement stabilized; and pre-fabricated door and window frames have been used. The mosaic floor has been done by a mixture of slag, portland cement, and lime.
Load test in accordance with the British Standard Code of Practice C.P:110:1972 (the structural use of concrete) has been performed on the roof of the house and the house passed the load test, and as such is fit for habitation.

A titre de démonstration, on a construit une maison expérimentale où les bétons et mortiers contiennent des cendres de balle de riz et de la chaux pour remplacer le ciment.
Le toit préfabriqué comprend des tuiles, des liteaux et un mortier de pose où le ciment a été remplacé par la cendre de balle de riz dans une proportion de 30 %. Le sol de fondation et la couche de base sont stabilisés au ciment, tandis que le carrelage au sol est posé sur une chape constituée d'une mélange de laitier, de ciment Portland et de chaux.
La maison a subi avec succès l'essai de chargement prévu au règlement britannique CP 110 : 1972, elle est donc certifiée conforme.

PROPERTIES OF POZZOLANIC CEMENTS OBTAINED BY MIDDLE-TEMPERATURE
CALCINING OF CLAYS. CASE OF METAKAOLINITE CEMENTS.

M.MURAT, J. AMBROISE, J. PERA

SUMMARY

With the aim at using solar reactors to manufacture middle-temperature pozzolanic cements from local raw-materials in Developing Countries, the hydration reaction and hardening of metakaolinites obtained by thermal decomposition of natural kaolinites in different electricaly heated reactors (fixed-bed, stirred-bed or fluidized bed reactors) have been studied. In a first series of experiments, it was shown that at 28 days, compressive strengths of about 100-150 Bars can be obtained when the raw-kaolinite is calcined between 700°C and 800°C and the metakaolinite activated with calcium hydroxide. However, mechanical strengths greatly depends on the type of reactor used to realize the déhydration of kaolinite, hydration conditions and mineralogical properties of the raw-material. A second series of experiments on the optimization of short-time (28 days) strengths, implying a judicious choice of sample curing and of both Water/Solid and Metakaolinite/Calcium hydroxide ratios has allowed to obtain compressive strengths up to 280 Bars, what is largely sufficient for individual housing in Developping Countries. But metakaolinite is certainly the more reactive thermally-dehydrated clay and must be considered as a " model ". So, an extension of the research to other clay minerals laterites and red-soils constituting local raw-materials, is envisaged.

APPLICATION OF FERROCEMENT FOR LOW COST HOUSING IN INDIA

MADHAVA RAO A.G., Structural Engineering Research Centre, Madras, India
MURTHY D.S.R.,   Structural Engineering Research Centre, Madras, India

Abstract

Ferrocement is a highly versatile construction material which has
established itself as an appropriate material for socially-relevant
applications in developing countries. Among the reasons why it is
suitable is the fact that the raw materials are available there as are
the skills necessary for the construction of ferrocement units.
The ferrocement applications described in this paper have good potential for applications in low-income housing schemes.
Ferrocement service modules can be used for the sites and services
schemes where the low-income groups are provided with a developed plot
with a service core unit.
The SERC Madras has developed sanitary service modules in ferrocement
for bath rooms and toilets and these have shown themselves to be
economical when compared to those made out of conventional materials.
Another important application for ferrocement cyclone resistant core
units is as an economical and practical solution for housing in
disaster prone units.

Le ferrociment est un matériau universel maintenant accepté comme
une solution appropriée à l'habitat pour les populations à faible revenu dans les pays en voie de développement, puisque l'on trouve sur place les matières brutes et la main d'oeuvre pour la fabrication des éléments de construction. Les modules décrits conviennent à des projets de
lotissements de terrains aménagés avec branchements et noyaux de service
Le Centre de Recherche des structures de Madrid a mis au point les modules sanitaires en ferrociment de prix économique par rapport aux installations en matériaux courants.
Une autre application du ferrociment est celle des unités centrales
de construction résistant aux cyclones, ce qui présente une solution
économique et pratique pour l'habitat dans les zones exposées.

THE USE OF BLENDED CEMENT IN CONCRETE

IBRAHIM A. ELDARWISH, Ph.D.
Prof. & Director, Testing of Materials Laboratories
MOSTAFA E. SHEHATA, Ph.D.
Assistant Prof., Structural Engineering Department

Faculty of Engineering, Alexandria University, Egypt

Abstract

Blended cement is a mixture of ordinary portland cement klinker
together with active or inactive material ground finely to produce
the required cement. It is being produced in many countries all over
the world. Different materials being added are Pozzolana, Slag, Fly
ash and Sand. In Egypt it is being produced under the trade name
of karnak cement which is obtained by blending together ordinary
portland cement klinker with 25% silicous sand after being finely
ground. The blended cement has less mechanical properties but it is
cheaper in cost.
Several mix proportions of sand have been added to the portland
cement klinker that range between 5% and 25%. It was found that the
addition of 20% sand in the form of ground materials represents
the most effective percentage regarding the mechanical properties of
cement mortar.
If the concrete Mix is carefully designed with good graded aggregate,
low water cement ratio, perhaps by the use of plasticizers and good
compaction, a concrete cube compressive strength that ranges from
206 to 325 kg/cm2 has been achieved. Splitting cylinder tensile
strength of maximum value of approximately 27 kg/cm2 has been obtained
while the maximum modulus of rupture was about 27 kg/cm2. Bond
strength of concrete with steel reinforcement was virtually independent of compressive strength of concrete and lay in the range of 24
kg/cm2. The fresh concrete properties were similar to those of concrete made with ordinary portland cement. It could be that the sulphate
resistance of the blended cement is higher than the ordinary one.
Tests on reinforced concrete columns and beams made with blended cement
showed that they can withstand ultimate loads in the range between
9.7% to 32% for R.C. columns and between 10% to 25.9% for R.C. beams
as compared to the values obtained when computed by the plastic theory.

UTILISATION DU CIMENT MELANGE
I.A ELDARWISH M.E. SHEHATA Université d'alexandrie, Egypte

En Egypte on fabrique un ciment mélangé sous l'appellation "Karnak",
constitué de clinker de ciment Portland et de sable siliceux (25 %).
Avec un dosage et une granulométrie appropriés, un rapport eau/ciment
peu élevé réalisé peut-être au moyen de plastifiants et d'un bon compactage, on obtient des résultats suivants : résistance à la compression sur cube entre 206 et 325 kg/cm2, résistance à traction par fendage sur cylindre d'une valeur maximale de 27kg/cm2, module de rupture
27kg/cm2, adhérence aux armatures 24kg/cm2. Les propriétés du béton
frais se comparent favorablement à celles du ciment Portland. Il se
peut même que la résistance aux sulfates soit améliorée.

PROPERTIES OF PASTES MORTARS AND CONCRETES MIXED WITH SEA WATERS
AND CONTAINING TURKISH CEMENTS

ASIM YEGINOBALI, Yarmouk University, Irbid, Jordan

Abstract

An extensive study has been carried to investigate the effects of sea
waters on some cement paste, mortar and concrete properties when used
as mixing water. As in most countries having sea coasts, sea waters
are occasionally used in Turkey to mix concrete due to the lack of
more suitable water. Although natural sea waters with a wide range
of salinity (17-39 g/ℓt) exist along the Turkish coasts, the Turkish
code puts relatively strict limitations on the mixing water compositions. The study was further prompted after a review of the related
literature and noting some conflicting results obtained by the previous investigators.

In the experiments sea waters from the Mediterranean, Marmara
and Black Sea were used together with four common Turkish cements;
ordinary portland, trass cements with 10% and 20% trass additions and
slag cement with 30% blast furnace slag addition. Cement properties
were somewhat different from similar cements in other countries.
Keeping the type of aggregate and mixing proportions constant and
using tap water for control mixes, altogether 16 mixing water-cement
combinations were possible. A total of 16 paste, mortar and concrete
properties were investigated forming specimens from the different
mixes and comparing the results with those obtained with tap water.
The study was conducted at the Middle East Technical University in
Ankara, Turkey.

According to the experimental results, mixing the sea waters did
not have significant effects on the consistency and soundness of the
pastes; workability, air content and sulfate resistance of mortars
and concretes. Sea waters caused slightly higher heat of hydration
and lower porosity in the pastes. The setting times were shortened
by up to 22% in proportion with salinity. With all cements compressive strengths were higher at 7,28 and 90 days, the latters by 15-25%.
Increases in split tensile and flexural strengths were smaller. Effects of sea water mixing on the corrosion of steel reinforcement were
investigated on mortar and concrete specimens with steel bars embedded
at different cover thicknesses. In loosely compacted mortars probability of corrosion increased, especially with Mediterranean water.
The test with dense concrete specimens is still underway. However,
after two years there were no visual signs indicating any adverse
effect of mixing with sea water.

The effects of sea water mixing could partially be explained by
the results of a parallel study involving the x-ray diffraction
analyses of some cement pastes mixed with sea water. The results are
discussed in detail and some recommendations have been made for further research on this subject.

PROPRIETES DES PATES DE CIMENT ET DES BETONS GACHEES AVEC L'EAU DE MER
ET CONTENANT DES CIMENTS DE FABRICATION TURQUE.
A. YEGINOBALI Irbid, Jordanie.

L'université technique du Moyen Orient à Ankara, Turquie a entrepris
une étude des effets du gâchage aux eaux de mers sur les propriétés des
pâtes de ciments et des bétons.

Bien que les eaux de mer le long des côtes turques présentent des
salinités de 17 à 39 g/litre, la réglementation turque prévoit des res-
trictions vigoureuses.

16 éprouvettes ont été fabriquées à partir d'eaux de mer (la Méditer-
ranée, la mer de Marmara et la mer Noire) et de ciments turcs (portland,
trass et laitier), à dosages et à type de granulat constants. Les résultats ne montrent aucun effet significatif de la présence des eaux de mer
sur la consistance et les résistances des pâtes, sur l'ouvrabilité, la
teneur en air et la résistance aux sulfates des mortiers en béton.
L'eau de mer provoque une chaleur d'hydratation plus élevée et une porosité moins prononcée dans les pâtes. Les temps de prise sont jusqu'à
22 % moins longs en fonction de la salinité. Avec tous les ciments les
résistances à la compression sont plus élevées à 7, 28 et 90 jours, ces
dernières de 15 - 25 %. Les améliorations dans les résistances en
flexion et à la traction par fendage sont moins prononcées. On a également examiné l'effet sur la corrosion des armatures avec des variations
de compactage et d'enrobage.

Le rapport comprend également les résultats d'analyses par diffraction
aux rayons X de certaines pâtes, permettant la formulation de recommandations pour un programme de recherche.

USE OF CONCRETES WITH LOW CEMENT CONTENT FOR HOUSING IN THE
IVORY COAST
M. SIMONNET   M. TITECAT   L.B.T.P. Ivory Coast

Use of low content of cement concrete is a means of reducing the cost of elementary housing. The tests undertaken
at the L.B.T.P. (Ivory Coast) show that to obtain concrete of
satisfactory workability, the low cement content of concrete
must be compensated by adding a filler. This additive can be
obtained more simply by replacing the aggregate normally used
by a crusher run product. This leads to a product which we
could call a gravel concrete. The cost of this concrete is
40 % lower than that of a classical concrete with 350 kg/m3
mix. 28 % of the saving is due to lowering the cement content
and 12 % to the replacement of aggregate by crusher-run
material. Feasibility tests on site have shown that such a
product using 150 kg/m3 cement and containing 100-150 kg/m3
filler could be transported by mixer truck and placed by
pumping in formwork made of planks 2.75 x 0.10 m. The surface aspect after demoulding is satisfactory. No shrinkage
cracks are visible on the test walls.
A pilot study in progress concerns 88 dwellings at
Abidjan and complementary tests in the laboratory contribute
to a better definition of the specifications for use of gravel
concrete, taking into account the requirements on strength
and durability.

L'emploi de béton à dosage en ciment réduit est un moyen d'abaisser
le coût des constructions simples
   Les essais menés au LBTP montrent que pour obtenir un béton ma-
niable, il convient de compenser la baisse du dosage en ciment par un
ajout de filler. Cet ajout de filler peut-être obtenu plus simplement en remplaçant les granulats habituellement utilisés par un "tout-
venant" de concassage. On obtient ainsi un produit que l'on pourrait
appeler "grave béton".
   Le coût de "cette grave béton" est de 40 % inférieur à celui d'un
béton classique dosé à 350 kg de ciment par m^3. L'économie provient
pour 28 % de la diminution du dosage en ciment et pour 12 % du remplacement des granulats par le tout-venant.
   Les essais de faisabilité sur chantier ont montré qu'un tel pro-
produit dosé à 150 kg de ciment/m^3 et contenant de 100 à 150 kg de
filler/m^3, pouvait être transporté par camion malaxeur et mis en oeuvre à la pompe à béton dans des banches de 2 m 75 de hauteur et de
10 cm de largeur. L'aspect au décoffrage était satisfaisant. Aucune
fissure de retrait n'était visible sur les murs d'essai.
   Les résistances mécaniques atteintes en compression à 28 jours se
situent entre 2 MPa et 4 MPa. Elles permettent d'envisager la construction de maisons à 1 ou 2 niveaux constituant le type d'habitation
économique le plus courant en Côte d'Ivoire.
   Une opération pilote en cours portant sur 88 logements à Abidjan et
des essais complémentaires au laboratoire, permettront de mieux définir les spécifications d'emploi de la "grave béton" compte tenu des
exigences en matière de résistance et de durabilité.

USE OF KENAF FIBRES FOR REINFORCEMENT OF RICH-CEMENT-SAND
CORRUGATED SHEETS

OMER M.E. FAGEIRI, Building & Road Research Institute, University of
Khartoum

Abstract

An experimental investigation on the possibility of using kenaf
fibres to reinforce rich cement-sand mortar to produce corrugated
sheets was carried out in the Building and Research Institute (BRRI),
University of Khartoum, Sudan. The findings of the investigation
revealed that the tensile properties of kenaf fibres are comparable
to those of some natural fibres (sisal) and synthetic fibres (polypropylene) that are used to reinforce a low tensile strength matrix.
It, also, revealed that the addition of these fibres (1.6% by wt.)
to rich cement-sand mortar (1 1/2:1 by wt.) to produce corrugated
sheets has substantially improved the bending moment capacity and
impact resistance of similar corrugated plain rich cement-sand
sheets, but has slightly increased their water absorption capacity.
The effect of these fibres on the density of plain sheets has been
found to be very slight. It is, also, worth mentioning that the
bending moment and water absorption capacities of the 10.7 mm thick
kenaf reinforced corrugated rich cement-sand sheets are found to
lie within the ASTM specifications for Grade A corrugated asbestos-
cement sheets.
The findings of the investigation were assessed at BRRI and were
found promising to pursue phase 2 of the kenaf-reinforced building
components project at BRRI.
In phase 2 of this project investigations will be carried out to
determine an optimum sheet size (width-length and thickness), optimum
cement/sand and water/cement ratios for the sheets to comply with the
bending moment and water absorption capacities standards specified
by ASTM for Grade A corrugated asbestos-cement sheets. Also the
investigation shall include the long term structural and environmental behaviour of kenaf fibres and sheets in service, a comprehensive evaluation for their physical and mechanical properties and
a techno-economic appraisal for a small project to produce these
sheets using simple manual techniques.

UTILIZATION OF BAMBOO AS A
LOW COST STRUCTURAL MATERIAL

Abang Abdullah Abang Ali
Universiti Pertanian Malaysia

ABSTRACT

The bamboos are very important plants in most part of Asia and
in many parts of the world. Despite being an easily replenishable
material having some noted strengths, bamboo has not been fully
utilized as a building material. However with the current rate of
consumption of the traditional materials by the building industry,
it is anticipated that bamboo shall become increasingly important
in the near future. Mechanical testing of local species of bamboo
is being carried out and a pilot project on cultivation of the
various species has been started at Universiti Pertanian Malaysia.
This paper presents the work which is being carried out at the
University on the utilization of bamboo as a low-cost material of
construction.

Le bambou est une plante très répandue dans la plupart des régions
asiatiques. Malgré les quantités disponibles et ses résistances appré-
ciables, il n'est pas encore pleinement exploité comme matériau de construction. Cependant, en vue de la consommation des matériaux traditionnels par l'industrie du bâtiment, on prévoit pour le bambou un rôle plus
important à l'avenir. L'article évoque les essais mécaniques en cours
sur les espèces locales du bambou et le projet-pilote concernant la culture de diverses espèces qui a débuté à l'Université Pertanian, Malaisie
Ces travaux s'étendent vers l'étude de l'utilisation du bambou en tant
que matériau de construction économique.

THE ROLE OF FORESTRY RESEARCH INSTITUTE, IBADAN IN THE USE OF
INDIGENOUS RAW MATERIALS FOR LOW COST HOUSING

E.O. ADEMILUYI & S.O.O. BADEJO
FORESTRY RESEARCH INSTITUTE OF NIGERIA, P.M.B. 5054, IBADAN

Abstract

About 70% of the Nigerian population are rural dwellers whose housing
problems as well as those of the low income workers have been accorded
very low priority in National Planning. One of the Government's
policy statements is that every Nigerian has a right to healthy and
habitable accommodation and for this, the Federal Government budgeted
about $4.5 billion under the 1975-80 Development Plan Period and even
a greater amount under the current plan period. However, the ever increasing cost of land, building materials, mortgage finance, housing
maintenance and global inflationary trends in all spheres of the economy hampers the realisation of these housing projects.
In the light of the present soaring cost of housing therefore, it was
considered that research into the use of locally available raw materials for the production of certain wood-based panels, which could
serve as basic building components would go a long way towards ensuring the Government's housing projects. The Forest Products Research
Laboratory, Ibadan, is therefore researching into the suitability of
sawmill wood wastes, plantation woods, agricultural residues and
certain prolific weeds for the production of wood-cement board composites and particle board.
As a construction material, wood-cement boards possess engineering
properties acceptable for commercial, residential and public house
buildings. They are low-cost; capable of mass production; resistant
to insect, fungi and fire attack; have very low moisture absorption
rate; with thermal insulating property which makes them versatile
building components under a wide range of weather conditions. These
properties make the boards well suited for walling and ceiling. Their
use for the latter could help cut back on the importation of asbestos
thereby saving some foreign exchange earnings for the country.
From the on-going investigations carried out in the Institute, excellent and technically suitable boards have been fabricated from the
country's sawmill using several species, having applied one or more
wood pretreatments.

LE ROLE DE L'INSTITUT DE RECHERCHE FORESTIERE Ibadan Nigéria, DANS
L'UTILISATION DES MATERIAUX LOCAUX POUR L'HABITAT ECONOMIQUE.
E.O. ADEMILUYI   S.O.O. BADEJO   Ibadan, Nigéria.

En raison de la hausse de prix des matériaux de construction et de
la pénurie de logement au Nigéria, les autorités ont chargé l'Institut
de Recherche Forestière d'une étude sur la possibilité d'utilisation
des produits de rebuts de scierie, les déchets agricoles et certaines
mauvaises herbes pour la fabrication de matériaux composites à base de
bois (agglomérés, panneaux de particules etc.)
Les panneaux composites bois-ciment présentent les propriétés mécaniques acceptables. De prix modique, ils résistent à l'humidité et au
feu et à l'attaque des insectes et sont particulièrement adaptés pour
les murs et plafonds. La recherche se poursuit sur l'utilisation de la
sciure et des résidus agricoles, bagasse, déchêts d'arachides, tiges de
maïs etc.

MATERIAUX LOCAUX EN TUNISIE.
A. FRIAA Tunis

   L'article présente un ensemble de résultats obtenus dans les labora-
toires du Département de Génie Civil de l'Ecole Nationale d'Ingénieurs
de Tunis par une équipe de jeunes chercheurs.
   Les thèmes qui seront abordés sont :
- La brique de terre pressé avec ou sans stabilisant : propriétés physiques et mécaniques et son utilisation dans le domaine du bâtiment.
- L'argile et le verre expansés : Technologie de fabrication et mode
  d'utilisation notamment en isolation thermique.
- Le tuf Tunisien ; ses propriétés de liant et applications
- La margine (sous produit de l'huile d'olive) : Propriétés hydrauli-
  ques, et mécaniques et perspectives d'utilisation en Génie Civil.

This report presents a survey of results obtained in the Civil
Engineering Department of the Tunisian National School of Engin--
eers by a team of young research scientists. The topics discussed
are as follows : compressed earth bricks with or without stabilizer,
physical and mechnical properties and their use in building, expanded
clay and glass, manufacturing technology and use especially in thermal insulation, Tunisian tuf, properties as a binder and applications, margine (by-product from olive oil) hydraulic and mechanical
properties for use in civil engineering.

RESEARCH PROGRAMME ON SECCO ROOFING
M. MARIOTTI   C.E.B.T.P.   Paris

The C.E.B.T.P. has been commissioned with a technological study to draw up the inventory of local materials and to suggest possible solutions for using these materials.

As regards roofing, the ancestral method in rural areas consists of using a grass roof made from secco placed on a steep slope. It is proposed to revalorize this type of secco roofing in order to improve the rate of production, promote manufacture of rolls of secco, ensure good waterproofing on gentle slopes under rain action with or without wind, ensure appropriate strength under self-weight with or without humidity, provide sufficiently strong means of fixingwhich resist wind pressures and improve the behaviour of secco against biological attacks by means of chemical treatment.

LES SUBSTANCES VEGETALES AU SERVICE DE L'HABITAT ECONOMIQUE.
C.S. CISSE S.N.E.D. Bamako

A Bamako les maisons sont construites en briques d'adobe fabriquées
à la main et séchées au soleil, avec une couverture en tôle ondulée.
Les enduits au mortier de terre stabilisée au ciment adhèrent mal et se
dégradent rapidement, et la tôle n'apporte aucune isolation thermique,
elle est sonore sous la pluie.
Les améliorations envisagées portent principalement sur deux points :
- remplacement des enduits extérieurs par des badigeons plus faciles à
réaliser et plus économiques (mélange de ciment et de chaux) appliqués
à la brosse en deux couches. Le mur est préparé au préalable par une
humidification et un brossage. Après badigeonnage on applique une solution à 5 % d'un hydrobant ;
- utilisation de toitures végétales pour remplacer la tôle. Le "secco"
est une herbe de la savane qui est transformée en panneaux de 1,55 m en
la ligaturant avant trempage dans un bain chimique pour améliorer la
résistance à l'eau, aux moisissures et aux insectes. Un film de polyé-
thylène inséré entre deux couches assure l'étanchéité de la couverture.

In Bamako the houses are built of adobe bricks made by
hand and dried in the sun with a corrugated iron roof. The
mortars and rendering have unsatisfactory bond and deteriorate quickly. The improvements planned concern two
points : replacing external renderings by coatings which are
easier to apply and more economical (mixture of cement and
lime) applied by brush in two coats. After whitewashing a
5 % hydrophobant solution is applied. The second topic concerns the use of grass roofs to remplace metal sheeting.
Secco in a savana grass which is transformed into 1.55 m
panels by binding them together before dipping into a chemical bath to improve waterproofing, resistance to mildew and
insects. A polyethylene sheet inserted between two layers
ensures watertight roofing.

TECHNOLOGY ALTERNATIVES FOR PRODUCING BRICKS IN DEVELOPING COUNTRIES

A A HAMMOND, Head, Materials Division, Building and Road Research
Institute (Council for Scientific and Industrial Research), Kumasi.

Abstract

The purpose of this paper is to discuss appropriate technologies
for brick making in the construction of low cost housing, while
bearing in mind the availability of capital and labour.
Three production methods are identified: Labour intensive; Semi-
mechanized and Fully mechanized. The advantages and disadvantages
of each are discussed as well as the results obtained.
The author concludes that highly mechanized processes do not lend
themselves readily for application in African countries and it is
preferable to utilize the labour intensive or semi-mechanized
methods. He advises that where there are suitable clays, fuel and
waterbricks should be produced by these methods.

Cet exposé rappelle les technologies appropriées à la fabrication des
briques pour la construction des logements pour les économiquement faibles. L'auteur indique trois méthodes :
- production par travail manuel intensif
- production semi mécanisée
- production complètement mécanisée

Il examine les avantages et les inconvenients de chaque technologie
ainsi que les résultats.
A condition de disposer de matériaux de base et de sources d'énergie
appropriés, il est recommandé d'adopter les méthodes de fabrication par
travail manuel intensif ou semi mécanisée.

BUILDING MATERIALS FOR HOUSING OF LOW-INCOME SECTOR IN EGYPT

Dr. AHMED A. EL-ERIAN and Dr. MAHMOUD A. REDA YOUSSEF

Abstract

This paper presents an overview of the housing problem in Egypt, and reports the present situation and future trends and development of building materials used in housing, especially for low-income sector. The basic building materials used in housing construction for low-income sector in Egypt are reviewed, and related problems and implications are identified.
Examples are given of recent undertaken research and development of building materials appropriate for low-cost housing, and recommended technical solutions and trends are presented for future development and implementation.
A special recommendation is given for the immediate integration of resources and technical expertise within the African region. A regional research center, chosen from among the pioneering research institutes and universities in the area, may be established to stimulate and co-ordinate further research and development, to implement research findings for practical applications, and to foster exchanging ideas and expertise within and outside Africa.

On présente la situation actuelle de l'habitat en Egypte et les problèmes qu'il pose, ainsi que le développement et les perspectives des matériaux de construction utilisés plus spécialement dans le secteur des faibles revenus.
Les recherches récentes entreprises dans ce but sont illustrées. Elles visent à l'intégration immédiate des ressources et de l'expérience technique dans la région africaine. Un centre de recherche en pointe doit être désigné pour mettre en pratique les conclusions, ainsi que pour encourager l'échange d'idées et d'expériences.

ELEMENTS D'ASSEMBLAGE EN CIMENT ET EN BETON POUR CONSTRUCTION D'HABITAT
ECONOMIQUE : L'EXPERIENCE DU PROJET COOPERATIF EN THAILANDE.
A.B. ETHERINGTON Asian Institute of Technology - University of Hawai

Ce système de construction est basé sur des éléments modulaires à
emboitement, permettant une pose rapide par une main d'oeuvre non
qualifiée.
L'auteur évoque la phase de production des éléments en béton armé
pour fondation, murs, planchers, ouvertures, escaliers, etc, dans une
usine sur chantier, ensuite l'assemblage avec l'incorporation d'éléments de toiture achetés ailleurs. On réalise une économie de 25 %
avec des constructions qui présentent des caractéristiques de qualité
et de résistance comparables à la construction conventionnelle. Ces
bâtiments résistent aux vents de 200 K/h et aux séismes d'une force
de 7,8 sur l'échelle Richter.

BUILDING MATERIALS AND CONSTRUCTION METHODS IN LIBYAN
JAMAHIRIYA

SALEH BARONY, Assoc. Professor
AYAD GALLAL, Assist. Professor
MUSTAFA TAWIL, Assoc. Professor
Civil Engineering Department, University of Al-Fateh, Tripoli.

Abstract

Traditional housing systems in Libya depending on local materials,
expertise and environment enjoyed wide application in the country
up to the Italian invasion and occupation at the beginning of this
century. Nowadays many of the building materials are imported even
though they are expensive and tend to have shortcomings from the
environmental and social points of view.
There is a housing programme which aims at giving almost every
family a modern residence by the year 1990.
Within the present set-up of the construction industry the materials
commonly used can be summarized according to their structural
functions as follows:

Wall Units: Gargaresh blocks
            Concrete blocks
            Clay bricks
            Sand limebricks
            Light weight blocks

Roof Units: Reinforced concrete
            Hollow blocks

The paper discusses past and present developments in construction
methods in Libya and ends with a series of conclusions in the form
of an appraisal and general recommendations which strongly advocate
using locally developed materials and systems in the planning,
design and construction processes.

MATERIAUX ET METHODES DE CONSTRUCTION EN JAMAHIRIYA
LIBYENNE

Saleh Barony, Professeur Associe

Ayad Gallal, Professeur Assistant

Mustafa Tawil, Professeur Associé

Departement de Génie Civil
AL FATEH UNIVERSITE, Tripoli

Résumé

Les empreintes de la civilisation en Libye datent de plusieurs
milliers d´annees et divers materiaux et systemes de const -
ruction furent utilisés . Quoiqu´aujourd´huit la Libye est
faiblement peuplée et les trois quarts de sa superficie
considéré comme désertique, la contrée fut un jour fortement
peuplée et richement cultivée.

La Jamahiriya en tant que pays en voie de développement fait
de grands efforts pour augmenter le niveau de vie de ses
habitants dans tous les domaines. Une de nos principales
priorités est le développement de systemes de construction
relativement bon marché, dépendant de matériaux locaux
et de technologies propres au pays ou parfaitement adaptées.

Nous essayons dans cette présentation de donner un apercu
des systemes d´habitation et des matériaux et méthodes de
construction depuis le traditionnel jusqu´aux procédés en
préfabriqué nouvellement introduits. Une discussion générale
de ces systemes et méthodes est présentée donnant des indi -
cations et recommandations sous forme de conclusion. Celle - ci
insiste sur l´utilisation de matériaux et procédés de construction
developpés localement et recommande leur inclusion lors de la
planification, la conception et la réalisation.

USE OF RICE HUSK AS FUEL FOR FIRING BUILDING BRICKS

Satya Prakash & F.U.Ahmed
Central Building Research Institute, Roorkee, India

Abstract

Bull's Trench Kilns using coal as fuel are very common
all over the world for firing bricks. This is employed
in India and other developing countries also for its
simple design and easy techniques. Some of the developing
countries who do not have fossil fuel are faced with the
acute problem of firing of bricks. However, some of them
are rich in agricultural and forest resources. Biomass
like rice husk, saw dust, firewood, groundnut husk etc.
are found there in plenty. Attempts have been made to use
these materials as fuel for firing bricks on small and
commercial scales. Field trials have shown that coal can
be substituted up to 30-40% in mixed feed firing. It has
been also found that bricks can be fired using rice husk
and firewood without any use of coal.

Les fours "Bull Trench" alimentés en charbon, sont exploités partout
dans le monde pour la cuisson des briques.On les utilise également en Inde
et dans d'autres pays en voie de développement pour leur simplicité tant
de conception que de technique.

La cuisson des briques pose un problème sérieux aux pays en voie de
développement, pauvres en combustibles fossils. Quelques uns sont néanmoins riches en ressources agricoles, d'où une biomasse élevée (balle
de riz, sciure, déchets d'arachide, bois de chauffage etc).

Dans une étude d'utilisation de ces matériaux comme combustibles pour
la cuisson des briques, on constate la possibilité de leur emploi pour
remplacer jusqu'à 40 % du charbon. Il est également possible d'alimenter
les fours uniquement en balle de riz et bois de chauffage, sans charbon.

LOW COST HOUSING IN CHINA USING INDIGENOUS MATERIALS

BAN ZHUO, Chinese Academy of Building Research

Abstract

The greater part of the urban housing in China, costing 100-170 yuan per square metres, belongs in the category of low cost housing. There is a fine tradition in the utilization of local materials in Chinese housing.
The importance of using indigenous raw materials has been accorded considerable attention in housing construction in recent years. Currently the following three kinds of materials are used most frequently for walls:
a. Brick
b. Concrete blocks
c. Insulating materials for industrial exterior panel wall.
The paper discusses certain new topics which merit research as well as new tasks confronting the building materials industry in China. As an example of the former the paper shows how residents are demanding higher qualities for their homes in the form of coloured wall paints that will not easily fade. The latter includes the need to change over from producing single-material components to composite components.

Sont considérés en Chine comme logements à faible coût les logements d'un prix de 100 - 170 yuan le m2.
On poursuit la tradition de l'usage des matériaux locaux qui s'est notablement développée ces dernières années pour la confection des briques, blocs de béton, isolation extérieure. Leur introduction dans des panneaux composites indique une voie pour leur utilisation. Mais de nouvelles questions se posent qui exigent des études : exigences des usagers relatives à leur habitation, utilisation des matériaux de finition et de matériaux de construction légers.

LES MATERIAUX LOCAUX A FAIBLE COUT ENERGETIQUE ET LEUR PROCEDES
DE FABRICATION.
S. BOUBEKEUR   GRET ERA-CNRS Lyon

La substitution des matériaux locaux au ciment représente un véritable enjeu économique pour le logement social. Selon les experts de
l'ONUDI elle permettrait à terme une réduction de 15 à 20 % des coûts
globaux des constructions. L'industrialisation de ces matériaux entrai-
nerait des effets positifs dans le système productif des pays en développement. Les travaux du GRET insistent sur la complémentarité des matériaux lourds (ciment, acier) et des matériaux locaux et sur la complémentarité des technologies modernes et locales. Dès lors, la gamme
importante de matériaux et de technologies disponibles autorisent à
faire des choix en fonction de la nature des travaux. Il faut cependant
observer les limites d'une telle sélection. Ainsi on présente les procédés PLATBROOD et STRAMIT, accompagnés d'un tableau d'identification
d'autres procédés qui feront l'objet de futures recherches.

Replacing cement by local materials is a truly economic
stake for social housing. According to UNIDO experts, it would
ensure a reduction of 15-20 % of overall building cost. The industrialization of these materials would underline the positive
effects in the productive system of developing countries. Work
at the GRET underlines the complementarity of heavy materials
(cement, steel) and local materials and on the blend of modern
and local technologies. The wide range of materials and technologies available facilitates a choice according to the type of
work. Two materials are presented, accompanied by a table to
identify other processes for future research.

DEVELOPING A BUILDING MATERIALS SECTOR IN THE CIRCUMSTANCES
OF HOUSING FOR THE URBAN POOR

F.I.A. TACKIE, Building and Road Research Institute, Ghana

Abstract

Of all the vital inputs required for the output of Housing, building
materials and components have posed the most dominant constraint
in third world countries. The special requirements of the urban
majority in this regard remain an even more complex problem.
If well developed, such an appropriate building materials sector
will offer at least three benefits (a) Shelter   (b) Basic Infrastructure and services   (c) Employment generation including inter-
sectorial multiplier effects.
Incidentally, the importance of housing to the urban poor, may be
measured by these same benefits.
In order to develop an effective building materials sector in ful-
filment of the requirements of the housing for the urban poor,
certain criteria must be met, even though some may seem contra-
dictory. These include (a) minimum cost especially foreign exchange
(b) public health, safety and durability   (c) adaptability to
building codes and the existing construction practices.
Experience has shown that one major constraint which may have
hindred any progress in this direction is the inability of central
governments to motivate private investment in the sector.
Ineffective international co-operation is yet another.
Some strategies are needed urgently. Incentives from both National
and International Sources to the private sector as well as indigenous Research organisations need to be considered.
Specifically, priority should be given to roofing materials.

VERS DES PRESCRIPTIONS ET DES REGLES APPROPRIES   POUR UNE POLITIOUE
D'HABITAT A FAIBLE COUT.

F.I.A TACKIE   Port Harcourt

Le problème de l'habitat dans le tiers monde est caractérisé par les
insuffisances en quantité et en qualité du milieu bâti existant. Le
coût de production constitue également une contrainte majeure, d'où le
besoin pressant d'une politique d'habitat économique.
    Ceci exige également la mise au point de matériaux économiques, mais
on constate que la plupart des prescriptions et des règles ne tiennent
par compte des solutions informelles que constituent des taudis et des
installations de fortune.
    Mais prescriptions et règles sont indispensables au développement
de tout habitat, formel ou informel. Ce point de vue est exprimé depuis
longtemps au niveau national et international, ainsi la demande d'une
révision radicale des règlements pour les rendre appropriés au tiers
monde est actuelle.
    Pour être efficace, cette révision doit engager les organisations
nationales et internationales, prenant en considération les problèmes
de recherche et de diffusion :
mise au point des matériaux appropriés et une utilisation, significa-
tion économique et l'espace autour de l'habitat, services communaux et
infrastructure de base.

MAISON ECONOMIQUE ·A CHARPENTE EN BOIS ADAPTEE AUX CONDITIONS ZAMBIENNES
M. LAAKKONEN Forest Department, Zambia.

Actuellement en Zambie, les maisons économiques sont construites en parpaings; mais leur prix est trop excessif pour la grande majorité de la population. Depuis que les plantations d'eucalyptus et de pins exotiques sont prospères dans le pays, un essai a été tenté afin d'utiliser ces bois exotiques pour la construction de maisons.

Les maisons proposées ont : deux chambres, un séjour, une cuisine, le sous-sol est protégé avec des toles d'acier galvanisées, empoisonnées, formant barrière dans le périmètre de la construction afin d'éviter les attaques de termites. La charpente de bois est de 50 X 100 mm, c/c montant 575 mm, mur 50 x 100 mm plaques provenant des plantations d'eucalyptus grandis et de plaques de fibrociment de 6 mm d'épaisseur sur 1200 mm de largeur sont clouées sur l'extérieur de la charpente, empiétant de 50 mm sur les montants. Un essai d'arrachement a été fait sur les clous dont l'espacement est déterminé d'après cette épreuve; vitesse du vent 31.7 m/s pour une force de vent à l'horizontal. Le toit est fait de plaques de fibrociment fixées sur la travée d'eucalyptus des extrémités des combles au milieu de la maison (aucun renforcement n'est utilisé).

SYMBOLS, SECURITY AND SALESMANSHIP AS FACTORS IN TECHNOLOGY REJECTION

RICHARD MARTIN, Technical Adviser, United States Agency for International Development, Regional Housing and Urban Development Office, Nairobi

Abstract

In spite of considerable investment in research, many demonstration projects and years of experience in attempting to introduce new technologies in the field of low income housing, there is a consistent lack of response from the public, even when there are demonstrable advantages in changing technologies. The paper argues that this phenomenon is due to three factors:
1. In self help housing (which, in one way or another almost all low income housing is) all risks of adopting a new technology are at the owner/builder's expense, and adoption of unknown technology therefore poses unwelcome financial risks.
2. Building technologies are almost always invented or developed outside the social and cultural group that will use them. They therefore have to be "sold" to the intended beneficiaries, a process that arouses deep suspicions, and is in itself a source of rejection.
3. In the urban areas of Africa, housing has great importance as a symbol of material and social status, and therefore building materials and technology are likely to be selected for their symbolic value. This causes the poor to prefer materials normally used by upper income groups to any which might be specially developed to suit their own situation.
The paper suggests possible alternative methods for developing better technologies in low income housing: these include working closely with the beneficiaries to identify their real needs, and taking note of the process by which the poor assemble their housing: their technical terms of reference, their financial constraints, their priorities and their perception of what shelter should really do.

SYMBOLES, SECURITE ET VENTE COMME FACTEURS DE REJET TECHNOLOGIQUE

RICHARD MARTIN, Conseilleur technique, U.S.A.I.D., Bureau Régional
du Logement et de l'Urbanisme, à Nairobi.

Résumé

Malgré d'importants investissements dans la recherche, beaucoup
de projets pilotes et des années d'expérience pour essayer d'intro-
duire des technologies nouvelles dans le domaine de l'habitat économique, il y a un fort manque de réponse de la part du public, même
lorsque il y a des avantages flagrants à changer de technologie.
La communication prétend que ce phénomène est dû à trois facteurs:

1. Dans l'auto-construction de logement (qui est d'une manière
   ou d'une autre presque le cas général de l'habitat économique)
   tous les risques d'adopter une technologie nouvelle sont aux
   frais du propriétaire ou du constructeur, et l'adoption d'une
   technologie inconnue amène donc des risques financiers malvenus.

2. Les technologies de la construction sont presque toujours inventées
   et développées en dehors du groupe social et culturel qui les
   utilisera. Elles doivent donc être "vendues" aux bénéficiaires
   supposés, un procédé qui lève de profondes suspicions, et qui
   est en lui même une source de rejet.

3. Dans les régions urbaines africaines, le logement possède une
   grande importance en tant que symbole de statut matériel et
   social, et donc les matériaux de construction et la technologie
   seront probablement choisis pour leur valeur symbolique. Ceci
   amène le pauvre à préférer des matériaux normalement utilisés par
   la classe nantie pour laquelle ils ont été spéciallement générés
   afin de répondre à leur propre situation.

La communication suggère des alternatives possibles aux méthodes
de développement de meilleures technologies destinées à l'habitat
économique: incluant un travail proche des bénéficiaires afin d'identifier leurs besoins réels et notant le processus d'assemblage du
logement du pauvre, de ses termes techniques de référence, de ses
contraintes financières, de ses priorités et de sa perception de ce
que l'abri doit réellement être.

LOW COST HOUSING BEGINS WITH AN OVERALL ASSESSMENT OF POSSIBLE
MATERIALS

NEVILLE R. HILL, Consultant, United Kingdom

Abstract

Projects for "low cost housing" are still tending to result in improved living standards for people in the middle income group.
Instead they should be providing truly low cost houses giving satisfactory living standards for the low and no income people so that
they will want to remain in the rural areas. To be low cost they
must be based primarily on the proper use of locally available
materials.
Rural housing needs materials whose delivered cost is low in proportion to its bulk or else makes a worthwhile improvement to the performance of the building. There has to be the proper exploitation
of the locally occurring raw materials taking into account stone,
clay/earth/mud, limestone for limemaking, pozzolanic materials of
all kinds, vegetation of all types, any agricultural and industrial
by-products and alternative fuels where needed. The existing availability and delivered price of brought in building materials has
also to be considered though seldom will Portland cement be cheap
enough to use in rural housing. Similarly the possible benefits of
recently developed materials and systems will have to be judged in
relation to the conditions found at the proposed site.
Increasingly, fuel costs, both for firing kilns such as for making
cement, lime, bricks and tiles and for transportation of building
materials, will govern what use is made of particular materials and
systems, as well as pointing to where R&D should be directed.
A general problem is that the established industrial research institutes (IRIs) have not been oriented to the housing problems of
the poorest people or to assisting the existing small scale industries in producing building materials.
The provision of the materials and the system of building has to be
within the capability of the local people otherwise the houses will
not be built in the numbers needed; nor will they be properly maintained.
Examples are given of various approaches to materials for rural building work from Ethiopia, Malawi and Botswana as well as selected
locations outside Africa.
The paper also identifies at least three areas where either greater
dissemination of appropriate existing techniques is required or the
development of new systems is warranted.

EVALUATION GLOBALE DES MATERIAUX POSSIBLES - POINT DE DEPART D'UNE
POLITIQUE D'HABITAT ECONOMIQUE.
N.R. HILL, Royaume Uni.

L'habitat économique est basé sur l'utilisation appropriée des matériaux locaux. Les responsables doivent être capables d'une évaluation
globale des matériaux disponibles - minéraux, produits de rebut agricole
ou industriel. Le coût de l'énergie nécessaire pour la cuisson des briques etc et pour le transport, aura une influence croissante sur l'utilisation des matériaux, en accentuant les secteurs pour la recherche et
le développement.
L'auteur souligne l'importance des rôles de chaque expert dans
l'équipe responsable d'un projet, ainsi que des sources d'information
et de coopération, car il faut une approche multi-disciplinaire à la
situation et à l'utilisation des matériaux.

MATERIALS FOR BUILDING HOUSES - SOME CASE HISTORIES FROM HOME AND
OVERSEAS

NEVILLE R HILL, Consultant, United Kingdom

Abstract

Case histories drawn from the author's own experience over the past
decade are given with the objective of showing ways to develop and
apply local building materials.
The examples have been chosen not only to illustrate certain inappropriate situations which have developed but also to give wider
publicity to what appear to be correct approaches to making use
of the local resources which exist.
The case histories have been taken from Central Southern England,
Caroline Islands in the Pacific Ocean, South-East Asia, East
Caribbean, Paraguay, Ethiopia, Malawi and Botswana.
A point that emerges from the examples given is the wide range of
materials and type of problem that have to be dealt with in making
appropriate building materials for low cost housing.
By way of an introduction to the situations he describes, the author
puts forward the suggestion that all workers in the field should
take a look at the materials that have been used for building houses
in one's own home area and try to judge what adjustments may have
to be made as regards the present situation if there is a change
in conditions in the future.

   L'auteur examine des situations tirées de son expérience sur dix ans
afin d'identifier les moyens pour la mise au point de l'utilisation des
matériaux locaux. Il suggère que les responsables de l'habitat économique commence leur étude par un examen de leur propre région pour définir les possibilités d'ajustement aux conditions changeantes. Après un
aperçu des matériaux utilisés dans le sud de l'Angleterre, on évoque la
situation aux îles Carolines (Pacifique), dans le Sud-Est de l'Asie,
les Caraibes, le Paraguay, l'Ethiopie, le Malawi et le Botswana.

L'UTILISATION DES GRANULATS LOCAUX POUR LE DEVELOPPEMENT DE L'HABITAT
ECONOMIQUE EN JORDANIE.
R. SHARIF   Building Research Center, Jordanie

Tout système d'habitat économique doit être basé sur l'utilisation
des matériaux locaux de résistance et de durabilité satisfaisantes.
On réduit les coûts par une efficacité améliorée de la main d'oeuvre et
par un minimum de gaspillage au stade de la conception.

L'auteur décrit le système élaboré par le centre de recherche du bâtiment (BRC) qui participe également à un projet de contrôle de qualité
des blocs en béton et un relevé des carrières. Ce travail permet la for
mulation de plusieurs recommandations concernant les méthodes d'exploitation, la substitution d'autres granulats aux calcaires, le renforcement des contrôles de qualité, l'étude de l'entretien et l'organisation
d'un séminaire pour l'échange des expériences et le transfert de techno
logie.

THE ECONOMICS OF BUILDING MATERIALS RESEARCH

PETER A. ERKELENS, Eindhoven University of Technology, The Netherlands

Abstract

The importance of the building industry compared to other industries is discussed and also the contribution of the building materials industry for low-cost housing.
It is shown that a good sound long term research programme into cheaper, more durable building materials will lower the building costs. Furthermore research into locally available materials may result in a decrease of the foreign currency component.
It will be indicated that a research programme should cover firstly those low cost housing items which form the most costly part of the bill of quantities both in terms of materials costs and trained labour costs. These may differ for the various countries.
Building research can be carried out in both developing and developed countries. The scope may be different. In the developed countries in general more sophisticated equipment tends to be available, which makes it possible to carry out durability tests and other long term tests. While in the developing countries research can be carried out based only on short term results and requiring less sophisticated equipment and trained personnel.
It is also emphasized that it is not only technical research that has to be carried out. It is also of importance to investigate the acceptability of certain materials. For example in Kenya the acceptance of timber for housing construction is not large. The use of low cost materials in other buildings like public buildings should increase the acceptance of these materials by the public. Appropriate does not necessarily mean appropriate in the opinion of the public. Finally it is stressed that the designer of low cost houses should be aware of the (im)possibilities of the use of low cost materials. This may require him to alter the design to stimulate their use.

L'ECONOMIE DANS LA RECHERCHE DES MATERIAUX DE CONSTRUCTION
P.A ERKELENS, Université de Technologie, Eindhoven, Pays Bas.

L'industrie du bâtiment et de la construction est de la plus haute
importance.(Au Kenya l'industrie du bâtiment représentait 48,3 % des
investissements en 1976), La part des matériaux s'élevait à 3.9 % du
Produit National Brut. Pour l'Afrique entière c'est entre 4 et 6 %.

Dans la recherche des matériaux de construction il faut tenir compte
des problèmes spécifiques des pays en voie de développement : c'est-à-
dire le niveau professiomel des artisans, le transport, l'entretien, les
matériaux appropriés et les devises.

Le champ de recherches en matière de matériaux et de constructions
est vaste. Cependant, en ce qui concerne les logements à bas prix, seule
une certaine catégorie des matériaux et des constructions est importante.
On peut commencer l'analyse sur plusieurs plans : elle peut se faire en
fonction des éléments utilisés et en fonction du prix à payer. Il est
possible par là de cataloguer des matériaux et des éléments moins chers
pour une recherche approfondie.

Les pays en voie de développement ont besoin de laboratoires pour la
recherche mais en général ils sont mal équipés en matériel. C'est pourquoi pour le moment la coopération avec les pays développés est souhaitable. Entretemps il est important que les premiers s'occupent d'abord :
- de la rédaction de spécifications
- de la vérification de la concordance des matériaux avec les spécifications
- des expériences simples qui ne requièrent pas beaucoup d'outillage ni
d'artisans qualifiés.

IS IT LOW COST HOUSING, OR LOWER THE COST OF HOUSING?

A. Nagabhushana Rau (Individual Member - CIB)
Jt. Managing Director, The Hindustan Construction Co.Ltd.,Bombay.

Abstract

The basic issue is how to lower the cost of housing as what is
'low cost' is ambiguous and varies from country to country.

The objective of research has to be to improve the living condition
of people by better shelter, within the cost affordable by them,
developing local materials, skills and technology available,
instead of considering other imported or capital intensive
materials.

In the present times, the life style changes so fast and hence is
it not worth considering buildings with lower life by evolving
specifications and codes consistent with safety?

The examples of Indian experience in construction project housing
have been detailed.

Reduction in cost has to be achieved by better management not only
at workers level, but at policy makers, project planners and project
managers levels.

The objective of research has to be to improve the cost of houses
with better management, better use of local materials and change in
the approach to life of buildings, change in the specifications and
codes, but keeping in view the safety of the structures.

S'AGIT-IL D'HABITAT A COUT REDUIT OU DE REDUIRE LES COUTS ?
A.N. RAU, Bombay.

Le problème de base consiste à diminuer le coût de l'habitat, car
l'expression ambigue "à bas coût" varie de pays en pays. L'objectif de
la recherche doit être l'amélioration des conditions de vie des populations
au moyen d'un abri convenable à un prix abordable qui met en oeuvre
les matériaux, la technologie et la main d'oeuvre disponibles localement,
au lieu d'utiliser des matériaux importés et coûteux.

Puisque le mode de vie change si rapidement, ne serait-il pas judicieux
d'étudier des bâtiments de durée de vie courte, néanmoins conformes
aux spécifications et aux prescriptions de sécurité?

APPROPRIATE TECHNOLOGY AND LOCAL CONTROL:
The Development of the Grenada Indigenous Housing Program

KEY WORDS

Low-Cost Housing, Community Development, Local Building Materials
(Pozzolan Cement, Bamboo, Forest Products), Local Energy Sources
(Micro-Hydropower, Biogas), Education, Employment, Citizen Participa-
tion and Local Control.

SUMMARY

In many developing countries, the least expensive low-cost housing
technology that is imported from the first world is unaffordable by
a great majority of the population. This is certainly true for
Grenada, a small island 70 miles north of Venezuela where the average
monthly income is less than $100 dollars per month and the low-cost
housing sells for more than $10,000 dollars.

In 1981, the Center for Environmental Change in conjunction with Huck
Rorick Associates entered into an agreement with the Peoples Revolu-
tionary Government to undertake a pilot program in community development and low cost housing. The program has begun community education,
design, and construction in the village of Waltham and ultimately
will construct a small village consisting of 50 low-cost dwellings,
community buildings, and infrastructure including sewage and waste
management systems, roads, and alternate energy systems.

The village and housing program are based on concepts of sustainability, ecological balance, local control, and participation. Energy
for the village will be derived from domestic sources such as biogas
and small scale hydropower. Construction will be based on local
materials. Waste will be handled as part of an integrated system,
including use for energy and fertilizer. The project is structured
to provide lasting benefits in education and employment, particularly
in local building material and construction industries.

The focus is on housing because in Grenada, housing is a critical
problem. From 1970 census data, 46% of the population lives in overcrowded conditions, 56% of households lack electricity, 64% lack
running water, and 77% lack indoor toilets. The population has increased since 1970 and there has been no new housing constructed.
The present conditions are much worse and the rising cost of imports,
especially energy, has significantly impacted the situation. The
cost of lumber rose 246% in the last 8 years, and cement, an energy
intensive material, rose 480%.

It is clear that locally self-sufficient housing ia an issue of major
importance, not only for Grenada, but world-wide. This paper will
describe the technical progress we have achieved with biogas, timber
bamboo and stone, based on local community participation.

TECHNOLOGIE APPROPRIEE ET CONTROLE LOCAL, DEVELOPPEMENT DU PROGRAMME DE
LOGEMENT INDIGENE DE GRENADE.
M.C. COMERIO University of California, Berkeley

Dans beaucoup de pays en voie de développement la technologie de
construction de logements importée du premier monde est inabordable
pour la majorité de la population. Ceci est certainement vrai pour
Grenada, une petite île à 70 milles au nord du Vénézuela, où le revenu
mensuel moyen est de moins de US $ 100 et où le logement à prix modéré
se vend pour plus de US $ 10,000.

En 1981, le "Center for Environmental Change", en collaboration avec
"Huck Rorick Associates", a signé un contrat avec le gouvernement révo-
lutionaire populaire pour entreprendre un programme pilote de dévelcp-
pement communautaire et de logement à prix modéré. Le programme a ccm-
mencé par l'éducation de la communauté, le projet et la construction
dans le village de Waltham et finalement construira un petit village de
50 logements à prix modéré, des bâtiments communautaires et une infrastructure consistant d'un système de disposition des égouts et des ordures, des routes et des systèmes d'énergie alternative.

Le village et le programme de logements sont basés sur les idées
d'autonomie, de balance écologique et de contrôle et de participation
locaux. L'énergie pour le village sera extraite de sources indigènes,
tels que biogaz et centrale hydraulique à petite échelle. La construction se fera avec des matériaux indigènes. Les ordures feront partie
d'un système intégral comprenant leur utilisation pour la production
d'énergie et d'engrais. Le projet est structuré pour produire des béné-
fices durables en éducation et en emploi, en particulier dans les indus
tries des matériaux indigènes et de la construction.

LA TECHNIQUE DE L'OPTIMISATION DES COUTS APPLIQUEE AU BATIMENT

A. HAKIMI, Directeur du Laboratoire Public d'Essais et d'Études,
Casablanca, Maroc
LA GROUPE RILEM-MAROC

Résumé

On ne peut pas aller à contre courant par rapport au theme central
consacré aux matériaux en disant qu'il n'est pas nécessaire d'attendre que des révolutions technologiques introduisent au Maroc
des matériaux nouveaux ou des techniques nouvelles pour optimiser
les coûts en bâtiment.
Certes l'optimisation des coûts comporte une importante composante
technique mais ne se résume pas en cela. Au fur et à mesure de l'accroissement de la taille d'un projet, la fonction gestion prend
de plus en plus d'importance au point de reléguer la technique au
second plan ou plus exactement d'en faire un outil parmi d'autres
d'élaboration des études, analyses, synthèses etc... indispensables
à toute prise de décision.

It does not run counter to the central theme of the Symposium if
one states that technological innovations do not automatically bring
Morocco new materials or new techniques for optimising building
costs.
Certainly the optimisation of costs is an important technical
constituent.
The control function assumes an increasing importance according
as the size of the project grows. Indeed the position can be reached
when the technology is pushed into second place or more precisely
when it becomes a tool, among several others, for elaborating studies,
analyses, syntheses etc... indispensable for all aspects of decision
making.

LE PLATRE, UN MATERIAU APPROPRIE A LA CONSTRUCTION ECONOMIQUE ?

MARC NOLHIER - PLAN CONSTRUCTION - FRANCE

Des recherches et expérimentations sur la construction économique à base de plâtre sont menées, depuis 1982, par la France et plusieurs pays africains, dans le cadre du programme REXCOOP "Réalisation Expérimentales en Coopération".
La communication présente l'actualité technique de ce type de construction et, après avoir proposé des critères de définition des technologies appropriées, elle s'inspire de l'exemple sénégalais pour évaluer, en fonction de ces critères, la technique des blocs de plâtre.

GYPSUM, AN APPROPRIATE MATERIAL FOR LOW COST HOUSING?

MARC NOLHIER - PLAN CONSTRUCTION - FRANCE

Since 1982, research and experimentation on low cost building based on gypsum are undertaken by France and several african countries, within the framework of the REXCOOP programme (Experimental Realizations in Cooperation).
The following report sums up today's technique on this type of building, and after proposing criteria for defining appropriate technologies, it uses the Senegal example in order to evaluate, according to these criteria, the gypsum blocks technique.

METHODS FOR REDUCING THE TENDENCY TOWARDS EMBRITTLEMENT IN NATURAL
FIBRE CONCRETE

HANS-ERIK GRAM, Swedish Cement and Concrete Research Institute

Abstract

Concrete reinforced with natural fibres has been studied in Sweden
since 1971. The aim was to develop a low cost, appropriate and durable
roofing sheet made of locally available materials. In collaboration
with organisations in Tanzania roofing sheets of sisal fibre concrete
has been developed. The durability of natural fibre concrete has been
studied at the Swedish Cement and Concrete Research Institute since
1979 in collaboration with the University of Dar es Salaam in Tanzania.
It was found that sisal fibre concrete becomes brittle in tropical
climates. The reason for this is that the sisal fibre is attacked by
the alkaline pore water in the concrete. This breakdown of the sisal
fibre has been assumed to occur as a result of a dissolution of the
lignin which binds the sisal fibre cells together. Instead of the
original lengthy fibre, a number of thin 2-3 mm long fibre cells are
obtained and these no longer interact with the surrounding concrete
matrix.
Different approaches to prevent the observed embrittlement of natural
fibre concrete have been tested:

a) Impregnating the fibre with various salts with the purpose of blocking the lignin molecules, b) impregnating the fibres with water-
   repellent agents to prevent the alkaline pore water from penetrating
   the fibre, c) combinations of fibre impregnations with salts and
   water-repellent agents, d) lowering the alkalinity of the pore
   water through various admixtures to the concrete matrix, e) sealing the pore system in the concrete so as to prevent the transport
   of alkaline pore water to the fibre, f) combination of c and d,
   and g) embedding twisted fibre bundles in the concrete instead
   of individual fibres which are completely surrounded by the matrix.

The results obtained so far show that impregnating the fibres with
salts or water-repellent agents has no more than a limited effect.
Combinations of impregnations with salt and water-repellent agents
give a certain effect. The best results were obtained with not impregnated fibres in a matrix with lowered alkalinity. Not impregnated
fibres in a matrix with a sealed pore system also showed positive
effects.

METHODES POUR PALLIER LA FRAGILISATION DU BETON DE FIBRES NATURELLES.
H.E GRAM, Swedish Ciment and Concret Institute.

Les plaques minces de béton armé de fibres de sisal, exposées au
climat tropical montrent des signes de fragilisation au bout de 6 mois.
Il s'avère que l'eau interstitielle et alcaline dans le béton dissout
les constituants des fibres.
Ce rapport explique les efforts pour remédier à cette fragilisation
les résultats expérimentaux indiquent une amélioration au moyen de
substitution des cendres de traitement de fumées siliceuses au ciment
Portland.
On peut également réduire l'alcalinité de l'eau interstitielle en
remplaçant le liant par un ciment fondu, ce qui retarde la fragilisation. Un résultat semblable est obtenu en obturant les pores du béton
par une application de cire ou par traitement des fibres avec des
agents d'imprégnation.

PROTECTION OF CLAY-EARTH HOUSES IN TOGO
F. EPHOEVI-GA   C.C.L.   Togo

Waterproofing products generally used in the rural areas can be
classified in two main categories : imported or local. In the C.C.L.
research centre such products have been used with success on adobe
walls specially built as specimens. The coating of these walls is
just a clay-earth plaster, protected with the waterproofing under
test.
Through accelerated tests which consist of sprinkling the walls
with water running from a movable sprayer used to measure air infiltration and water penetration in the various materials of the house,
it is possible to evaluate the efficiency of the treatment with regard
to a reference wall.
Though kapok oil provides a certain protection to clay-earth
buildings, it is less effective than mixed mortar or calcium palmitate.

ANALYSE DE LA VIE UTILE DES MATERIAUX POUR L'ENVELOPPE DU BATIMENT

CHRISTER SJÖSTRÖM
L'Institut National Suédois de Recherches sur la Construction
et l'Urbanisme, Suède

SOMMAIRE

La présente communication décrit les principaux facteurs de vieillissement affectant les matériaux de construction extérieurs. De
plus elle illustre par des exemples le processus de désintégration
propre à divers types de matériaux. Y figure aussi un bref exposé
portant sur l'examen des méthodes de pré-laquage de la toile. Ainsi
sont analysés une sélection de maisons, une exposition d'échantillons
de matériaux et un vieillissement accéléré. En tête de communication figure une courte présentation de certaines méthodes d'attaque
systématique du problème de la prévision de la vie utile.

ANALYSIS OF SERVICE LIFE OF MATERIALS FOR THE BUILDING ENVELOPE

Abstract

The paper describes the essential deteriorating agents (climatic
factors and normal air constituents, pollutants and other environmental factors) and how they effect materials in the building envelope.
The most important deteriorating agents, and combinations of agents,
for different classes of materials are pointed out.Within this context
some of the likely deterioration processes are outlined together with
a review of what properties might be used as indicators of ageing.
Organic materials, metals and ceramic materials are dealt with, both
in general terms and with specific examples.
The complex but important question of the relationship between environment and micro-environment (climate and micro-climate) is discussed
but it is not subjected to an in-depth analysis. Techniques and equipment for measuring and describing different parameters of the environment are presented.
Finally a look is taken at certain principles for durability testing.

COLLAPSE MECHANISMS OF RURAL HOUSE FRAMES IN SOUTHERN CAMEROON

NJOCK LIBII, Josué, Ecole Polytechnique,
University of Yaounde, Cameroon

In this paper, we have studied the collapse mechanisms of Basic
traditional and modern traditional house types. By dividing each
house into three components: the foundation, the wall frame and the
roof, we have identified eleven important collapse mechanisms and
associated collapse modes. We have also postulated the Agents responsible for the mechanisms.
By comparing the frequency of occurrence of the mechanisms in both
house types it was found that the order of importance of the
mechanisms is the same for both but that the magnitudes of the frequencies themselves are, in general, twenty five percent lower in
Modern houses than in Basic traditional houses. Finally, the aging
curves have been drawn. From these it is seen that the Basic traditional houses age five times as fast as Modern ones and the latter last
five times as long as the former. These differences are due essentially to the nature of the construction materials rather than to
the structure of the frame. The exact connection between Aging curves
and collapse mechanisms remains the subject of current investigations.

Dans cet article, nous avons étudié les mécanismes qui contribuent
au vieillissement de deux types de maisons: le traditionnel et le
semi-dur.
Pour ce faire, nous avions décomposé la maison en trois parties essentielles: la fondation, les murs, et la toiture. Nous avons iden-
tifié onze mécanismes principaux avec les déformations qu'ils
entraînent. Nous avons aussi avancé les causes probables de ces
mécanismes.
L'analyse des fréquences des mécanismes a révélé que leur ordre
d'importance était exactement le même dans les deux types de maisons.
Cependant, ces mécanismes sont beaucoup plus fréquents dans les maisons traditionnelles de l'ordre de 25%, au moins.
Nous avons tracé les courbes de vieillissement pour les deux types
de maisons. Celles-ci ont la même allure. Cependant, les maisons
traditionnelles vieillissent cinq fois plus vite que les semi-durs
alors que ces derniers durent cinq fois plus long.
Les différences ainsi trouvées sont essentiellement dues au matériaux
de construction plutôt qu'à la différence de structures qui n'est
pas très grande. La relation exacte entre les mécanismes sus-mention-
nés et le processus de vieillissement demeure l'objet de nos recherches actuelles.

DEVELOPMENT OF MATERIALS OF CONSTRUCTION IN SAUDI ARABIA

ABDUL HAMID J.ALTAYYEB, Department of Civil Engineering, University of Petroleum and Minerals, Dhahran.

WAJAHAT H.MIRZA, Department of Civil Engineering, King Abdulaziz University, Jeddah.

ABSTRACT:

This paper describes the efforts being made in developing materials of construction from local resources. An extensive survey of the potential reserves has been carried out and samples of aggregates, sands and clays have been collected. Physical properties of these raw materials have been determined and their use in mortars, bricks and tiles has been investigated. Encouraging results are obtained regarding the production of strong and durable materials of construction.

Cet article décrit les efforts accomplis dans la mise au point de matériaux de construction à partir des ressources locales. On a entrepris une investigation étendue des gisements avec collecte d'échantillons de granulats, de sables et d'argiles. L'étude permet de déterminer les propriétés physiques de ces matériaux et leur utilisation dans les mortiers, les briques et les tuiles. Les résultats indiquent la possibilité de produire des matériaux de résistances et de disponibilité satisfaisantes.

LIME AND CEMENT COATINGS - TEST PROGRAMME
M. MARIOTTI   C.E.B.T.P. Paris

The C.E.B.T.P. has undertaken tests to improve the application
of lime and cement based coatings to protect earth walls made of
compacted blocks without cement stabilization (except when placed
at wall corners). The aim of this reserach was to ensure a more -
economical protection than the traditional rendering, with a material
easy to apply and maintain. The composition and the consistency of
the coating were studied as well as the conditions for preparing
the substrate and placing the material to achieve satisfactory covering power, good bond to the substrate during application and after
hardening, sufficient waterproofing of the wall to avoid cyclic
deformation due to shrinkage and swelling of the substrate and
satisfactory performance under ageing cycles.

CONTRIBUTION A LA DEFINITION DES EXIGENCES REGLEMENTS ET NORMES DE
CONSTRUCTION DANS UN PAYS DONNE ; EXEMPLE DU CAMEROUN.

JOSE FONTAN, CENTRE SCIENTIFIQUE ET TECHNIQUE DU BATIMENT -PARIS-

RESUME

Quelles sont les exigences auxquelles doivent répondre les maisons
d'habitation dans un pays ou un groupe de pays donné ? Le rapport
présente comment des rencontres avec les responsables gouvernementaux
en matière d'habitat, les maîtres d'ouvrage, les maîtres d'oeuvre, les
industriels, les entrepreneurs et la population locale ont pu permettre
de définir les exigences techniques et économiques relatives à l'habitat au Cameroun.
    Il a ensuite été possible dans le cas particulier de maisons indi-
viduelles en bois, de déterminer sous la forme d'un guide de conception
les règles de construction qu'il sera nécessaire d'appliquer afin de
satisfaire à ces exigences.

ABSTRACT

What are the requirements concerning housing in a country or
a group of countries ? This reports presents how meetings with
thoseresponsible for housing, architecture and building to discuss with manufacturers and local population can foster the defi -
nition of technical and economical requirements about Cameroon
housing. It was then possible to ascertain the quality rules for
wood building in order to satisfy these requirements.

TESTS AND TECHNICAL SPECIFICATIONS FOR CONCRETES IN SOMALIA

G. AUGUSTI, University of Florence
C. BLASI, Technical University of Milan
A. CECCOTTI, University of Palermo
A. FONTANA, University of Calabria
G. SACCHI, National Somali University

National Somali University - Mogadishu, School of Engineering

Abstract

The results obtained by the authors together with C. Polizotto,
G. Sara, H. Mohamud and A. Adan within the framework of the Technical
Cooperation Programme between Italy and Somalia are given.
Since no national code for reinforced concrete buildings exists in
Somalia and foreign standards, (which are sometimes unsuited to local
conditions), are applied, the authors felt that there was a risk cf
poor quality of most concretes.
So it was decided to commence extensive tests on concretes in common
use in the Mogadishu area where most of the reinforced concrete build-
ing activity is carried on. The actual research was undertaken at the
Laboratory for Structures and Building Materials of the Engineering
School of the National Somali University in Mogadishu.
After a brief description of the materials commonly used in the
Mogadishu area (Benadir), a standard mortar is proposed to allow the
identification of the cement's strength. Then, results on destructive
and non-destructive tests of concrete, made with the materials available in Somalia are reported; finally, a cost-strength comparison is
made between commonly used concretes·, obtained from coral aggregates,
and concretes made with siliceous materials, which can only be found
outside the Mogadishu area and so are seldom applied in practice.
The paper concludes by detailing the research objectives which have
been set for the immediate future in the National Somali University.
The aim of these investigations is to facilitate within a reasonable
period, a set of Technical Instructions for the acceptance and control
of materials and for the design of reinforced concrete structures in
Somalia.

ESSAIS ET RECOMMANDATIONS TECHNIQUES POUR LES BETONS CONFECTIONNES EN SOMALIE

G. AUGUSTI, C. BLASI, A. CECCOTTI, Université Nationale de Somalie

Dans le cadre de la coopération technique entre la Somalie et l'Italie, on présente ici les résultats obtenus après deux dernières années d'études et d'essais dans le Laboratoire de Matériaux et Construction de l'Ecole des Ingénieurs en Somalì.

Après une brève description des caractéristiques des matériaux courants dans la région de Mogodishu (Benadir), on propose un mortier normalisé pour l'identification des bétons.

Ensuite on donne les résultats d'essais destructifs et non-destructifs sur des bétons confectionnés avec des matériaux courants.

Enfin, on compare, sous le rapport coût-résistance, les bétons confectionnés avec granulats ordinaires (corallins) et les bétons obtenus avec granulats quartzeux qui ne sont pas employés, n'étant pas disponibles près de la capitale.

Cette recherche a pour but de donner les premières références pour un Code Technique somalien pour les constructions en béton armé.

EVOLVING APPROPRIATE BUILDING CODES AND REGULATIONS AS A BASIS FOR
LOW COST HOUSING

F.I.A. TACKIE, Building and Road Research Institute, Ghana.

Abstract

The housing problem in most third world countries is characterizec
by gross inadequacies both in quantity of stock and quality of the
total housing environment. Cost of output is one major constraint
hence the relevance of Low Cost Housing Policies.
To achieve this there is the need for the development of equal
Low Cost building materials amongst other inputs.
Some efforts have been made, notably the housing stock of the slums
and squatter settlements as well as the rural housing stock.
Ironically, most of the building codes and regulations have either
ignored or have not been sympathetic with such informal solutions
to the housing problem.
However, building codes and regulations are indispensable to the
development of any housing environment whether formal or informal.
Such a view has over a long time been expressed at both the National
and International levels. Thus the call for the drastic revision
of all codes and regulations to suit the peculiar circumstances of
the third world is very timely.
What is lacking is an action oriented strategy which will transform
expectations into reality. For the revision to materialise, it
should involve both National and International bodies and above all
should consider several and interrelated issues including (a) Research
and dissemination, (b) Promotion of appropriate building materials
and its utilisation, (c) Economic significance of space around the
home, (d) Communal services and basic infrastructure.

DEVELOPPEMENT D'UN SECTEUR DE MATERIAUX DE CONSTRUCTION POUR L'HABITAT
DES POPULATIONS URBAINES A FAIBLE REVENU,
F.I.A. TACKIE Port Harcourt

De tous les apports nécessaires pour l'habitat, ce sont les matériaux et les éléments de construction qui ont constitué la contrainte
prédominante dans les pays du tiers monde, surtout pour les bâtiments
urbains.

Un secteur bien développé de matériaux de construction appropriés
aurait au moins trois avantages : il offrirait des abris, l'infrastructure et les équipements de base et des emplois.

Les critères à respecter dans le développement d'un tel secteur comprennent : un coût minimal, surtout en devises étrangères, la santé publique, la sécurité et la durabilité et l'adaptabilité aux prescriptions et pratiques existantes,

L'expérience montre que les entraves au progrès dans cette direction
sont l'impuissance des gouvernements à motiver l'investissement privé
et le manque d'efficacité de la coopération internationale. Une politique doit être formulée d'urgence accompagnée d'incitations de sources
nationales et internationales vers le secteur privé et les organismes
de recherche régionaux. Une priorité doit être accordée aux matériaux
de couverture.

QUALITY ASSURANCE FOR BUILDING CONSTRUCTION

By

Assistant Professor Musa R. Resheidat
Civil Engineering Department
Yarmouk University
Irbid - Jordan

ABSTRACT

Building is an old-established, highly traditional regionally and locally conditioned activity, bound by a variety of cultural, social, climatic, as well as technical parameters. The search for an optimal criteria for the use of the available local building materials, selection of the structural system, method of construction, and human skills in developing countries should be realized.

Quality assurance is an integrated system of quality controls, applied to all stages of building process, based on the right decision which takes into account the economical, cultural, social, environmental and technical aspects.

This paper treats quality assurance with respect to safety, serviceability and durability of structures. The principles of quality assurance are applied to the entire building process, viz. planning, design, selection of materials, construction, testing procedure, inspection and control and use of structures. These principles aim at ensuring that the structural performance requirements are fulfilled in an economical manner.

Considering that concrete is a leading construction material in developing countries because of its strength, durability, and social acceptance, quality assurance subsystems such as acceptance of testing will be presented. Accordingly, the role of specifications should be aimed at getting the quality needed rather than a probability of rejection. A specification must be practical, realistic, fair, and in tune with the nature's laws.

Construction is the area where the payoff from quality assurance and quality control is perhaps the greatest. With the best designs and specifications, one can still have a poor structure if things go wrong in the field. Therefore, inspection and proper control are of vital importance. The activities of inspection in the field are outlined.

The system of quality assurance for building construction is presented. Interaction among the technical aspects in the building process is also outlined. The social factors play a main role in this system.

This paper intends to answer the first of the following two questions: "Are we doing the right things?" and "Are we doing things right?"

L'ASSURANCE DE QUALITE POUR LA CONSTRUCTION.
M.R RESHAIDAT   Université du Yarmouk Irbid -- Jordanie

Le bâtiment est une vieille tradition régionale et locale en rapport
avec les conditions culturelles sociales et naturelles et les paramêtres
techniques. Dans les pays développés, des recherches ont été entreprises
pour un meilleur critère des méthodes de constructions et des matériaux
utilisés. L'assurance de la qualité est liée au système du contrôle employé à tous les stades de la construction qui tient compte des aspects
économiques, sociaux, culturels de l'environnement et des aspects techniques. Cette étude examine l'assurance de qualité en accord avec la
sécurité, l'utilisation et la durée des structures : choix des matériaux
calcul, essais, construction, et contrôle de la façon la plus économique.
La construction est l'étape qui demande le plus de contrôle, d'attention
et d'assurance.